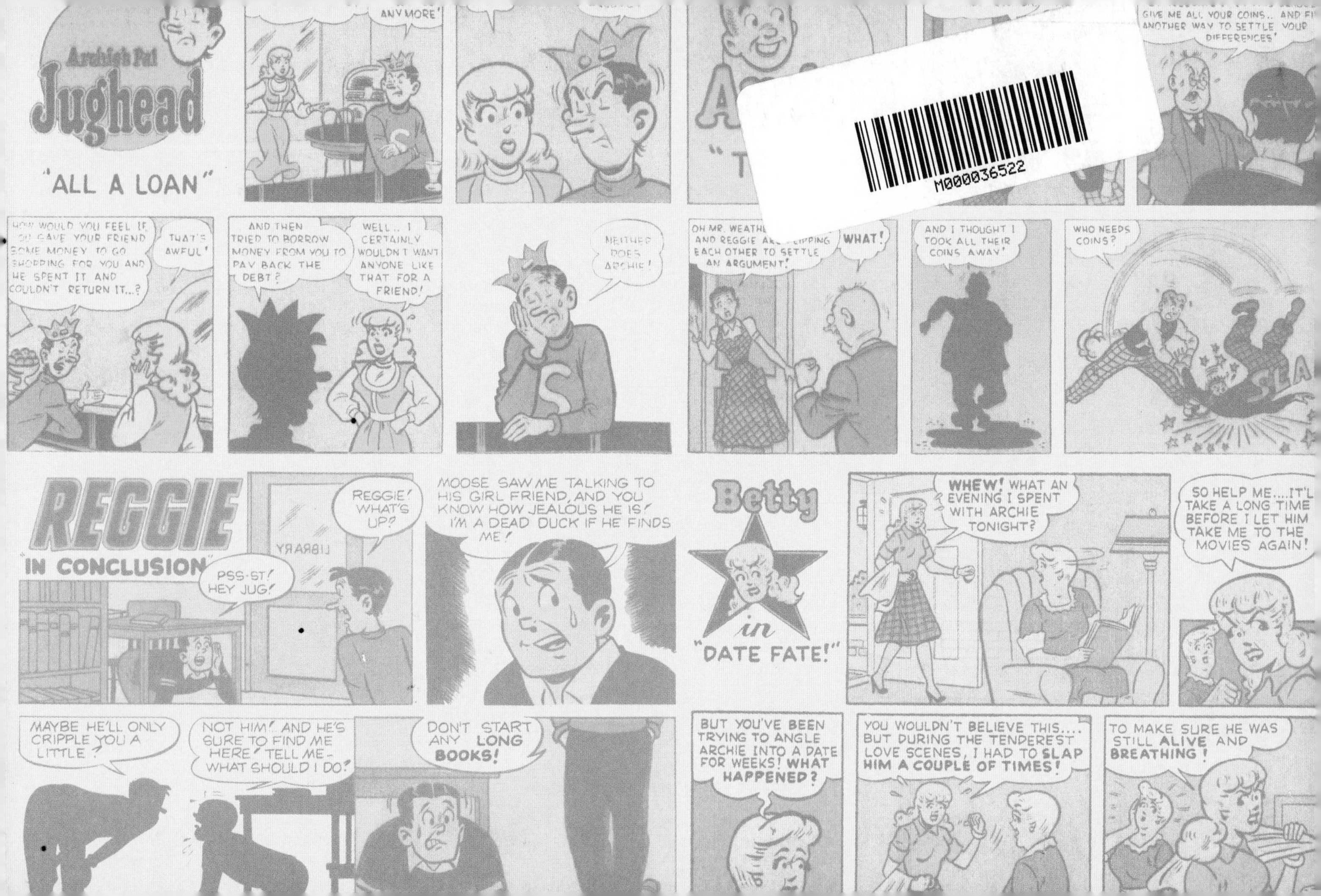
Archie's Pal
Jughead
"ALL A LOAN"
ANY MORE!
GIVE ME ALL YOUR COINS.. AND
ANOTHER WAY TO SETTLE YOUR DIFFERENCES!
HOW WOULD YOU FEEL IF YOU GAVE YOUR FRIEND SOME MONEY TO GO SHOPPING FOR YOU AND HE SPENT IT AND COULDN'T RETURN IT...?
THAT'S AWFUL!
AND THEN TRIED TO BORROW MONEY FROM YOU TO PAY BACK THE DEBT?
WELL.. I CERTAINLY WOULDN'T WANT ANYONE LIKE THAT FOR A FRIEND!
NEITHER DOES ARCHIE!
AND REGGIE ARE
EACH OTHER TO SETTLE AN ARGUMENT!
WHAT!
AND I THOUGHT I TOOK ALL THEIR COINS AWAY!
WHO NEEDS COINS?
REGGIE
"IN CONCLUSION"
REGGIE! WHAT'S UP?
LIBRARY
PSS-ST! HEY JUG!
MOOSE SAW ME TALKING TO HIS GIRL FRIEND, AND YOU KNOW HOW JEALOUS HE IS! I'M A DEAD DUCK IF HE FINDS ME!
Betty
in
"DATE FATE!"
WHEW! WHAT AN EVENING I SPENT WITH ARCHIE TONIGHT?
SO HELP ME....IT'LL TAKE A LONG TIME BEFORE I LET HIM TAKE ME TO THE MOVIES AGAIN!
MAYBE HE'LL ONLY CRIPPLE YOU A LITTLE?
NOT HIM! AND HE'S SURE TO FIND ME HERE! TELL ME - WHAT SHOULD I DO?
DON'T START ANY LONG BOOKS!
BUT YOU'VE BEEN TRYING TO ANGLE ARCHIE INTO A DATE FOR WEEKS! WHAT HAPPENED?
YOU WOULDN'T BELIEVE THIS.... BUT DURING THE TENDEREST LOVE SCENES, I HAD TO SLAP HIM A COUPLE OF TIMES!
TO MAKE SURE HE WAS STILL ALIVE AND BREATHING!

Archie

Joke Book

VOLUME ONE

Great Gags From Great Archie Artists!

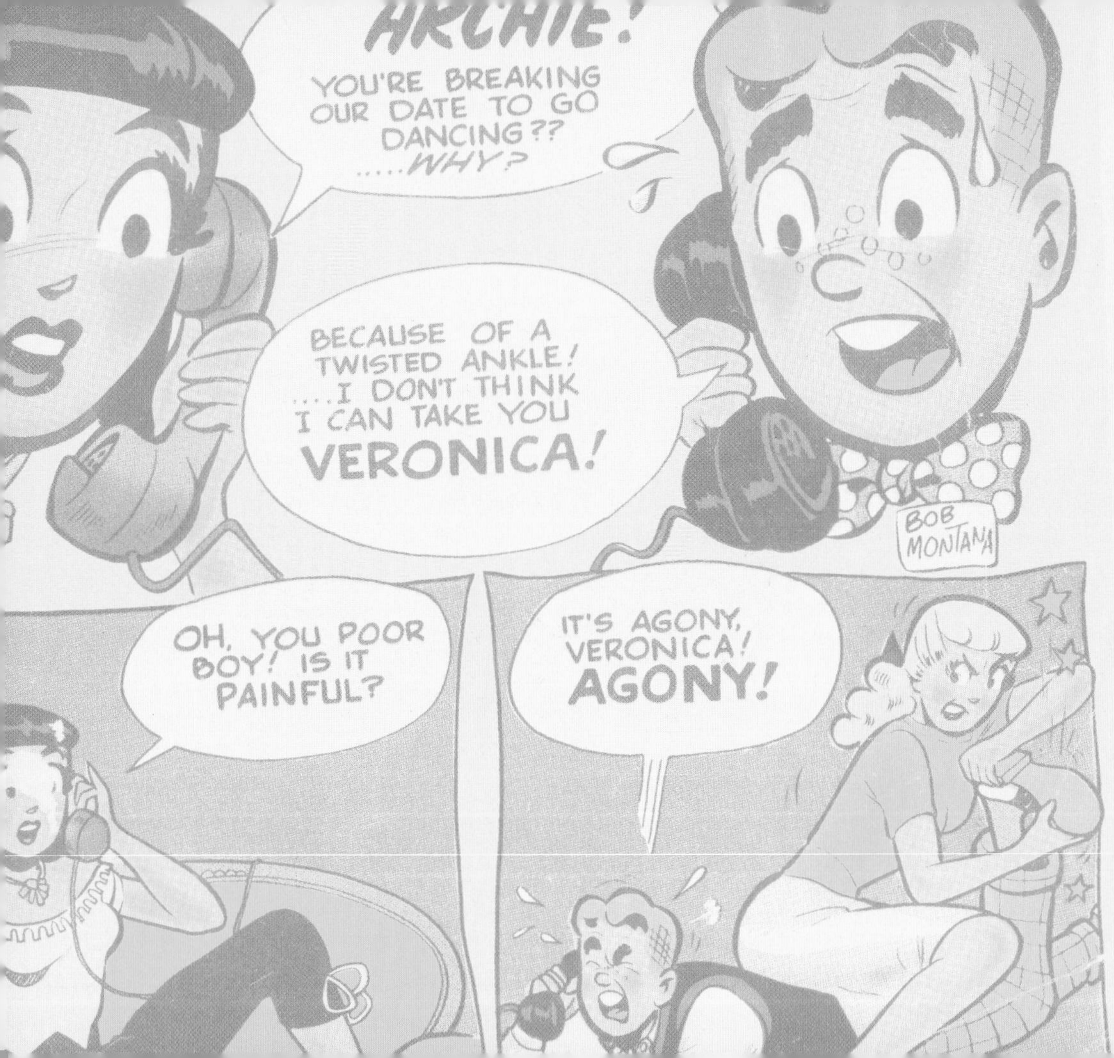
ARCHIE!
YOU'RE BREAKING OUR DATE TO GO DANCING?? .....WHY?
BECAUSE OF A TWISTED ANKLE! ....I DON'T THINK I CAN TAKE YOU VERONICA!
BOB MONTANA
OH, YOU POOR BOY! IS IT PAINFUL?
IT'S AGONY, VERONICA! AGONY!

IDW

Operations:

Ted Adams, CEO & Publisher

Greg Goldstein, Chief Operating Officer

Robbie Robbins, EVP/Sr. Graphic Artist

Chris Ryall, Chief Creative Officer

Matthew Ruzicka, CPA, Chief Financial Officer

Alan Payne, VP of Sales

Art by **Bob Montana, Samm Schwartz, Tom Moore, Dan DeCarlo, and Friends!**

Collection Edited by **Justin Eisinger & Greg Goldstein**

Collection Cover Designed by **David Boswell**

Collection Design by **Bill Tortolini**

Special thanks to Jon Goldwater, Nancy Silberkleit, Mike Pellerito, Victor Gorelick and Carlos Antunes of Archie Comics for their invaluable assistance.

Additional thanks to Chloe Zuanich for her assistance in preparing this volume.

ISBN: 978-1-60010-958-4 www.IDWPUBLISHING.com 14 13 12 11 1 2 3 4

ARCHIE'S JOKE BOOK, VOL. 1: GREAT GAGS FROM GREAT ARCHIE ARTISTS! JULY 2011. FIRST PRINTING.

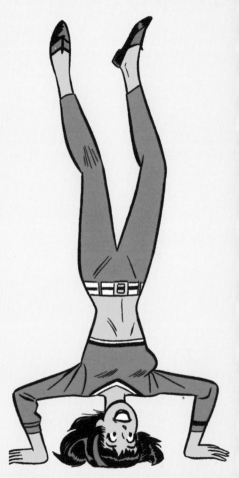

Originally published by Archie Comic Publications as ARCHIE'S JOKE BOOK Issues #1–11.

Great Gags From Great Archie Artists!

Everybody has favorites. Either it's Archie, Jughead, Big Moose... or the eternal question—Betty or Veronica? Some people even love Reggie... Why? I don't know; he's such a pain! Archie readers have favorites for the stories, too. Some like the pure comedy, or romance, even the bizarre worlds of *Archie's Madhouse* and *Jughead's Dipsy Doodles*, while others want the classic five-page story, and some want to read big multi-part story arcs collected in graphic novels. But my favorites are the Archie gags contained within the pages of the book you have in your hands right now.

There is something pure about the newspaper strip style of joke telling. There's the setup, the joke, and then right on to the next joke. It's rapid-fire comics at their best, featuring some of the best gag people in comics. Greats like Bob Montana, Samm Schwartz, Dan DeCarlo and other Archie greats like George Gladir, Tom Moore, Joe Edwards, Dick Malmgren, Stan Goldberg and more are all featured here. Each gag selected by the fine folks (and Archie fans) at IDW from the many published over the years.

The quick gags are a perfect glimpse into the world of *Archie* and why it is so appealing. Archie is like a vortex of constant excitement and we all get to go along for the ride of a lifetime as things quickly get out of hand. You can see how two of the best looking girls in comics could become so taken with him. Throw in the best pal any guy could want—Jughead—and it's easy to see how Archie has been the epitome of teen life for seven generations.

Mike Pellerito
President, Archie Comic Publications, Inc.
April 2011

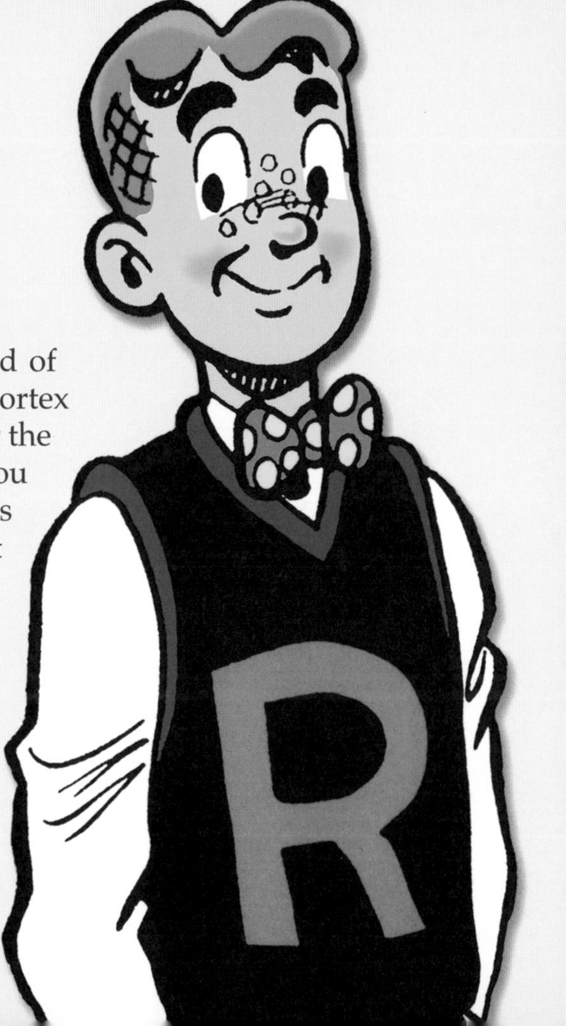
R

Archie

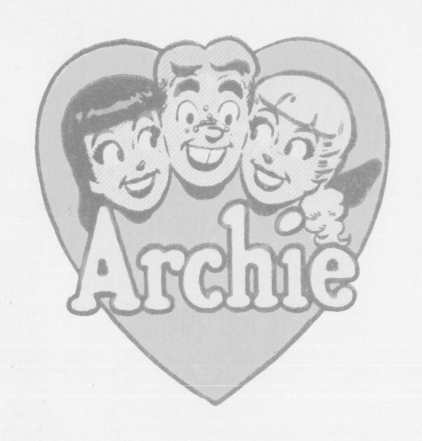

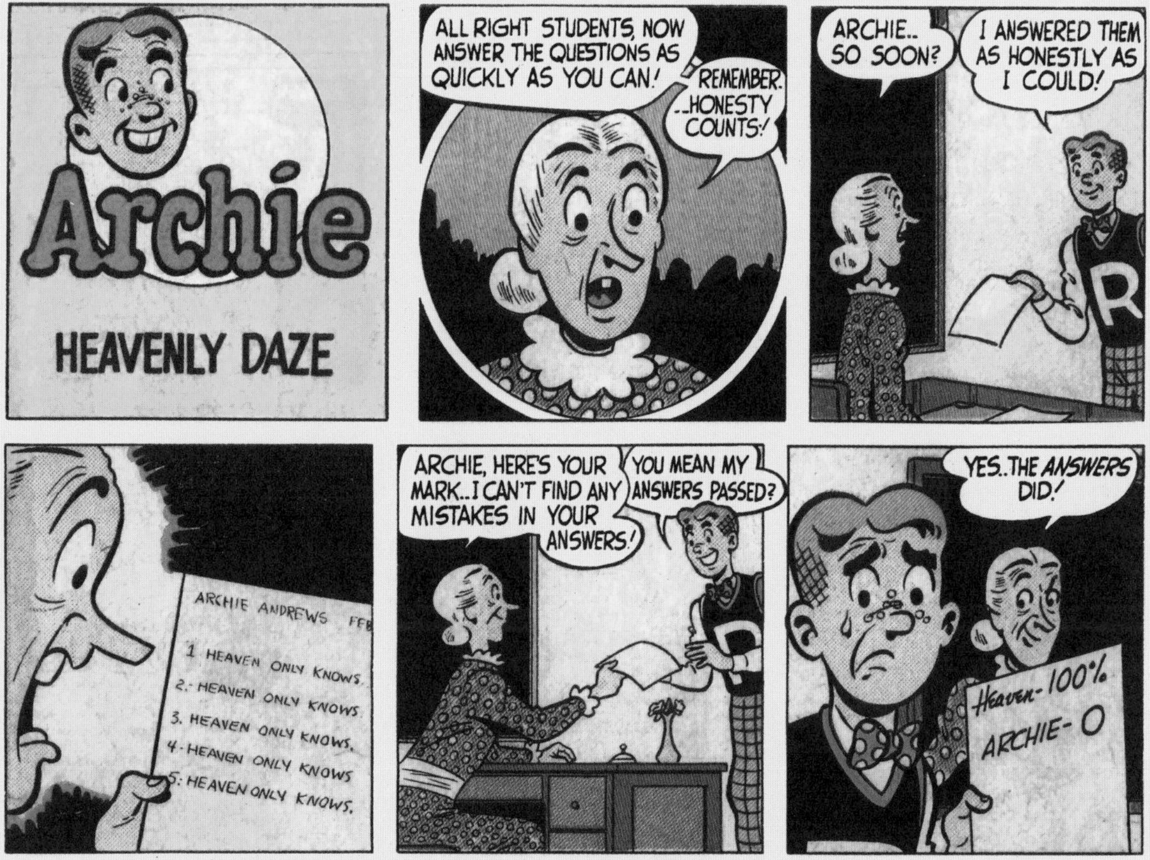
Archie
HEAVENLY DAZE
ALL RIGHT STUDENTS, NOW ANSWER THE QUESTIONS AS QUICKLY AS YOU CAN!
REMEMBER. ..HONESTY COUNTS!
ARCHIE.. SO SOON?
I ANSWERED THEM AS HONESTLY AS I COULD!
ARCHIE ANDREWS FEB
1 HEAVEN ONLY KNOWS.
2.- HEAVEN ONLY KNOWS
3. HEAVEN ONLY KNOWS.
4.- HEAVEN ONLY KNOWS
5: HEAVEN ONLY KNOWS.
ARCHIE, HERE'S YOUR MARK..I CAN'T FIND ANY MISTAKES IN YOUR ANSWERS!
YOU MEAN MY ANSWERS PASSED?
YES..THE ANSWERS DID!
Heaven-100%
ARCHIE-O

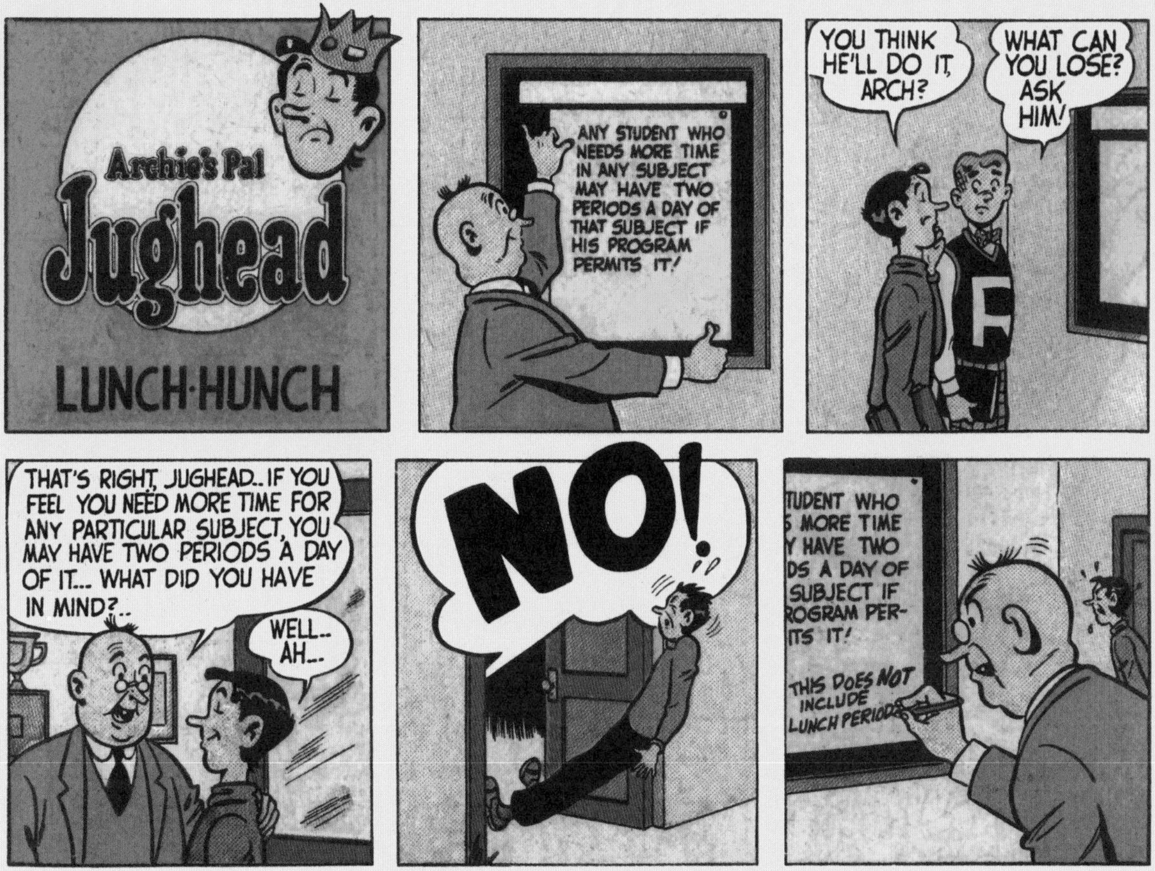
Archie's Pal
Jughead
LUNCH·HUNCH
ANY STUDENT WHO NEEDS MORE TIME IN ANY SUBJECT MAY HAVE TWO PERIODS A DAY OF THAT SUBJECT IF HIS PROGRAM PERMITS IT!
YOU THINK HE'LL DO IT, ARCH?
WHAT CAN YOU LOSE? ASK HIM!
THAT'S RIGHT, JUGHEAD.. IF YOU FEEL YOU NEED MORE TIME FOR ANY PARTICULAR SUBJECT, YOU MAY HAVE TWO PERIODS A DAY OF IT... WHAT DID YOU HAVE IN MIND?..
WELL.. AH...
NO!
THIS DOES NOT INCLUDE LUNCH PERIODS

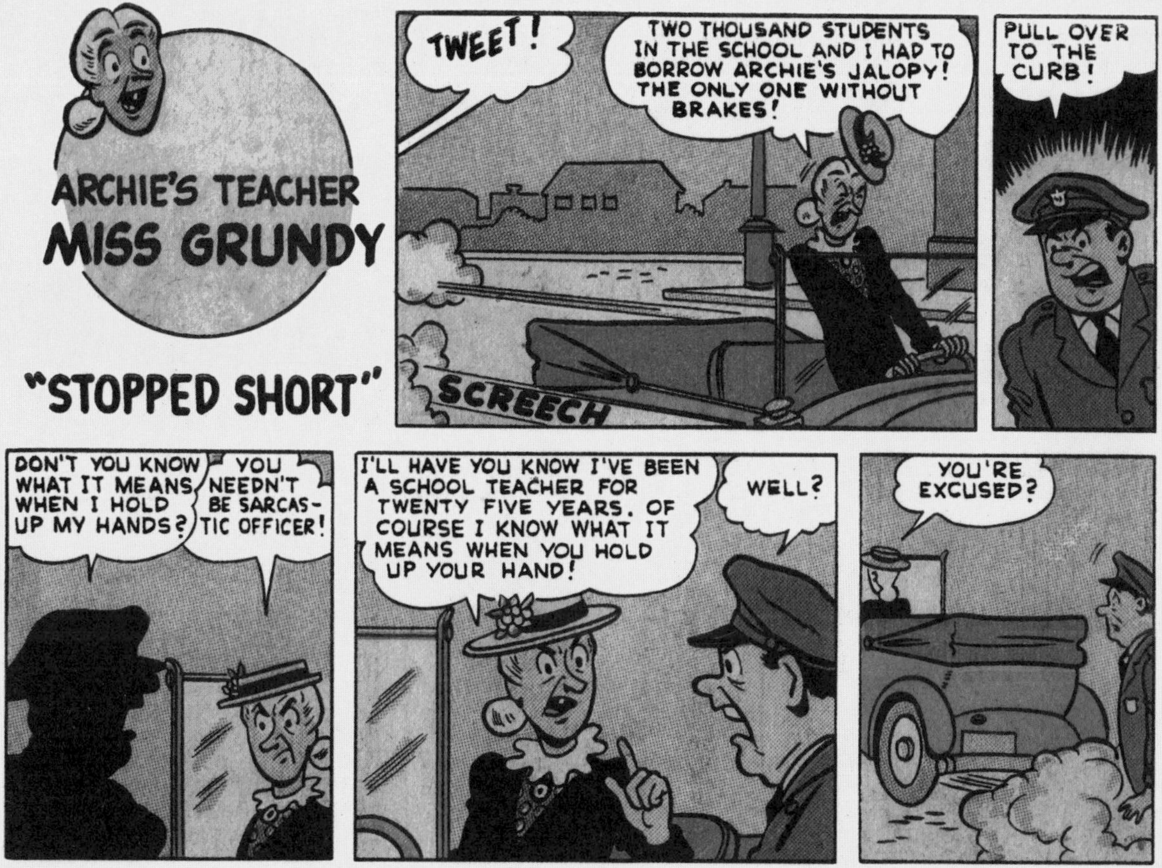
ARCHIE'S TEACHER
MISS GRUNDY
"STOPPED SHORT"
TWEET!
TWO THOUSAND STUDENTS IN THE SCHOOL AND I HAD TO BORROW ARCHIE'S JALOPY! THE ONLY ONE WITHOUT BRAKES!
SCREECH
PULL OVER TO THE CURB!
DON'T YOU KNOW WHAT IT MEANS WHEN I HOLD UP MY HANDS?
YOU NEEDN'T BE SARCAS-TIC OFFICER!
I'LL HAVE YOU KNOW I'VE BEEN A SCHOOL TEACHER FOR TWENTY FIVE YEARS. OF COURSE I KNOW WHAT IT MEANS WHEN YOU HOLD UP YOUR HAND!
WELL?
YOU'RE EXCUSED?

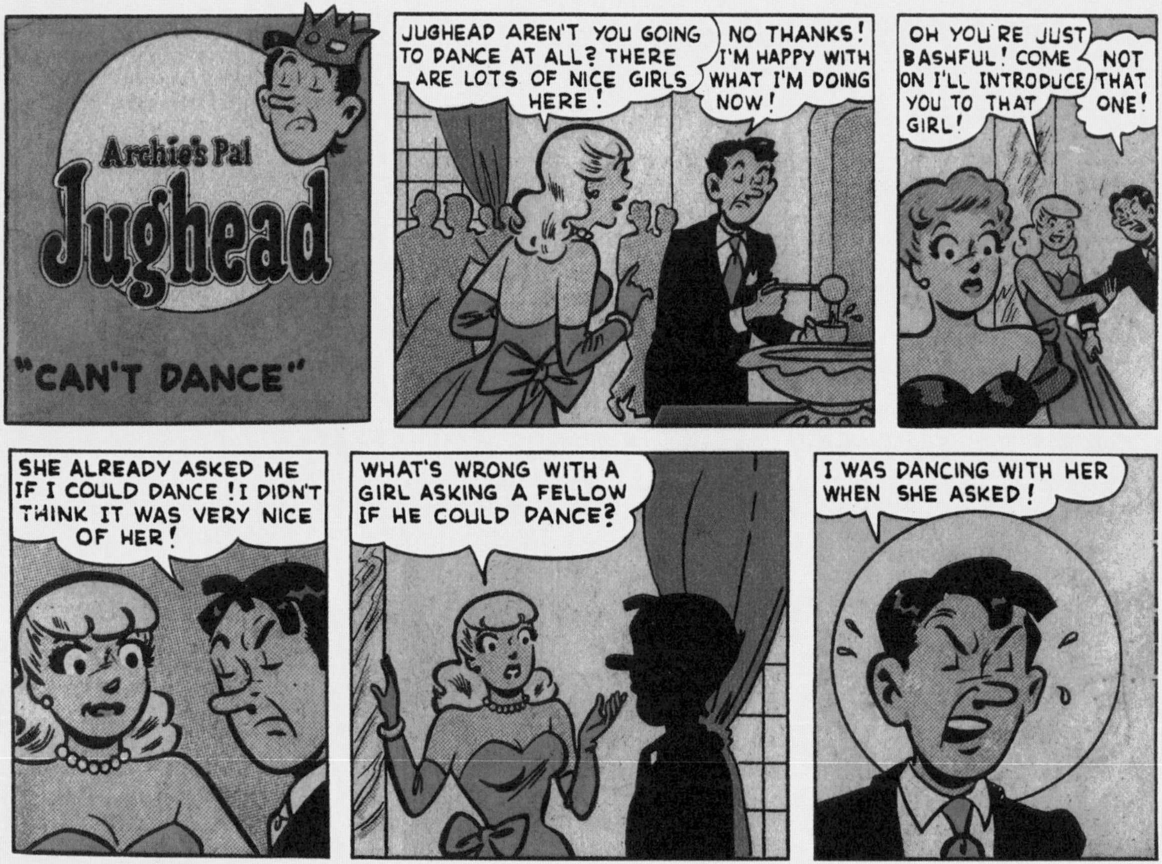
Archie's Pal
Jughead
"CAN'T DANCE"
JUGHEAD AREN'T YOU GOING TO DANCE AT ALL? THERE ARE LOTS OF NICE GIRLS HERE!
NO THANKS! I'M HAPPY WITH WHAT I'M DOING NOW!
OH YOU'RE JUST BASHFUL! COME ON I'LL INTRODUCE YOU TO THAT GIRL!
NOT THAT ONE!
SHE ALREADY ASKED ME IF I COULD DANCE! I DIDN'T THINK IT WAS VERY NICE OF HER!
WHAT'S WRONG WITH A GIRL ASKING A FELLOW IF HE COULD DANCE?
I WAS DANCING WITH HER WHEN SHE ASKED!

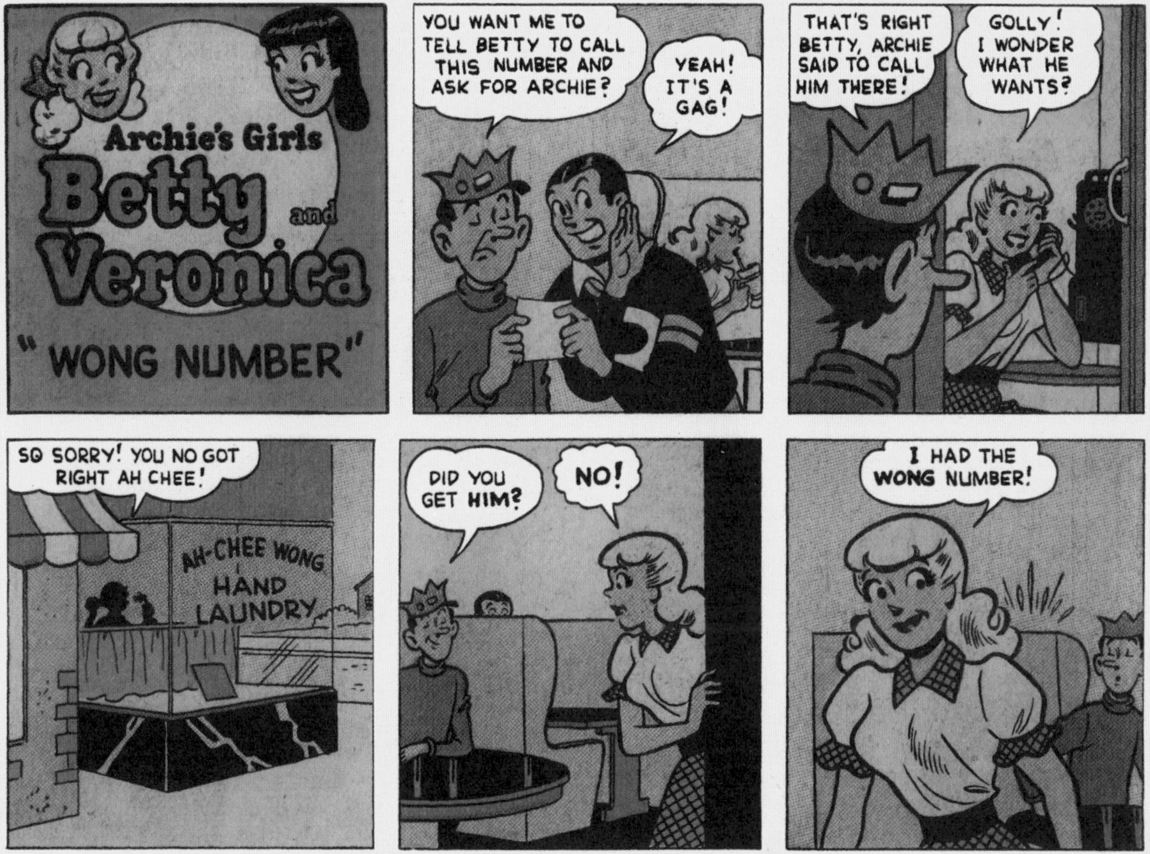
Archie's Girls
Betty and Veronica
"WONG NUMBER"
YOU WANT ME TO TELL BETTY TO CALL THIS NUMBER AND ASK FOR ARCHIE?
YEAH! IT'S A GAG!
THAT'S RIGHT BETTY, ARCHIE SAID TO CALL HIM THERE!
GOLLY! I WONDER WHAT HE WANTS?
SO SORRY! YOU NO GOT RIGHT AH CHEE!
AH-CHEE WONG
HAND LAUNDRY
DID YOU GET HIM?
NO!
I HAD THE WONG NUMBER!

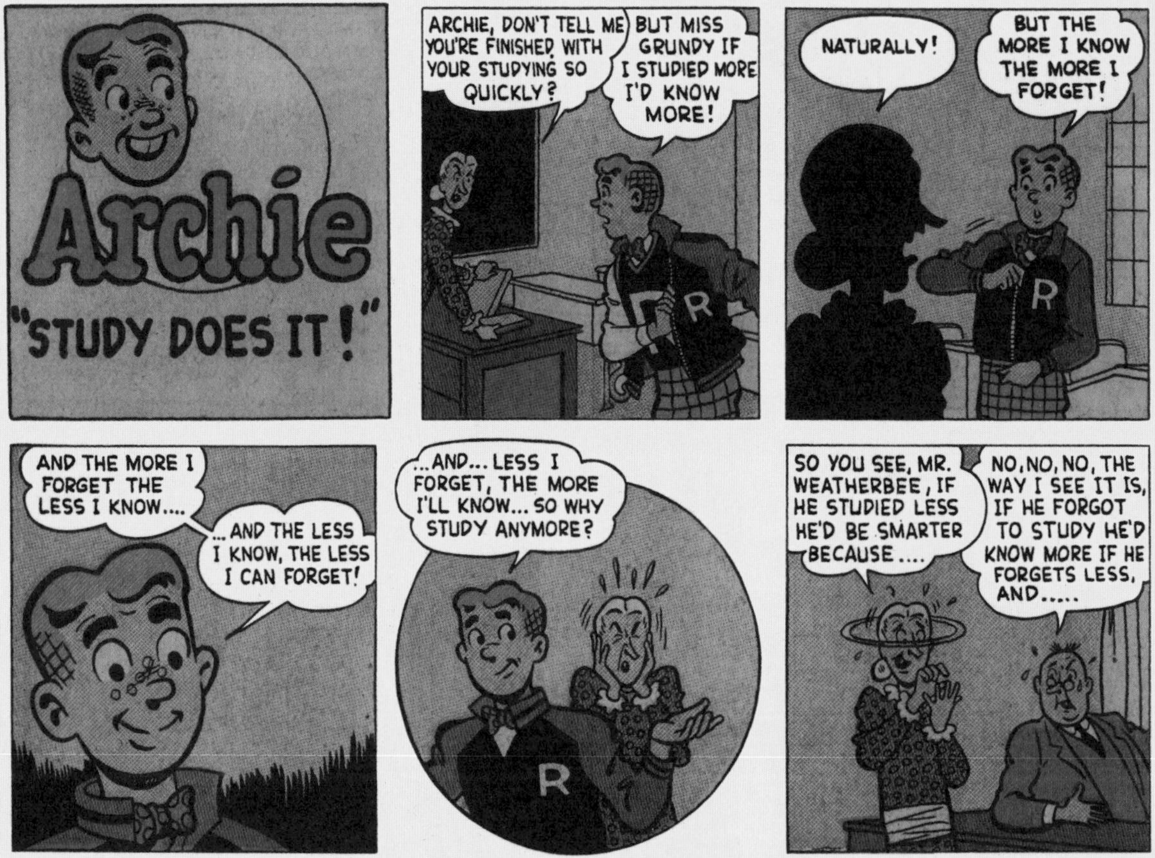
Archie
"STUDY DOES IT!"
ARCHIE, DON'T TELL ME YOU'RE FINISHED WITH YOUR STUDYING SO QUICKLY?
BUT MISS GRUNDY IF I STUDIED MORE I'D KNOW MORE!
NATURALLY!
BUT THE MORE I KNOW THE MORE I FORGET!
AND THE MORE I FORGET THE LESS I KNOW....
...AND THE LESS I KNOW, THE LESS I CAN FORGET!
...AND... LESS I FORGET, THE MORE I'LL KNOW... SO WHY STUDY ANYMORE?
SO YOU SEE, MR. WEATHERBEE, IF HE STUDIED LESS HE'D BE SMARTER BECAUSE....
NO, NO, NO, THE WAY I SEE IT IS, IF HE FORGOT TO STUDY HE'D KNOW MORE IF HE FORGETS LESS, AND.....

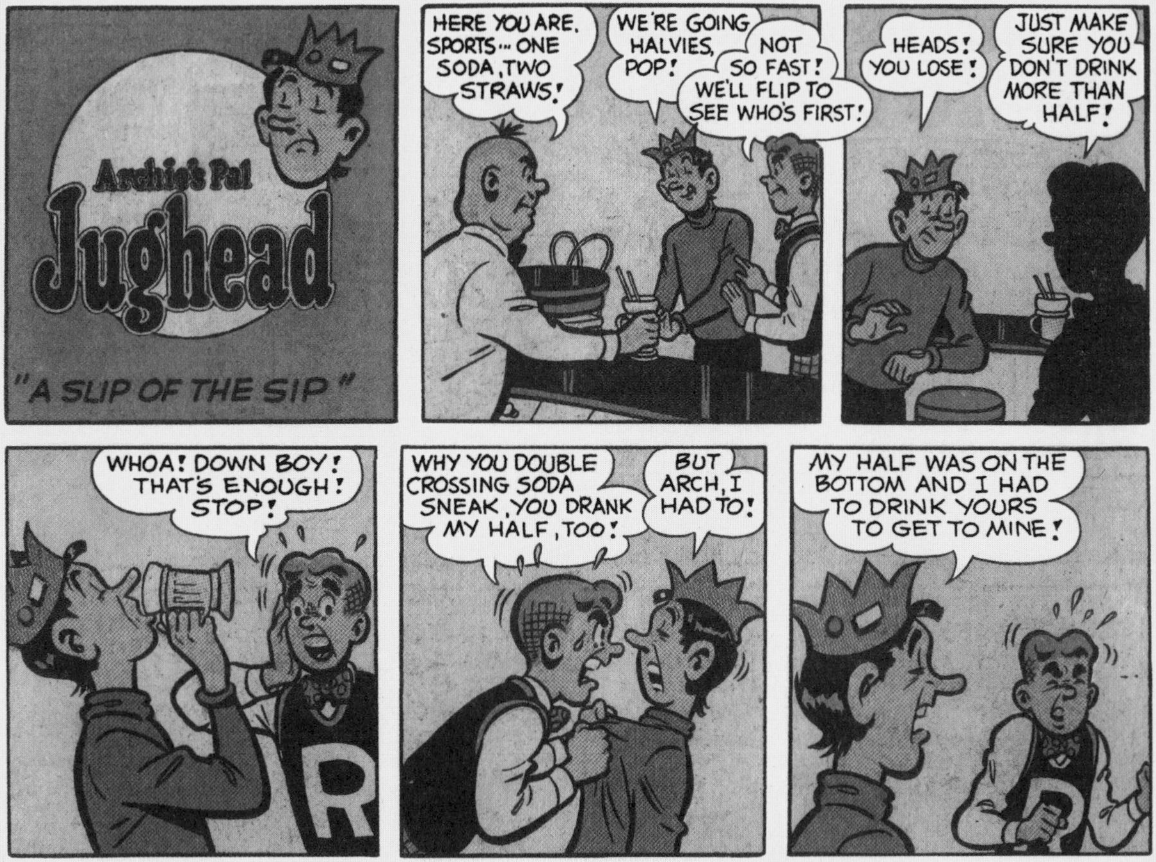
Archie's Pal
Jughead
"A SLIP OF THE SIP"
HERE YOU ARE, SPORTS... ONE SODA, TWO STRAWS!
WE'RE GOING HALVIES, POP!
NOT SO FAST! WE'LL FLIP TO SEE WHO'S FIRST!
HEADS! YOU LOSE!
JUST MAKE SURE YOU DON'T DRINK MORE THAN HALF!
WHOA! DOWN BOY! THAT'S ENOUGH! STOP!
WHY YOU DOUBLE CROSSING SODA SNEAK, YOU DRANK MY HALF, TOO!
BUT ARCH, I HAD TO!
MY HALF WAS ON THE BOTTOM AND I HAD TO DRINK YOURS TO GET TO MINE!

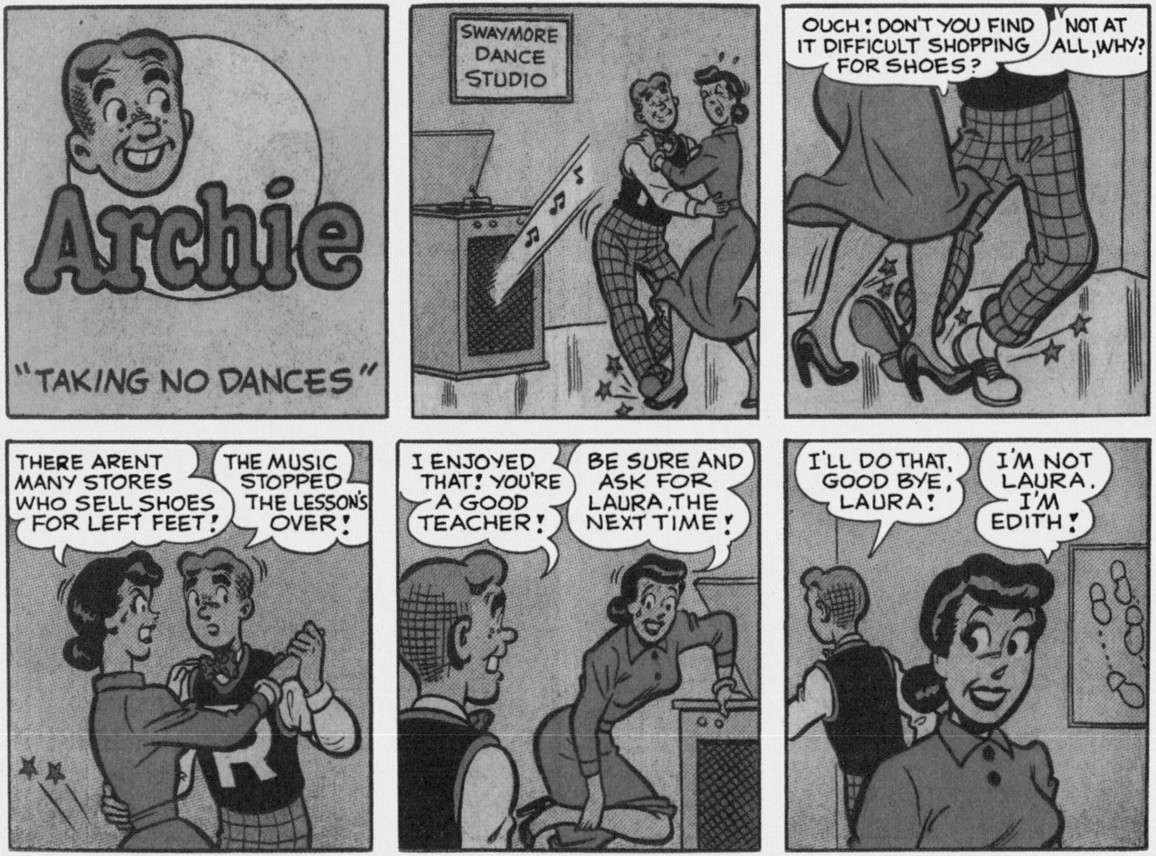
Archie
"TAKING NO DANCES"
SWAYMORE DANCE STUDIO
OUCH! DON'T YOU FIND IT DIFFICULT SHOPPING FOR SHOES?
NOT AT ALL, WHY?
THERE ARENT MANY STORES WHO SELL SHOES FOR LEFT FEET!
THE MUSIC STOPPED THE LESSON'S OVER!
I ENJOYED THAT! YOU'RE A GOOD TEACHER!
BE SURE AND ASK FOR LAURA, THE NEXT TIME!
I'LL DO THAT. GOOD BYE, LAURA!
I'M NOT LAURA. I'M EDITH!

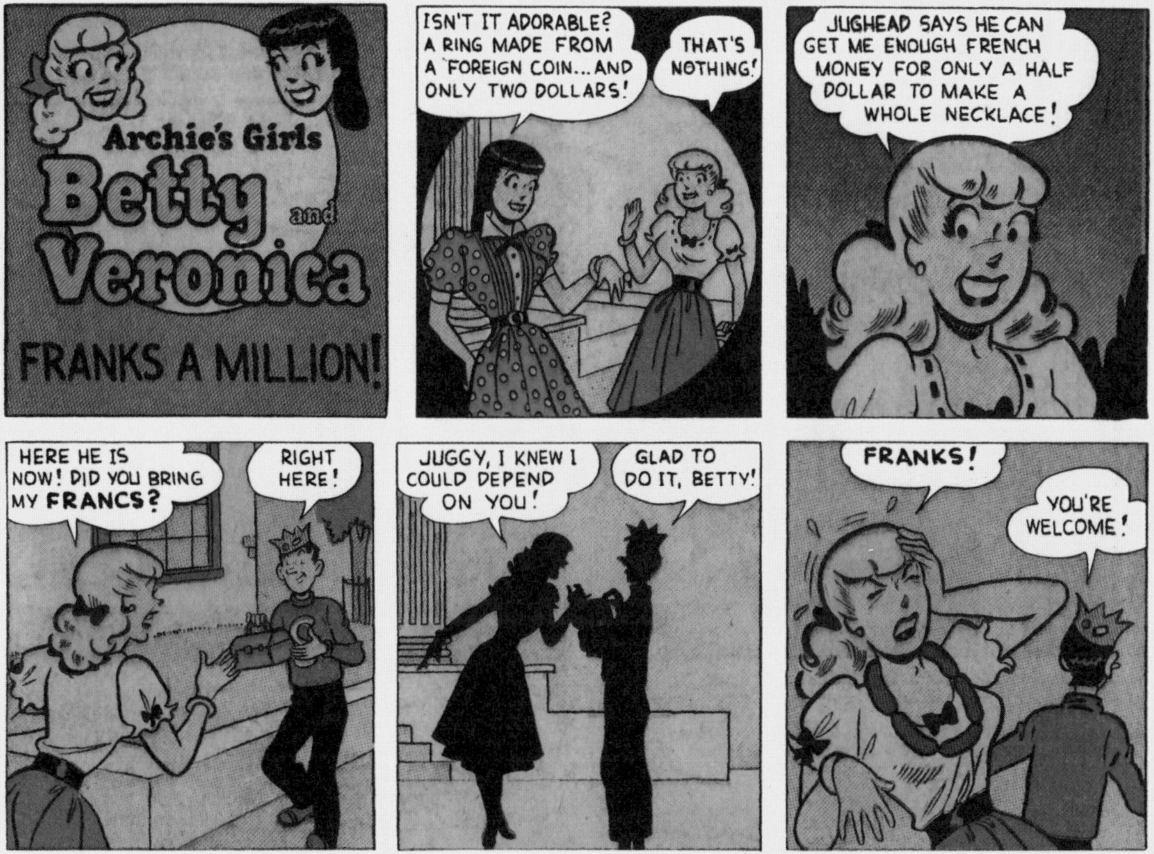
Archie's Girls
Betty and Veronica
FRANKS A MILLION!
ISN'T IT ADORABLE? A RING MADE FROM A "FOREIGN COIN... AND ONLY TWO DOLLARS!
THAT'S NOTHING!
JUGHEAD SAYS HE CAN GET ME ENOUGH FRENCH MONEY FOR ONLY A HALF DOLLAR TO MAKE A WHOLE NECKLACE!
HERE HE IS NOW! DID YOU BRING MY FRANCS?
RIGHT HERE!
JUGGY, I KNEW I COULD DEPEND ON YOU!
GLAD TO DO IT, BETTY!
FRANKS!
YOU'RE WELCOME!

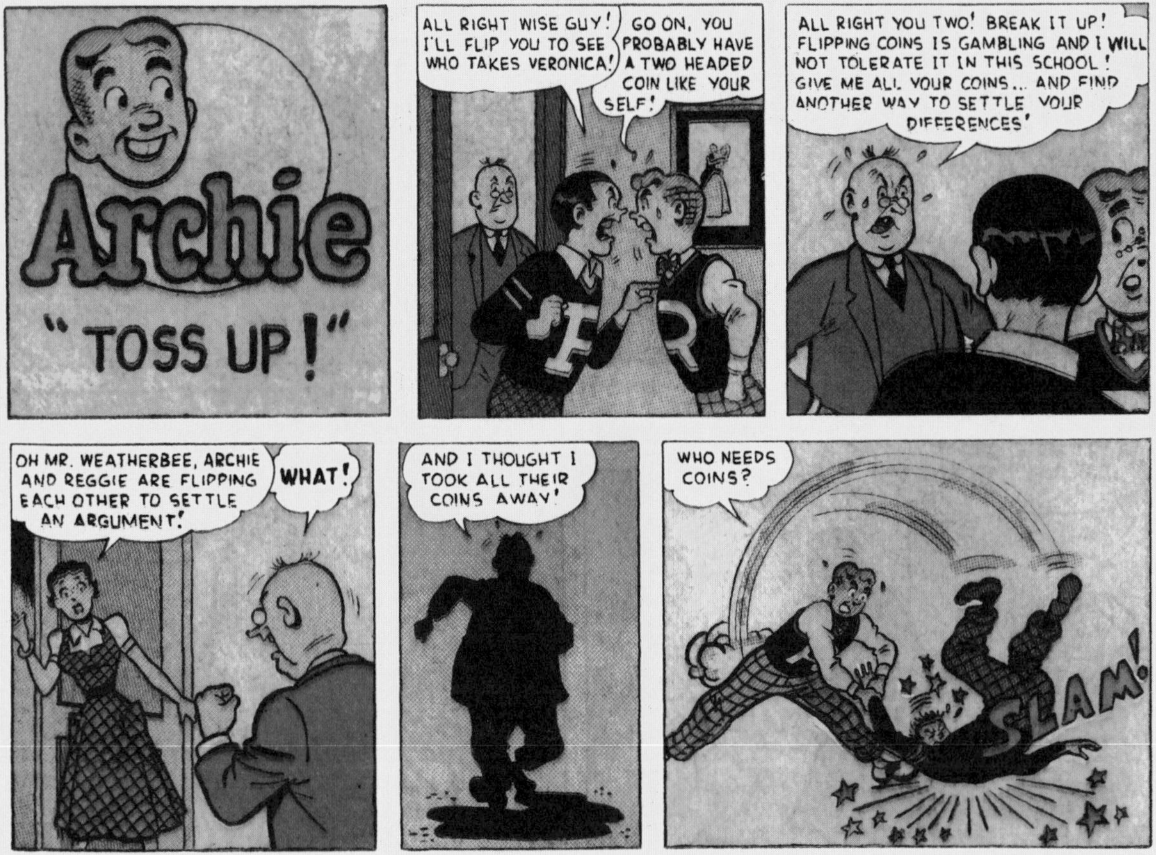
Archie
"TOSS UP!"
ALL RIGHT WISE GUY! I'LL FLIP YOU TO SEE WHO TAKES VERONICA!
GO ON, YOU PROBABLY HAVE A TWO HEADED COIN LIKE YOURSELF!
ALL RIGHT YOU TWO! BREAK IT UP! FLIPPING COINS IS GAMBLING AND I WILL NOT TOLERATE IT IN THIS SCHOOL! GIVE ME ALL YOUR COINS... AND FIND ANOTHER WAY TO SETTLE YOUR DIFFERENCES!
OH MR. WEATHERBEE, ARCHIE AND REGGIE ARE FLIPPING EACH OTHER TO SETTLE AN ARGUMENT!
WHAT!
AND I THOUGHT I TOOK ALL THEIR COINS AWAY!
WHO NEEDS COINS?
SLAM!

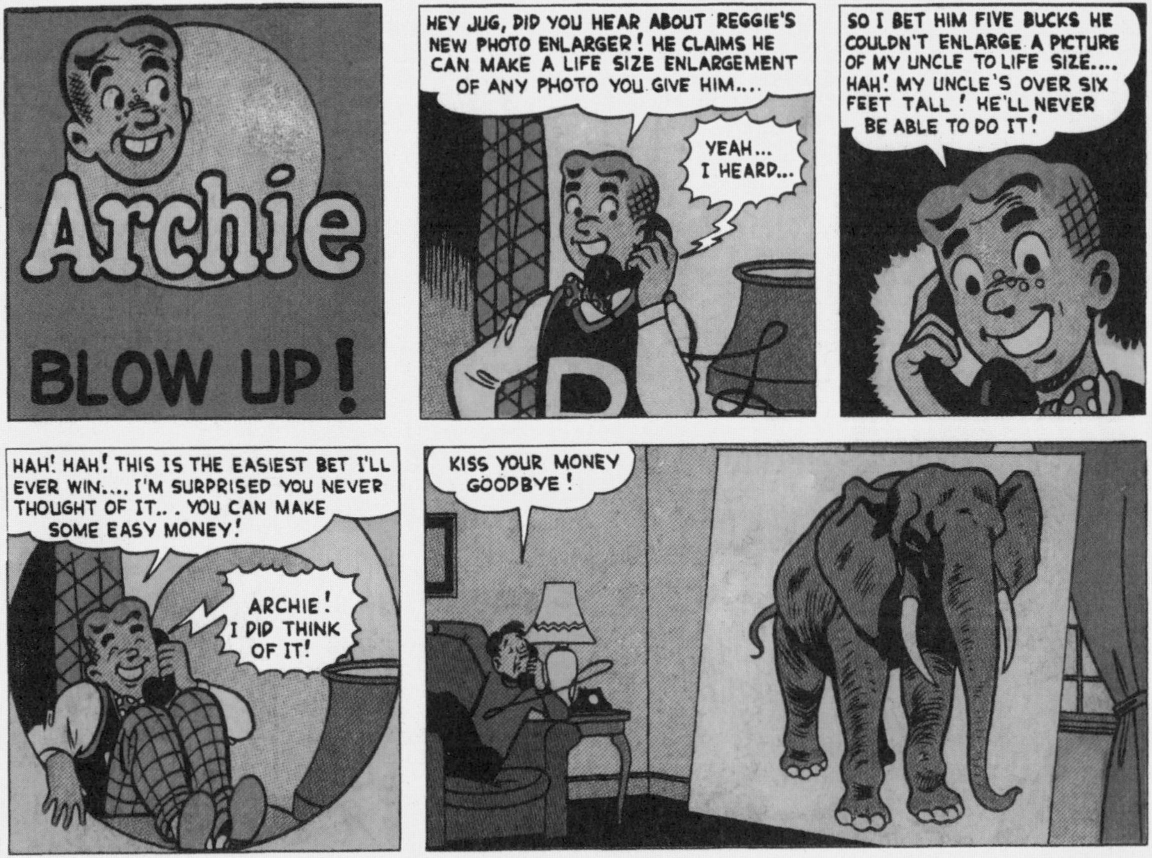

Archie
BLOW UP!
HEY JUG, DID YOU HEAR ABOUT REGGIE'S NEW PHOTO ENLARGER! HE CLAIMS HE CAN MAKE A LIFE SIZE ENLARGEMENT OF ANY PHOTO YOU GIVE HIM....
YEAH... I HEARD...
SO I BET HIM FIVE BUCKS HE COULDN'T ENLARGE A PICTURE OF MY UNCLE TO LIFE SIZE.... HAH! MY UNCLE'S OVER SIX FEET TALL! HE'LL NEVER BE ABLE TO DO IT!
HAH! HAH! THIS IS THE EASIEST BET I'LL EVER WIN.... I'M SURPRISED YOU NEVER THOUGHT OF IT... YOU CAN MAKE SOME EASY MONEY!
ARCHIE! I DID THINK OF IT!
KISS YOUR MONEY GOODBYE!

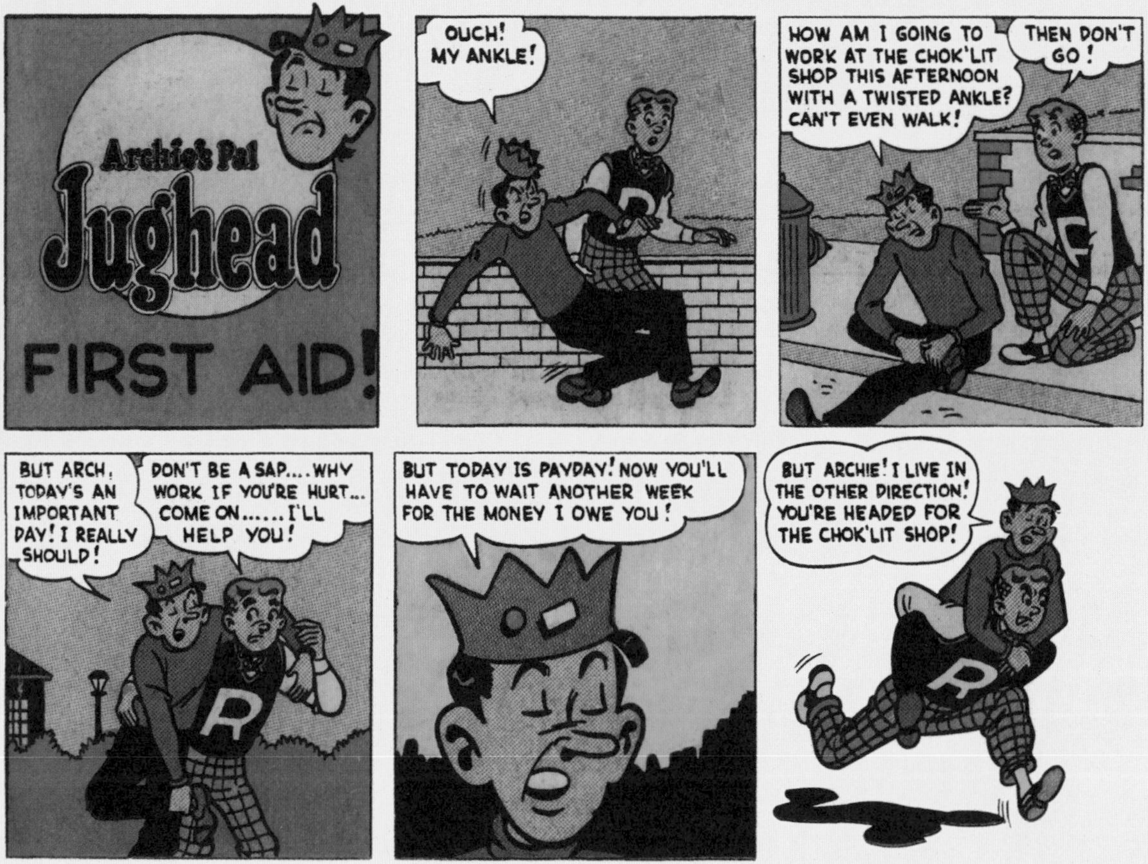
Archie's Pal
Jughead
FIRST AID!
OUCH! MY ANKLE!
HOW AM I GOING TO WORK AT THE CHOK'LIT SHOP THIS AFTERNOON WITH A TWISTED ANKLE? CAN'T EVEN WALK!
THEN DON'T GO!
BUT ARCH, TODAY'S AN IMPORTANT DAY! I REALLY SHOULD!
DON'T BE A SAP....WHY WORK IF YOU'RE HURT... COME ON......I'LL HELP YOU!
BUT TODAY IS PAYDAY! NOW YOU'LL HAVE TO WAIT ANOTHER WEEK FOR THE MONEY I OWE YOU!
BUT ARCHIE! I LIVE IN THE OTHER DIRECTION! YOU'RE HEADED FOR THE CHOK'LIT SHOP!

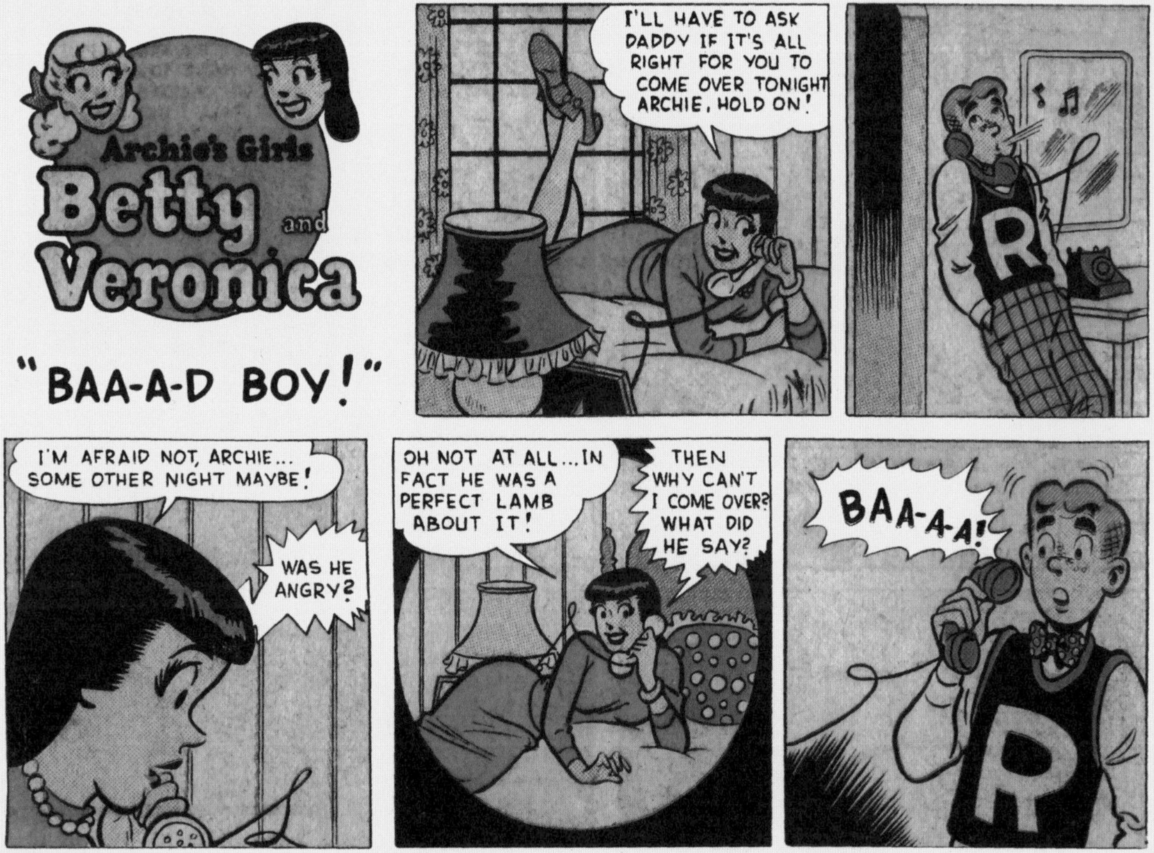
Archie's Girls
Betty and Veronica
"BAA-A-D BOY!"
I'LL HAVE TO ASK DADDY IF IT'S ALL RIGHT FOR YOU TO COME OVER TONIGHT ARCHIE, HOLD ON!
I'M AFRAID NOT, ARCHIE... SOME OTHER NIGHT MAYBE!
WAS HE ANGRY?
OH NOT AT ALL... IN FACT HE WAS A PERFECT LAMB ABOUT IT!
THEN WHY CAN'T I COME OVER? WHAT DID HE SAY?
BAA-A-A!

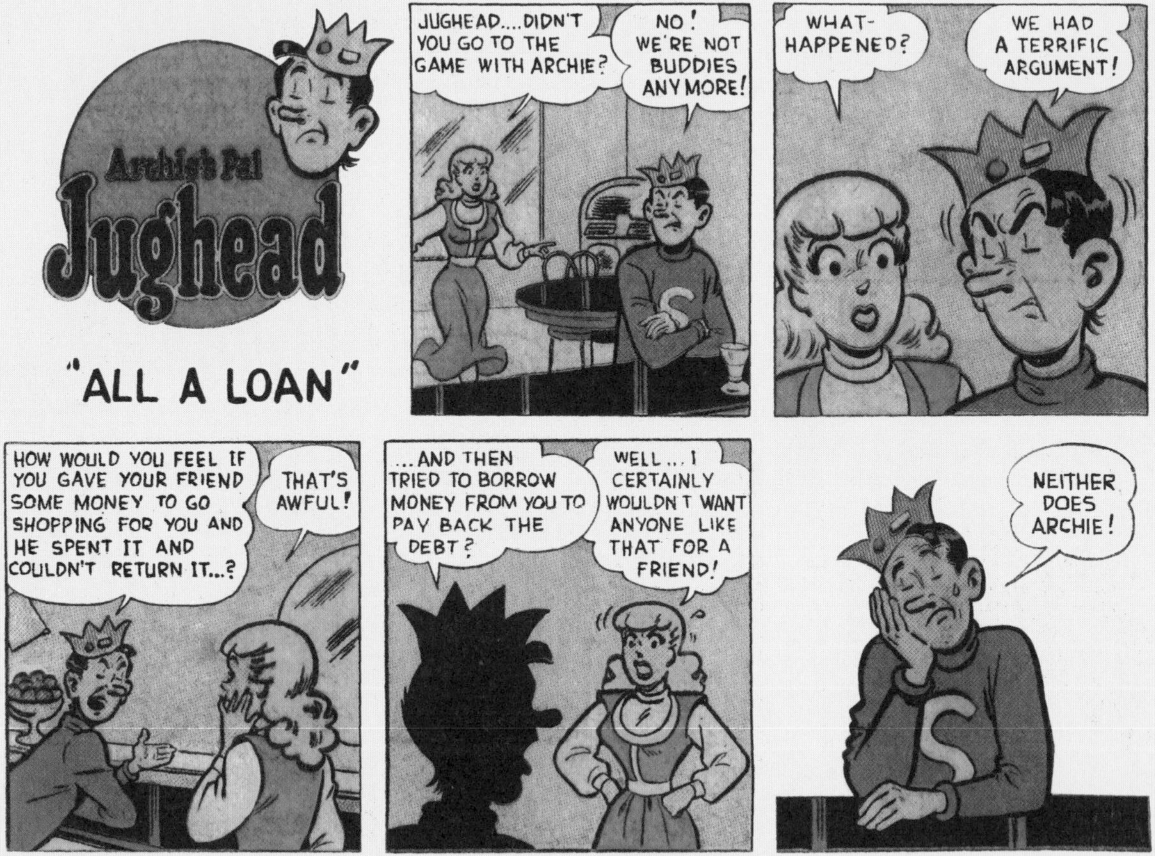
Archie's Pal
Jughead
"ALL A LOAN"
JUGHEAD....DIDN'T YOU GO TO THE GAME WITH ARCHIE?
NO! WE'RE NOT BUDDIES ANYMORE!
WHAT-HAPPENED?
WE HAD A TERRIFIC ARGUMENT!
HOW WOULD YOU FEEL IF YOU GAVE YOUR FRIEND SOME MONEY TO GO SHOPPING FOR YOU AND HE SPENT IT AND COULDN'T RETURN IT...?
THAT'S AWFUL!
...AND THEN TRIED TO BORROW MONEY FROM YOU TO PAY BACK THE DEBT?
WELL... I CERTAINLY WOULDN'T WANT ANYONE LIKE THAT FOR A FRIEND!
NEITHER DOES ARCHIE!

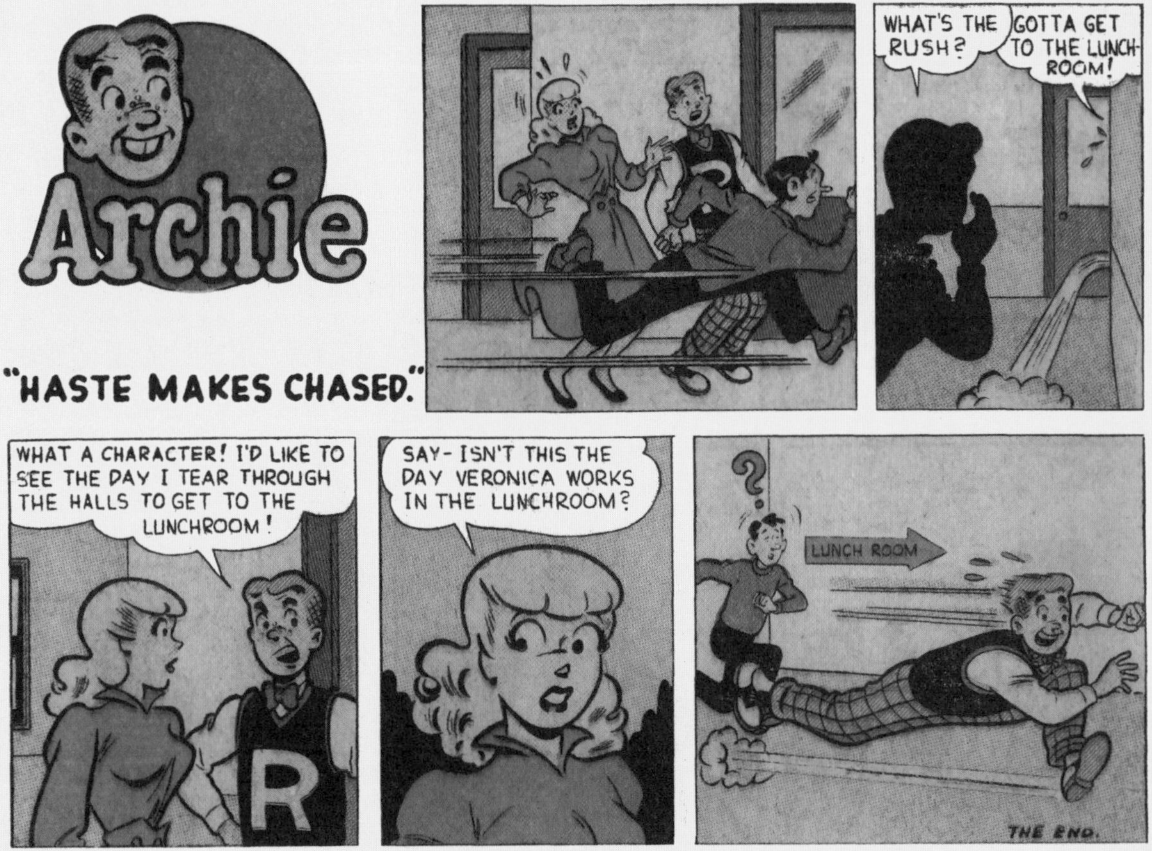
Archie
"HASTE MAKES CHASED."
WHAT'S THE RUSH?
GOTTA GET TO THE LUNCH-ROOM!
WHAT A CHARACTER! I'D LIKE TO SEE THE DAY I TEAR THROUGH THE HALLS TO GET TO THE LUNCHROOM!
R
SAY- ISN'T THIS THE DAY VERONICA WORKS IN THE LUNCHROOM?
?
LUNCH ROOM
THE END.

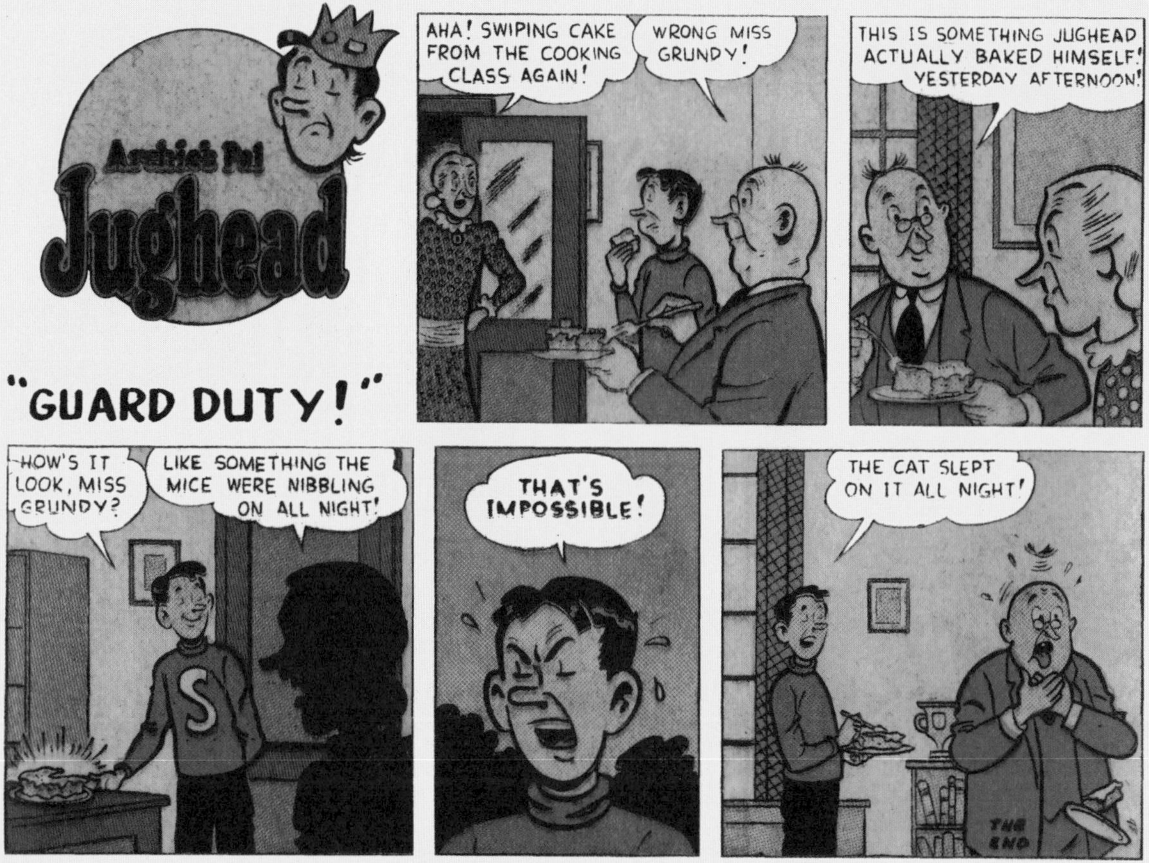
Archie's Pal
Jughead
"GUARD DUTY!"
AHA! SWIPING CAKE FROM THE COOKING CLASS AGAIN!
WRONG MISS GRUNDY!
THIS IS SOMETHING JUGHEAD ACTUALLY BAKED HIMSELF! YESTERDAY AFTERNOON!
HOW'S IT LOOK, MISS GRUNDY?
LIKE SOMETHING THE MICE WERE NIBBLING ON ALL NIGHT!
THAT'S IMPOSSIBLE!
THE CAT SLEPT ON IT ALL NIGHT!
THE END

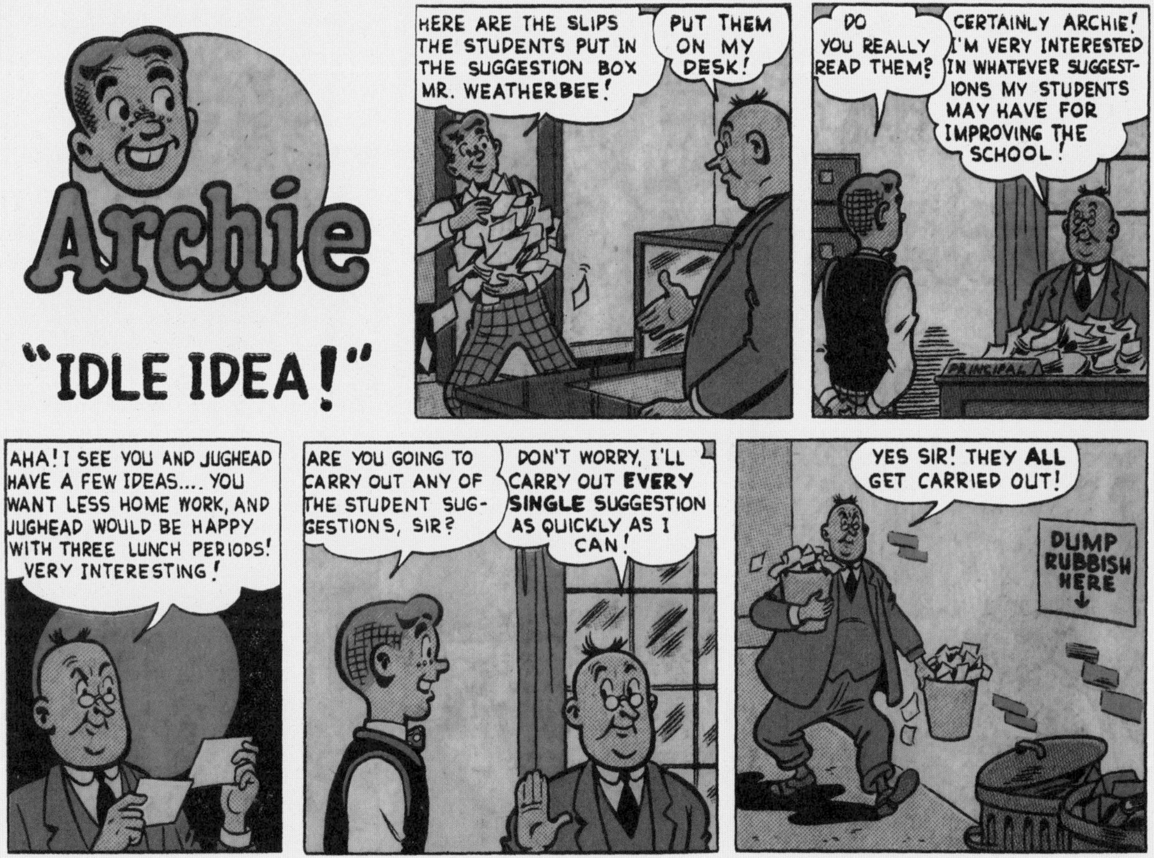
Archie
"IDLE IDEA!"
HERE ARE THE SLIPS THE STUDENTS PUT IN THE SUGGESTION BOX MR. WEATHERBEE!
PUT THEM ON MY DESK!
DO YOU REALLY READ THEM?
CERTAINLY ARCHIE! I'M VERY INTERESTED IN WHATEVER SUGGESTIONS MY STUDENTS MAY HAVE FOR IMPROVING THE SCHOOL!
PRINCIPAL
AHA! I SEE YOU AND JUGHEAD HAVE A FEW IDEAS.... YOU WANT LESS HOME WORK, AND JUGHEAD WOULD BE HAPPY WITH THREE LUNCH PERIODS! VERY INTERESTING!
ARE YOU GOING TO CARRY OUT ANY OF THE STUDENT SUGGESTIONS, SIR?
DON'T WORRY, I'LL CARRY OUT EVERY SINGLE SUGGESTION AS QUICKLY AS I CAN!
YES SIR! THEY ALL GET CARRIED OUT!
DUMP RUBBISH HERE

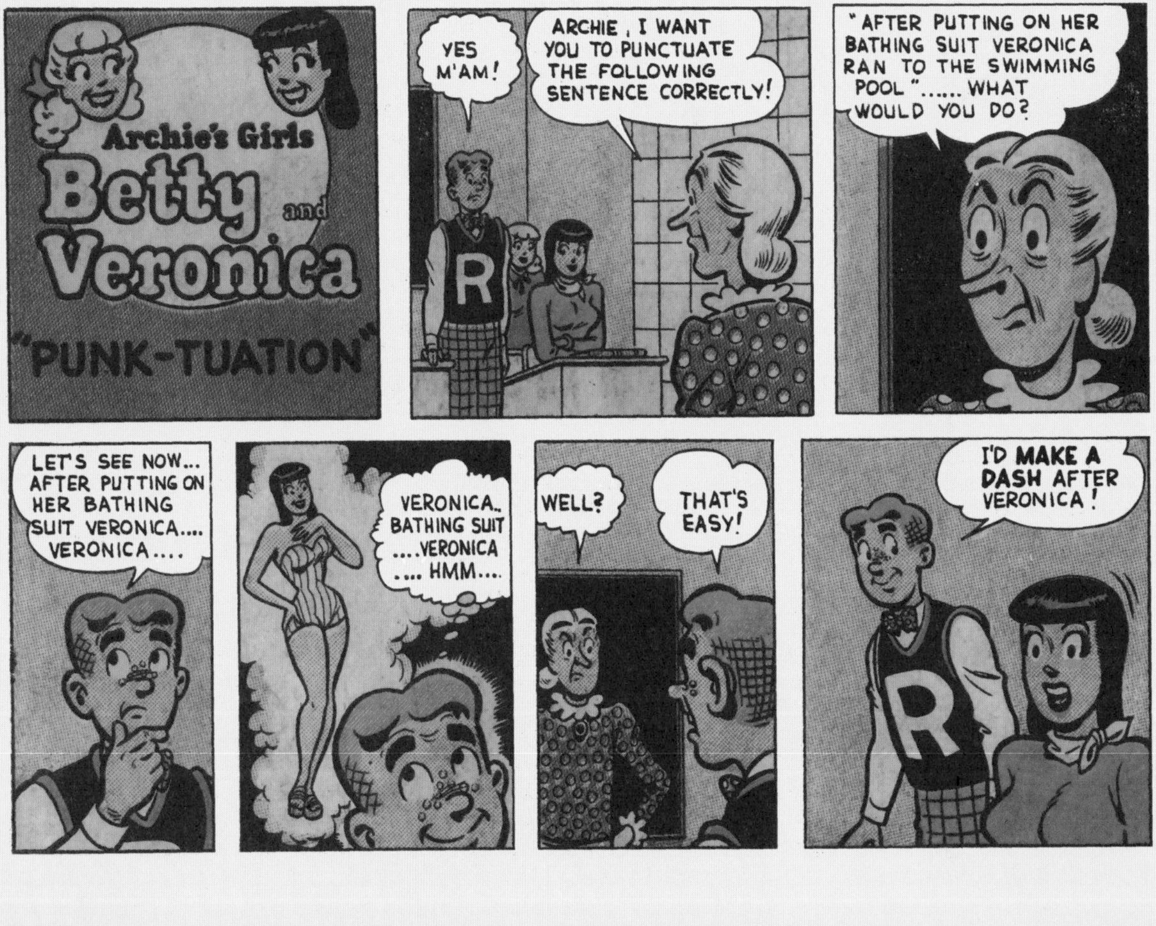
Archie's Girls
Betty and Veronica
"PUNK-TUATION"
YES M'AM!
ARCHIE, I WANT YOU TO PUNCTUATE THE FOLLOWING SENTENCE CORRECTLY!
"AFTER PUTTING ON HER BATHING SUIT VERONICA RAN TO THE SWIMMING POOL"...... WHAT WOULD YOU DO?
LET'S SEE NOW... AFTER PUTTING ON HER BATHING SUIT VERONICA.... VERONICA....
VERONICA.. BATHING SUIT ....VERONICA .... HMM....
WELL?
THAT'S EASY!
I'D MAKE A DASH AFTER VERONICA!

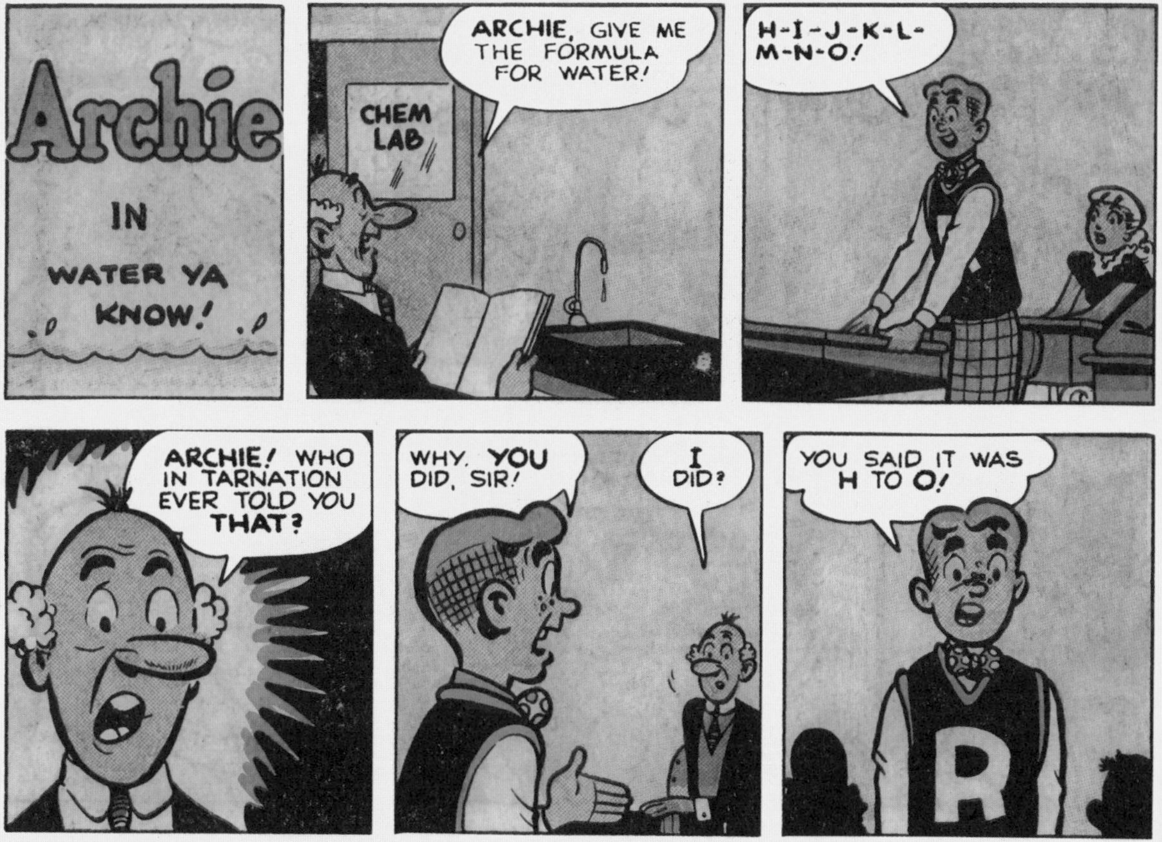
Archie
IN
WATER YA
KNOW!
CHEM
LAB
ARCHIE, GIVE ME THE FORMULA FOR WATER!
H-I-J-K-L-M-N-O!
ARCHIE! WHO IN TARNATION EVER TOLD YOU THAT?
WHY, YOU DID, SIR!
I DID?
YOU SAID IT WAS H TO O!

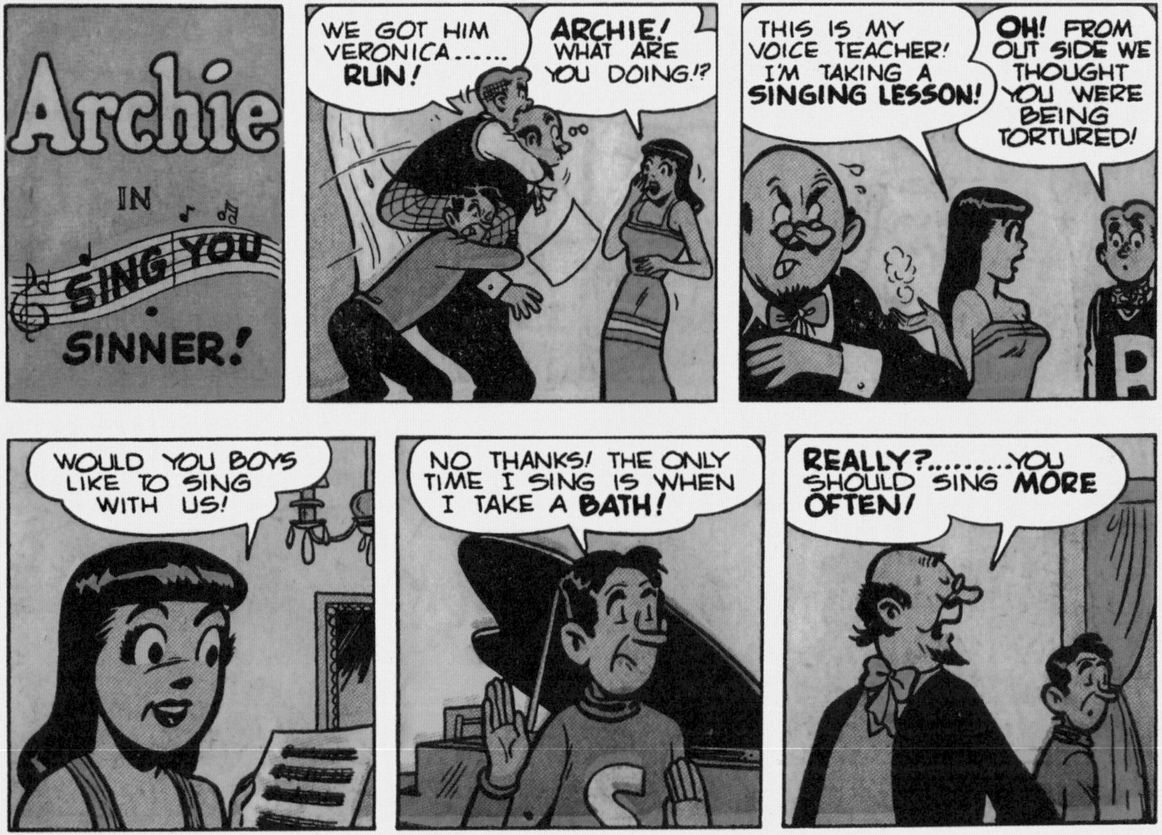
Archie
IN
SING YOU SINNER!
WE GOT HIM VERONICA...... RUN!
ARCHIE! WHAT ARE YOU DOING!?
THIS IS MY VOICE TEACHER! I'M TAKING A SINGING LESSON!
OH! FROM OUT SIDE WE THOUGHT YOU WERE BEING TORTURED!
WOULD YOU BOYS LIKE TO SING WITH US!
NO THANKS! THE ONLY TIME I SING IS WHEN I TAKE A BATH!
REALLY?........YOU SHOULD SING MORE OFTEN!

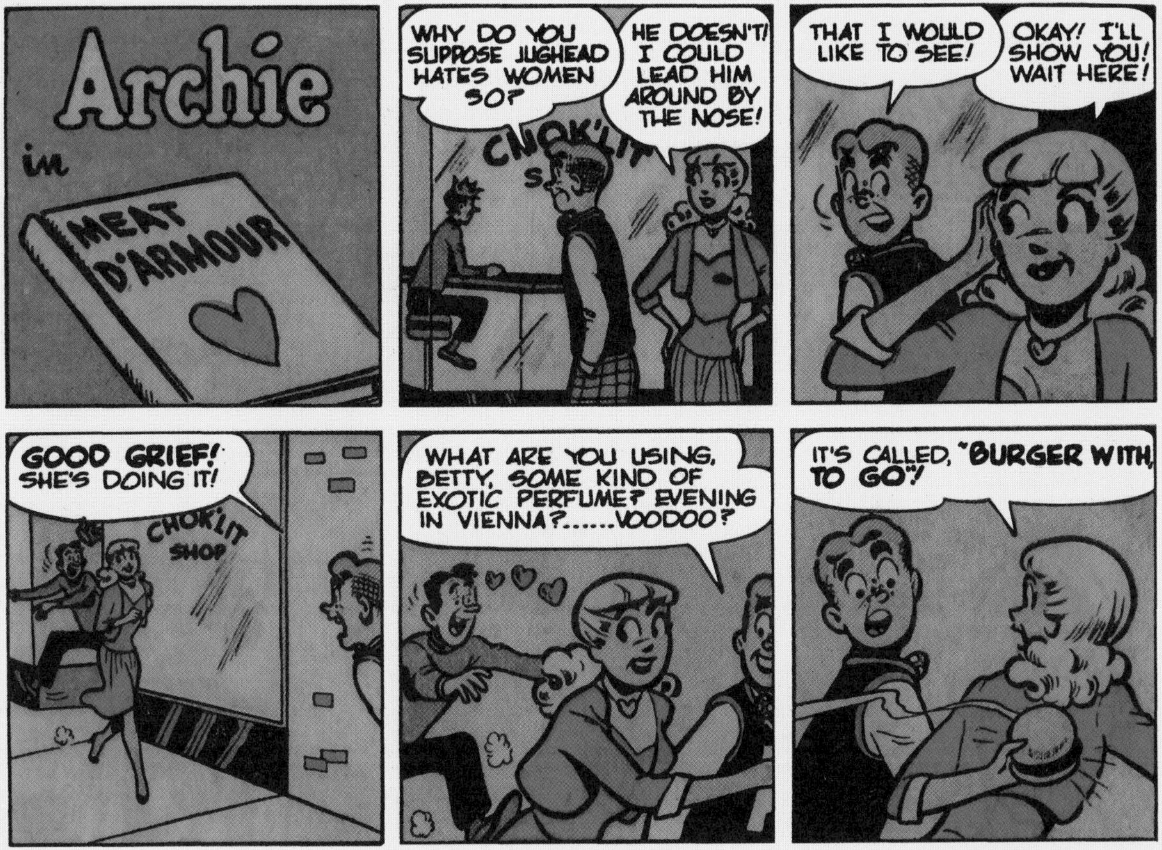
Archie
in
MEAT D'ARMOUR
WHY DO YOU SUPPOSE JUGHEAD HATES WOMEN SO?
HE DOESN'T! I COULD LEAD HIM AROUND BY THE NOSE!
CHOK'LIT S
THAT I WOULD LIKE TO SEE!
OKAY! I'LL SHOW YOU! WAIT HERE!
GOOD GRIEF! SHE'S DOING IT!
CHOK'LIT SHOP
WHAT ARE YOU USING, BETTY, SOME KIND OF EXOTIC PERFUME? EVENING IN VIENNA?......VOODOO?
IT'S CALLED, "BURGER WITH, TO GO"!

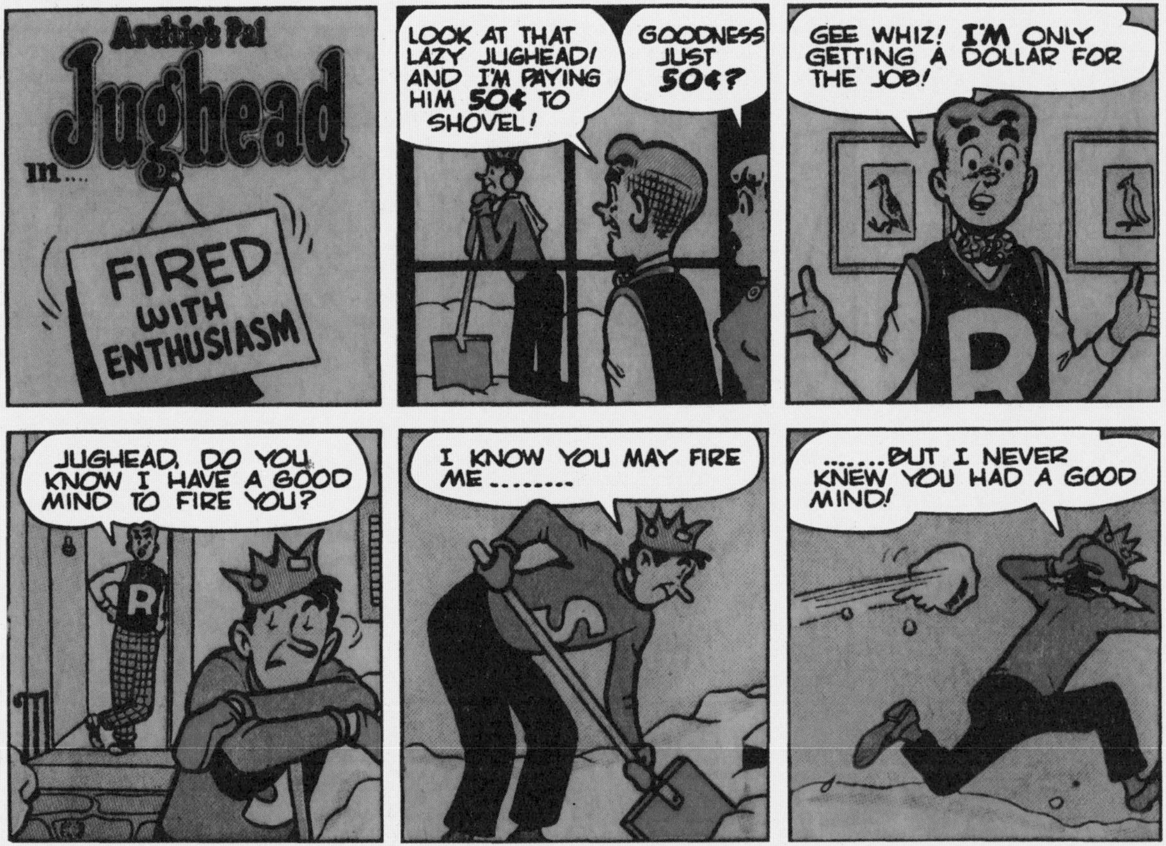
Archie's Pal
Jughead
in....
FIRED WITH ENTHUSIASM
LOOK AT THAT LAZY JUGHEAD! AND I'M PAYING HIM 50¢ TO SHOVEL!
GOODNESS JUST 50¢?
GEE WHIZ! I'M ONLY GETTING A DOLLAR FOR THE JOB!
JUGHEAD, DO YOU KNOW I HAVE A GOOD MIND TO FIRE YOU?
I KNOW YOU MAY FIRE ME ....
.......BUT I NEVER KNEW YOU HAD A GOOD MIND!

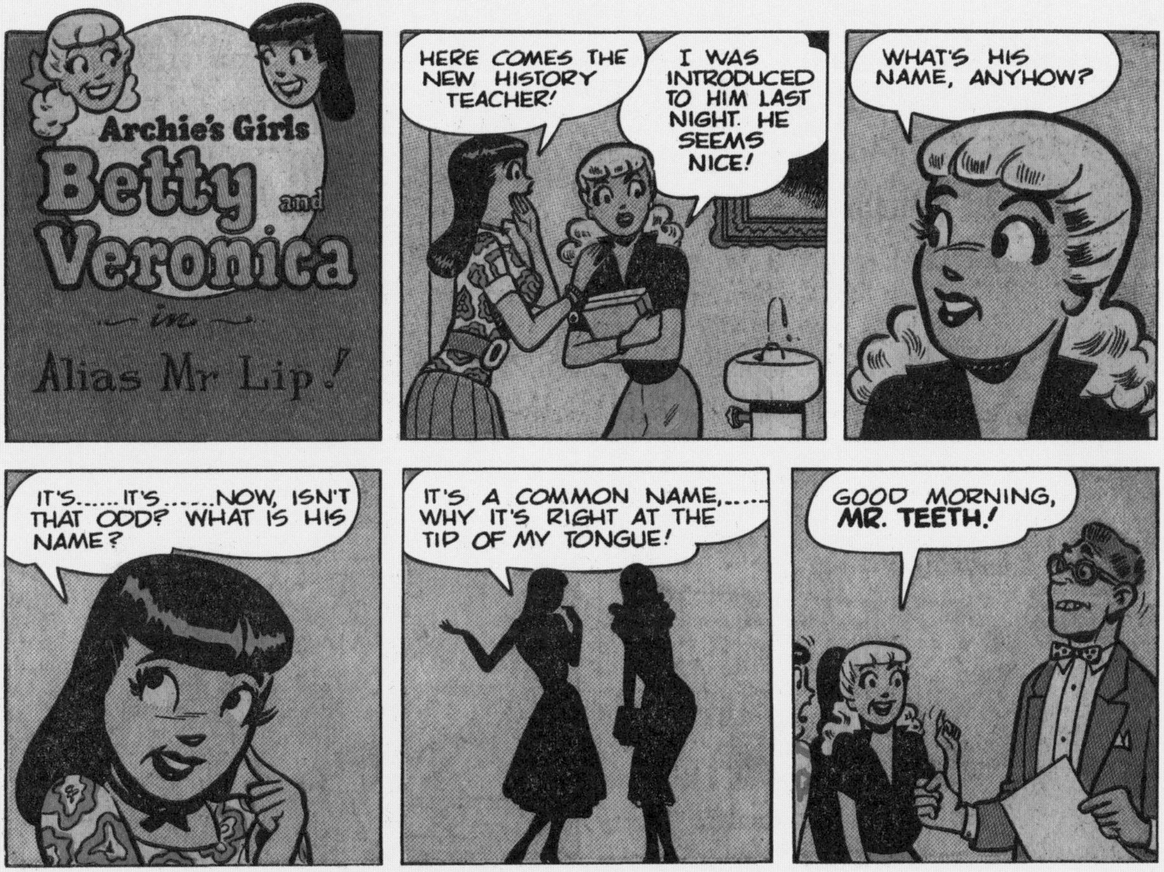
Archie's Girls
Betty and Veronica
in
Alias Mr Lip!
HERE COMES THE NEW HISTORY TEACHER!
I WAS INTRODUCED TO HIM LAST NIGHT. HE SEEMS NICE!
WHAT'S HIS NAME, ANYHOW?
IT'S......IT'S......NOW, ISN'T THAT ODD? WHAT IS HIS NAME?
IT'S A COMMON NAME,...... WHY IT'S RIGHT AT THE TIP OF MY TONGUE!
GOOD MORNING, MR. TEETH!

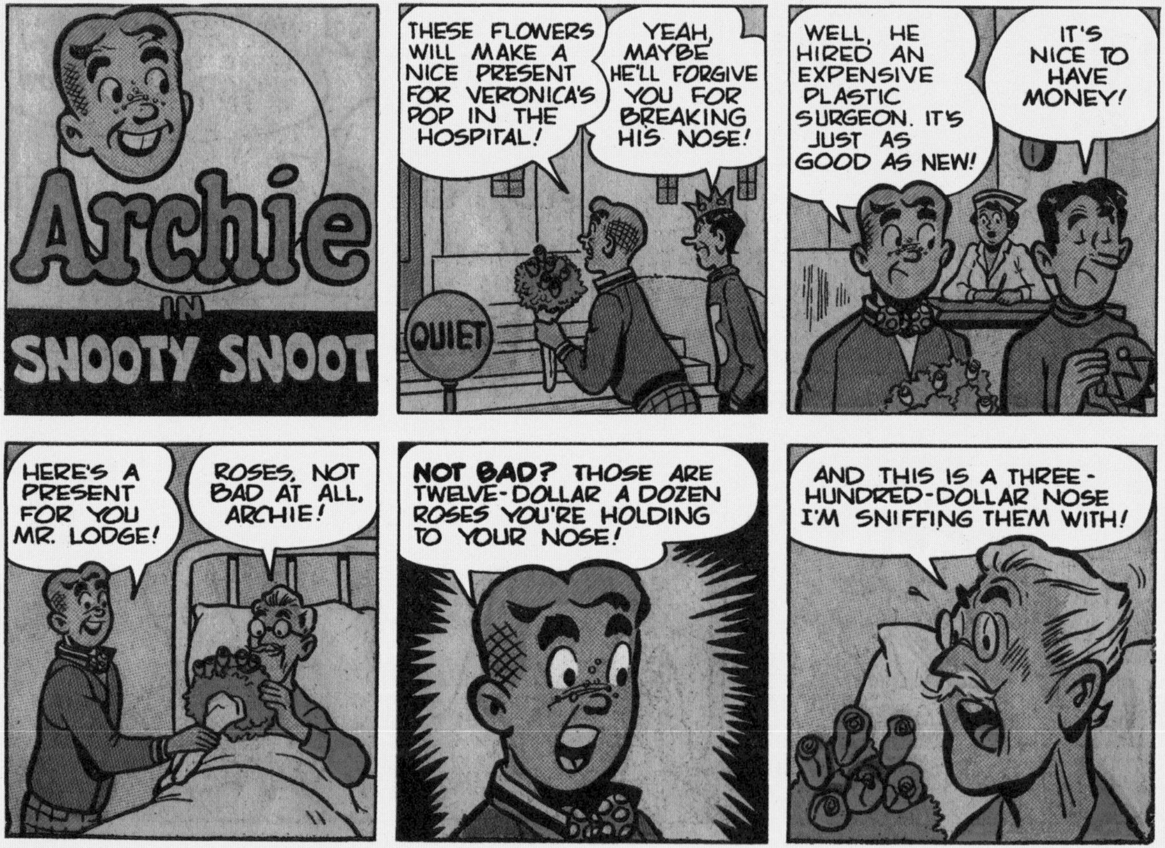
Archie
IN
SNOOTY SNOOT
THESE FLOWERS WILL MAKE A NICE PRESENT FOR VERONICA'S POP IN THE HOSPITAL!
YEAH, MAYBE HE'LL FORGIVE YOU FOR BREAKING HIS NOSE!
QUIET
WELL, HE HIRED AN EXPENSIVE PLASTIC SURGEON. IT'S JUST AS GOOD AS NEW!
IT'S NICE TO HAVE MONEY!
HERE'S A PRESENT FOR YOU MR. LODGE!
ROSES, NOT BAD AT ALL, ARCHIE!
NOT BAD? THOSE ARE TWELVE-DOLLAR A DOZEN ROSES YOU'RE HOLDING TO YOUR NOSE!
AND THIS IS A THREE-HUNDRED-DOLLAR NOSE I'M SNIFFING THEM WITH!

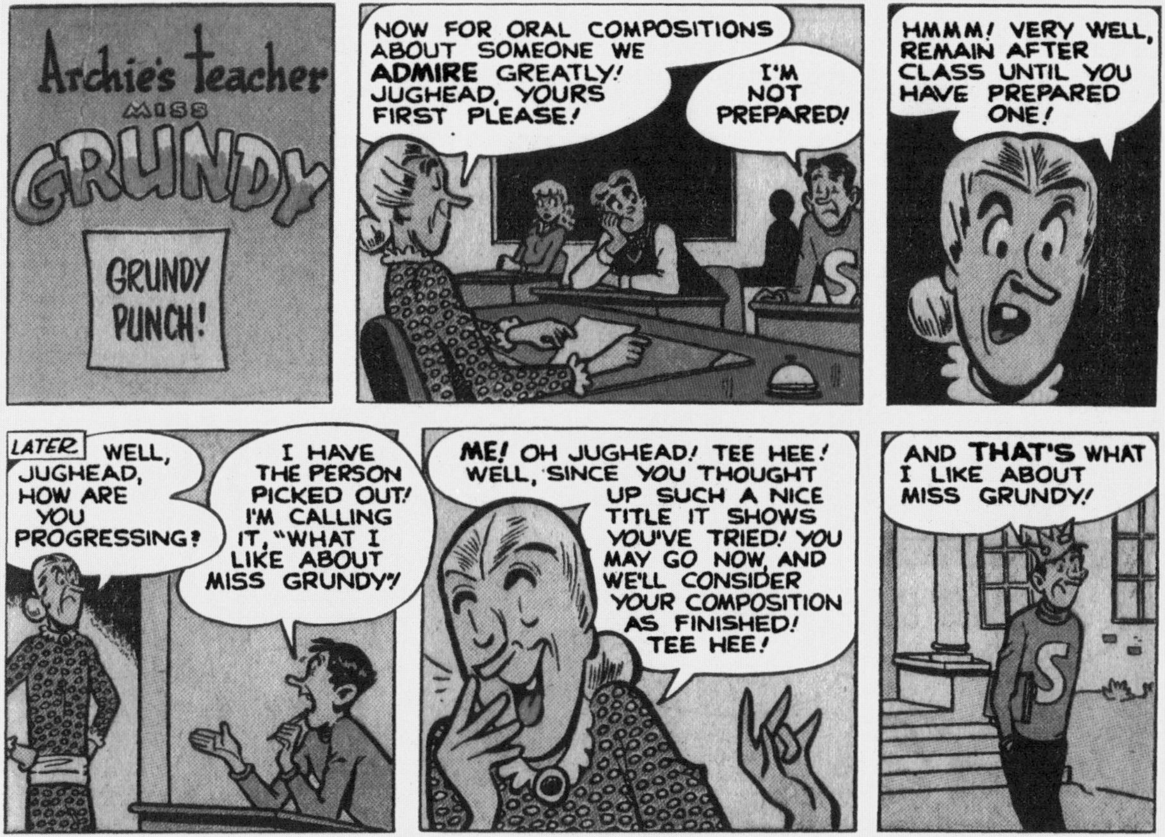
Archie's teacher MISS GRUNDY
GRUNDY PUNCH!
NOW FOR ORAL COMPOSITIONS ABOUT SOMEONE WE ADMIRE GREATLY! JUGHEAD, YOURS FIRST PLEASE!
I'M NOT PREPARED!
HMMM! VERY WELL, REMAIN AFTER CLASS UNTIL YOU HAVE PREPARED ONE!
LATER
WELL, JUGHEAD, HOW ARE YOU PROGRESSING?
I HAVE THE PERSON PICKED OUT! I'M CALLING IT, "WHAT I LIKE ABOUT MISS GRUNDY"!
ME! OH JUGHEAD! TEE HEE! WELL, SINCE YOU THOUGHT UP SUCH A NICE TITLE IT SHOWS YOU'VE TRIED! YOU MAY GO NOW, AND WE'LL CONSIDER YOUR COMPOSITION AS FINISHED! TEE HEE!
AND THAT'S WHAT I LIKE ABOUT MISS GRUNDY!

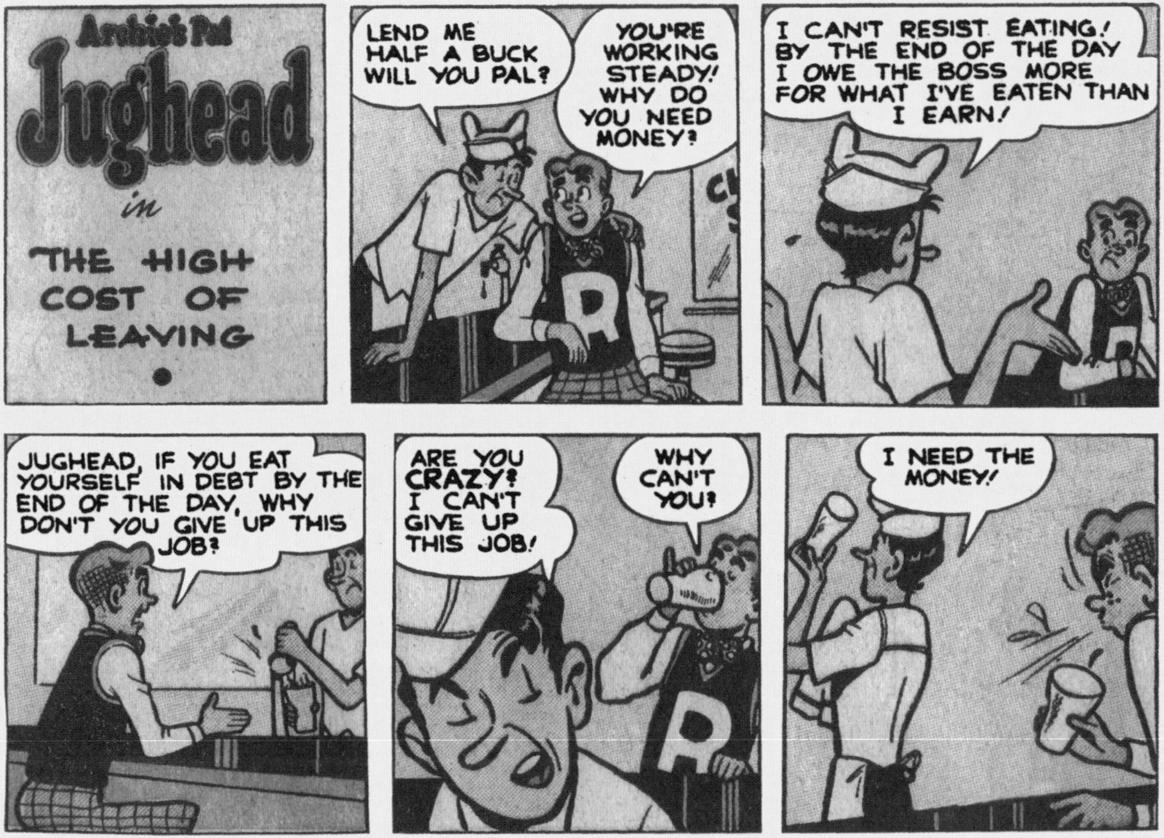
Archie's Pal
Jughead
in
THE HIGH COST OF LEAVING
LEND ME HALF A BUCK WILL YOU PAL?
YOU'RE WORKING STEADY! WHY DO YOU NEED MONEY?
I CAN'T RESIST EATING! BY THE END OF THE DAY I OWE THE BOSS MORE FOR WHAT I'VE EATEN THAN I EARN!
JUGHEAD, IF YOU EAT YOURSELF IN DEBT BY THE END OF THE DAY, WHY DON'T YOU GIVE UP THIS JOB?
ARE YOU CRAZY? I CAN'T GIVE UP THIS JOB!
WHY CAN'T YOU?
I NEED THE MONEY!

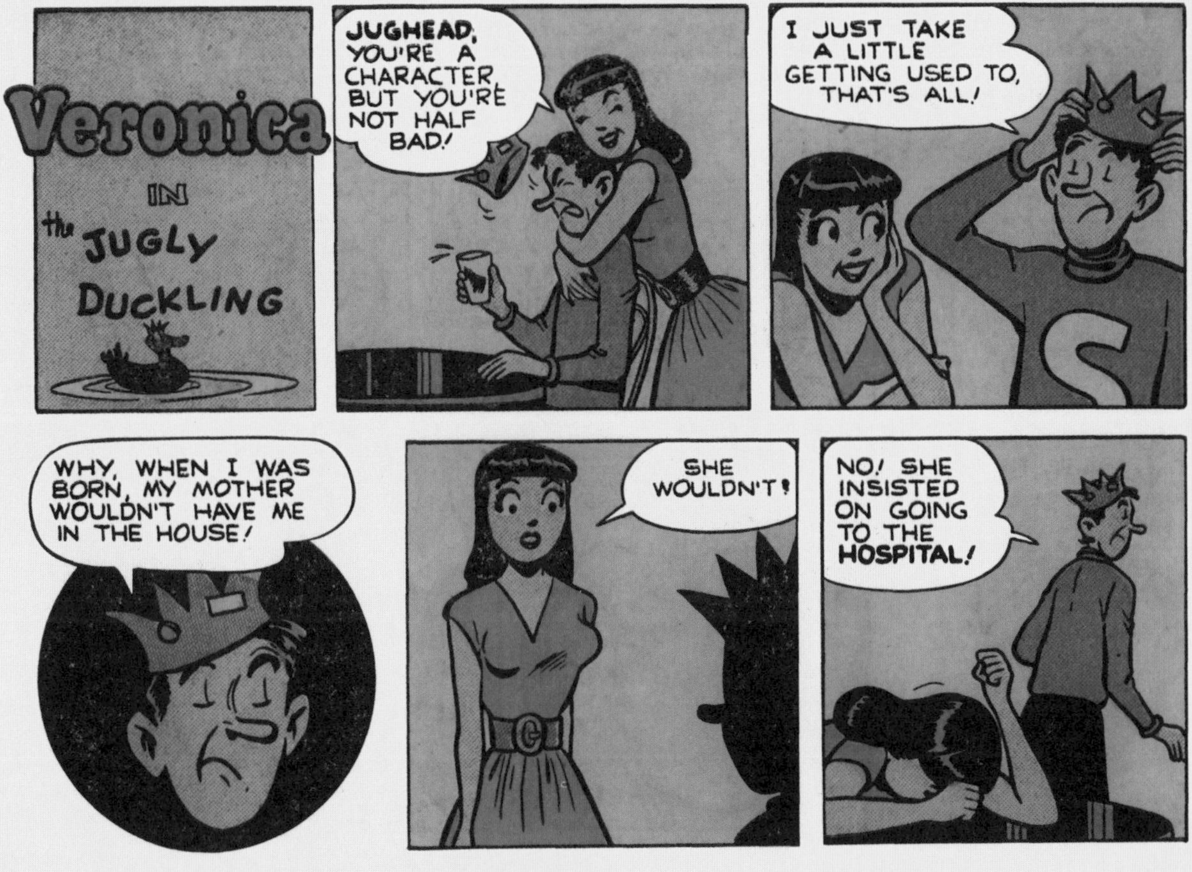
Veronica
IN
the JUGLY DUCKLING
JUGHEAD, YOU'RE A CHARACTER, BUT YOU'RE NOT HALF BAD!
I JUST TAKE A LITTLE GETTING USED TO, THAT'S ALL!
WHY, WHEN I WAS BORN, MY MOTHER WOULDN'T HAVE ME IN THE HOUSE!
SHE WOULDN'T!
NO! SHE INSISTED ON GOING TO THE HOSPITAL!

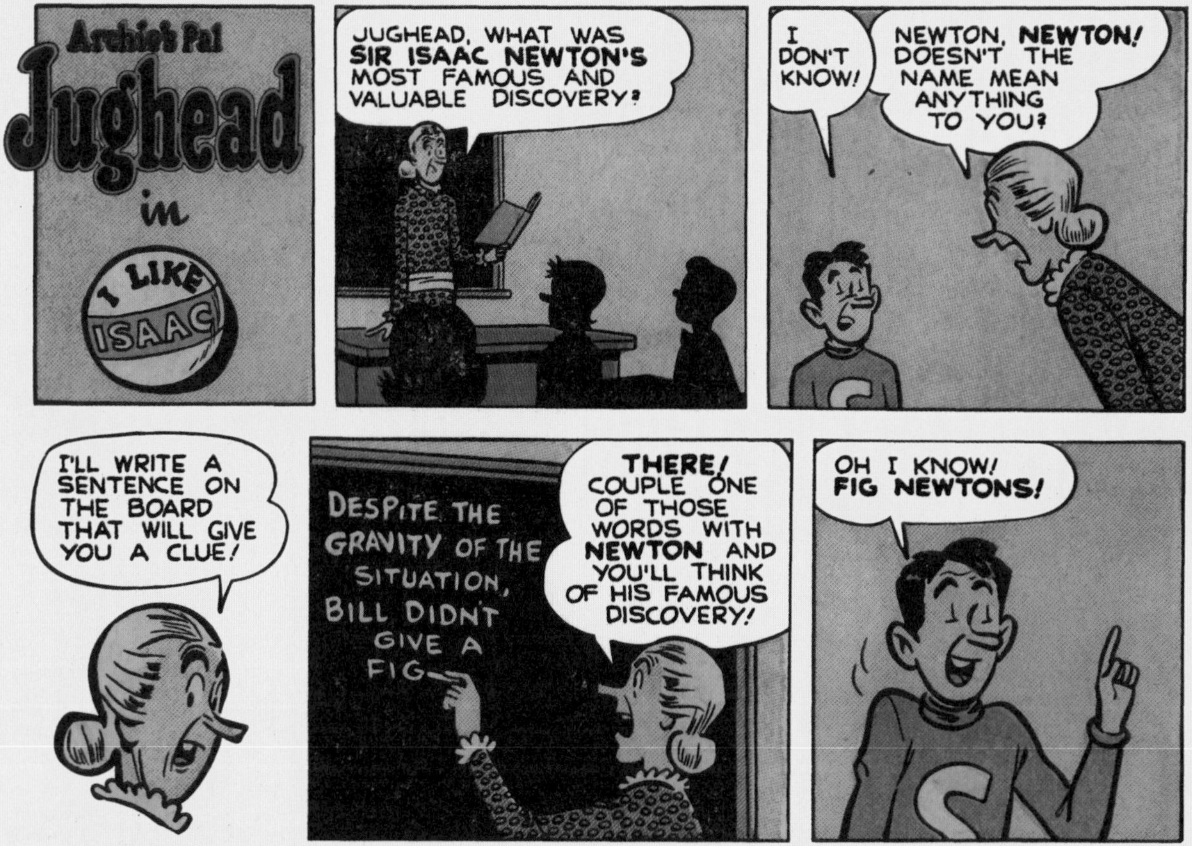
Archie's Pal
Jughead
in
I LIKE ISAAC
JUGHEAD, WHAT WAS **SIR ISAAC NEWTON'S** MOST FAMOUS AND VALUABLE DISCOVERY?
I DON'T KNOW!
NEWTON, **NEWTON!** DOESN'T THE NAME MEAN ANYTHING TO YOU?
I'LL WRITE A SENTENCE ON THE BOARD THAT WILL GIVE YOU A CLUE!
DESPITE THE GRAVITY OF THE SITUATION, BILL DIDN'T GIVE A FIG.
THERE! COUPLE ONE OF THOSE WORDS WITH **NEWTON** AND YOU'LL THINK OF HIS FAMOUS DISCOVERY!
OH I KNOW! **FIG NEWTONS!**

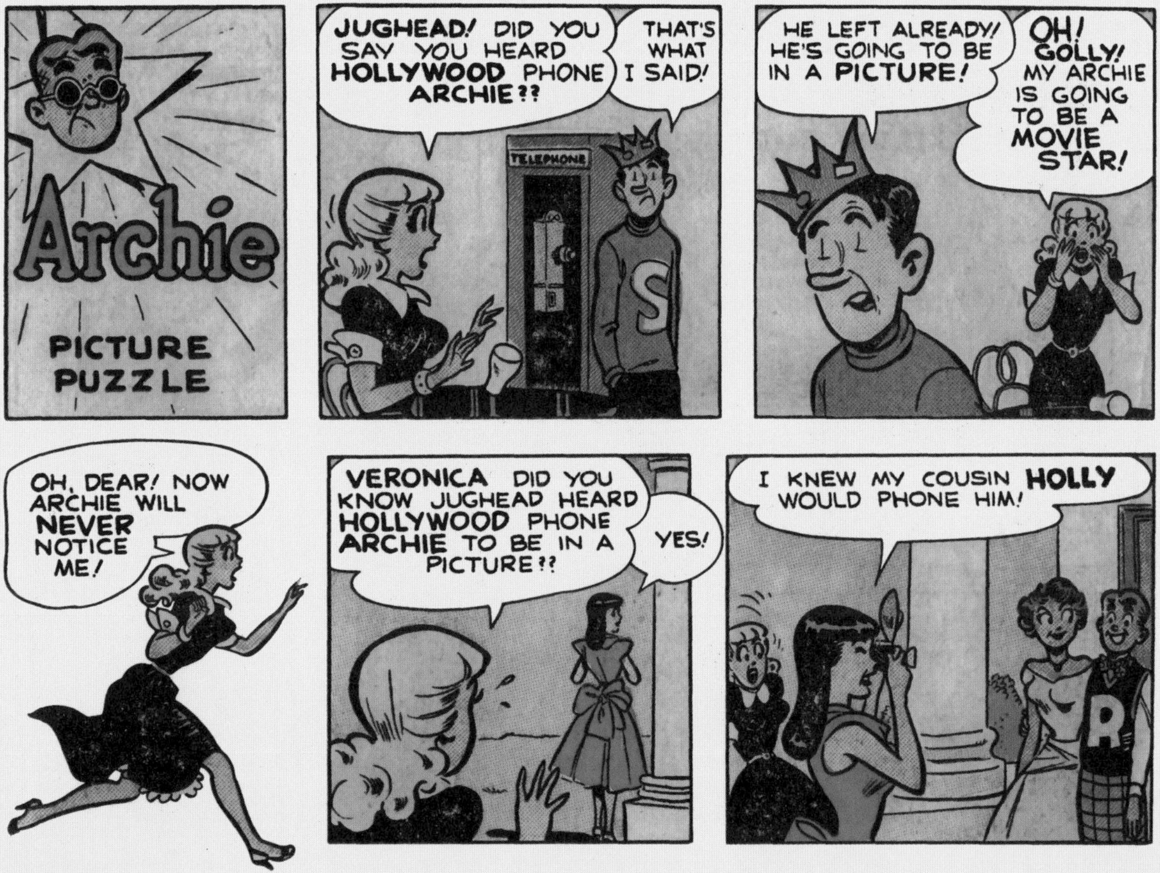
Archie
PICTURE PUZZLE
JUGHEAD! DID YOU SAY YOU HEARD HOLLYWOOD PHONE ARCHIE??
THAT'S WHAT I SAID!
TELEPHONE
HE LEFT ALREADY! HE'S GOING TO BE IN A PICTURE!
OH! GOLLY! MY ARCHIE IS GOING TO BE A MOVIE STAR!
OH, DEAR! NOW ARCHIE WILL NEVER NOTICE ME!
VERONICA DID YOU KNOW JUGHEAD HEARD HOLLYWOOD PHONE ARCHIE TO BE IN A PICTURE??
YES!
I KNEW MY COUSIN HOLLY WOULD PHONE HIM!

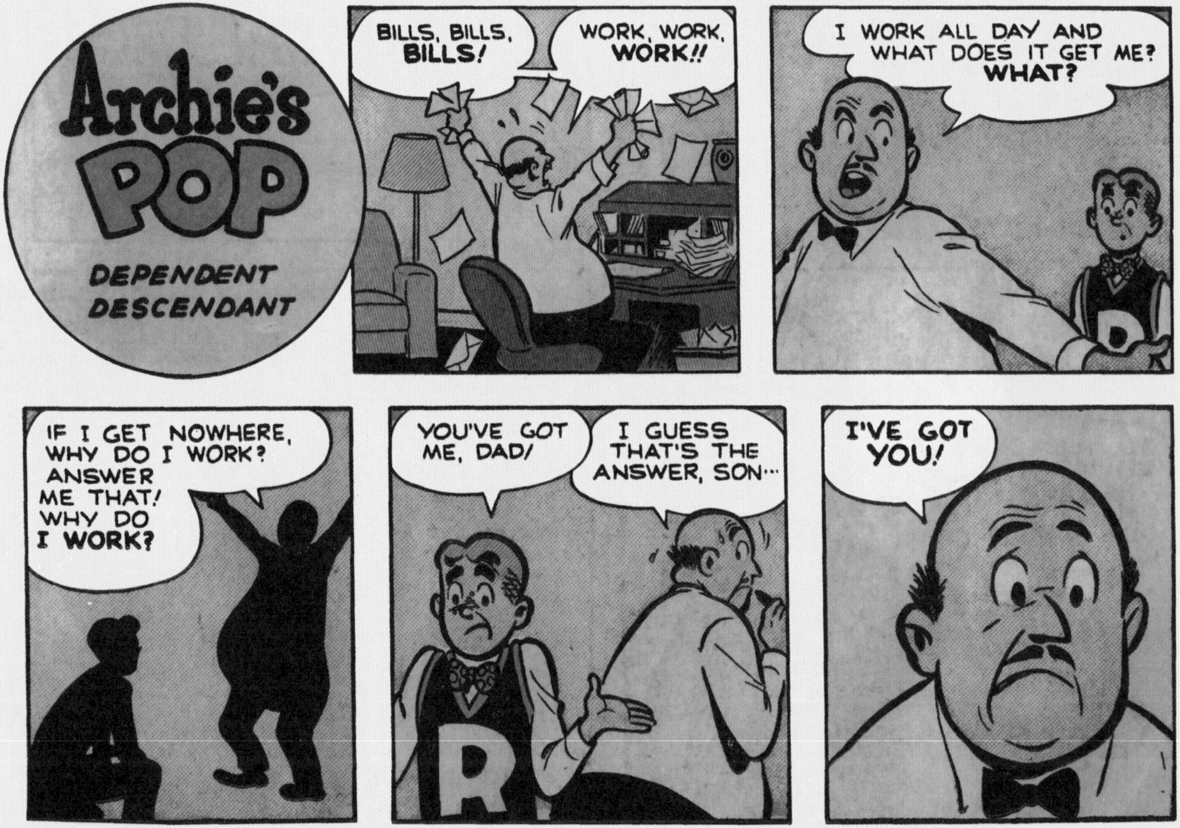
Archie's POP
DEPENDENT DESCENDANT
BILLS, BILLS, BILLS!
WORK, WORK, WORK!!
I WORK ALL DAY AND WHAT DOES IT GET ME? WHAT?
IF I GET NOWHERE, WHY DO I WORK? ANSWER ME THAT! WHY DO I WORK?
YOU'VE GOT ME, DAD!
I GUESS THAT'S THE ANSWER, SON...
I'VE GOT YOU!

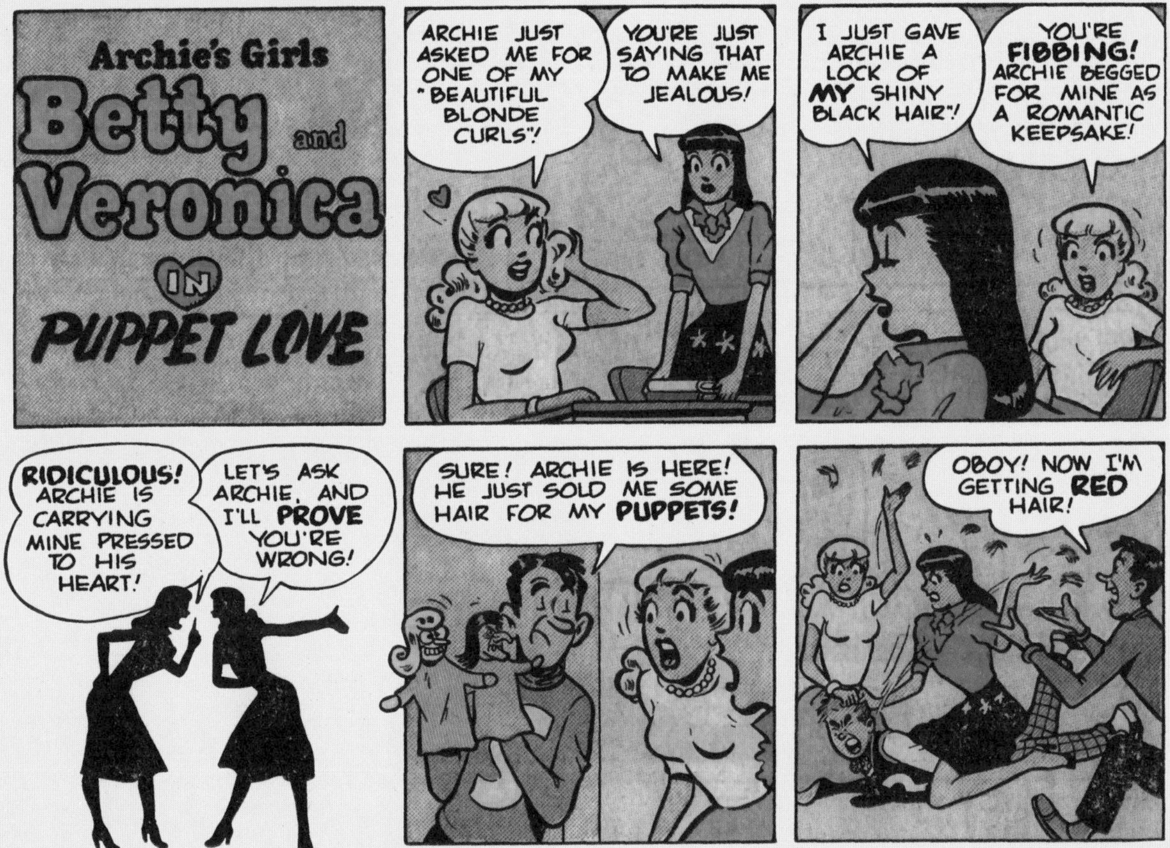
Archie's Girls
Betty and Veronica
IN
PUPPET LOVE
ARCHIE JUST ASKED ME FOR ONE OF MY "BEAUTIFUL BLONDE CURLS"!
YOU'RE JUST SAYING THAT TO MAKE ME JEALOUS!
I JUST GAVE ARCHIE A LOCK OF MY SHINY BLACK HAIR"!
YOU'RE FIBBING! ARCHIE BEGGED FOR MINE AS A ROMANTIC KEEPSAKE!
RIDICULOUS! ARCHIE IS CARRYING MINE PRESSED TO HIS HEART!
LET'S ASK ARCHIE, AND I'LL PROVE YOU'RE WRONG!
SURE! ARCHIE IS HERE! HE JUST SOLD ME SOME HAIR FOR MY PUPPETS!
OBOY! NOW I'M GETTING RED HAIR!

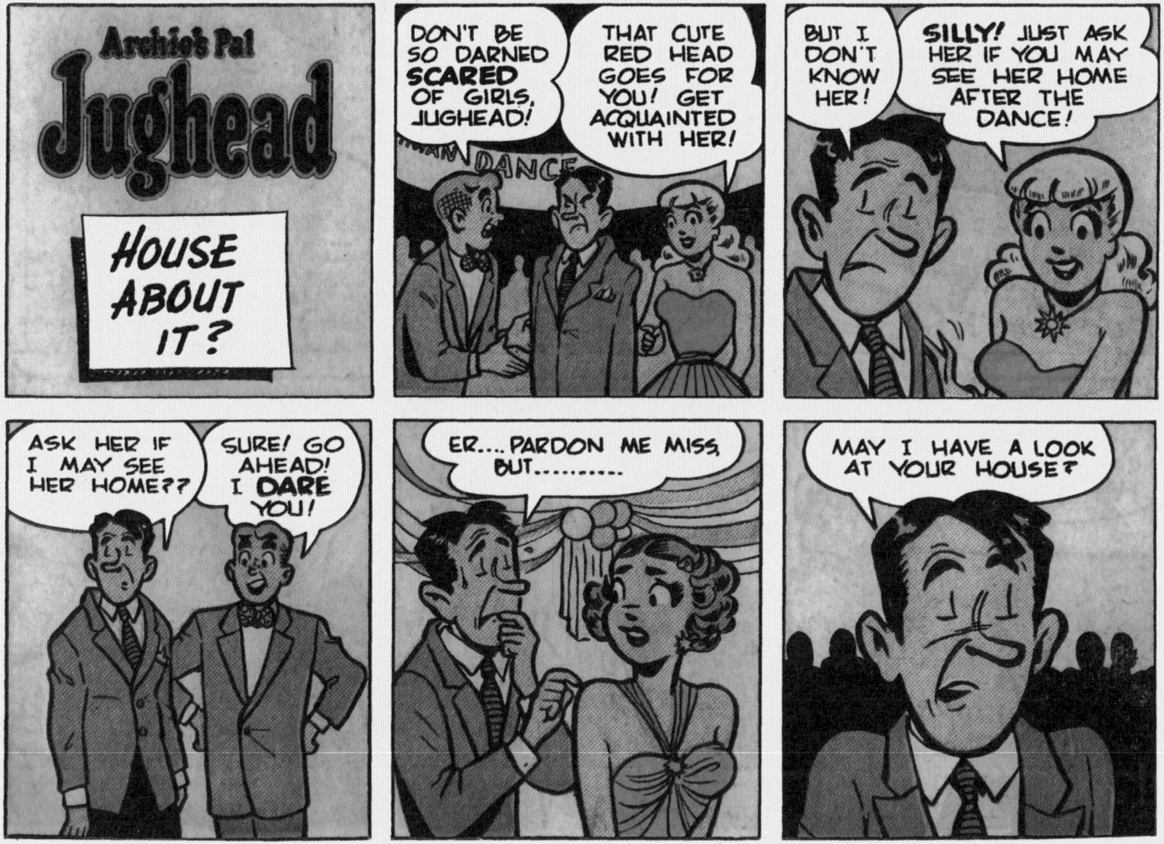
Archie's Pal
Jughead
HOUSE ABOUT IT?
DON'T BE SO DARNED SCARED OF GIRLS, JUGHEAD!
THAT CUTE RED HEAD GOES FOR YOU! GET ACQUAINTED WITH HER!
DANCE
BUT I DON'T KNOW HER!
SILLY! JUST ASK HER IF YOU MAY SEE HER HOME AFTER THE DANCE!
ASK HER IF I MAY SEE HER HOME??
SURE! GO AHEAD! I DARE YOU!
ER.... PARDON ME MISS, BUT..........
MAY I HAVE A LOOK AT YOUR HOUSE?

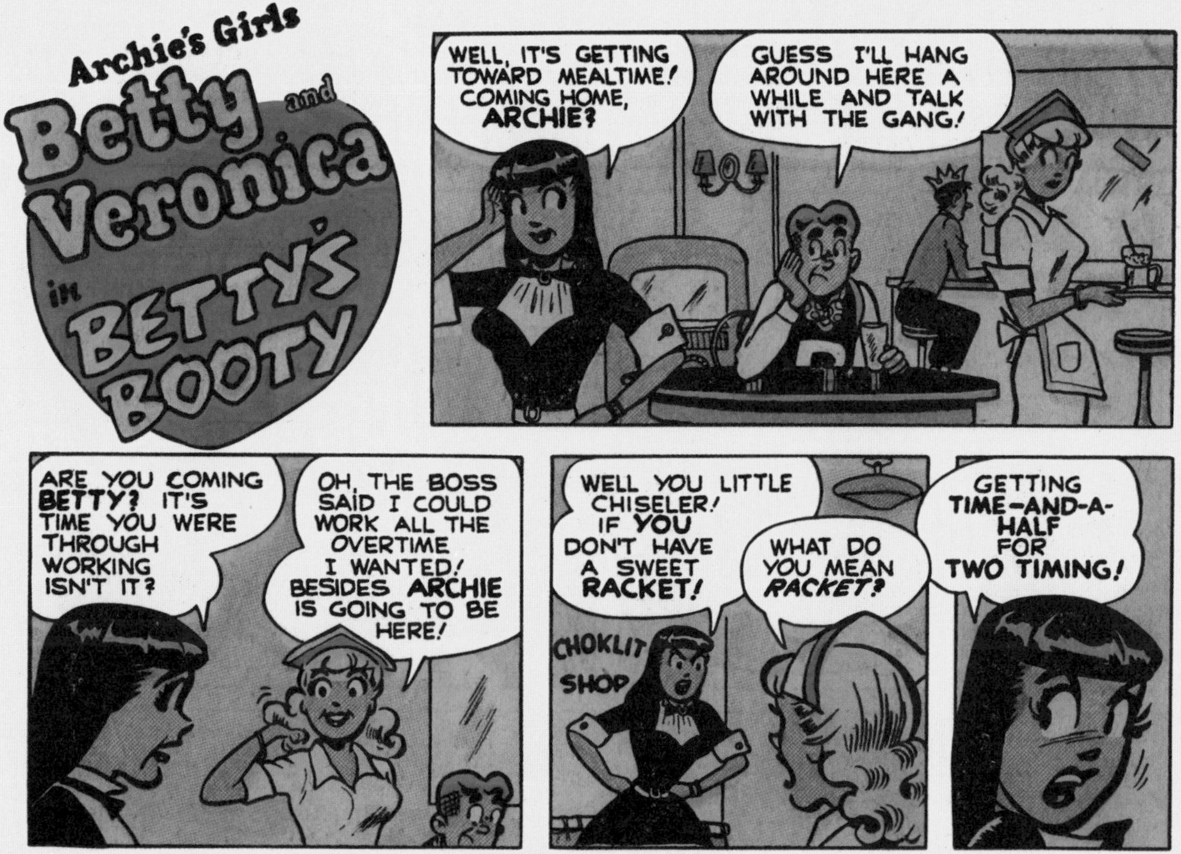
Archie's Girls
Betty and Veronica
in BETTY'S BOOTY
WELL, IT'S GETTING TOWARD MEALTIME! COMING HOME, ARCHIE?
GUESS I'LL HANG AROUND HERE A WHILE AND TALK WITH THE GANG!
ARE YOU COMING BETTY? IT'S TIME YOU WERE THROUGH WORKING ISN'T IT?
OH, THE BOSS SAID I COULD WORK ALL THE OVERTIME I WANTED! BESIDES ARCHIE IS GOING TO BE HERE!
WELL YOU LITTLE CHISELER! IF YOU DON'T HAVE A SWEET RACKET!
CHOKLIT SHOP
WHAT DO YOU MEAN RACKET?
GETTING TIME-AND-A-HALF FOR TWO TIMING!

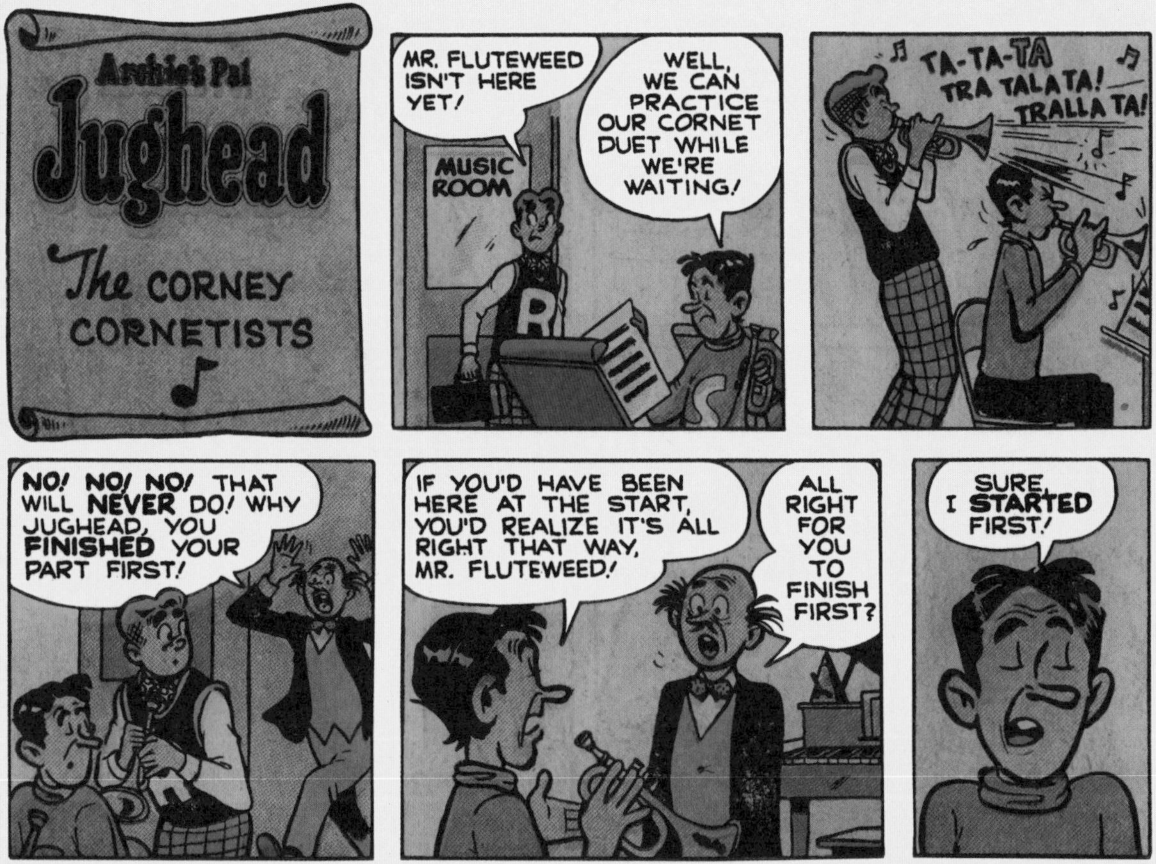
Archie's Pal
Jughead
The CORNEY CORNETISTS
MR. FLUTEWEED ISN'T HERE YET!
WELL, WE CAN PRACTICE OUR CORNET DUET WHILE WE'RE WAITING!
MUSIC ROOM
TA-TA-TA
TRA TALA TA!
TRALLA TA!
NO! NO! NO! THAT WILL NEVER DO! WHY JUGHEAD, YOU FINISHED YOUR PART FIRST!
IF YOU'D HAVE BEEN HERE AT THE START, YOU'D REALIZE IT'S ALL RIGHT THAT WAY, MR. FLUTEWEED!
ALL RIGHT FOR YOU TO FINISH FIRST?
SURE, I STARTED FIRST!

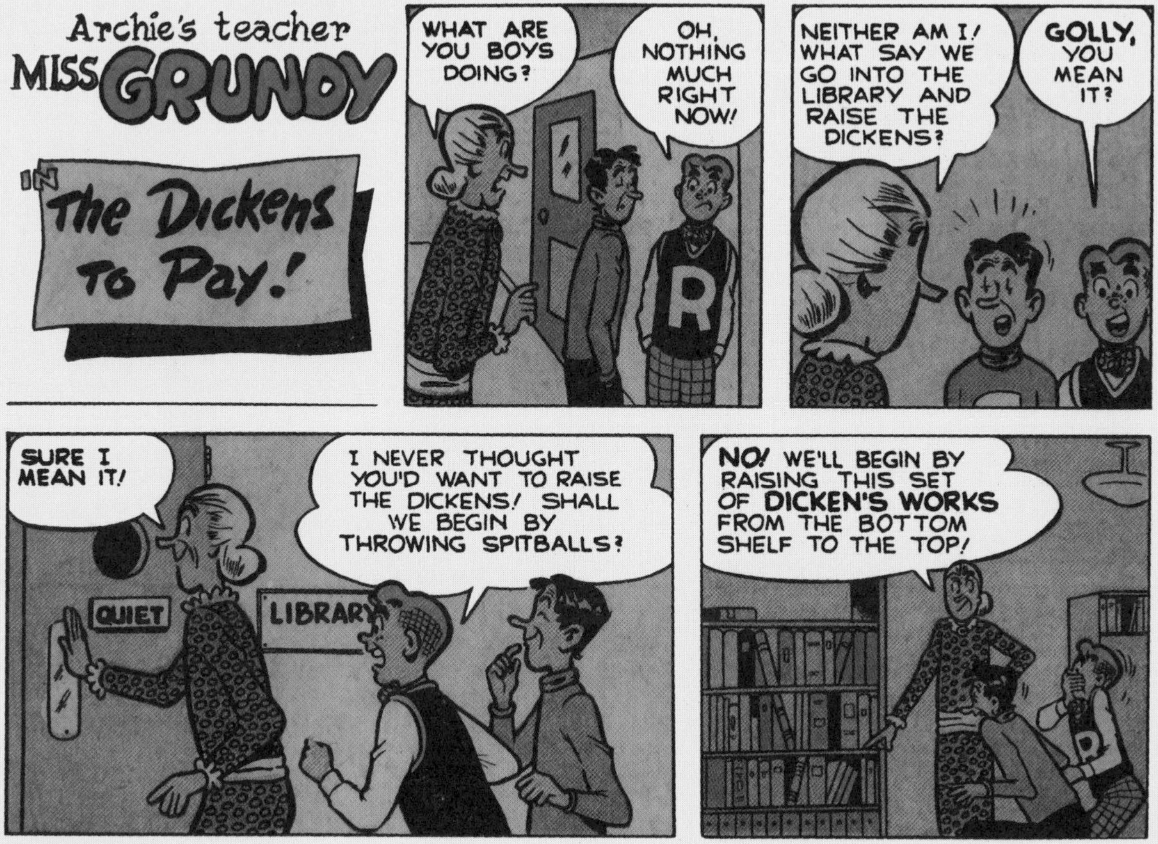
Archie's teacher
MISS GRUNDY
IN "The Dickens to Pay!"
WHAT ARE YOU BOYS DOING?
OH, NOTHING MUCH RIGHT NOW!
NEITHER AM I! WHAT SAY WE GO INTO THE LIBRARY AND RAISE THE DICKENS?
GOLLY, YOU MEAN IT?
SURE I MEAN IT!
I NEVER THOUGHT YOU'D WANT TO RAISE THE DICKENS! SHALL WE BEGIN BY THROWING SPITBALLS?
QUIET
LIBRARY
NO! WE'LL BEGIN BY RAISING THIS SET OF DICKEN'S WORKS FROM THE BOTTOM SHELF TO THE TOP!

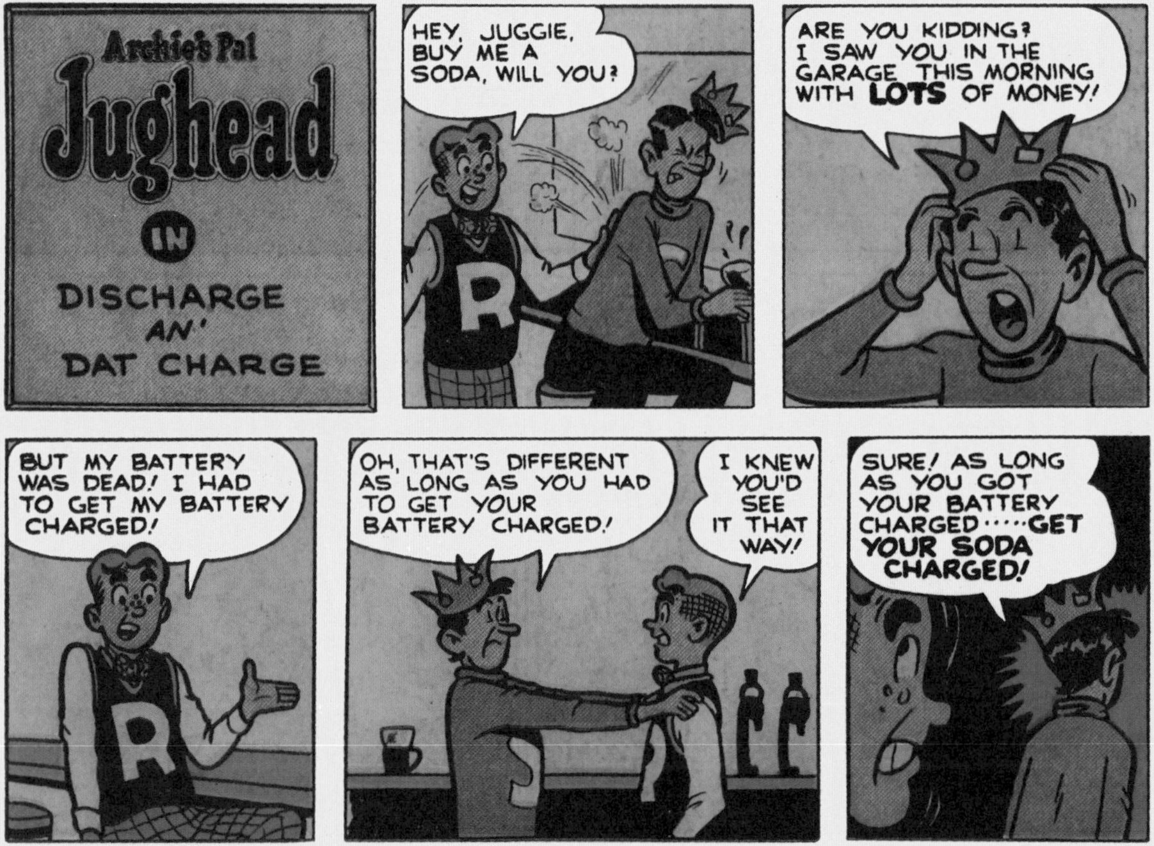

Archie's Pal
Jughead
IN
DISCHARGE AN' DAT CHARGE
HEY, JUGGIE, BUY ME A SODA, WILL YOU?
ARE YOU KIDDING? I SAW YOU IN THE GARAGE THIS MORNING WITH LOTS OF MONEY!
BUT MY BATTERY WAS DEAD! I HAD TO GET MY BATTERY CHARGED!
OH, THAT'S DIFFERENT AS LONG AS YOU HAD TO GET YOUR BATTERY CHARGED!
I KNEW YOU'D SEE IT THAT WAY!
SURE! AS LONG AS YOU GOT YOUR BATTERY CHARGED.....GET YOUR SODA CHARGED!

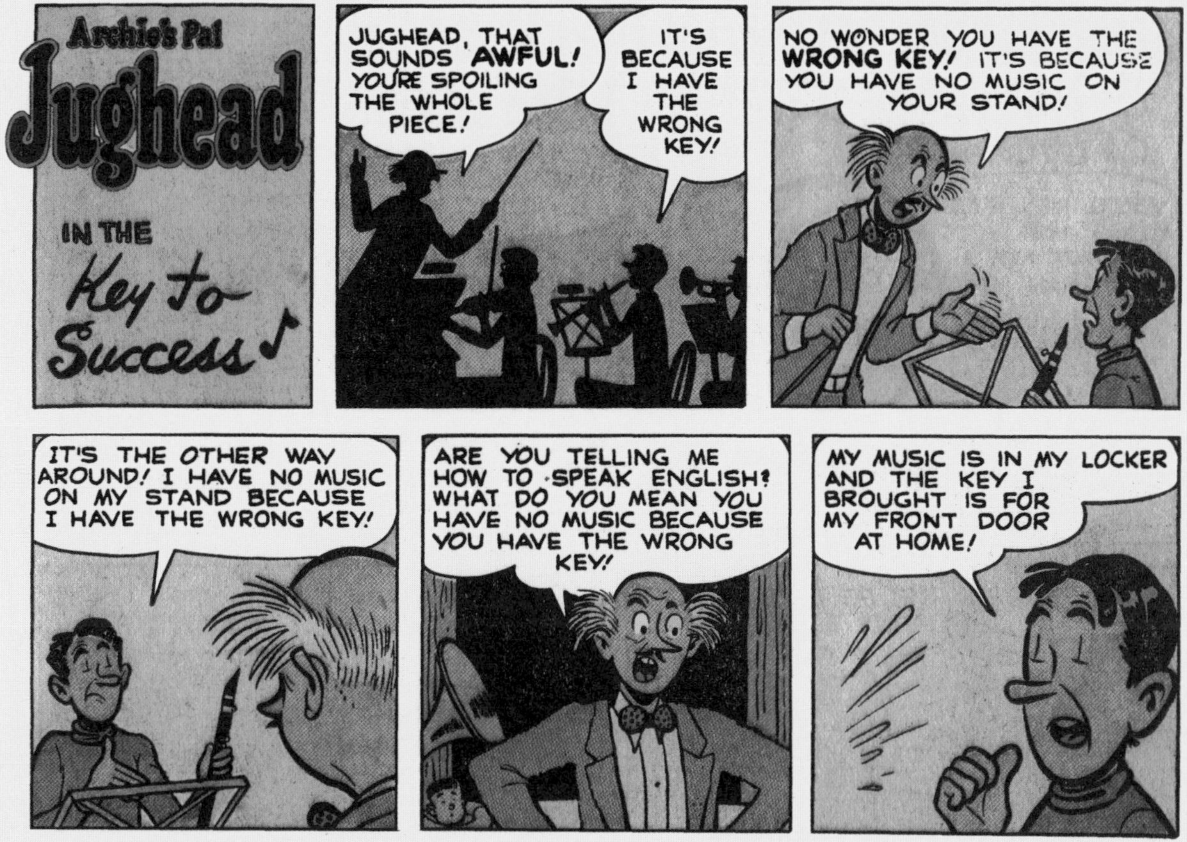

Archie's Pal
Jughead
IN THE
Key to Success
JUGHEAD, THAT SOUNDS AWFUL! YOU'RE SPOILING THE WHOLE PIECE!
IT'S BECAUSE I HAVE THE WRONG KEY!
NO WONDER YOU HAVE THE WRONG KEY! IT'S BECAUSE YOU HAVE NO MUSIC ON YOUR STAND!
IT'S THE OTHER WAY AROUND! I HAVE NO MUSIC ON MY STAND BECAUSE I HAVE THE WRONG KEY!
ARE YOU TELLING ME HOW TO SPEAK ENGLISH? WHAT DO YOU MEAN YOU HAVE NO MUSIC BECAUSE YOU HAVE THE WRONG KEY!
MY MUSIC IS IN MY LOCKER AND THE KEY I BROUGHT IS FOR MY FRONT DOOR AT HOME!

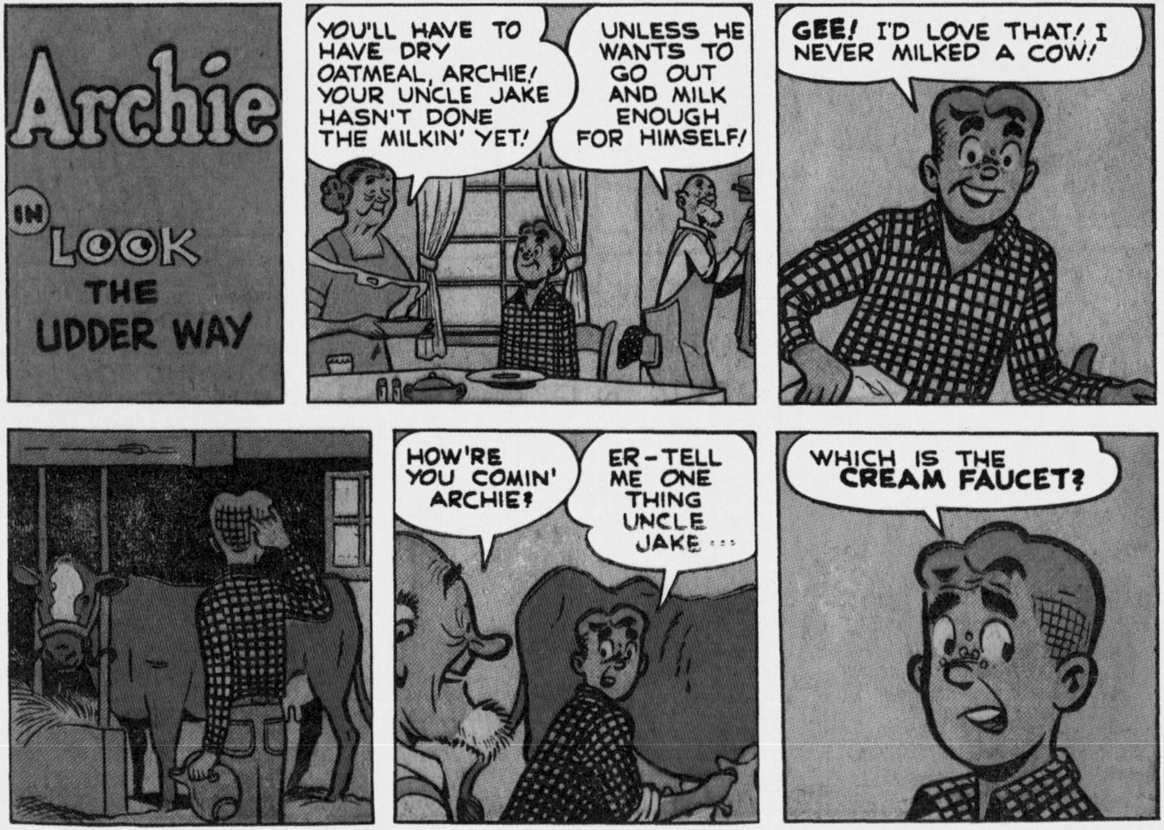
Archie
IN LOOK THE UDDER WAY
YOU'LL HAVE TO HAVE DRY OATMEAL, ARCHIE! YOUR UNCLE JAKE HASN'T DONE THE MILKIN' YET!
UNLESS HE WANTS TO GO OUT AND MILK ENOUGH FOR HIMSELF!
GEE! I'D LOVE THAT! I NEVER MILKED A COW!
HOW'RE YOU COMIN' ARCHIE?
ER-TELL ME ONE THING UNCLE JAKE...
WHICH IS THE CREAM FAUCET?

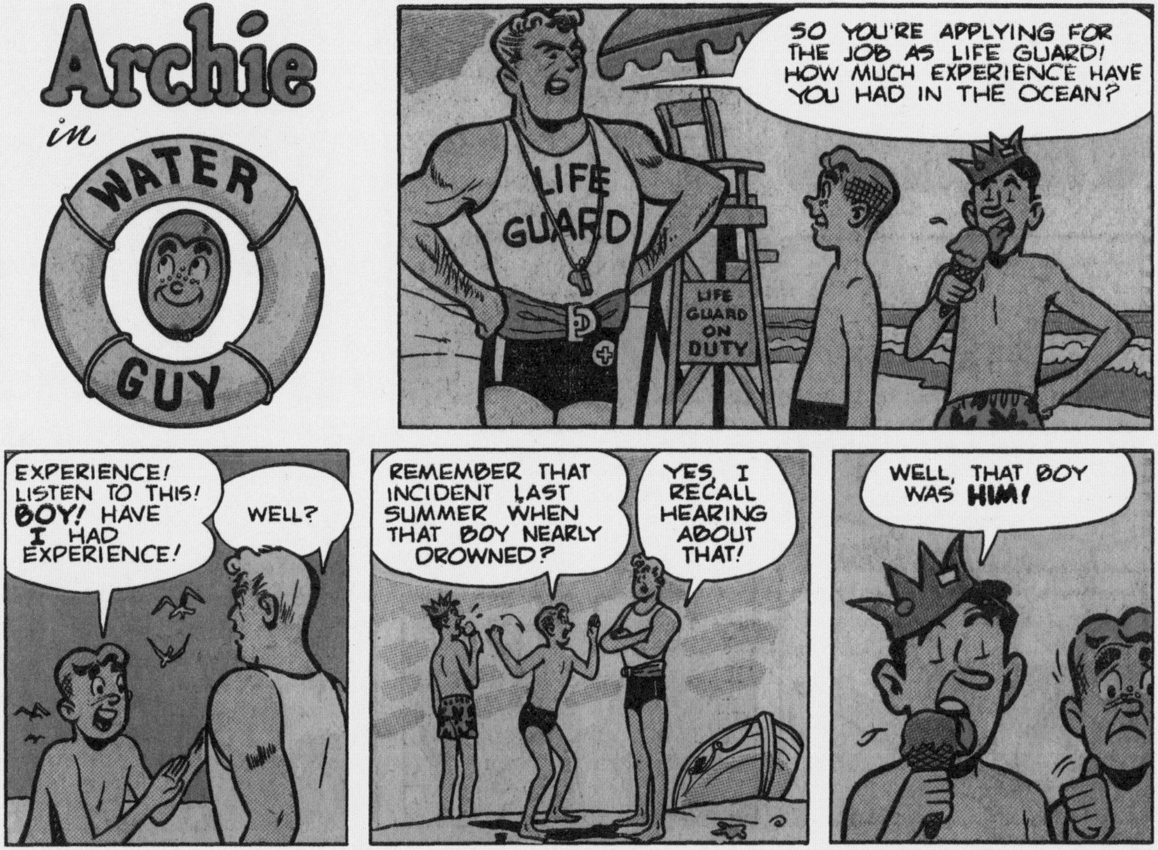
Archie
in
WATER GUY
SO YOU'RE APPLYING FOR THE JOB AS LIFE GUARD! HOW MUCH EXPERIENCE HAVE YOU HAD IN THE OCEAN?
LIFE GUARD
LIFE GUARD ON DUTY
EXPERIENCE! LISTEN TO THIS! BOY! HAVE I HAD EXPERIENCE!
WELL?
REMEMBER THAT INCIDENT LAST SUMMER WHEN THAT BOY NEARLY DROWNED?
YES, I RECALL HEARING ABOUT THAT!
WELL, THAT BOY WAS HIM!

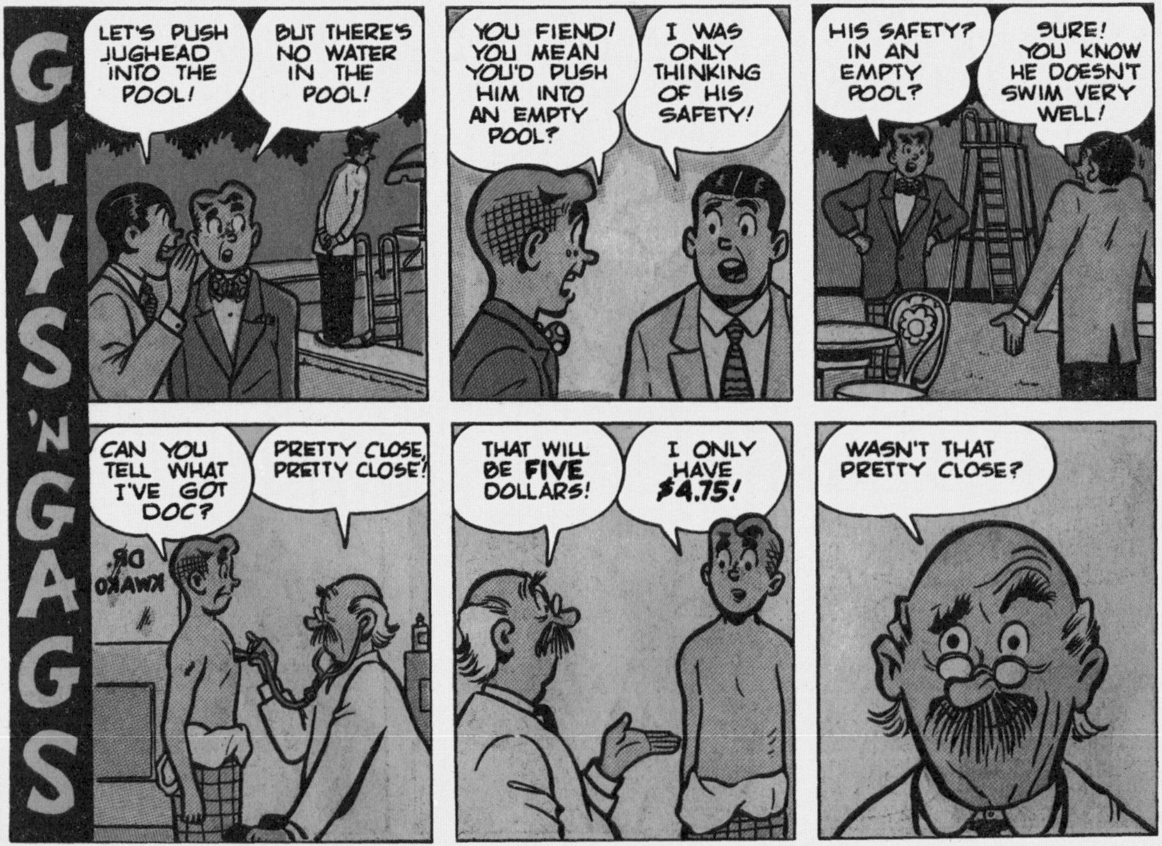
GUYS 'N GAGS
LET'S PUSH JUGHEAD INTO THE POOL!
BUT THERE'S NO WATER IN THE POOL!
YOU FIEND! YOU MEAN YOU'D PUSH HIM INTO AN EMPTY POOL?
I WAS ONLY THINKING OF HIS SAFETY!
HIS SAFETY? IN AN EMPTY POOL?
SURE! YOU KNOW HE DOESN'T SWIM VERY WELL!
CAN YOU TELL WHAT I'VE GOT DOC?
PRETTY CLOSE, PRETTY CLOSE!
THAT WILL BE FIVE DOLLARS!
I ONLY HAVE $4.75!
WASN'T THAT PRETTY CLOSE?

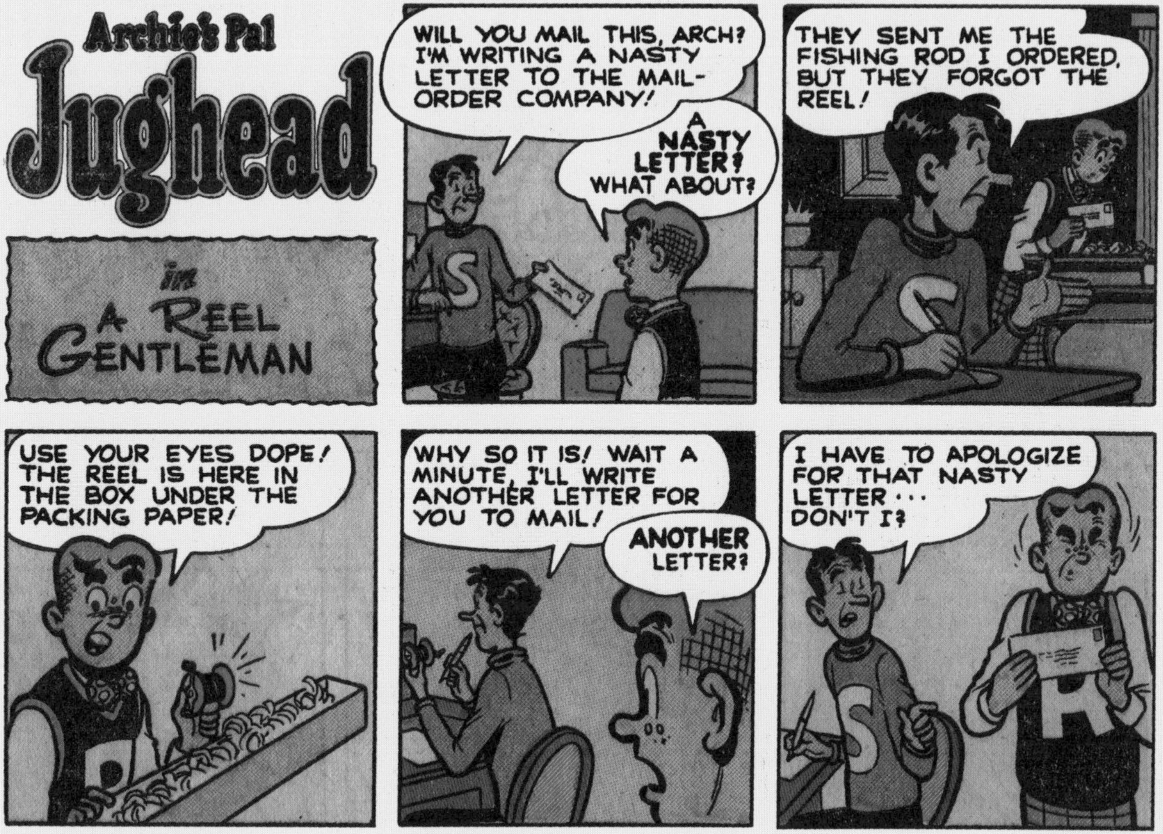

Archie's Pal
Jughead
in
A REEL GENTLEMAN
WILL YOU MAIL THIS, ARCH? I'M WRITING A NASTY LETTER TO THE MAIL-ORDER COMPANY!
A NASTY LETTER? WHAT ABOUT?
THEY SENT ME THE FISHING ROD I ORDERED, BUT THEY FORGOT THE REEL!
USE YOUR EYES DOPE! THE REEL IS HERE IN THE BOX UNDER THE PACKING PAPER!
WHY SO IT IS! WAIT A MINUTE, I'LL WRITE ANOTHER LETTER FOR YOU TO MAIL!
ANOTHER LETTER?
I HAVE TO APOLOGIZE FOR THAT NASTY LETTER ... DON'T I?

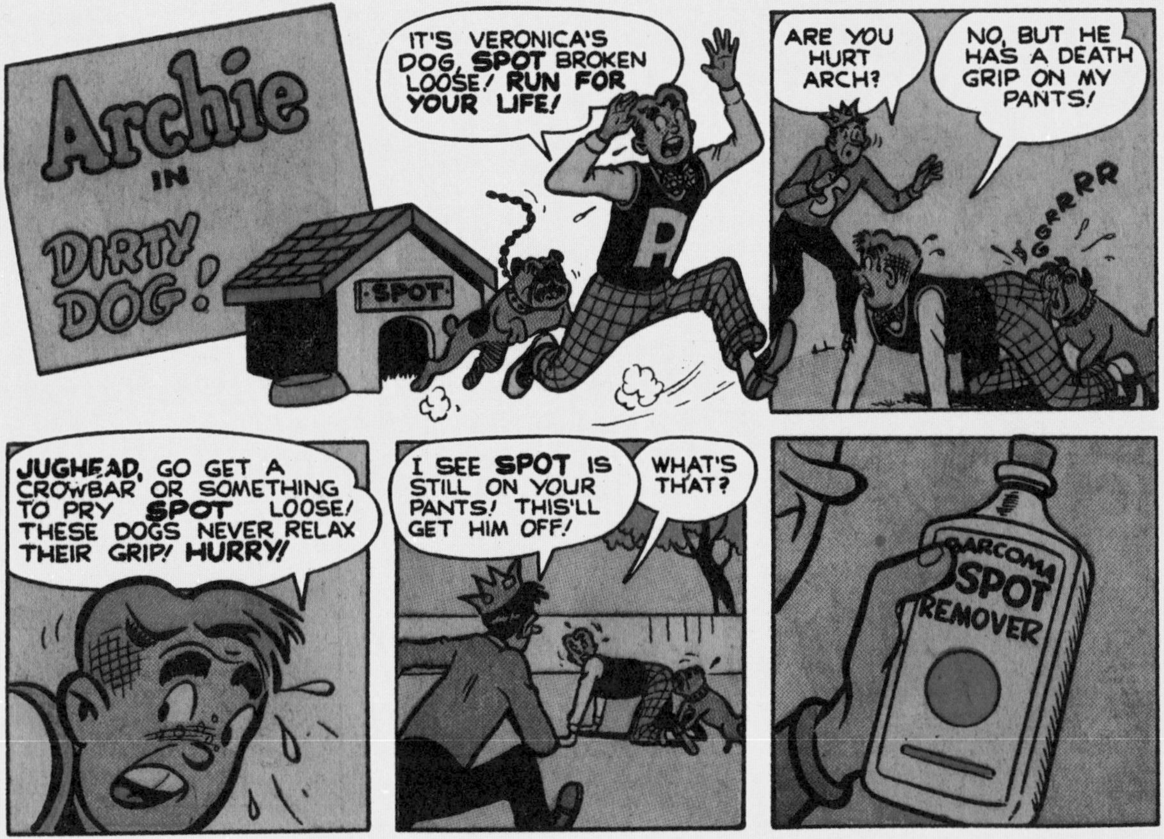
Archie
IN
DIRTY DOG!
SPOT
IT'S VERONICA'S DOG, SPOT BROKEN LOOSE! RUN FOR YOUR LIFE!
ARE YOU HURT ARCH?
NO, BUT HE HAS A DEATH GRIP ON MY PANTS!
GGRRRRR
JUGHEAD, GO GET A CROWBAR OR SOMETHING TO PRY SPOT LOOSE! THESE DOGS NEVER RELAX THEIR GRIP! HURRY!
I SEE SPOT IS STILL ON YOUR PANTS! THIS'LL GET HIM OFF!
WHAT'S THAT?
BARCOMA SPOT REMOVER

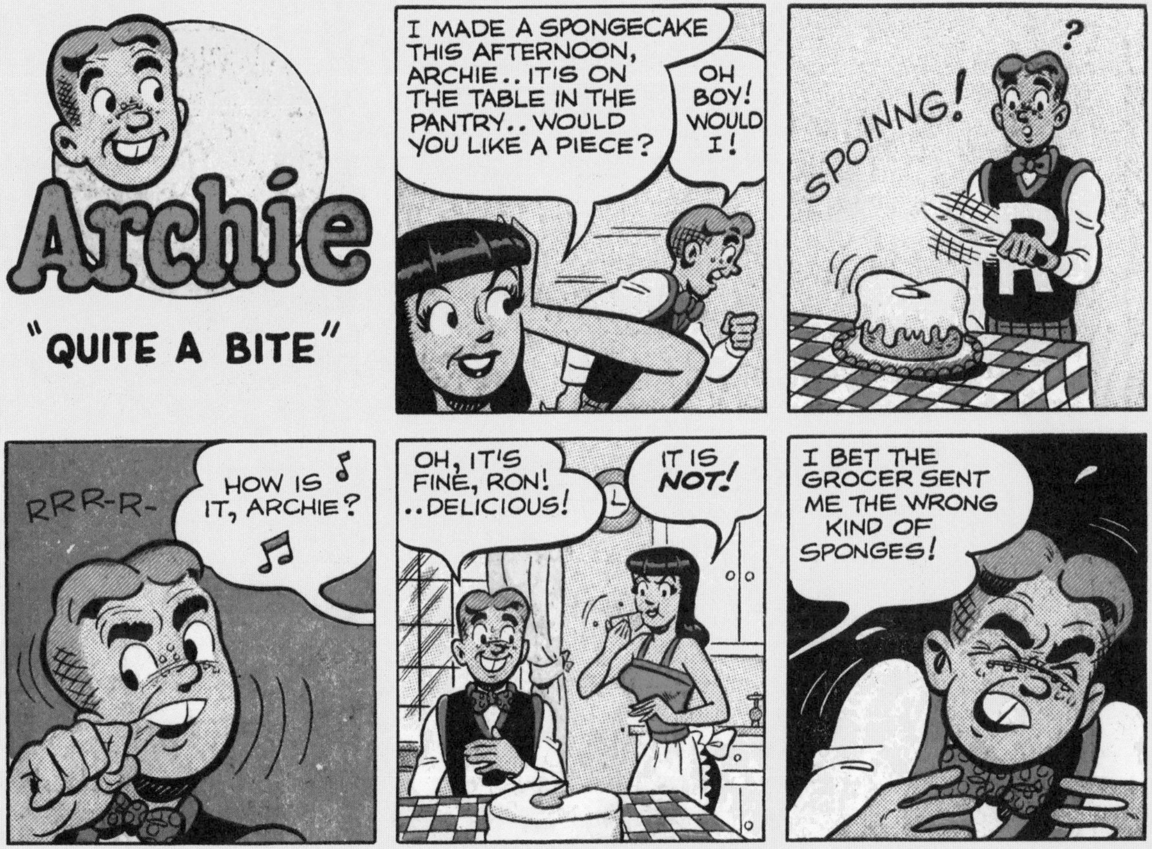
Archie
"QUITE A BITE"
I MADE A SPONGECAKE THIS AFTERNOON, ARCHIE.. IT'S ON THE TABLE IN THE PANTRY.. WOULD YOU LIKE A PIECE?
OH BOY! WOULD I!
?
SPOINNG!
RRR-R-
HOW IS IT, ARCHIE?
OH, IT'S FINE, RON! ..DELICIOUS!
IT IS NOT!
I BET THE GROCER SENT ME THE WRONG KIND OF SPONGES!

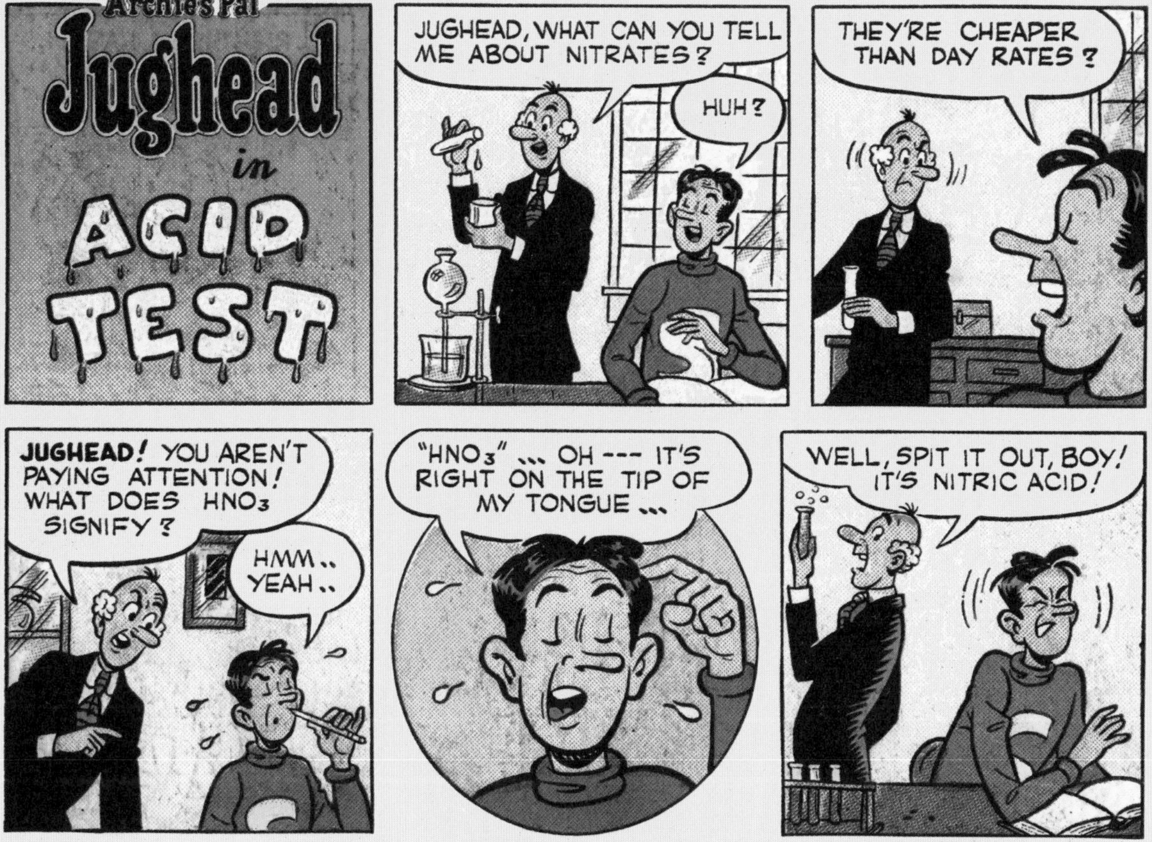
Archie's Pal
Jughead
in
ACID TEST
JUGHEAD, WHAT CAN YOU TELL ME ABOUT NITRATES?
HUH?
THEY'RE CHEAPER THAN DAY RATES?
JUGHEAD! YOU AREN'T PAYING ATTENTION! WHAT DOES HNO3 SIGNIFY?
HMM.. YEAH..
"HNO3" ... OH --- IT'S RIGHT ON THE TIP OF MY TONGUE ...
WELL, SPIT IT OUT, BOY! IT'S NITRIC ACID!

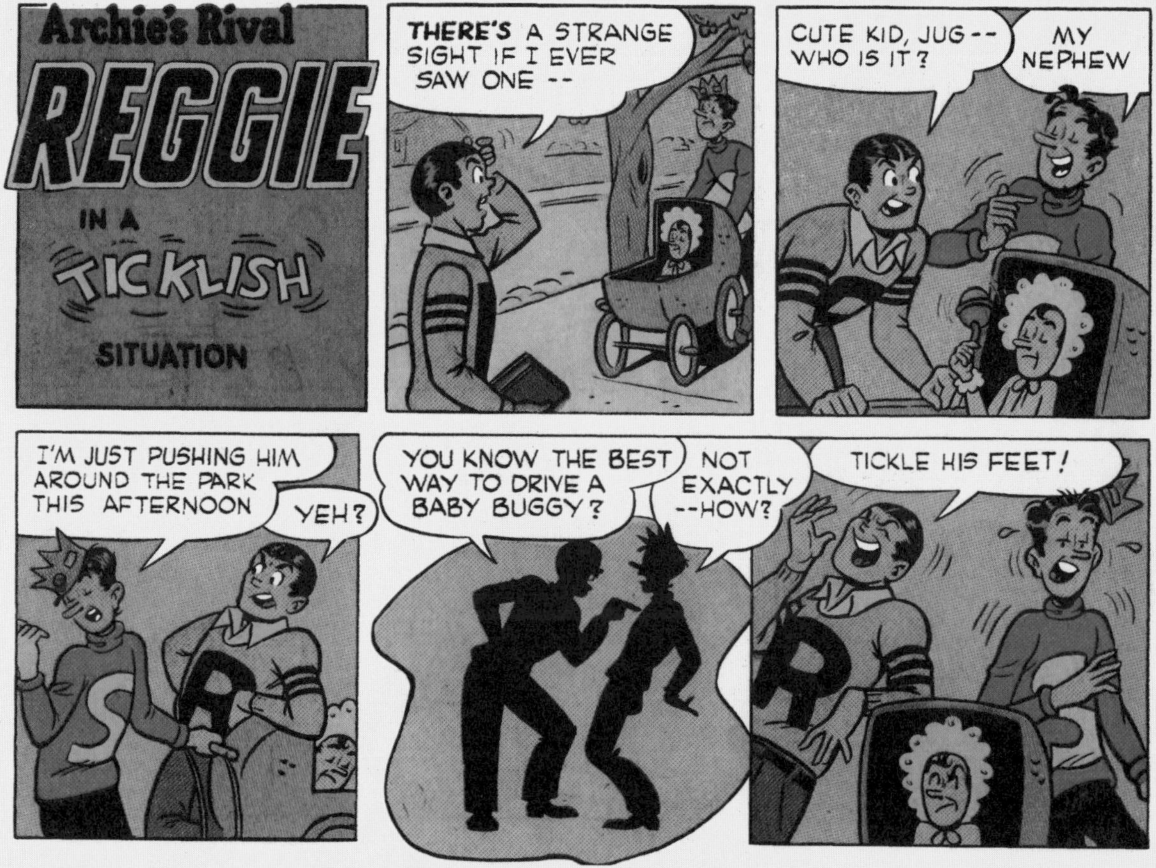

Archie's Rival
REGGIE
IN A TICKLISH SITUATION
THERE'S A STRANGE SIGHT IF I EVER SAW ONE --
CUTE KID, JUG -- WHO IS IT ?
MY NEPHEW
I'M JUST PUSHING HIM AROUND THE PARK THIS AFTERNOON
YEH ?
YOU KNOW THE BEST WAY TO DRIVE A BABY BUGGY ?
NOT EXACTLY --HOW?
TICKLE HIS FEET!

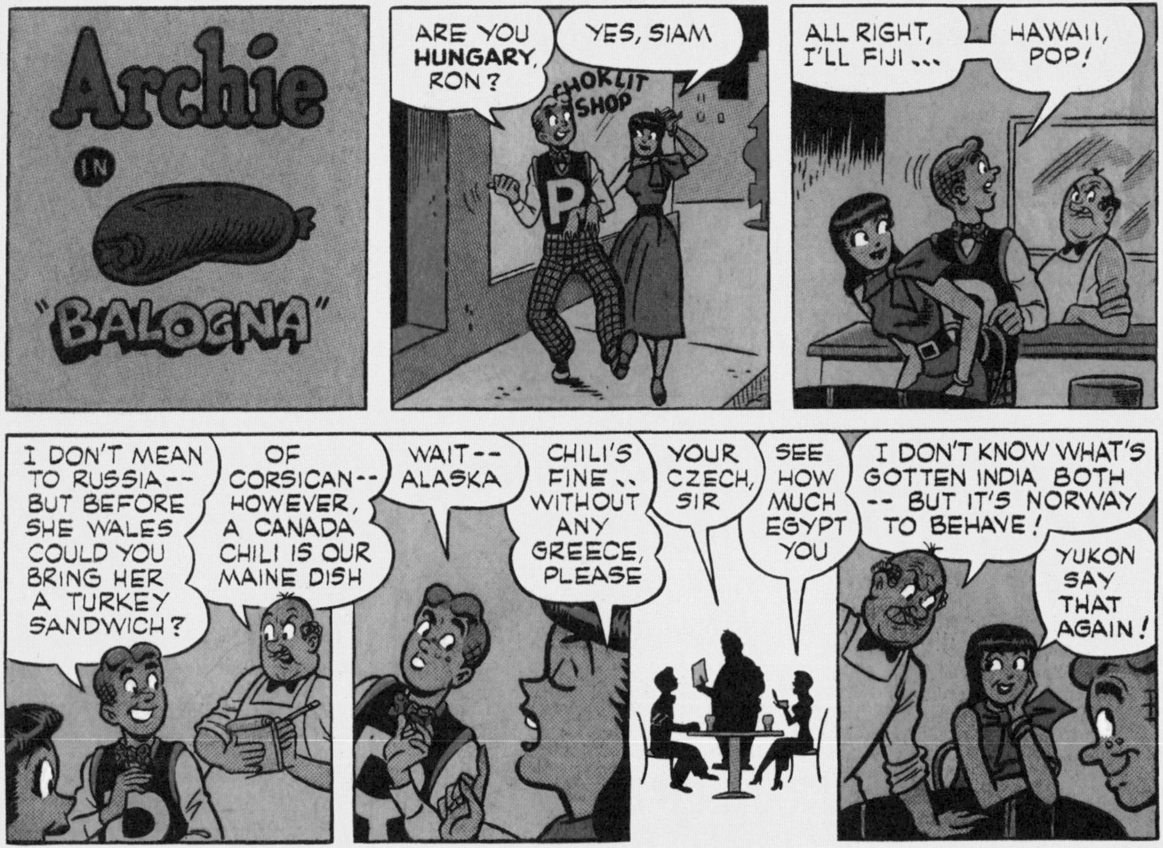
Archie
IN
"BALOGNA"
ARE YOU HUNGARY, RON?
YES, SIAM
CHOKLIT SHOP
ALL RIGHT, I'LL FIJI ...
HAWAII, POP!
I DON'T MEAN TO RUSSIA-- BUT BEFORE SHE WALES COULD YOU BRING HER A TURKEY SANDWICH?
OF CORSICAN-- HOWEVER, A CANADA CHILI IS OUR MAINE DISH
WAIT-- ALASKA
CHILI'S FINE .. WITHOUT ANY GREECE, PLEASE
YOUR CZECH, SIR
SEE HOW MUCH EGYPT YOU
I DON'T KNOW WHAT'S GOTTEN INDIA BOTH -- BUT IT'S NORWAY TO BEHAVE!
YUKON SAY THAT AGAIN!

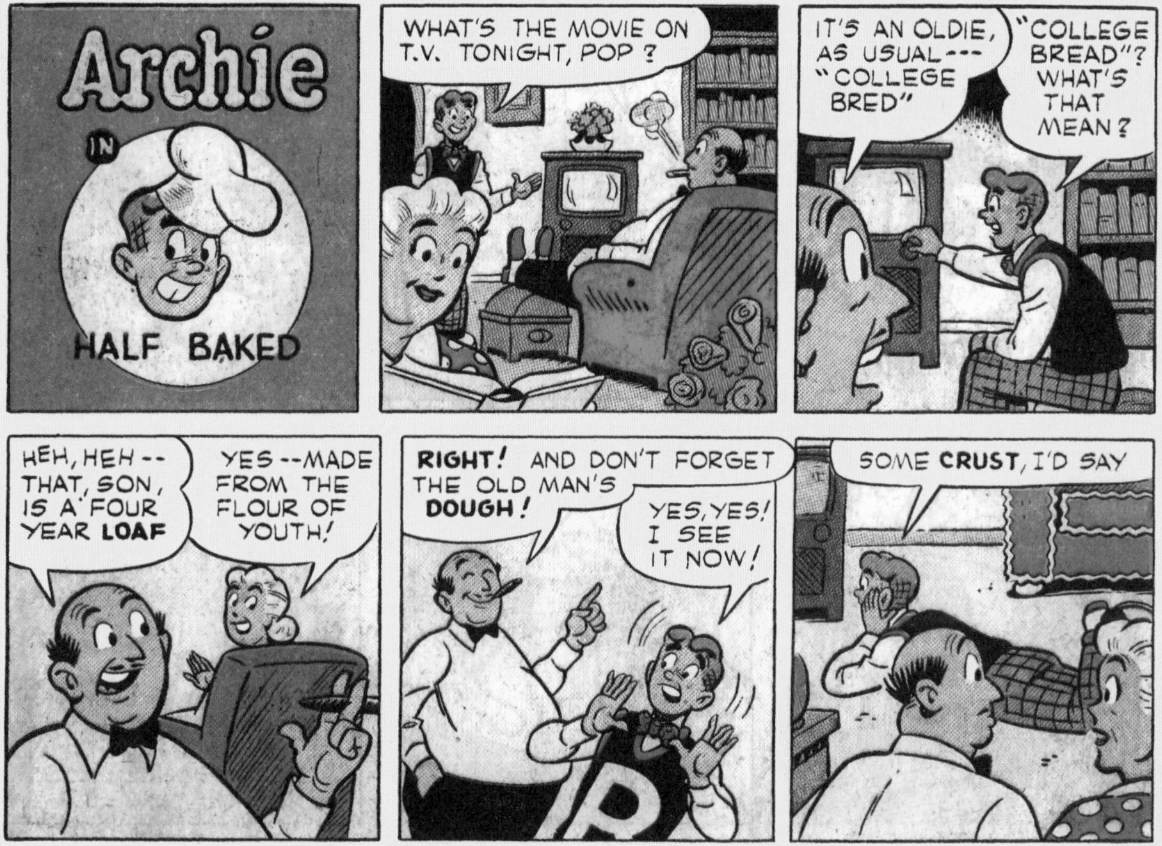
Archie
IN
HALF BAKED
WHAT'S THE MOVIE ON T.V. TONIGHT, POP ?
IT'S AN OLDIE, AS USUAL--- "COLLEGE BRED"
"COLLEGE BREAD"? WHAT'S THAT MEAN ?
HEH, HEH -- THAT, SON, IS A FOUR YEAR LOAF
YES --MADE FROM THE FLOUR OF YOUTH!
RIGHT! AND DON'T FORGET THE OLD MAN'S DOUGH!
YES, YES! I SEE IT NOW!
SOME CRUST, I'D SAY

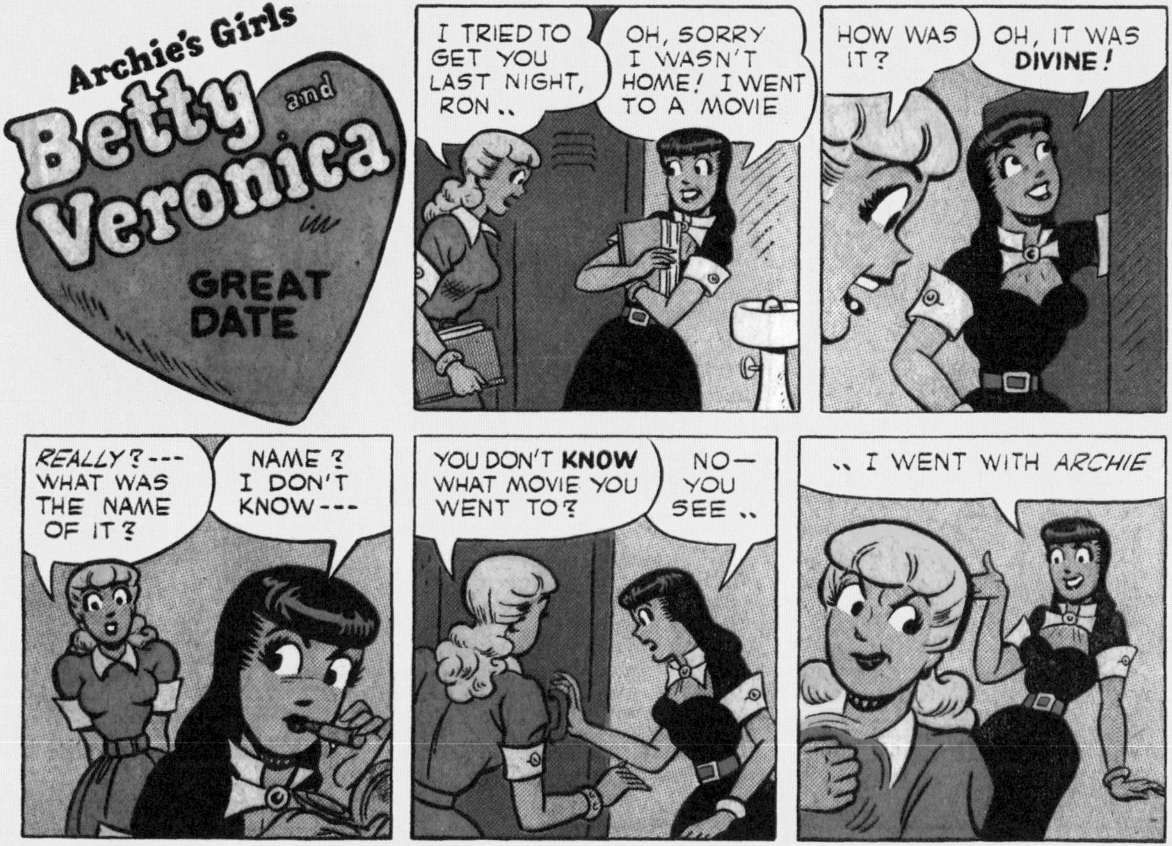
Archie's Girls
Betty and Veronica
in
GREAT DATE
I TRIED TO GET YOU LAST NIGHT, RON ..
OH, SORRY I WASN'T HOME! I WENT TO A MOVIE
HOW WAS IT?
OH, IT WAS **DIVINE**!
REALLY? --- WHAT WAS THE NAME OF IT?
NAME? I DON'T KNOW---
YOU DON'T **KNOW** WHAT MOVIE YOU WENT TO?
NO— YOU SEE ..
.. I WENT WITH *ARCHIE*

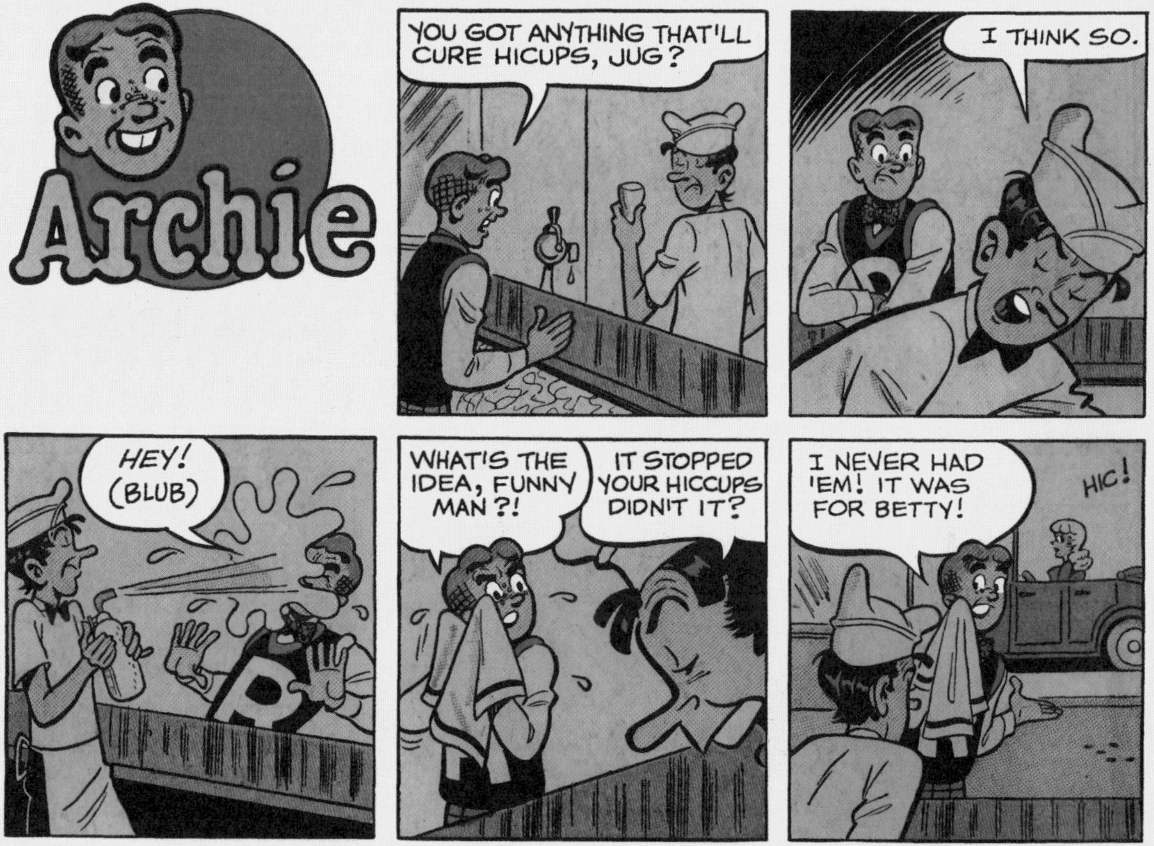
Archie
YOU GOT ANYTHING THAT'LL CURE HICUPS, JUG?
I THINK SO.
HEY! (BLUB)
WHAT'S THE IDEA, FUNNY MAN?!
IT STOPPED YOUR HICCUPS DIDN'T IT?
I NEVER HAD 'EM! IT WAS FOR BETTY!
HIC!

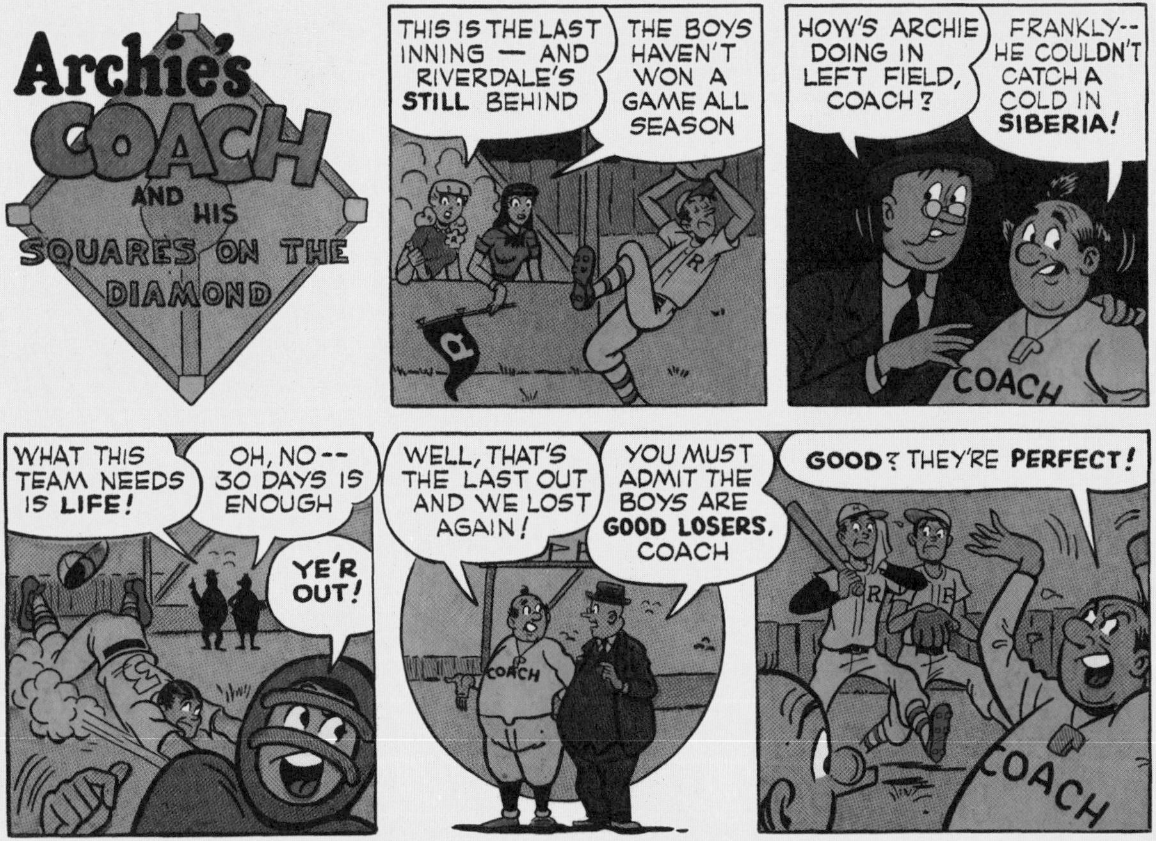
Archie's COACH AND HIS SQUARES ON THE DIAMOND
THIS IS THE LAST INNING — AND RIVERDALE'S STILL BEHIND
THE BOYS HAVEN'T WON A GAME ALL SEASON
HOW'S ARCHIE DOING IN LEFT FIELD, COACH?
FRANKLY-- HE COULDN'T CATCH A COLD IN SIBERIA!
COACH
WHAT THIS TEAM NEEDS IS LIFE!
OH, NO-- 30 DAYS IS ENOUGH
YE'R OUT!
WELL, THAT'S THE LAST OUT AND WE LOST AGAIN!
YOU MUST ADMIT THE BOYS ARE GOOD LOSERS, COACH
COACH
GOOD? THEY'RE PERFECT!
COACH

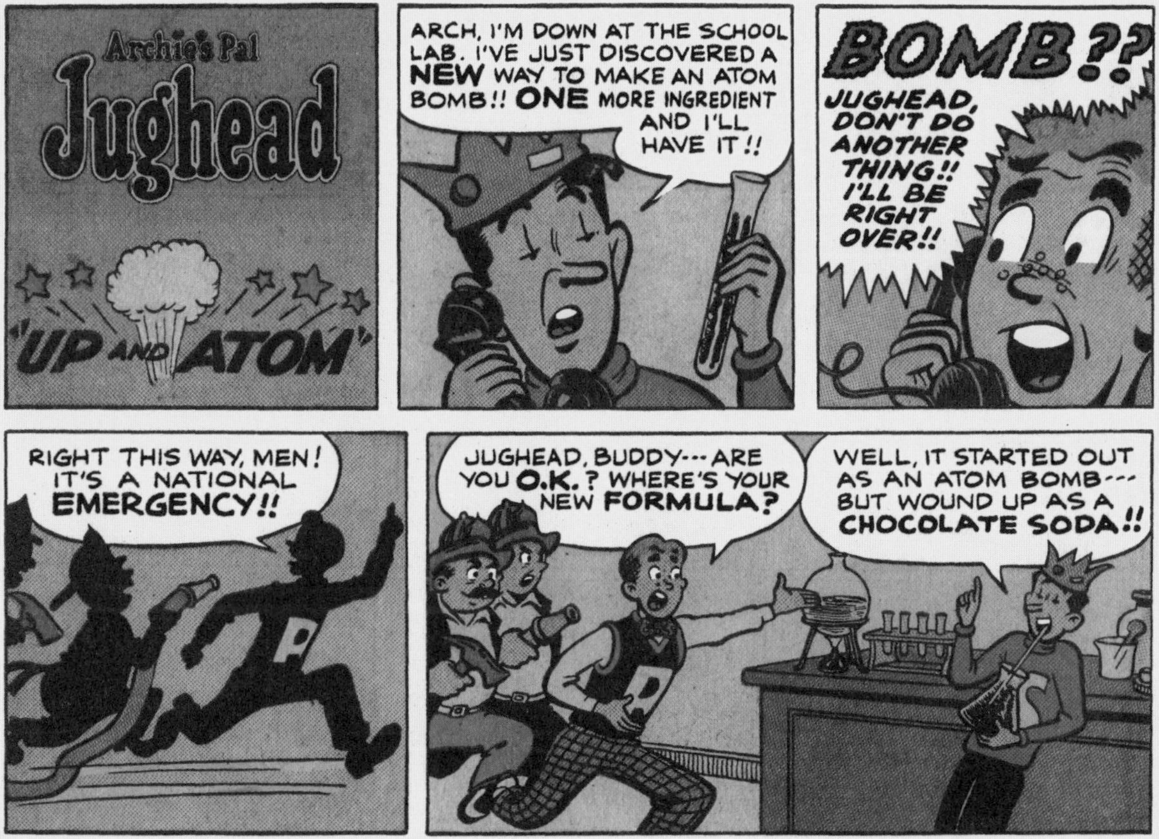
Archie's Pal
Jughead
"UP AND ATOM"
ARCH, I'M DOWN AT THE SCHOOL LAB. I'VE JUST DISCOVERED A NEW WAY TO MAKE AN ATOM BOMB!! ONE MORE INGREDIENT AND I'LL HAVE IT!!
BOMB??
JUGHEAD, DON'T DO ANOTHER THING!! I'LL BE RIGHT OVER!!
RIGHT THIS WAY, MEN! IT'S A NATIONAL EMERGENCY!!
JUGHEAD, BUDDY--- ARE YOU O.K.? WHERE'S YOUR NEW FORMULA?
WELL, IT STARTED OUT AS AN ATOM BOMB--- BUT WOUND UP AS A CHOCOLATE SODA!!

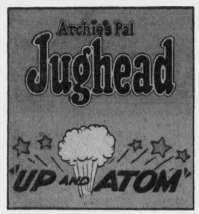

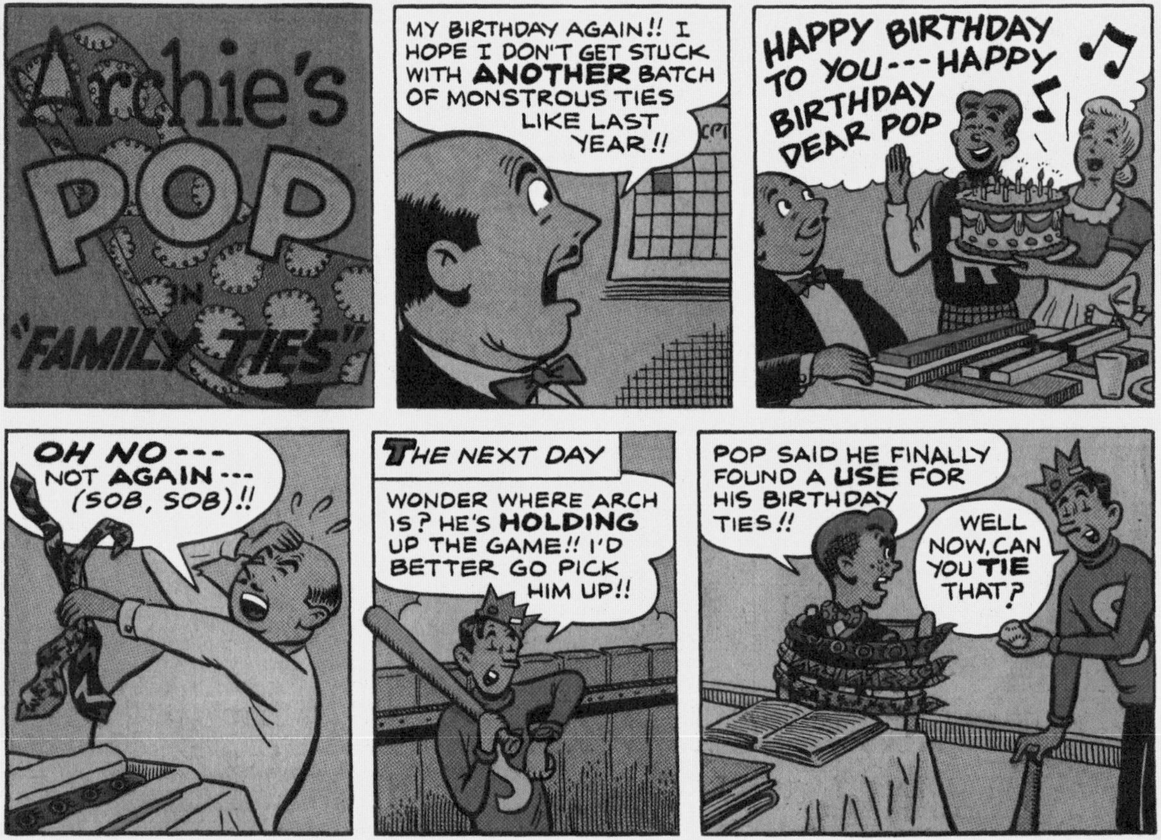
Archie's POP IN "FAMILY TIES"
MY BIRTHDAY AGAIN!! I HOPE I DON'T GET STUCK WITH ANOTHER BATCH OF MONSTROUS TIES LIKE LAST YEAR!!
HAPPY BIRTHDAY TO YOU---HAPPY BIRTHDAY DEAR POP
OH NO--- NOT AGAIN--- (SOB, SOB)!!
THE NEXT DAY
WONDER WHERE ARCH IS? HE'S HOLDING UP THE GAME!! I'D BETTER GO PICK HIM UP!!
POP SAID HE FINALLY FOUND A USE FOR HIS BIRTHDAY TIES!!
WELL NOW, CAN YOU TIE THAT?

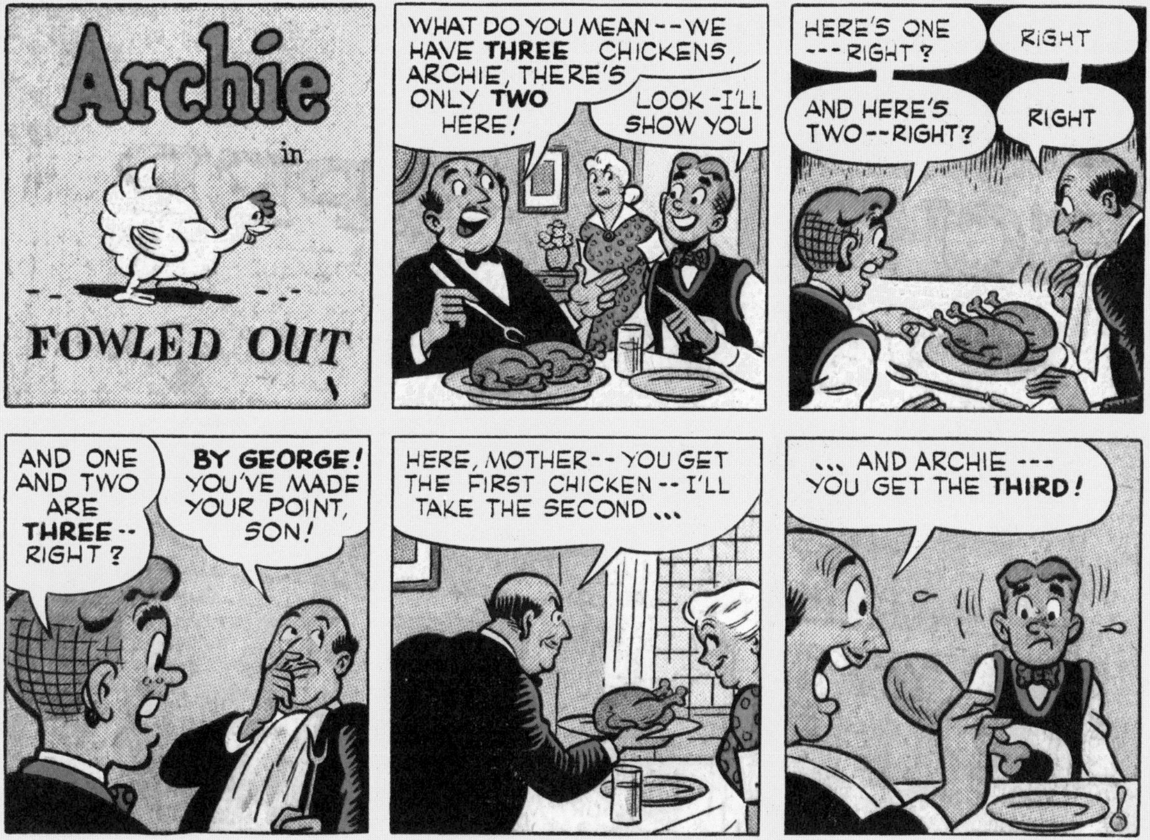
Archie
in
FOWLED OUT
WHAT DO YOU MEAN--WE HAVE THREE CHICKENS, ARCHIE, THERE'S ONLY TWO HERE!
LOOK-I'LL SHOW YOU
HERE'S ONE ---RIGHT?
RIGHT
AND HERE'S TWO--RIGHT?
RIGHT
AND ONE AND TWO ARE THREE-- RIGHT?
BY GEORGE! YOU'VE MADE YOUR POINT, SON!
HERE, MOTHER--YOU GET THE FIRST CHICKEN--I'LL TAKE THE SECOND...
... AND ARCHIE --- YOU GET THE THIRD!

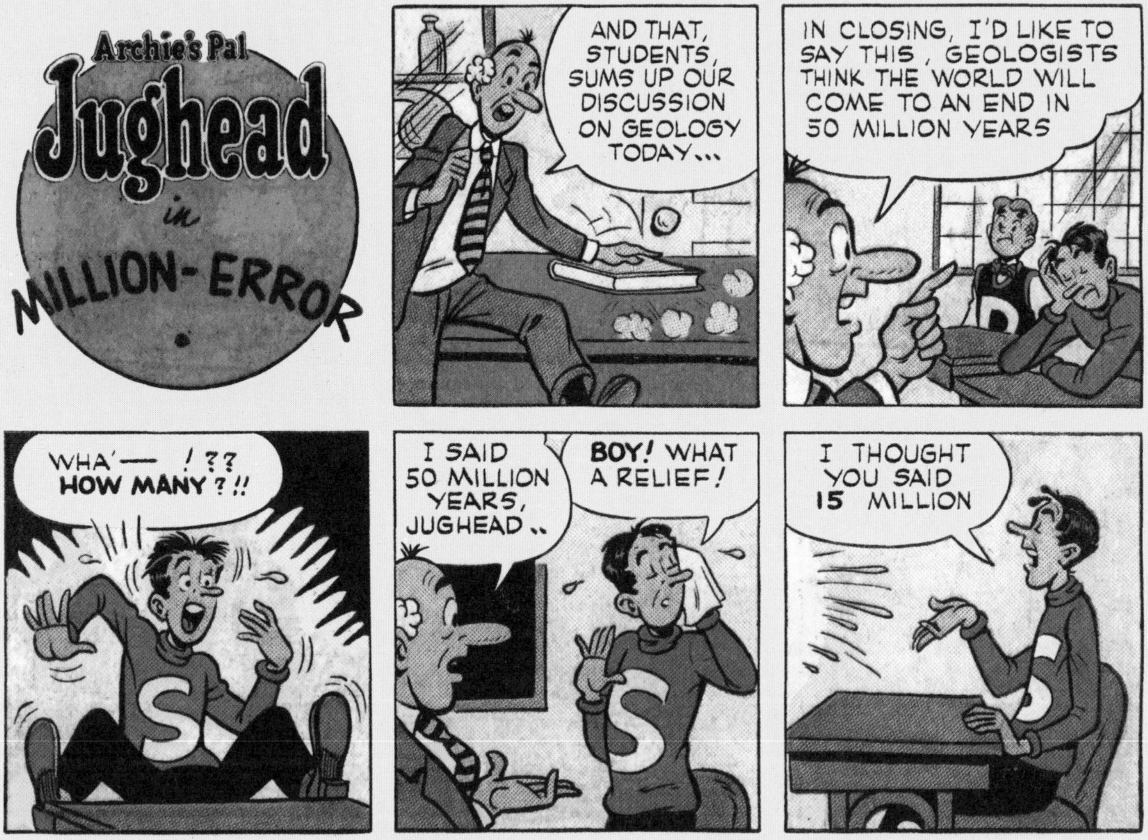

Archie's Pal
Jughead
in
MILLION-ERROR
AND THAT, STUDENTS, SUMS UP OUR DISCUSSION ON GEOLOGY TODAY...
IN CLOSING, I'D LIKE TO SAY THIS, GEOLOGISTS THINK THE WORLD WILL COME TO AN END IN 50 MILLION YEARS
WHA'— !?? HOW MANY ?!!
I SAID 50 MILLION YEARS, JUGHEAD..
BOY! WHAT A RELIEF!
I THOUGHT YOU SAID 15 MILLION

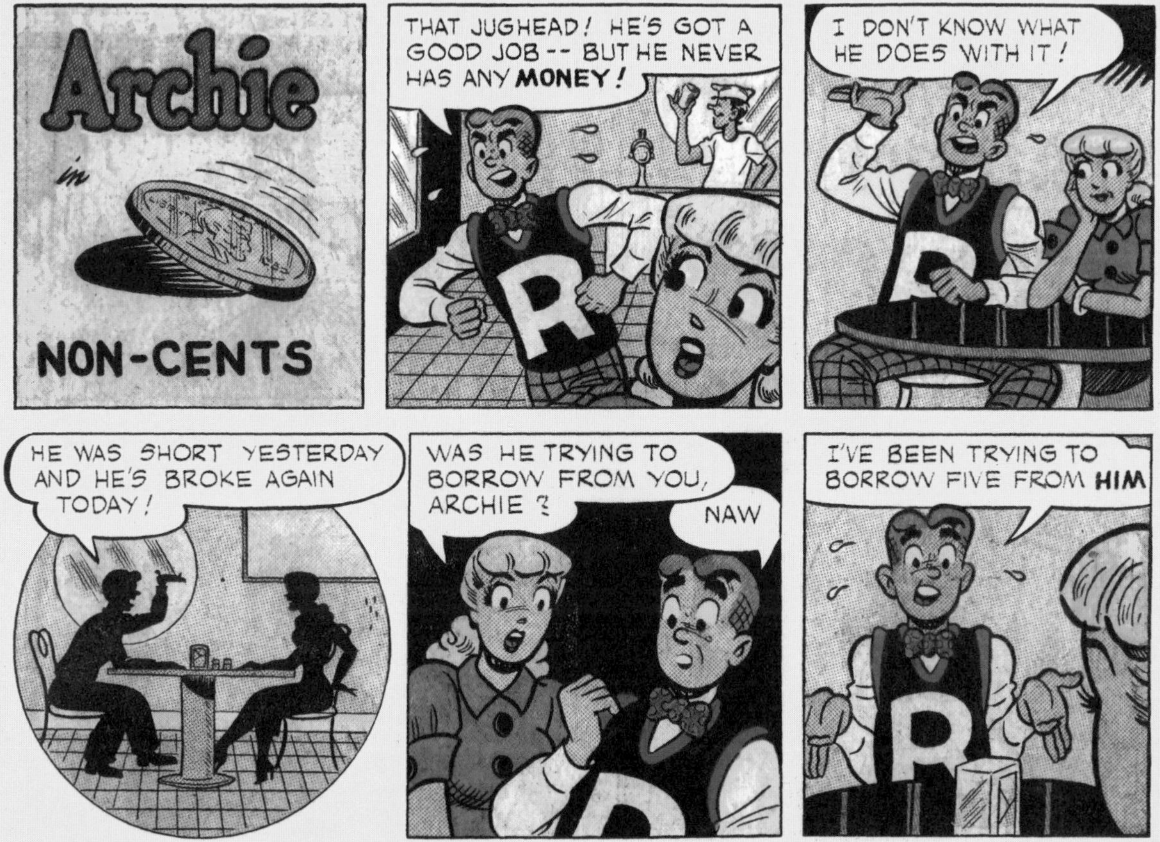
Archie
in
NON-CENTS
THAT JUGHEAD! HE'S GOT A GOOD JOB -- BUT HE NEVER HAS ANY MONEY!
I DON'T KNOW WHAT HE DOES WITH IT!
HE WAS SHORT YESTERDAY AND HE'S BROKE AGAIN TODAY!
WAS HE TRYING TO BORROW FROM YOU, ARCHIE ?
NAW
I'VE BEEN TRYING TO BORROW FIVE FROM HIM

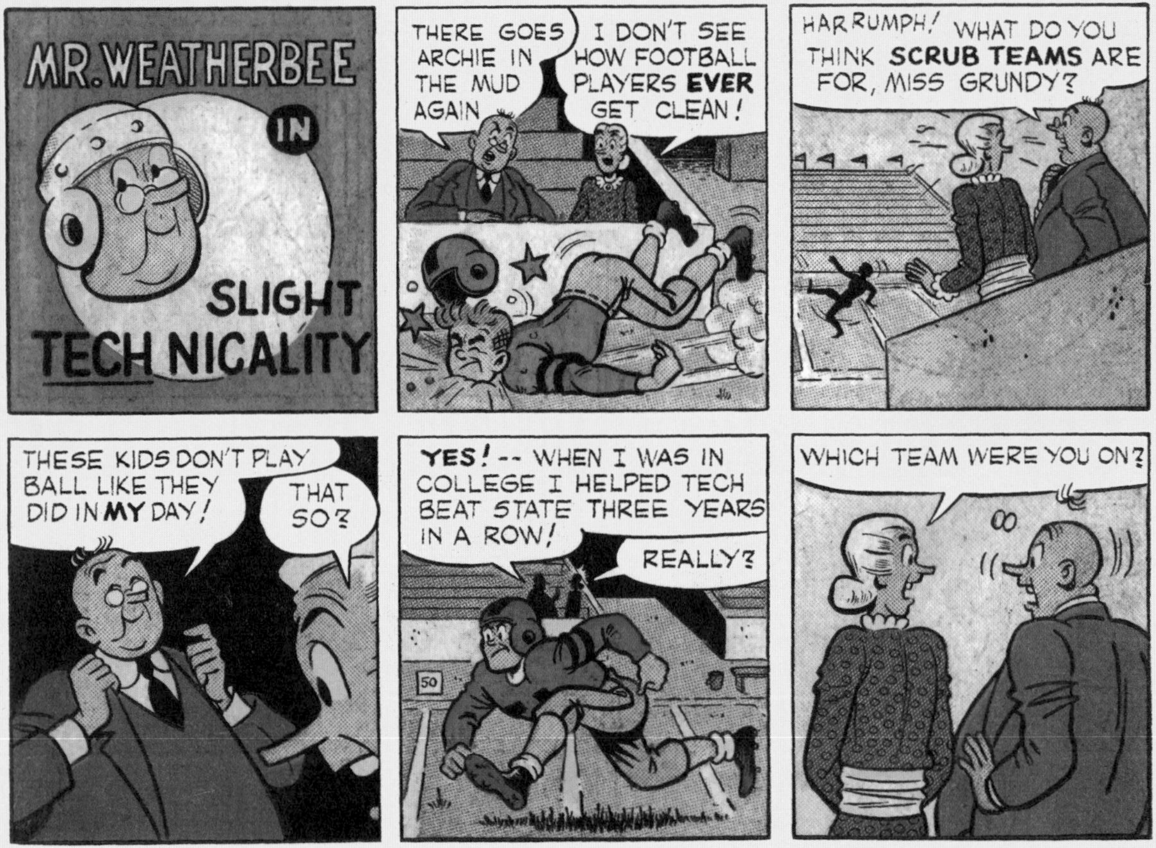
MR. WEATHERBEE
IN
SLIGHT TECH NICALITY
THERE GOES ARCHIE IN THE MUD AGAIN
I DON'T SEE HOW FOOTBALL PLAYERS EVER GET CLEAN!
HARRUMPH! WHAT DO YOU THINK SCRUB TEAMS ARE FOR, MISS GRUNDY?
THESE KIDS DON'T PLAY BALL LIKE THEY DID IN MY DAY!
THAT SO?
YES! -- WHEN I WAS IN COLLEGE I HELPED TECH BEAT STATE THREE YEARS IN A ROW!
REALLY?
50
WHICH TEAM WERE YOU ON?

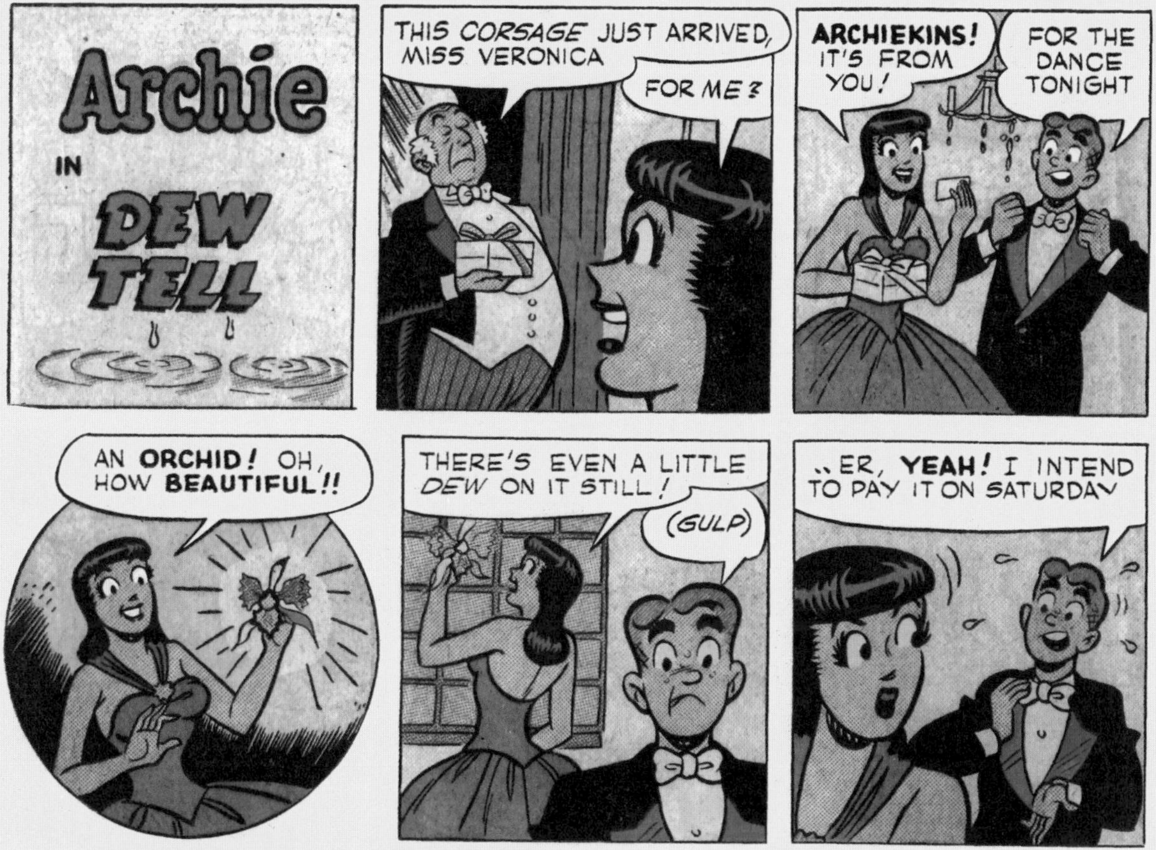
Archie
IN
DEW TELL
THIS CORSAGE JUST ARRIVED, MISS VERONICA
FOR ME?
ARCHIEKINS! IT'S FROM YOU!
FOR THE DANCE TONIGHT
AN ORCHID! OH, HOW BEAUTIFUL!!
THERE'S EVEN A LITTLE DEW ON IT STILL!
(GULP)
..ER, YEAH! I INTEND TO PAY IT ON SATURDAY

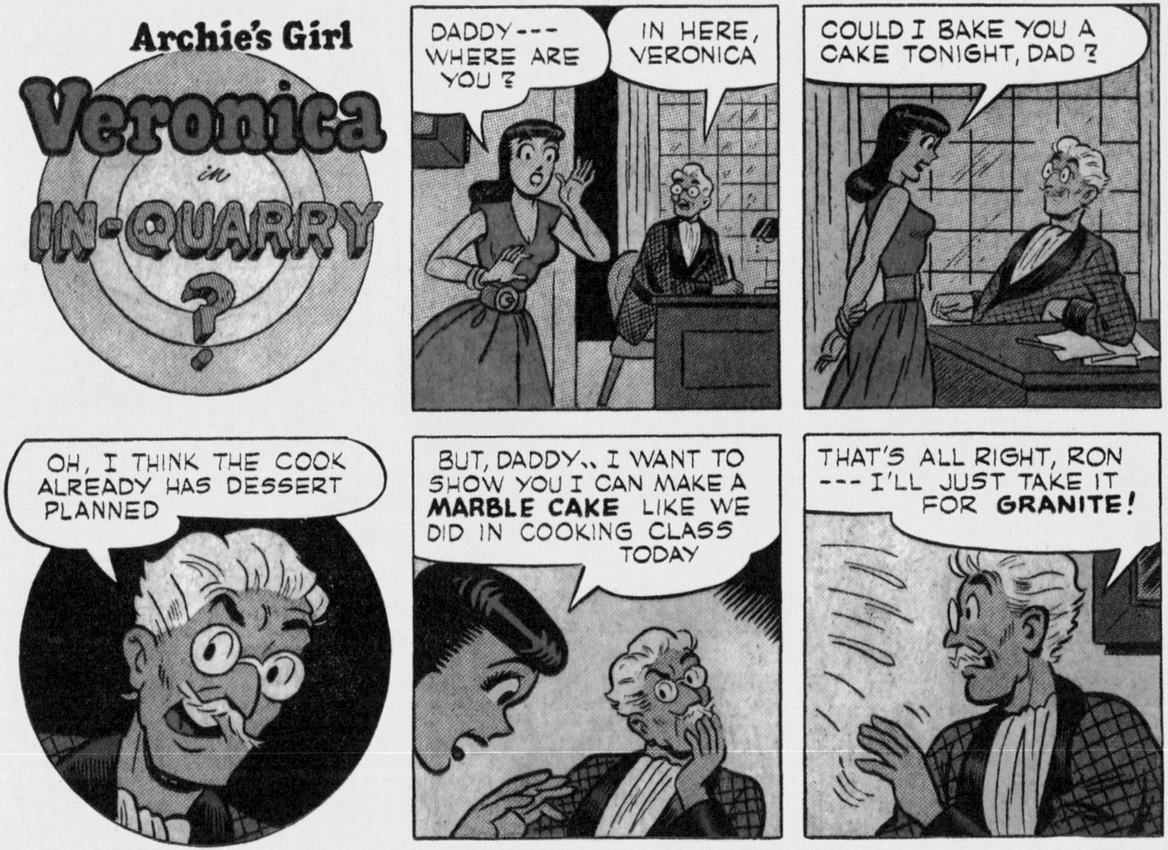
Archie's Girl
Veronica
in
IN-QUARRY
DADDY--- WHERE ARE YOU ?
IN HERE, VERONICA
COULD I BAKE YOU A CAKE TONIGHT, DAD ?
OH, I THINK THE COOK ALREADY HAS DESSERT PLANNED
BUT, DADDY.. I WANT TO SHOW YOU I CAN MAKE A MARBLE CAKE LIKE WE DID IN COOKING CLASS TODAY
THAT'S ALL RIGHT, RON --- I'LL JUST TAKE IT FOR GRANITE!

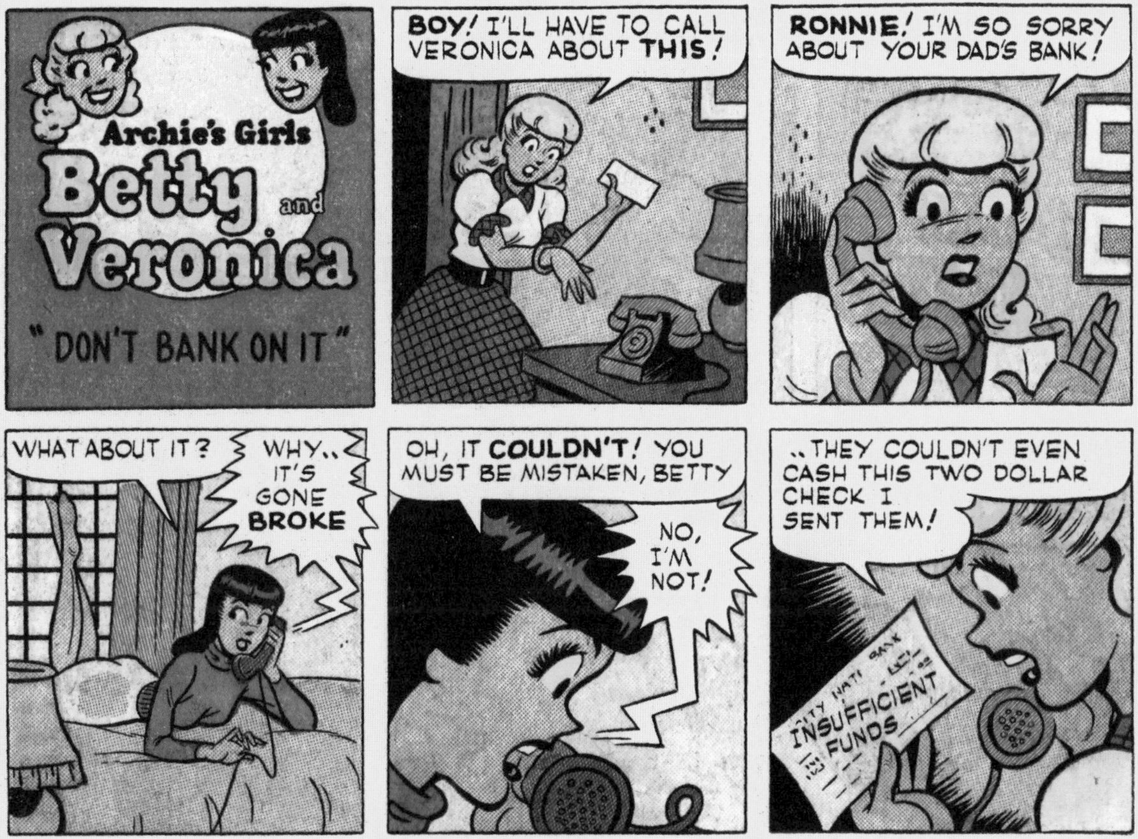

Archie's Girls
Betty and Veronica
"DON'T BANK ON IT"
BOY! I'LL HAVE TO CALL VERONICA ABOUT THIS!
RONNIE! I'M SO SORRY ABOUT YOUR DAD'S BANK!
WHAT ABOUT IT?
WHY.. IT'S GONE BROKE
OH, IT COULDN'T! YOU MUST BE MISTAKEN, BETTY
NO, I'M NOT!
..THEY COULDN'T EVEN CASH THIS TWO DOLLAR CHECK I SENT THEM!
INSUFFICIENT FUNDS

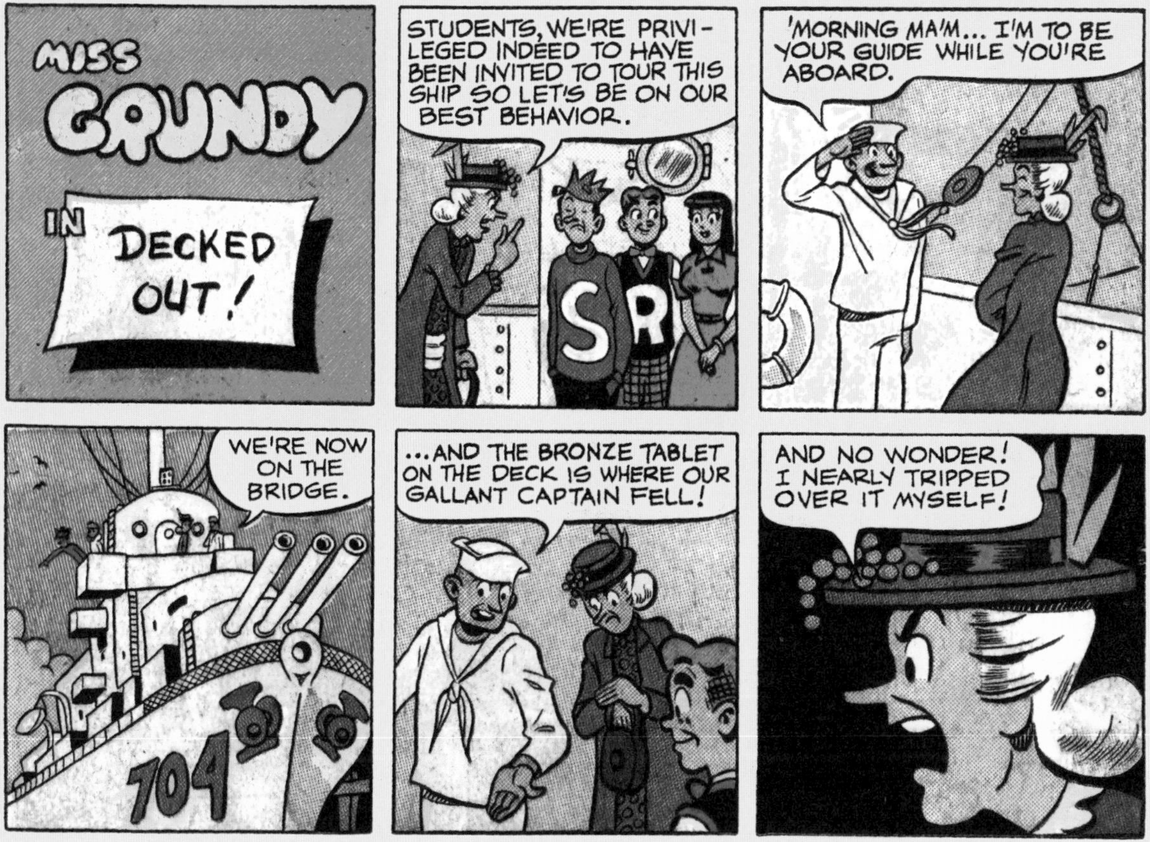
MISS GRUNDY
IN DECKED OUT!
STUDENTS, WE'RE PRIVI-LEGED INDEED TO HAVE BEEN INVITED TO TOUR THIS SHIP SO LET'S BE ON OUR BEST BEHAVIOR.
S
R
'MORNING MA'M... I'M TO BE YOUR GUIDE WHILE YOU'RE ABOARD.
WE'RE NOW ON THE BRIDGE.
704
...AND THE BRONZE TABLET ON THE DECK IS WHERE OUR GALLANT CAPTAIN FELL!
AND NO WONDER! I NEARLY TRIPPED OVER IT MYSELF!

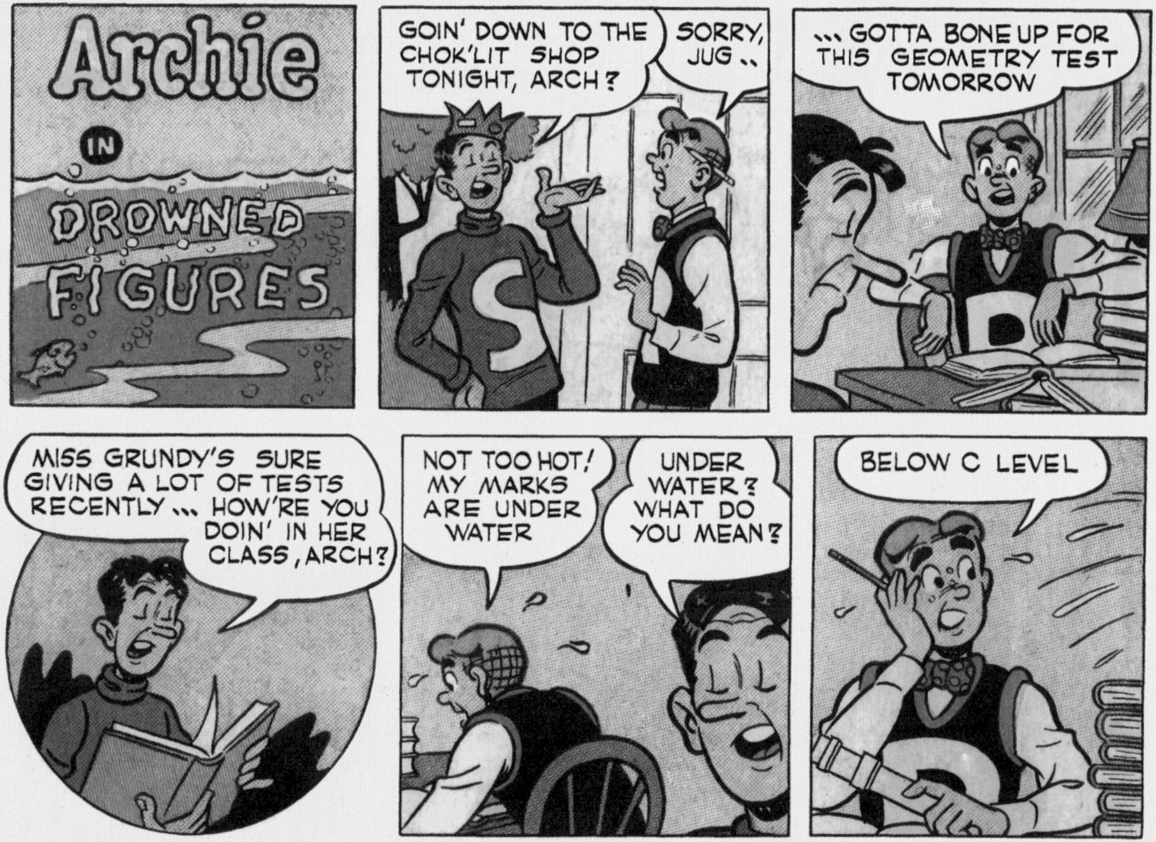
Archie
IN
DROWNED FIGURES
GOIN' DOWN TO THE CHOK'LIT SHOP TONIGHT, ARCH?
SORRY, JUG..
... GOTTA BONE UP FOR THIS GEOMETRY TEST TOMORROW
MISS GRUNDY'S SURE GIVING A LOT OF TESTS RECENTLY ... HOW'RE YOU DOIN' IN HER CLASS, ARCH?
NOT TOO HOT! MY MARKS ARE UNDER WATER
UNDER WATER? WHAT DO YOU MEAN?
BELOW C LEVEL

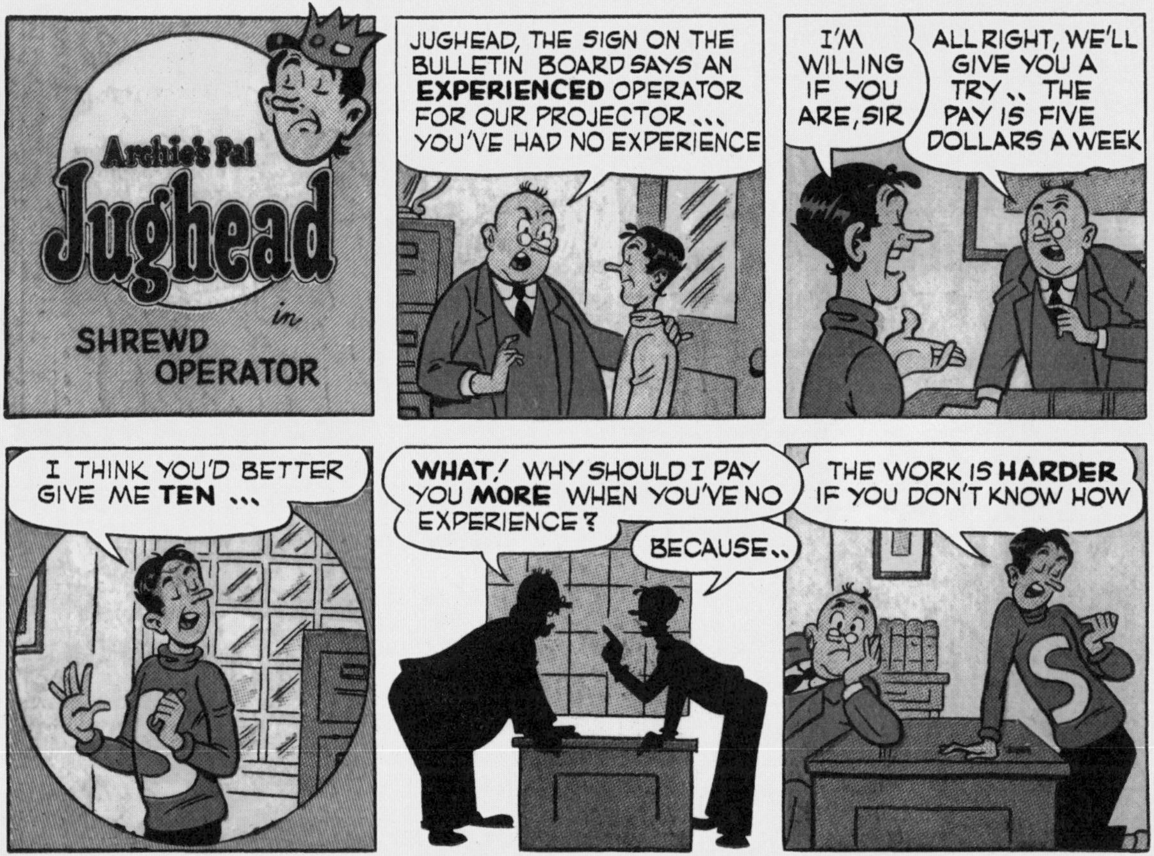

Archie's Pal
Jughead
in
SHREWD OPERATOR
JUGHEAD, THE SIGN ON THE BULLETIN BOARD SAYS AN **EXPERIENCED** OPERATOR FOR OUR PROJECTOR ... YOU'VE HAD NO EXPERIENCE
I'M WILLING IF YOU ARE, SIR
ALL RIGHT, WE'LL GIVE YOU A TRY .. THE PAY IS FIVE DOLLARS A WEEK
I THINK YOU'D BETTER GIVE ME **TEN** ...
WHAT! WHY SHOULD I PAY YOU **MORE** WHEN YOU'VE NO EXPERIENCE?
BECAUSE..
THE WORK IS **HARDER** IF YOU DON'T KNOW HOW

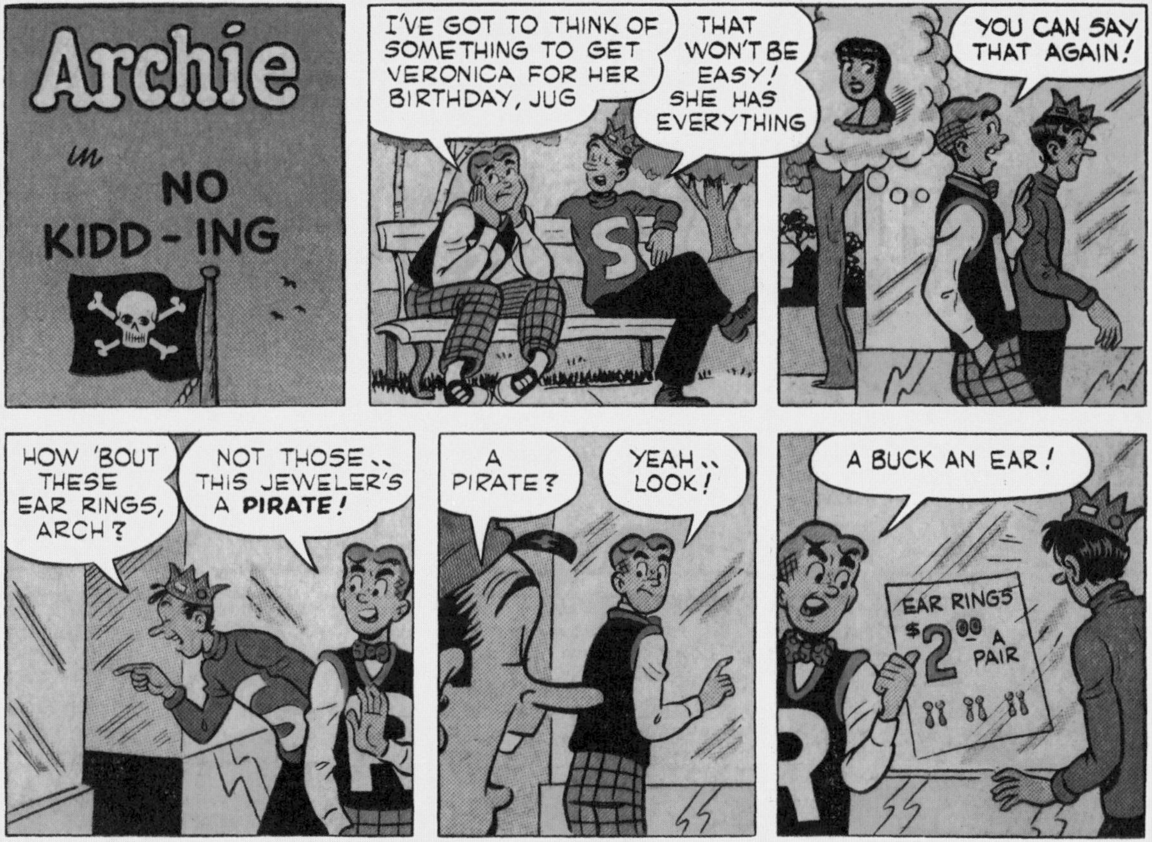
Archie
in
NO KIDD-ING
I'VE GOT TO THINK OF SOMETHING TO GET VERONICA FOR HER BIRTHDAY, JUG
THAT WON'T BE EASY! SHE HAS EVERYTHING
YOU CAN SAY THAT AGAIN!
HOW 'BOUT THESE EAR RINGS, ARCH?
NOT THOSE .. THIS JEWELER'S A PIRATE!
A PIRATE?
YEAH .. LOOK!
A BUCK AN EAR!
EAR RINGS $2.00 A PAIR

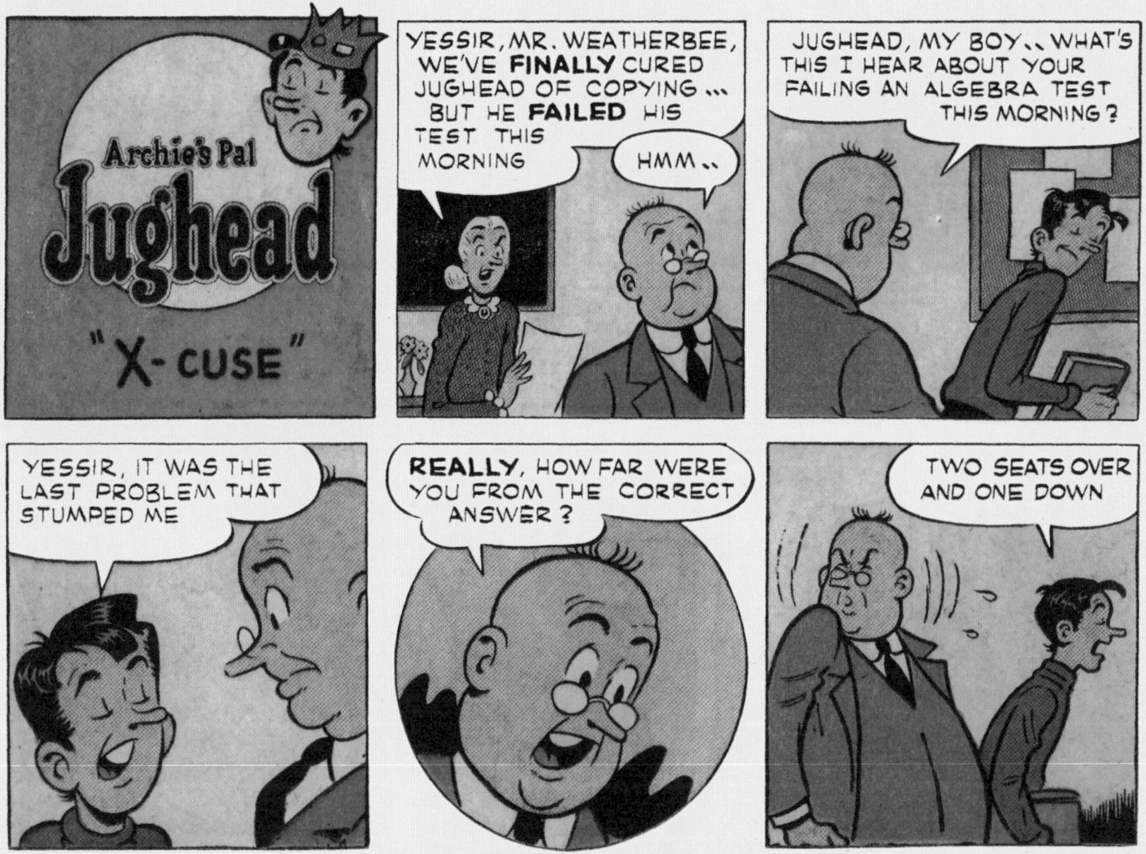
Archie's Pal
Jughead
"X-CUSE"
YESSIR, MR. WEATHERBEE, WE'VE FINALLY CURED JUGHEAD OF COPYING ... BUT HE FAILED HIS TEST THIS MORNING
HMM ..
JUGHEAD, MY BOY .. WHAT'S THIS I HEAR ABOUT YOUR FAILING AN ALGEBRA TEST THIS MORNING ?
YESSIR, IT WAS THE LAST PROBLEM THAT STUMPED ME
REALLY, HOW FAR WERE YOU FROM THE CORRECT ANSWER ?
TWO SEATS OVER AND ONE DOWN

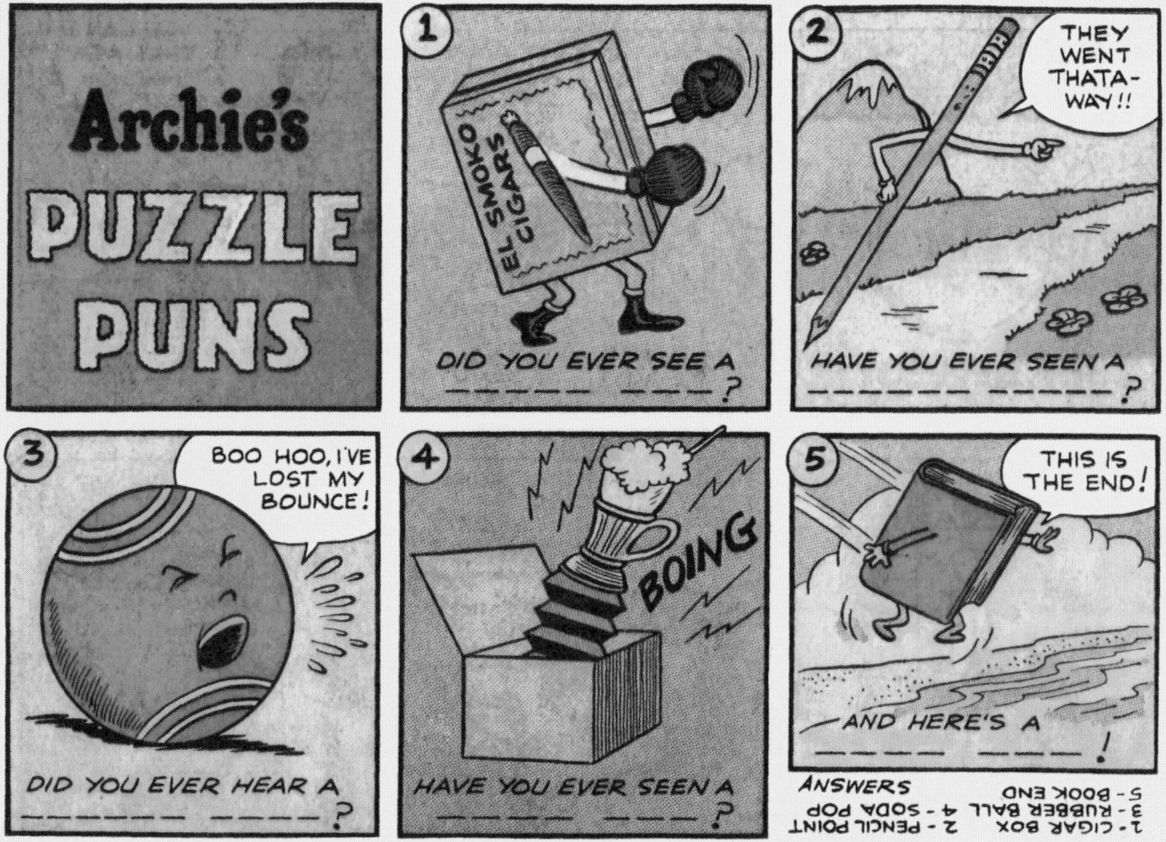
Archie's
PUZZLE
PUNS
1
EL SMOKO CIGARS
DID YOU EVER SEE A
_ _ _ _ _ _ _ _ _ ?
2
THEY WENT THATA-WAY!!
HAVE YOU EVER SEEN A
_ _ _ _ _ _ _ _ _ _ _ ?
3
BOO HOO, I'VE LOST MY BOUNCE!
DID YOU EVER HEAR A
_ _ _ _ _ _ _ _ _ _ ?
4
BOING
HAVE YOU EVER SEEN A
_ _ _ _ _ _ _ ?
5
THIS IS THE END!
AND HERE'S A
_ _ _ _ _ _ _ !

ANSWERS

1 - CIGAR BOX 2 - PENCIL POINT
3 - RUBBER BALL 4 - SODA POP
5 - BOOK END

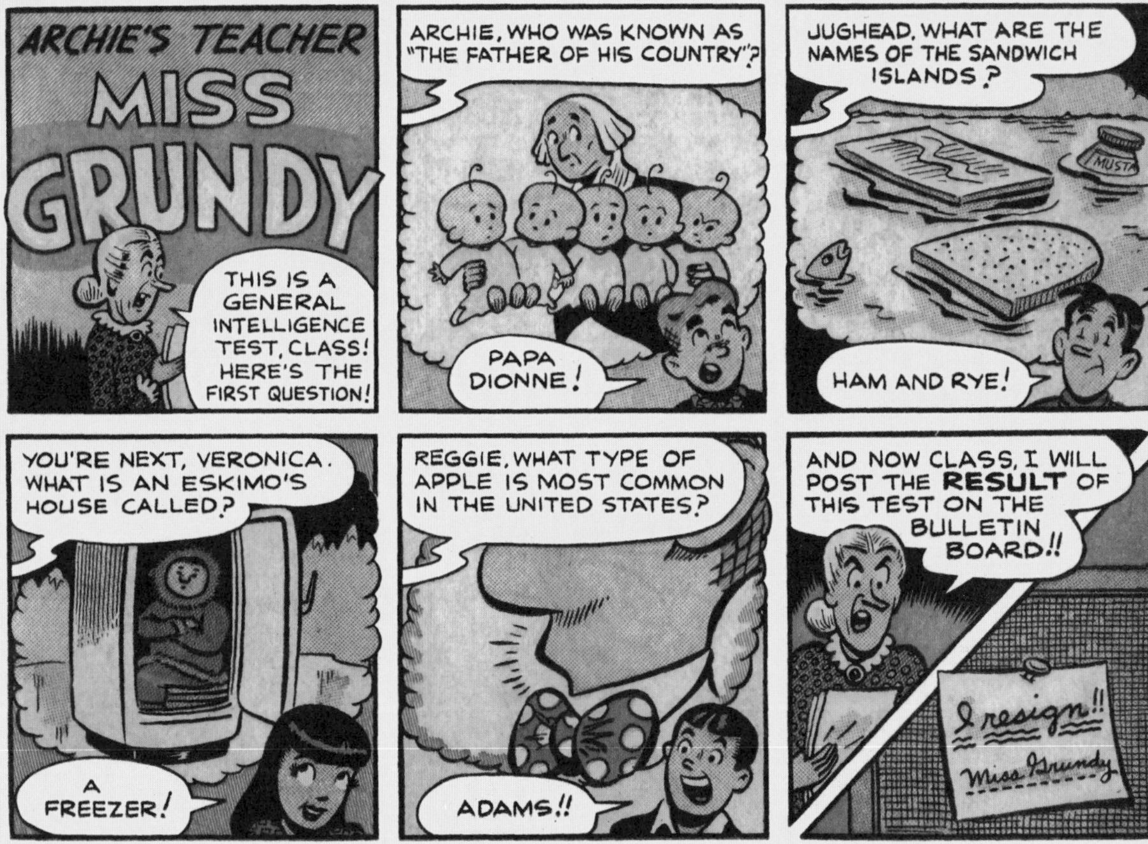
ARCHIE'S TEACHER
MISS GRUNDY
THIS IS A GENERAL INTELLIGENCE TEST, CLASS! HERE'S THE FIRST QUESTION!
ARCHIE, WHO WAS KNOWN AS "THE FATHER OF HIS COUNTRY"?
PAPA DIONNE!
JUGHEAD, WHAT ARE THE NAMES OF THE SANDWICH ISLANDS?
MUSTA
HAM AND RYE!
YOU'RE NEXT, VERONICA. WHAT IS AN ESKIMO'S HOUSE CALLED?
A FREEZER!
REGGIE, WHAT TYPE OF APPLE IS MOST COMMON IN THE UNITED STATES?
ADAMS!!
AND NOW CLASS, I WILL POST THE RESULT OF THIS TEST ON THE BULLETIN BOARD!!
I resign!!
Miss Grundy

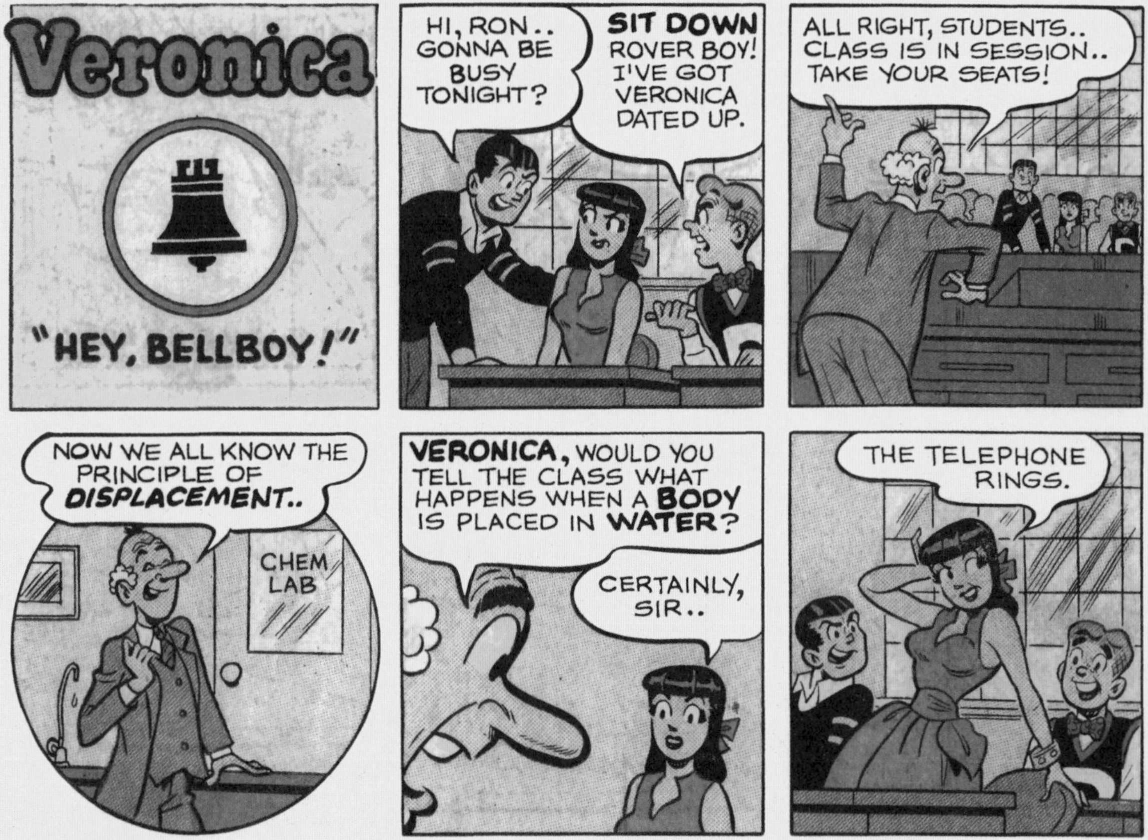
Veronica
"HEY, BELLBOY!"
HI, RON.. GONNA BE BUSY TONIGHT?
SIT DOWN ROVER BOY! I'VE GOT VERONICA DATED UP.
ALL RIGHT, STUDENTS.. CLASS IS IN SESSION.. TAKE YOUR SEATS!
NOW WE ALL KNOW THE PRINCIPLE OF DISPLACEMENT..
CHEM LAB
VERONICA, WOULD YOU TELL THE CLASS WHAT HAPPENS WHEN A BODY IS PLACED IN WATER?
CERTAINLY, SIR..
THE TELEPHONE RINGS.

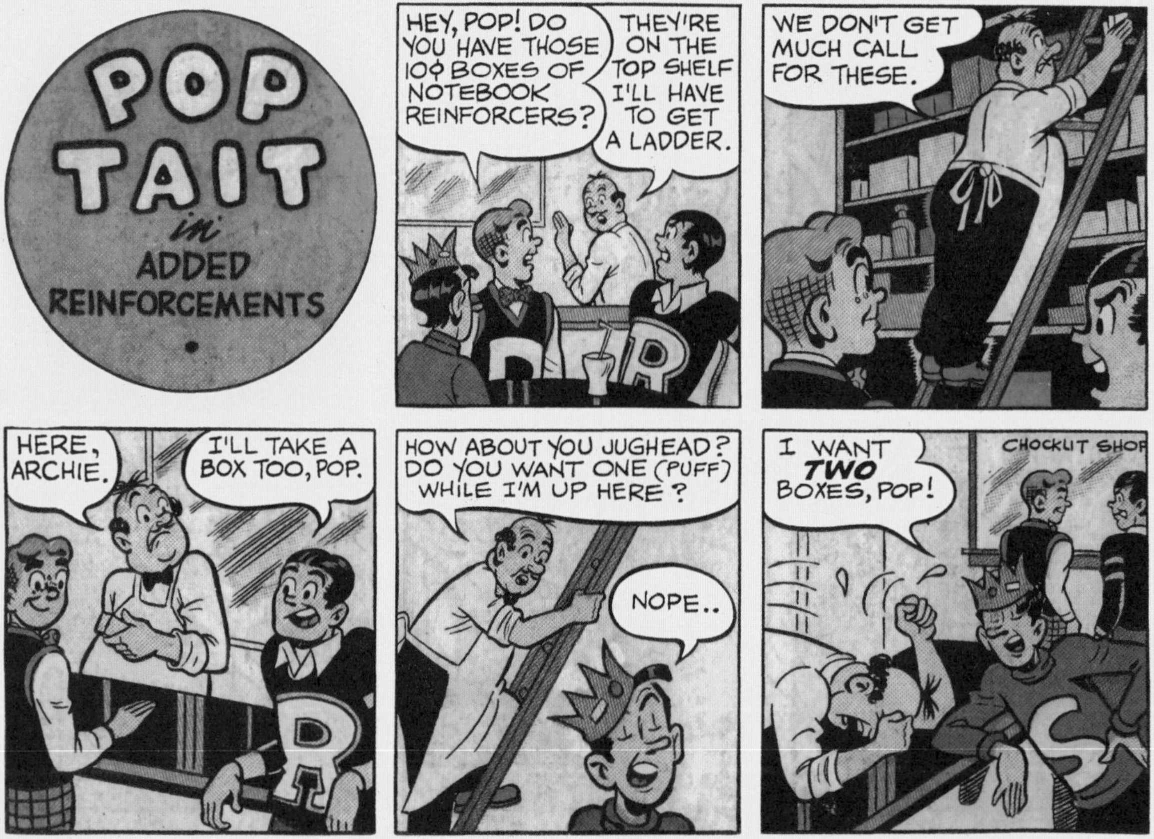
POP TAIT in ADDED REINFORCEMENTS
HEY, POP! DO YOU HAVE THOSE 10¢ BOXES OF NOTEBOOK REINFORCERS?
THEY'RE ON THE TOP SHELF I'LL HAVE TO GET A LADDER.
WE DON'T GET MUCH CALL FOR THESE.
HERE, ARCHIE.
I'LL TAKE A BOX TOO, POP.
HOW ABOUT YOU JUGHEAD? DO YOU WANT ONE (PUFF) WHILE I'M UP HERE?
NOPE..
I WANT TWO BOXES, POP!
CHOCKLIT SHOP

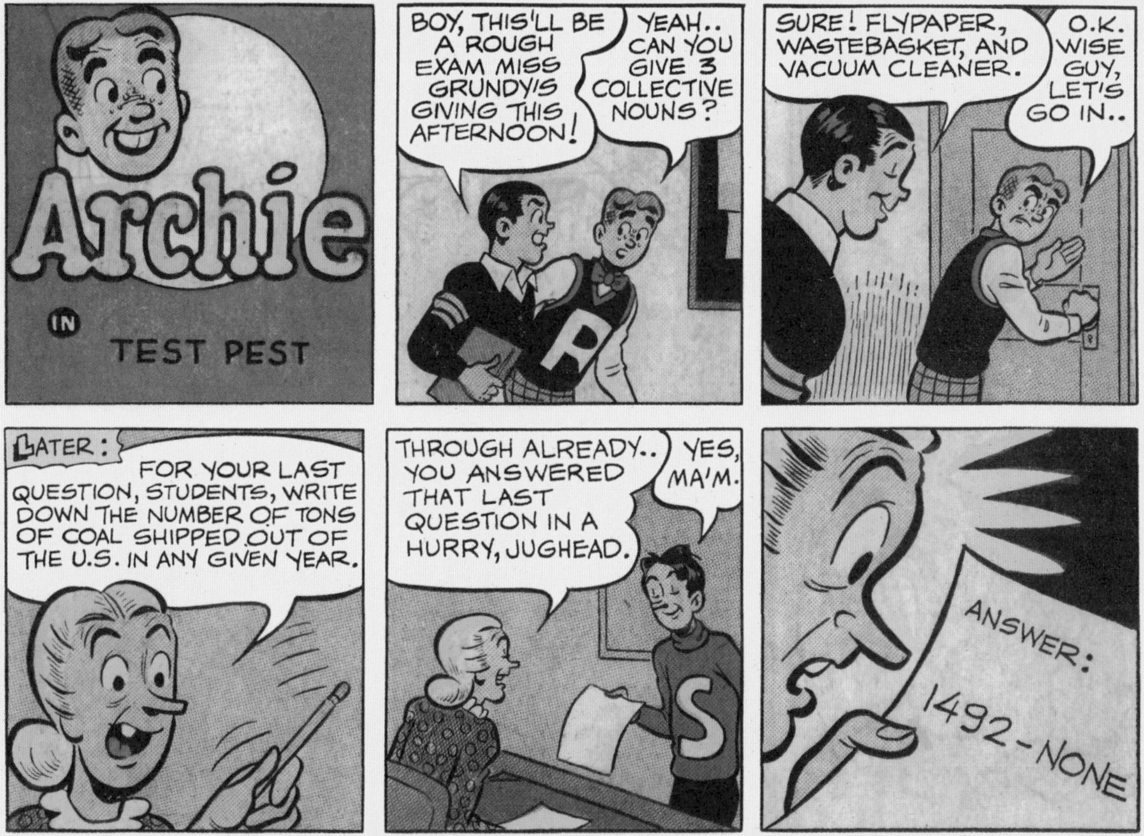
Archie
IN
TEST PEST
BOY, THIS'LL BE A ROUGH EXAM MISS GRUNDY'S GIVING THIS AFTERNOON!
YEAH.. CAN YOU GIVE 3 COLLECTIVE NOUNS?
SURE! FLYPAPER, WASTEBASKET, AND VACUUM CLEANER.
O.K. WISE GUY, LET'S GO IN..
LATER:
FOR YOUR LAST QUESTION, STUDENTS, WRITE DOWN THE NUMBER OF TONS OF COAL SHIPPED OUT OF THE U.S. IN ANY GIVEN YEAR.
THROUGH ALREADY.. YOU ANSWERED THAT LAST QUESTION IN A HURRY, JUGHEAD.
YES, MA'M.
ANSWER:
1492-NONE

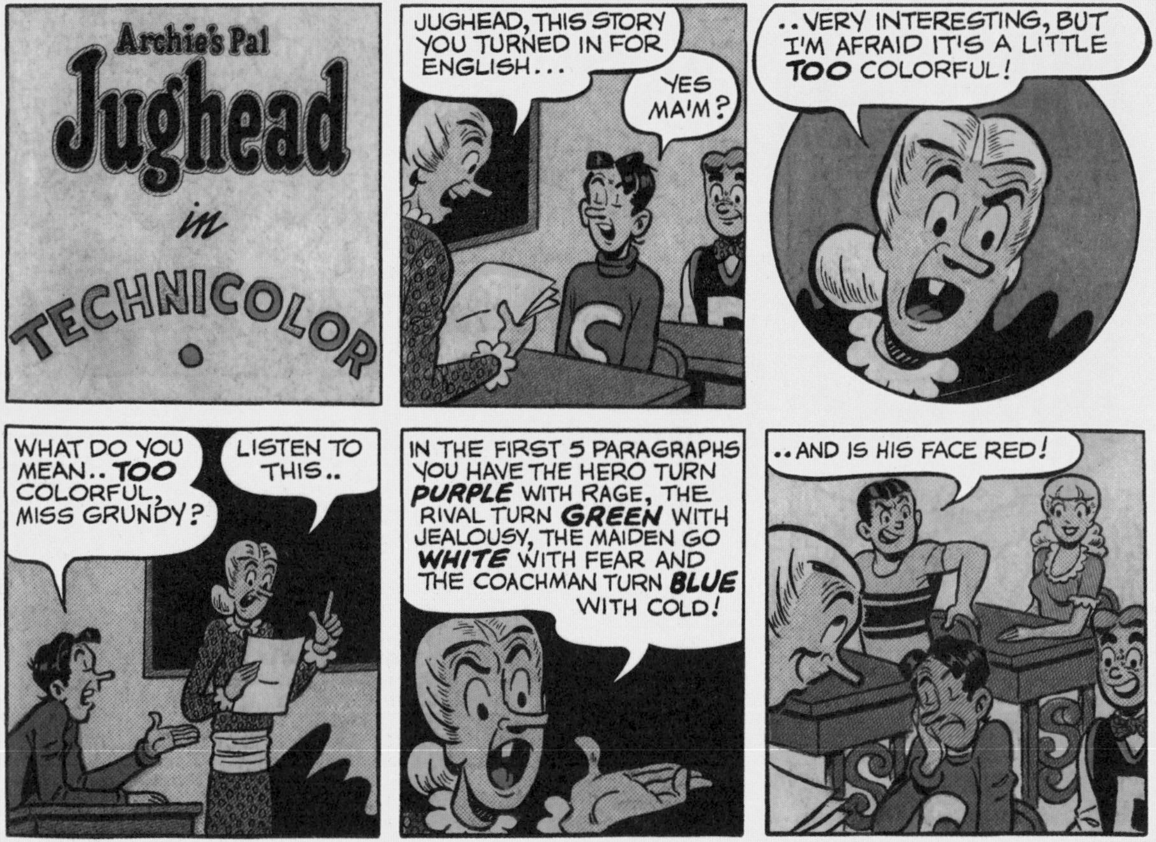
Archie's Pal
Jughead
in
TECHNICOLOR
JUGHEAD, THIS STORY YOU TURNED IN FOR ENGLISH...
YES MA'M?
..VERY INTERESTING, BUT I'M AFRAID IT'S A LITTLE TOO COLORFUL!
WHAT DO YOU MEAN.. TOO COLORFUL, MISS GRUNDY?
LISTEN TO THIS..
IN THE FIRST 5 PARAGRAPHS YOU HAVE THE HERO TURN PURPLE WITH RAGE, THE RIVAL TURN GREEN WITH JEALOUSY, THE MAIDEN GO WHITE WITH FEAR AND THE COACHMAN TURN BLUE WITH COLD!
..AND IS HIS FACE RED!

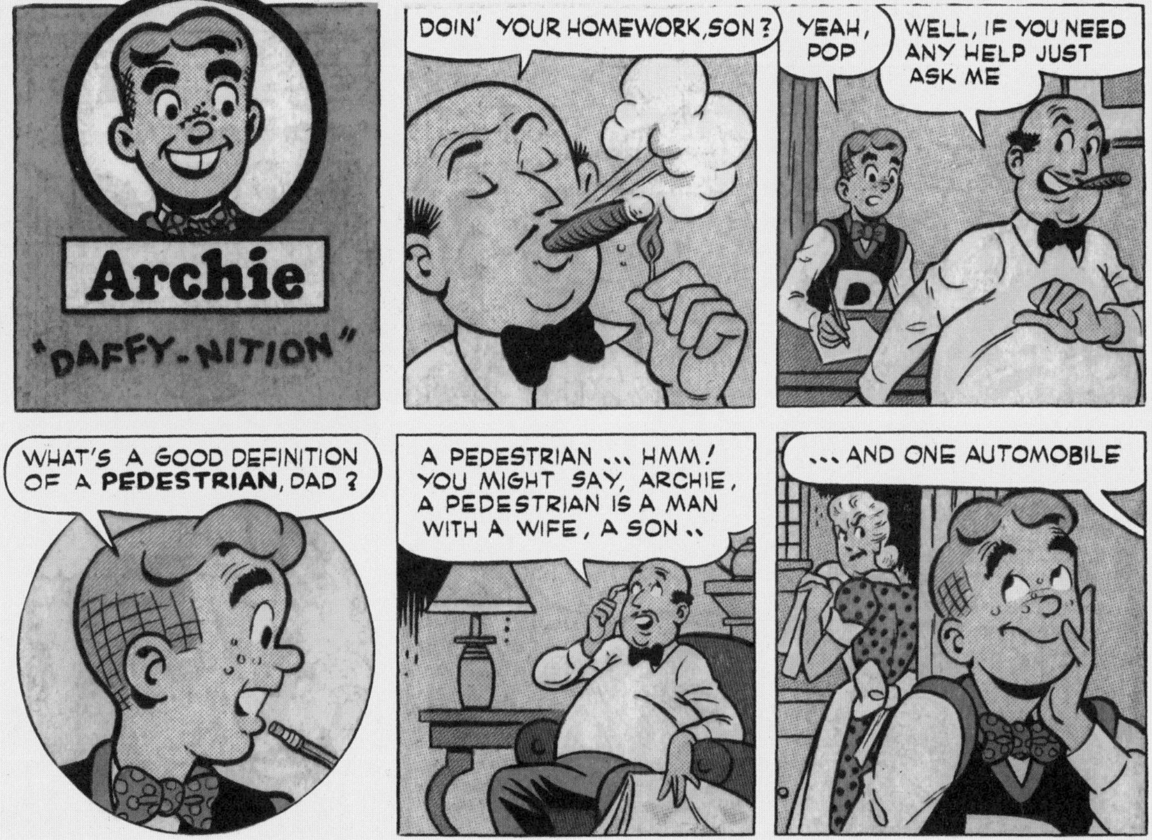
Archie
"DAFFY-NITION"
DOIN' YOUR HOMEWORK, SON?
YEAH, POP
WELL, IF YOU NEED ANY HELP JUST ASK ME
WHAT'S A GOOD DEFINITION OF A **PEDESTRIAN**, DAD?
A PEDESTRIAN ... HMM! YOU MIGHT SAY, ARCHIE, A PEDESTRIAN IS A MAN WITH A WIFE, A SON ..
... AND ONE AUTOMOBILE

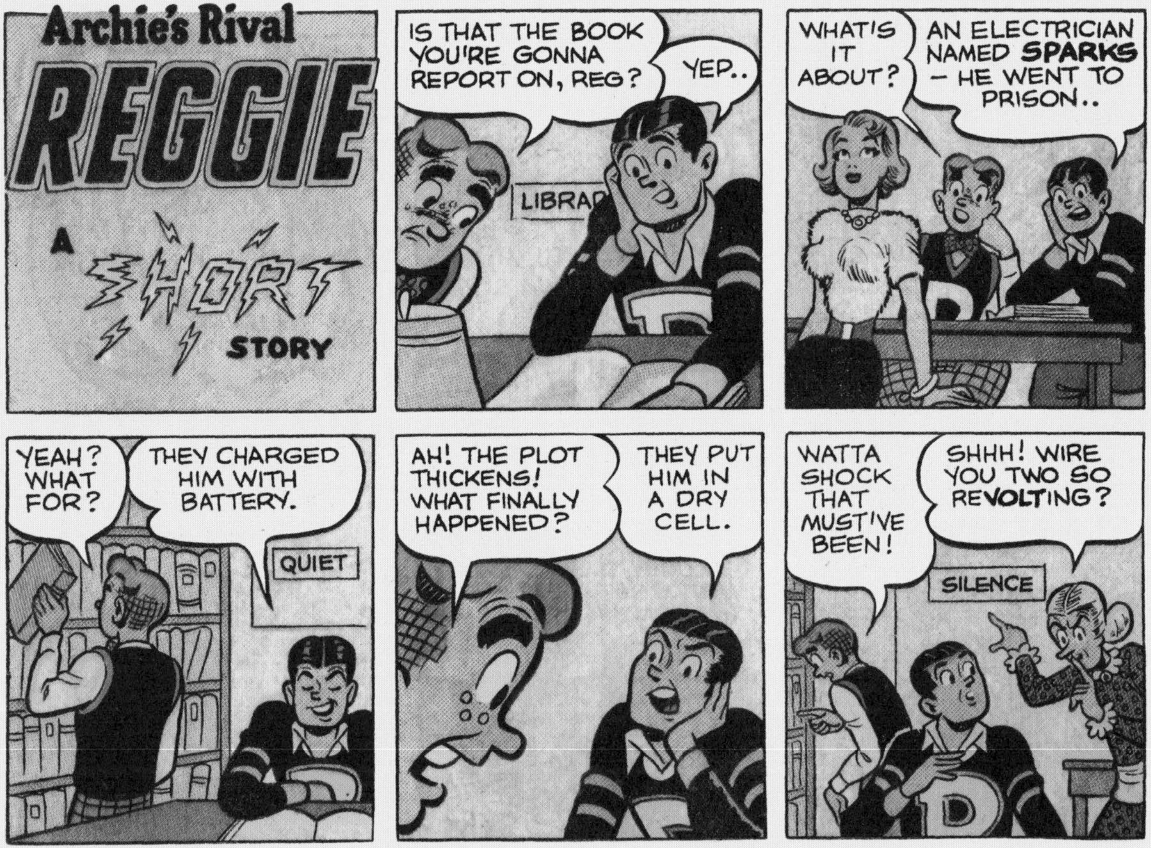
Archie's Rival
REGGIE
A SHORT STORY
IS THAT THE BOOK YOU'RE GONNA REPORT ON, REG?
YEP..
LIBRAR
WHAT'S IT ABOUT?
AN ELECTRICIAN NAMED SPARKS – HE WENT TO PRISON..
YEAH? WHAT FOR?
THEY CHARGED HIM WITH BATTERY.
QUIET
AH! THE PLOT THICKENS! WHAT FINALLY HAPPENED?
THEY PUT HIM IN A DRY CELL.
WATTA SHOCK THAT MUST'VE BEEN!
SHHH! WIRE YOU TWO SO REVOLTING?
SILENCE

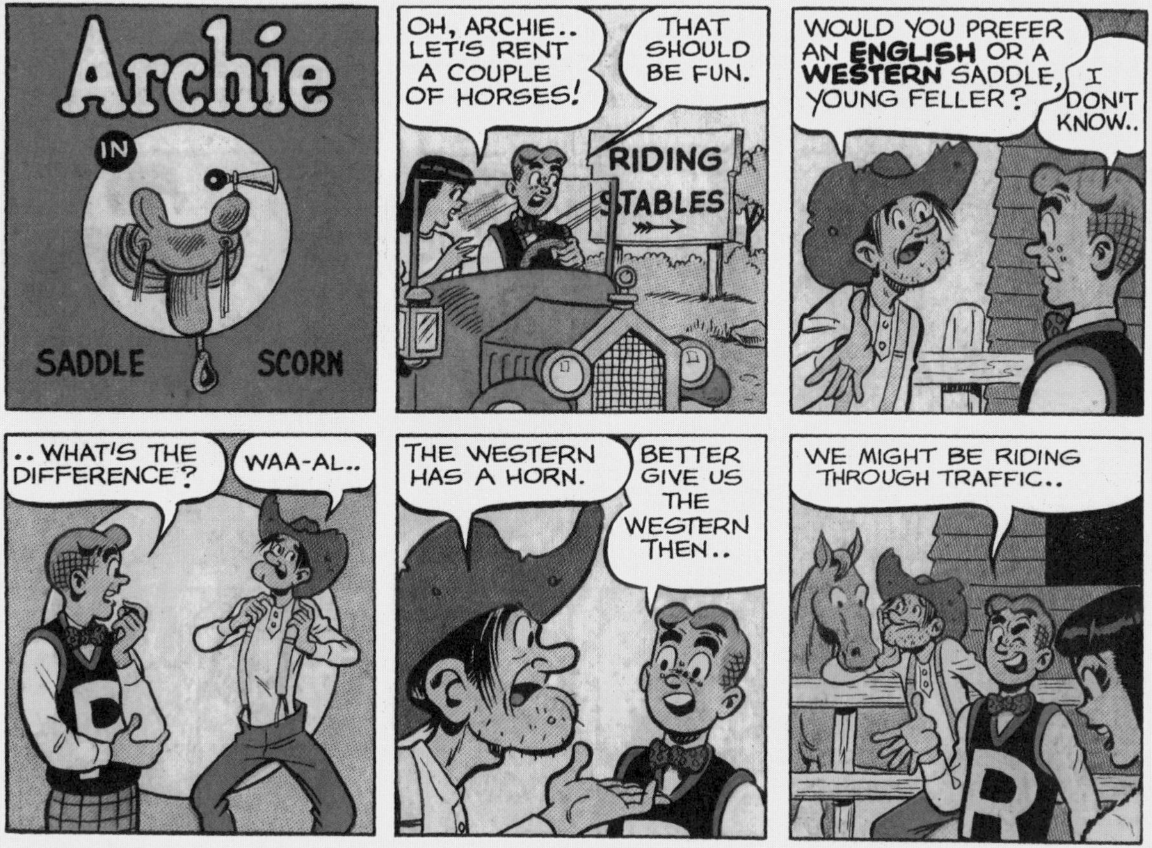
Archie
IN
SADDLE SCORN
OH, ARCHIE.. LET'S RENT A COUPLE OF HORSES!
THAT SHOULD BE FUN.
RIDING STABLES
WOULD YOU PREFER AN **ENGLISH** OR A **WESTERN** SADDLE, YOUNG FELLER?
I DON'T KNOW..
..WHAT'S THE DIFFERENCE?
WAA-AL..
THE WESTERN HAS A HORN.
BETTER GIVE US THE WESTERN THEN..
WE MIGHT BE RIDING THROUGH TRAFFIC..

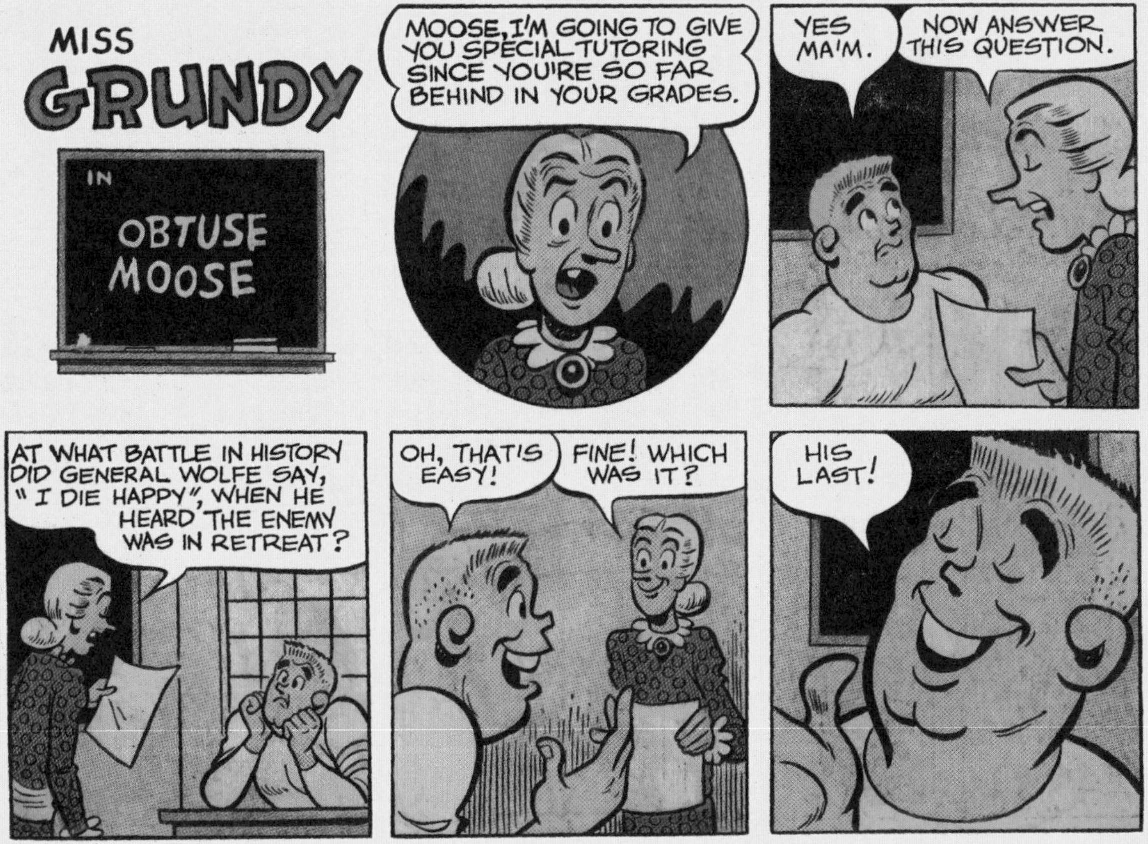
MISS
GRUNDY
IN
OBTUSE MOOSE
MOOSE, I'M GOING TO GIVE YOU SPECIAL TUTORING SINCE YOU'RE SO FAR BEHIND IN YOUR GRADES.
YES MA'M.
NOW ANSWER THIS QUESTION.
AT WHAT BATTLE IN HISTORY DID GENERAL WOLFE SAY, "I DIE HAPPY", WHEN HE HEARD THE ENEMY WAS IN RETREAT?
OH, THAT'S EASY!
FINE! WHICH WAS IT?
HIS LAST!

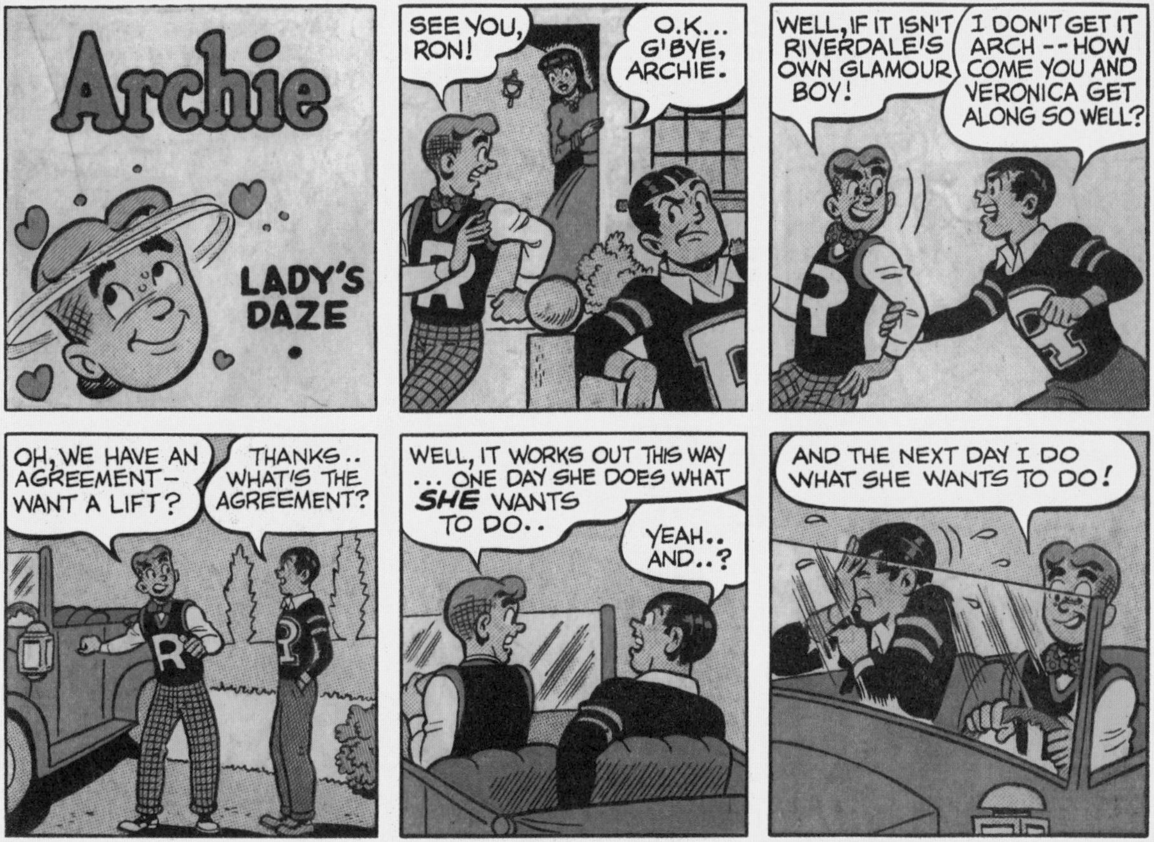
Archie
LADY'S DAZE
SEE YOU, RON!
O.K... G'BYE, ARCHIE.
WELL, IF IT ISN'T RIVERDALE'S OWN GLAMOUR BOY!
I DON'T GET IT ARCH -- HOW COME YOU AND VERONICA GET ALONG SO WELL?
OH, WE HAVE AN AGREEMENT- WANT A LIFT?
THANKS.. WHAT'S THE AGREEMENT?
WELL, IT WORKS OUT THIS WAY ... ONE DAY SHE DOES WHAT SHE WANTS TO DO..
YEAH.. AND..?
AND THE NEXT DAY I DO WHAT SHE WANTS TO DO!

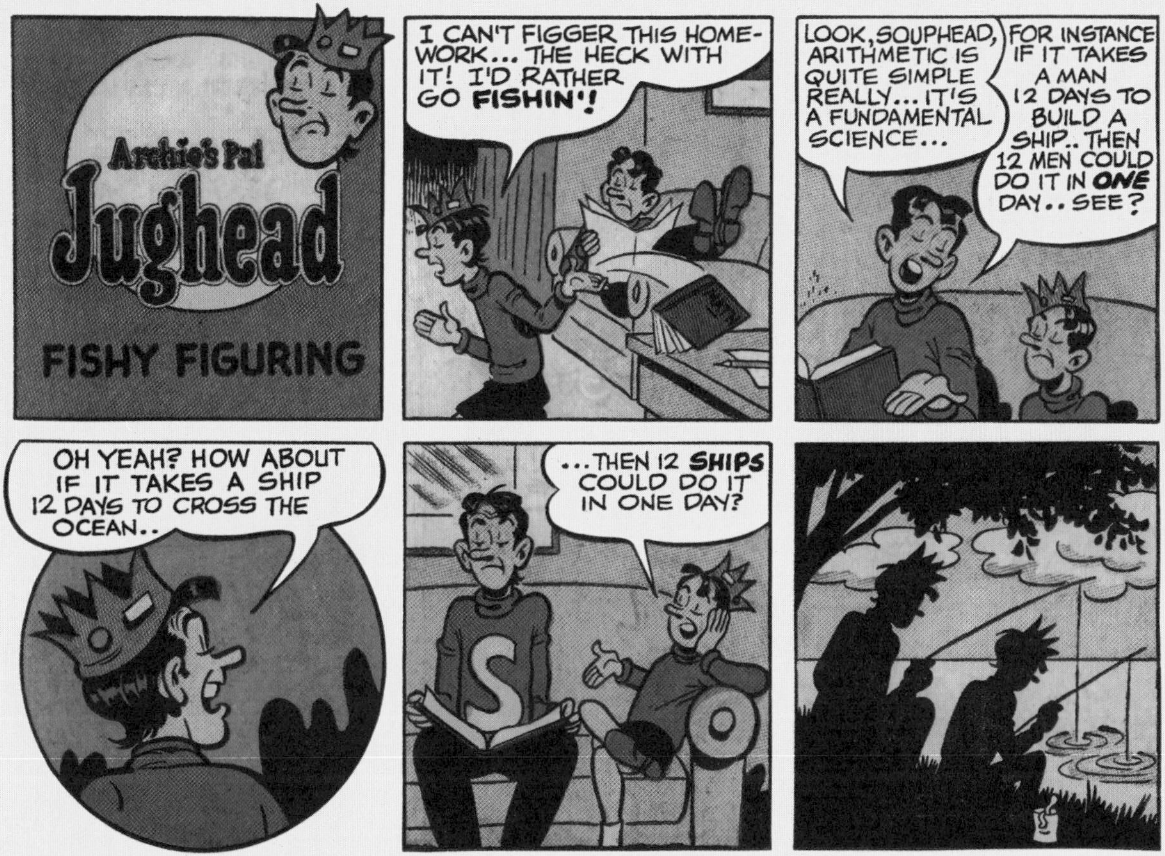
Archie's Pal
Jughead
FISHY FIGURING
I CAN'T FIGGER THIS HOME-WORK... THE HECK WITH IT! I'D RATHER GO FISHIN'!
LOOK, SOUPHEAD, ARITHMETIC IS QUITE SIMPLE REALLY... IT'S A FUNDAMENTAL SCIENCE...
FOR INSTANCE IF IT TAKES A MAN 12 DAYS TO BUILD A SHIP.. THEN 12 MEN COULD DO IT IN ONE DAY.. SEE?
OH YEAH? HOW ABOUT IF IT TAKES A SHIP 12 DAYS TO CROSS THE OCEAN..
...THEN 12 SHIPS COULD DO IT IN ONE DAY?

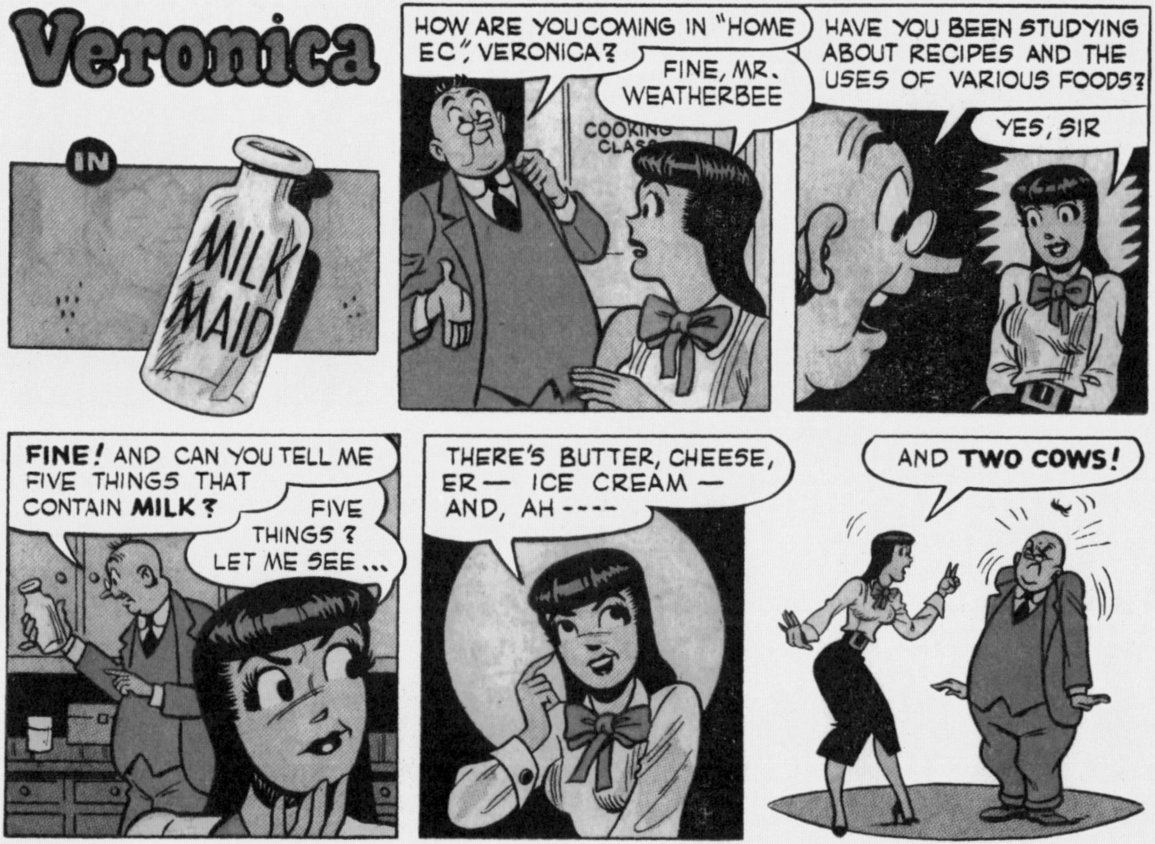

Veronica
IN
MILK MAID
COOKING CLASS
HOW ARE YOU COMING IN "HOME EC", VERONICA?
FINE, MR. WEATHERBEE
HAVE YOU BEEN STUDYING ABOUT RECIPES AND THE USES OF VARIOUS FOODS?
YES, SIR
FINE! AND CAN YOU TELL ME FIVE THINGS THAT CONTAIN MILK?
FIVE THINGS? LET ME SEE...
THERE'S BUTTER, CHEESE, ER— ICE CREAM — AND, AH ----
AND TWO COWS!

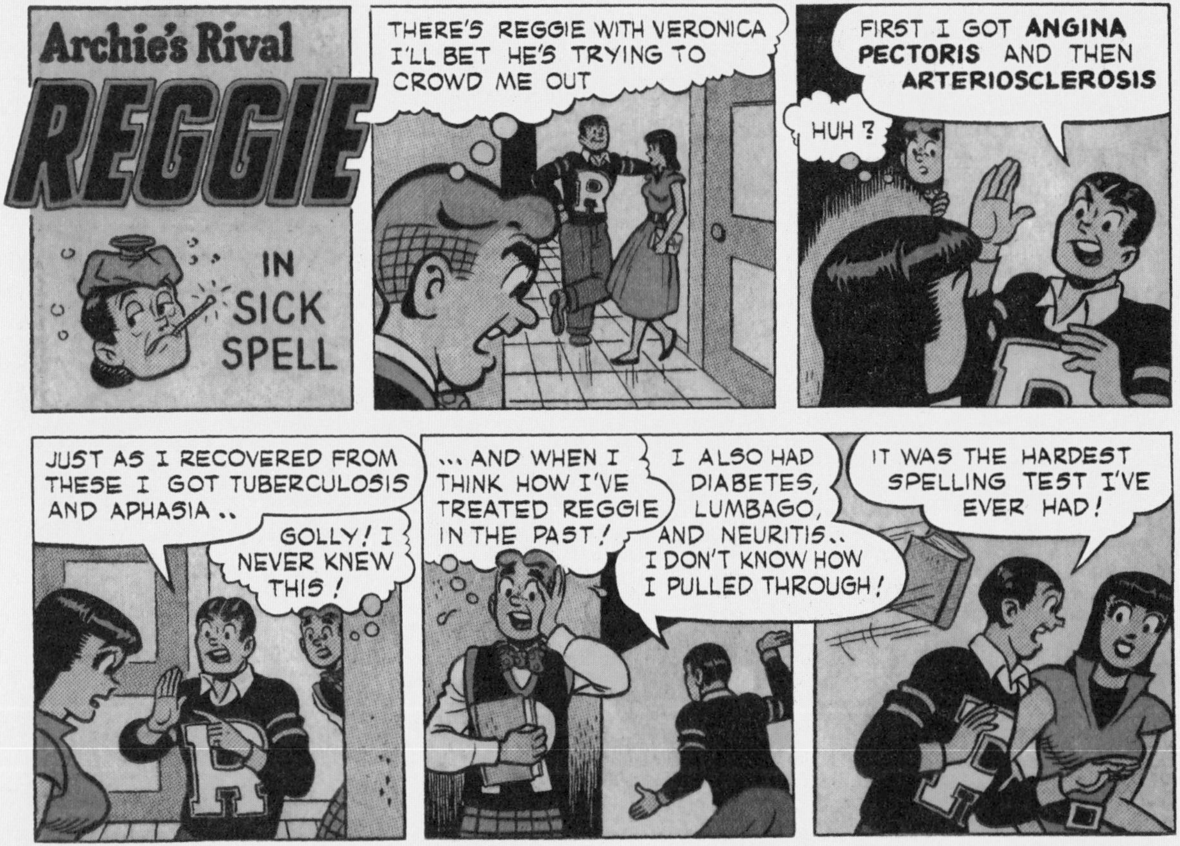
Archie's Rival
REGGIE
IN SICK SPELL
THERE'S REGGIE WITH VERONICA I'LL BET HE'S TRYING TO CROWD ME OUT
FIRST I GOT ANGINA PECTORIS AND THEN ARTERIOSCLEROSIS
HUH ?
JUST AS I RECOVERED FROM THESE I GOT TUBERCULOSIS AND APHASIA ..
GOLLY! I NEVER KNEW THIS!
... AND WHEN I THINK HOW I'VE TREATED REGGIE IN THE PAST!
I ALSO HAD DIABETES, LUMBAGO, AND NEURITIS.. I DON'T KNOW HOW I PULLED THROUGH!
IT WAS THE HARDEST SPELLING TEST I'VE EVER HAD!

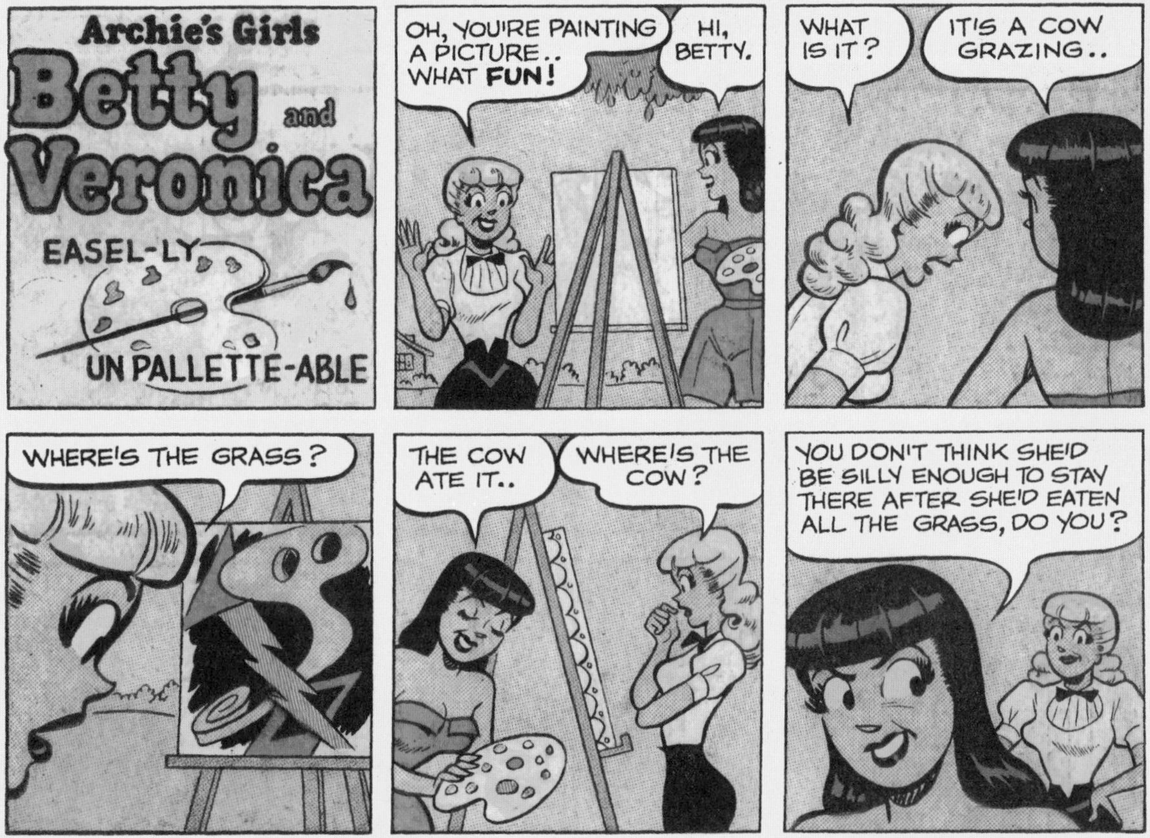
Archie's Girls
Betty and Veronica
EASEL-LY
UN PALLETTE-ABLE
OH, YOU'RE PAINTING A PICTURE.. WHAT FUN!
HI, BETTY.
WHAT IS IT?
IT'S A COW GRAZING..
WHERE'S THE GRASS?
THE COW ATE IT..
WHERE'S THE COW?
YOU DON'T THINK SHE'D BE SILLY ENOUGH TO STAY THERE AFTER SHE'D EATEN ALL THE GRASS, DO YOU?

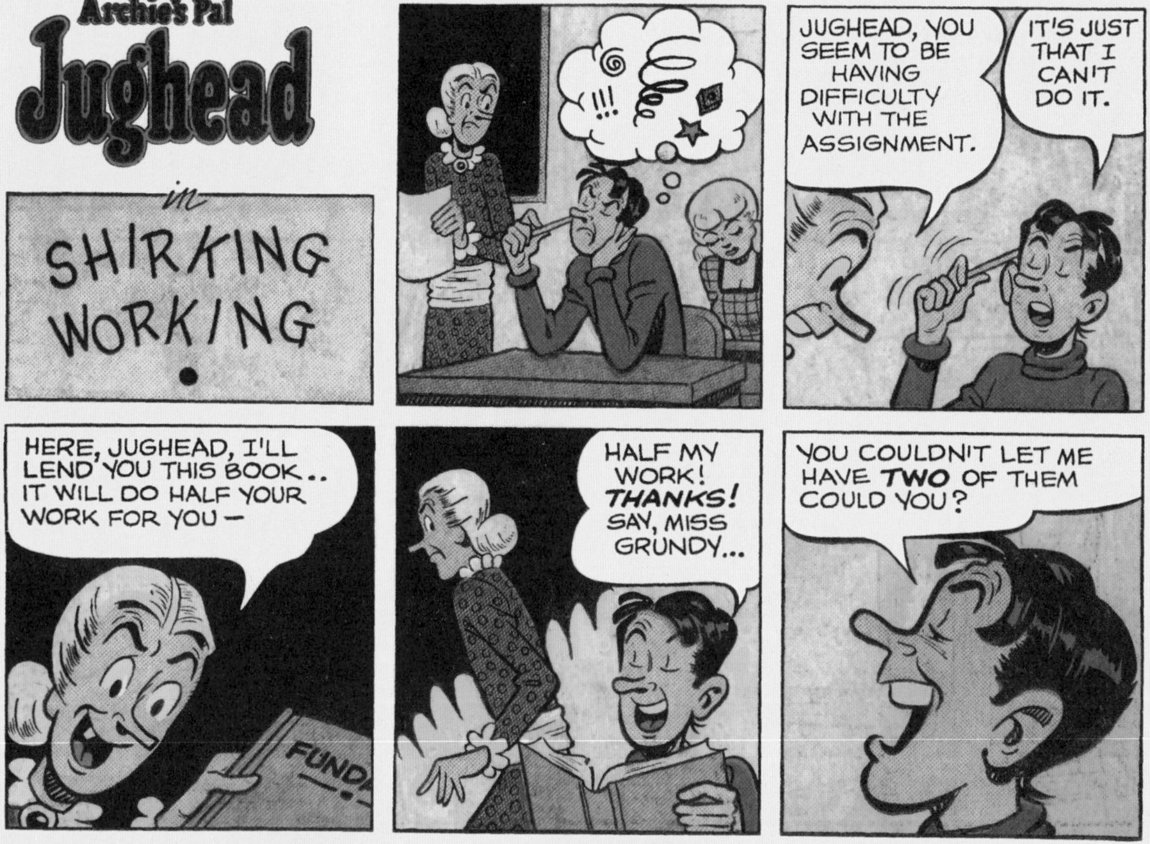
Archie's Pal
Jughead
in
SHIRKING WORKING
!!!
JUGHEAD, YOU SEEM TO BE HAVING DIFFICULTY WITH THE ASSIGNMENT.
IT'S JUST THAT I CAN'T DO IT.
HERE, JUGHEAD, I'LL LEND YOU THIS BOOK.. IT WILL DO HALF YOUR WORK FOR YOU —
FUND
HALF MY WORK! THANKS! SAY, MISS GRUNDY...
YOU COULDN'T LET ME HAVE TWO OF THEM COULD YOU?

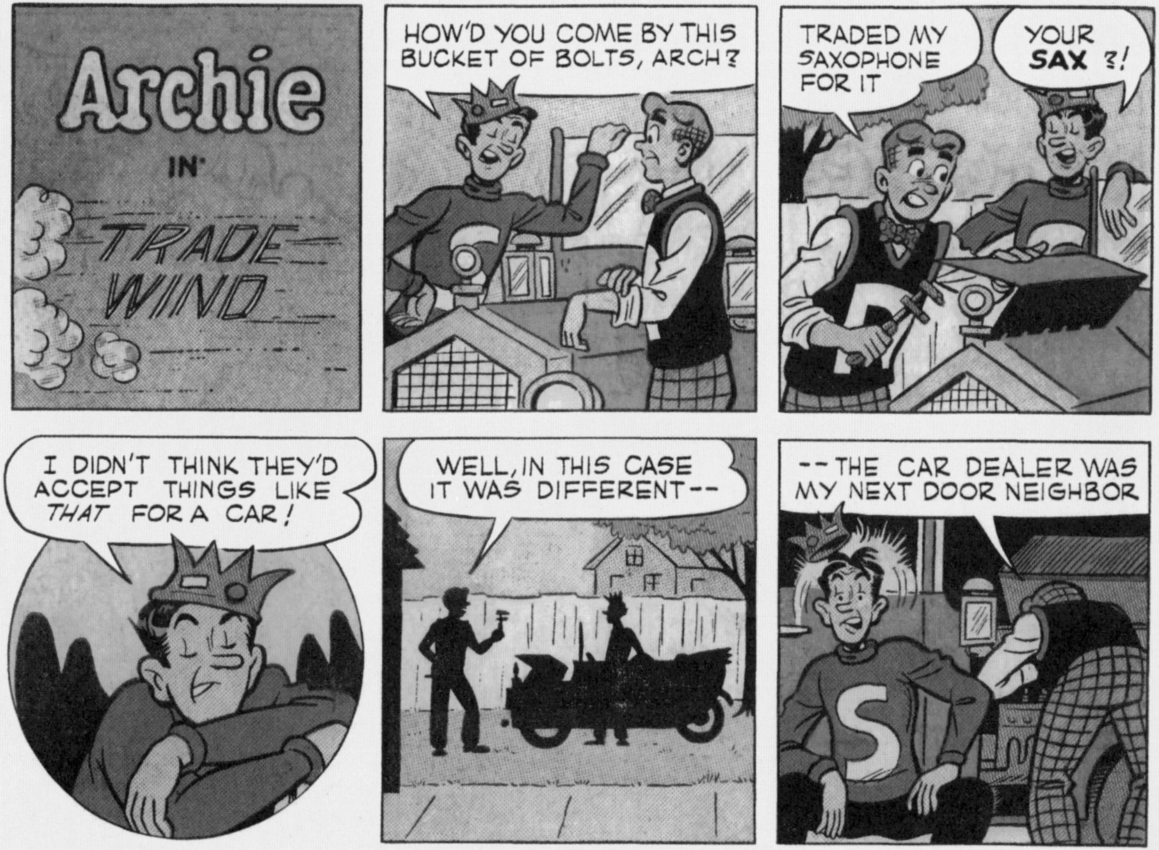
Archie
IN
TRADE WIND
HOW'D YOU COME BY THIS BUCKET OF BOLTS, ARCH?
TRADED MY SAXOPHONE FOR IT
YOUR SAX ?!
I DIDN'T THINK THEY'D ACCEPT THINGS LIKE THAT FOR A CAR!
WELL, IN THIS CASE IT WAS DIFFERENT--
--THE CAR DEALER WAS MY NEXT DOOR NEIGHBOR

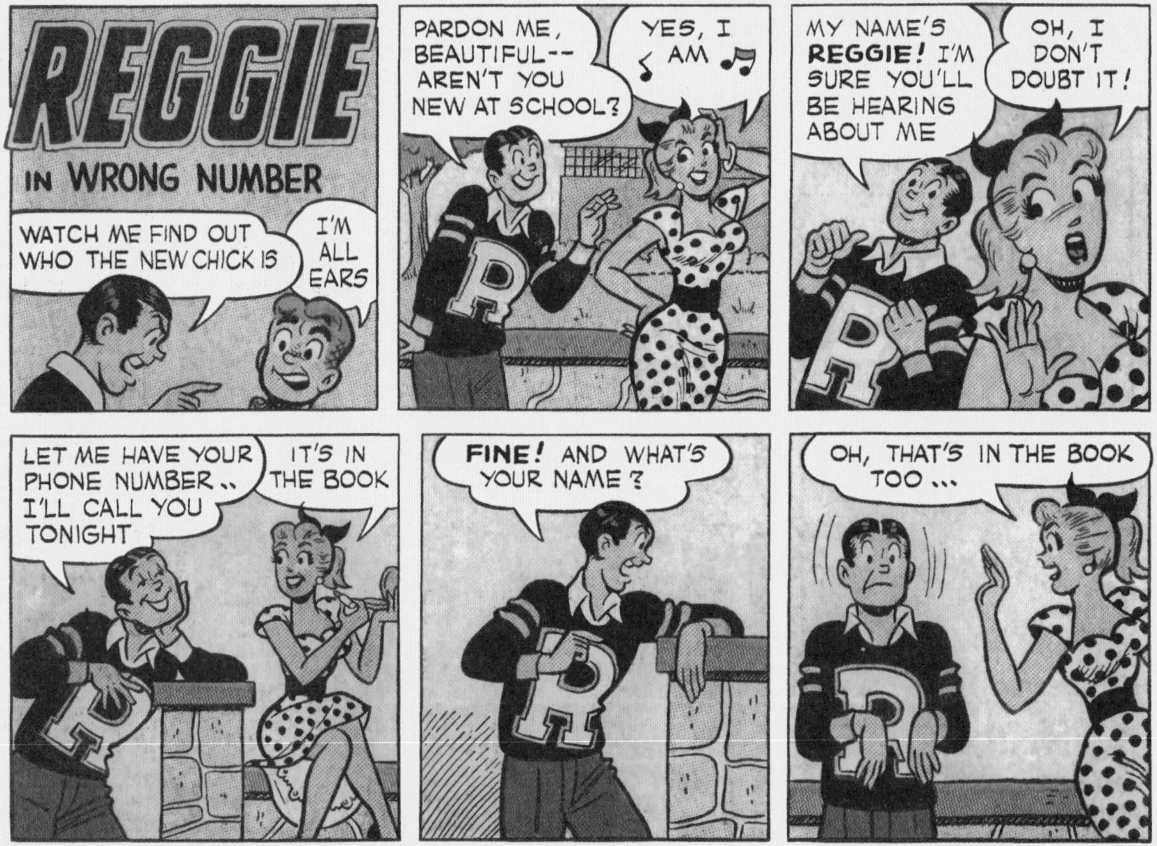
REGGIE
IN WRONG NUMBER
WATCH ME FIND OUT WHO THE NEW CHICK IS
I'M ALL EARS
PARDON ME, BEAUTIFUL-- AREN'T YOU NEW AT SCHOOL?
YES, I AM
MY NAME'S REGGIE! I'M SURE YOU'LL BE HEARING ABOUT ME
OH, I DON'T DOUBT IT!
LET ME HAVE YOUR PHONE NUMBER.. I'LL CALL YOU TONIGHT
IT'S IN THE BOOK
FINE! AND WHAT'S YOUR NAME?
OH, THAT'S IN THE BOOK TOO ...

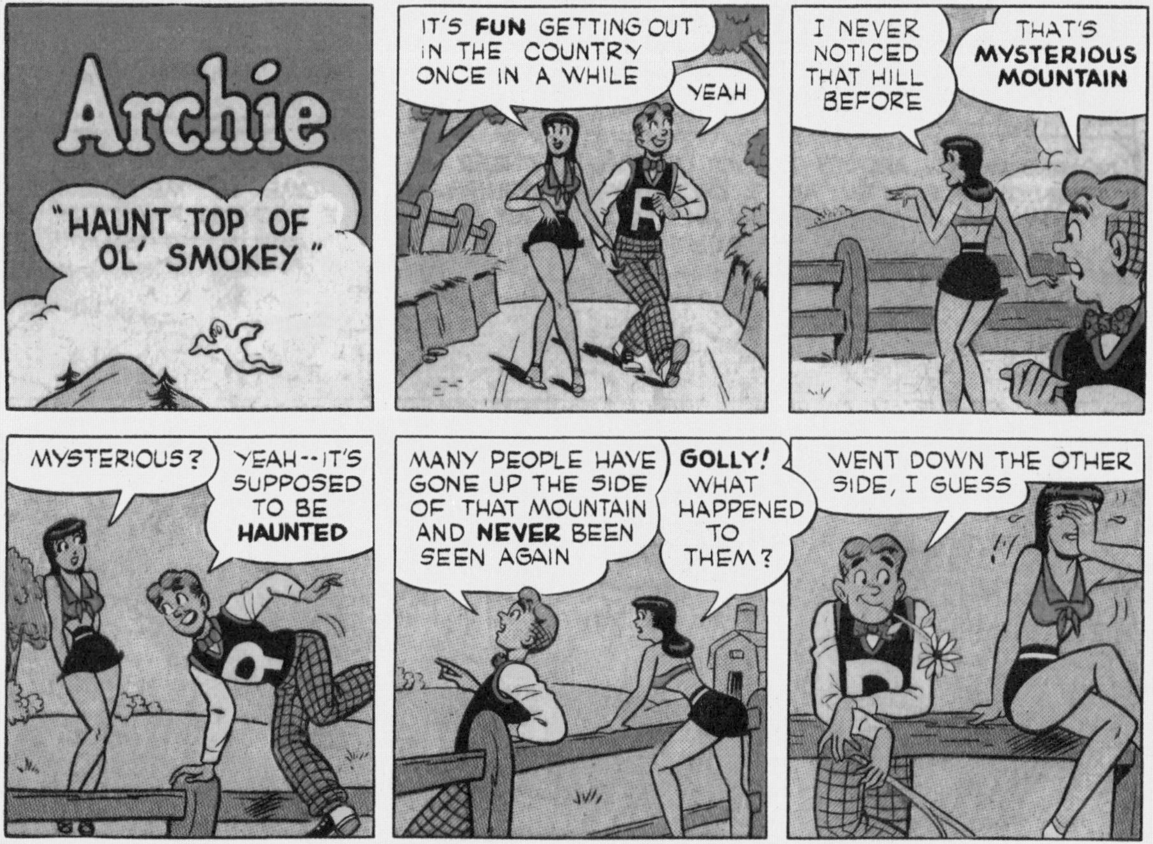
Archie
"HAUNT TOP OF OL' SMOKEY"
IT'S FUN GETTING OUT IN THE COUNTRY ONCE IN A WHILE
YEAH
I NEVER NOTICED THAT HILL BEFORE
THAT'S MYSTERIOUS MOUNTAIN
MYSTERIOUS?
YEAH--IT'S SUPPOSED TO BE HAUNTED
MANY PEOPLE HAVE GONE UP THE SIDE OF THAT MOUNTAIN AND NEVER BEEN SEEN AGAIN
GOLLY! WHAT HAPPENED TO THEM?
WENT DOWN THE OTHER SIDE, I GUESS

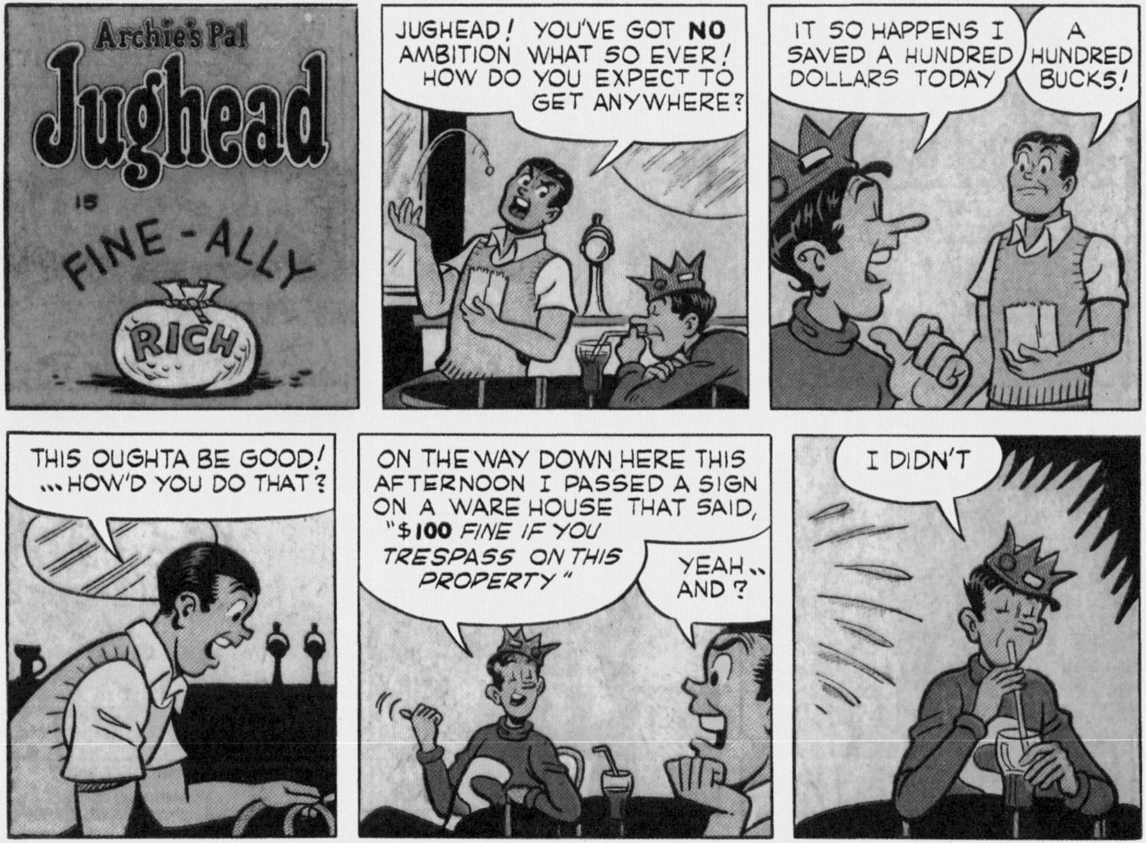
Archie's Pal
Jughead
IS
FINE-ALLY
RICH
JUGHEAD! YOU'VE GOT NO AMBITION WHAT SO EVER! HOW DO YOU EXPECT TO GET ANYWHERE?
IT SO HAPPENS I SAVED A HUNDRED DOLLARS TODAY
A HUNDRED BUCKS!
THIS OUGHTA BE GOOD! ...HOW'D YOU DO THAT?
ON THE WAY DOWN HERE THIS AFTERNOON I PASSED A SIGN ON A WARE HOUSE THAT SAID, "$100 FINE IF YOU TRESPASS ON THIS PROPERTY"
YEAH.. AND?
I DIDN'T

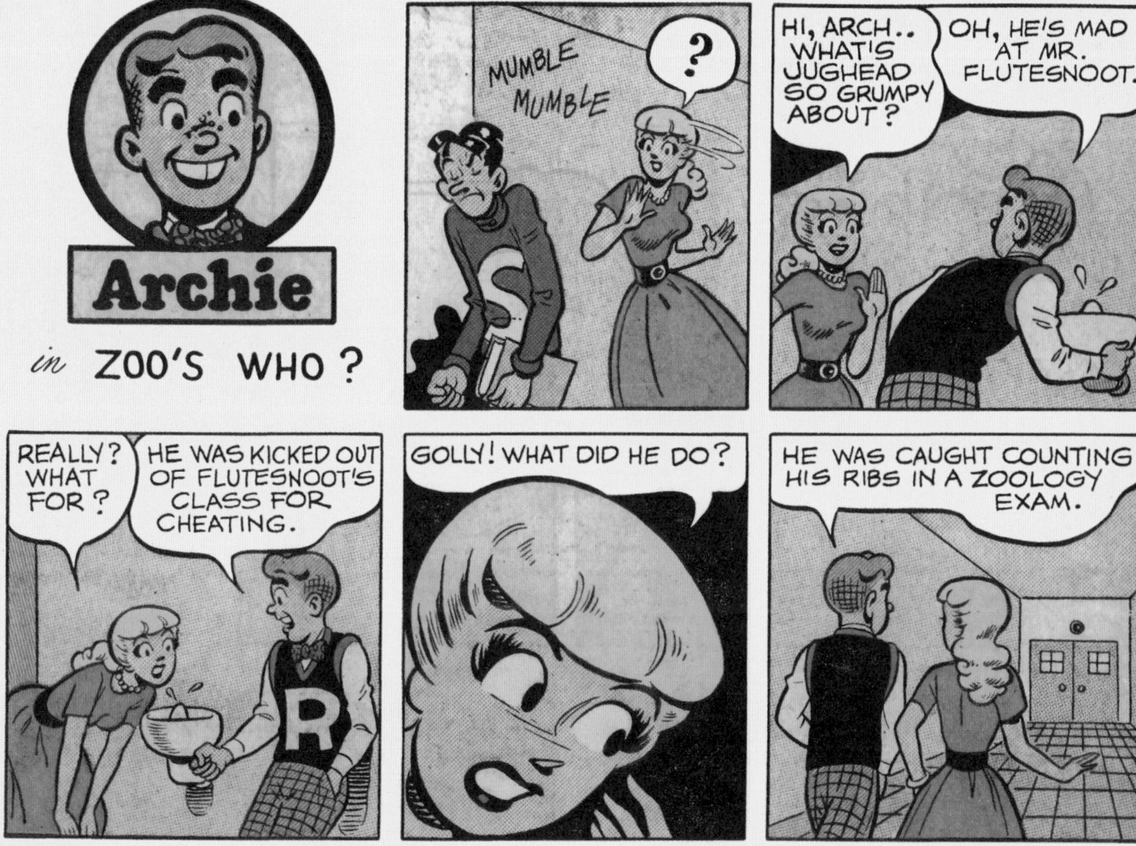
Archie
in ZOO'S WHO?
MUMBLE MUMBLE
?
HI, ARCH.. WHAT'S JUGHEAD SO GRUMPY ABOUT?
OH, HE'S MAD AT MR. FLUTESNOOT.
REALLY? WHAT FOR?
HE WAS KICKED OUT OF FLUTESNOOT'S CLASS FOR CHEATING.
GOLLY! WHAT DID HE DO?
HE WAS CAUGHT COUNTING HIS RIBS IN A ZOOLOGY EXAM.

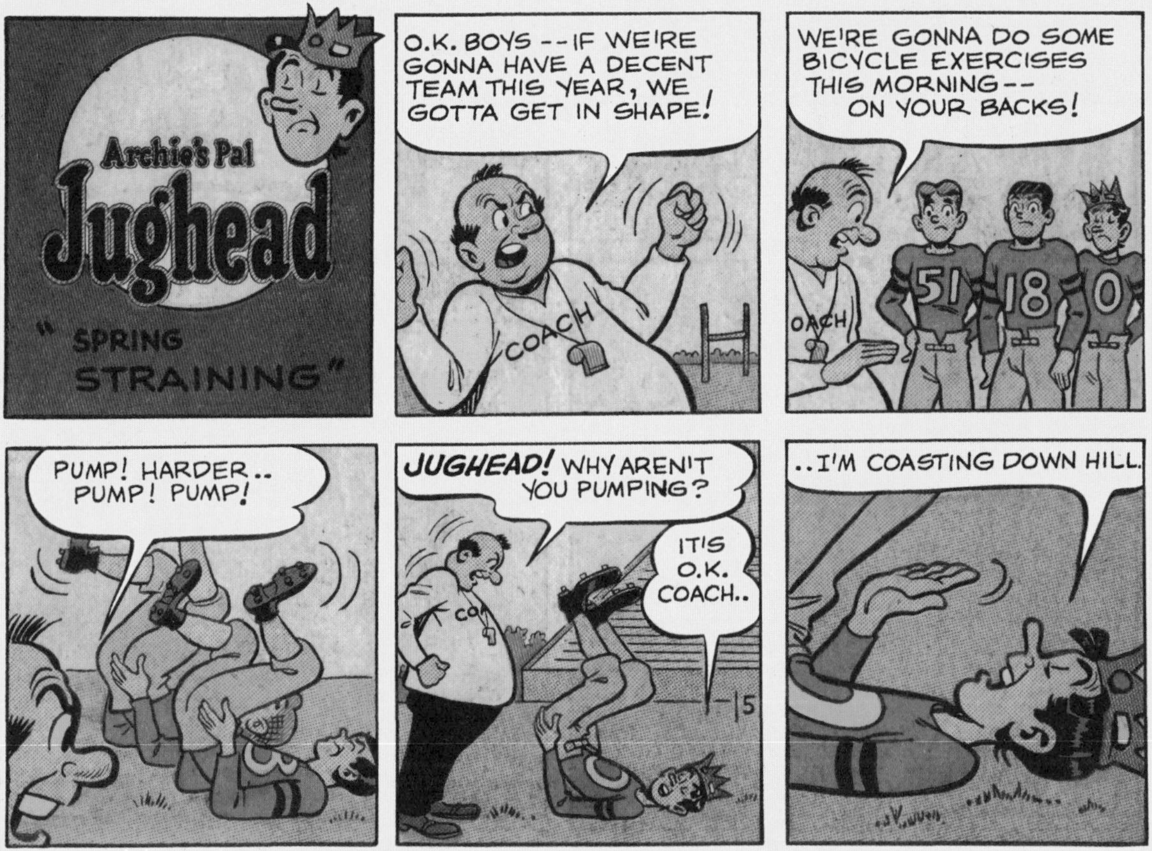
Archie's Pal
Jughead
"SPRING STRAINING"
O.K. BOYS --IF WE'RE GONNA HAVE A DECENT TEAM THIS YEAR, WE GOTTA GET IN SHAPE!
COACH
WE'RE GONNA DO SOME BICYCLE EXERCISES THIS MORNING-- ON YOUR BACKS!
51
18
0
PUMP! HARDER.. PUMP! PUMP!
JUGHEAD! WHY AREN'T YOU PUMPING?
IT'S O.K. COACH..
..I'M COASTING DOWN HILL.

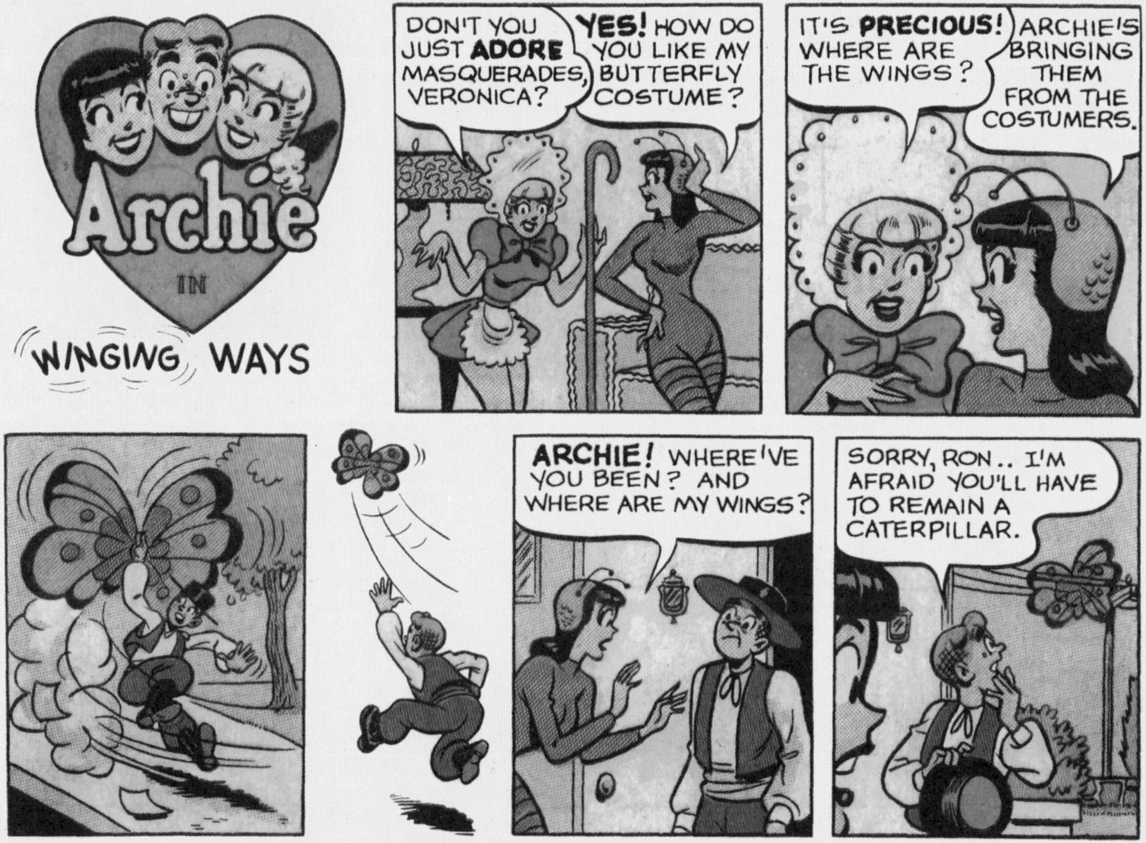
Archie
IN
WINGING WAYS
DON'T YOU JUST ADORE MASQUERADES, VERONICA?
YES! HOW DO YOU LIKE MY BUTTERFLY COSTUME?
IT'S PRECIOUS! WHERE ARE THE WINGS?
ARCHIE'S BRINGING THEM FROM THE COSTUMERS.
ARCHIE! WHERE'VE YOU BEEN? AND WHERE ARE MY WINGS?
SORRY, RON.. I'M AFRAID YOU'LL HAVE TO REMAIN A CATERPILLAR.

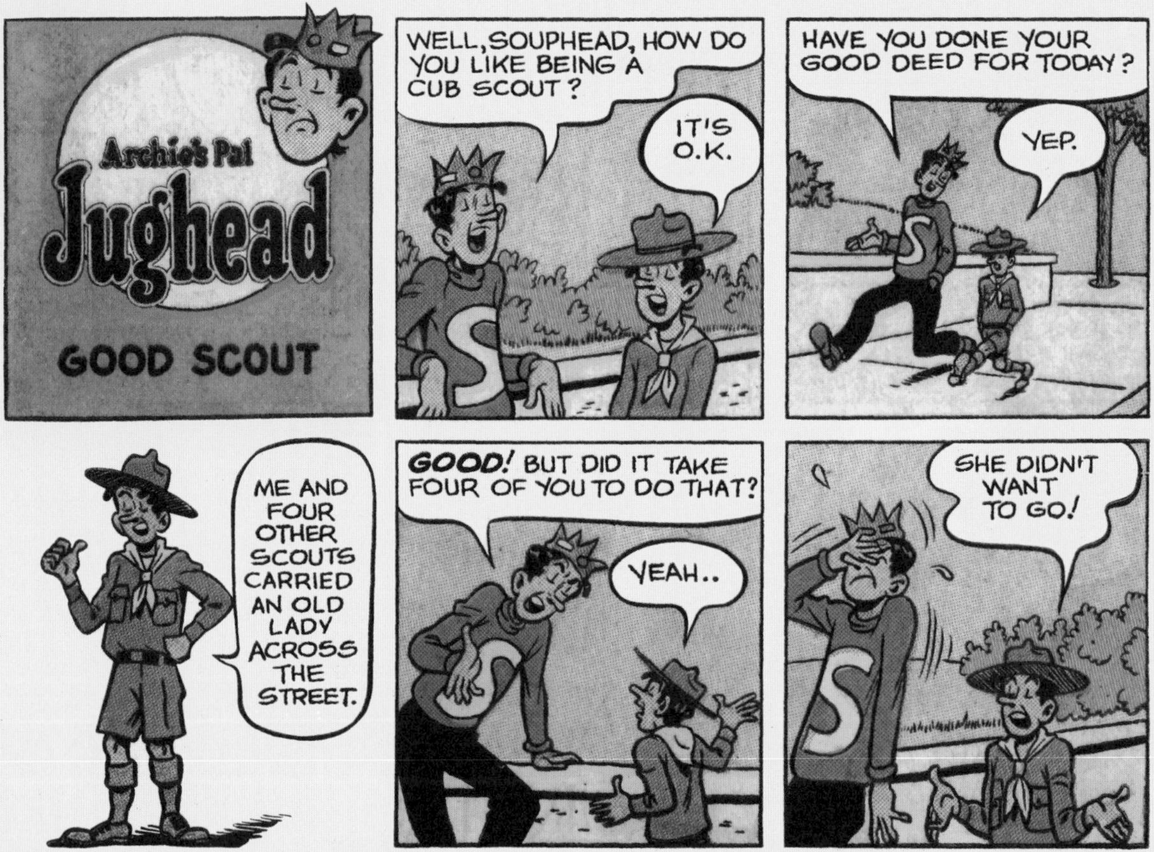
Archie's Pal
Jughead
GOOD SCOUT
WELL, SOUPHEAD, HOW DO YOU LIKE BEING A CUB SCOUT?
IT'S O.K.
HAVE YOU DONE YOUR GOOD DEED FOR TODAY?
YEP.
ME AND FOUR OTHER SCOUTS CARRIED AN OLD LADY ACROSS THE STREET.
GOOD! BUT DID IT TAKE FOUR OF YOU TO DO THAT?
YEAH..
SHE DIDN'T WANT TO GO!

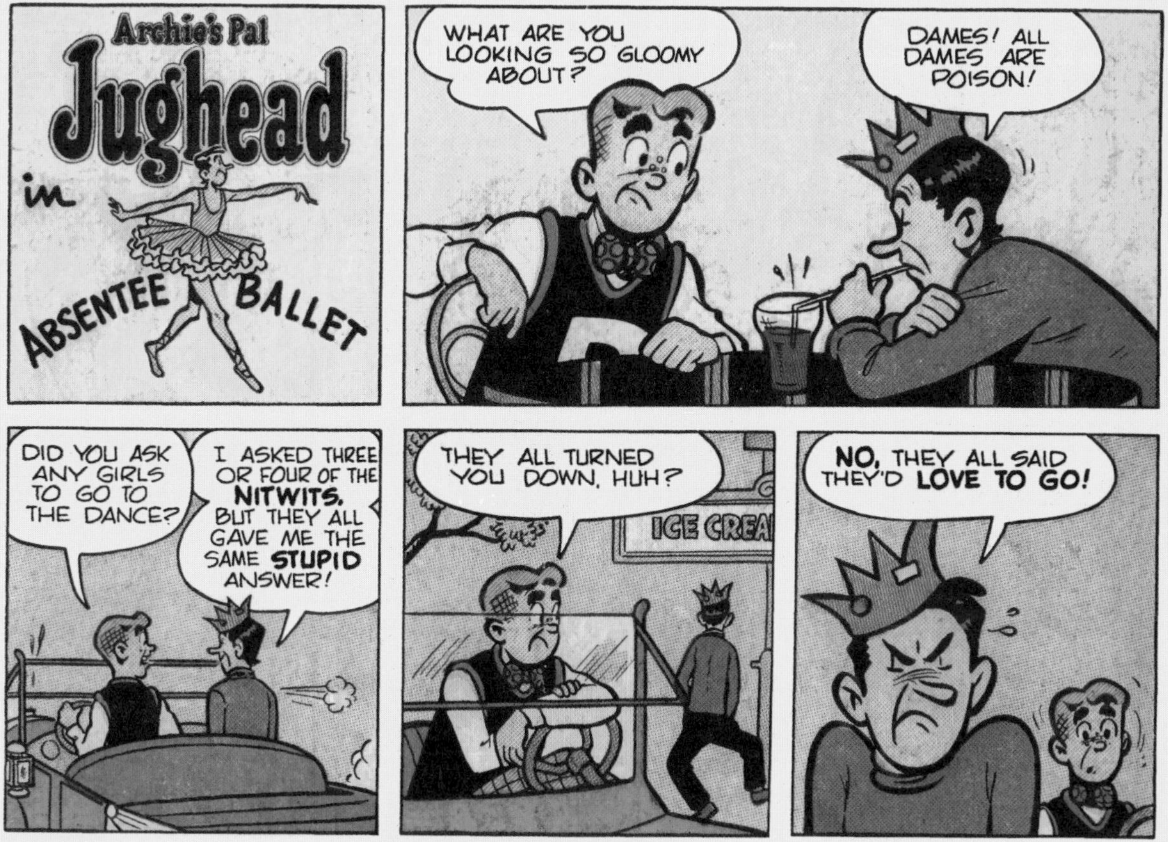
Archie's Pal
Jughead
in
ABSENTEE BALLET
WHAT ARE YOU LOOKING SO GLOOMY ABOUT?
DAMES! ALL DAMES ARE POISON!
DID YOU ASK ANY GIRLS TO GO TO THE DANCE?
I ASKED THREE OR FOUR OF THE NITWITS. BUT THEY ALL GAVE ME THE SAME STUPID ANSWER!
THEY ALL TURNED YOU DOWN, HUH?
ICE CREA
NO, THEY ALL SAID THEY'D LOVE TO GO!

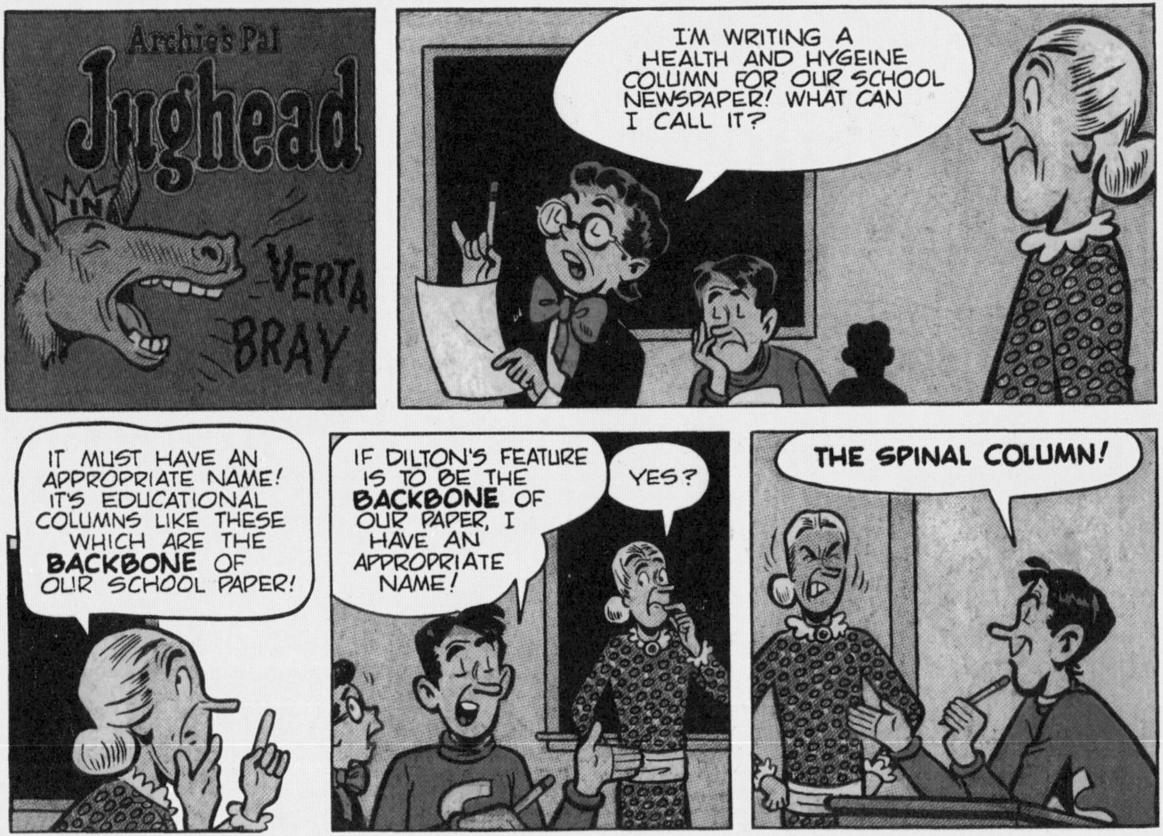
Archie's Pal
Jughead
IN
VERTA BRAY
I'M WRITING A HEALTH AND HYGEINE COLUMN FOR OUR SCHOOL NEWSPAPER! WHAT CAN I CALL IT?
IT MUST HAVE AN APPROPRIATE NAME! IT'S EDUCATIONAL COLUMNS LIKE THESE WHICH ARE THE BACKBONE OF OUR SCHOOL PAPER!
IF DILTON'S FEATURE IS TO BE THE BACKBONE OF OUR PAPER, I HAVE AN APPROPRIATE NAME!
YES?
THE SPINAL COLUMN!

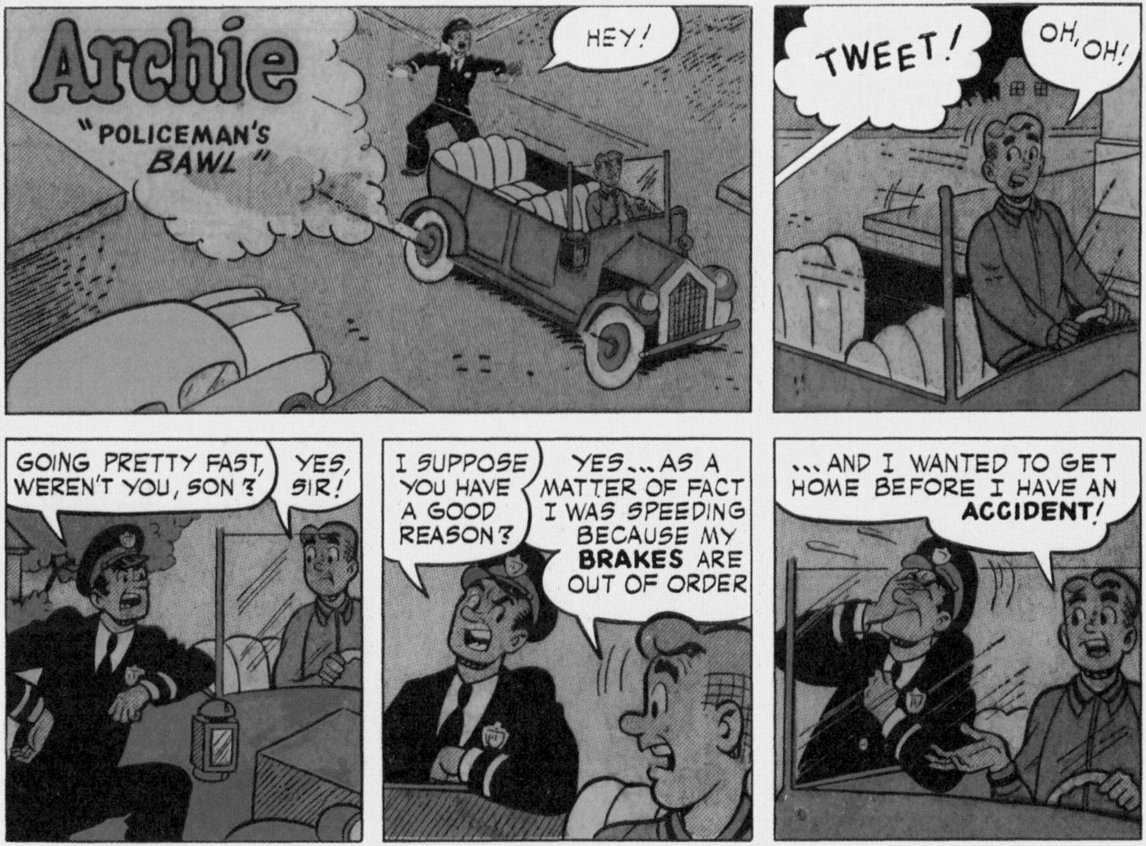
Archie
"POLICEMAN'S BAWL"
HEY!
TWEET!
OH, OH!
GOING PRETTY FAST, WEREN'T YOU, SON?
YES, SIR!
I SUPPOSE YOU HAVE A GOOD REASON?
YES... AS A MATTER OF FACT I WAS SPEEDING BECAUSE MY BRAKES ARE OUT OF ORDER
...AND I WANTED TO GET HOME BEFORE I HAVE AN ACCIDENT!

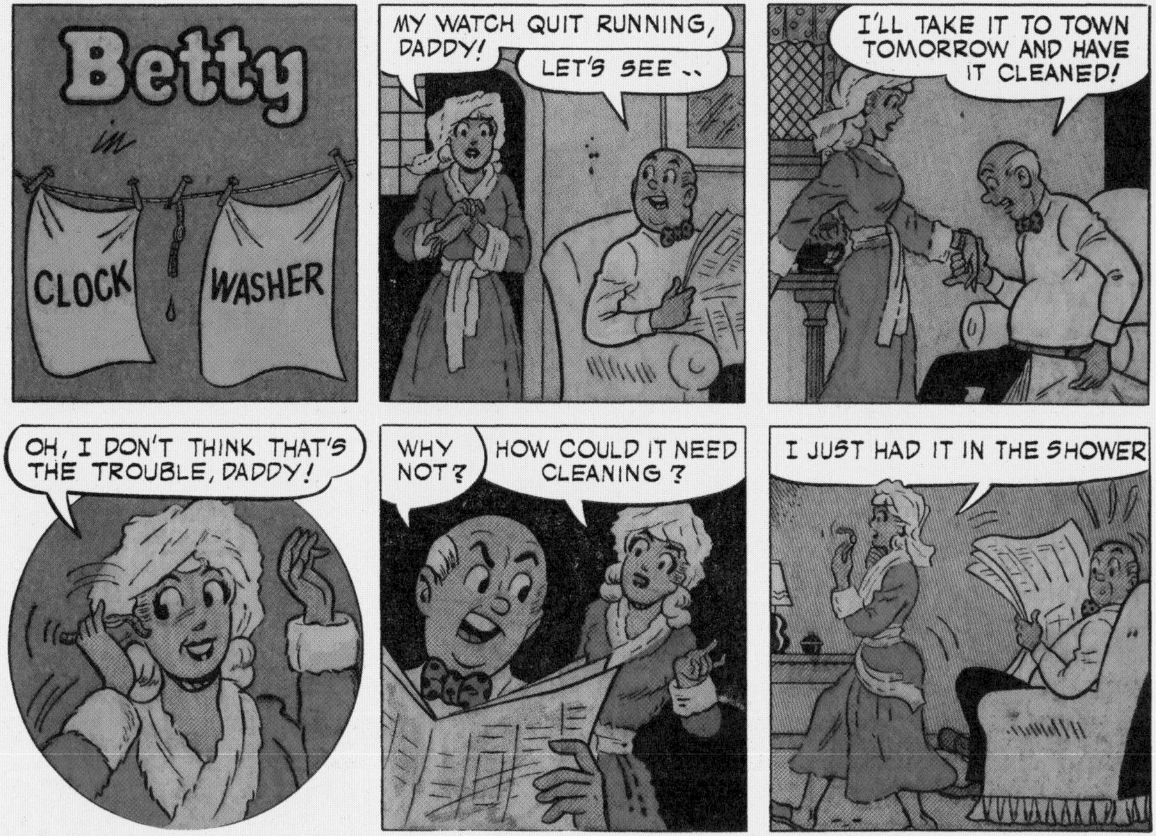
Betty
in
CLOCK
WASHER
MY WATCH QUIT RUNNING, DADDY!
LET'S SEE ..
I'LL TAKE IT TO TOWN TOMORROW AND HAVE IT CLEANED!
OH, I DON'T THINK THAT'S THE TROUBLE, DADDY!
WHY NOT?
HOW COULD IT NEED CLEANING?
I JUST HAD IT IN THE SHOWER

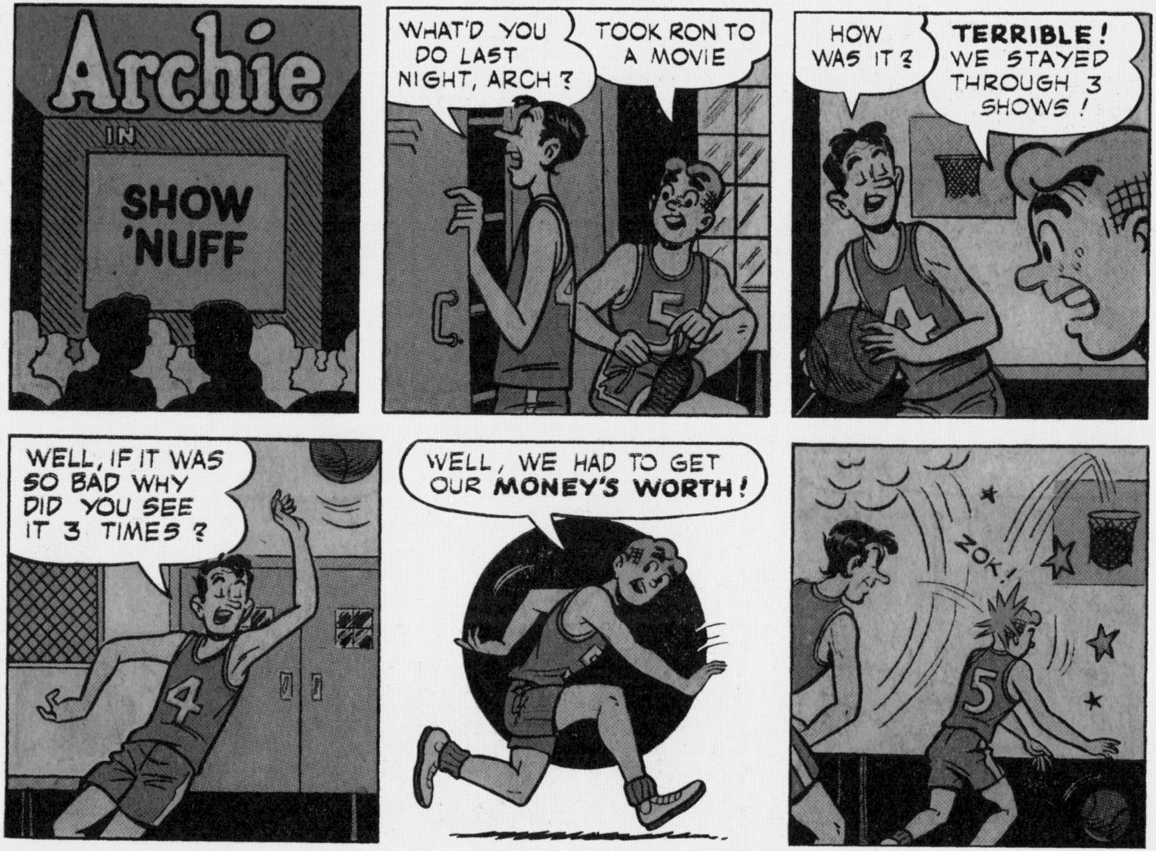
Archie
IN
SHOW 'NUFF
WHAT'D YOU DO LAST NIGHT, ARCH ?
TOOK RON TO A MOVIE
HOW WAS IT ?
TERRIBLE! WE STAYED THROUGH 3 SHOWS !
WELL, IF IT WAS SO BAD WHY DID YOU SEE IT 3 TIMES ?
WELL, WE HAD TO GET OUR MONEY'S WORTH !
ZOK!

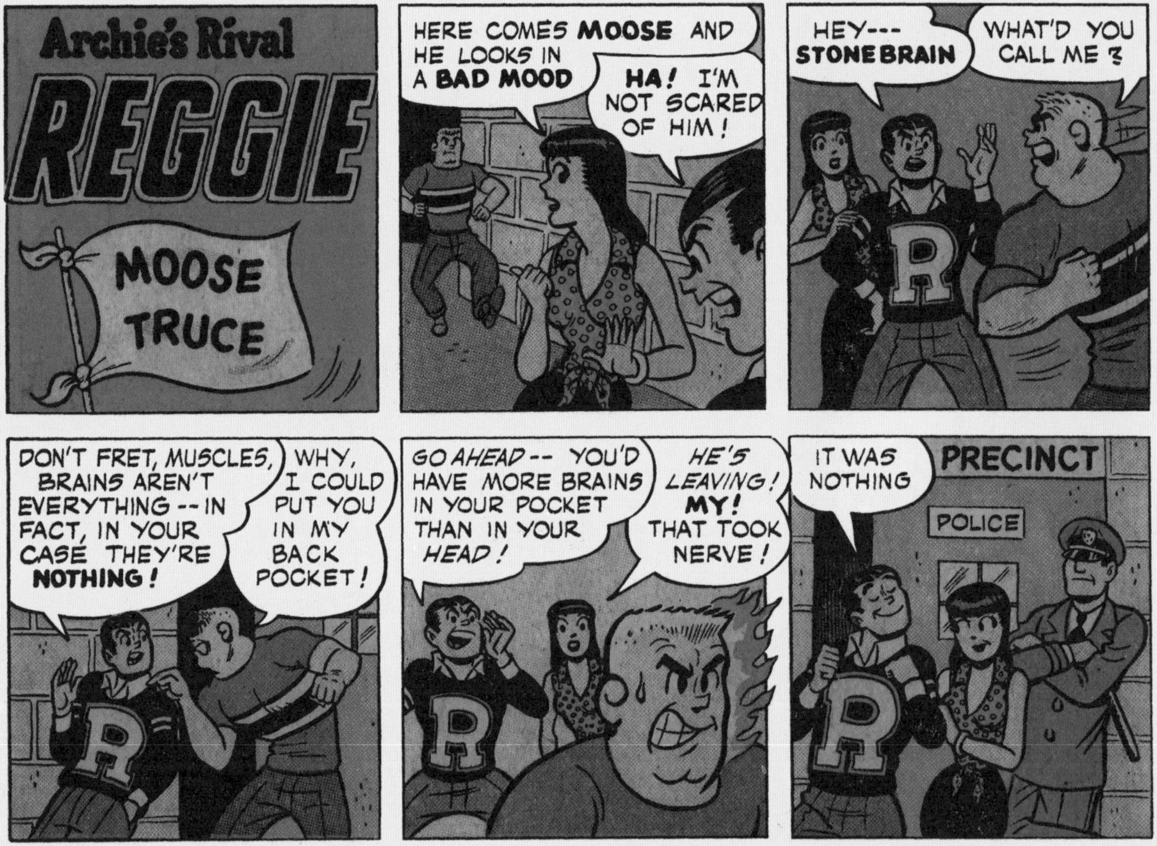
Archie's Rival
REGGIE
MOOSE TRUCE
HERE COMES MOOSE AND HE LOOKS IN A BAD MOOD
HA! I'M NOT SCARED OF HIM!
HEY--- STONEBRAIN
WHAT'D YOU CALL ME ?
DON'T FRET, MUSCLES, BRAINS AREN'T EVERYTHING -- IN FACT, IN YOUR CASE THEY'RE NOTHING!
WHY, I COULD PUT YOU IN MY BACK POCKET!
GO AHEAD -- YOU'D HAVE MORE BRAINS IN YOUR POCKET THAN IN YOUR HEAD!
HE'S LEAVING! MY! THAT TOOK NERVE!
IT WAS NOTHING
PRECINCT
POLICE

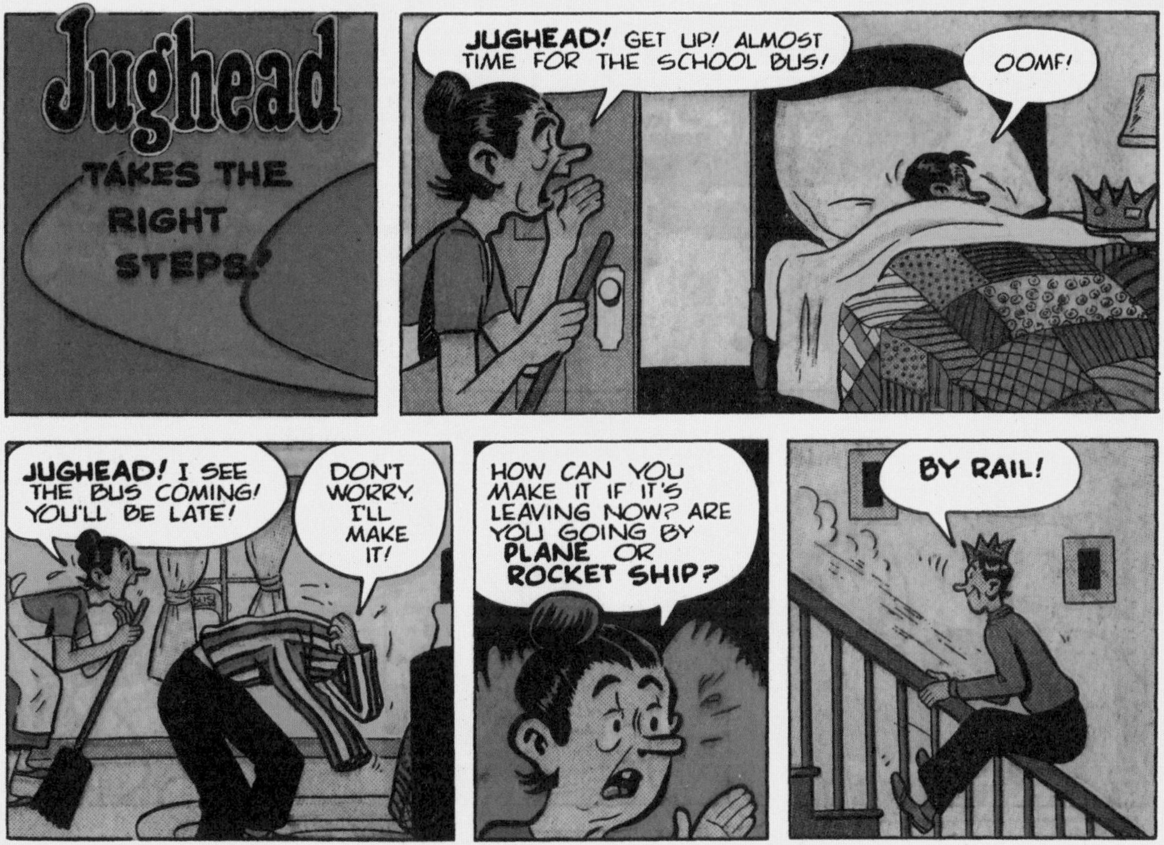
Jughead
TAKES THE RIGHT STEPS!
JUGHEAD! GET UP! ALMOST TIME FOR THE SCHOOL BUS!
OOMF!
JUGHEAD! I SEE THE BUS COMING! YOU'LL BE LATE!
DON'T WORRY. I'LL MAKE IT!
HOW CAN YOU MAKE IT IF IT'S LEAVING NOW? ARE YOU GOING BY PLANE OR ROCKET SHIP?
BY RAIL!

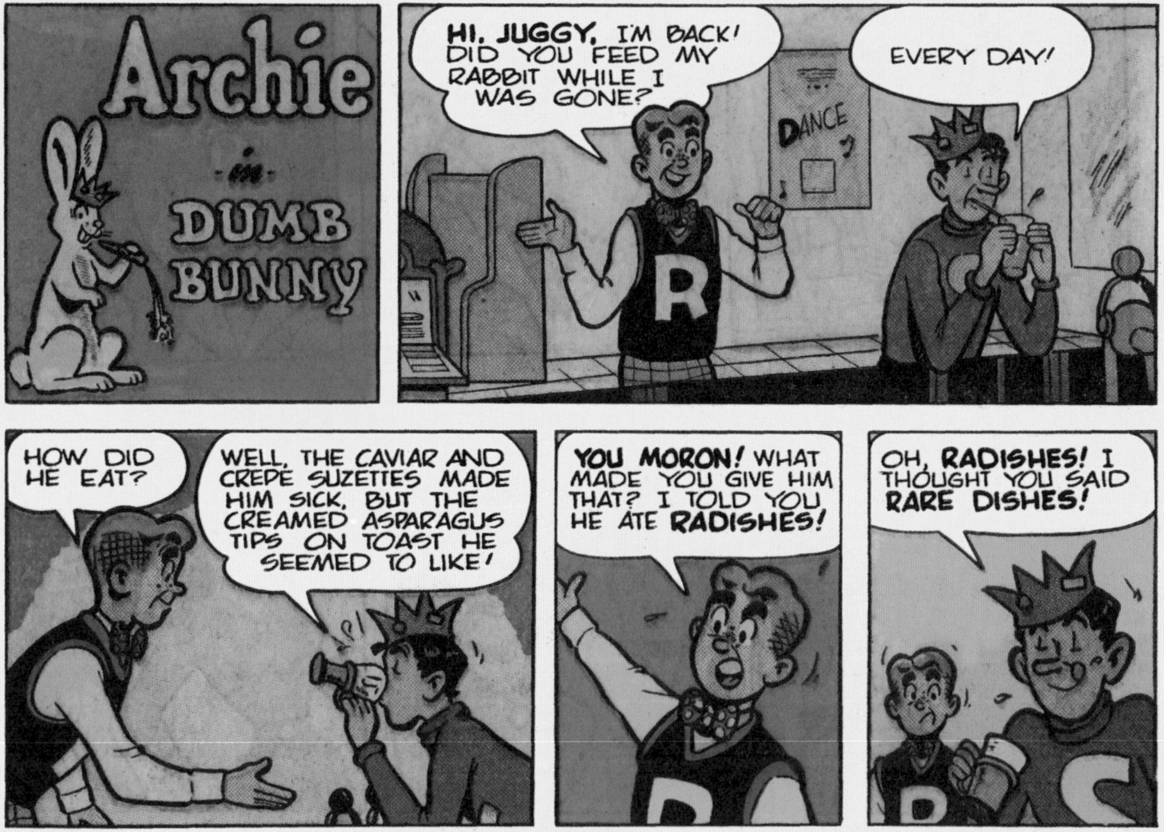
Archie
-in-
DUMB BUNNY
HI, JUGGY, I'M BACK! DID YOU FEED MY RABBIT WHILE I WAS GONE?
EVERY DAY!
DANCE
HOW DID HE EAT?
WELL, THE CAVIAR AND CREPE SUZETTES MADE HIM SICK, BUT THE CREAMED ASPARAGUS TIPS ON TOAST HE SEEMED TO LIKE!
YOU MORON! WHAT MADE YOU GIVE HIM THAT? I TOLD YOU HE ATE RADISHES!
OH, RADISHES! I THOUGHT YOU SAID RARE DISHES!

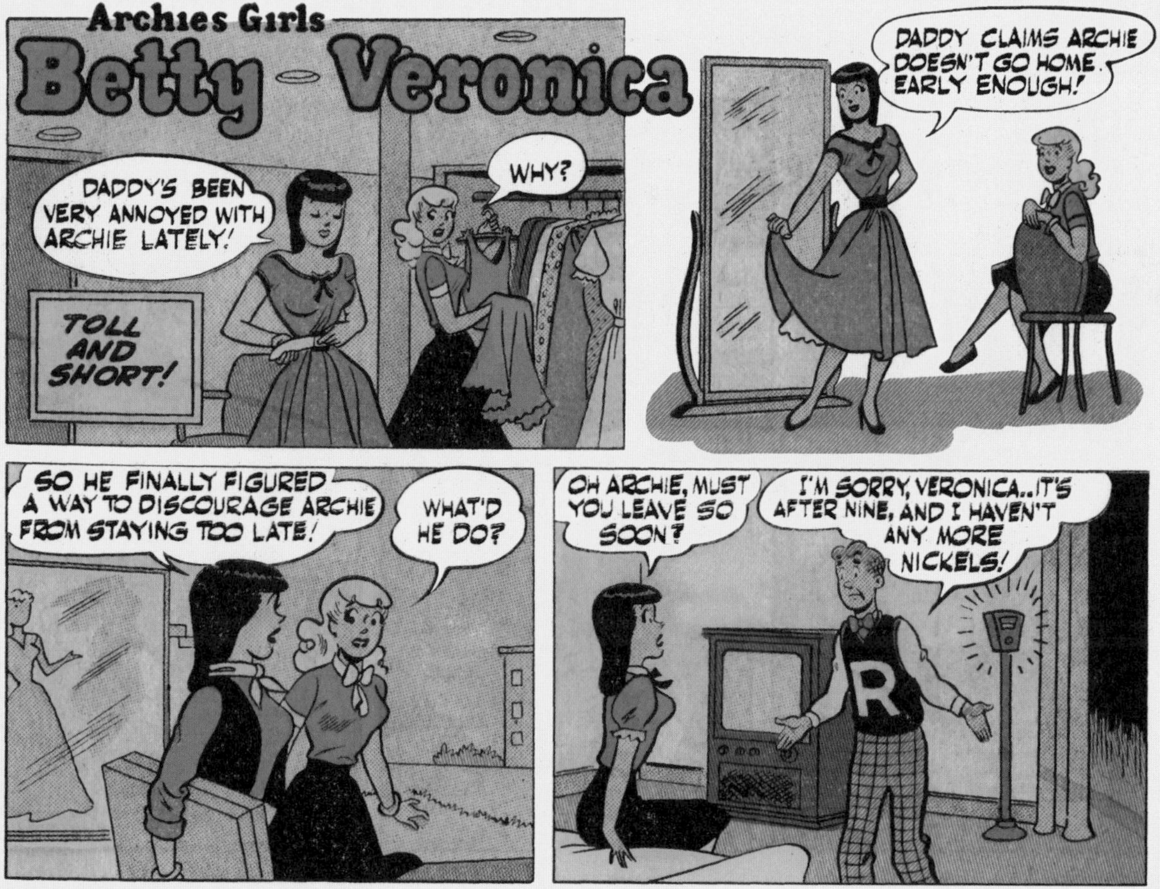
Archies Girls
Betty Veronica
DADDY'S BEEN VERY ANNOYED WITH ARCHIE LATELY!
WHY?
TOLL AND SHORT!
DADDY CLAIMS ARCHIE DOESN'T GO HOME EARLY ENOUGH!
SO HE FINALLY FIGURED A WAY TO DISCOURAGE ARCHIE FROM STAYING TOO LATE!
WHAT'D HE DO?
OH ARCHIE, MUST YOU LEAVE SO SOON?
I'M SORRY, VERONICA..IT'S AFTER NINE, AND I HAVEN'T ANY MORE NICKELS!
R

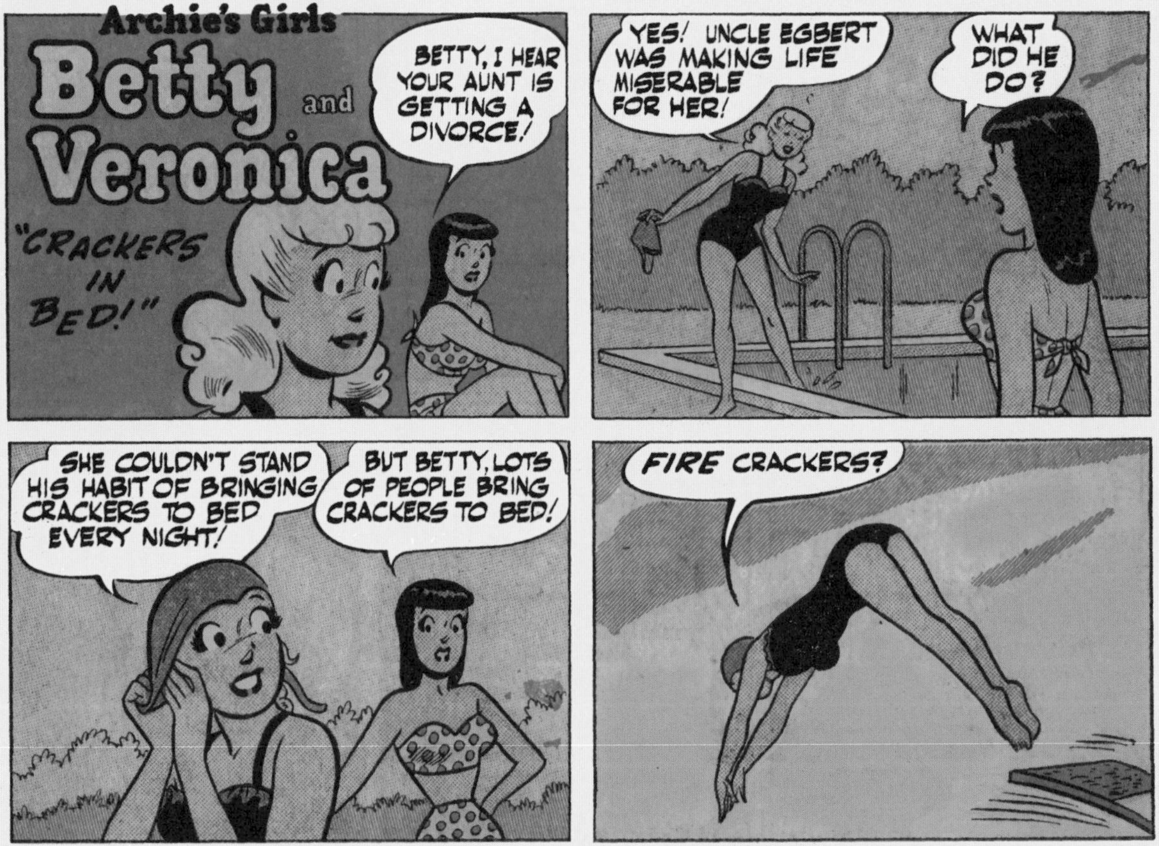
Archie's Girls
Betty and Veronica
"CRACKERS IN BED!"
BETTY, I HEAR YOUR AUNT IS GETTING A DIVORCE!
YES! UNCLE EGBERT WAS MAKING LIFE MISERABLE FOR HER!
WHAT DID HE DO?
SHE COULDN'T STAND HIS HABIT OF BRINGING CRACKERS TO BED EVERY NIGHT!
BUT BETTY, LOTS OF PEOPLE BRING CRACKERS TO BED!
FIRE CRACKERS?

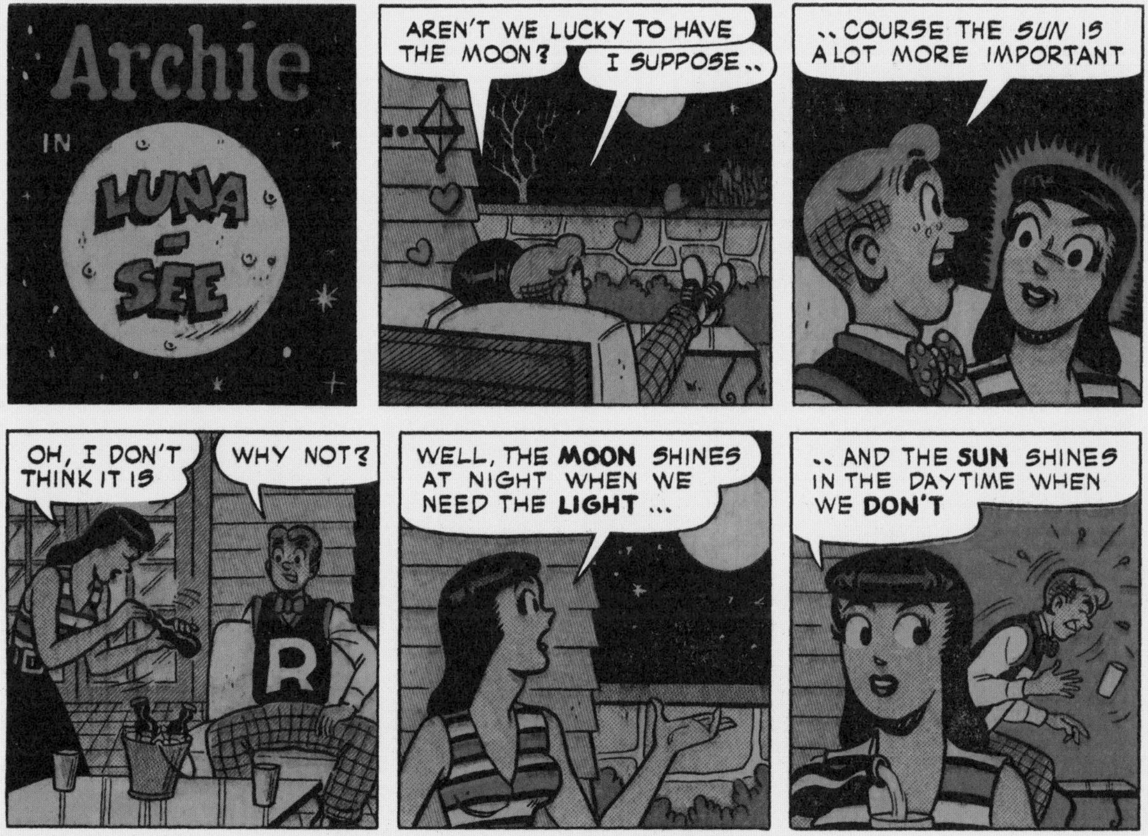
Archie
IN
LUNA - SEE
AREN'T WE LUCKY TO HAVE THE MOON?
I SUPPOSE ..
.. COURSE THE SUN IS A LOT MORE IMPORTANT
OH, I DON'T THINK IT IS
WHY NOT?
WELL, THE MOON SHINES AT NIGHT WHEN WE NEED THE LIGHT ...
.. AND THE SUN SHINES IN THE DAYTIME WHEN WE DON'T
R

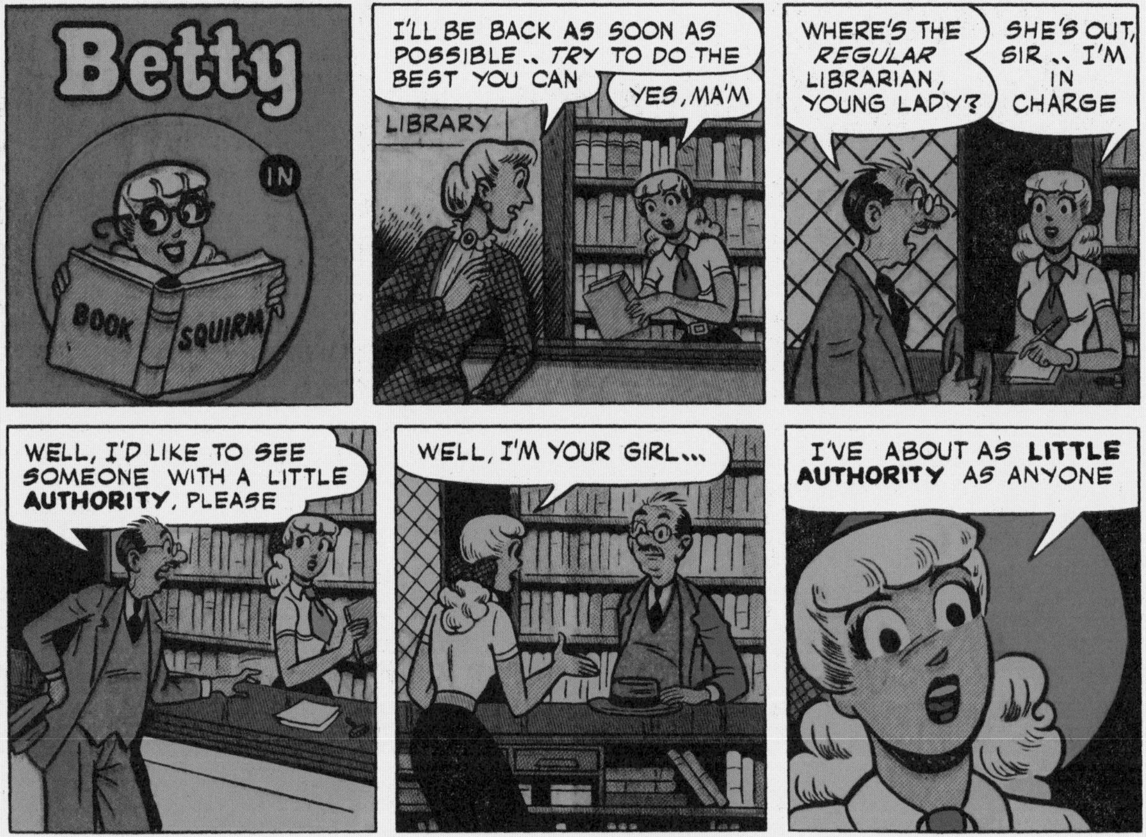
Betty
IN
BOOK SQUIRM
I'LL BE BACK AS SOON AS POSSIBLE .. *TRY* TO DO THE BEST YOU CAN
YES, MA'M
LIBRARY
WHERE'S THE *REGULAR* LIBRARIAN, YOUNG LADY?
SHE'S OUT, SIR .. I'M IN CHARGE
WELL, I'D LIKE TO SEE SOMEONE WITH A LITTLE **AUTHORITY**, PLEASE
WELL, I'M YOUR GIRL...
I'VE ABOUT AS **LITTLE AUTHORITY** AS ANYONE

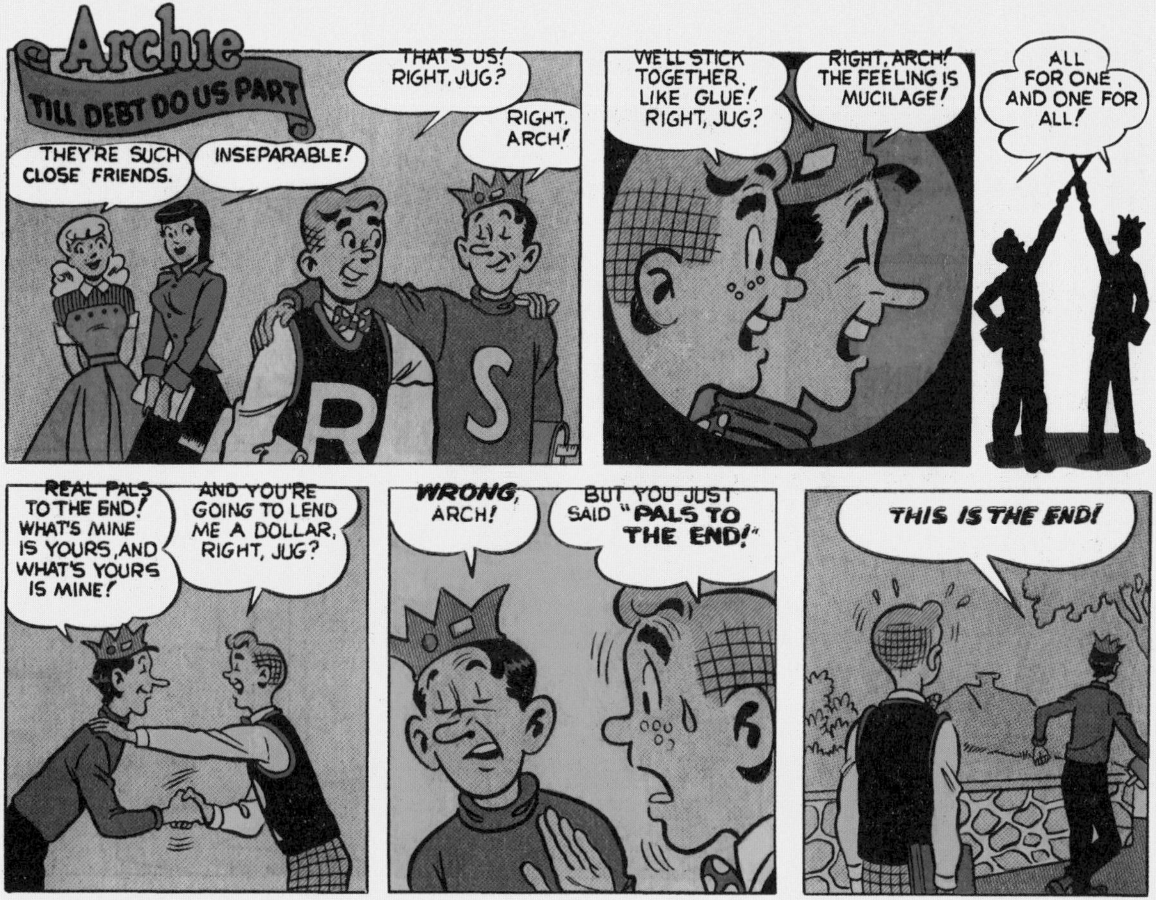
Archie
TILL DEBT DO US PART
THEY'RE SUCH CLOSE FRIENDS.
INSEPARABLE!
THAT'S US! RIGHT, JUG?
RIGHT, ARCH!
WE'LL STICK TOGETHER, LIKE GLUE! RIGHT, JUG?
RIGHT, ARCH! THE FEELING IS MUCILAGE!
ALL FOR ONE, AND ONE FOR ALL!
REAL PALS TO THE END! WHAT'S MINE IS YOURS, AND WHAT'S YOURS IS MINE!
AND YOU'RE GOING TO LEND ME A DOLLAR, RIGHT, JUG?
WRONG, ARCH!
BUT YOU JUST SAID "PALS TO THE END!"
THIS IS THE END!

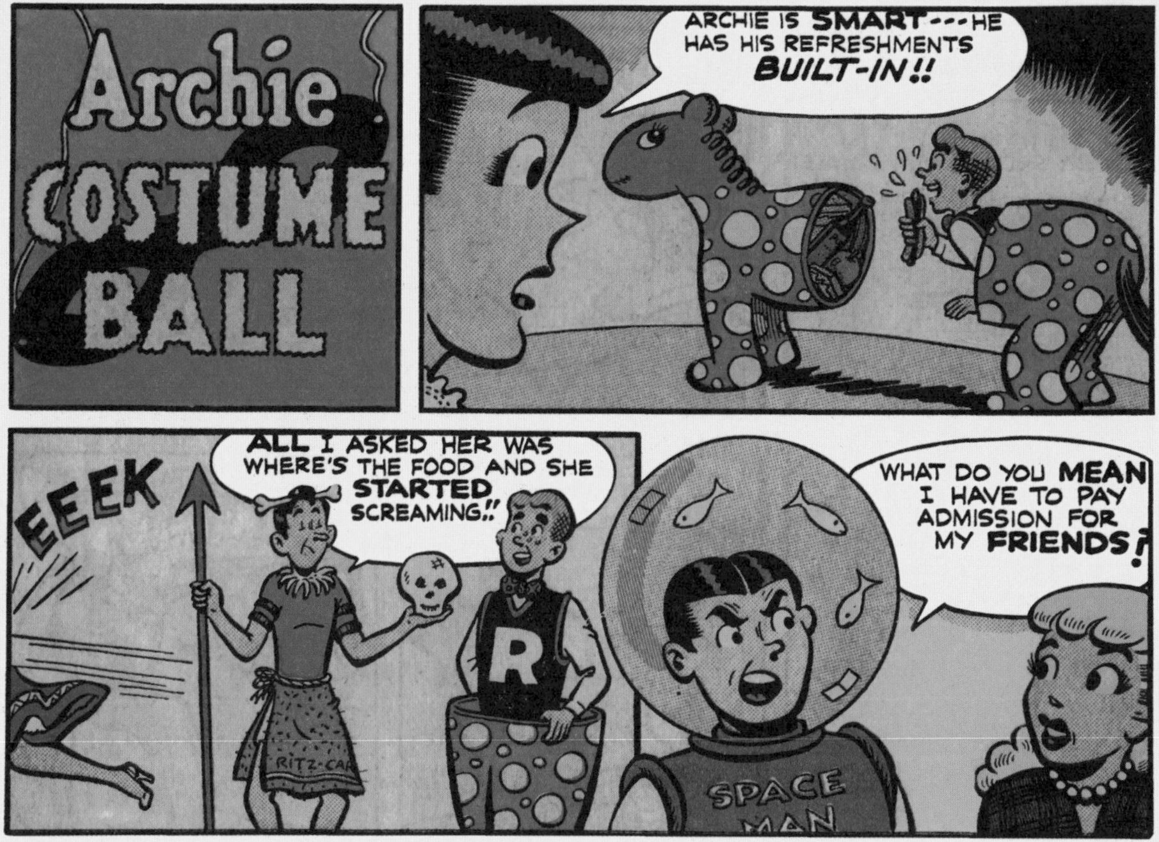
Archie COSTUME BALL
ARCHIE IS SMART---HE HAS HIS REFRESHMENTS BUILT-IN!!
EEEK
ALL I ASKED HER WAS WHERE'S THE FOOD AND SHE STARTED SCREAMING!!
RITZ-CA
R
WHAT DO YOU MEAN I HAVE TO PAY ADMISSION FOR MY FRIENDS?
SPACE MAN

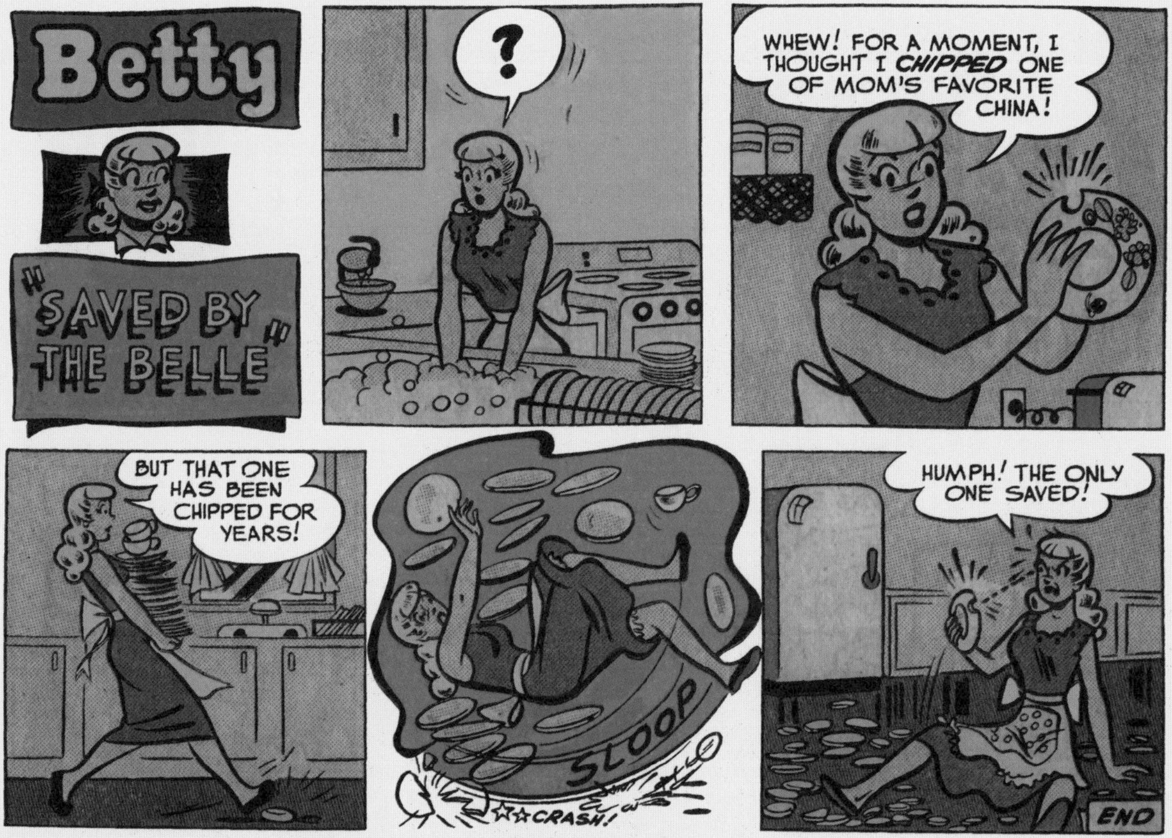
Betty
"SAVED BY THE BELLE"
?
WHEW! FOR A MOMENT, I THOUGHT I CHIPPED ONE OF MOM'S FAVORITE CHINA!
BUT THAT ONE HAS BEEN CHIPPED FOR YEARS!
SLOOP
CRASH!
HUMPH! THE ONLY ONE SAVED!
END

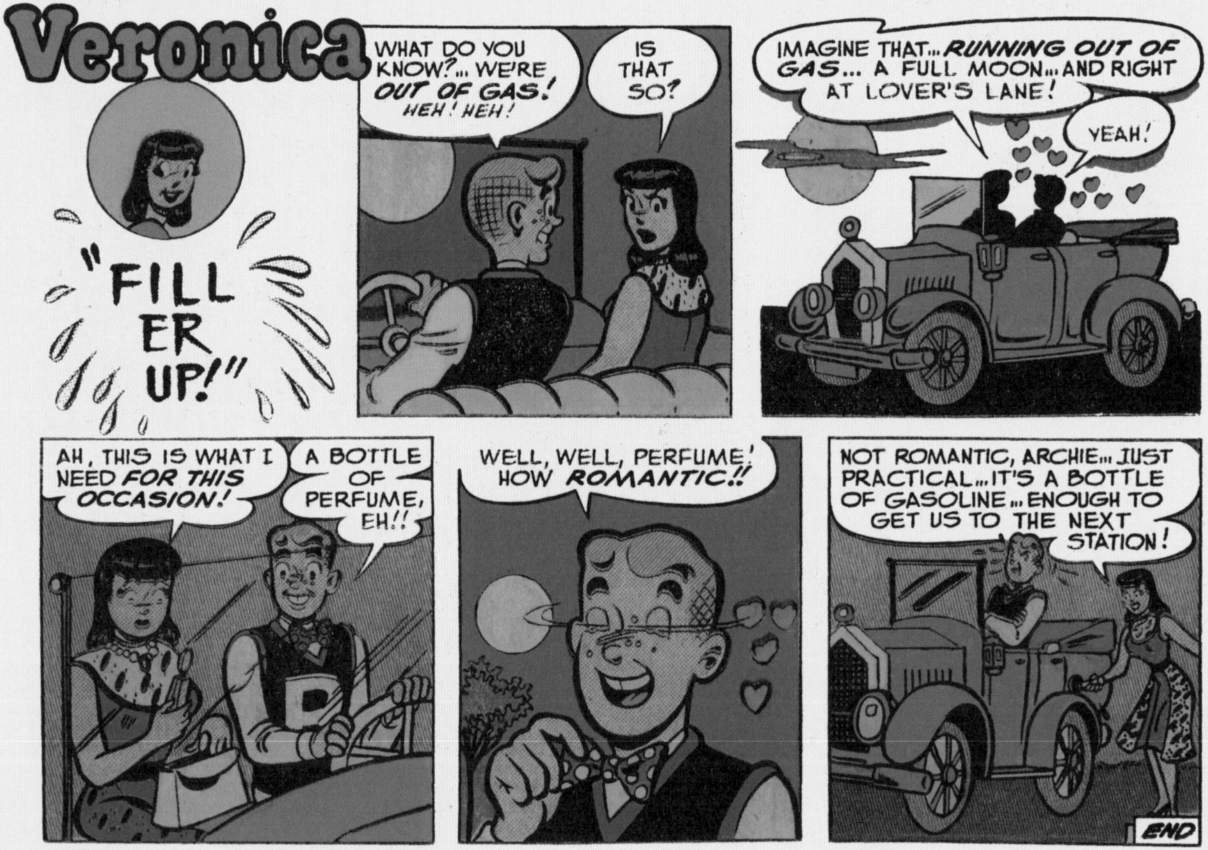

Veronica
"FILL ER UP!"
WHAT DO YOU KNOW?... WE'RE OUT OF GAS! HEH! HEH!
IS THAT SO?
IMAGINE THAT... RUNNING OUT OF GAS... A FULL MOON... AND RIGHT AT LOVER'S LANE!
YEAH!
AH, THIS IS WHAT I NEED FOR THIS OCCASION!
A BOTTLE OF PERFUME, EH!!
WELL, WELL, PERFUME! HOW ROMANTIC!!
NOT ROMANTIC, ARCHIE... JUST PRACTICAL... IT'S A BOTTLE OF GASOLINE... ENOUGH TO GET US TO THE NEXT STATION!
END

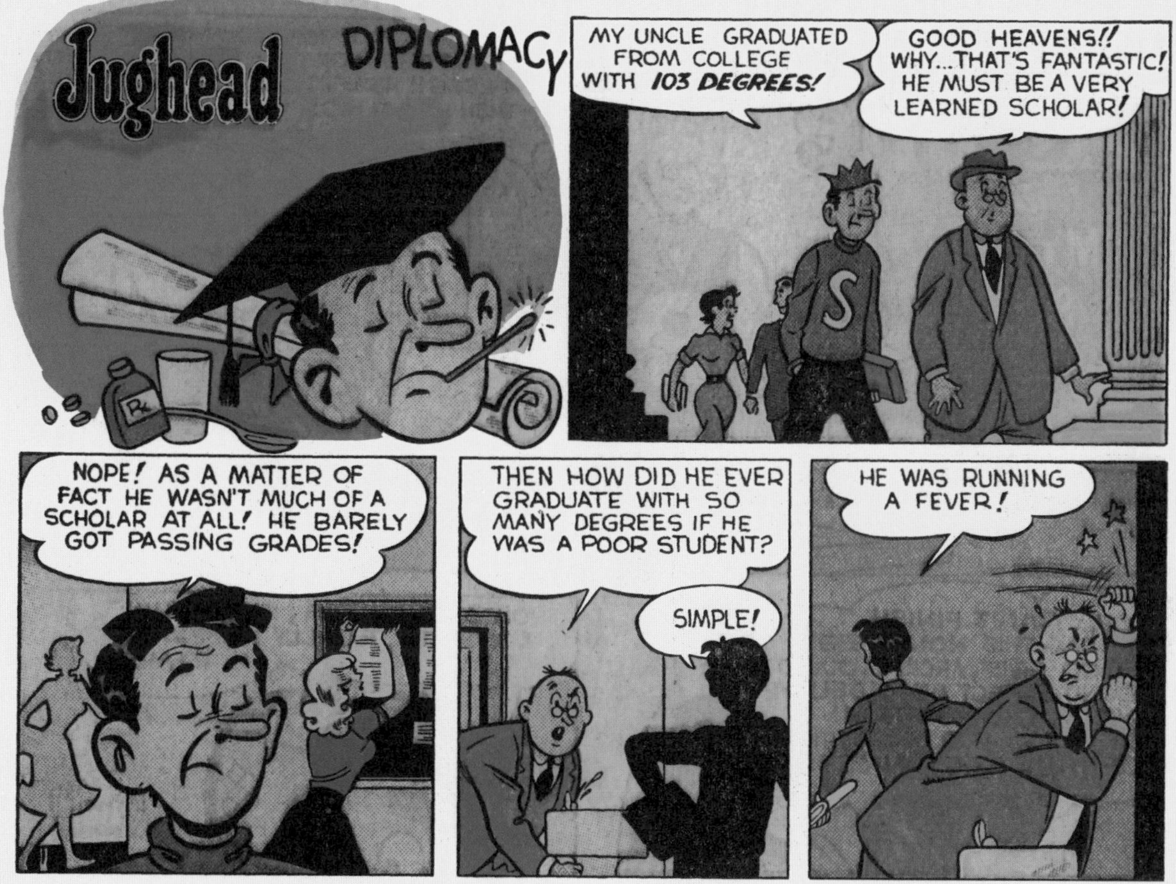
Jughead
DIPLOMACY
MY UNCLE GRADUATED FROM COLLEGE WITH 103 DEGREES!
GOOD HEAVENS!! WHY...THAT'S FANTASTIC! HE MUST BE A VERY LEARNED SCHOLAR!
NOPE! AS A MATTER OF FACT HE WASN'T MUCH OF A SCHOLAR AT ALL! HE BARELY GOT PASSING GRADES!
THEN HOW DID HE EVER GRADUATE WITH SO MANY DEGREES IF HE WAS A POOR STUDENT?
SIMPLE!
HE WAS RUNNING A FEVER!

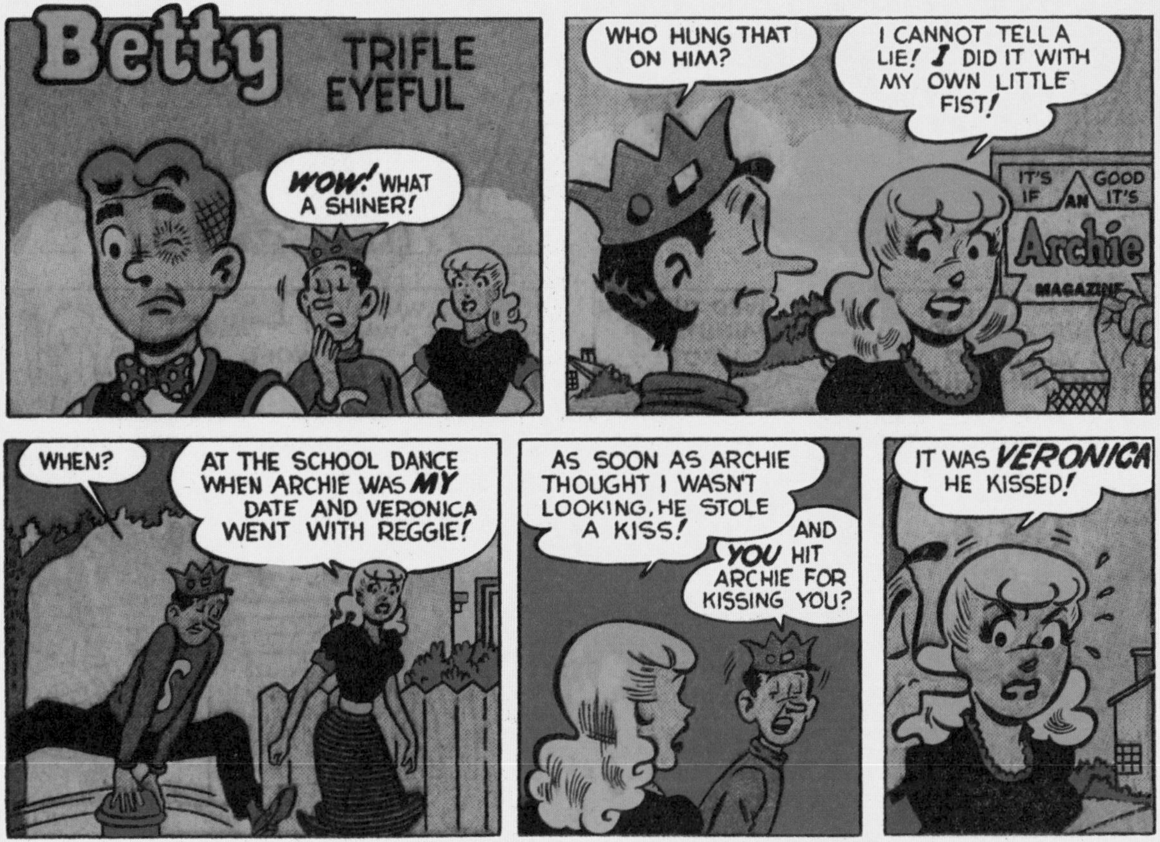
Betty
TRIFLE EYEFUL
WOW! WHAT A SHINER!
WHO HUNG THAT ON HIM?
I CANNOT TELL A LIE! I DID IT WITH MY OWN LITTLE FIST!
IT'S A GOOD IF AN IT'S Archie MAGAZINE
WHEN?
AT THE SCHOOL DANCE WHEN ARCHIE WAS MY DATE AND VERONICA WENT WITH REGGIE!
AS SOON AS ARCHIE THOUGHT I WASN'T LOOKING, HE STOLE A KISS!
AND YOU HIT ARCHIE FOR KISSING YOU?
IT WAS VERONICA HE KISSED!

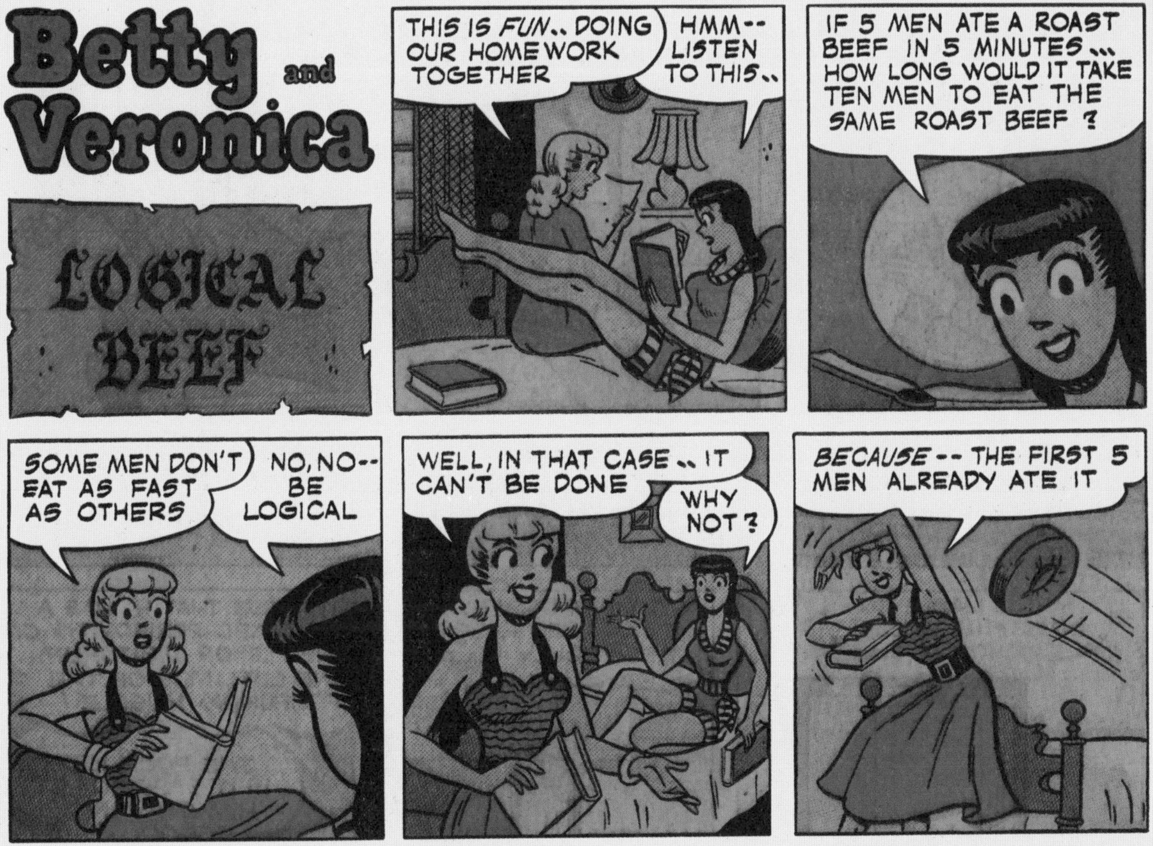
Betty and Veronica
LOGICAL BEEF
THIS IS FUN.. DOING OUR HOMEWORK TOGETHER
HMM-- LISTEN TO THIS..
IF 5 MEN ATE A ROAST BEEF IN 5 MINUTES... HOW LONG WOULD IT TAKE TEN MEN TO EAT THE SAME ROAST BEEF ?
SOME MEN DON'T EAT AS FAST AS OTHERS
NO, NO-- BE LOGICAL
WELL, IN THAT CASE .. IT CAN'T BE DONE
WHY NOT ?
BECAUSE -- THE FIRST 5 MEN ALREADY ATE IT

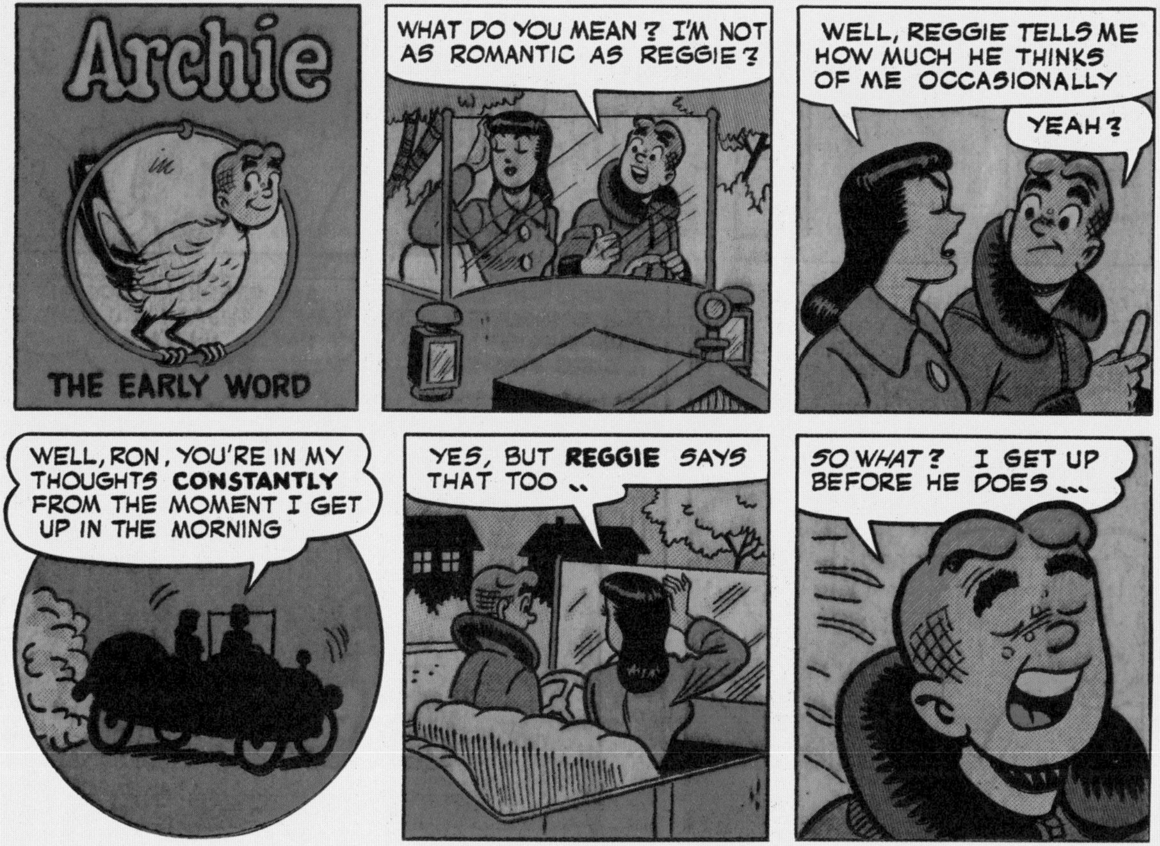
Archie
THE EARLY WORD
WHAT DO YOU MEAN ? I'M NOT AS ROMANTIC AS REGGIE ?
WELL, REGGIE TELLS ME HOW MUCH HE THINKS OF ME OCCASIONALLY
YEAH ?
WELL, RON, YOU'RE IN MY THOUGHTS CONSTANTLY FROM THE MOMENT I GET UP IN THE MORNING
YES, BUT REGGIE SAYS THAT TOO ..
SO WHAT ? I GET UP BEFORE HE DOES ...

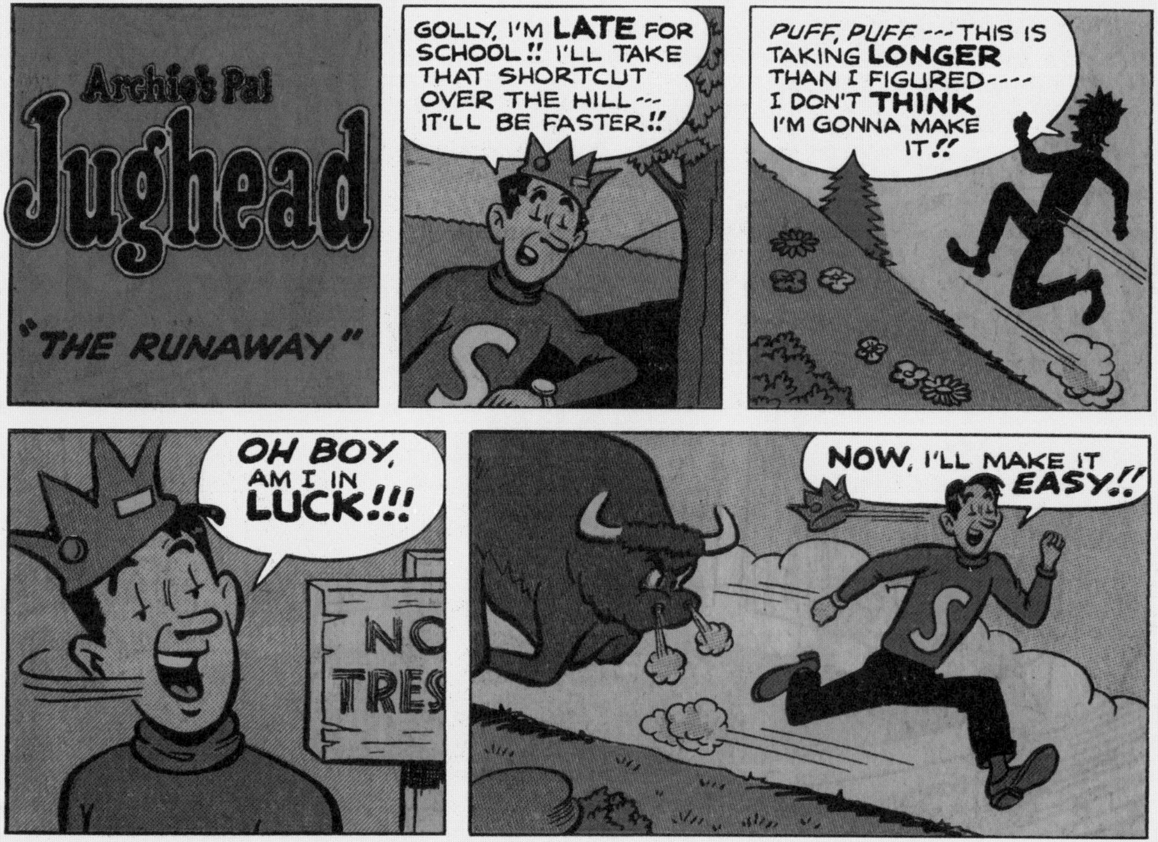
Archie's Pal
Jughead
"THE RUNAWAY"
GOLLY, I'M LATE FOR SCHOOL!! I'LL TAKE THAT SHORTCUT OVER THE HILL--- IT'LL BE FASTER!!
PUFF, PUFF ---THIS IS TAKING LONGER THAN I FIGURED---- I DON'T THINK I'M GONNA MAKE IT!!
OH BOY, AM I IN LUCK!!!
NO
TRES
NOW, I'LL MAKE IT EASY!!

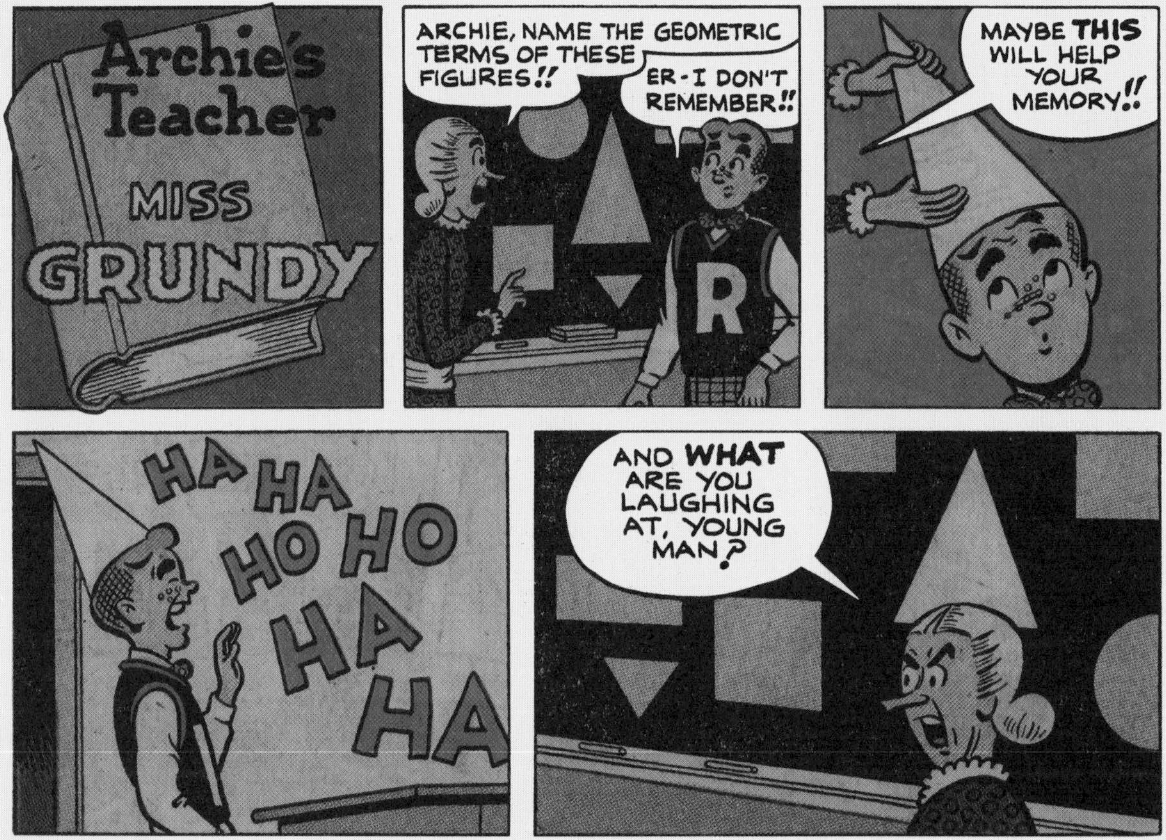
Archie's Teacher
MISS GRUNDY
ARCHIE, NAME THE GEOMETRIC TERMS OF THESE FIGURES!!
ER-I DON'T REMEMBER!!
MAYBE THIS WILL HELP YOUR MEMORY!!
HA HA HA HO HO HO HA HA HA
AND WHAT ARE YOU LAUGHING AT, YOUNG MAN?

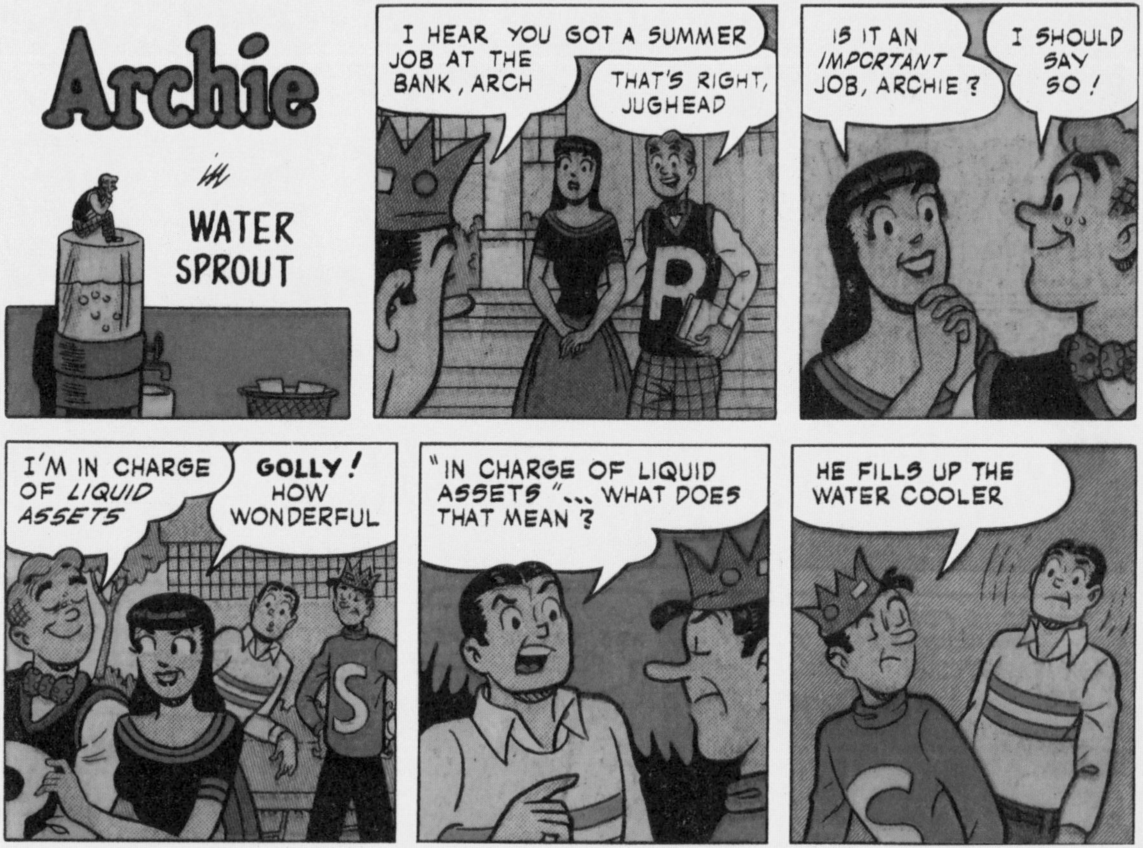
Archie
in
WATER SPROUT
I HEAR YOU GOT A SUMMER JOB AT THE BANK, ARCH
THAT'S RIGHT, JUGHEAD
IS IT AN IMPORTANT JOB, ARCHIE ?
I SHOULD SAY SO !
I'M IN CHARGE OF LIQUID ASSETS
GOLLY! HOW WONDERFUL
"IN CHARGE OF LIQUID ASSETS"... WHAT DOES THAT MEAN ?
HE FILLS UP THE WATER COOLER

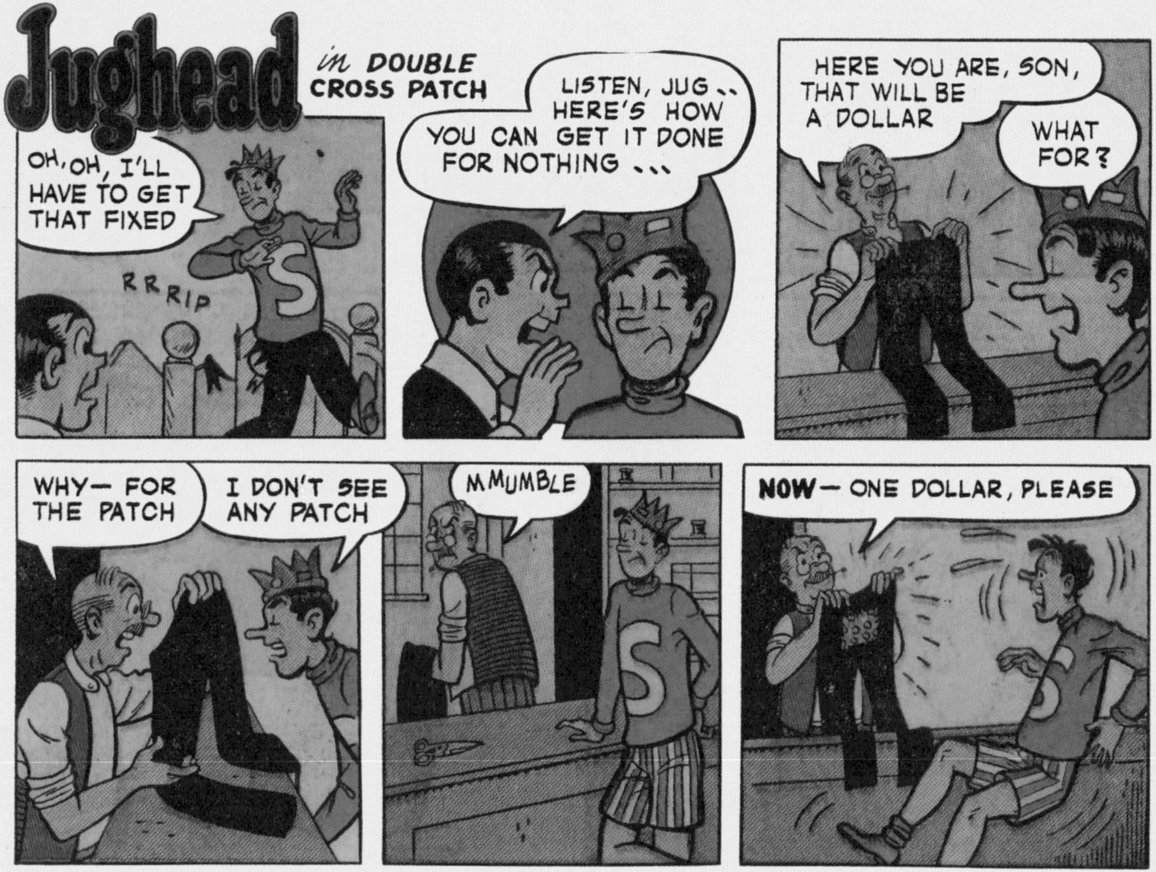
Jughead
in DOUBLE CROSS PATCH
OH, OH, I'LL HAVE TO GET THAT FIXED
RRRIP
LISTEN, JUG .. HERE'S HOW YOU CAN GET IT DONE FOR NOTHING ...
HERE YOU ARE, SON, THAT WILL BE A DOLLAR
WHAT FOR?
WHY— FOR THE PATCH
I DON'T SEE ANY PATCH
MMUMBLE
NOW— ONE DOLLAR, PLEASE

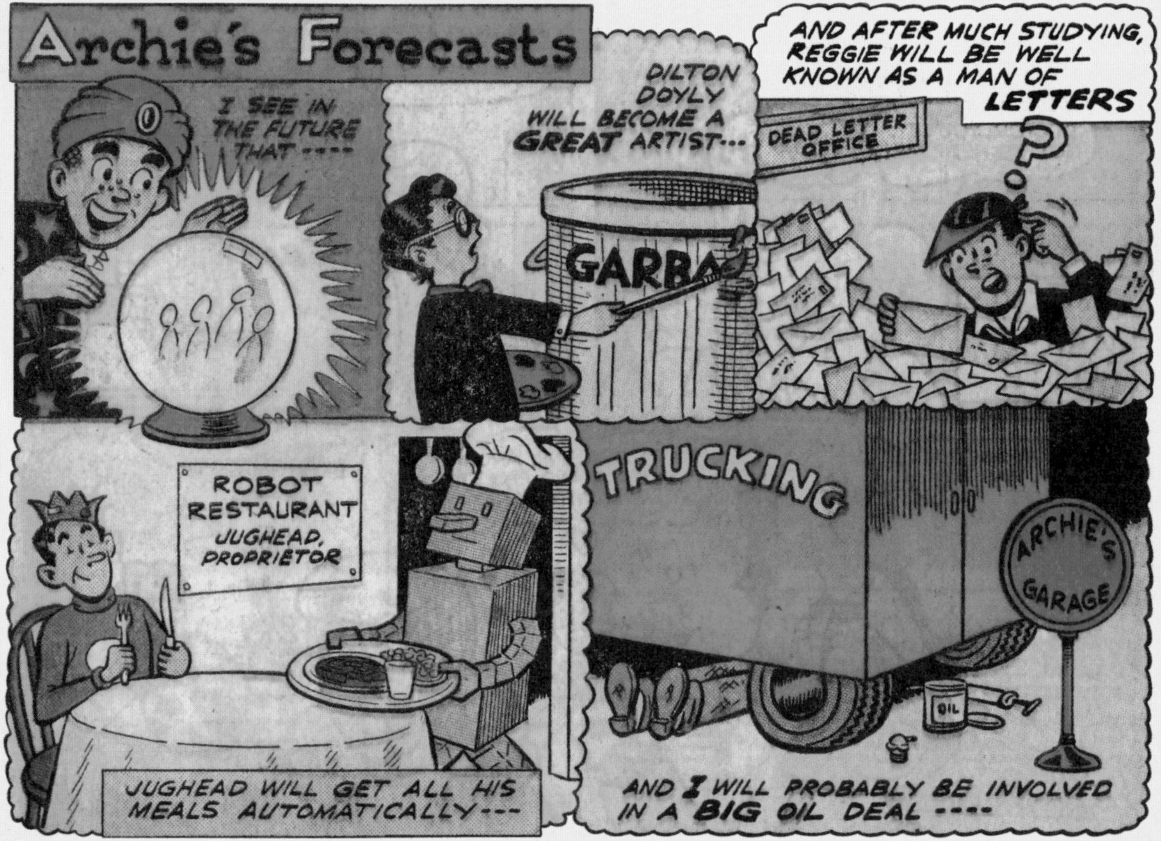
Archie's Forecasts
I SEE IN THE FUTURE THAT ----
DILTON DOYLY WILL BECOME A GREAT ARTIST...
GARBA
AND AFTER MUCH STUDYING, REGGIE WILL BE WELL KNOWN AS A MAN OF LETTERS
DEAD LETTER OFFICE
ROBOT RESTAURANT JUGHEAD, PROPRIETOR
JUGHEAD WILL GET ALL HIS MEALS AUTOMATICALLY---
TRUCKING
ARCHIE'S GARAGE
OIL
AND I WILL PROBABLY BE INVOLVED IN A BIG OIL DEAL ----

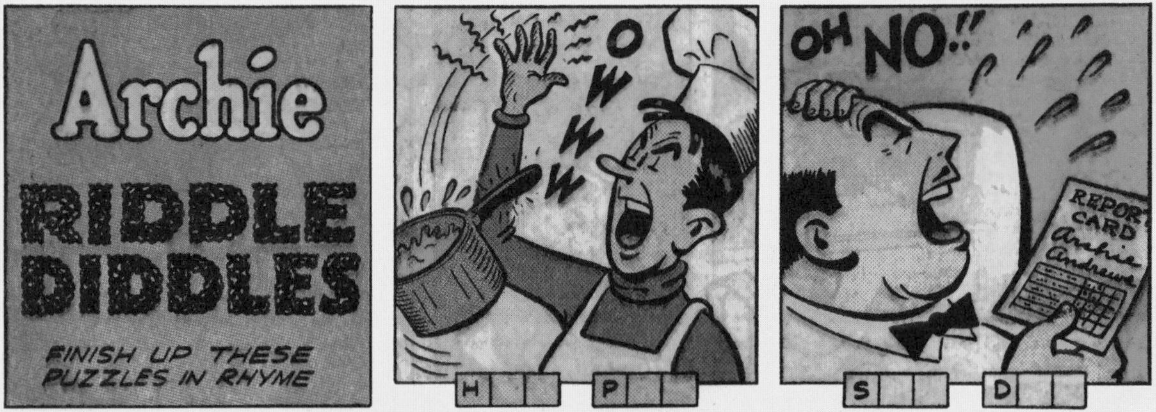
Archie
RIDDLE DIDDLES
FINISH UP THESE PUZZLES IN RHYME
OWWWWW
H P
OH NO!!
REPORT CARD
Archie Andrews
S D

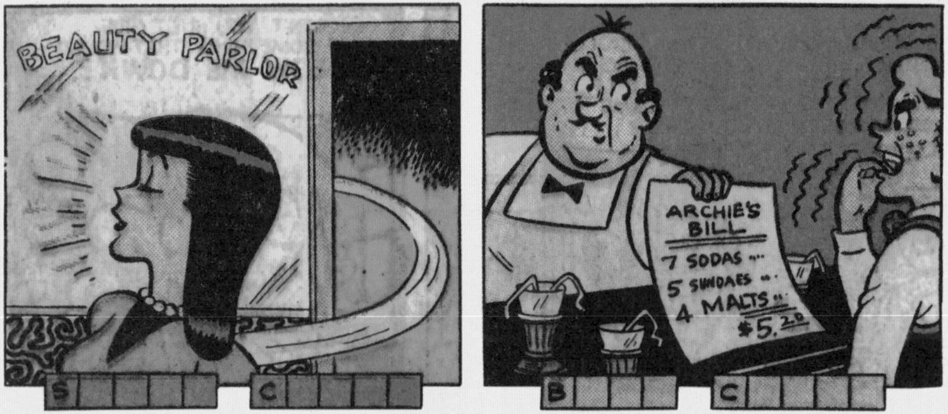
BEAUTY PARLOR
S C
ARCHIE'S BILL
7 SODAS
5 SUNDAES
4 MALTS
$5.20
B C

ANSWERS:

1 - HOT
POT

2 - SAD
DAD

3 - SLICK
CHICK

4 - BILL
CHILL

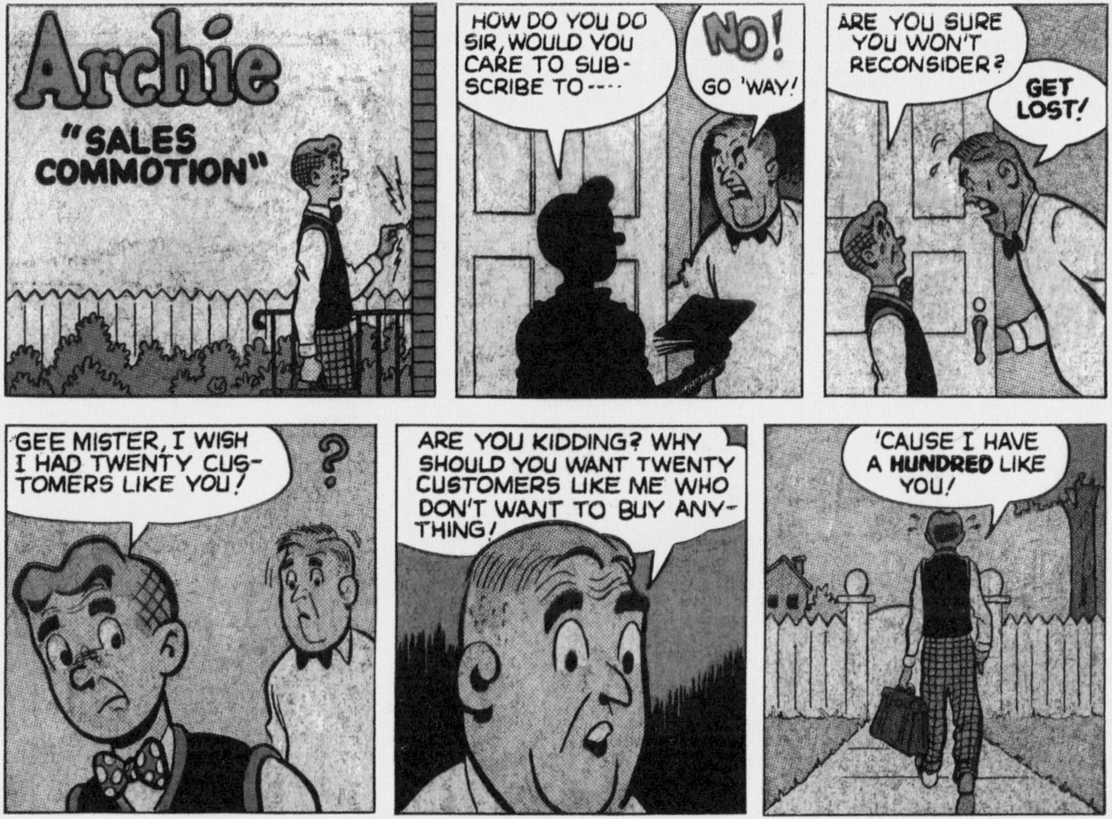
Archie
"SALES COMMOTION"
HOW DO YOU DO SIR, WOULD YOU CARE TO SUB-SCRIBE TO----
NO! GO 'WAY!
ARE YOU SURE YOU WON'T RECONSIDER?
GET LOST!
GEE MISTER, I WISH I HAD TWENTY CUS-TOMERS LIKE YOU!
?
ARE YOU KIDDING? WHY SHOULD YOU WANT TWENTY CUSTOMERS LIKE ME WHO DON'T WANT TO BUY ANY-THING!
'CAUSE I HAVE A HUNDRED LIKE YOU!

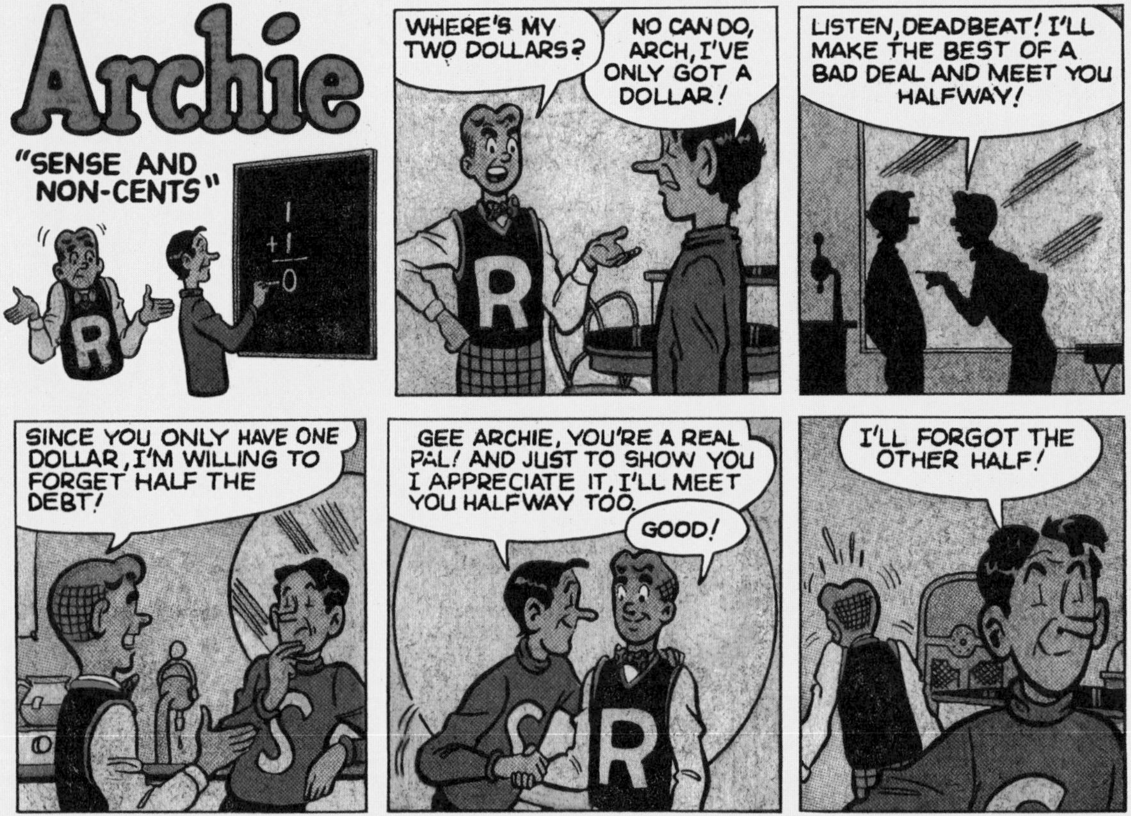
Archie
"SENSE AND NON-CENTS"
1
+1
0
WHERE'S MY TWO DOLLARS?
NO CAN DO, ARCH, I'VE ONLY GOT A DOLLAR!
LISTEN, DEADBEAT! I'LL MAKE THE BEST OF A BAD DEAL AND MEET YOU HALFWAY!
SINCE YOU ONLY HAVE ONE DOLLAR, I'M WILLING TO FORGET HALF THE DEBT!
GEE ARCHIE, YOU'RE A REAL PAL! AND JUST TO SHOW YOU I APPRECIATE IT, I'LL MEET YOU HALFWAY TOO.
GOOD!
I'LL FORGOT THE OTHER HALF!

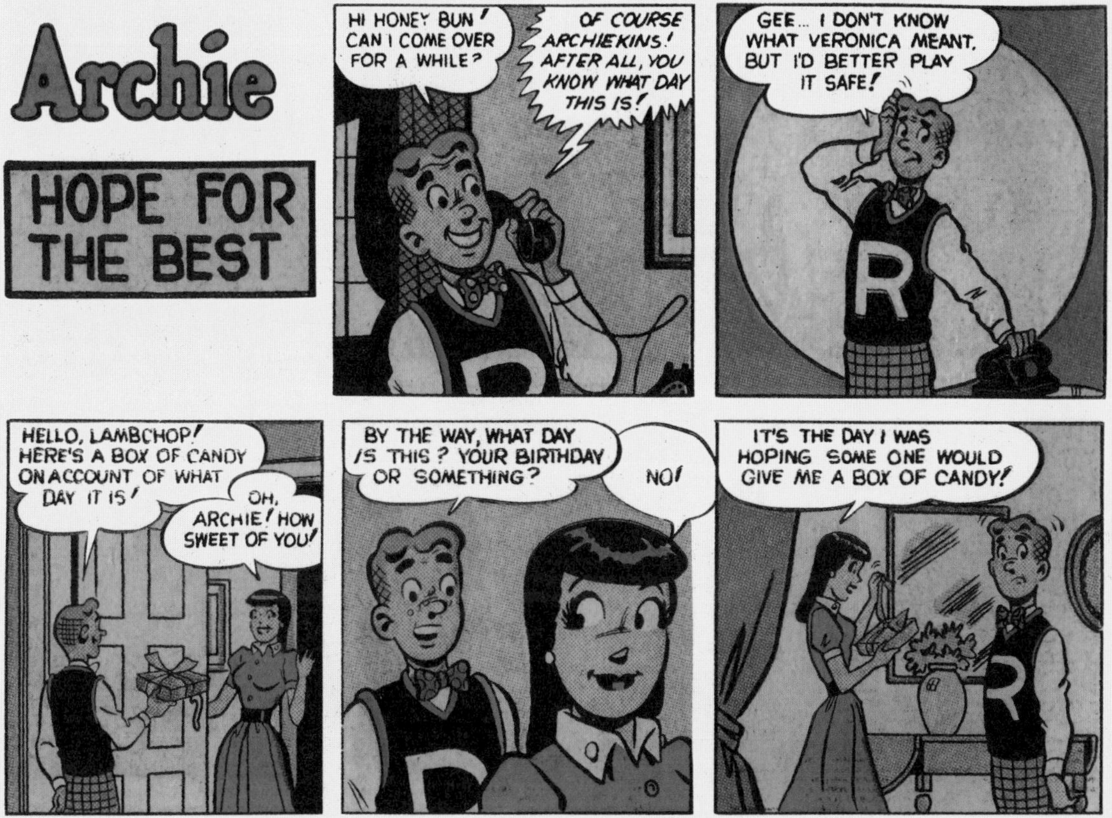
Archie
HOPE FOR THE BEST
HI HONEY BUN! CAN I COME OVER FOR A WHILE?
OF COURSE ARCHIEKINS! AFTER ALL, YOU KNOW WHAT DAY THIS IS!
GEE... I DON'T KNOW WHAT VERONICA MEANT, BUT I'D BETTER PLAY IT SAFE!
HELLO, LAMBCHOP! HERE'S A BOX OF CANDY ON ACCOUNT OF WHAT DAY IT IS!
OH, ARCHIE! HOW SWEET OF YOU!
BY THE WAY, WHAT DAY IS THIS? YOUR BIRTHDAY OR SOMETHING?
NO!
IT'S THE DAY I WAS HOPING SOME ONE WOULD GIVE ME A BOX OF CANDY!

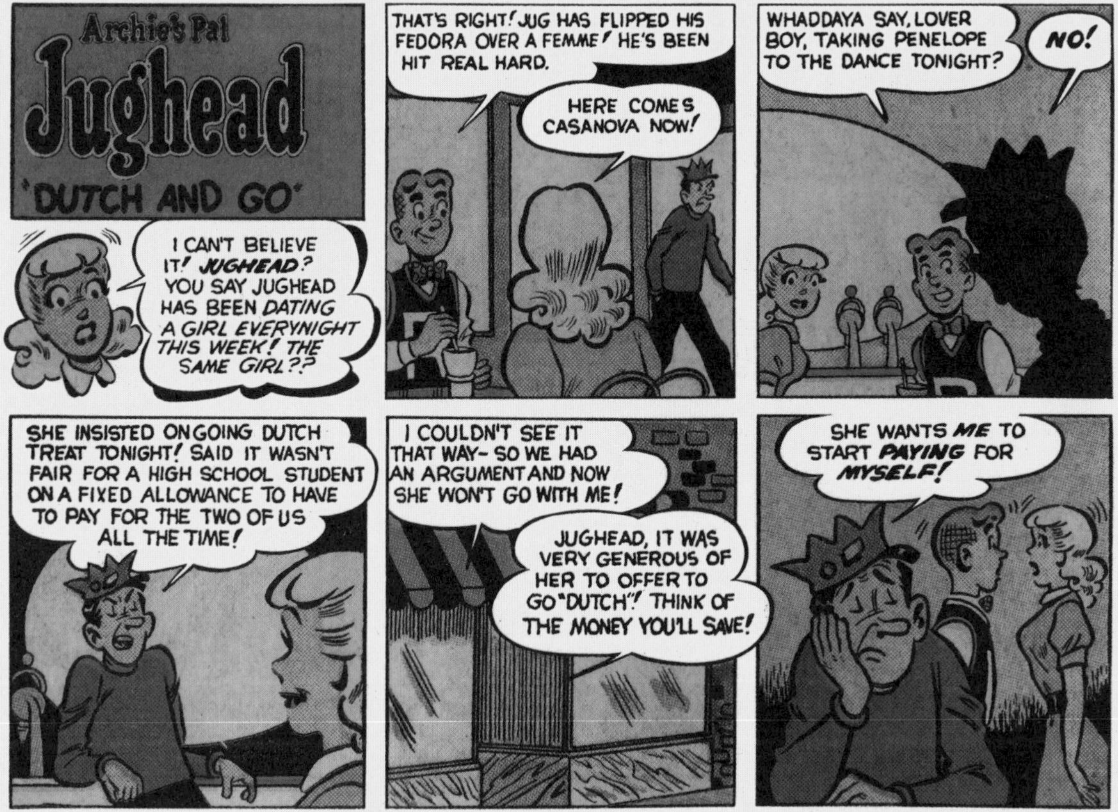
Archie's Pal
Jughead
"DUTCH AND GO"
I CAN'T BELIEVE IT! JUGHEAD? YOU SAY JUGHEAD HAS BEEN DATING A GIRL EVERYNIGHT THIS WEEK! THE SAME GIRL??
THAT'S RIGHT! JUG HAS FLIPPED HIS FEDORA OVER A FEMME! HE'S BEEN HIT REAL HARD.
HERE COMES CASANOVA NOW!
WHADDAYA SAY, LOVER BOY, TAKING PENELOPE TO THE DANCE TONIGHT?
NO!
SHE INSISTED ONGOING DUTCH TREAT TONIGHT! SAID IT WASN'T FAIR FOR A HIGH SCHOOL STUDENT ON A FIXED ALLOWANCE TO HAVE TO PAY FOR THE TWO OF US ALL THE TIME!
I COULDN'T SEE IT THAT WAY- SO WE HAD AN ARGUMENT AND NOW SHE WON'T GO WITH ME!
JUGHEAD, IT WAS VERY GENEROUS OF HER TO OFFER TO GO "DUTCH"! THINK OF THE MONEY YOU'LL SAVE!
SHE WANTS ME TO START PAYING FOR MYSELF!

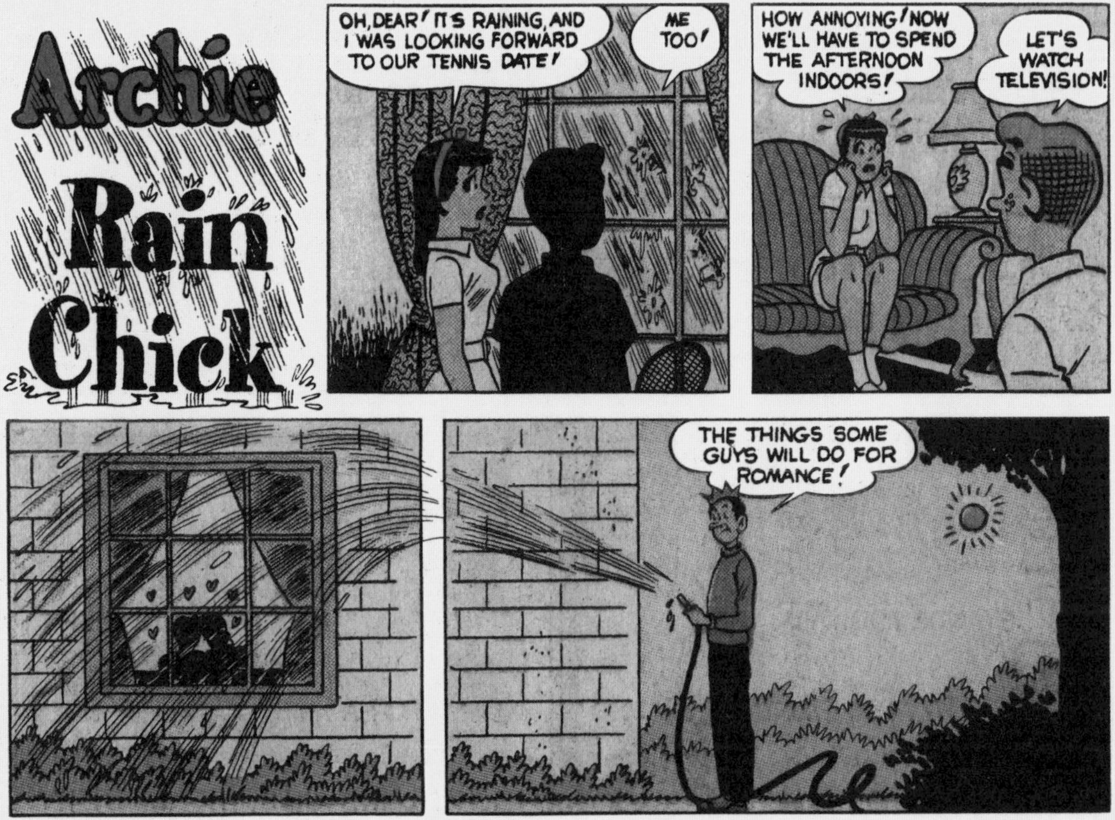
Archie
Rain Chick
OH, DEAR! IT'S RAINING, AND I WAS LOOKING FORWARD TO OUR TENNIS DATE!
ME TOO!
HOW ANNOYING! NOW WE'LL HAVE TO SPEND THE AFTERNOON INDOORS!
LET'S WATCH TELEVISION!
THE THINGS SOME GUYS WILL DO FOR ROMANCE!

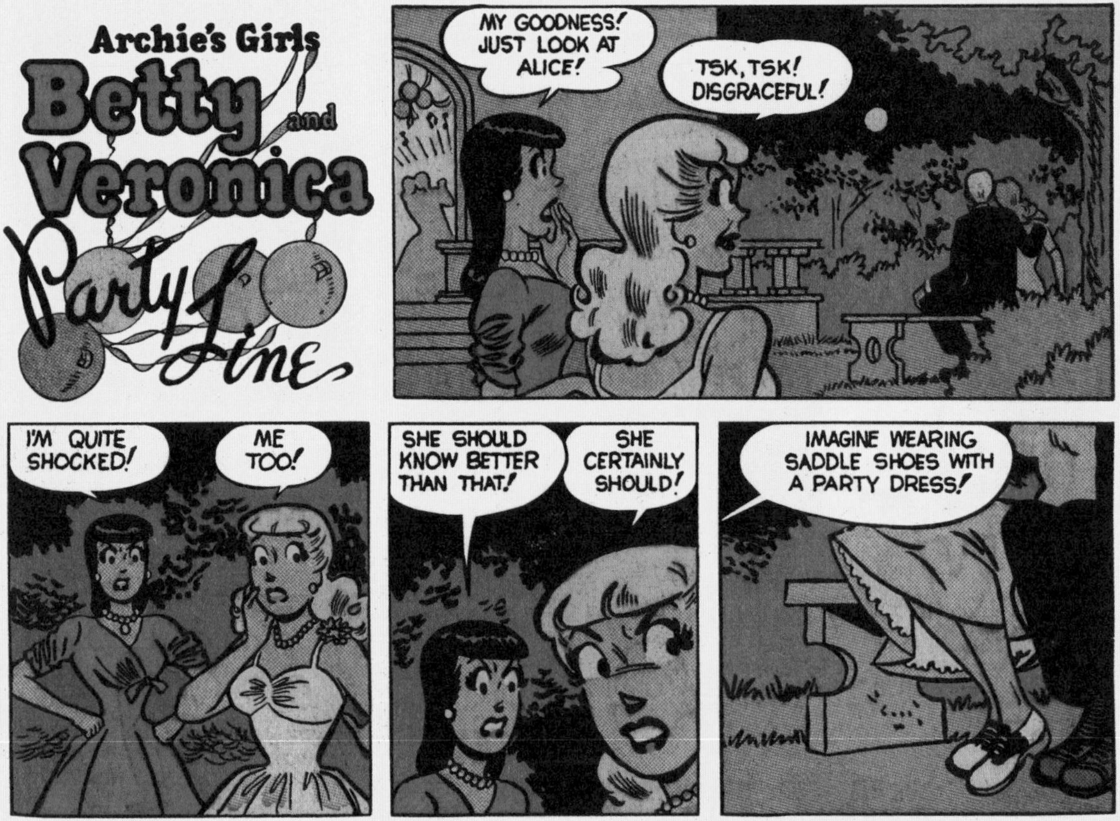
Archie's Girls
Betty and Veronica
Party Line
MY GOODNESS! JUST LOOK AT ALICE!
TSK, TSK! DISGRACEFUL!
I'M QUITE SHOCKED!
ME TOO!
SHE SHOULD KNOW BETTER THAN THAT!
SHE CERTAINLY SHOULD!
IMAGINE WEARING SADDLE SHOES WITH A PARTY DRESS!

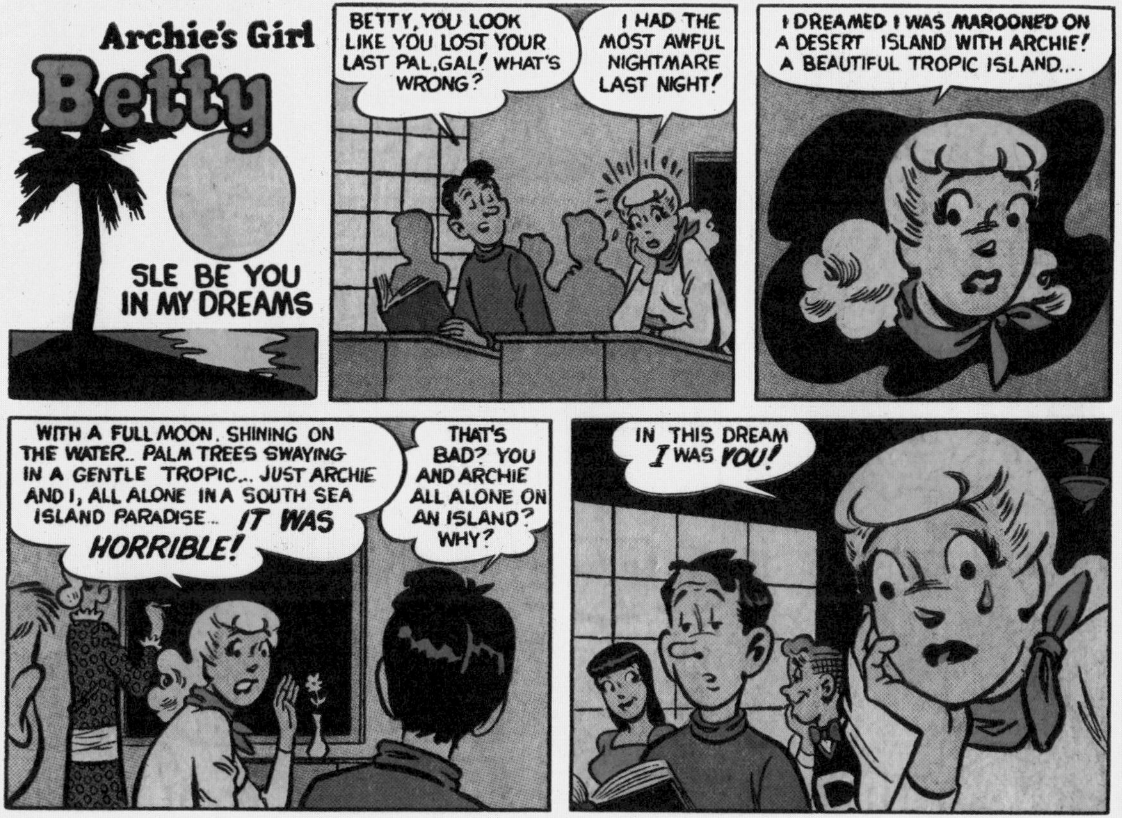
Archie's Girl
Betty
SLE BE YOU IN MY DREAMS
BETTY, YOU LOOK LIKE YOU LOST YOUR LAST PAL, GAL! WHAT'S WRONG?
I HAD THE MOST AWFUL NIGHTMARE LAST NIGHT!
I DREAMED I WAS MAROONED ON A DESERT ISLAND WITH ARCHIE! A BEAUTIFUL TROPIC ISLAND....
WITH A FULL MOON, SHINING ON THE WATER.. PALM TREES SWAYING IN A GENTLE TROPIC... JUST ARCHIE AND I, ALL ALONE IN A SOUTH SEA ISLAND PARADISE... IT WAS HORRIBLE!
THAT'S BAD? YOU AND ARCHIE ALL ALONE ON AN ISLAND? WHY?
IN THIS DREAM I WAS YOU!

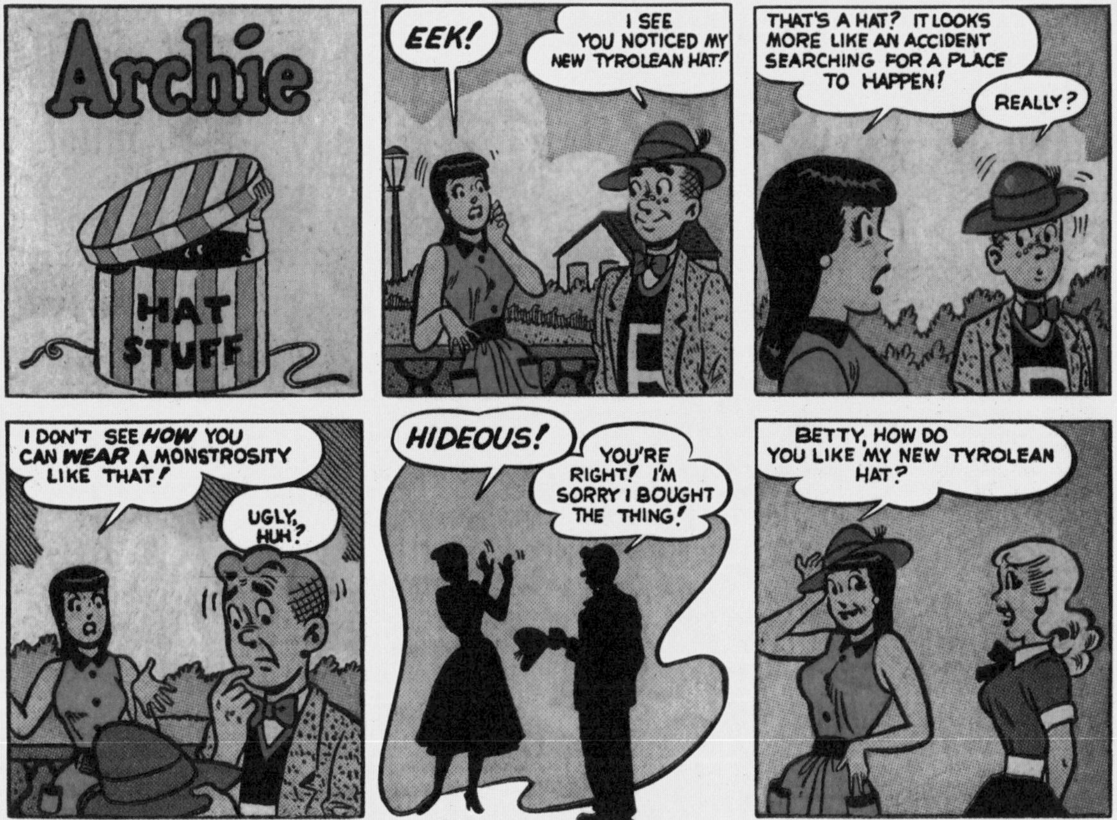
Archie
HAT STUFF
EEK!
I SEE YOU NOTICED MY NEW TYROLEAN HAT!
THAT'S A HAT? IT LOOKS MORE LIKE AN ACCIDENT SEARCHING FOR A PLACE TO HAPPEN!
REALLY?
I DON'T SEE HOW YOU CAN WEAR A MONSTROSITY LIKE THAT!
UGLY, HUH?
HIDEOUS!
YOU'RE RIGHT! I'M SORRY I BOUGHT THE THING!
BETTY, HOW DO YOU LIKE MY NEW TYROLEAN HAT?

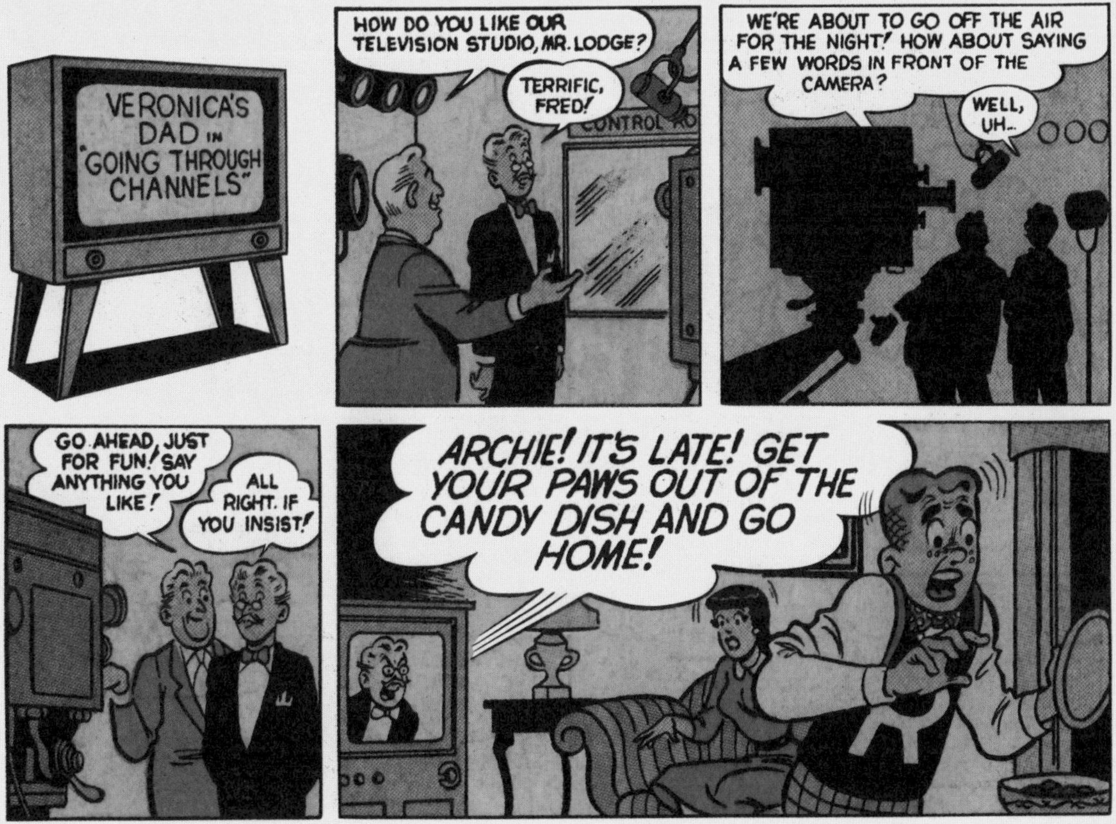
VERONICA'S DAD IN "GOING THROUGH CHANNELS"
HOW DO YOU LIKE OUR TELEVISION STUDIO, MR. LODGE?
TERRIFIC, FRED!
CONTROL RO
WE'RE ABOUT TO GO OFF THE AIR FOR THE NIGHT! HOW ABOUT SAYING A FEW WORDS IN FRONT OF THE CAMERA?
WELL, UH..
GO AHEAD, JUST FOR FUN! SAY ANYTHING YOU LIKE!
ALL RIGHT. IF YOU INSIST!
ARCHIE! IT'S LATE! GET YOUR PAWS OUT OF THE CANDY DISH AND GO HOME!

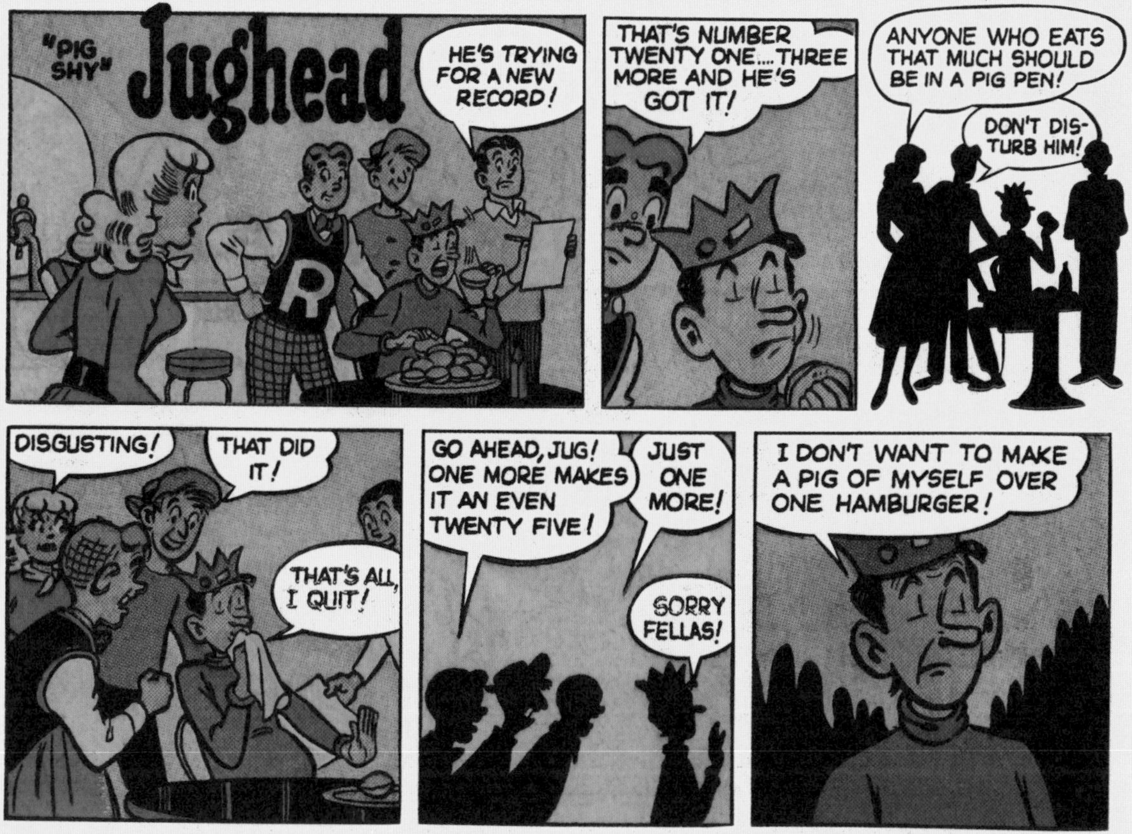
"PIG SHY"
Jughead
HE'S TRYING FOR A NEW RECORD!
THAT'S NUMBER TWENTY ONE....THREE MORE AND HE'S GOT IT!
ANYONE WHO EATS THAT MUCH SHOULD BE IN A PIG PEN!
DON'T DIS-TURB HIM!
DISGUSTING!
THAT DID IT!
THAT'S ALL, I QUIT!
GO AHEAD, JUG! ONE MORE MAKES IT AN EVEN TWENTY FIVE!
JUST ONE MORE!
SORRY FELLAS!
I DON'T WANT TO MAKE A PIG OF MYSELF OVER ONE HAMBURGER!

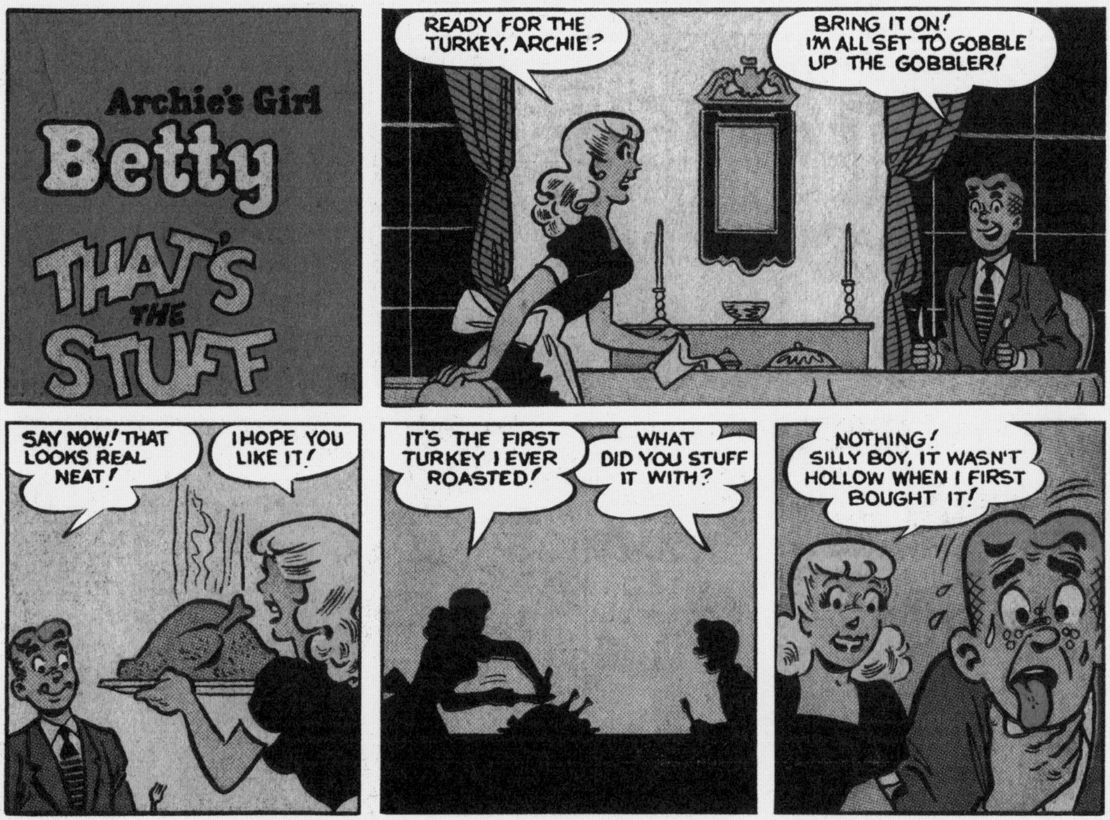
Archie's Girl
Betty
THAT'S THE STUFF
READY FOR THE TURKEY, ARCHIE?
BRING IT ON! I'M ALL SET TO GOBBLE UP THE GOBBLER!
SAY NOW! THAT LOOKS REAL NEAT!
I HOPE YOU LIKE IT!
IT'S THE FIRST TURKEY I EVER ROASTED!
WHAT DID YOU STUFF IT WITH?
NOTHING! SILLY BOY, IT WASN'T HOLLOW WHEN I FIRST BOUGHT IT!

hooky hogan

"LIVING UP TO HIS NAME"

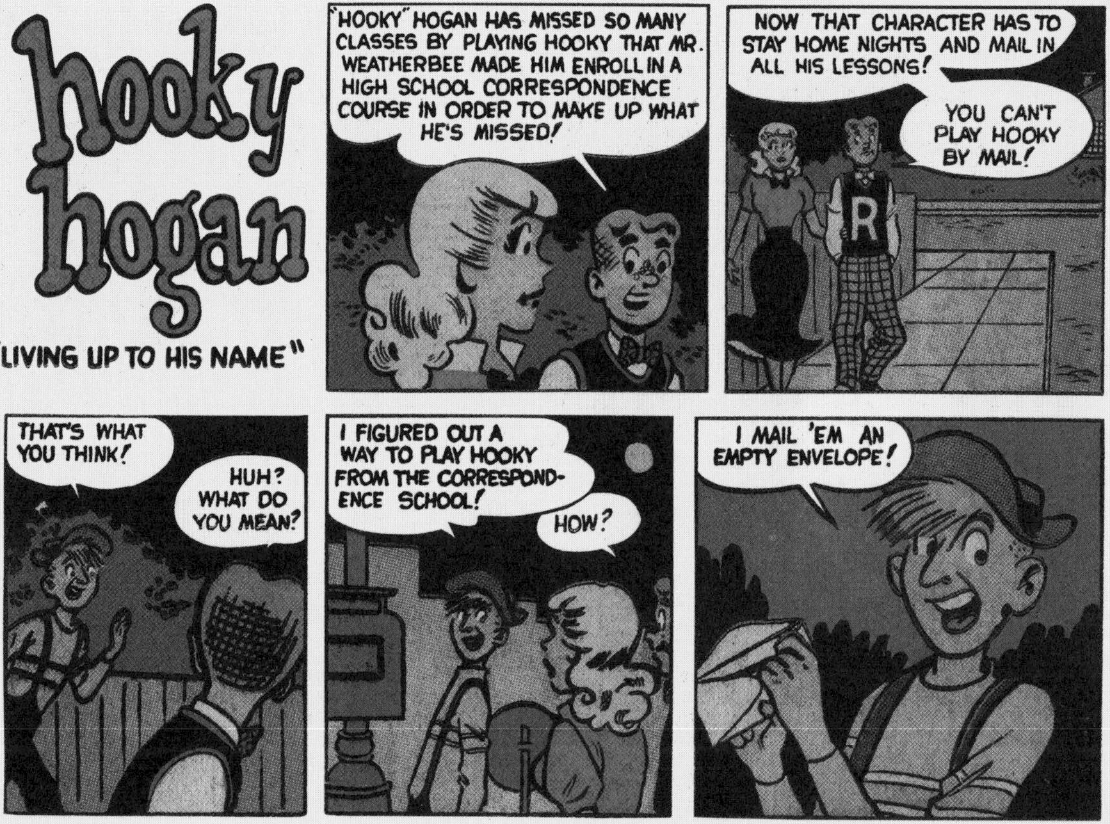
"HOOKY" HOGAN HAS MISSED SO MANY CLASSES BY PLAYING HOOKY THAT MR. WEATHERBEE MADE HIM ENROLL IN A HIGH SCHOOL CORRESPONDENCE COURSE IN ORDER TO MAKE UP WHAT HE'S MISSED!
NOW THAT CHARACTER HAS TO STAY HOME NIGHTS AND MAIL IN ALL HIS LESSONS!
YOU CAN'T PLAY HOOKY BY MAIL!
R
THAT'S WHAT YOU THINK!
HUH? WHAT DO YOU MEAN?
I FIGURED OUT A WAY TO PLAY HOOKY FROM THE CORRESPOND-ENCE SCHOOL!
HOW?
I MAIL 'EM AN EMPTY ENVELOPE!

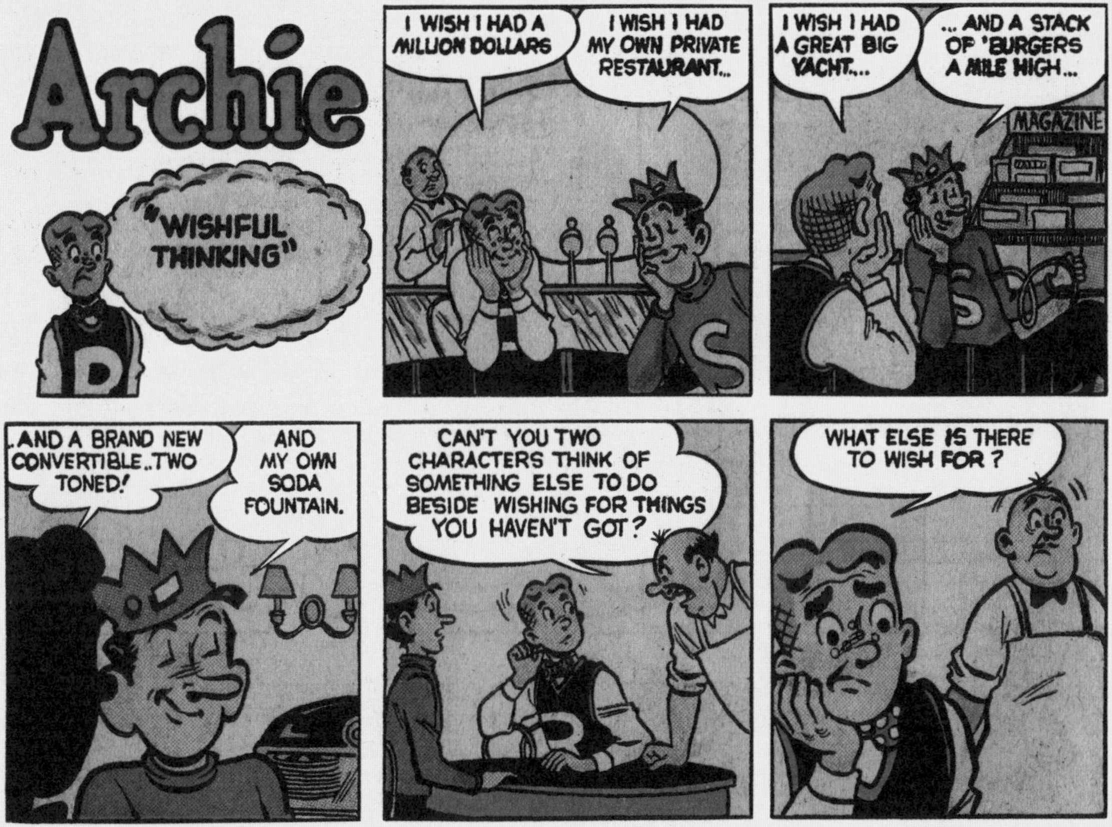
Archie
"WISHFUL THINKING"
I WISH I HAD A MILLION DOLLARS
I WISH I HAD MY OWN PRIVATE RESTAURANT...
I WISH I HAD A GREAT BIG YACHT...
... AND A STACK OF 'BURGERS A MILE HIGH...
MAGAZINE
..AND A BRAND NEW CONVERTIBLE..TWO TONED!
AND MY OWN SODA FOUNTAIN.
CAN'T YOU TWO CHARACTERS THINK OF SOMETHING ELSE TO DO BESIDE WISHING FOR THINGS YOU HAVEN'T GOT?
WHAT ELSE IS THERE TO WISH FOR?

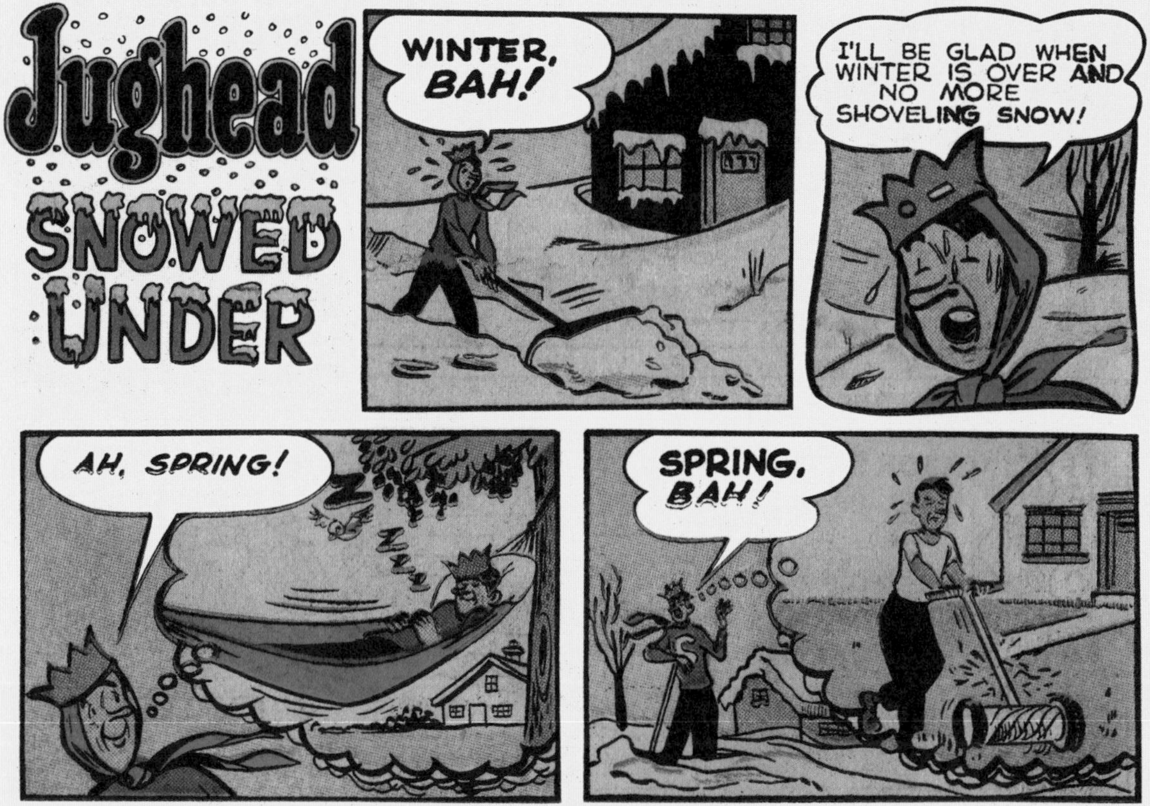
Jughead
SNOWED UNDER
WINTER, BAH!
I'LL BE GLAD WHEN WINTER IS OVER AND NO MORE SHOVELING SNOW!
AH, SPRING!
SPRING, BAH!

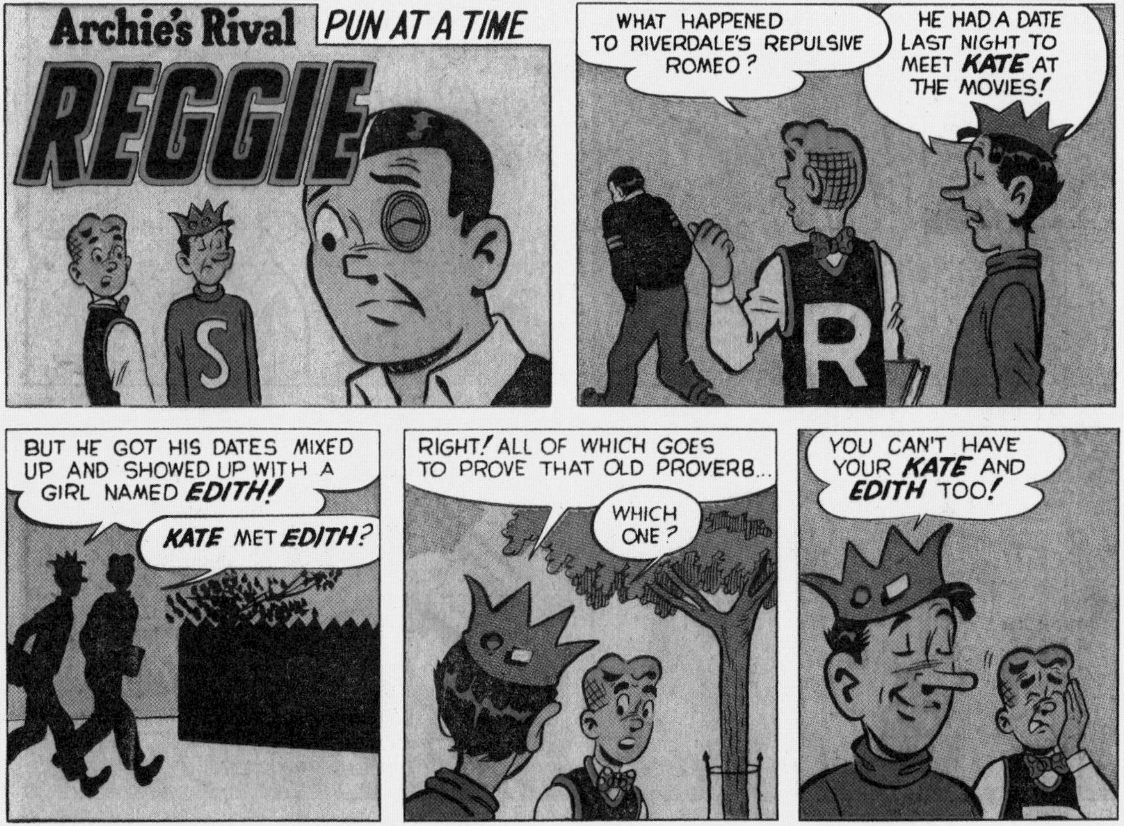

Archie's Rival
PUN AT A TIME
REGGIE
WHAT HAPPENED TO RIVERDALE'S REPULSIVE ROMEO?
HE HAD A DATE LAST NIGHT TO MEET KATE AT THE MOVIES!
BUT HE GOT HIS DATES MIXED UP AND SHOWED UP WITH A GIRL NAMED EDITH!
KATE MET EDITH?
RIGHT! ALL OF WHICH GOES TO PROVE THAT OLD PROVERB...
WHICH ONE?
YOU CAN'T HAVE YOUR KATE AND EDITH TOO!

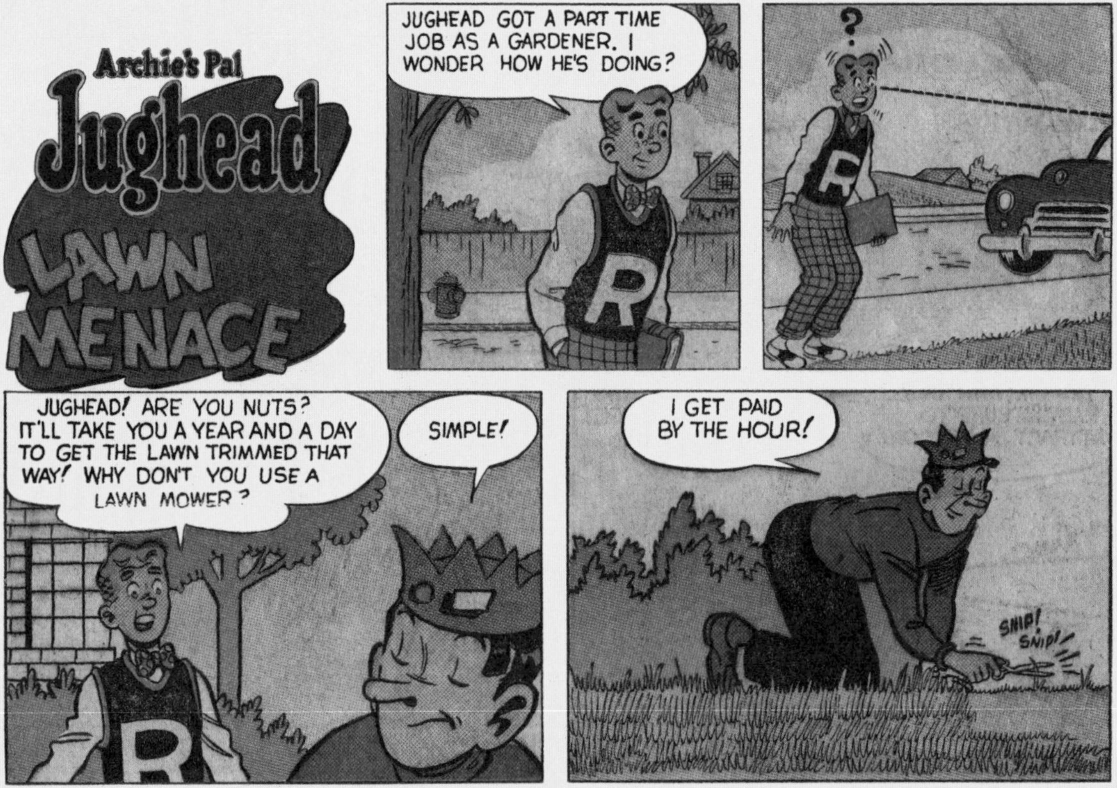
Archie's Pal
Jughead
LAWN MENACE
JUGHEAD GOT A PART TIME JOB AS A GARDENER. I WONDER HOW HE'S DOING?
?
JUGHEAD! ARE YOU NUTS? IT'LL TAKE YOU A YEAR AND A DAY TO GET THE LAWN TRIMMED THAT WAY! WHY DON'T YOU USE A LAWN MOWER?
SIMPLE!
I GET PAID BY THE HOUR!
SNIP! SNIP!

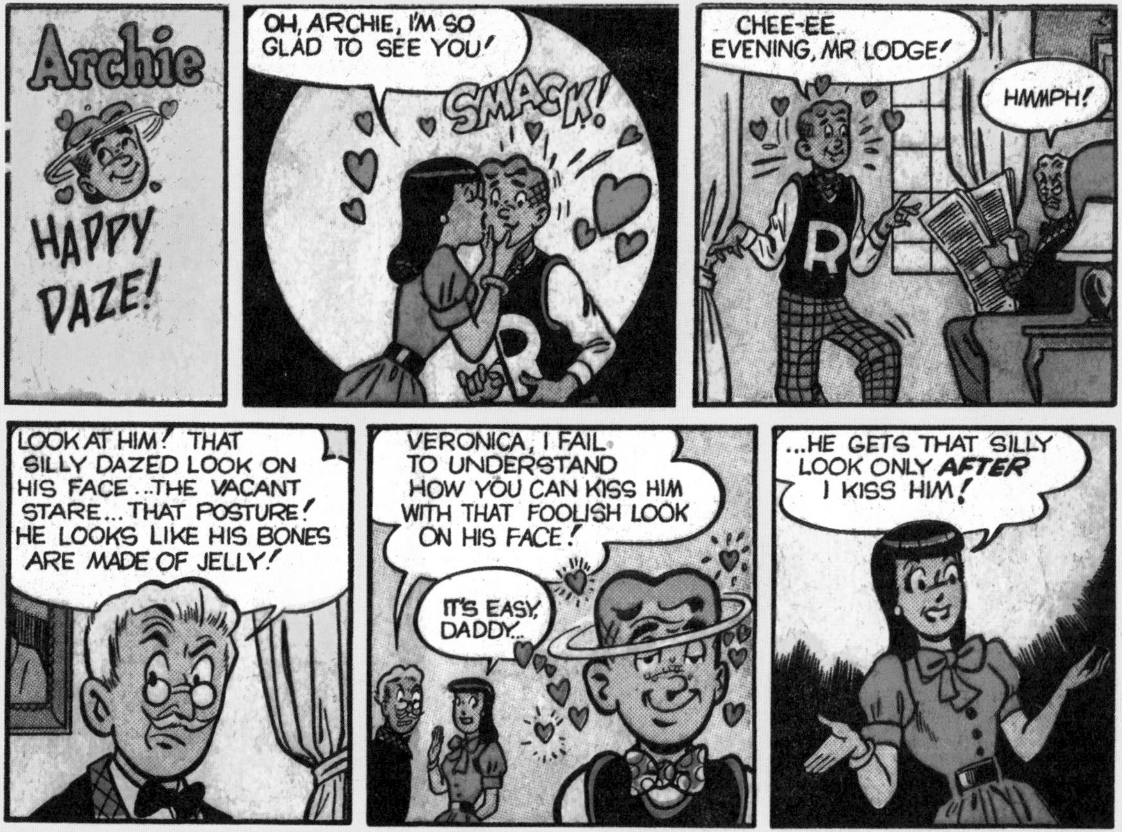
Archie
HAPPY DAZE!
OH, ARCHIE, I'M SO GLAD TO SEE YOU!
SMACK!
CHEE-EE EVENING, MR LODGE!
HMMPH!
LOOK AT HIM! THAT SILLY DAZED LOOK ON HIS FACE...THE VACANT STARE... THAT POSTURE! HE LOOKS LIKE HIS BONES ARE MADE OF JELLY!
VERONICA, I FAIL TO UNDERSTAND HOW YOU CAN KISS HIM WITH THAT FOOLISH LOOK ON HIS FACE!
IT'S EASY, DADDY...
...HE GETS THAT SILLY LOOK ONLY AFTER I KISS HIM!

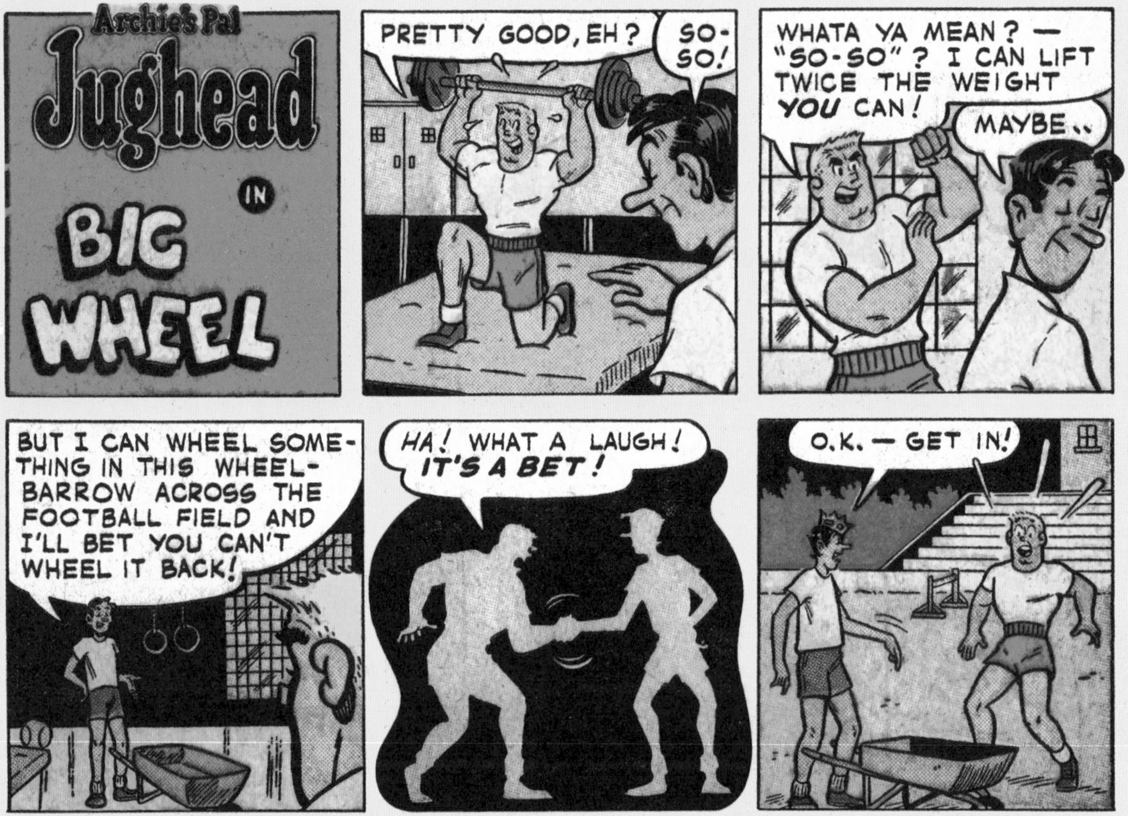
Archie's Pal
Jughead
IN
BIG WHEEL
PRETTY GOOD, EH?
SO-SO!
WHATA YA MEAN? — "SO-SO"? I CAN LIFT TWICE THE WEIGHT YOU CAN!
MAYBE..
BUT I CAN WHEEL SOMETHING IN THIS WHEELBARROW ACROSS THE FOOTBALL FIELD AND I'LL BET YOU CAN'T WHEEL IT BACK!
HA! WHAT A LAUGH! IT'S A BET!
O.K. — GET IN!

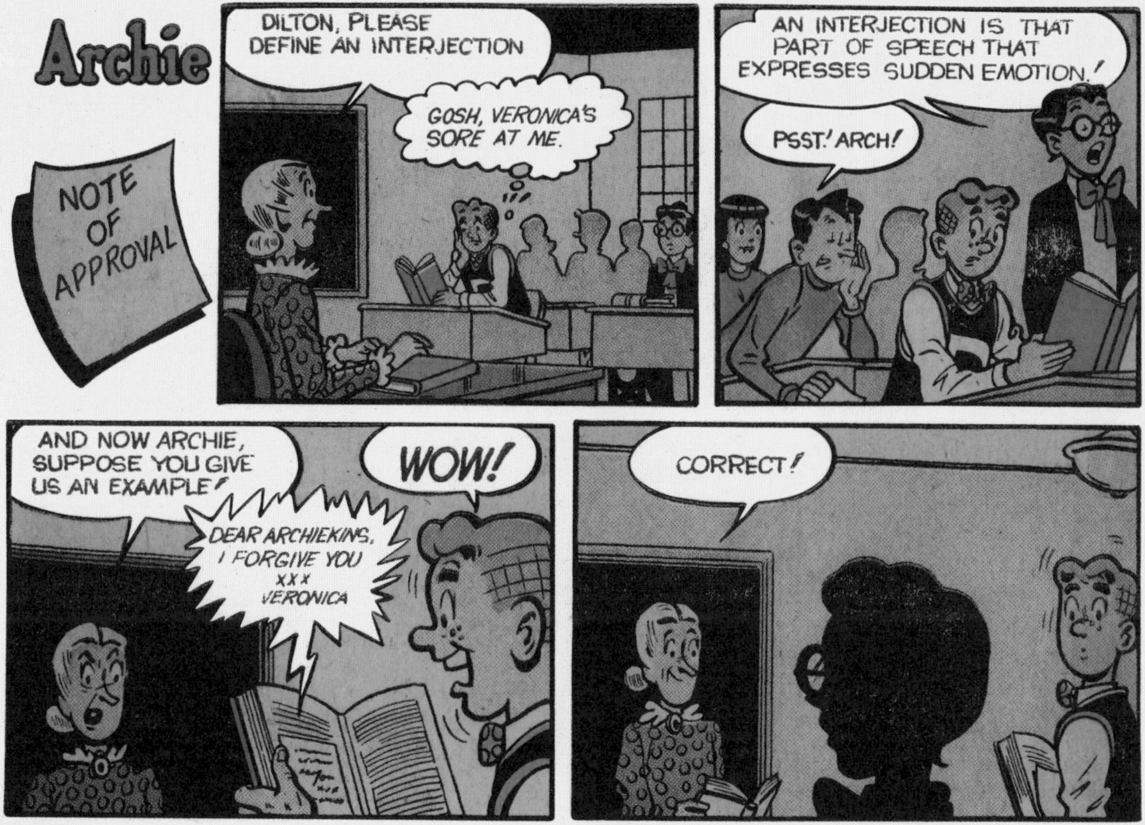
Archie
NOTE OF APPROVAL
DILTON, PLEASE DEFINE AN INTERJECTION
GOSH, VERONICA'S SORE AT ME.
AN INTERJECTION IS THAT PART OF SPEECH THAT EXPRESSES SUDDEN EMOTION!
PSST! ARCH!
AND NOW ARCHIE, SUPPOSE YOU GIVE US AN EXAMPLE!
WOW!
DEAR ARCHIEKINS, I FORGIVE YOU XXX VERONICA
CORRECT!

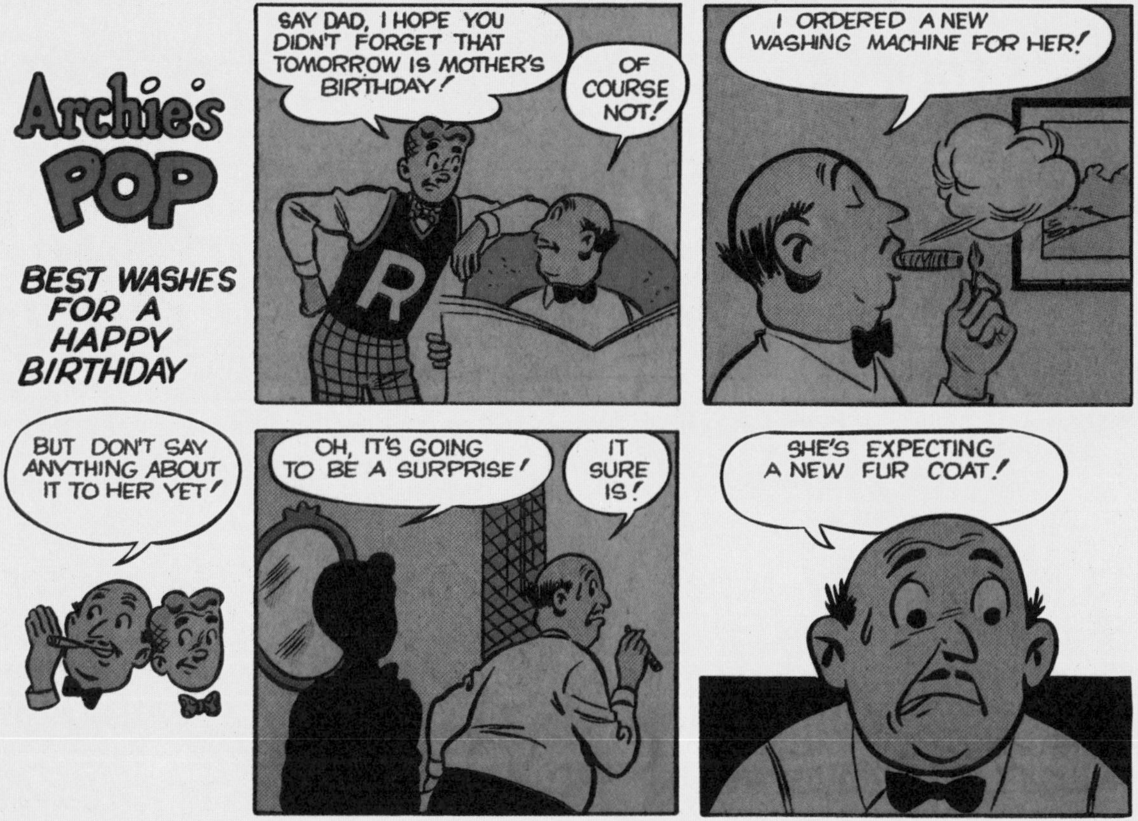
Archie's
POP
BEST WASHES FOR A HAPPY BIRTHDAY
SAY DAD, I HOPE YOU DIDN'T FORGET THAT TOMORROW IS MOTHER'S BIRTHDAY!
OF COURSE NOT!
I ORDERED A NEW WASHING MACHINE FOR HER!
BUT DON'T SAY ANYTHING ABOUT IT TO HER YET!
OH, IT'S GOING TO BE A SURPRISE!
IT SURE IS!
SHE'S EXPECTING A NEW FUR COAT!

Archie

From Dad To Worse

FRED, I WISH YOU'D HAVE A TALK WITH ARCHIE!
WHY? WHAT'D HE DO?
I HEARD HIM USING SOME RATHER STRONG LANGUAGE THIS AFTERNOON!
HE DID, EH!

WELL! I'LL TEACH HIM A THING OR TWO ABOUT USING THAT KIND OF TALK!
EEYOWWW!!
FRED! PLEASE! THAT'S ENOUGH FOR ONE LESSON!
OF ALL THE XX!! @☆ BLANKETY #!! BLANK ?!!@☆! ☆

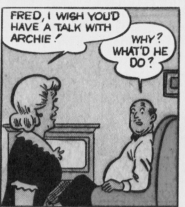

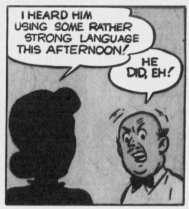

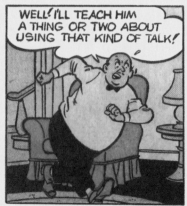

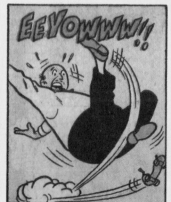

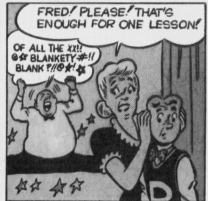

Archie's Pal

Jughead

MISSED-UNDERSTANDING

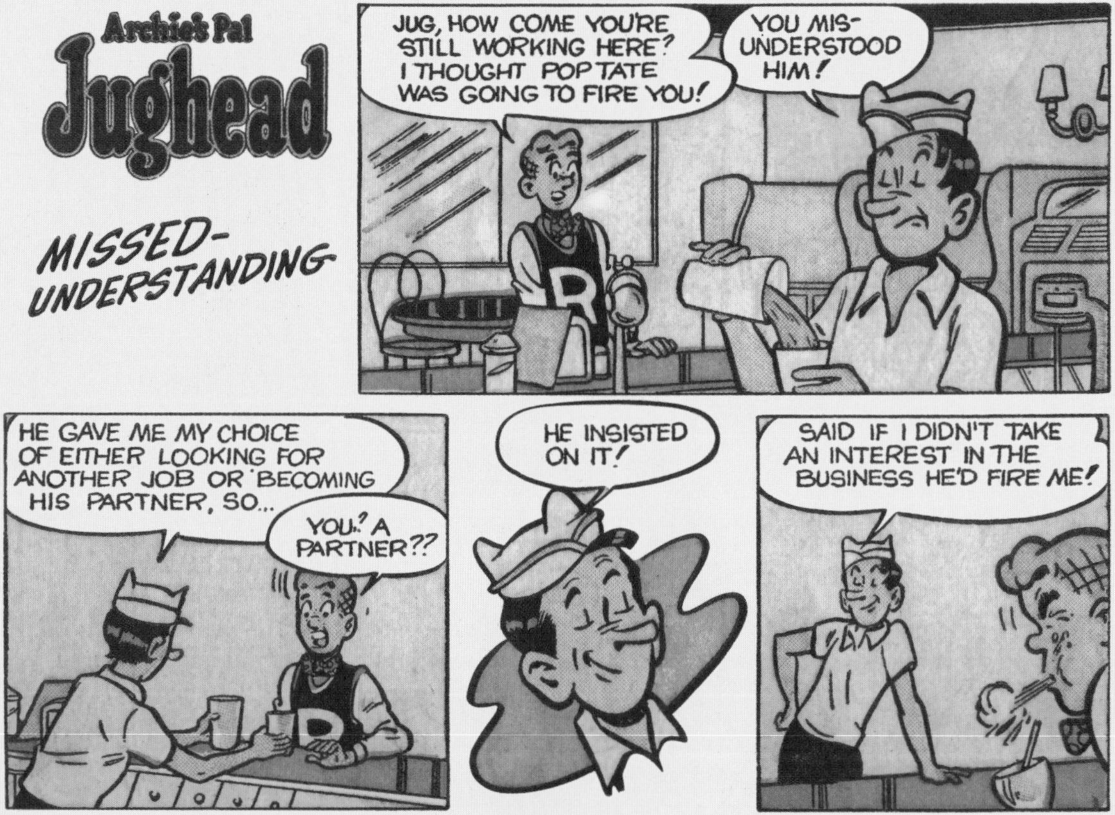

JUG, HOW COME YOU'RE STILL WORKING HERE? I THOUGHT POP TATE WAS GOING TO FIRE YOU!
YOU MIS-UNDERSTOOD HIM!
HE GAVE ME MY CHOICE OF EITHER LOOKING FOR ANOTHER JOB OR BECOMING HIS PARTNER, SO...
YOU..? A PARTNER??
HE INSISTED ON IT!
SAID IF I DIDN'T TAKE AN INTEREST IN THE BUSINESS HE'D FIRE ME!

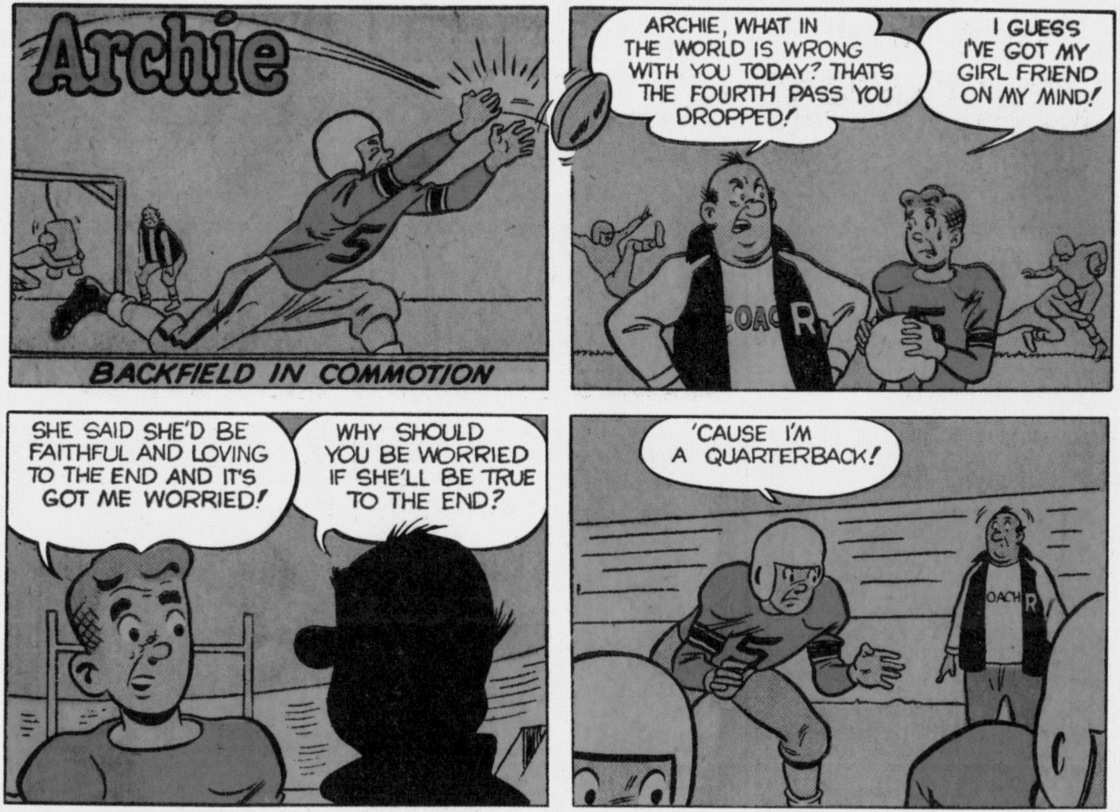
Archie
BACKFIELD IN COMMOTION
ARCHIE, WHAT IN THE WORLD IS WRONG WITH YOU TODAY? THAT'S THE FOURTH PASS YOU DROPPED!
I GUESS I'VE GOT MY GIRL FRIEND ON MY MIND!
COACH R
SHE SAID SHE'D BE FAITHFUL AND LOVING TO THE END AND IT'S GOT ME WORRIED!
WHY SHOULD YOU BE WORRIED IF SHE'LL BE TRUE TO THE END?
'CAUSE I'M A QUARTERBACK!
OACH R

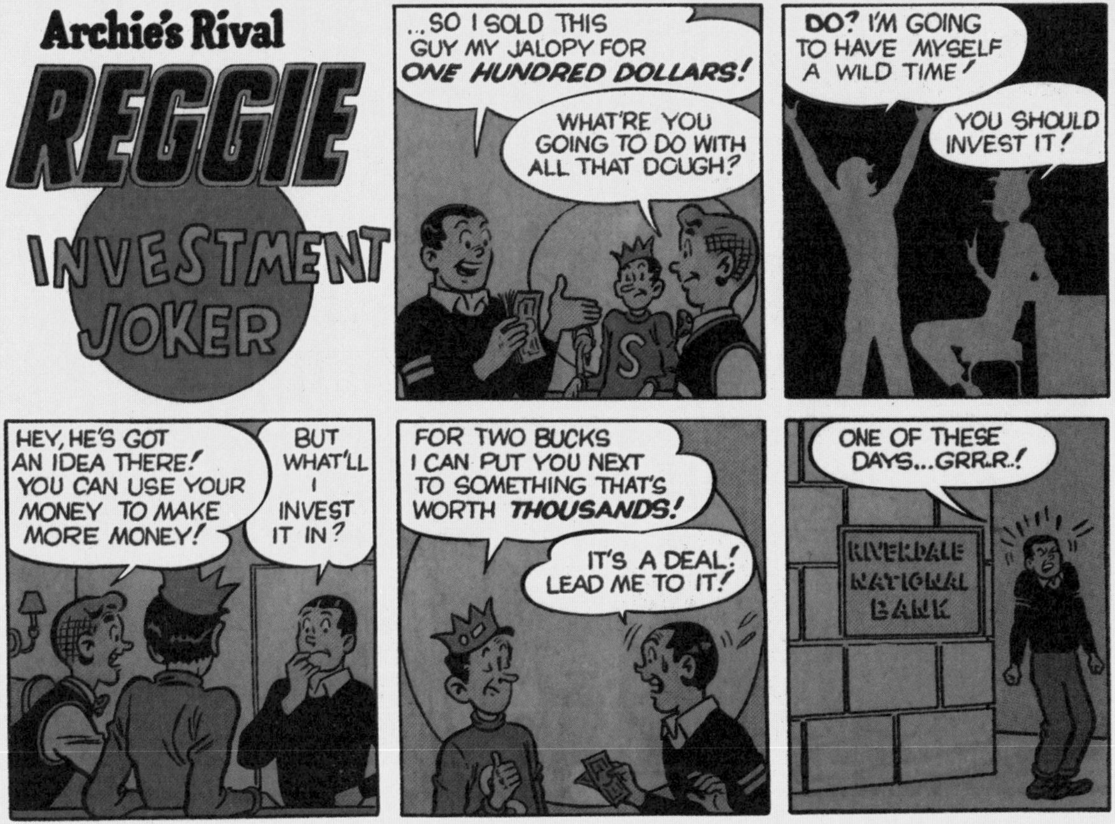

Archie's Rival
REGGIE
INVESTMENT JOKER
...SO I SOLD THIS GUY MY JALOPY FOR ONE HUNDRED DOLLARS!
WHAT'RE YOU GOING TO DO WITH ALL THAT DOUGH?
DO? I'M GOING TO HAVE MYSELF A WILD TIME!
YOU SHOULD INVEST IT!
HEY, HE'S GOT AN IDEA THERE! YOU CAN USE YOUR MONEY TO MAKE MORE MONEY!
BUT WHAT'LL I INVEST IT IN?
FOR TWO BUCKS I CAN PUT YOU NEXT TO SOMETHING THAT'S WORTH THOUSANDS!
IT'S A DEAL! LEAD ME TO IT!
RIVERDALE NATIONAL BANK
ONE OF THESE DAYS...GRR.R..!

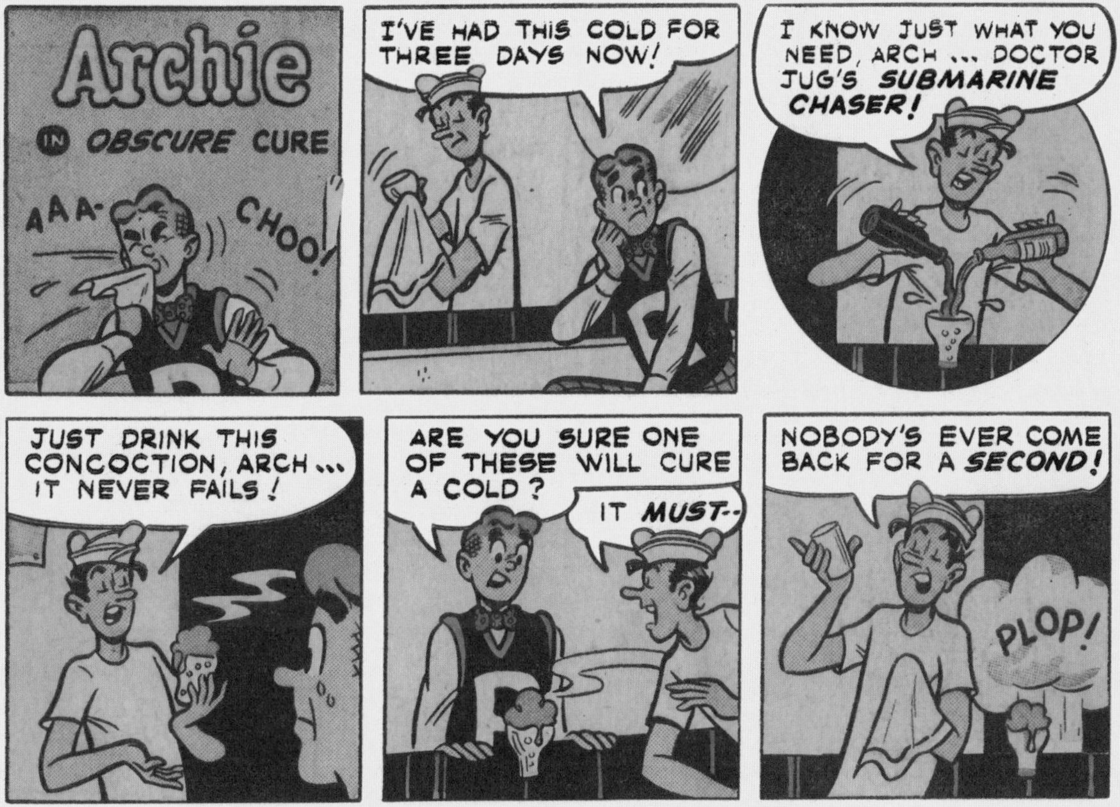
Archie
IN OBSCURE CURE
AAA-CHOO!
I'VE HAD THIS COLD FOR THREE DAYS NOW!
I KNOW JUST WHAT YOU NEED, ARCH ... DOCTOR JUG'S SUBMARINE CHASER!
JUST DRINK THIS CONCOCTION, ARCH ... IT NEVER FAILS!
ARE YOU SURE ONE OF THESE WILL CURE A COLD?
IT MUST--
NOBODY'S EVER COME BACK FOR A SECOND!
PLOP!

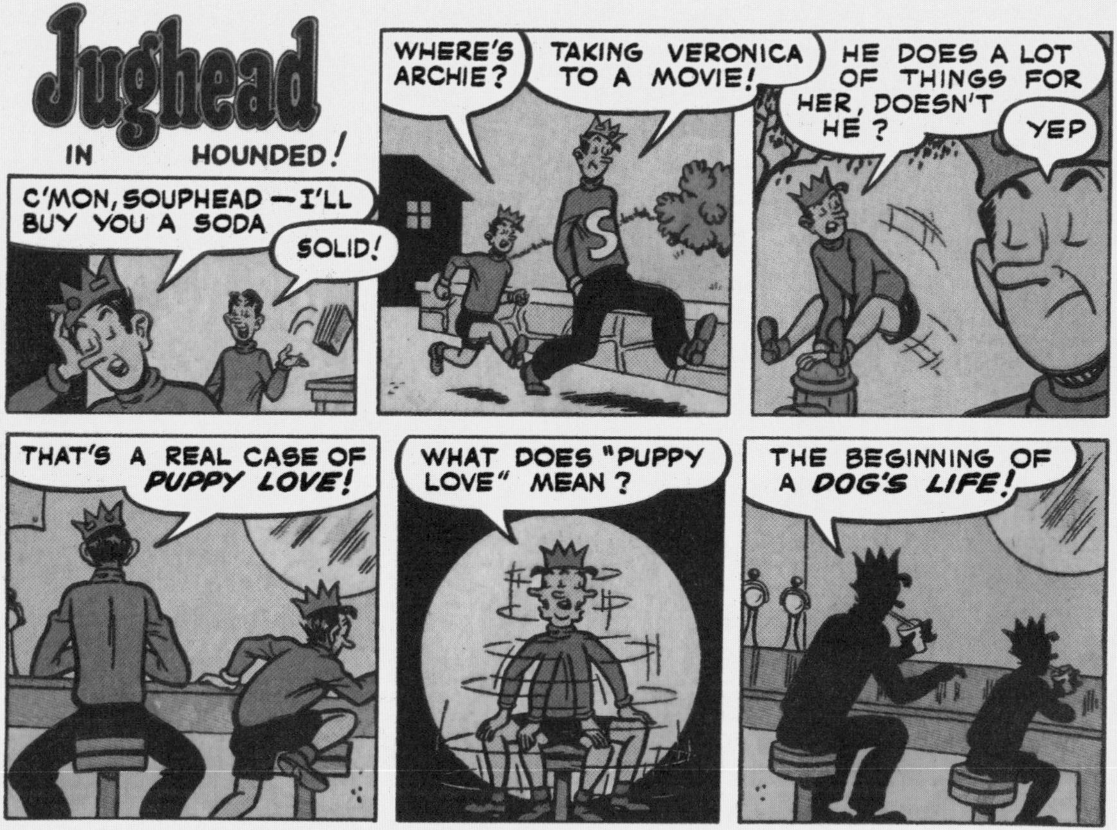

Jughead
IN HOUNDED!
C'MON, SOUPHEAD — I'LL BUY YOU A SODA
SOLID!
WHERE'S ARCHIE?
TAKING VERONICA TO A MOVIE!
HE DOES A LOT OF THINGS FOR HER, DOESN'T HE?
YEP
THAT'S A REAL CASE OF PUPPY LOVE!
WHAT DOES "PUPPY LOVE" MEAN?
THE BEGINNING OF A DOG'S LIFE!

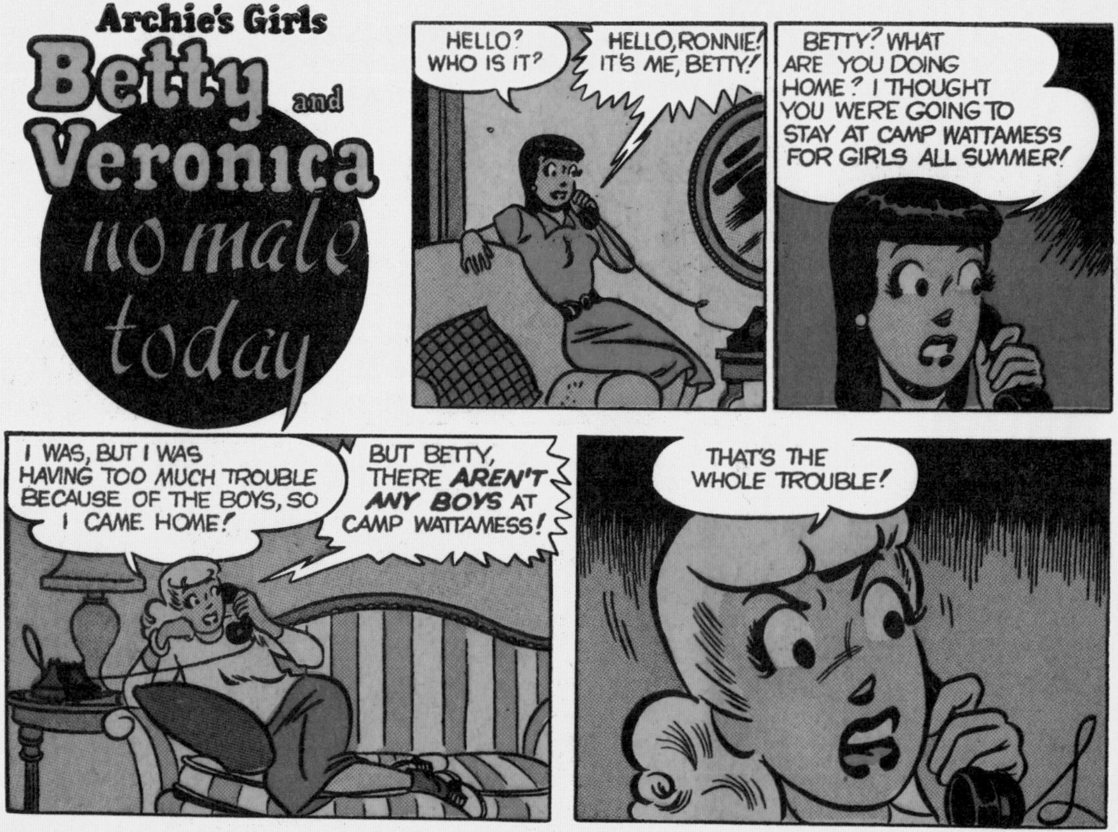
Archie's Girls
Betty and Veronica
no male today
HELLO? WHO IS IT?
HELLO, RONNIE! IT'S ME, BETTY!
BETTY? WHAT ARE YOU DOING HOME? I THOUGHT YOU WERE GOING TO STAY AT CAMP WATTAMESS FOR GIRLS ALL SUMMER!
I WAS, BUT I WAS HAVING TOO MUCH TROUBLE BECAUSE OF THE BOYS, SO I CAME HOME!
BUT BETTY, THERE AREN'T ANY BOYS AT CAMP WATTAMESS!
THAT'S THE WHOLE TROUBLE!

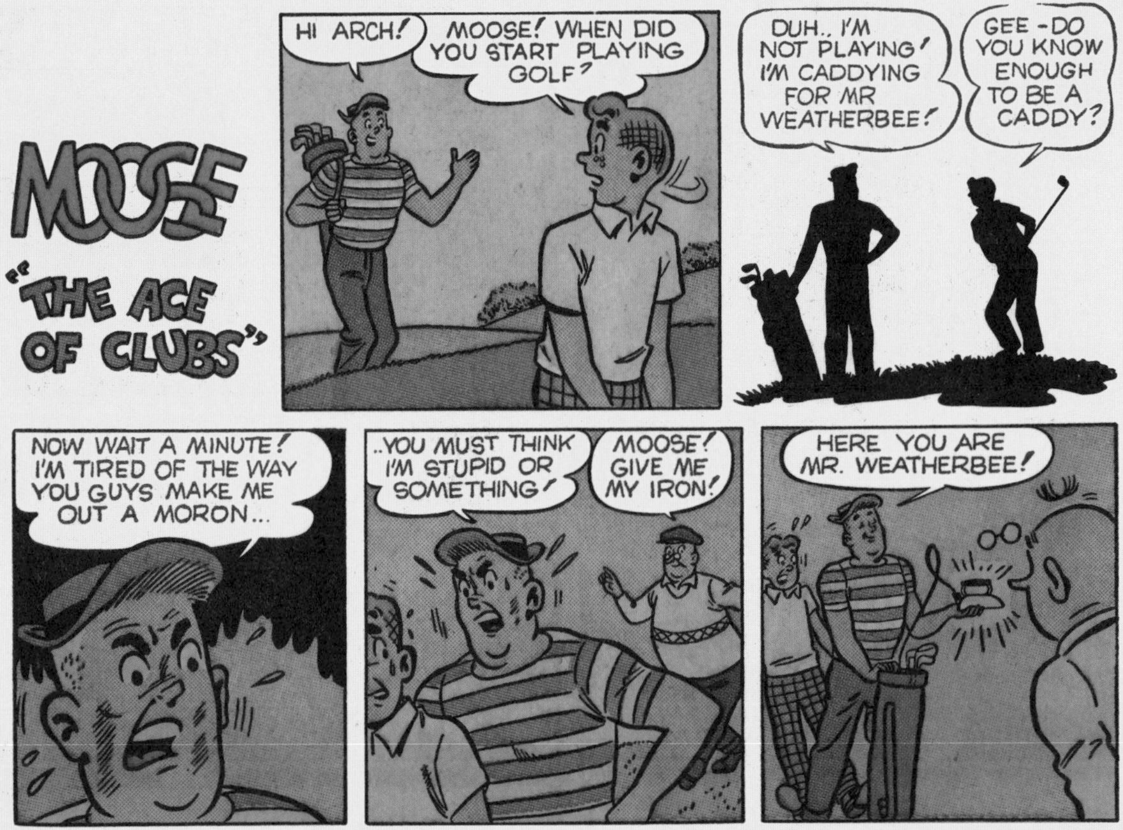
MOOSE
"THE ACE OF CLUBS"
HI ARCH!
MOOSE! WHEN DID YOU START PLAYING GOLF?
DUH.. I'M NOT PLAYING! I'M CADDYING FOR MR WEATHERBEE!
GEE -DO YOU KNOW ENOUGH TO BE A CADDY?
NOW WAIT A MINUTE! I'M TIRED OF THE WAY YOU GUYS MAKE ME OUT A MORON...
..YOU MUST THINK I'M STUPID OR SOMETHING!
MOOSE! GIVE ME MY IRON!
HERE YOU ARE MR. WEATHERBEE!

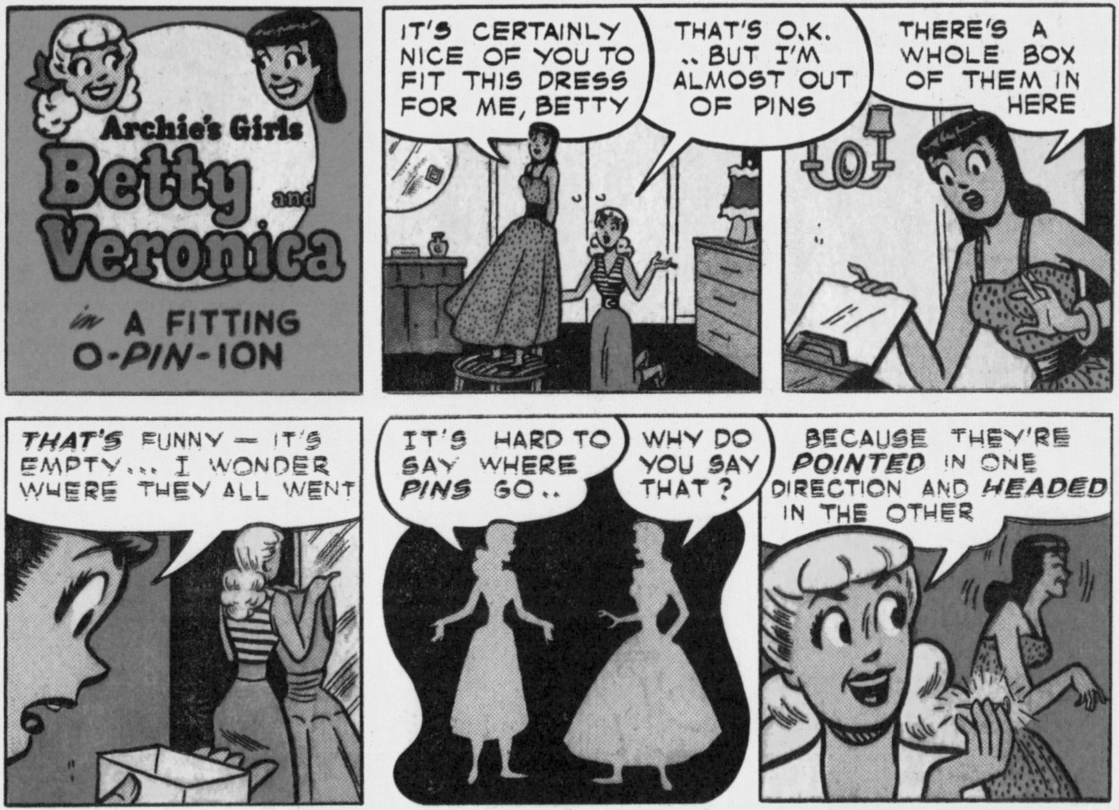
Archie's Girls
Betty and Veronica
in A FITTING O-PIN-ION
IT'S CERTAINLY NICE OF YOU TO FIT THIS DRESS FOR ME, BETTY
THAT'S O.K. .. BUT I'M ALMOST OUT OF PINS
THERE'S A WHOLE BOX OF THEM IN HERE
THAT'S FUNNY — IT'S EMPTY... I WONDER WHERE THEY ALL WENT
IT'S HARD TO SAY WHERE PINS GO..
WHY DO YOU SAY THAT?
BECAUSE THEY'RE POINTED IN ONE DIRECTION AND HEADED IN THE OTHER

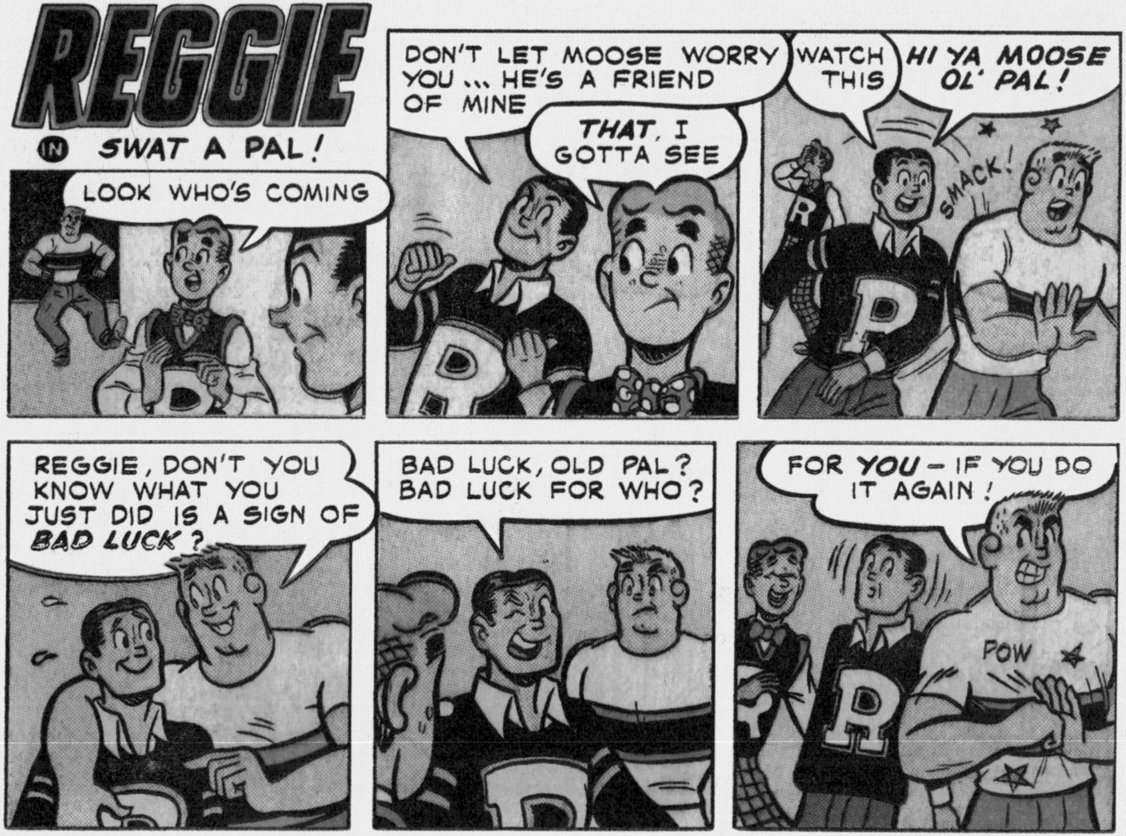
REGGIE
IN SWAT A PAL!
LOOK WHO'S COMING
DON'T LET MOOSE WORRY YOU ... HE'S A FRIEND OF MINE
THAT, I GOTTA SEE
WATCH THIS
HI YA MOOSE OL' PAL!
SMACK!
REGGIE, DON'T YOU KNOW WHAT YOU JUST DID IS A SIGN OF BAD LUCK?
BAD LUCK, OLD PAL? BAD LUCK FOR WHO?
FOR YOU - IF YOU DO IT AGAIN!
POW

ARCHIE'S
PICTURE DICTIONARY~
AVIATION SECTION

1... PROP WASH.
2... JET ACE.
3... CABIN MODEL.
4... TAXIING.
5... PLANE HANGER.

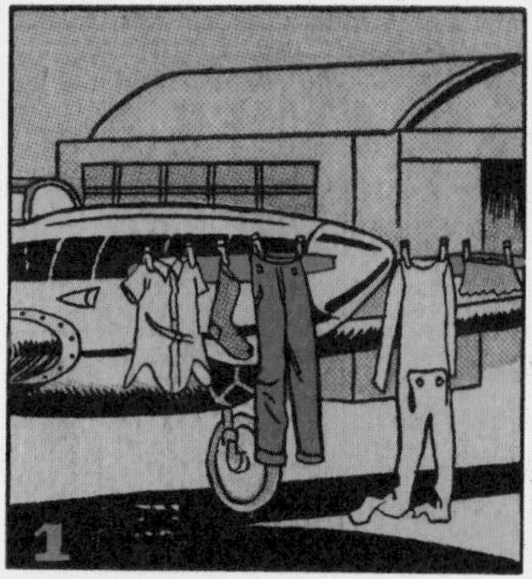
1

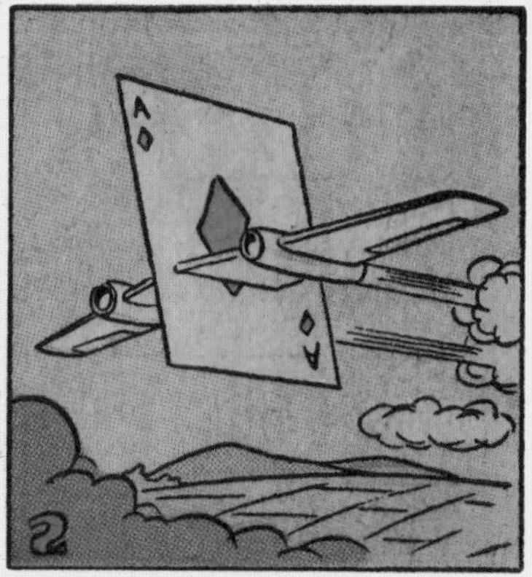
2

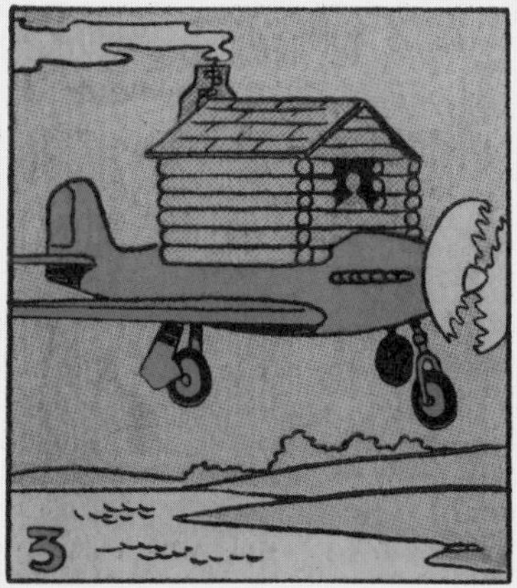
3

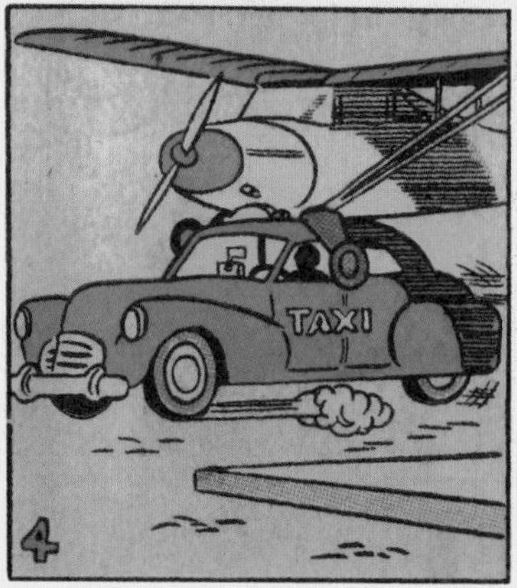
TAXI
4

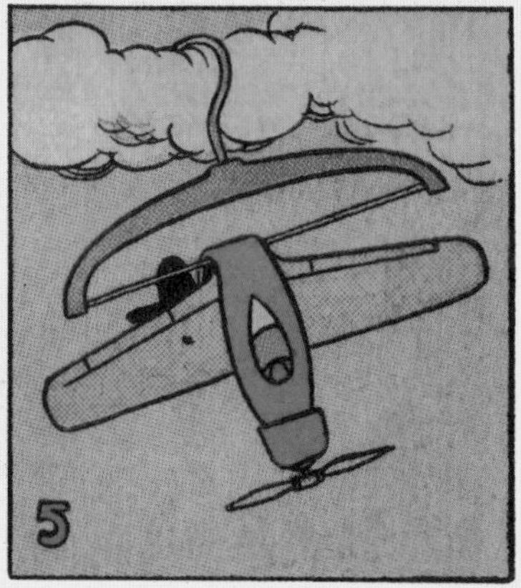
5

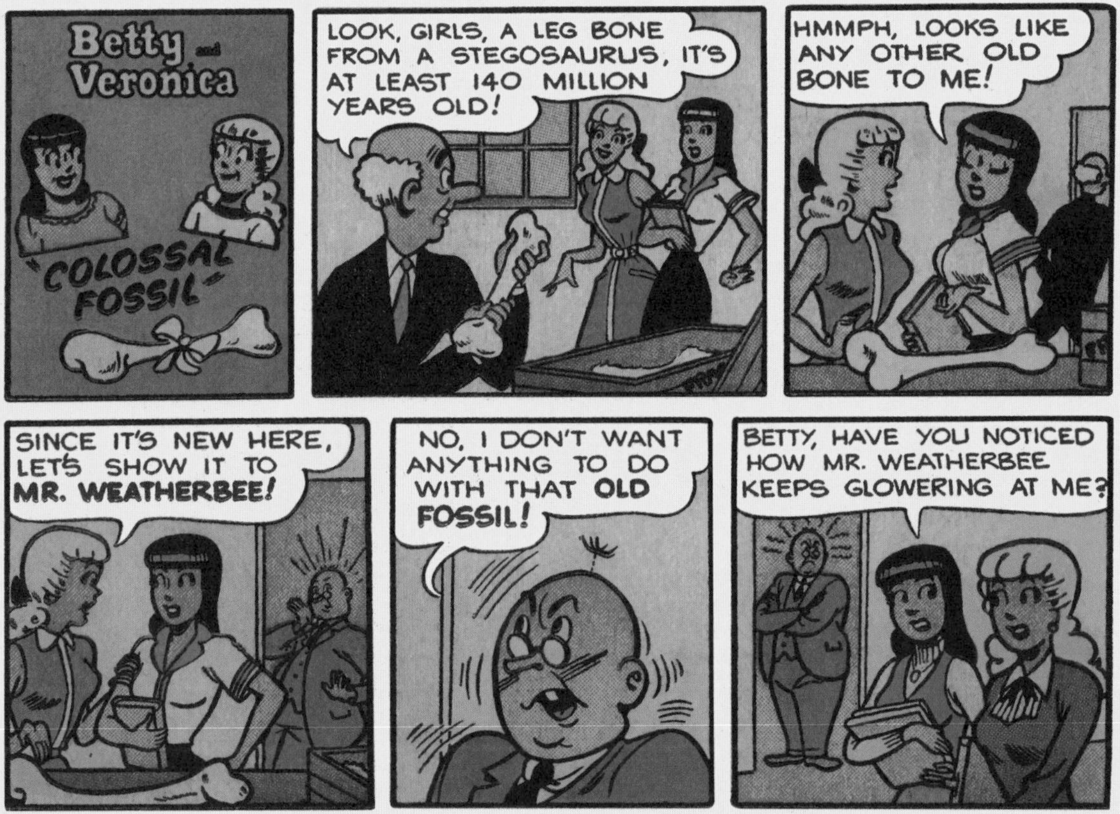
Betty and Veronica
"COLOSSAL FOSSIL"
LOOK, GIRLS, A LEG BONE FROM A STEGOSAURUS, IT'S AT LEAST 140 MILLION YEARS OLD!
HMMPH, LOOKS LIKE ANY OTHER OLD BONE TO ME!
SINCE IT'S NEW HERE, LET'S SHOW IT TO MR. WEATHERBEE!
NO, I DON'T WANT ANYTHING TO DO WITH THAT OLD FOSSIL!
BETTY, HAVE YOU NOTICED HOW MR. WEATHERBEE KEEPS GLOWERING AT ME?

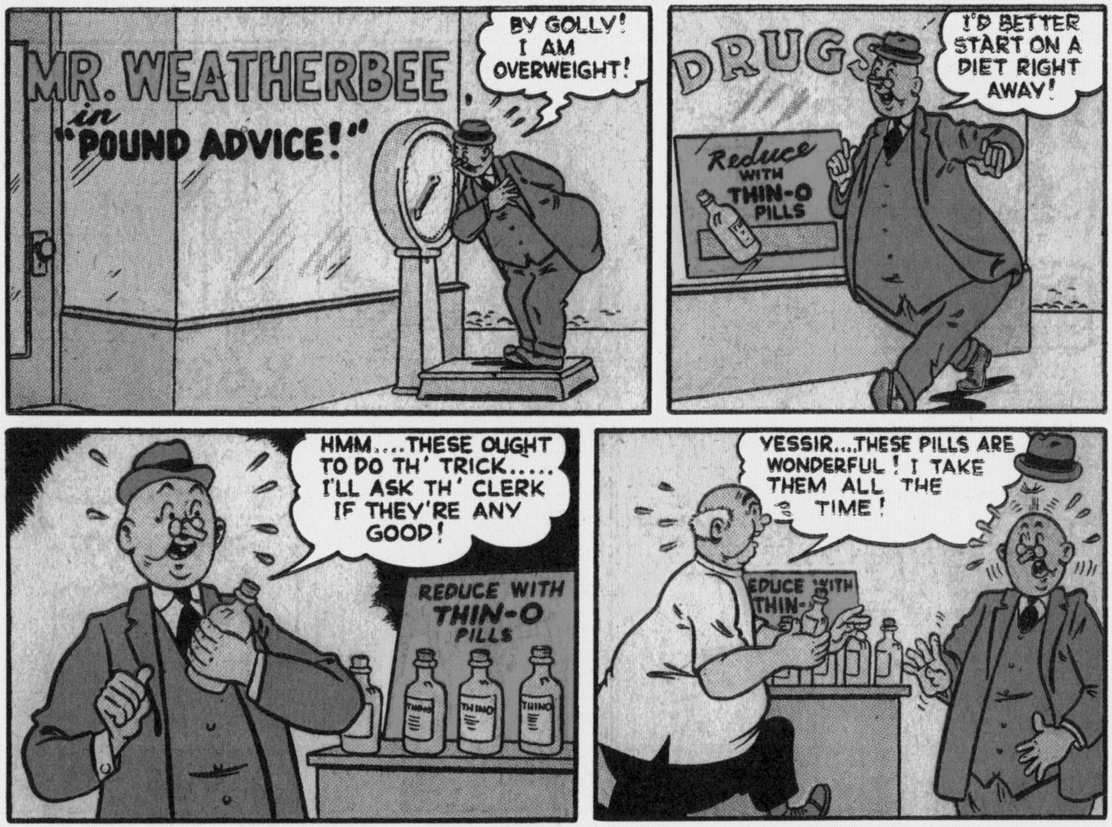
MR. WEATHERBEE
in
"POUND ADVICE!"
BY GOLLY! I AM OVERWEIGHT!
DRUGS
Reduce WITH THIN-O PILLS
I'D BETTER START ON A DIET RIGHT AWAY!
HMM....THESE OUGHT TO DO TH' TRICK..... I'LL ASK TH' CLERK IF THEY'RE ANY GOOD!
REDUCE WITH THIN-O PILLS
YESSIR....THESE PILLS ARE WONDERFUL! I TAKE THEM ALL THE TIME!

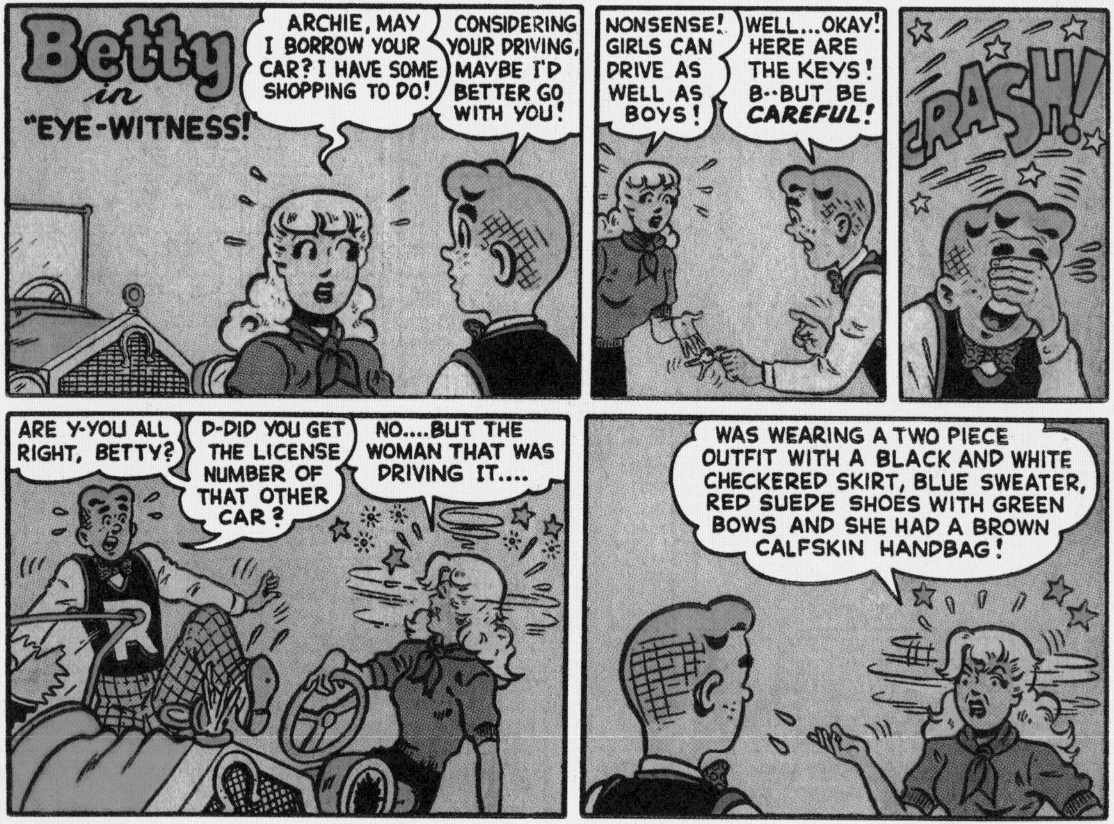
Betty in "EYE-WITNESS!
ARCHIE, MAY I BORROW YOUR CAR? I HAVE SOME SHOPPING TO DO!
CONSIDERING YOUR DRIVING, MAYBE I'D BETTER GO WITH YOU!
NONSENSE! GIRLS CAN DRIVE AS WELL AS BOYS!
WELL...OKAY! HERE ARE THE KEYS! B--BUT BE CAREFUL!
CRASH!
ARE Y-YOU ALL RIGHT, BETTY?
D-DID YOU GET THE LICENSE NUMBER OF THAT OTHER CAR?
NO....BUT THE WOMAN THAT WAS DRIVING IT....
WAS WEARING A TWO PIECE OUTFIT WITH A BLACK AND WHITE CHECKERED SKIRT, BLUE SWEATER, RED SUEDE SHOES WITH GREEN BOWS AND SHE HAD A BROWN CALFSKIN HANDBAG!

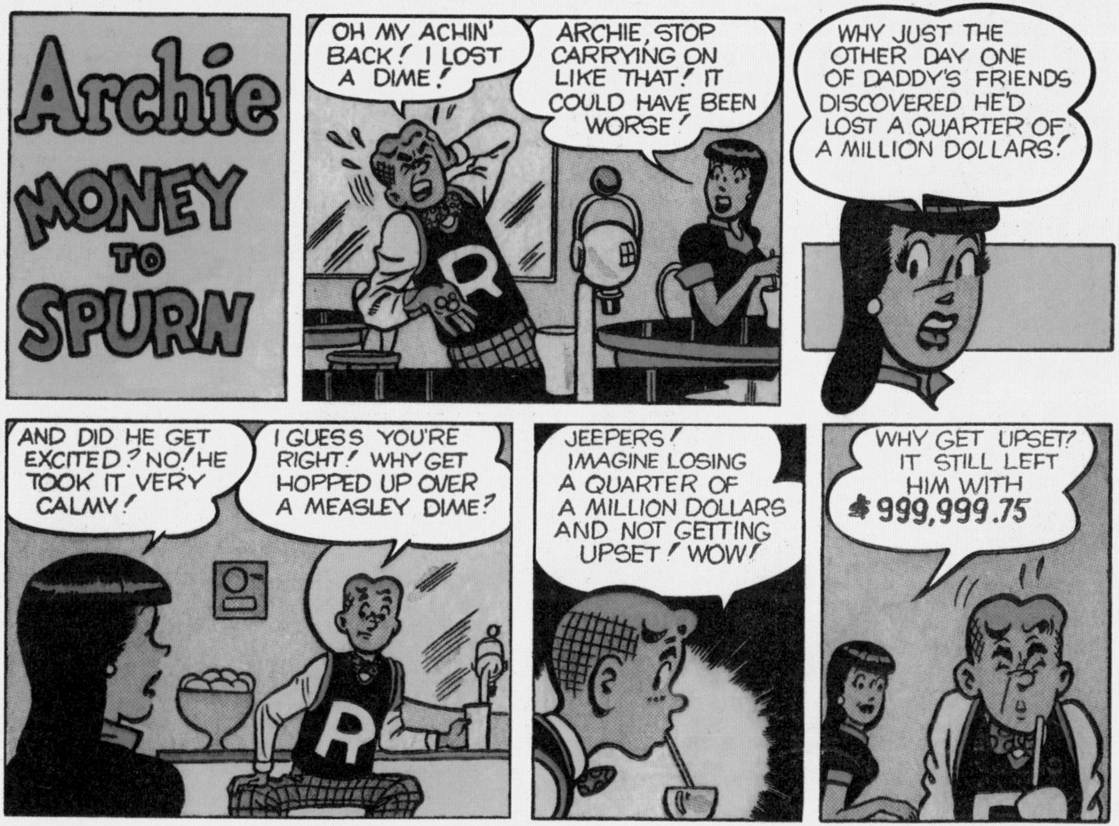
Archie
MONEY TO SPURN
OH MY ACHIN' BACK! I LOST A DIME!
ARCHIE, STOP CARRYING ON LIKE THAT! IT COULD HAVE BEEN WORSE!
WHY JUST THE OTHER DAY ONE OF DADDY'S FRIENDS DISCOVERED HE'D LOST A QUARTER OF A MILLION DOLLARS!
AND DID HE GET EXCITED? NO! HE TOOK IT VERY CALMY!
I GUESS YOU'RE RIGHT! WHY GET HOPPED UP OVER A MEASLEY DIME?
JEEPERS! IMAGINE LOSING A QUARTER OF A MILLION DOLLARS AND NOT GETTING UPSET! WOW!
WHY GET UPSET? IT STILL LEFT HIM WITH $999,999.75

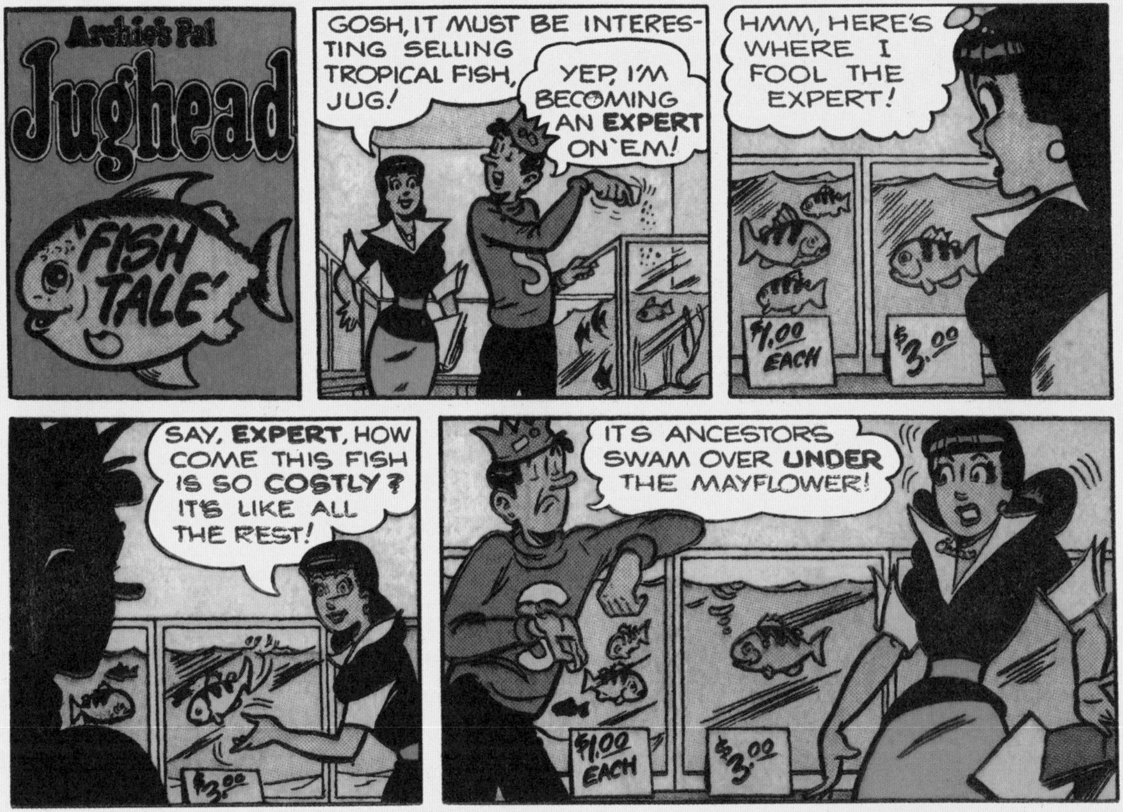
Archie's Pal
Jughead
"FISH TALE"
GOSH, IT MUST BE INTERESTING SELLING TROPICAL FISH, JUG!
YEP, I'M BECOMING AN **EXPERT** ON 'EM!
HMM, HERE'S WHERE I FOOL THE EXPERT!
$1.00 EACH
$3.00
SAY, **EXPERT**, HOW COME THIS FISH IS SO **COSTLY**? IT'S LIKE ALL THE REST!
$3.00
ITS ANCESTORS SWAM OVER **UNDER** THE MAYFLOWER!
$1.00 EACH
$3.00

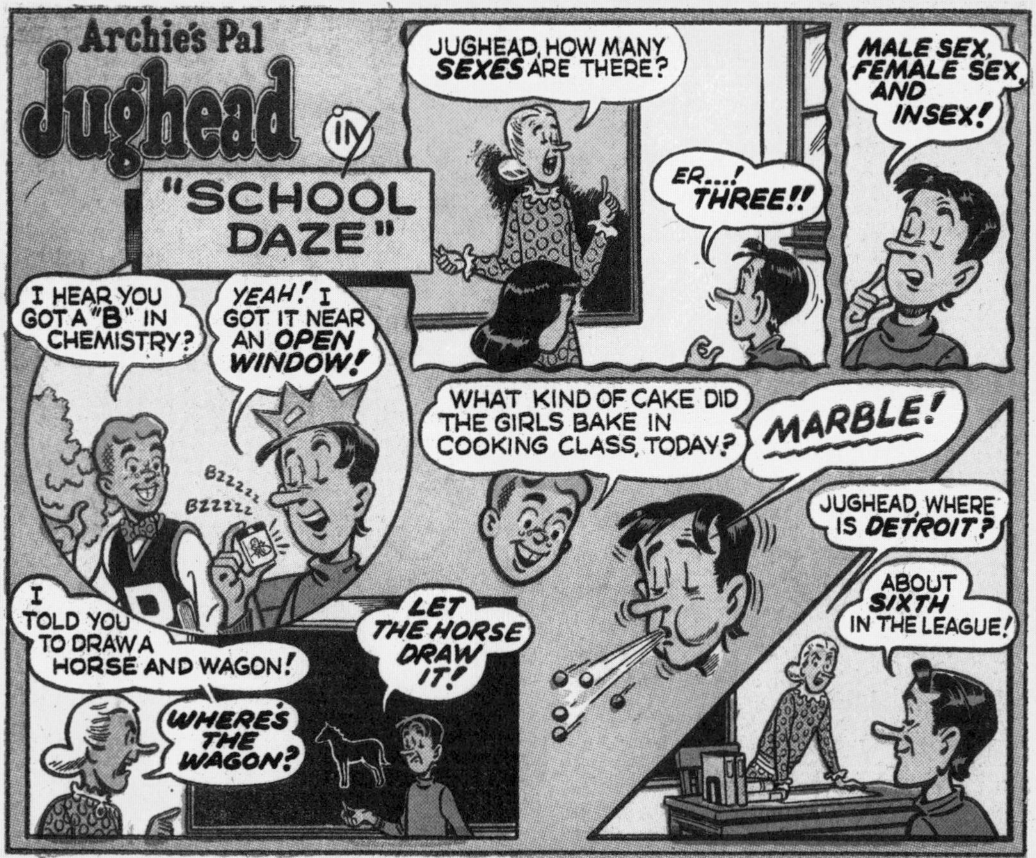
Archie's Pal
Jughead
IN
"SCHOOL DAZE"
JUGHEAD, HOW MANY SEXES ARE THERE?
ER....! THREE!!
MALE SEX, FEMALE SEX, AND INSEX!
I HEAR YOU GOT A "B" IN CHEMISTRY?
YEAH! I GOT IT NEAR AN OPEN WINDOW!
BZZZZZ
BZZZZZ
WHAT KIND OF CAKE DID THE GIRLS BAKE IN COOKING CLASS, TODAY?
MARBLE!
JUGHEAD, WHERE IS DETROIT?
ABOUT SIXTH IN THE LEAGUE!
I TOLD YOU TO DRAW A HORSE AND WAGON!
LET THE HORSE DRAW IT!
WHERE'S THE WAGON?

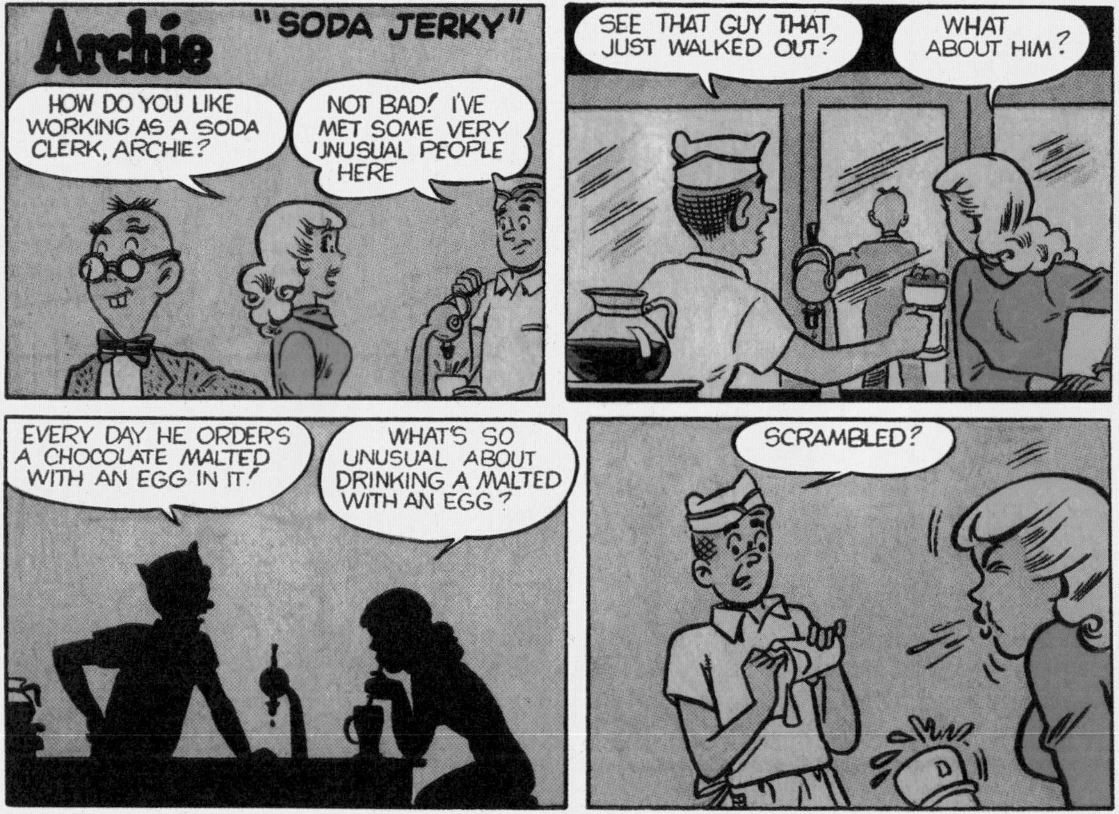
Archie
"SODA JERKY"
HOW DO YOU LIKE WORKING AS A SODA CLERK, ARCHIE?
NOT BAD! I'VE MET SOME VERY UNUSUAL PEOPLE HERE
SEE THAT GUY THAT JUST WALKED OUT?
WHAT ABOUT HIM?
EVERY DAY HE ORDERS A CHOCOLATE MALTED WITH AN EGG IN IT!
WHAT'S SO UNUSUAL ABOUT DRINKING A MALTED WITH AN EGG?
SCRAMBLED?

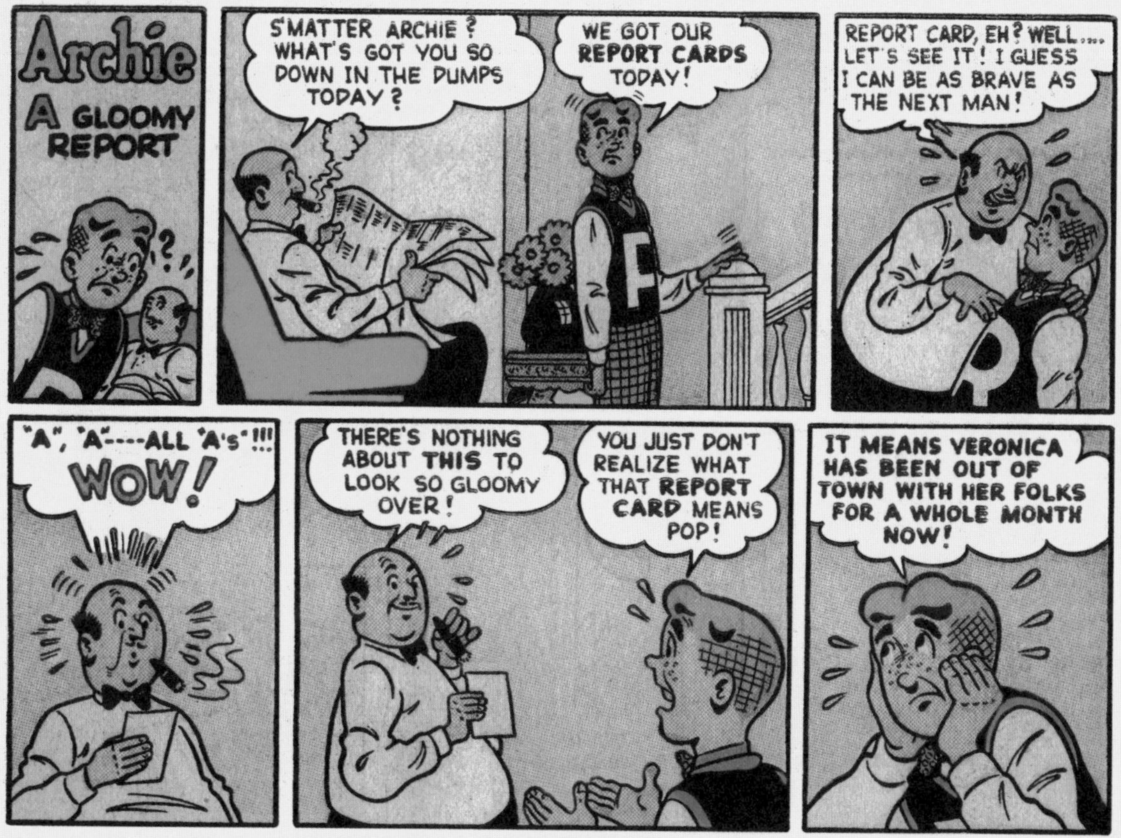
Archie
A GLOOMY REPORT
S'MATTER ARCHIE ? WHAT'S GOT YOU SO DOWN IN THE DUMPS TODAY ?
WE GOT OUR REPORT CARDS TODAY!
REPORT CARD, EH? WELL.... LET'S SEE IT! I GUESS I CAN BE AS BRAVE AS THE NEXT MAN!
"A", "A"----ALL "A's"!!! WOW!
THERE'S NOTHING ABOUT THIS TO LOOK SO GLOOMY OVER!
YOU JUST DON'T REALIZE WHAT THAT REPORT CARD MEANS POP!
IT MEANS VERONICA HAS BEEN OUT OF TOWN WITH HER FOLKS FOR A WHOLE MONTH NOW!

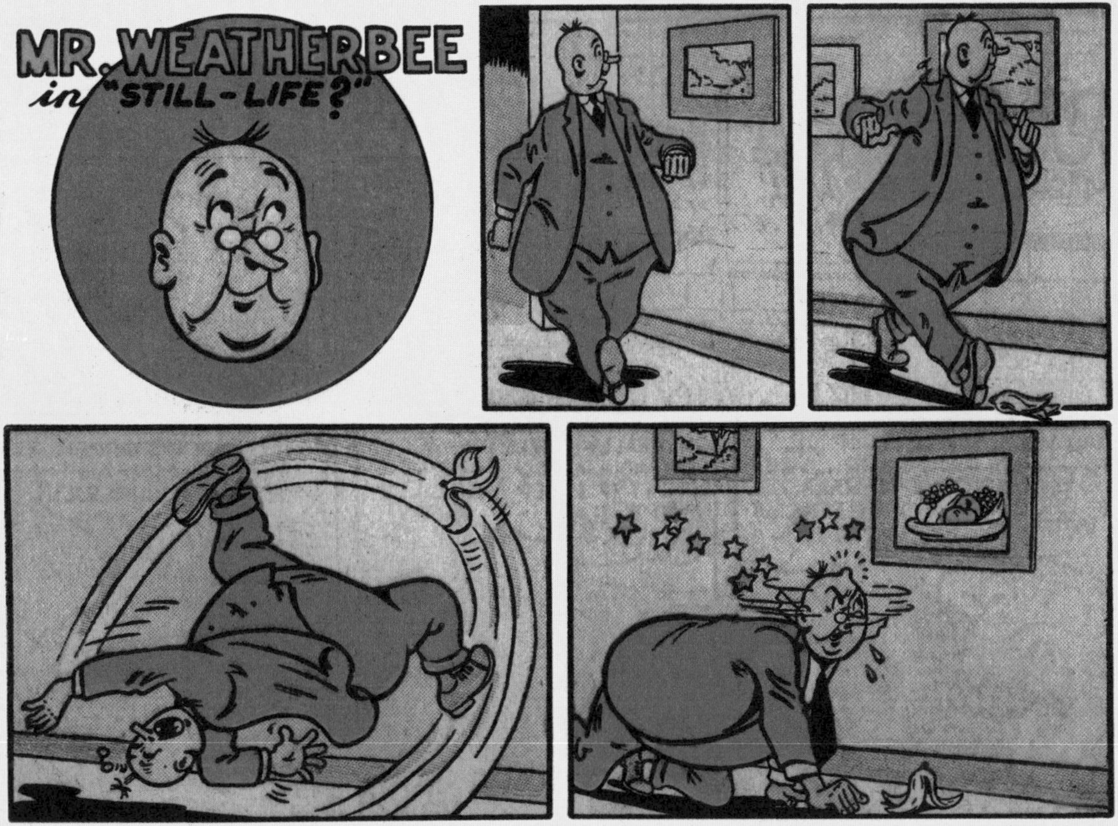
MR. WEATHERBEE
in "STILL-LIFE?"

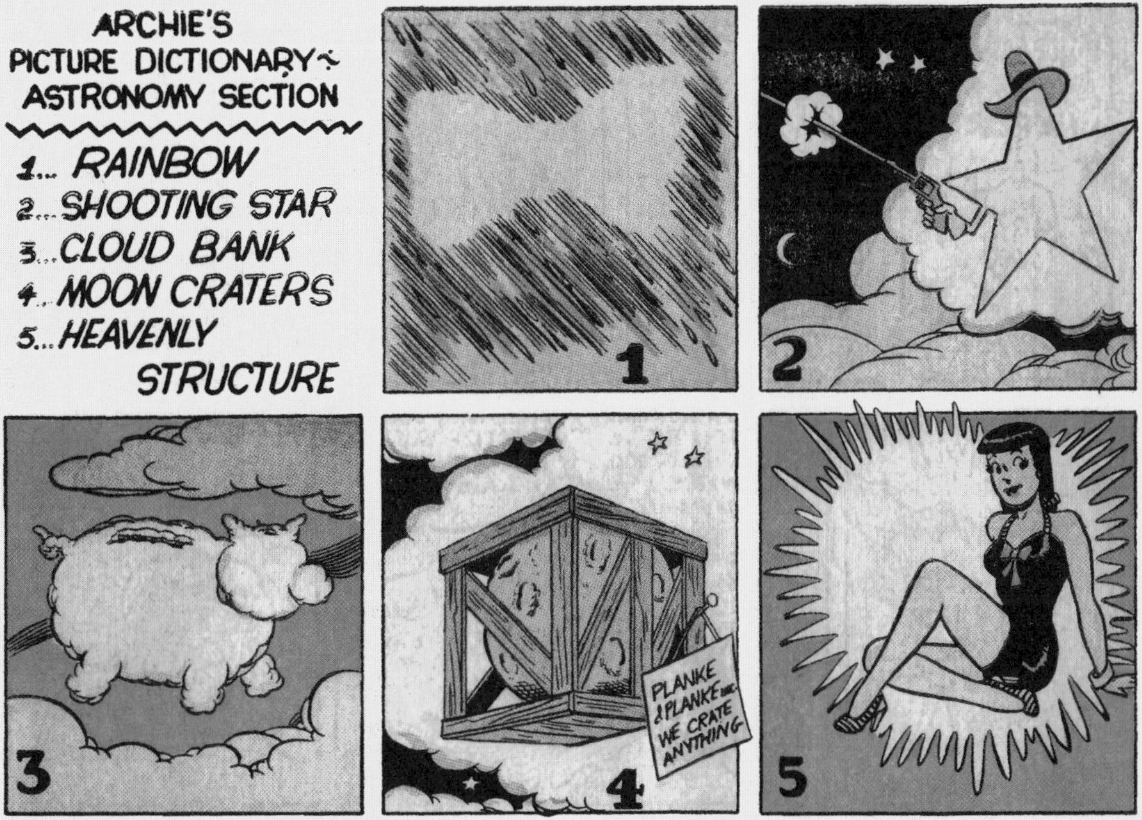
ARCHIE'S
PICTURE DICTIONARY~
ASTRONOMY SECTION
1... RAINBOW
2... SHOOTING STAR
3... CLOUD BANK
4... MOON CRATERS
5... HEAVENLY STRUCTURE
1
2
3
PLANKE & PLANKE INC. WE CRATE ANYTHING
4
5

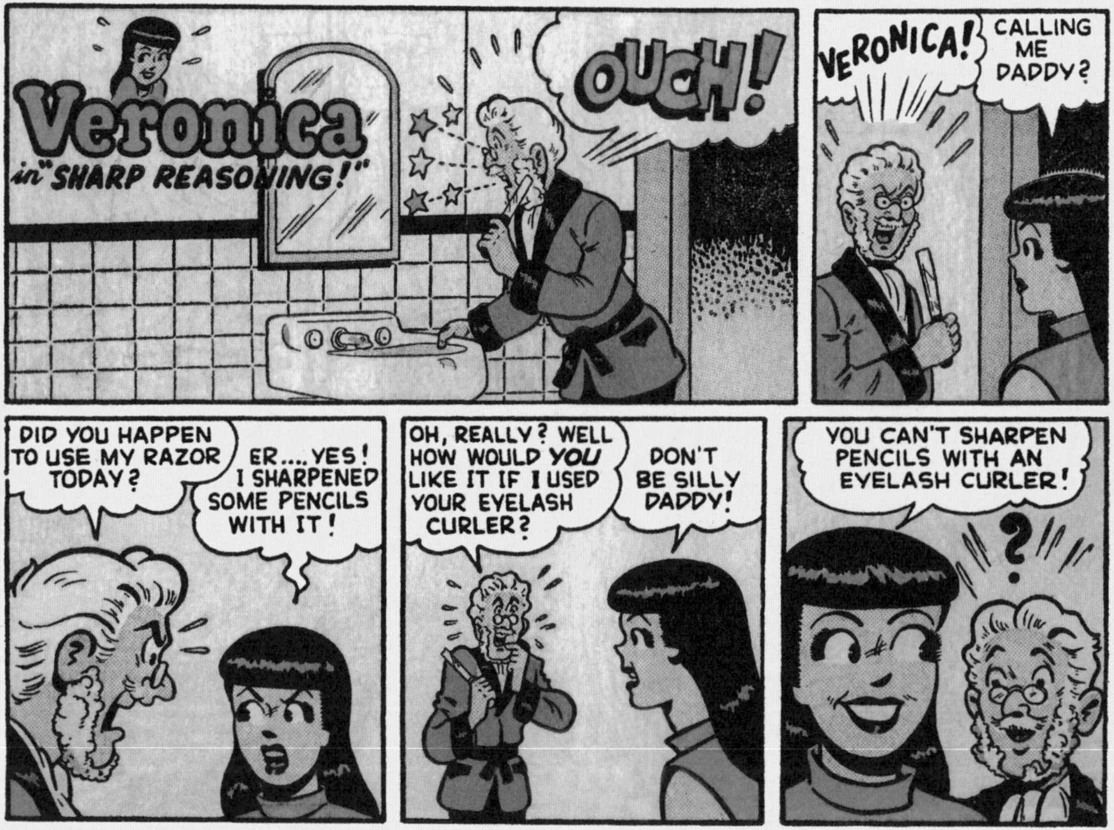

Veronica
in "SHARP REASONING!"
OUCH!
VERONICA!
CALLING ME DADDY?
DID YOU HAPPEN TO USE MY RAZOR TODAY?
ER.... YES! I SHARPENED SOME PENCILS WITH IT!
OH, REALLY? WELL HOW WOULD *YOU* LIKE IT IF I USED YOUR EYELASH CURLER?
DON'T BE SILLY DADDY!
YOU CAN'T SHARPEN PENCILS WITH AN EYELASH CURLER!
?

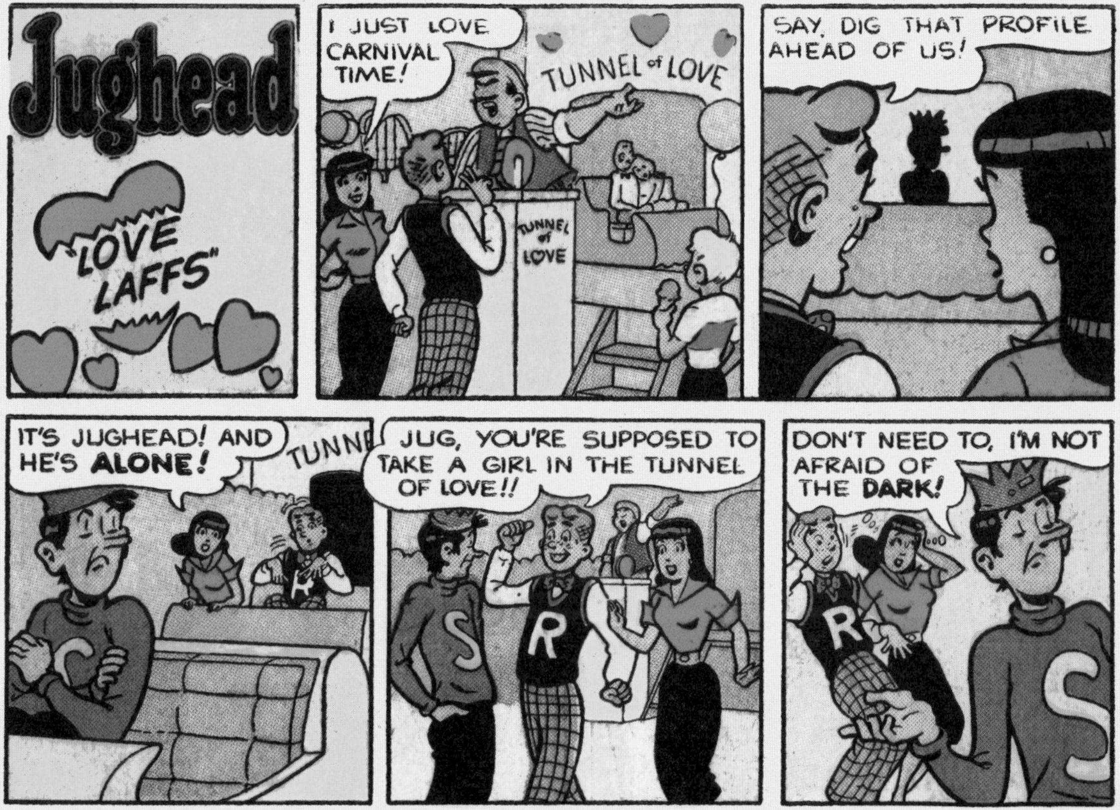
Jughead
"LOVE LAFFS"
I JUST LOVE CARNIVAL TIME!
TUNNEL of LOVE
TUNNEL of LOVE
SAY, DIG THAT PROFILE AHEAD OF US!
IT'S JUGHEAD! AND HE'S ALONE!
TUNN
JUG, YOU'RE SUPPOSED TO TAKE A GIRL IN THE TUNNEL OF LOVE!!
DON'T NEED TO, I'M NOT AFRAID OF THE DARK!

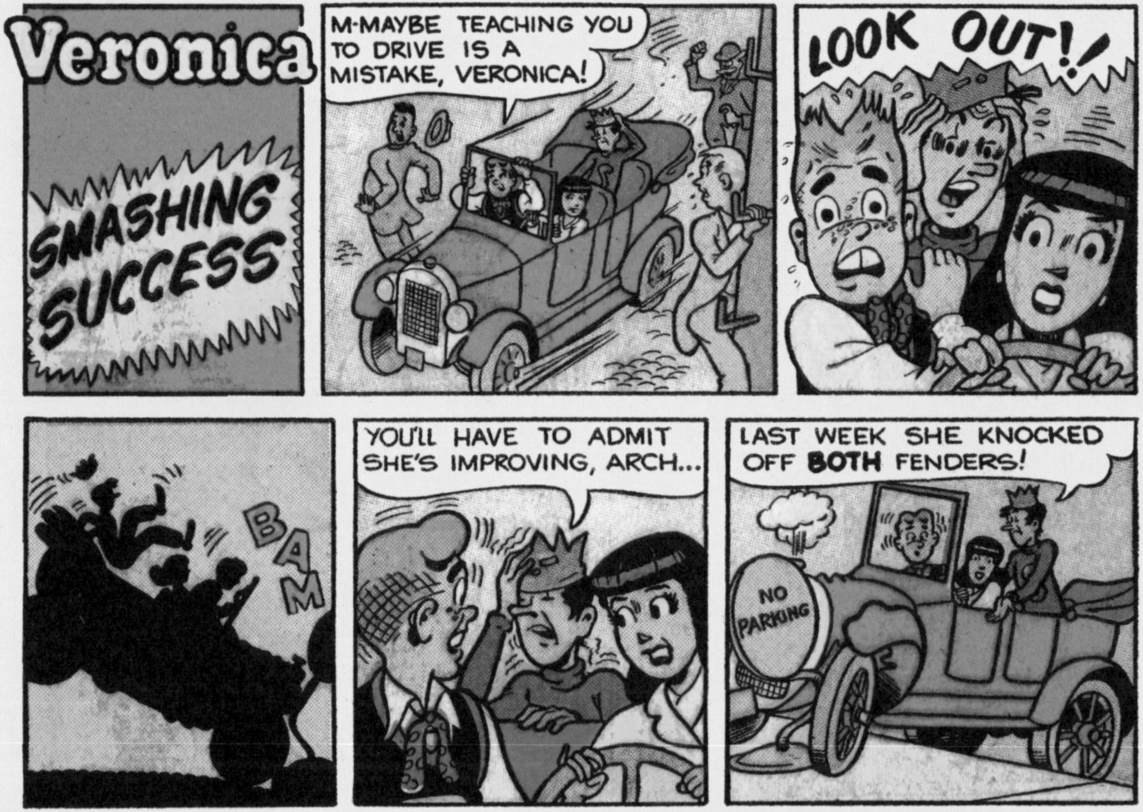
Veronica
SMASHING SUCCESS
M-MAYBE TEACHING YOU TO DRIVE IS A MISTAKE, VERONICA!
LOOK OUT!!
BAM
YOU'LL HAVE TO ADMIT SHE'S IMPROVING, ARCH...
LAST WEEK SHE KNOCKED OFF BOTH FENDERS!
NO PARKING

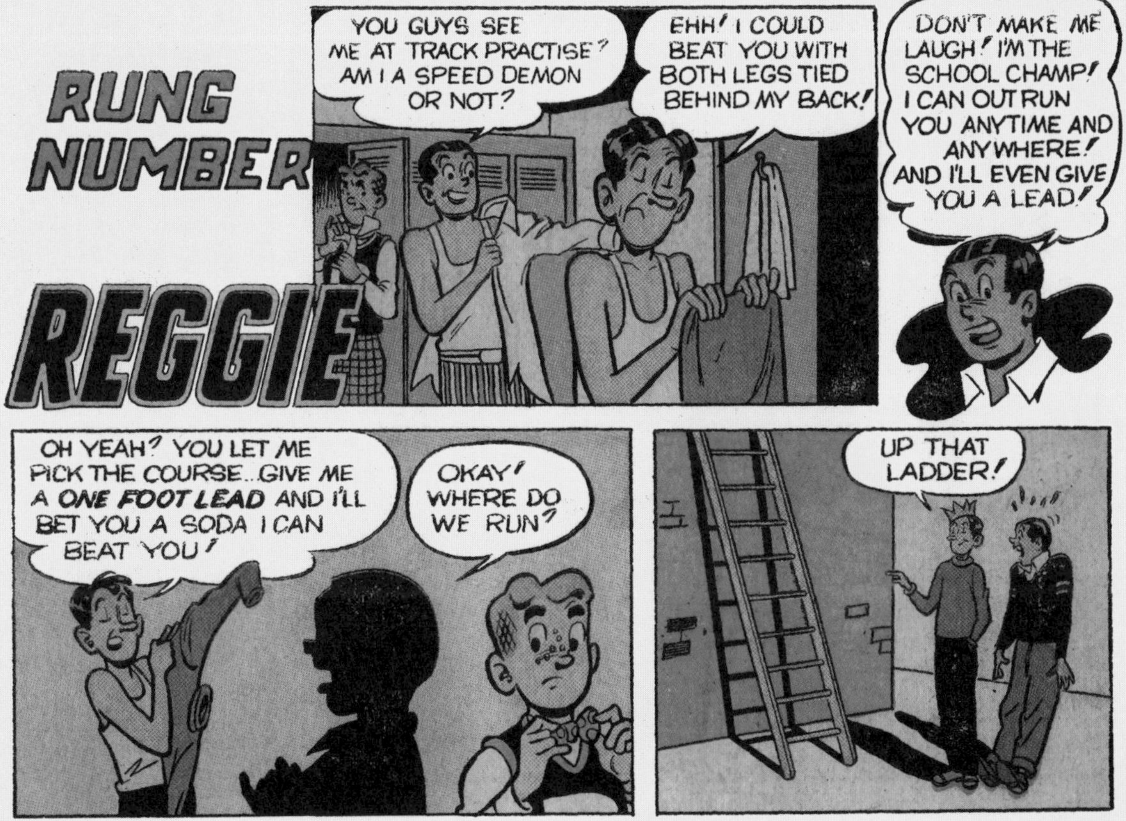
RUNG NUMBER
REGGIE
YOU GUYS SEE ME AT TRACK PRACTISE? AM I A SPEED DEMON OR NOT?
EHH! I COULD BEAT YOU WITH BOTH LEGS TIED BEHIND MY BACK!
DON'T MAKE ME LAUGH! I'M THE SCHOOL CHAMP! I CAN OUT RUN YOU ANYTIME AND ANYWHERE! AND I'LL EVEN GIVE YOU A LEAD!
OH YEAH? YOU LET ME PICK THE COURSE...GIVE ME A ONE FOOT LEAD AND I'LL BET YOU A SODA I CAN BEAT YOU!
OKAY! WHERE DO WE RUN?
UP THAT LADDER!

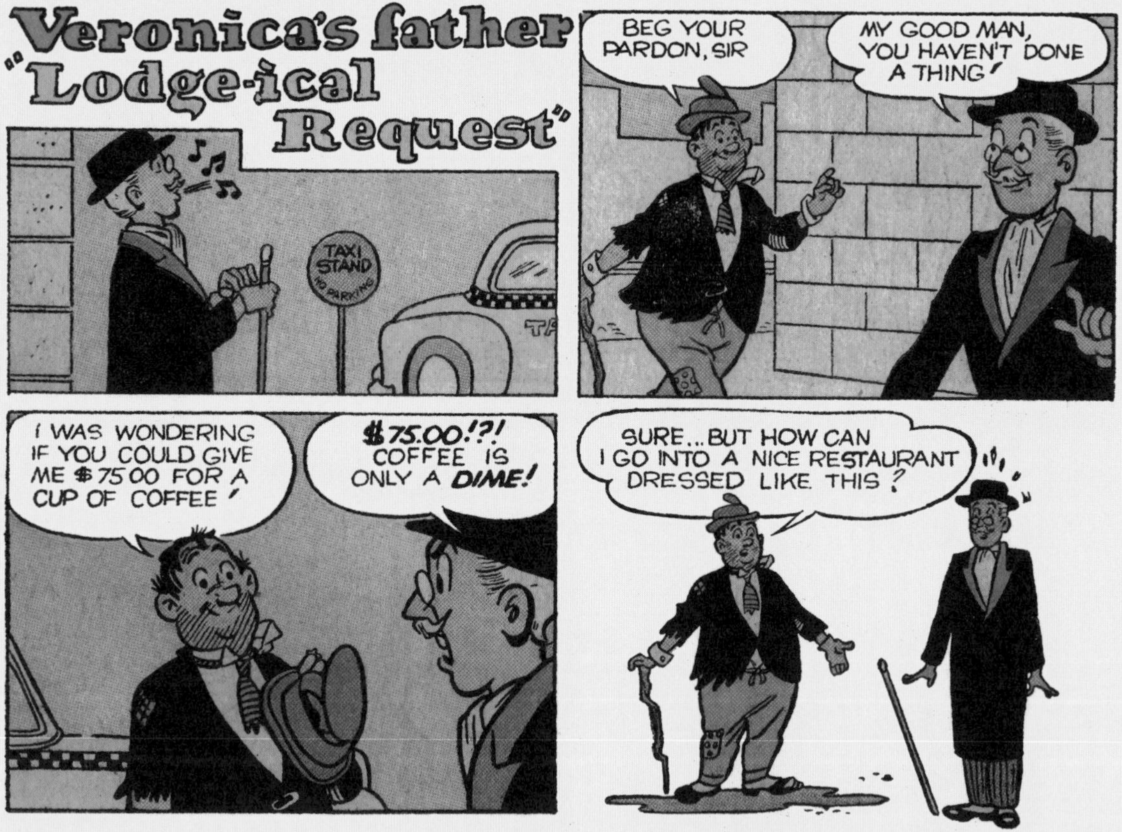
Veronica's father
"Lodge-ical Request"
TAXI STAND
NO PARKING
BEG YOUR PARDON, SIR
MY GOOD MAN, YOU HAVEN'T DONE A THING!
I WAS WONDERING IF YOU COULD GIVE ME $75.00 FOR A CUP OF COFFEE!
$75.00!?! COFFEE IS ONLY A DIME!
SURE... BUT HOW CAN I GO INTO A NICE RESTAURANT DRESSED LIKE THIS?

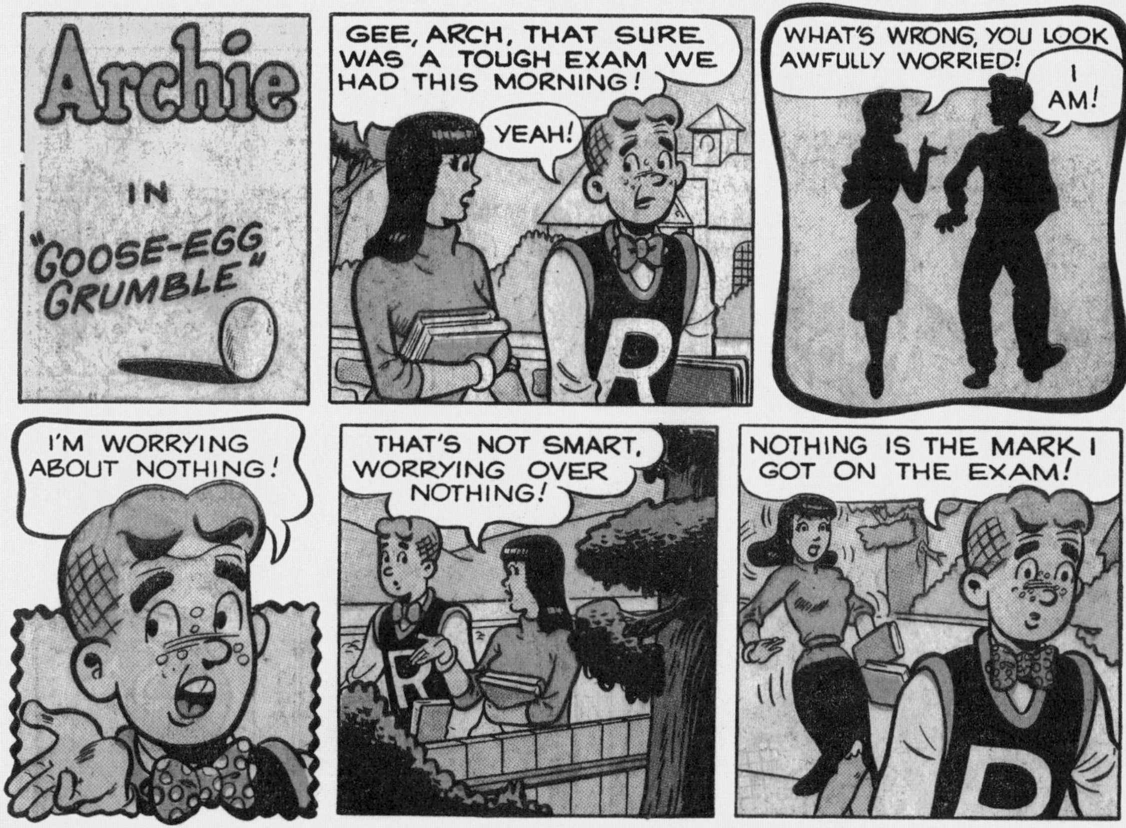
Archie
IN
"GOOSE-EGG GRUMBLE"
GEE, ARCH, THAT SURE WAS A TOUGH EXAM WE HAD THIS MORNING!
YEAH!
WHAT'S WRONG, YOU LOOK AWFULLY WORRIED!
I AM!
I'M WORRYING ABOUT NOTHING!
THAT'S NOT SMART, WORRYING OVER NOTHING!
NOTHING IS THE MARK I GOT ON THE EXAM!

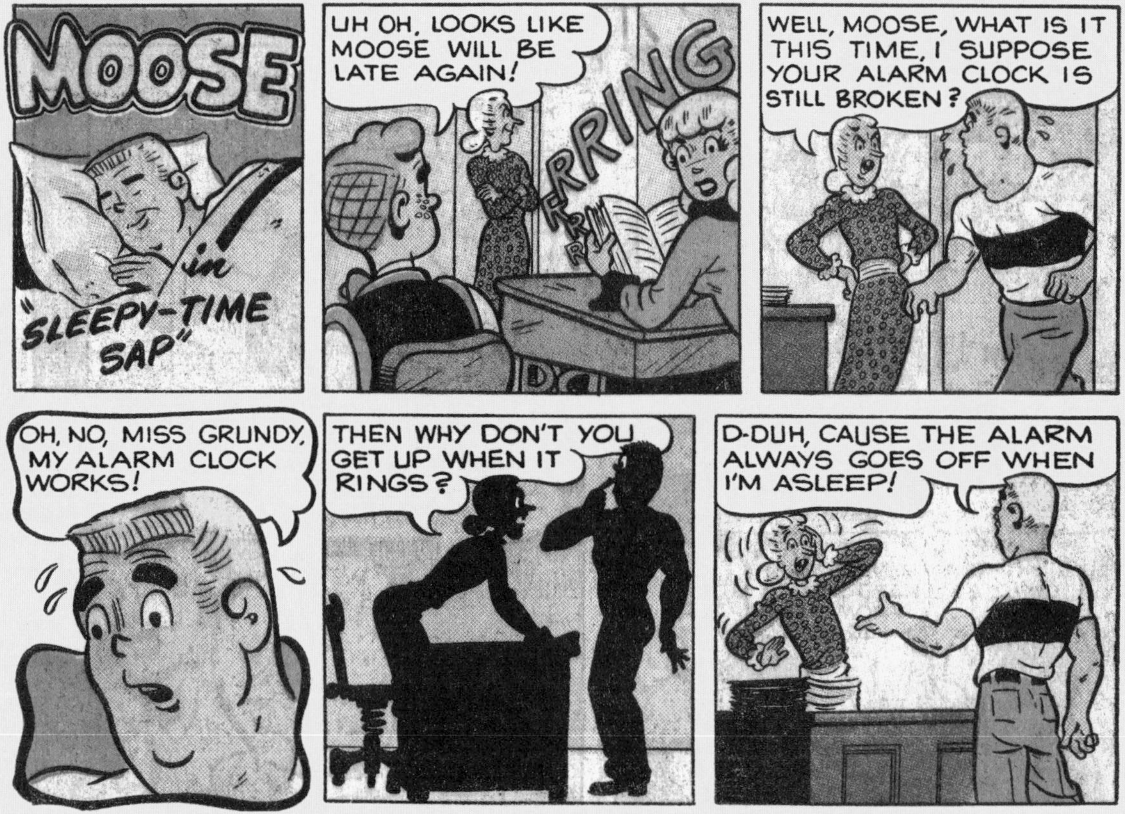
MOOSE
in
"SLEEPY-TIME SAP"
UH OH, LOOKS LIKE MOOSE WILL BE LATE AGAIN!
RRRRRING
WELL, MOOSE, WHAT IS IT THIS TIME, I SUPPOSE YOUR ALARM CLOCK IS STILL BROKEN?
OH, NO, MISS GRUNDY, MY ALARM CLOCK WORKS!
THEN WHY DON'T YOU GET UP WHEN IT RINGS?
D-DUH, CAUSE THE ALARM ALWAYS GOES OFF WHEN I'M ASLEEP!

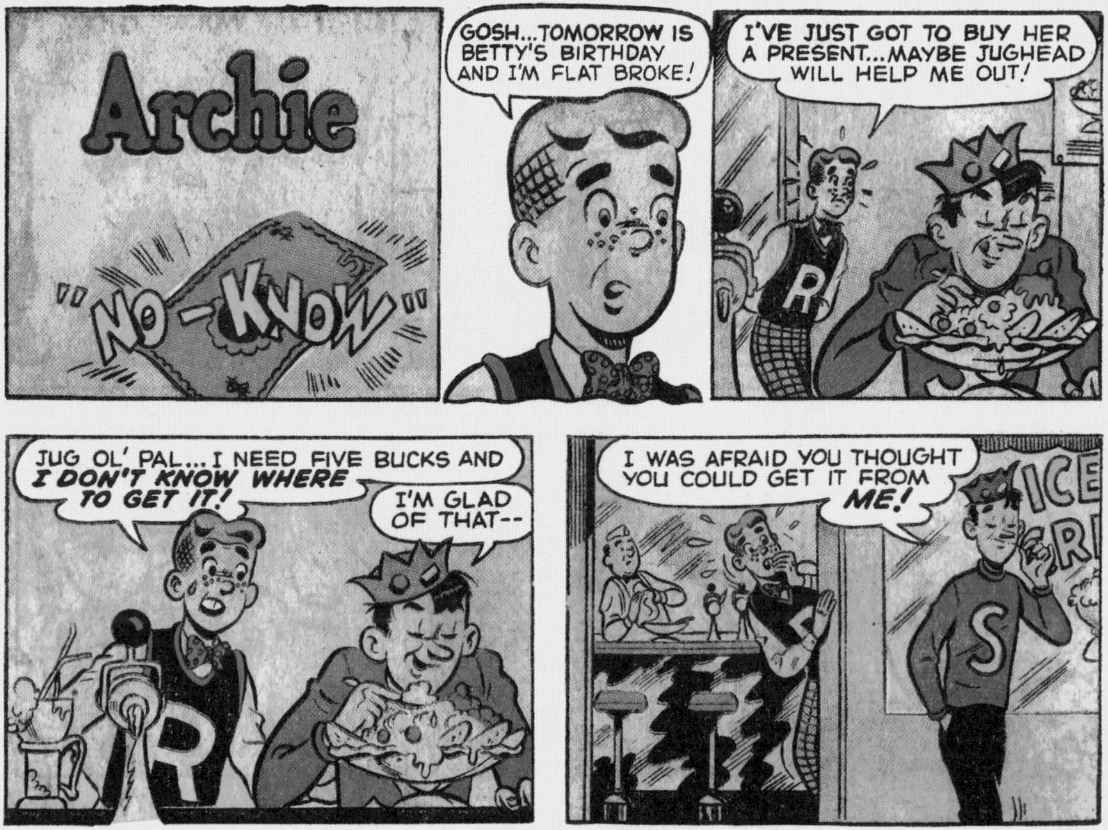
Archie
"NO-KNOW"
GOSH...TOMORROW IS BETTY'S BIRTHDAY AND I'M FLAT BROKE!
I'VE JUST GOT TO BUY HER A PRESENT...MAYBE JUGHEAD WILL HELP ME OUT!
JUG OL' PAL...I NEED FIVE BUCKS AND I DON'T KNOW WHERE TO GET IT!
I'M GLAD OF THAT--
I WAS AFRAID YOU THOUGHT YOU COULD GET IT FROM ME!
ICE CR

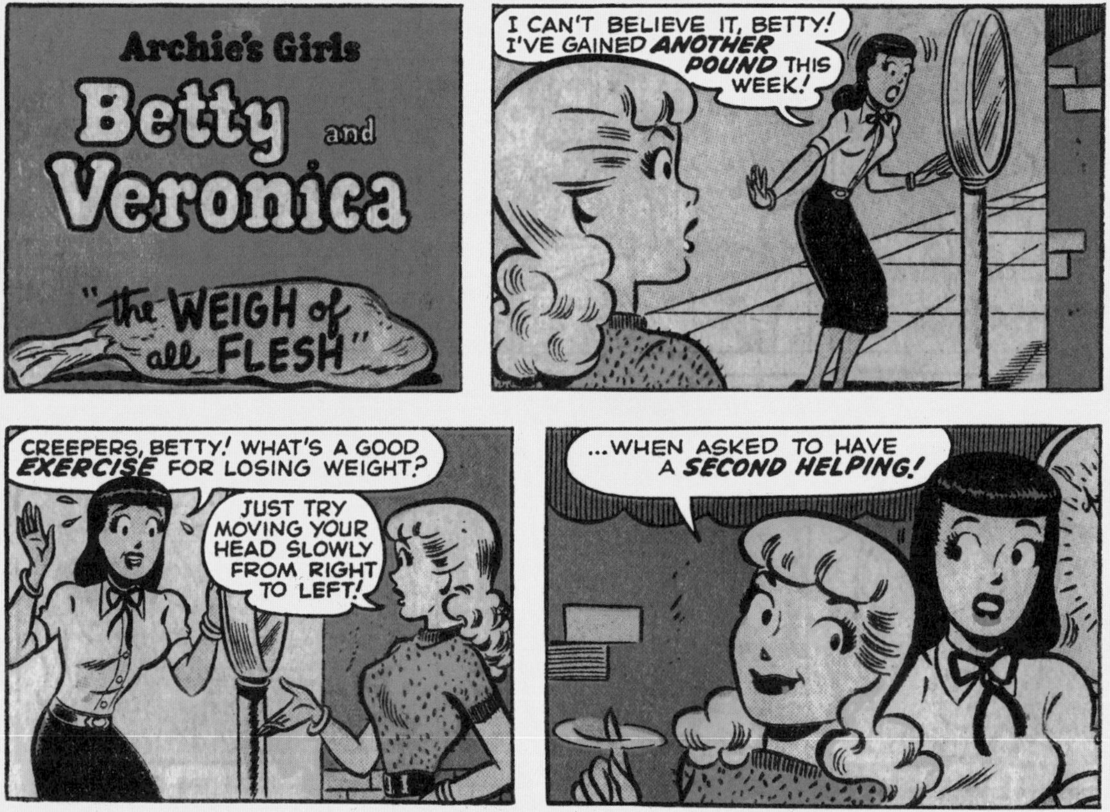
Archie's Girls
Betty and Veronica
"the WEIGH of all FLESH"
I CAN'T BELIEVE IT, BETTY! I'VE GAINED ANOTHER POUND THIS WEEK!
CREEPERS, BETTY! WHAT'S A GOOD EXERCISE FOR LOSING WEIGHT?
JUST TRY MOVING YOUR HEAD SLOWLY FROM RIGHT TO LEFT!
...WHEN ASKED TO HAVE A SECOND HELPING!

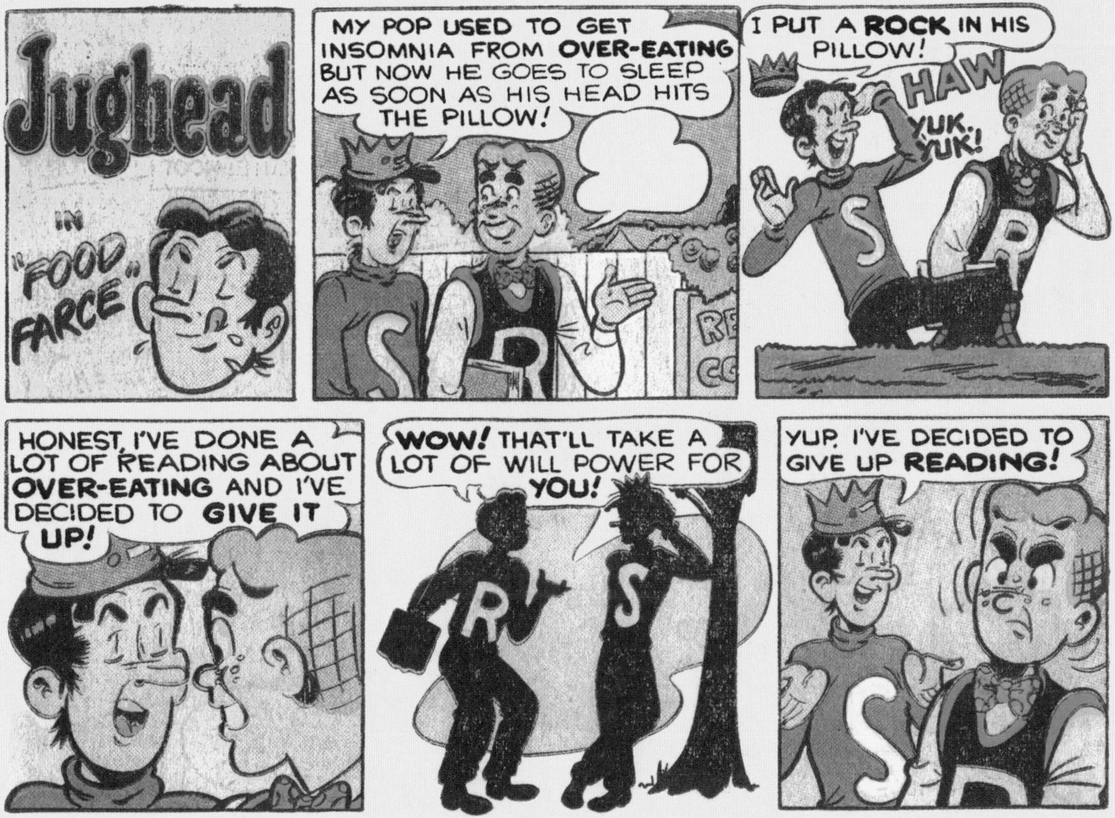
Jughead
IN "FOOD FARCE"
MY POP USED TO GET INSOMNIA FROM OVER-EATING BUT NOW HE GOES TO SLEEP AS SOON AS HIS HEAD HITS THE PILLOW!
I PUT A ROCK IN HIS PILLOW!
HAW
YUK, YUK!
HONEST, I'VE DONE A LOT OF READING ABOUT OVER-EATING AND I'VE DECIDED TO GIVE IT UP!
WOW! THAT'LL TAKE A LOT OF WILL POWER FOR YOU!
YUP, I'VE DECIDED TO GIVE UP READING!

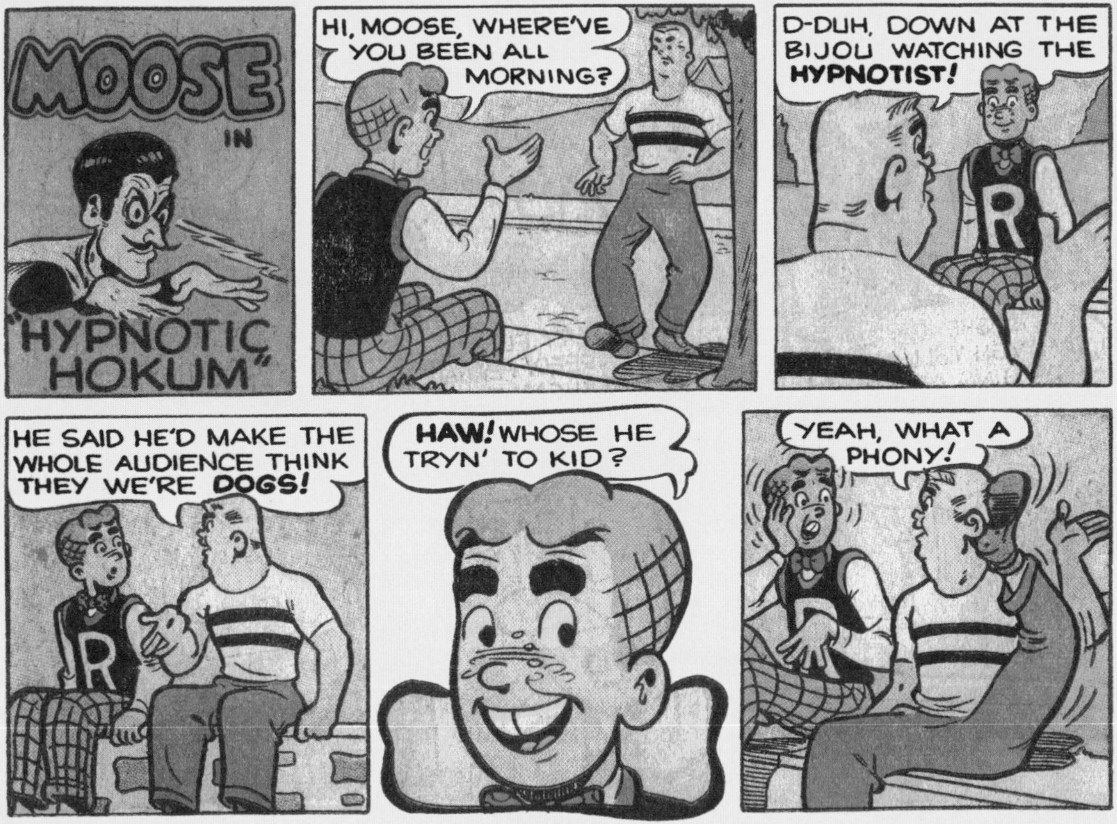
MOOSE
IN
"HYPNOTIC HOKUM"
HI, MOOSE, WHERE'VE YOU BEEN ALL MORNING?
D-DUH, DOWN AT THE BIJOU WATCHING THE **HYPNOTIST!**
HE SAID HE'D MAKE THE WHOLE AUDIENCE THINK THEY WE'RE **DOGS!**
HAW! WHOSE HE TRYN' TO KID?
YEAH, WHAT A PHONY!

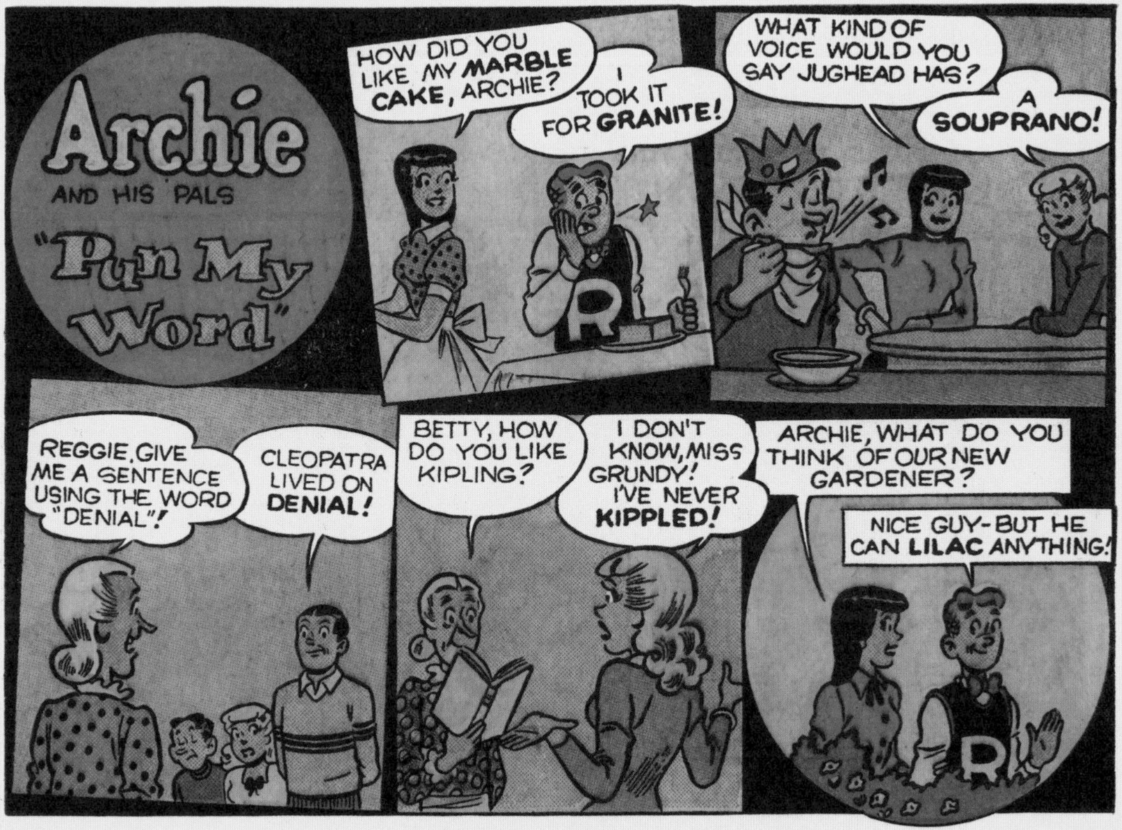

Archie
AND HIS PALS
"Pun My Word"
HOW DID YOU LIKE MY MARBLE CAKE, ARCHIE?
I TOOK IT FOR GRANITE!
WHAT KIND OF VOICE WOULD YOU SAY JUGHEAD HAS?
A SOUPRANO!
REGGIE, GIVE ME A SENTENCE USING THE WORD "DENIAL"!
CLEOPATRA LIVED ON DENIAL!
BETTY, HOW DO YOU LIKE KIPLING?
I DON'T KNOW, MISS GRUNDY! I'VE NEVER KIPPLED!
ARCHIE, WHAT DO YOU THINK OF OUR NEW GARDENER?
NICE GUY- BUT HE CAN LILAC ANYTHING!

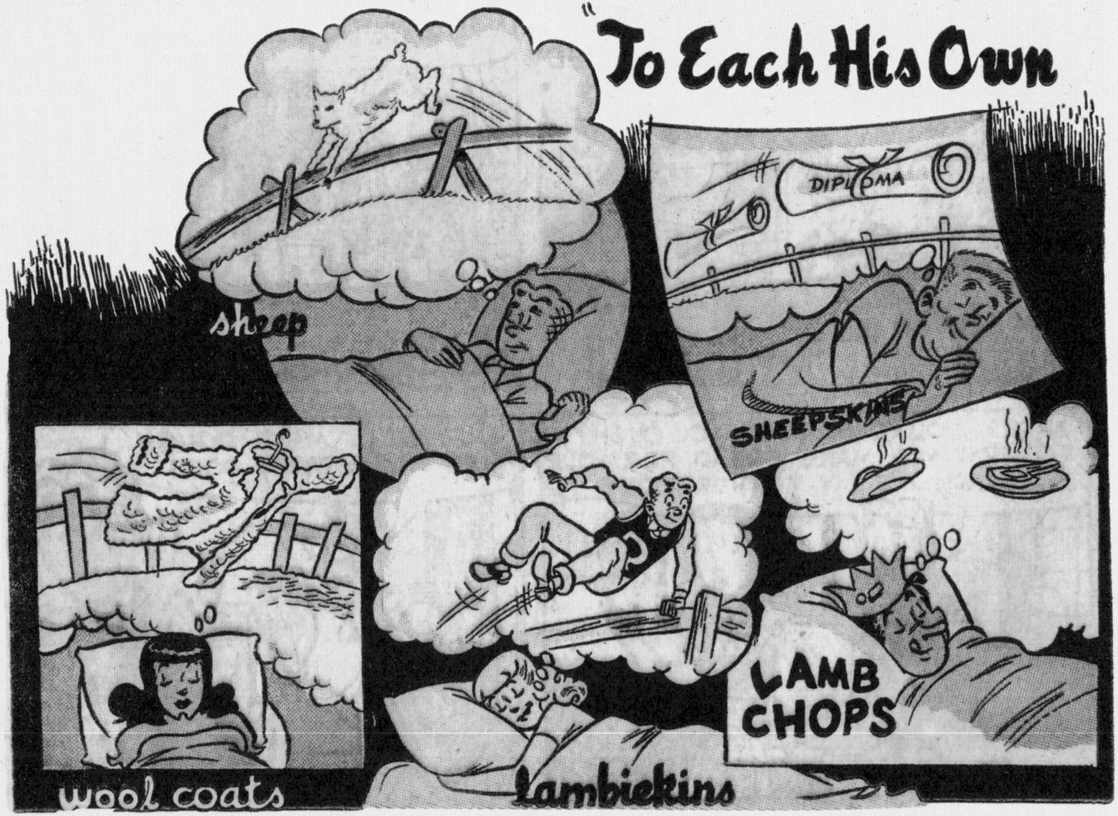
"To Each His Own
sheep
DIPLOMA
SHEEPSKINS
wool coats
lambiekins
LAMB CHOPS

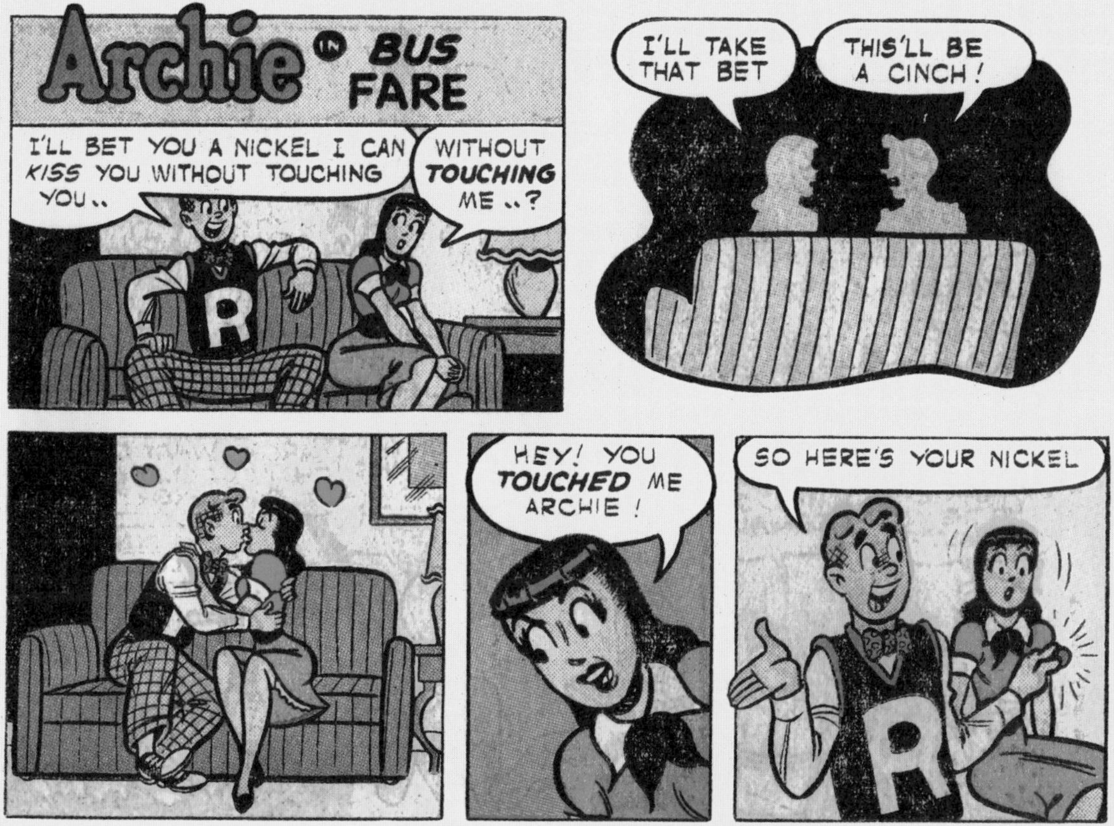
Archie IN BUS FARE
I'LL BET YOU A NICKEL I CAN KISS YOU WITHOUT TOUCHING YOU..
WITHOUT TOUCHING ME..?
I'LL TAKE THAT BET
THIS'LL BE A CINCH!
HEY! YOU TOUCHED ME ARCHIE!
SO HERE'S YOUR NICKEL

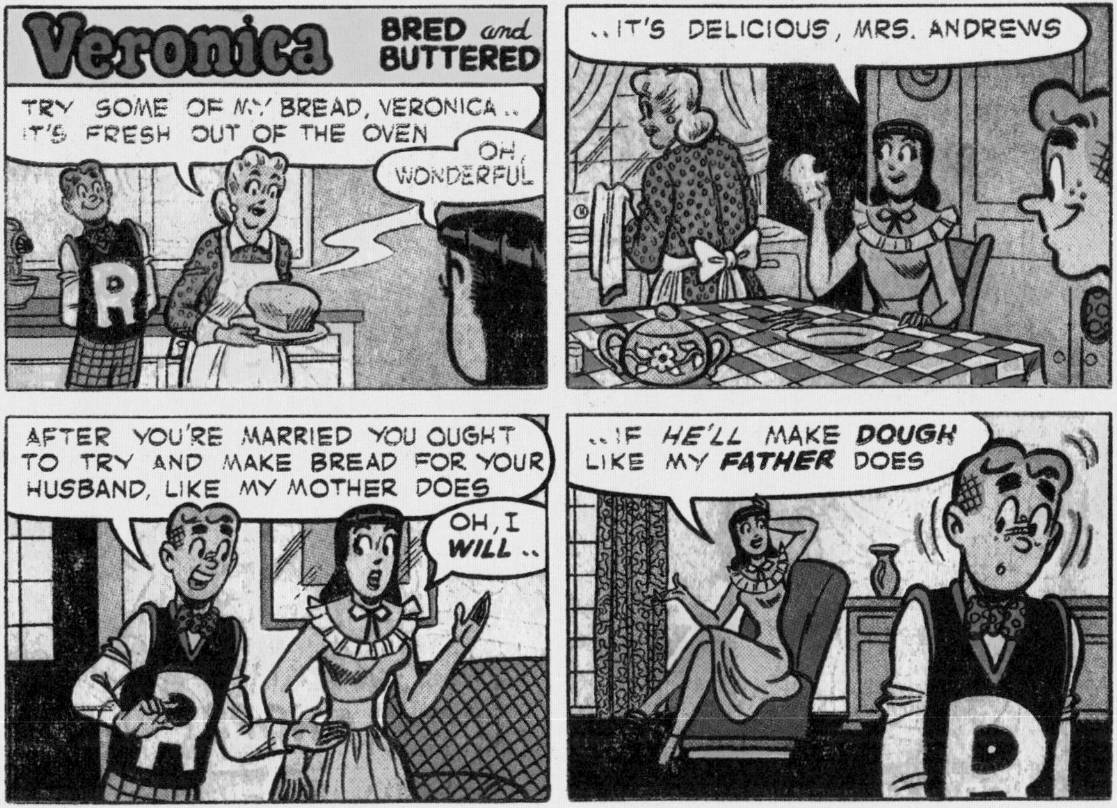
Veronica
BRED and BUTTERED
TRY SOME OF MY BREAD, VERONICA .. IT'S FRESH OUT OF THE OVEN
OH, WONDERFUL
.. IT'S DELICIOUS, MRS. ANDREWS
AFTER YOU'RE MARRIED YOU OUGHT TO TRY AND MAKE BREAD FOR YOUR HUSBAND, LIKE MY MOTHER DOES
OH, I WILL ..
.. IF HE'LL MAKE DOUGH LIKE MY FATHER DOES

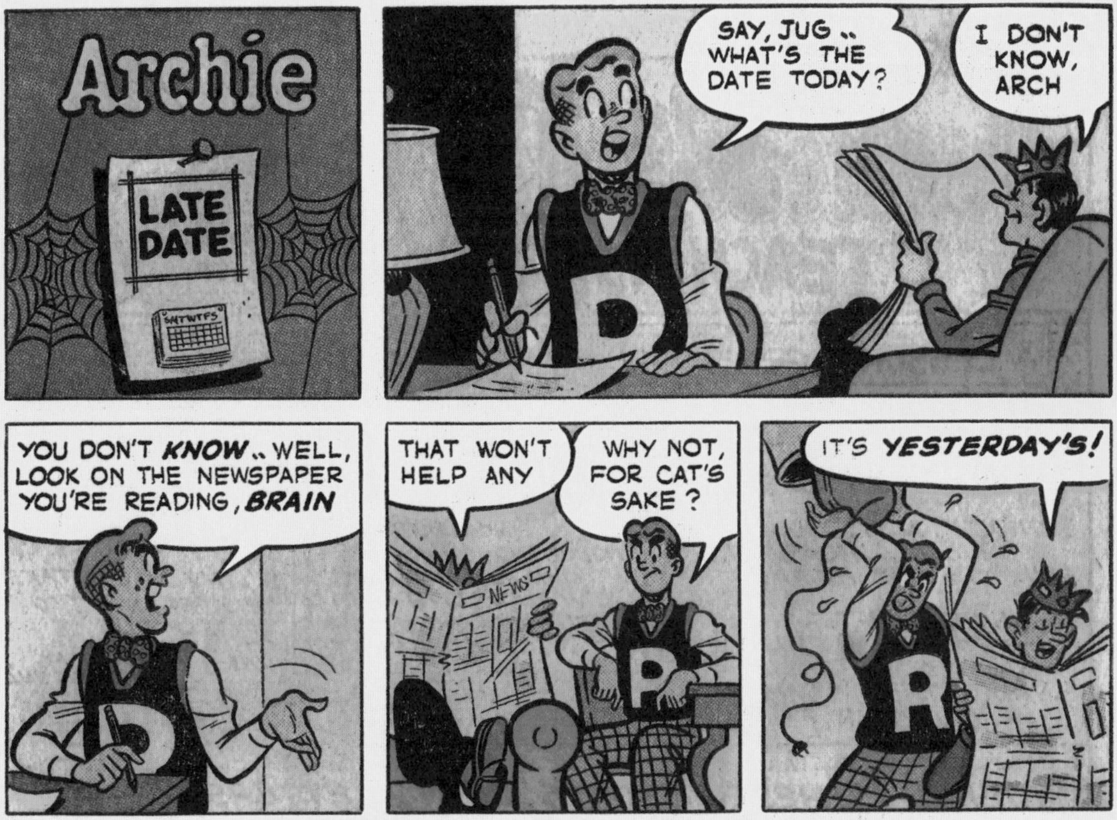
Archie
LATE DATE
SMTWTFS
SAY, JUG .. WHAT'S THE DATE TODAY?
I DON'T KNOW, ARCH
YOU DON'T KNOW .. WELL, LOOK ON THE NEWSPAPER YOU'RE READING, BRAIN
THAT WON'T HELP ANY
WHY NOT, FOR CAT'S SAKE?
NEWS
IT'S YESTERDAY'S!

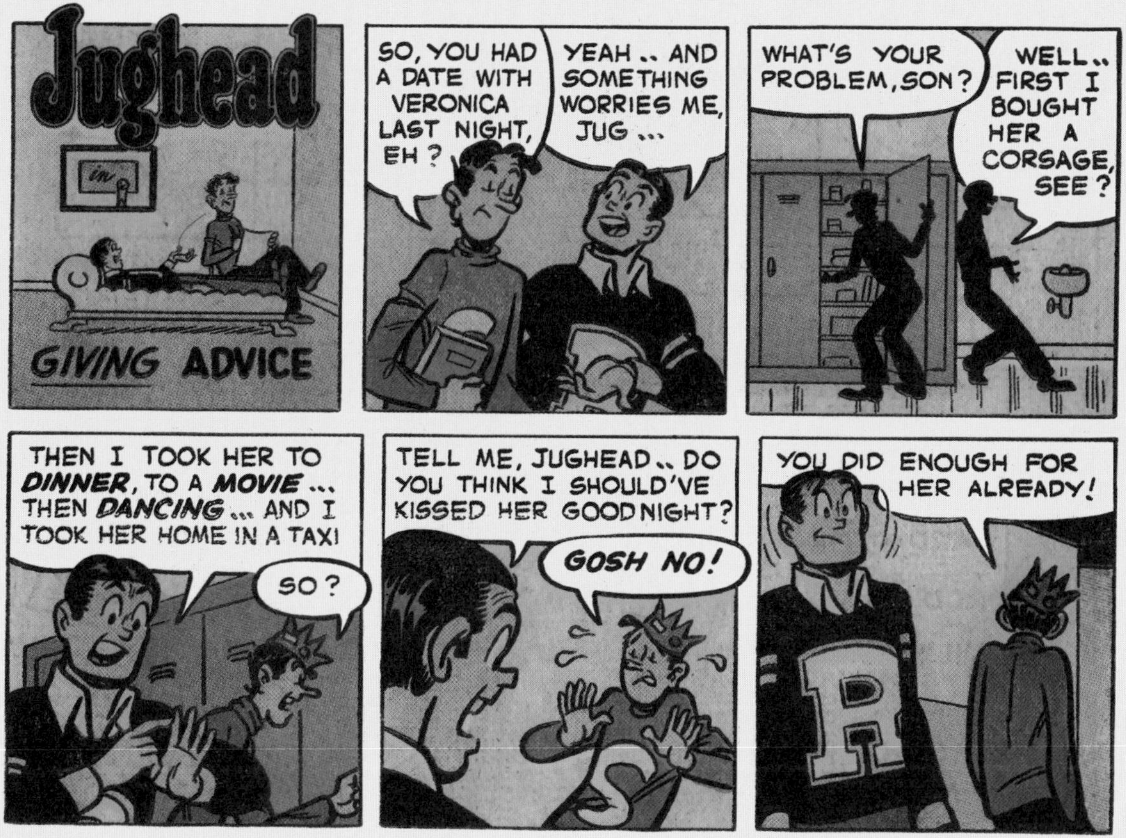
Jughead
in
GIVING ADVICE
SO, YOU HAD A DATE WITH VERONICA LAST NIGHT, EH ?
YEAH .. AND SOMETHING WORRIES ME, JUG ...
WHAT'S YOUR PROBLEM, SON ?
WELL .. FIRST I BOUGHT HER A CORSAGE, SEE ?
THEN I TOOK HER TO DINNER, TO A MOVIE ... THEN DANCING ... AND I TOOK HER HOME IN A TAXI
SO ?
TELL ME, JUGHEAD .. DO YOU THINK I SHOULD'VE KISSED HER GOODNIGHT ?
GOSH NO!
YOU DID ENOUGH FOR HER ALREADY!

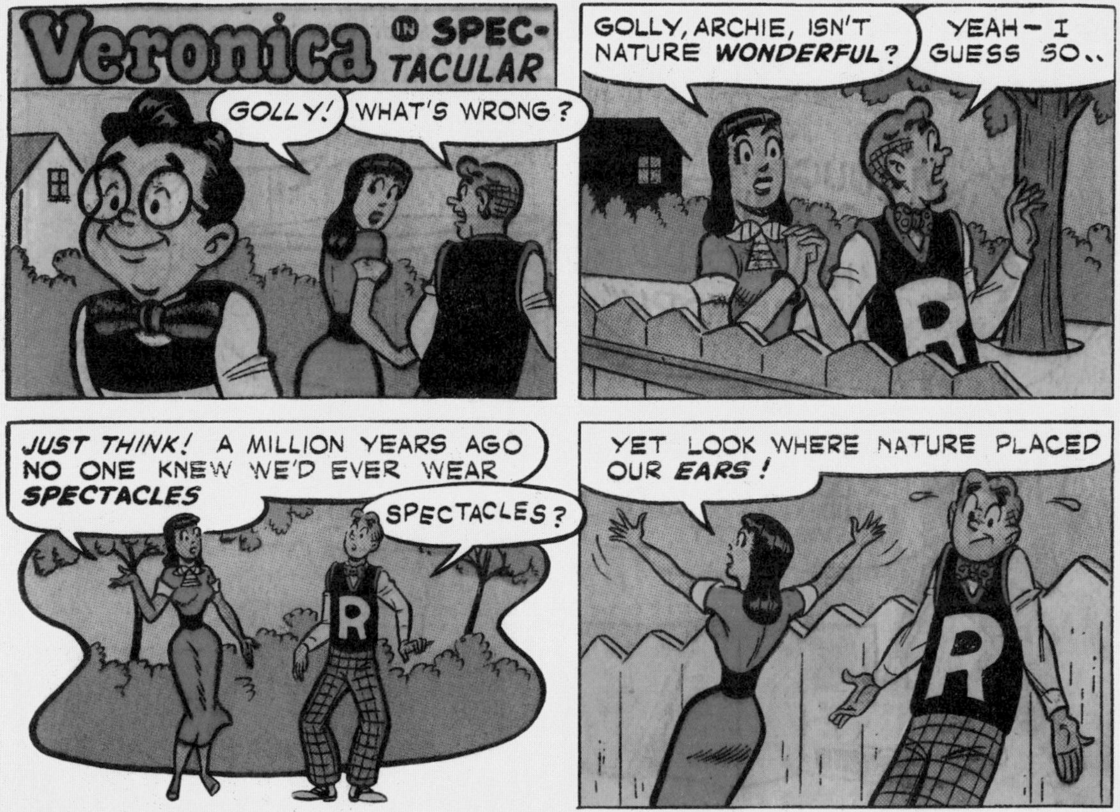
Veronica IN SPECTACULAR
GOLLY!
WHAT'S WRONG?
GOLLY, ARCHIE, ISN'T NATURE WONDERFUL?
YEAH — I GUESS SO..
JUST THINK! A MILLION YEARS AGO NO ONE KNEW WE'D EVER WEAR SPECTACLES
SPECTACLES?
YET LOOK WHERE NATURE PLACED OUR EARS!

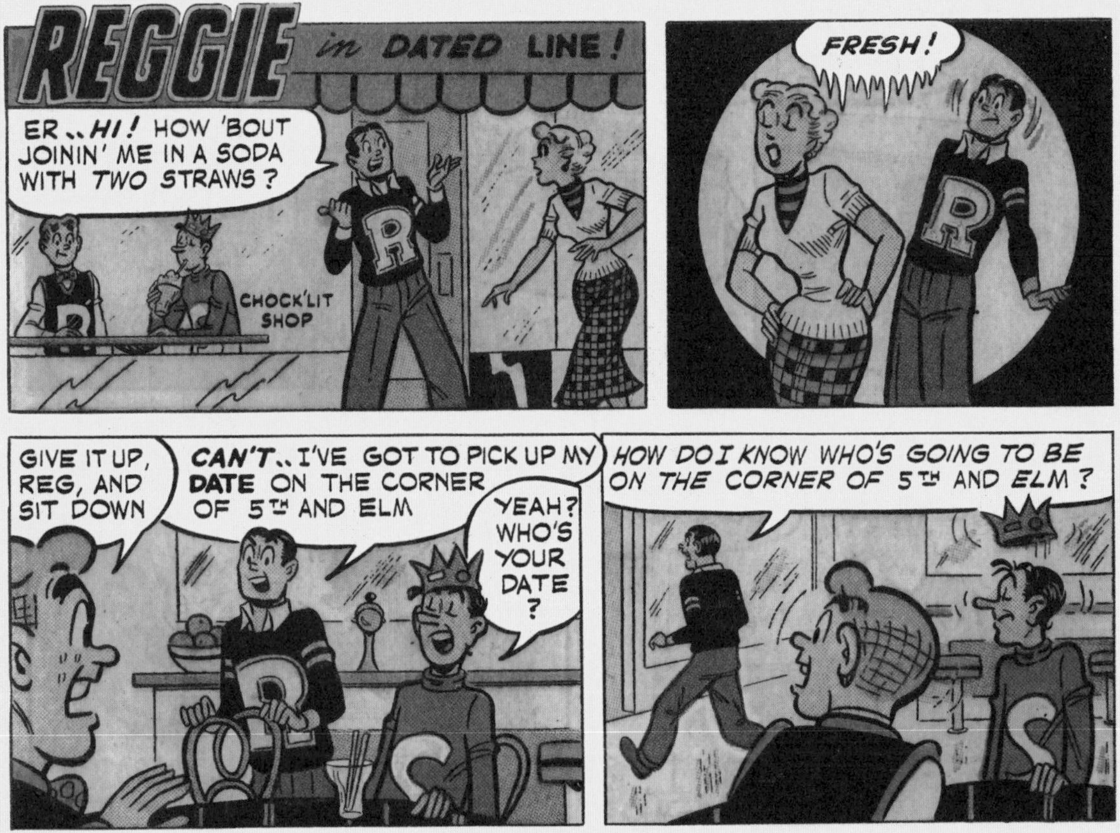
REGGIE in DATED LINE!
ER..HI! HOW 'BOUT JOININ' ME IN A SODA WITH TWO STRAWS?
CHOCK'LIT SHOP
FRESH!
GIVE IT UP, REG, AND SIT DOWN
CAN'T.. I'VE GOT TO PICK UP MY DATE ON THE CORNER OF 5TH AND ELM
YEAH? WHO'S YOUR DATE?
HOW DO I KNOW WHO'S GOING TO BE ON THE CORNER OF 5TH AND ELM?

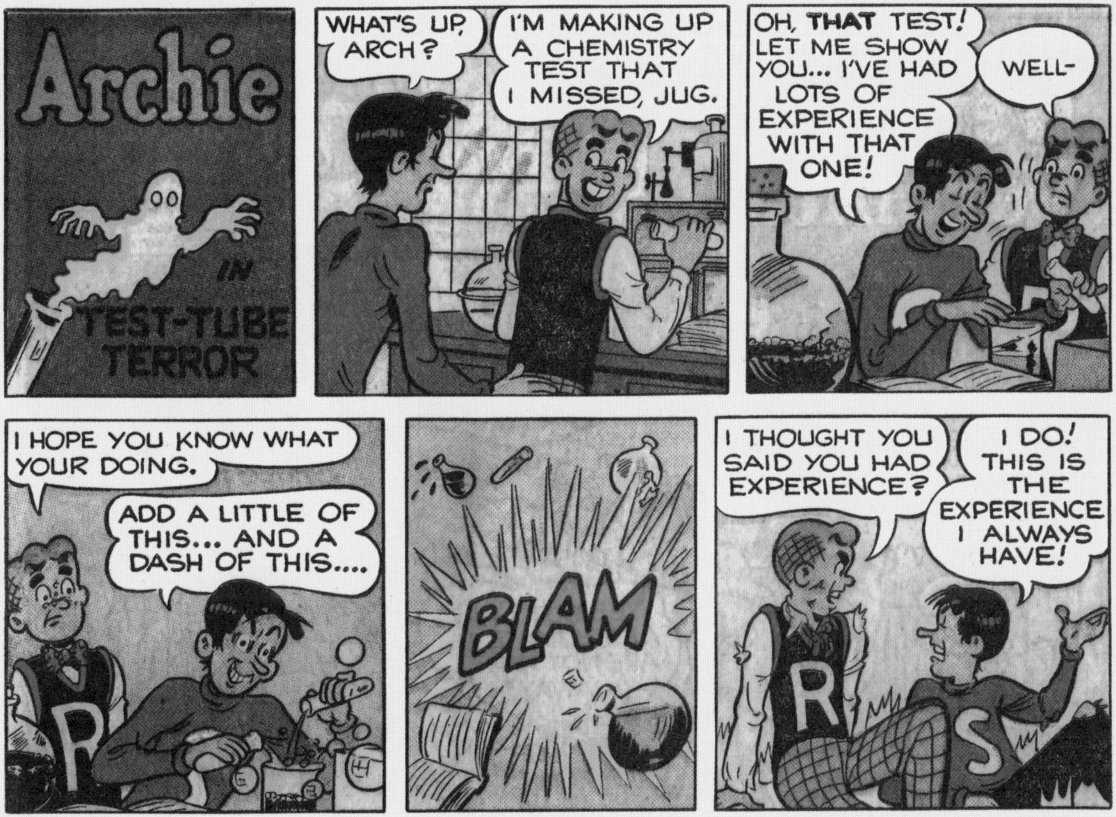
Archie
IN
TEST-TUBE TERROR
WHAT'S UP, ARCH?
I'M MAKING UP A CHEMISTRY TEST THAT I MISSED, JUG.
OH, THAT TEST! LET ME SHOW YOU... I'VE HAD LOTS OF EXPERIENCE WITH THAT ONE!
WELL-
I HOPE YOU KNOW WHAT YOUR DOING.
ADD A LITTLE OF THIS... AND A DASH OF THIS....
BLAM
I THOUGHT YOU SAID YOU HAD EXPERIENCE?
I DO! THIS IS THE EXPERIENCE I ALWAYS HAVE!

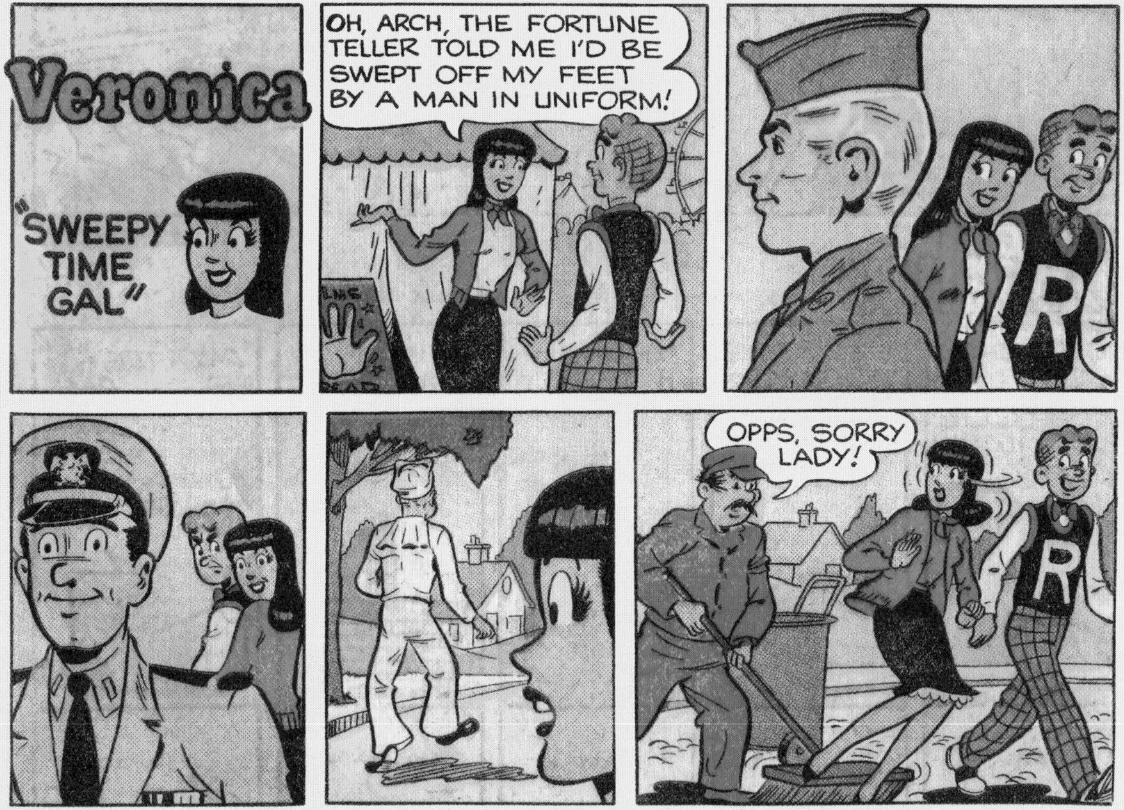
Veronica
"SWEEPY TIME GAL"
OH, ARCH, THE FORTUNE TELLER TOLD ME I'D BE SWEPT OFF MY FEET BY A MAN IN UNIFORM!
OPPS, SORRY LADY!

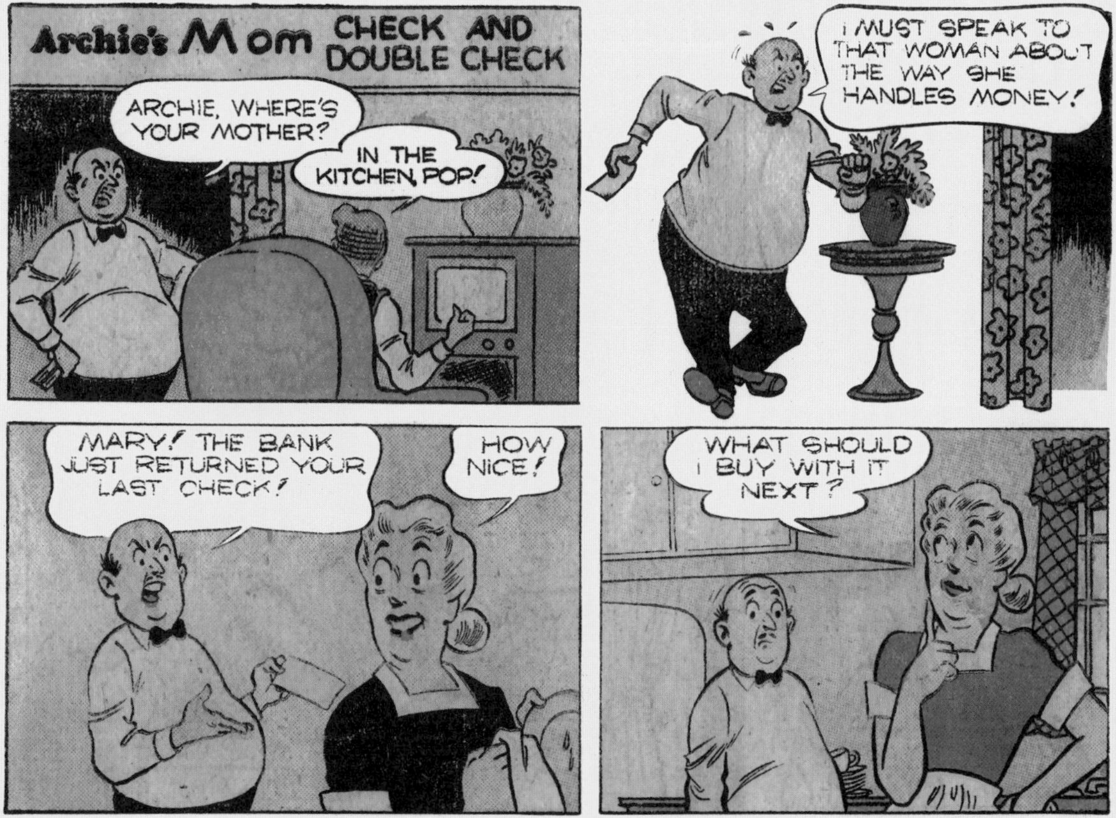
Archie's Mom
CHECK AND DOUBLE CHECK
ARCHIE, WHERE'S YOUR MOTHER?
IN THE KITCHEN, POP!
I MUST SPEAK TO THAT WOMAN ABOUT THE WAY SHE HANDLES MONEY!
MARY! THE BANK JUST RETURNED YOUR LAST CHECK!
HOW NICE!
WHAT SHOULD I BUY WITH IT NEXT?

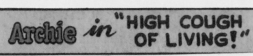

Archie in "HIGH COUGH OF LIVING!"

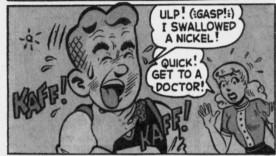

ULP! (:GASP!:) I SWALLOWED A NICKEL!

QUICK! GET TO A DOCTOR!

KAFF!

KAFF!

YOU CAN RELAX NOW ARCHIE! IT'S ALL OVER! HERE'S YOUR NICKEL!

WHEW! THAT WAS CLOSE!

ISN'T IT WONDERFUL ARCHIE, THE THINGS DOCTORS CAN DO TODAY... IT'S NOTHING SHORT OF MIRACULOUS!

IT SURE IS ·BETTY, IT SURE IS!

DR. BANDADE

I SWALLOWED A NICKEL AND HE MADE ME COUGH UP FIVE DOLLARS!

END.

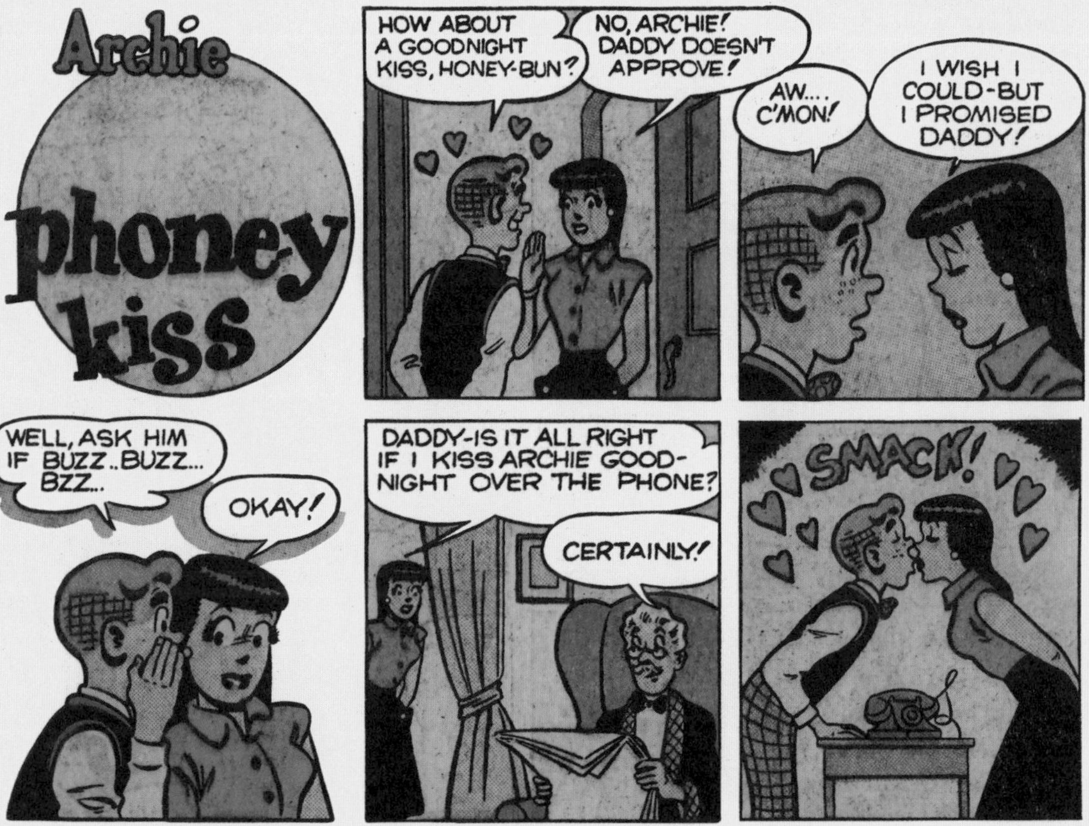
Archie
phoney kiss
HOW ABOUT A GOODNIGHT KISS, HONEY-BUN?
NO, ARCHIE! DADDY DOESN'T APPROVE!
AW.... C'MON!
I WISH I COULD-BUT I PROMISED DADDY!
WELL, ASK HIM IF BUZZ..BUZZ... BZZ...
OKAY!
DADDY-IS IT ALL RIGHT IF I KISS ARCHIE GOOD-NIGHT OVER THE PHONE?
CERTAINLY!
SMACK!

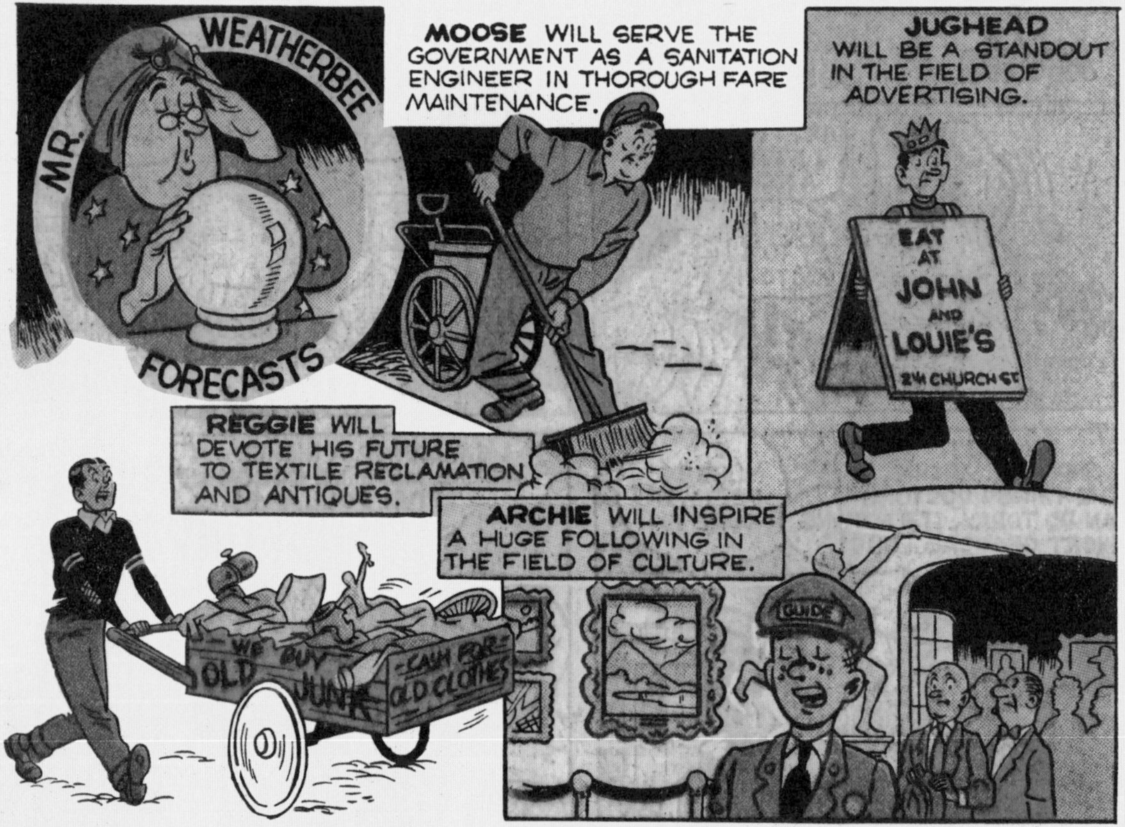
MR. WEATHERBEE FORECASTS
MOOSE WILL SERVE THE GOVERNMENT AS A SANITATION ENGINEER IN THOROUGH FARE MAINTENANCE.
JUGHEAD WILL BE A STANDOUT IN THE FIELD OF ADVERTISING.
EAT AT JOHN AND LOUIE'S
REGGIE WILL DEVOTE HIS FUTURE TO TEXTILE RECLAMATION AND ANTIQUES.
WE BUY OLD JUNK
CASH FOR OLD CLOTHES
ARCHIE WILL INSPIRE A HUGE FOLLOWING IN THE FIELD OF CULTURE.
GUIDE

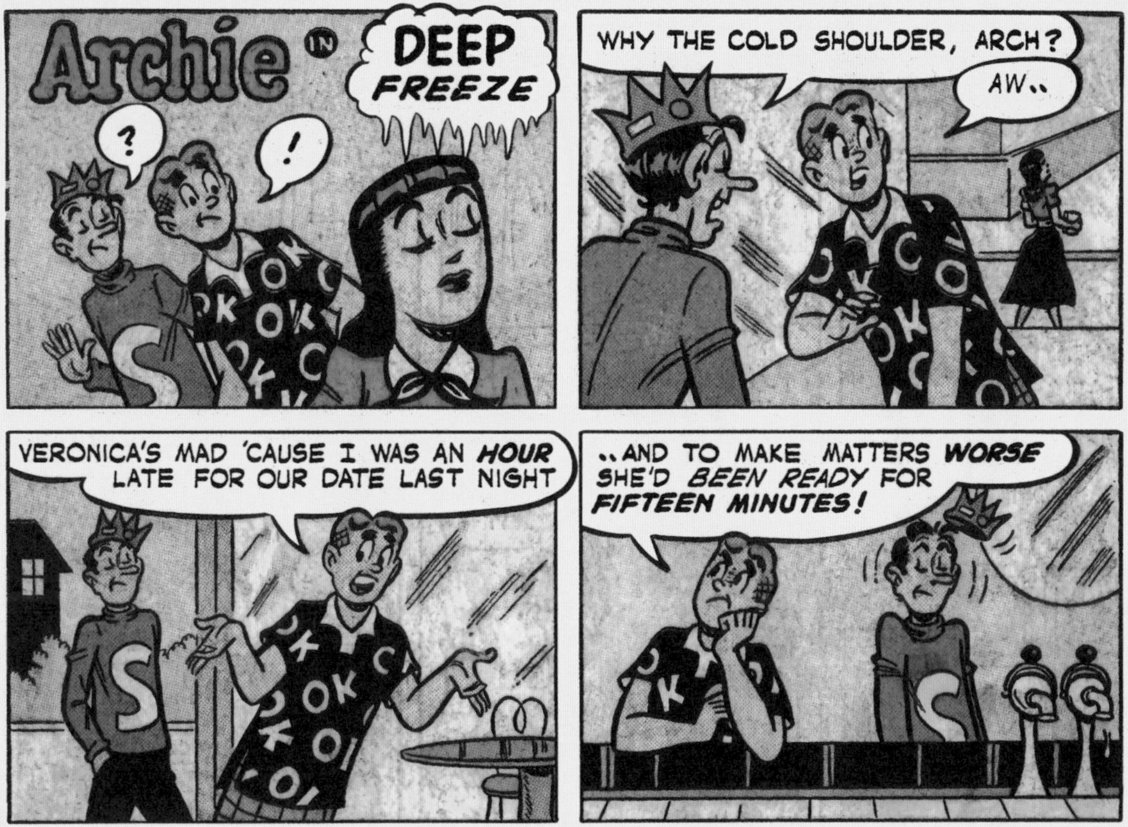
Archie IN
DEEP FREEZE
?
!
WHY THE COLD SHOULDER, ARCH?
AW..
VERONICA'S MAD 'CAUSE I WAS AN HOUR LATE FOR OUR DATE LAST NIGHT
..AND TO MAKE MATTERS WORSE SHE'D BEEN READY FOR FIFTEEN MINUTES!

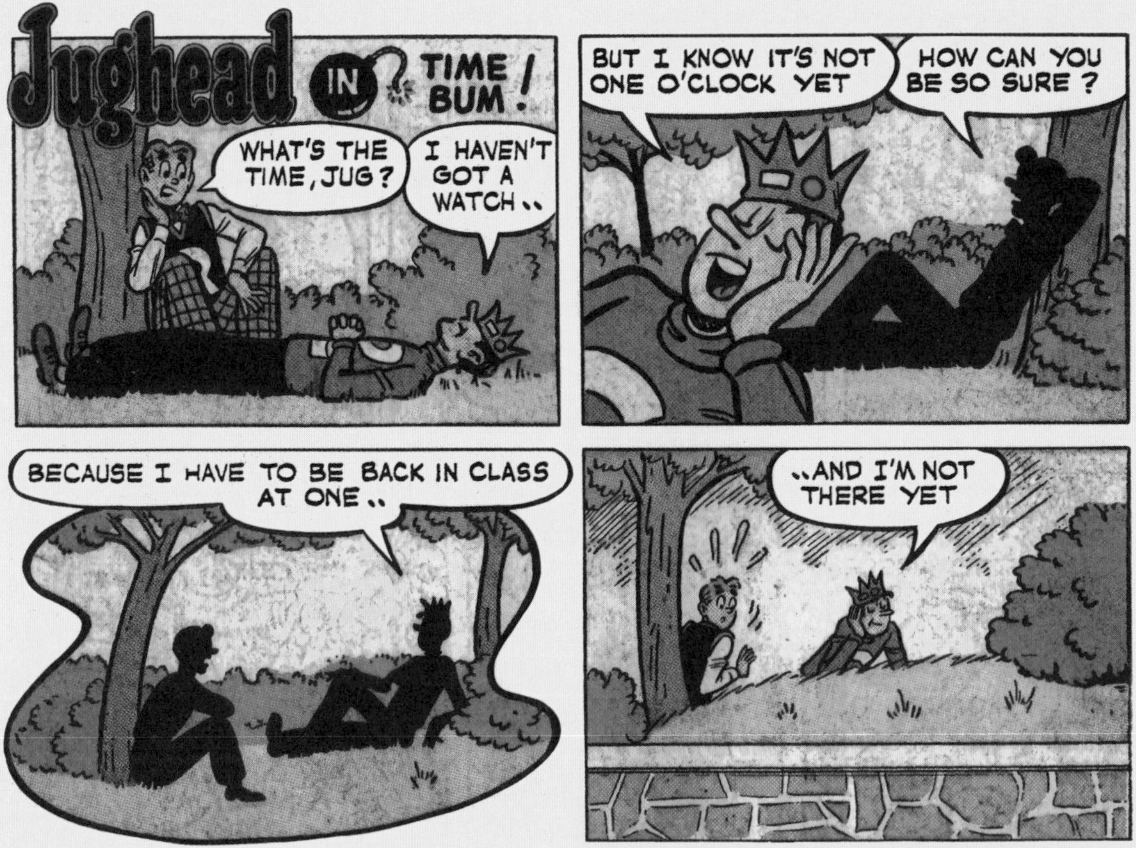
Jughead IN TIME BUM!
WHAT'S THE TIME, JUG?
I HAVEN'T GOT A WATCH ..
BUT I KNOW IT'S NOT ONE O'CLOCK YET
HOW CAN YOU BE SO SURE?
BECAUSE I HAVE TO BE BACK IN CLASS AT ONE ..
..AND I'M NOT THERE YET

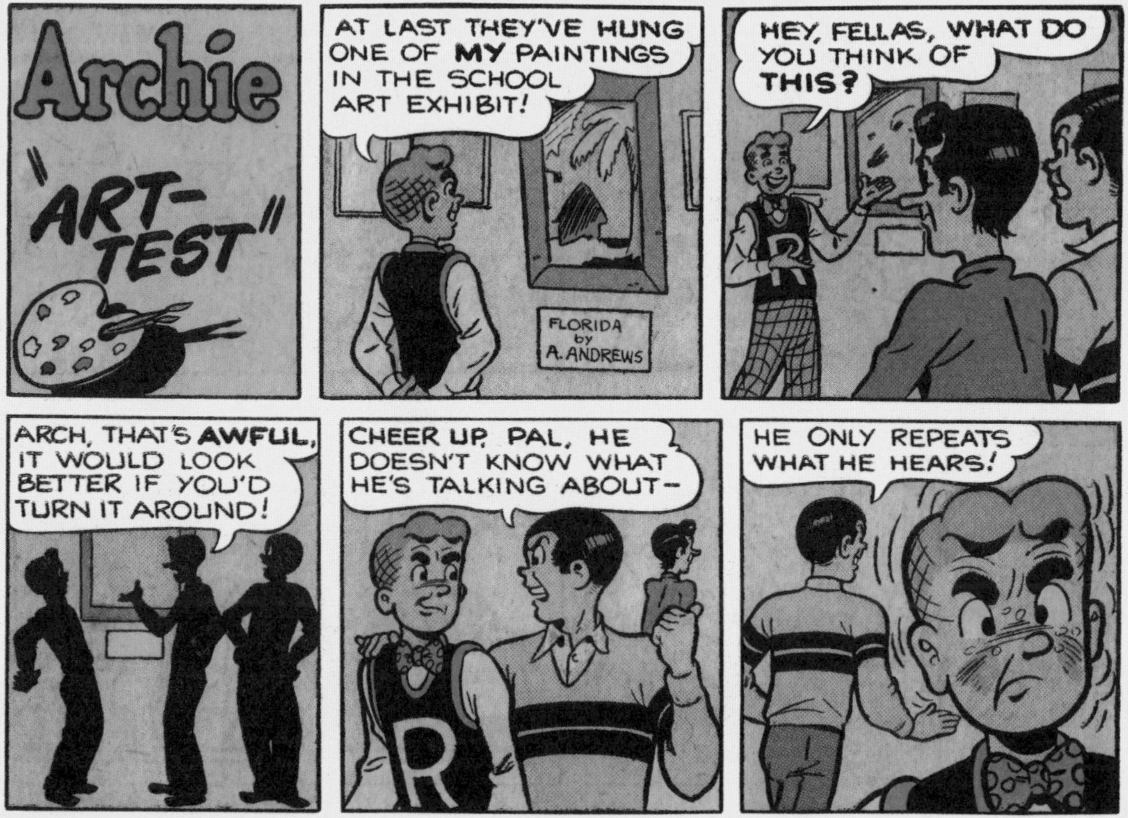

Archie
"ART-TEST"
AT LAST THEY'VE HUNG ONE OF MY PAINTINGS IN THE SCHOOL ART EXHIBIT!
FLORIDA by A. ANDREWS
HEY, FELLAS, WHAT DO YOU THINK OF THIS?
ARCH, THAT'S AWFUL, IT WOULD LOOK BETTER IF YOU'D TURN IT AROUND!
CHEER UP, PAL, HE DOESN'T KNOW WHAT HE'S TALKING ABOUT—
HE ONLY REPEATS WHAT HE HEARS!

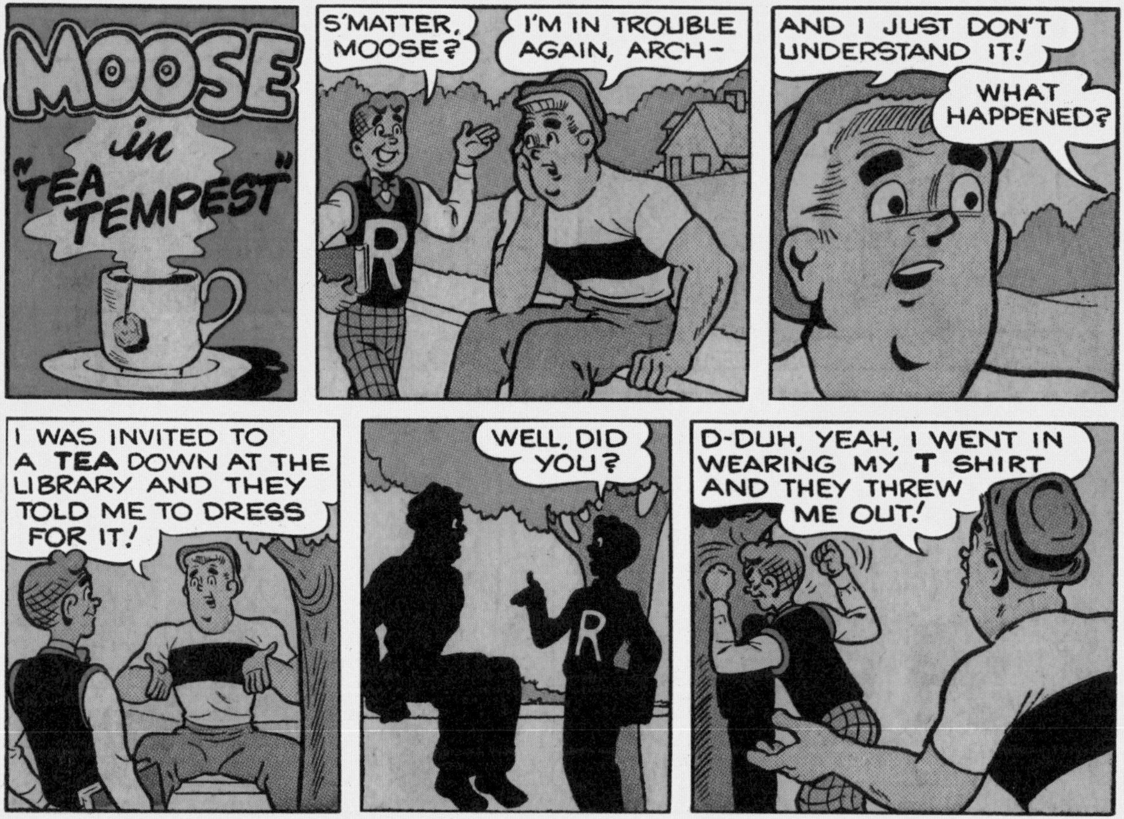
MOOSE
in
"TEA TEMPEST"
S'MATTER, MOOSE?
I'M IN TROUBLE AGAIN, ARCH-
AND I JUST DON'T UNDERSTAND IT!
WHAT HAPPENED?
I WAS INVITED TO A TEA DOWN AT THE LIBRARY AND THEY TOLD ME TO DRESS FOR IT!
WELL, DID YOU?
D-DUH, YEAH, I WENT IN WEARING MY T SHIRT AND THEY THREW ME OUT!

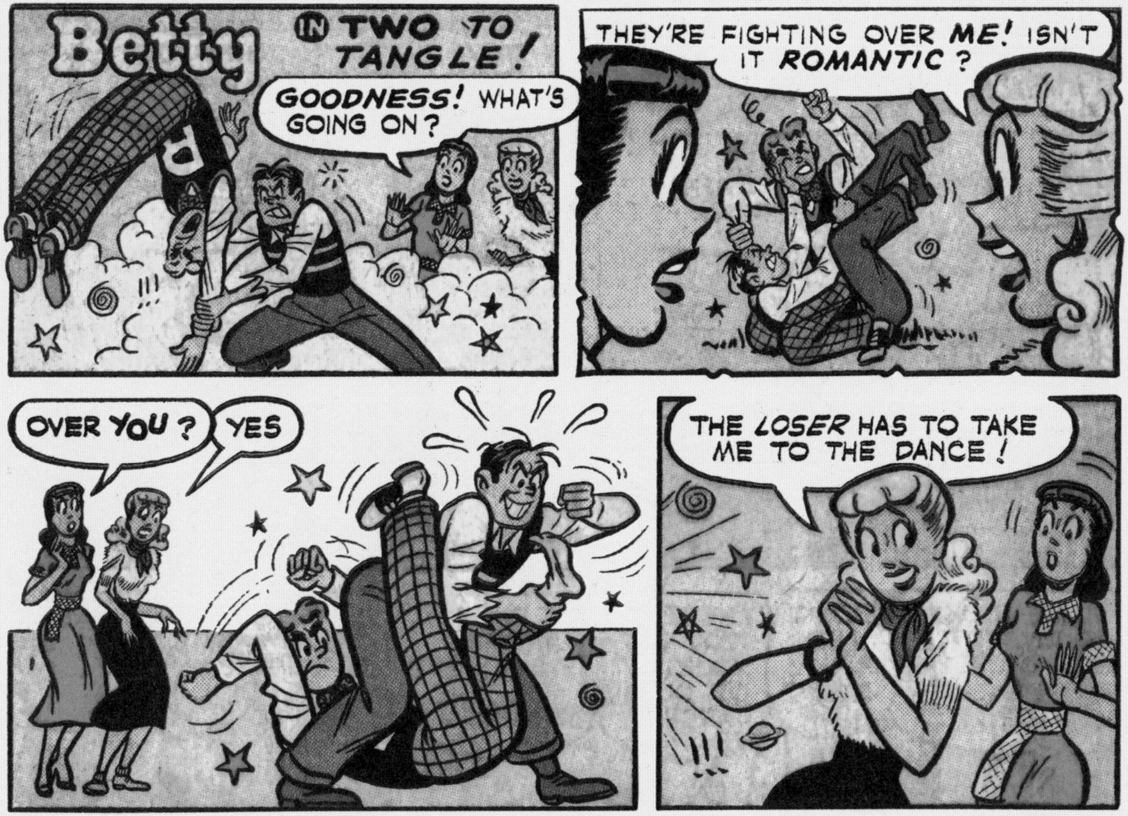
Betty
IN TWO TO TANGLE!
GOODNESS! WHAT'S GOING ON?
THEY'RE FIGHTING OVER ME! ISN'T IT ROMANTIC?
OVER YOU?
YES
THE LOSER HAS TO TAKE ME TO THE DANCE!

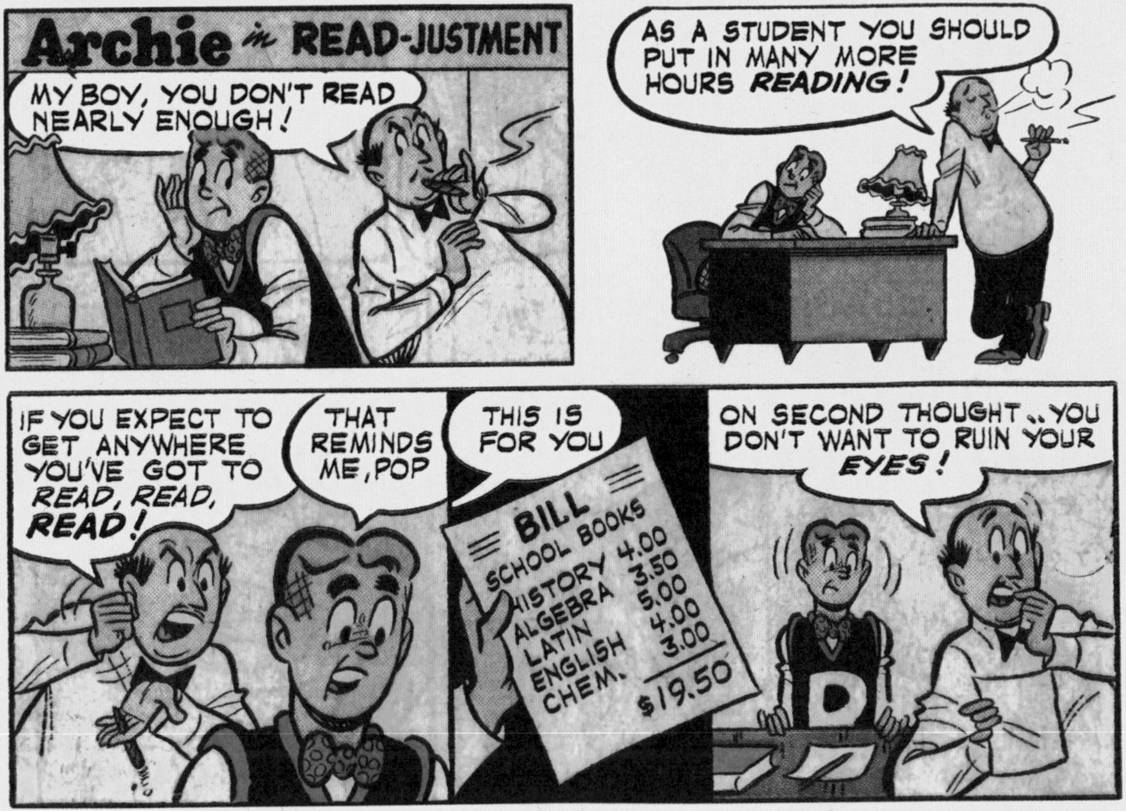
Archie in READ-JUSTMENT
MY BOY, YOU DON'T READ NEARLY ENOUGH!
AS A STUDENT YOU SHOULD PUT IN MANY MORE HOURS READING!
IF YOU EXPECT TO GET ANYWHERE YOU'VE GOT TO READ, READ, READ!
THAT REMINDS ME, POP
THIS IS FOR YOU
BILL
SCHOOL BOOKS
HISTORY 4.00
ALGEBRA 3.50
LATIN 5.00
ENGLISH 4.00
CHEM. 3.00
$19.50
ON SECOND THOUGHT.. YOU DON'T WANT TO RUIN YOUR EYES!
D

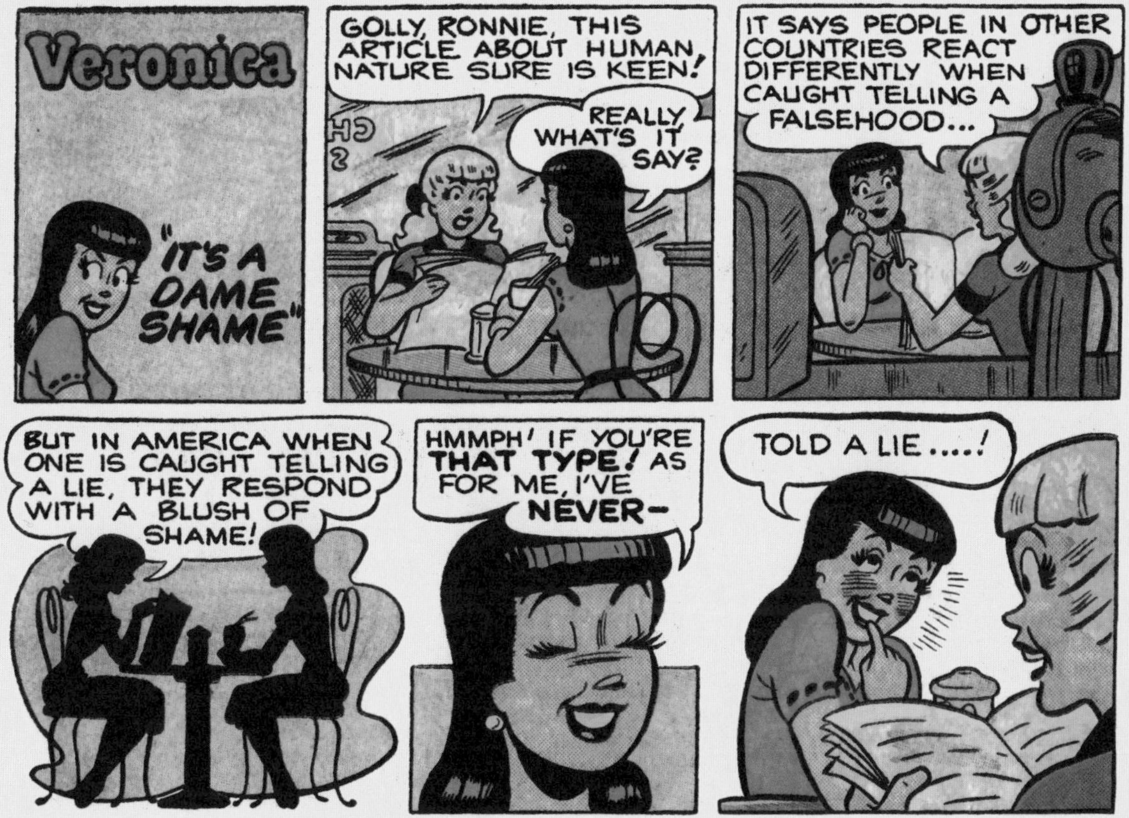
Veronica
"IT'S A DAME SHAME"
GOLLY, RONNIE, THIS ARTICLE ABOUT HUMAN NATURE SURE IS KEEN!
REALLY, WHAT'S IT SAY?
IT SAYS PEOPLE IN OTHER COUNTRIES REACT DIFFERENTLY WHEN CAUGHT TELLING A FALSEHOOD...
BUT IN AMERICA WHEN ONE IS CAUGHT TELLING A LIE, THEY RESPOND WITH A BLUSH OF SHAME!
HMMPH! IF YOU'RE THAT TYPE! AS FOR ME, I'VE NEVER—
TOLD A LIE....!

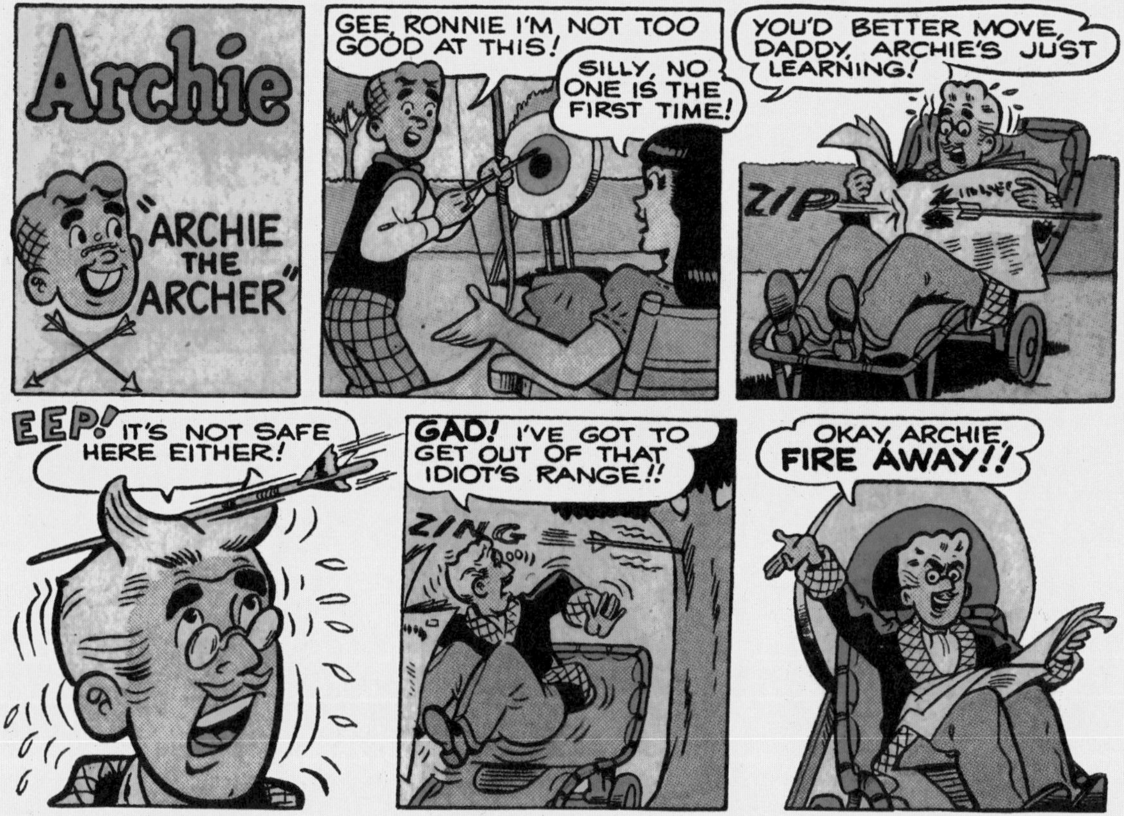
Archie
"ARCHIE THE ARCHER"
GEE, RONNIE I'M NOT TOO GOOD AT THIS!
SILLY, NO ONE IS THE FIRST TIME!
YOU'D BETTER MOVE, DADDY, ARCHIE'S JUST LEARNING!
ZIP
EEP! IT'S NOT SAFE HERE EITHER!
GAD! I'VE GOT TO GET OUT OF THAT IDIOT'S RANGE!!
ZING
OKAY, ARCHIE, FIRE AWAY!!

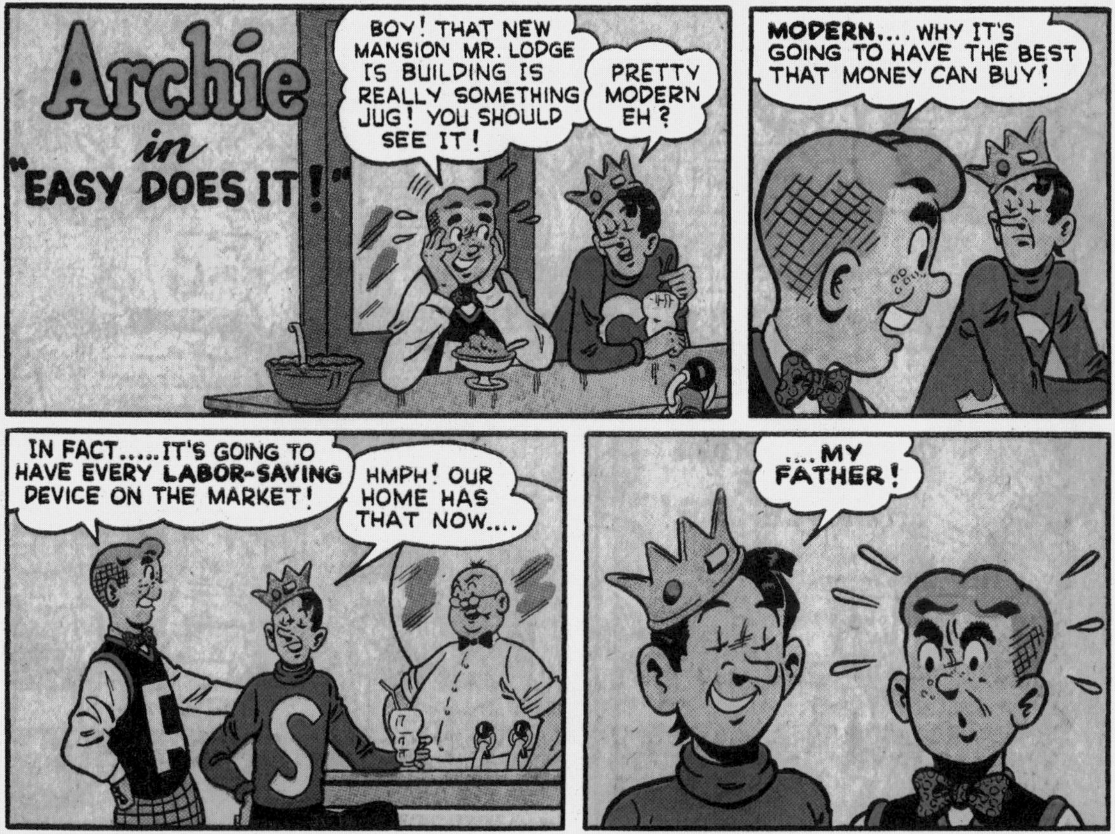
Archie in "EASY DOES IT!"
BOY! THAT NEW MANSION MR. LODGE IS BUILDING IS REALLY SOMETHING JUG! YOU SHOULD SEE IT!
PRETTY MODERN EH?
MODERN.... WHY IT'S GOING TO HAVE THE BEST THAT MONEY CAN BUY!
IN FACT.....IT'S GOING TO HAVE EVERY LABOR-SAVING DEVICE ON THE MARKET!
HMPH! OUR HOME HAS THAT NOW....
....MY FATHER!

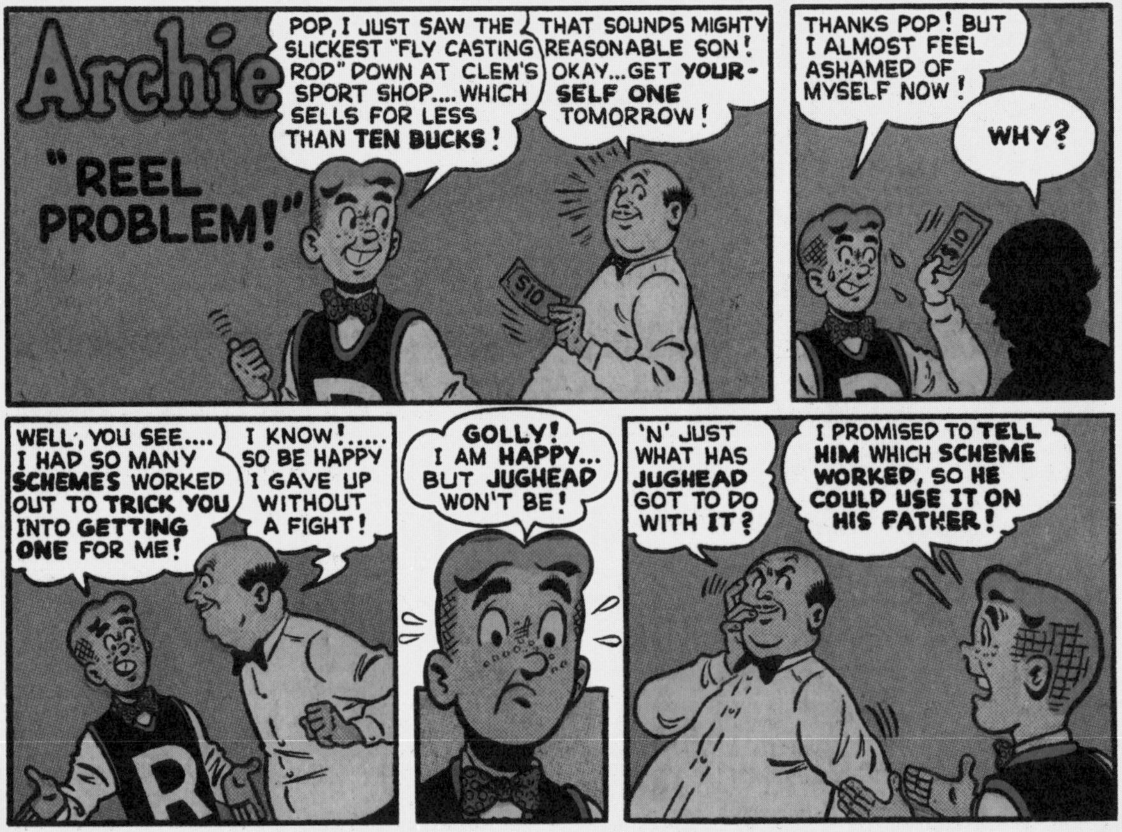
Archie
"REEL PROBLEM!"
POP, I JUST SAW THE SLICKEST "FLY CASTING ROD" DOWN AT CLEM'S SPORT SHOP.... WHICH SELLS FOR LESS THAN TEN BUCKS!
THAT SOUNDS MIGHTY REASONABLE SON! OKAY...GET YOURSELF ONE TOMORROW!
$10
THANKS POP! BUT I ALMOST FEEL ASHAMED OF MYSELF NOW!
WHY?
$10
WELL, YOU SEE.... I HAD SO MANY SCHEMES WORKED OUT TO TRICK YOU INTO GETTING ONE FOR ME!
I KNOW!..... SO BE HAPPY I GAVE UP WITHOUT A FIGHT!
GOLLY! I AM HAPPY... BUT JUGHEAD WON'T BE!
'N' JUST WHAT HAS JUGHEAD GOT TO DO WITH IT?
I PROMISED TO TELL HIM WHICH SCHEME WORKED, SO HE COULD USE IT ON HIS FATHER!

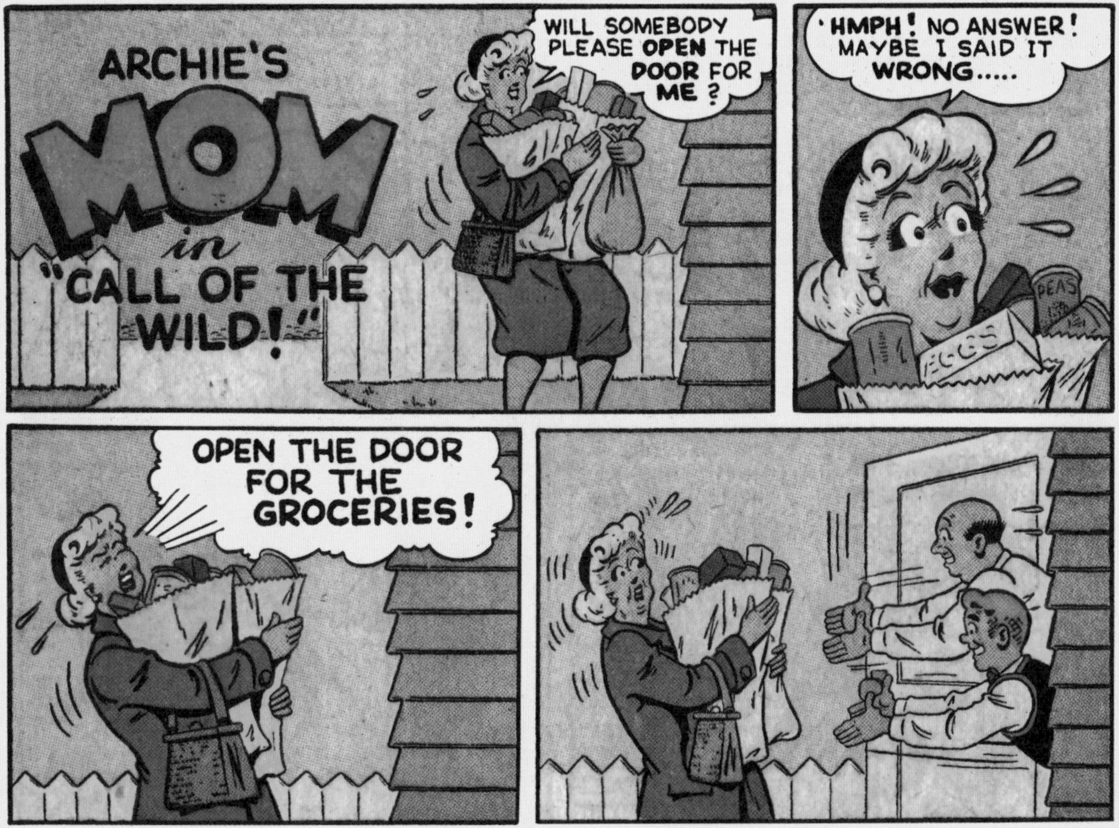
ARCHIE'S MOM in "CALL OF THE WILD!"
WILL SOMEBODY PLEASE OPEN THE DOOR FOR ME ?
'HMPH! NO ANSWER! MAYBE I SAID IT WRONG.....
EGGS
PEAS
OPEN THE DOOR FOR THE GROCERIES!

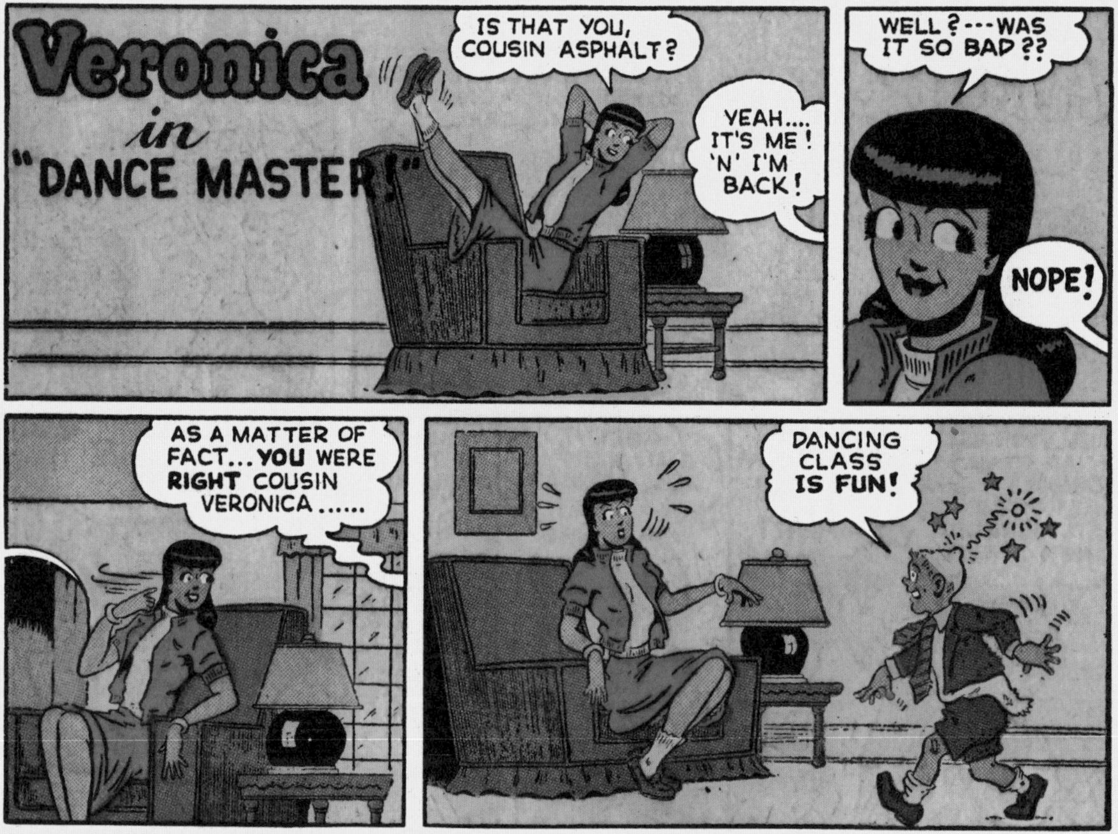
Veronica
in
"DANCE MASTER!"
IS THAT YOU, COUSIN ASPHALT?
YEAH.... IT'S ME! 'N' I'M BACK!
WELL?---WAS IT SO BAD??
NOPE!
AS A MATTER OF FACT...YOU WERE RIGHT COUSIN VERONICA......
DANCING CLASS IS FUN!

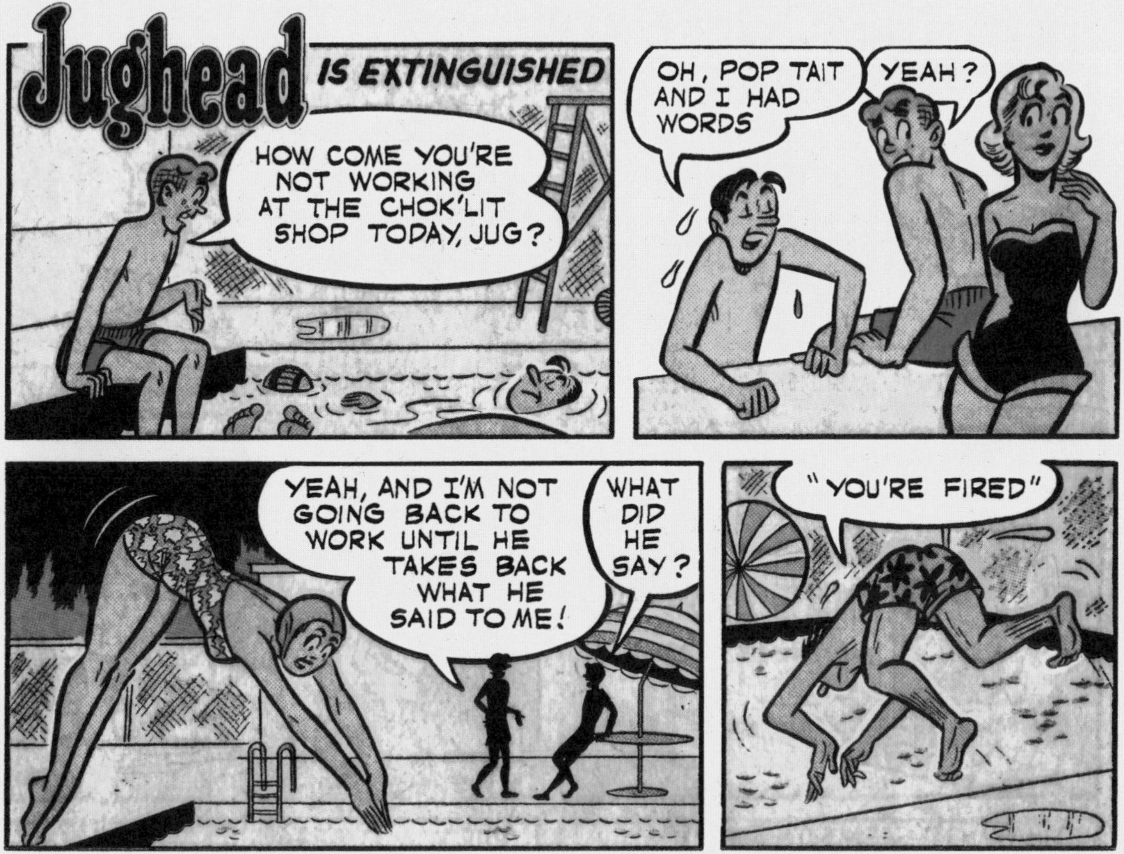
Jughead IS EXTINGUISHED
HOW COME YOU'RE NOT WORKING AT THE CHOK'LIT SHOP TODAY, JUG?
OH, POP TAIT AND I HAD WORDS
YEAH?
YEAH, AND I'M NOT GOING BACK TO WORK UNTIL HE TAKES BACK WHAT HE SAID TO ME!
WHAT DID HE SAY?
"YOU'RE FIRED"

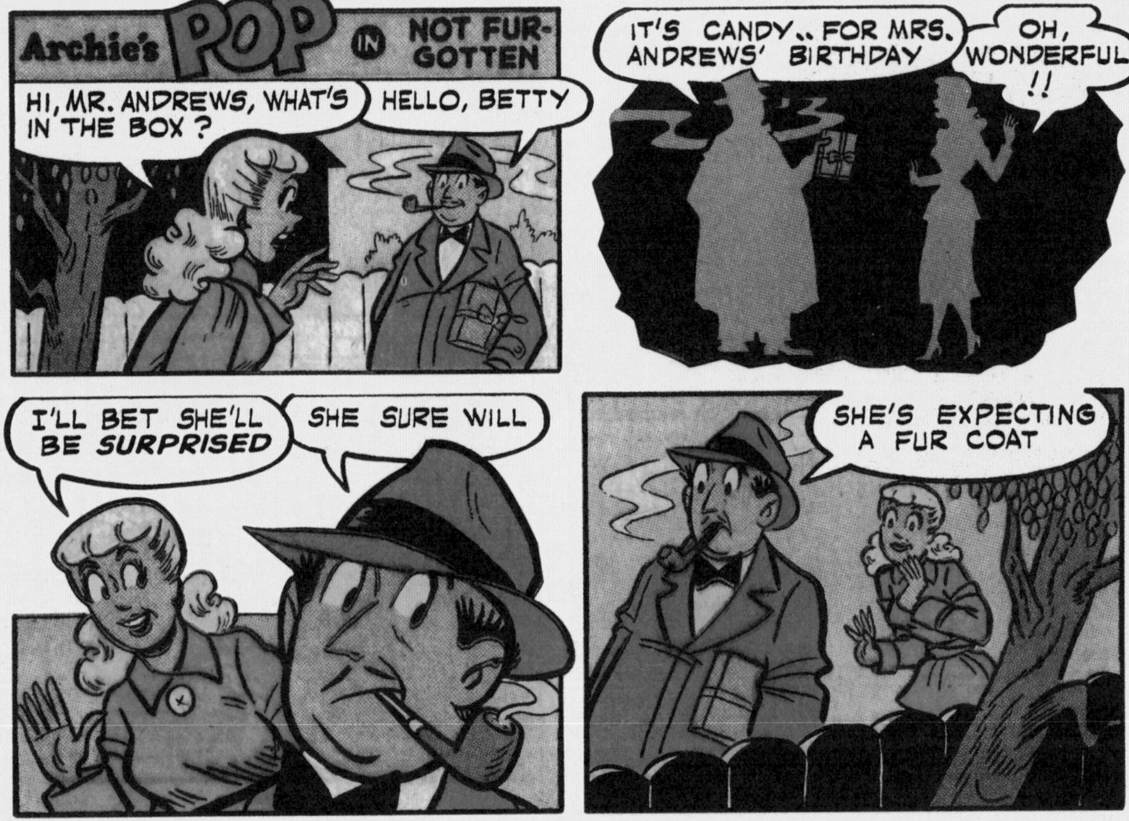
Archie's POP in NOT FUR-GOTTEN
HI, MR. ANDREWS, WHAT'S IN THE BOX ?
HELLO, BETTY
IT'S CANDY.. FOR MRS. ANDREWS' BIRTHDAY
OH, WONDERFUL !!
I'LL BET SHE'LL BE *SURPRISED*
SHE SURE WILL
SHE'S EXPECTING A FUR COAT

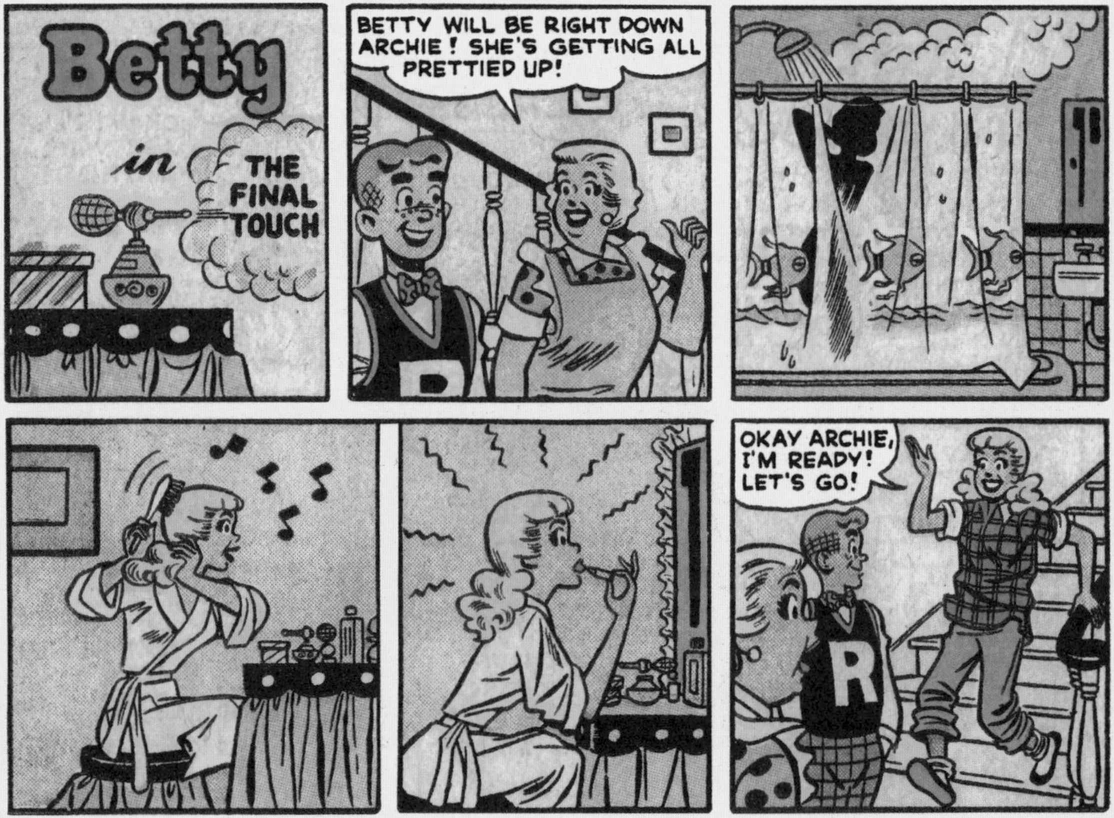
Betty
in
THE FINAL TOUCH
BETTY WILL BE RIGHT DOWN ARCHIE! SHE'S GETTING ALL PRETTIED UP!
OKAY ARCHIE, I'M READY! LET'S GO!

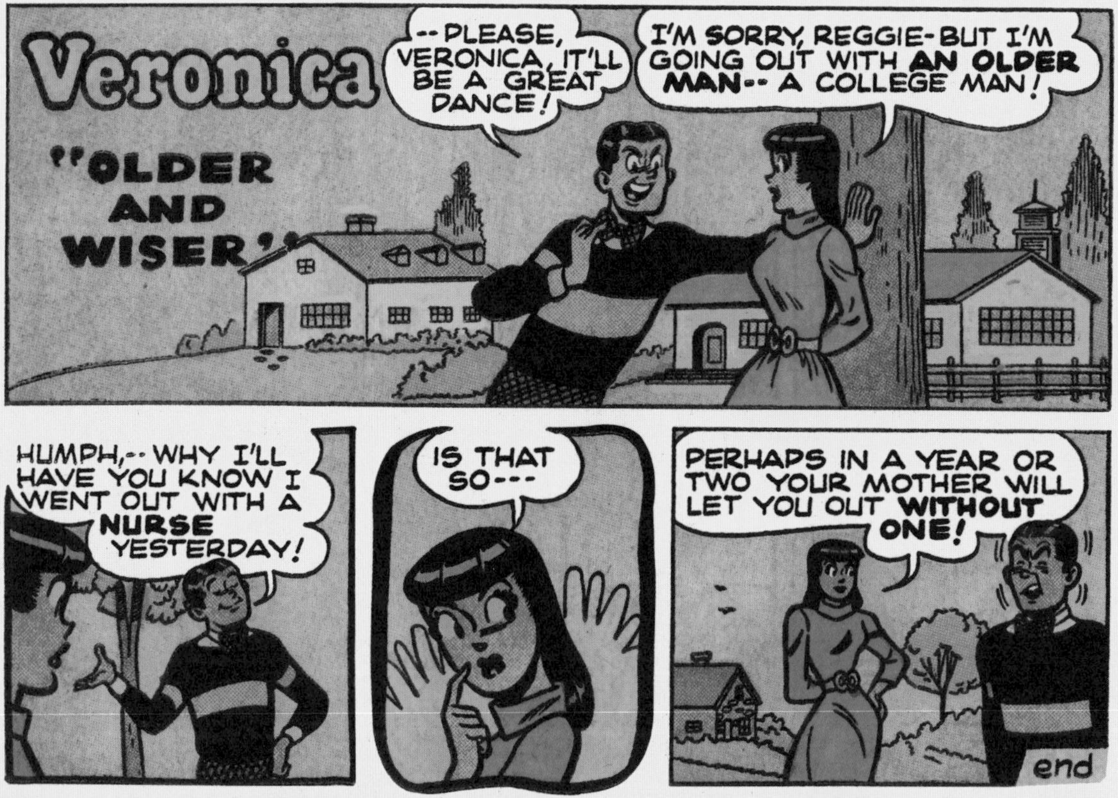
Veronica
"OLDER AND WISER"
-- PLEASE, VERONICA, IT'LL BE A GREAT DANCE!
I'M SORRY, REGGIE- BUT I'M GOING OUT WITH AN OLDER MAN-- A COLLEGE MAN!
HUMPH,-- WHY I'LL HAVE YOU KNOW I WENT OUT WITH A NURSE YESTERDAY!
IS THAT SO---
PERHAPS IN A YEAR OR TWO YOUR MOTHER WILL LET YOU OUT WITHOUT ONE!
end

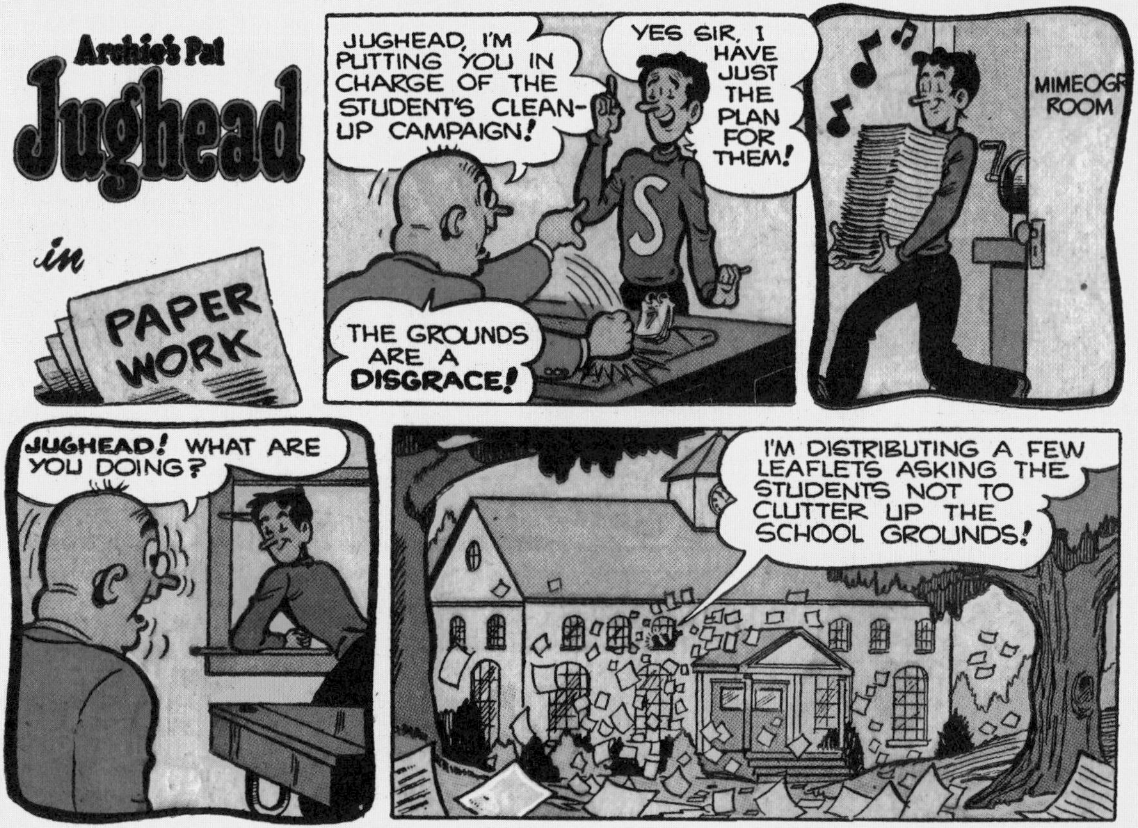

Archie's Pal
Jughead
in
PAPER WORK
JUGHEAD, I'M PUTTING YOU IN CHARGE OF THE STUDENT'S CLEAN-UP CAMPAIGN!
THE GROUNDS ARE A DISGRACE!
YES SIR, I HAVE JUST THE PLAN FOR THEM!
MIMEOGR ROOM
JUGHEAD! WHAT ARE YOU DOING?
I'M DISTRIBUTING A FEW LEAFLETS ASKING THE STUDENTS NOT TO CLUTTER UP THE SCHOOL GROUNDS!

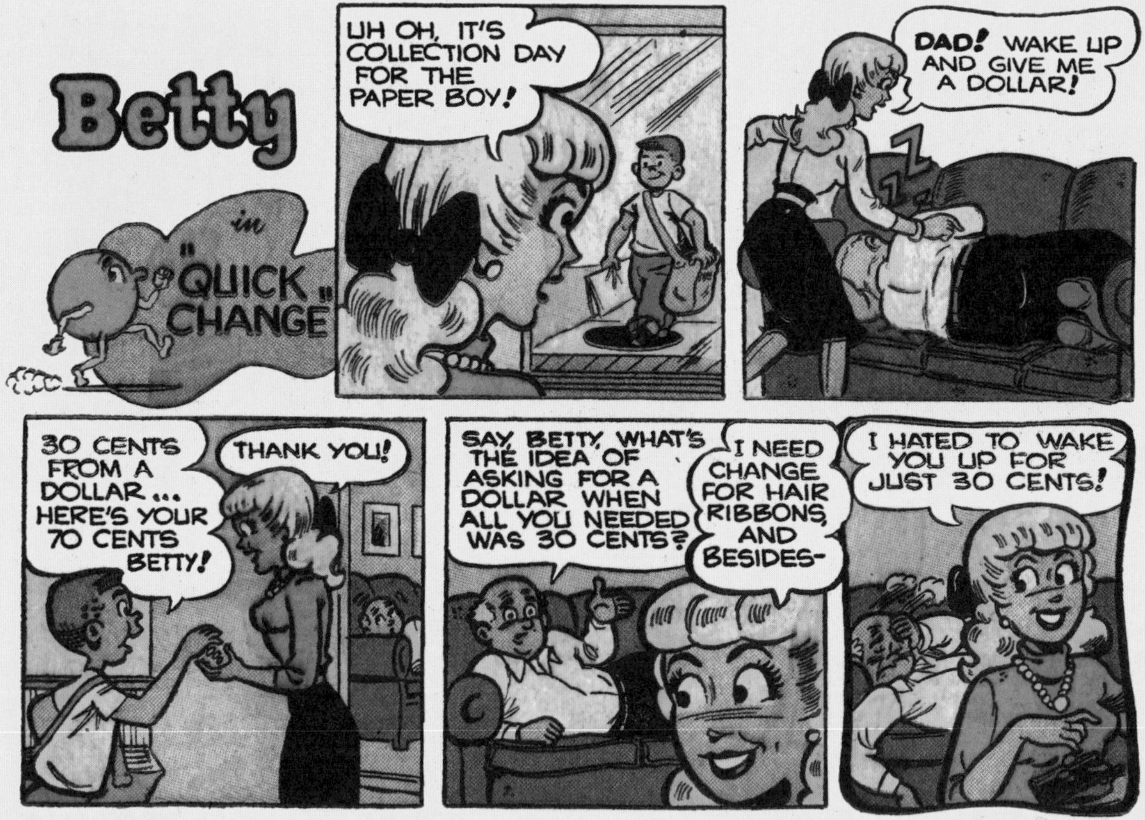
Betty
in
"QUICK CHANGE"
UH OH, IT'S COLLECTION DAY FOR THE PAPER BOY!
DAD! WAKE UP AND GIVE ME A DOLLAR!
Z Z Z
30 CENTS FROM A DOLLAR... HERE'S YOUR 70 CENTS BETTY!
THANK YOU!
SAY, BETTY, WHAT'S THE IDEA OF ASKING FOR A DOLLAR WHEN ALL YOU NEEDED WAS 30 CENTS?
I NEED CHANGE FOR HAIR RIBBONS, AND BESIDES-
I HATED TO WAKE YOU UP FOR JUST 30 CENTS!

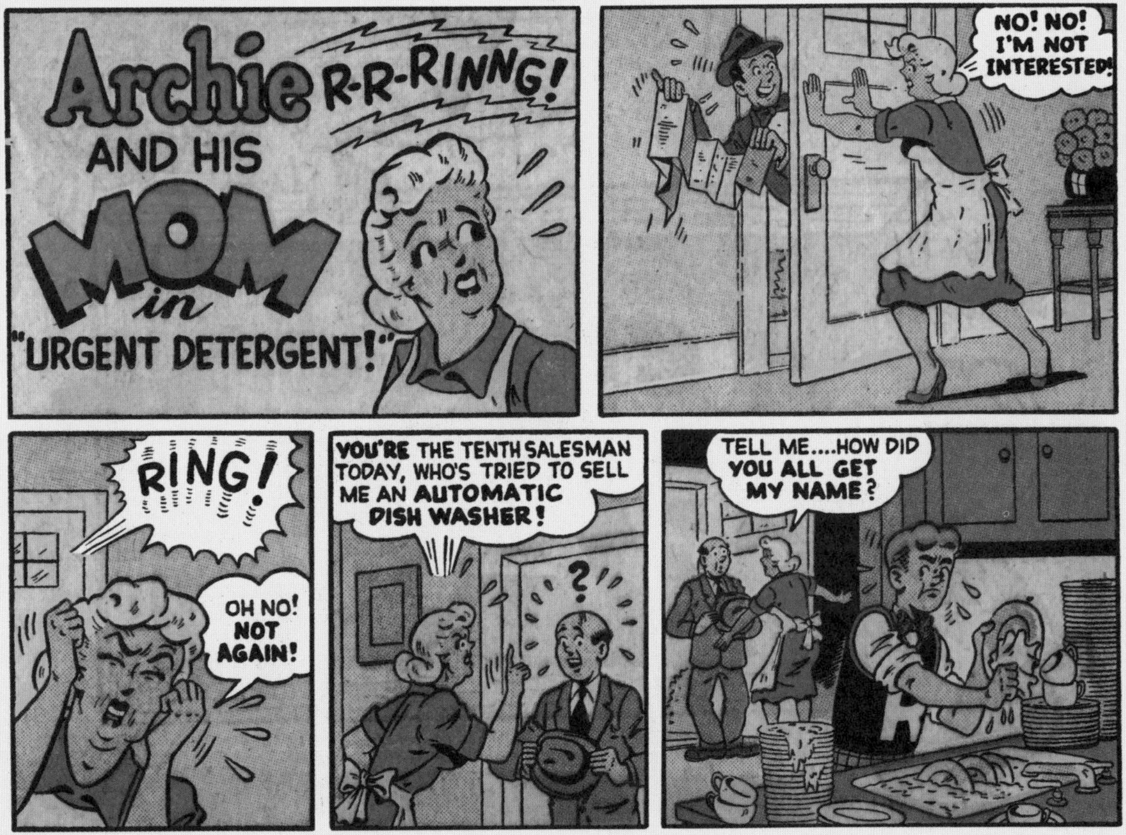
Archie
AND HIS
MOM
in
"URGENT DETERGENT!"
R-R-RINNG!
NO! NO! I'M NOT INTERESTED!
RING!
OH NO! NOT AGAIN!
YOU'RE THE TENTH SALESMAN TODAY, WHO'S TRIED TO SELL ME AN AUTOMATIC DISH WASHER!
?
TELL ME....HOW DID YOU ALL GET MY NAME?

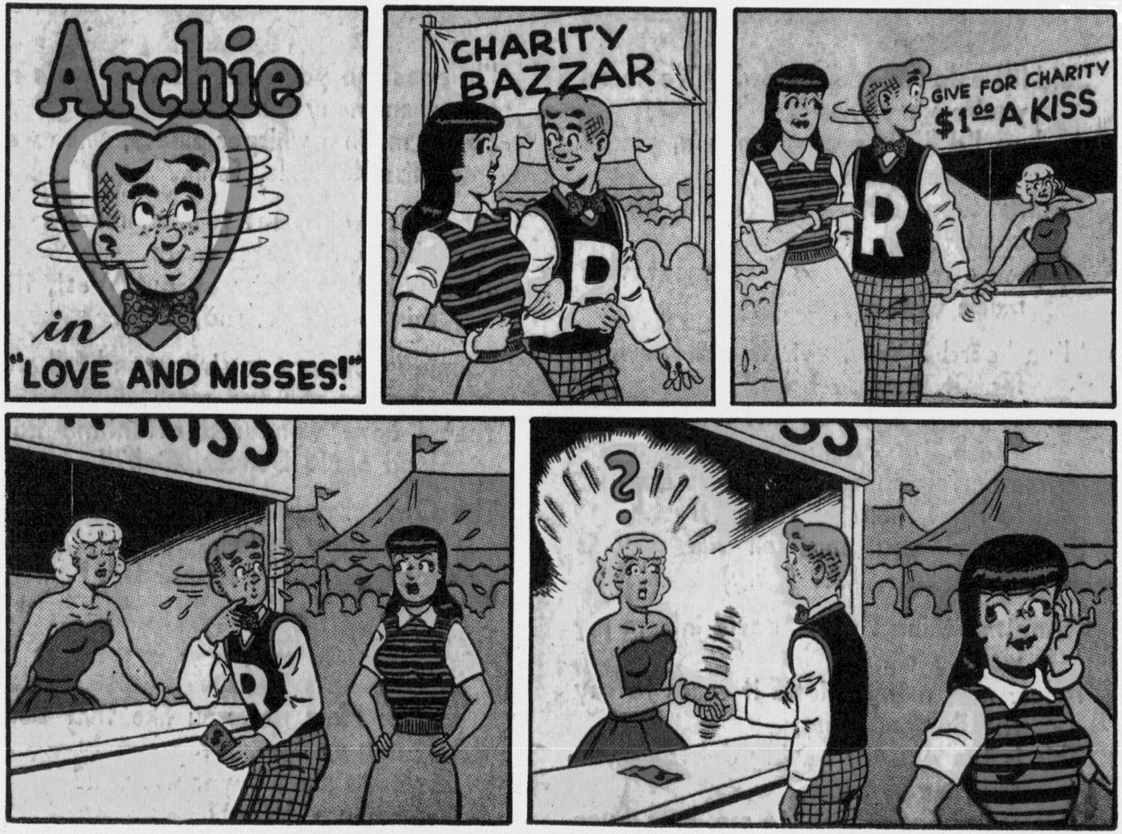
Archie
in
"LOVE AND MISSES!"
CHARITY BAZZAR
GIVE FOR CHARITY
$1.00 A KISS
?

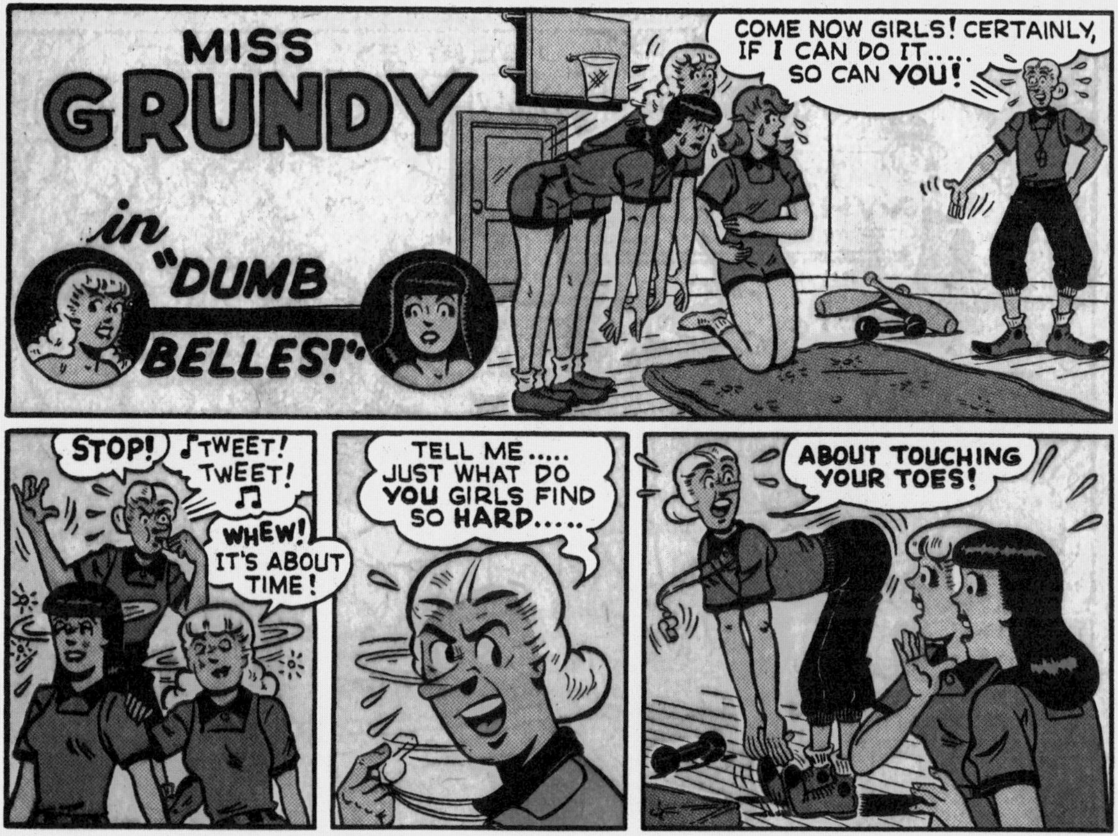
MISS GRUNDY
in "DUMB BELLES!"
COME NOW GIRLS! CERTAINLY, IF I CAN DO IT..... SO CAN YOU!
STOP!
TWEET! TWEET!
WHEW! IT'S ABOUT TIME!
TELL ME..... JUST WHAT DO YOU GIRLS FIND SO HARD.....
ABOUT TOUCHING YOUR TOES!

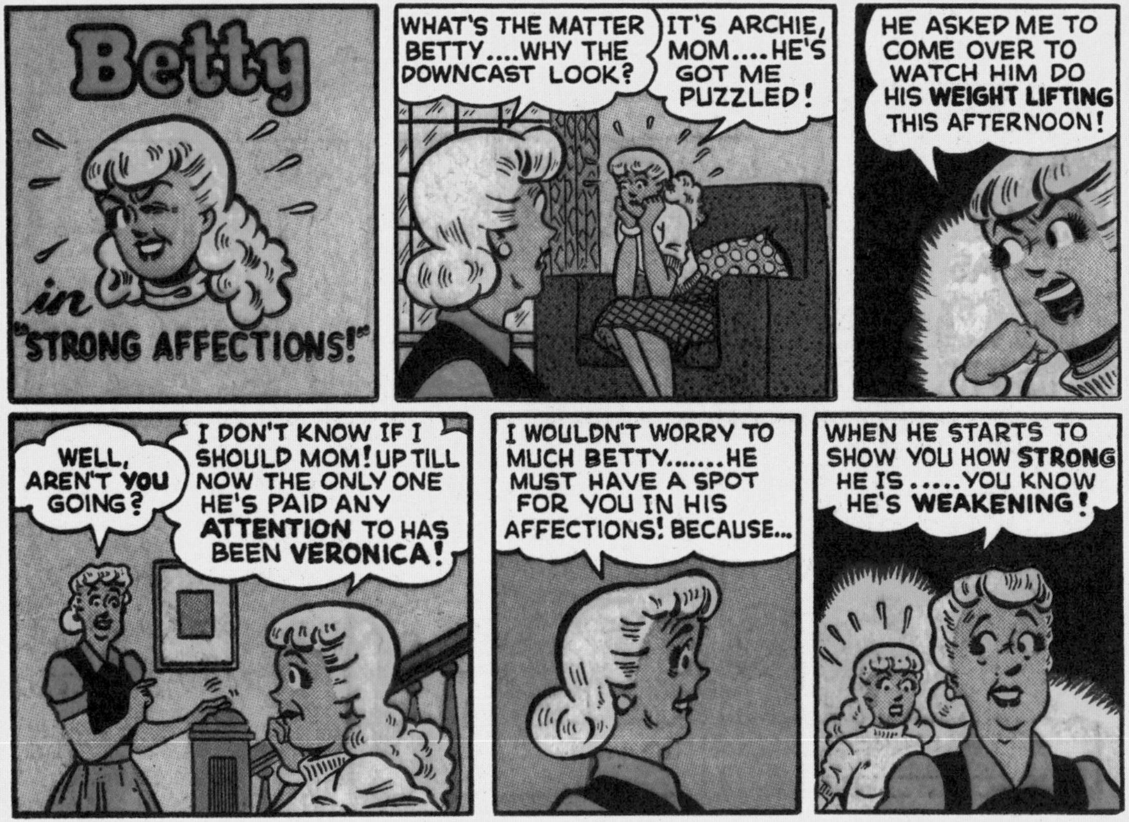
Betty
in
"STRONG AFFECTIONS!"
WHAT'S THE MATTER BETTY....WHY THE DOWNCAST LOOK?
IT'S ARCHIE, MOM....HE'S GOT ME PUZZLED!
HE ASKED ME TO COME OVER TO WATCH HIM DO HIS WEIGHT LIFTING THIS AFTERNOON!
WELL, AREN'T YOU GOING?
I DON'T KNOW IF I SHOULD MOM! UP TILL NOW THE ONLY ONE HE'S PAID ANY ATTENTION TO HAS BEEN VERONICA!
I WOULDN'T WORRY TO MUCH BETTY.......HE MUST HAVE A SPOT FOR YOU IN HIS AFFECTIONS! BECAUSE...
WHEN HE STARTS TO SHOW YOU HOW STRONG HE IS .....YOU KNOW HE'S WEAKENING!

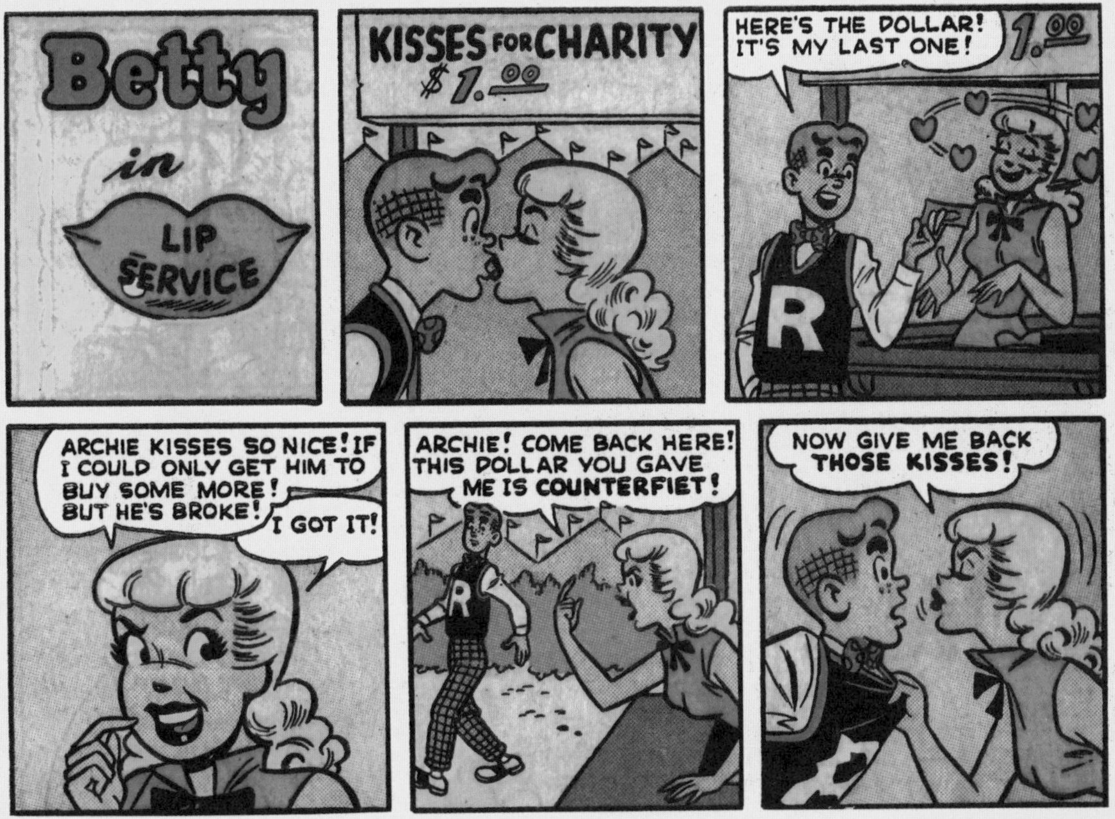
Betty
in
LIP SERVICE
KISSES FOR CHARITY
$1.00
HERE'S THE DOLLAR! IT'S MY LAST ONE!
1.00
ARCHIE KISSES SO NICE! IF I COULD ONLY GET HIM TO BUY SOME MORE! BUT HE'S BROKE!
I GOT IT!
ARCHIE! COME BACK HERE! THIS DOLLAR YOU GAVE ME IS COUNTERFIET!
NOW GIVE ME BACK THOSE KISSES!

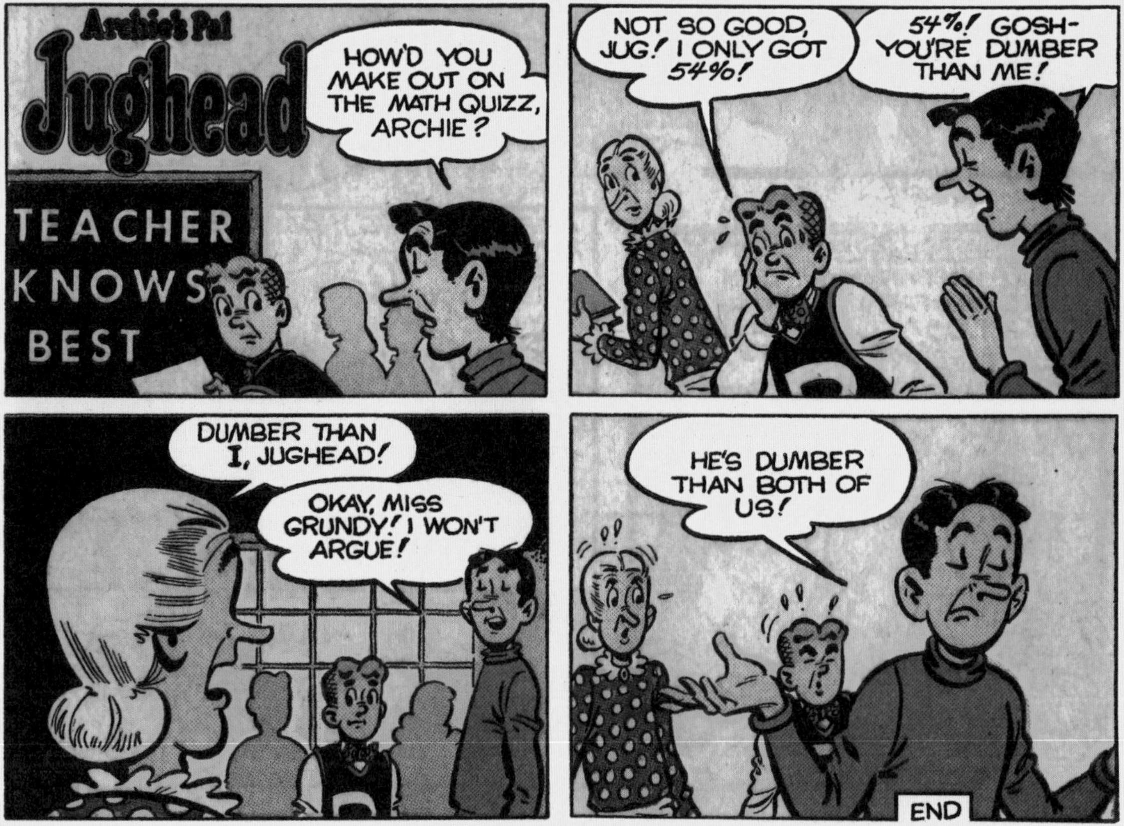
Archie's Pal
Jughead
TEACHER KNOWS BEST
HOW'D YOU MAKE OUT ON THE MATH QUIZZ, ARCHIE?
NOT SO GOOD, JUG! I ONLY GOT 54%!
54%! GOSH- YOU'RE DUMBER THAN ME!
DUMBER THAN I, JUGHEAD!
OKAY, MISS GRUNDY! I WON'T ARGUE!
HE'S DUMBER THAN BOTH OF US!
END

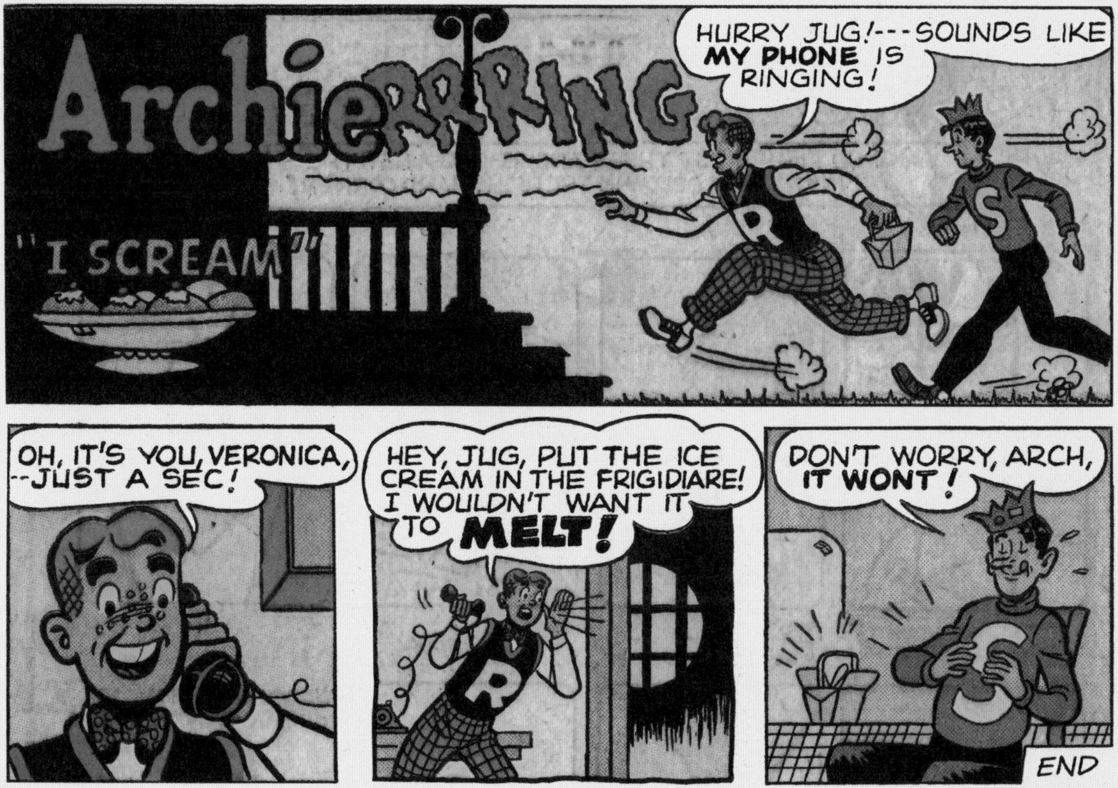
Archie
"I SCREAM"
RRRRING
HURRY JUG!---SOUNDS LIKE MY PHONE IS RINGING!
OH, IT'S YOU, VERONICA, --JUST A SEC!
HEY, JUG, PUT THE ICE CREAM IN THE FRIGIDIARE! I WOULDN'T WANT IT TO MELT!
DON'T WORRY, ARCH, IT WONT!
END

Archie Riddle Diddle

FINISH THESE PUZZLES IN RHYME

HISTORY TEST 100%
G L

W
H G

M D

B
S L

ANSWERS

1. GLAD LAD
2. HIGH GUY
3. MAD DAD
4. SWEATER LETTER

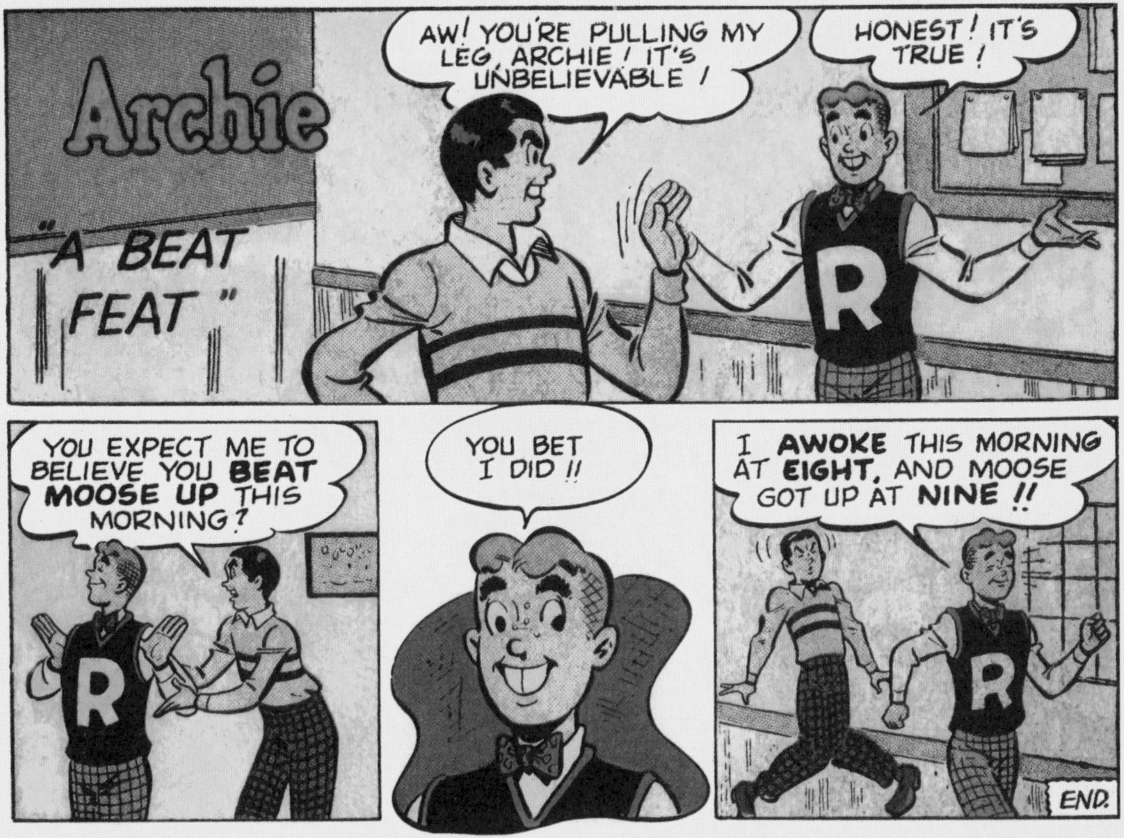
Archie
"A BEAT FEAT"
AW! YOU'RE PULLING MY LEG, ARCHIE! IT'S UNBELIEVABLE!
HONEST! IT'S TRUE!
YOU EXPECT ME TO BELIEVE YOU **BEAT MOOSE UP** THIS MORNING?
YOU BET I DID!!
I **AWOKE** THIS MORNING AT **EIGHT**, AND MOOSE GOT UP AT **NINE**!!
END.

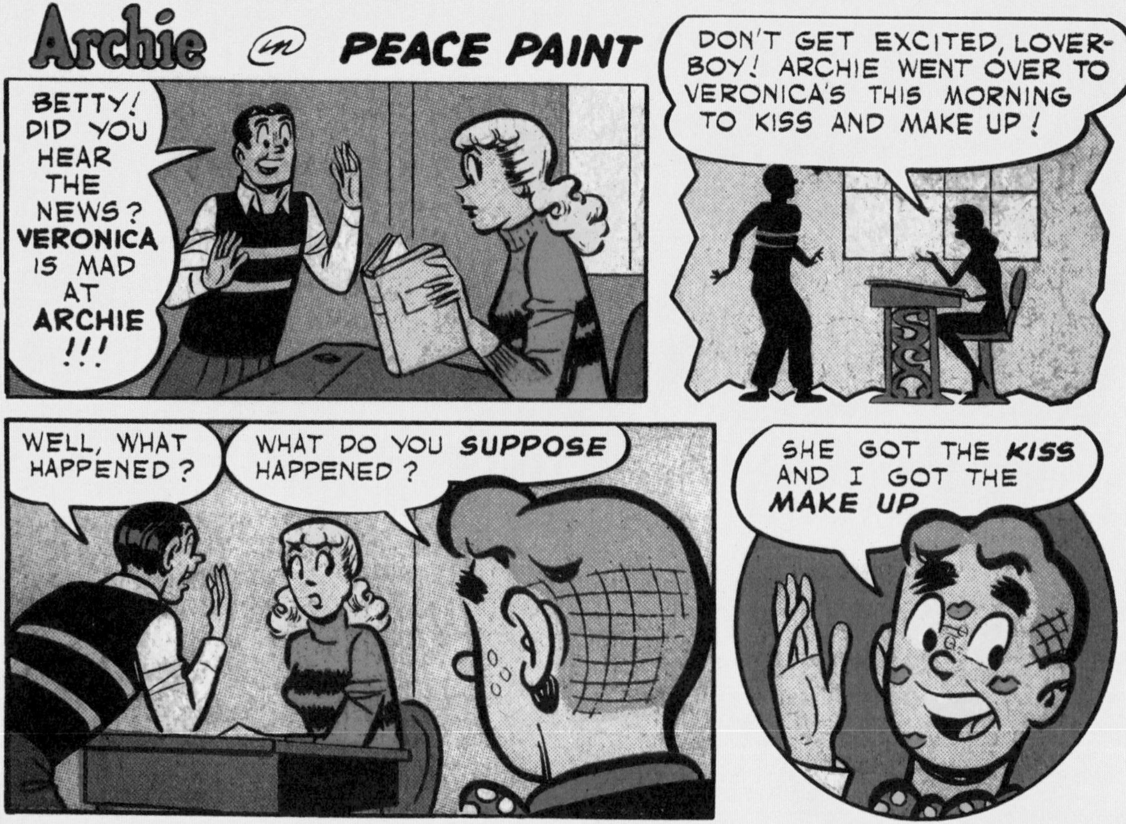
Archie in PEACE PAINT
BETTY! DID YOU HEAR THE NEWS? VERONICA IS MAD AT ARCHIE !!!
DON'T GET EXCITED, LOVER-BOY! ARCHIE WENT OVER TO VERONICA'S THIS MORNING TO KISS AND MAKE UP!
WELL, WHAT HAPPENED?
WHAT DO YOU SUPPOSE HAPPENED?
SHE GOT THE KISS AND I GOT THE MAKE UP

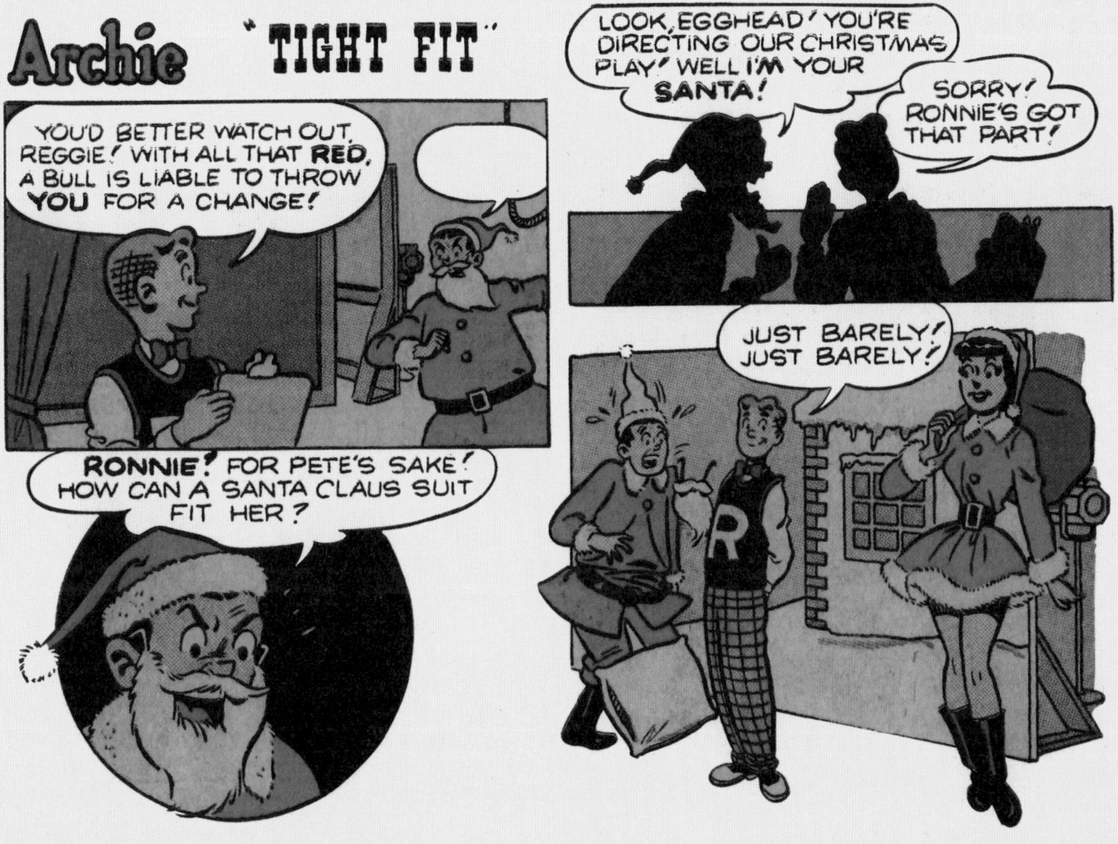
Archie "TIGHT FIT"
YOU'D BETTER WATCH OUT, REGGIE! WITH ALL THAT RED, A BULL IS LIABLE TO THROW YOU FOR A CHANGE!
RONNIE! FOR PETE'S SAKE! HOW CAN A SANTA CLAUS SUIT FIT HER?
LOOK, EGGHEAD! YOU'RE DIRECTING OUR CHRISTMAS PLAY! WELL I'M YOUR SANTA!
SORRY! RONNIE'S GOT THAT PART!
JUST BARELY! JUST BARELY!

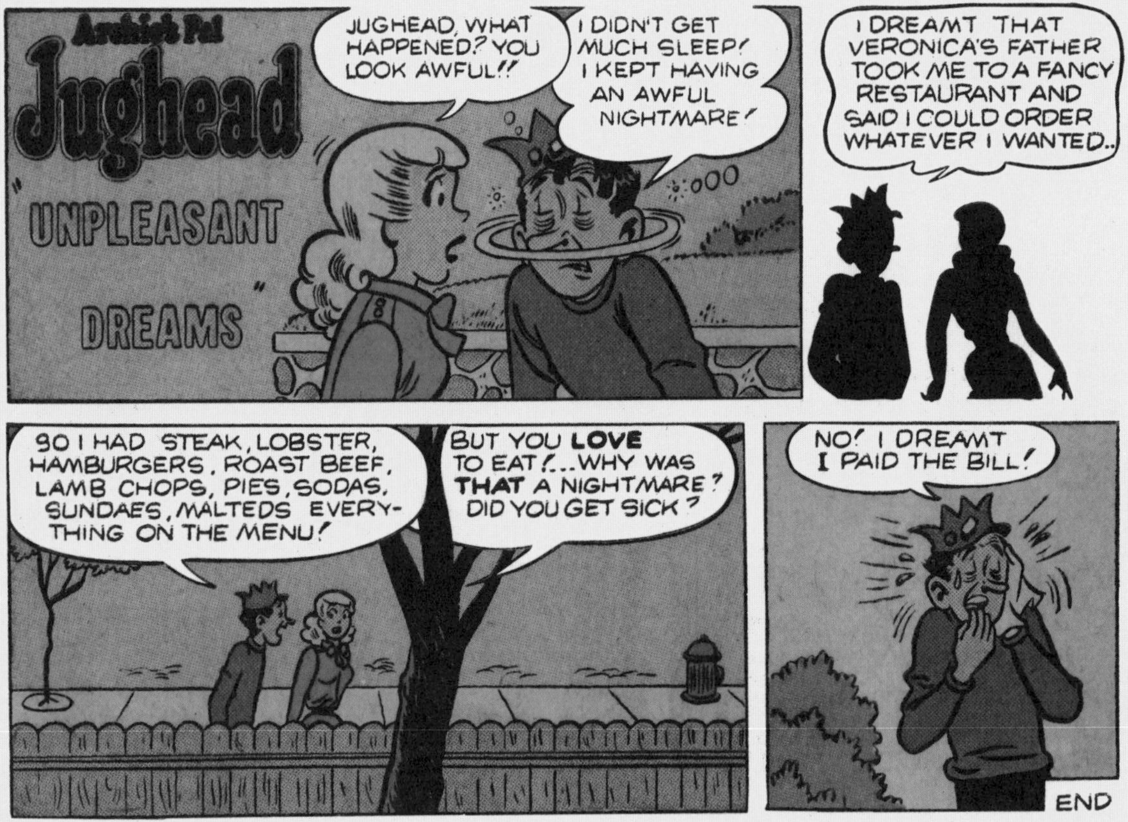
Archie's Pal
Jughead
"UNPLEASANT DREAMS"
JUGHEAD, WHAT HAPPENED? YOU LOOK AWFUL!!
I DIDN'T GET MUCH SLEEP! I KEPT HAVING AN AWFUL NIGHTMARE!
I DREAMT THAT VERONICA'S FATHER TOOK ME TO A FANCY RESTAURANT AND SAID I COULD ORDER WHATEVER I WANTED..
SO I HAD STEAK, LOBSTER, HAMBURGERS, ROAST BEEF, LAMB CHOPS, PIES, SODAS, SUNDAES, MALTEDS EVERY-THING ON THE MENU!
BUT YOU LOVE TO EAT!...WHY WAS THAT A NIGHTMARE? DID YOU GET SICK?
NO! I DREAMT I PAID THE BILL!
END

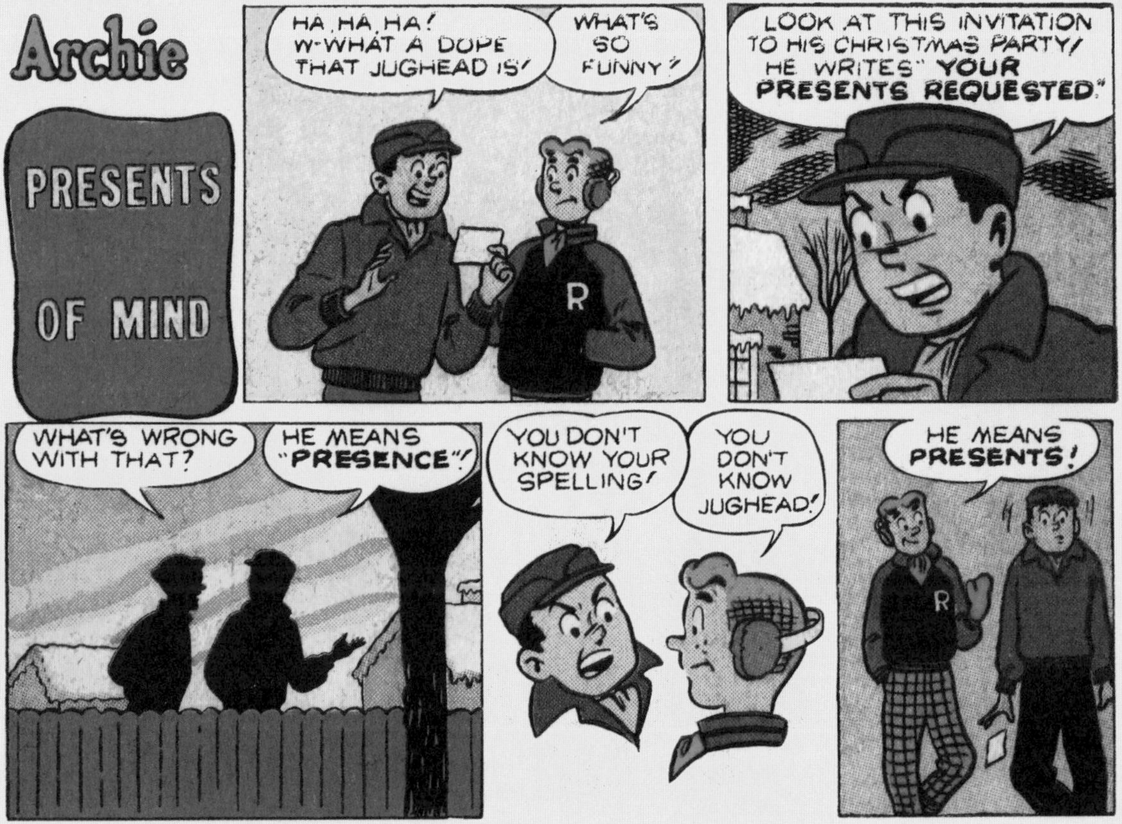

Archie
PRESENTS OF MIND
HA, HA, HA! W-WHAT A DOPE THAT JUGHEAD IS!
WHAT'S SO FUNNY?
LOOK AT THIS INVITATION TO HIS CHRISTMAS PARTY! HE WRITES "YOUR PRESENTS REQUESTED."
WHAT'S WRONG WITH THAT?
HE MEANS "PRESENCE"!
YOU DON'T KNOW YOUR SPELLING!
YOU DON'T KNOW JUGHEAD!
HE MEANS PRESENTS!

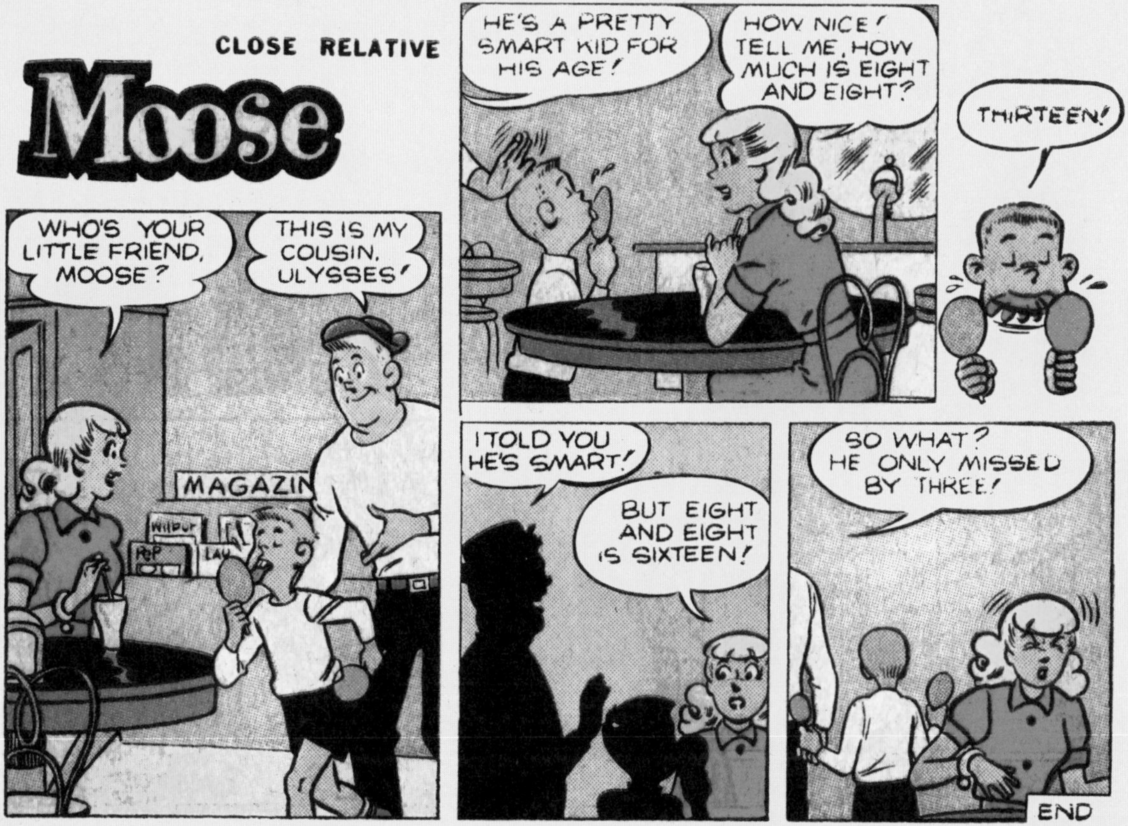
CLOSE RELATIVE
Moose
WHO'S YOUR LITTLE FRIEND, MOOSE?
THIS IS MY COUSIN, ULYSSES!
MAGAZIN
HE'S A PRETTY SMART KID FOR HIS AGE!
HOW NICE! TELL ME, HOW MUCH IS EIGHT AND EIGHT?
THIRTEEN!
I TOLD YOU HE'S SMART!
BUT EIGHT AND EIGHT IS SIXTEEN!
SO WHAT? HE ONLY MISSED BY THREE!
END

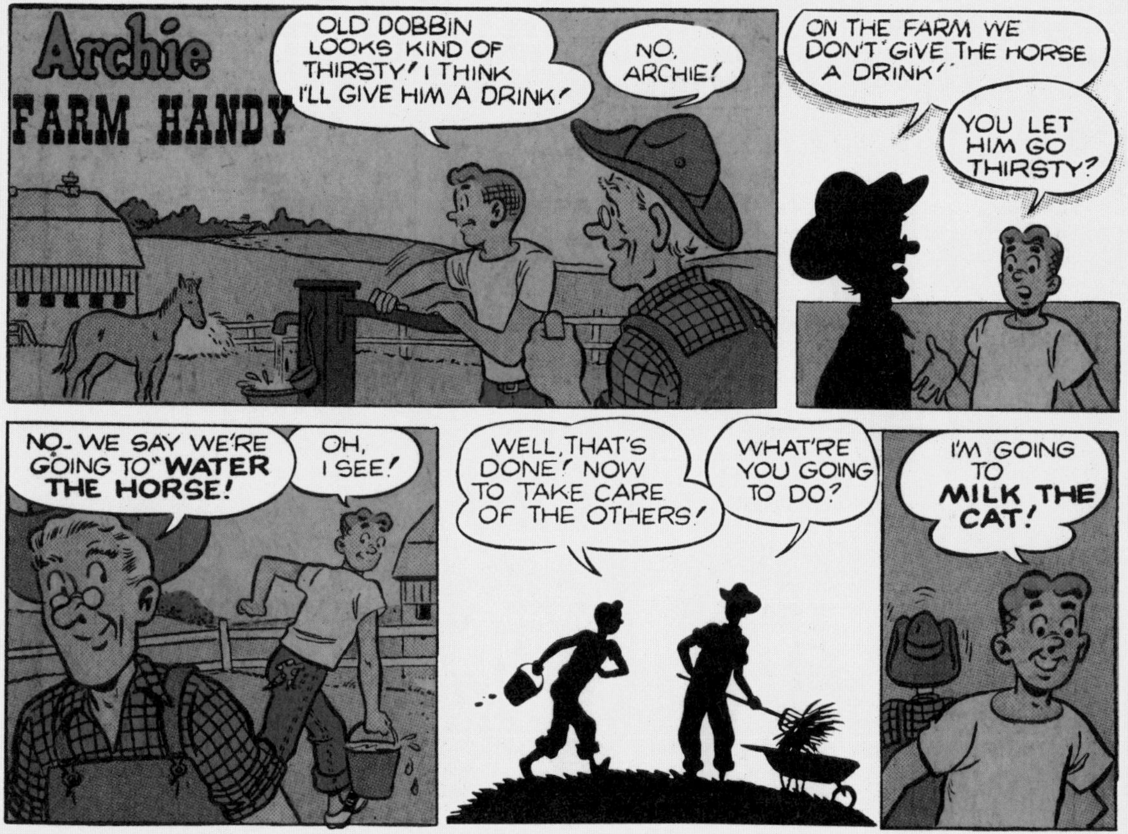
Archie
FARM HANDY
OLD DOBBIN LOOKS KIND OF THIRSTY! I THINK I'LL GIVE HIM A DRINK!
NO, ARCHIE!
ON THE FARM WE DON'T "GIVE THE HORSE A DRINK"
YOU LET HIM GO THIRSTY?
NO- WE SAY WE'RE GOING TO "WATER THE HORSE!
OH, I SEE!
WELL, THAT'S DONE! NOW TO TAKE CARE OF THE OTHERS!
WHAT'RE YOU GOING TO DO?
I'M GOING TO MILK THE CAT!

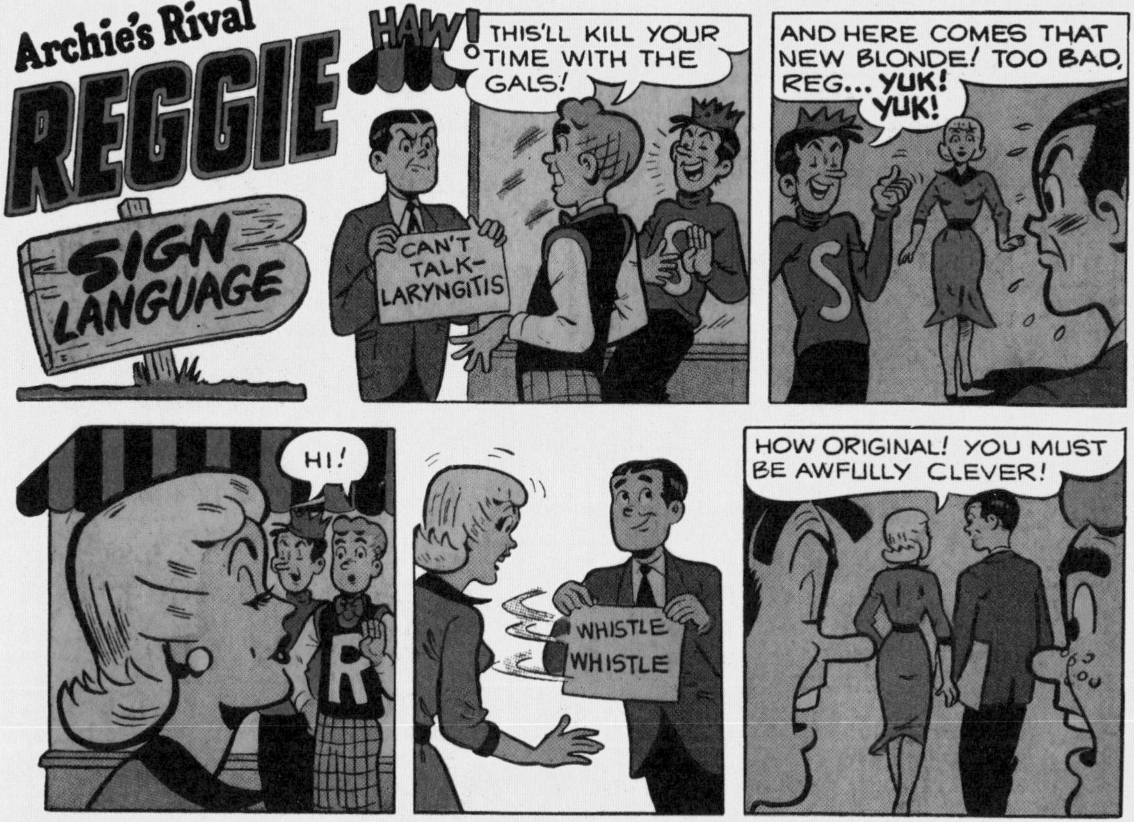

Archie's Rival
REGGIE
SIGN LANGUAGE
HAW!
THIS'LL KILL YOUR TIME WITH THE GALS!
CAN'T TALK-LARYNGITIS
AND HERE COMES THAT NEW BLONDE! TOO BAD, REG... YUK! YUK!
HI!
WHISTLE WHISTLE
HOW ORIGINAL! YOU MUST BE AWFULLY CLEVER!

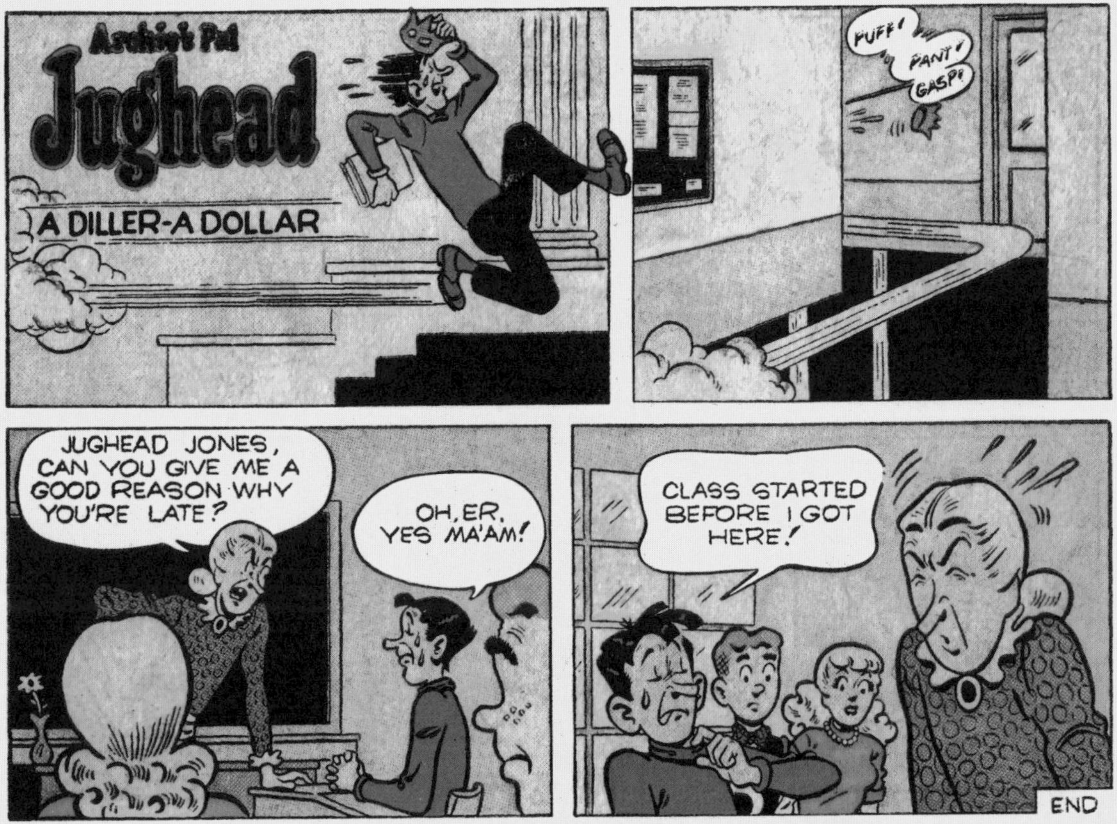
Archie's Pal
Jughead
A DILLER-A DOLLAR
PUFF!
PANT!
GASP!
JUGHEAD JONES, CAN YOU GIVE ME A GOOD REASON WHY YOU'RE LATE?
OH, ER, YES MA'AM!
CLASS STARTED BEFORE I GOT HERE!
END

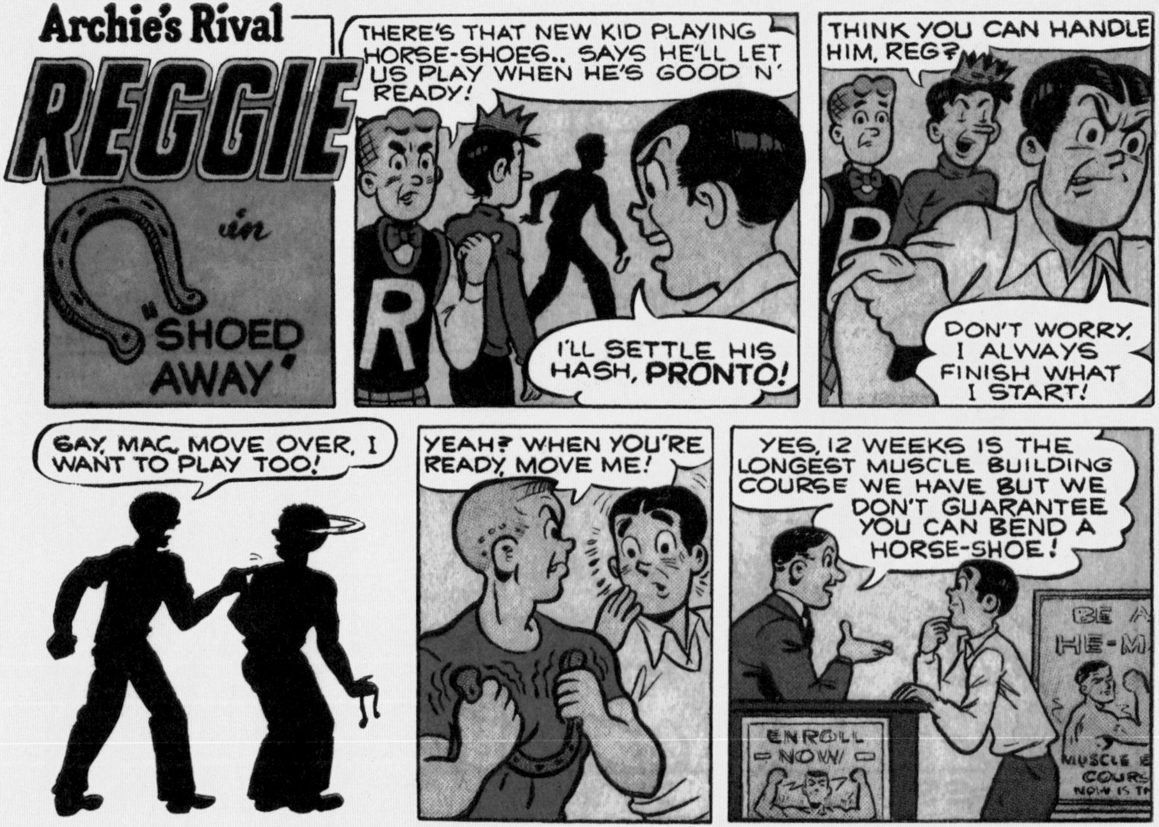
Archie's Rival
REGGIE
in
"SHOED AWAY"
THERE'S THAT NEW KID PLAYING HORSE-SHOES.. SAYS HE'LL LET US PLAY WHEN HE'S GOOD N' READY!
I'LL SETTLE HIS HASH, PRONTO!
THINK YOU CAN HANDLE HIM, REG?
DON'T WORRY, I ALWAYS FINISH WHAT I START!
SAY, MAC, MOVE OVER, I WANT TO PLAY TOO!
YEAH? WHEN YOU'RE READY, MOVE ME!
YES, 12 WEEKS IS THE LONGEST MUSCLE BUILDING COURSE WE HAVE BUT WE DON'T GUARANTEE YOU CAN BEND A HORSE-SHOE!
ENROLL NOW!

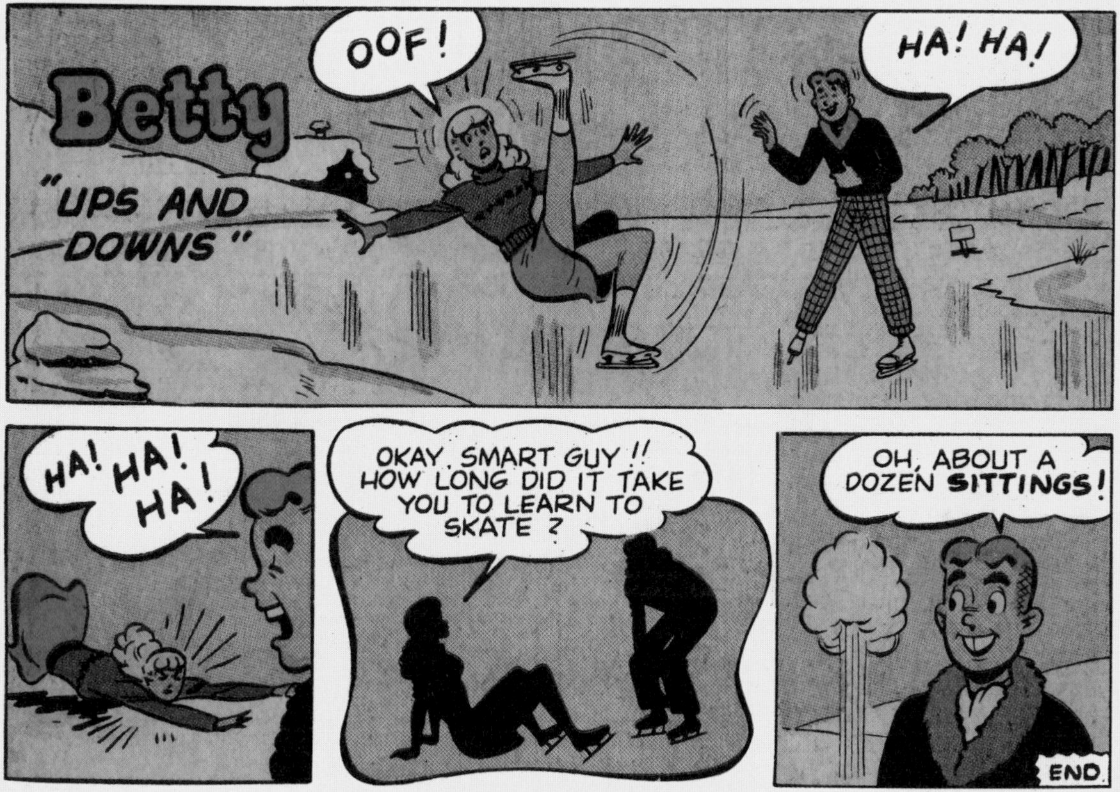
Betty
"UPS AND DOWNS"
OOF!
HA! HA!
HA! HA! HA!
OKAY, SMART GUY !! HOW LONG DID IT TAKE YOU TO LEARN TO SKATE ?
OH, ABOUT A DOZEN SITTINGS!
END

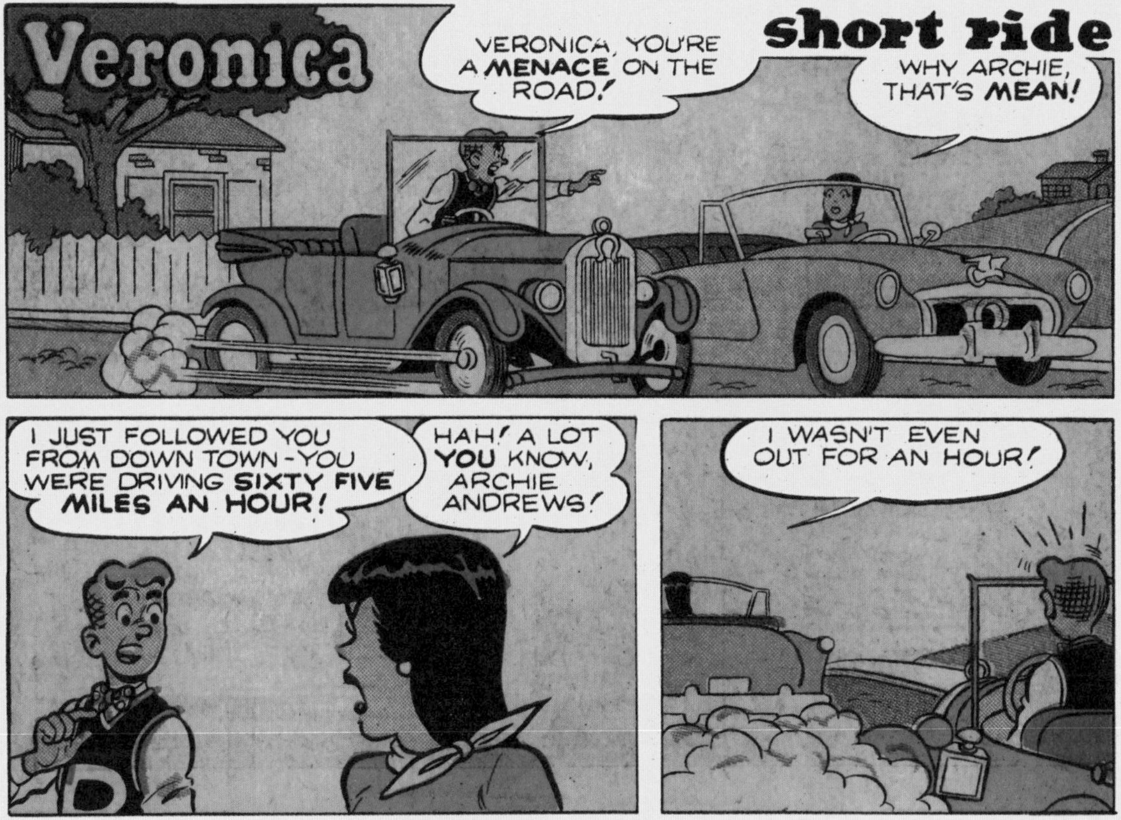
Veronica
short ride
VERONICA, YOU'RE A MENACE ON THE ROAD!
WHY ARCHIE, THAT'S MEAN!
I JUST FOLLOWED YOU FROM DOWN TOWN - YOU WERE DRIVING SIXTY FIVE MILES AN HOUR!
HAH! A LOT YOU KNOW, ARCHIE ANDREWS!
I WASN'T EVEN OUT FOR AN HOUR!

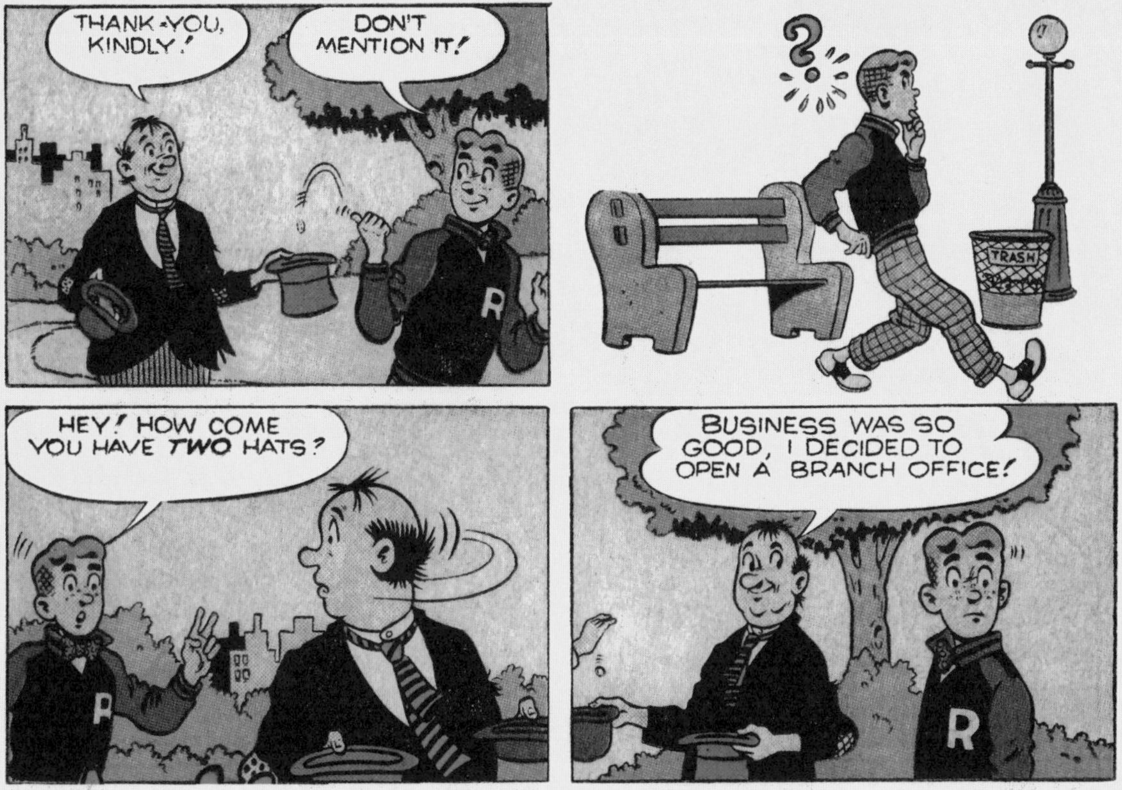
THANK-YOU, KINDLY!
DON'T MENTION IT!
TRASH
HEY! HOW COME YOU HAVE **TWO** HATS?
BUSINESS WAS SO GOOD, I DECIDED TO OPEN A BRANCH OFFICE!

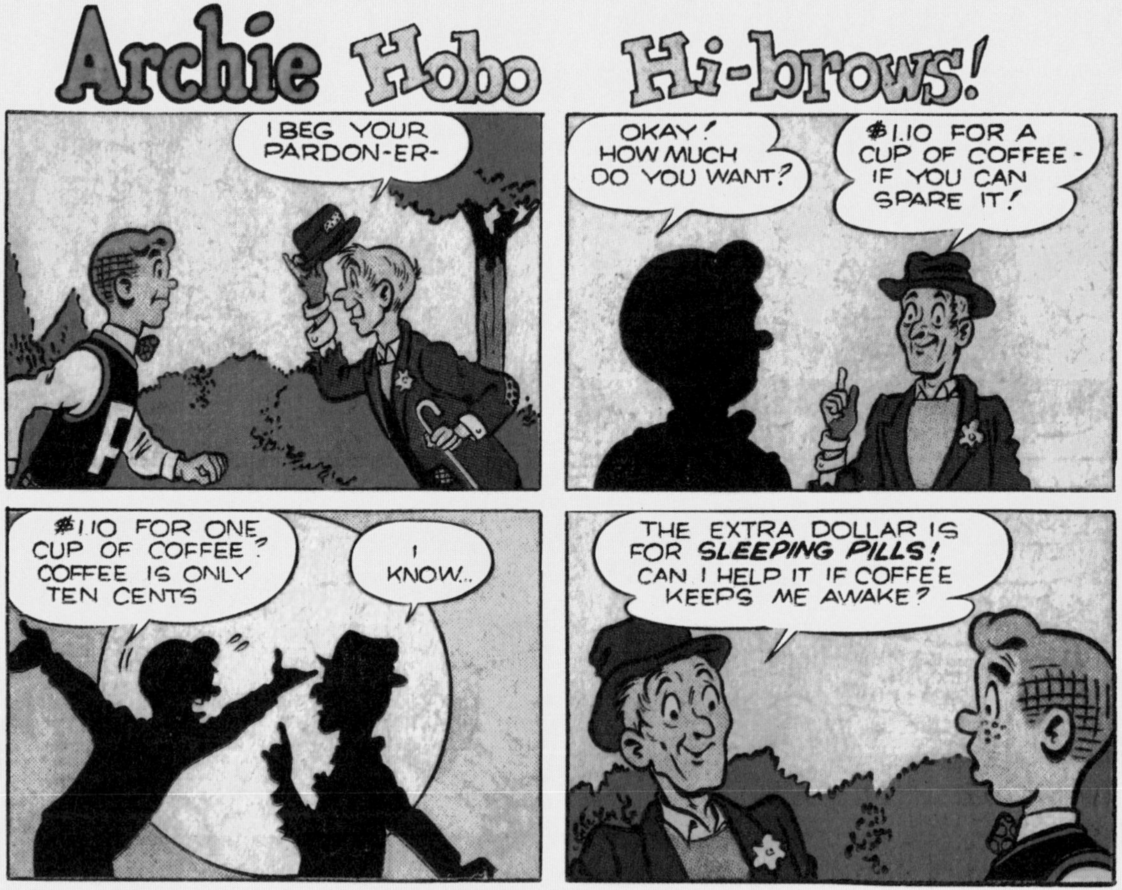
Archie Hobo Hi-brows!
I BEG YOUR PARDON-ER-
OKAY! HOW MUCH DO YOU WANT?
$1.10 FOR A CUP OF COFFEE - IF YOU CAN SPARE IT!
$1.10 FOR ONE CUP OF COFFEE? COFFEE IS ONLY TEN CENTS
I KNOW...
THE EXTRA DOLLAR IS FOR SLEEPING PILLS! CAN I HELP IT IF COFFEE KEEPS ME AWAKE?

MISS GRUNDY "DENTAL HYGIENE"
IN OUR LAST HYGIENE CLASS WE STUDIED SOME OF THE DISEASES TRANSMITTED BY VARIOUS INSECTS...
TODAY, WE SHALL STUDY MEANS OF COMBATING AND PREVENTING SUCH ILLNESS!
MOOSE, WHAT IS BEST MEANS OF PREVENTING INFECTION DUE TO BITING INSECTS?
HAW! 'AT'S AN EASY ONE!
DON'T BITE ANY!
END

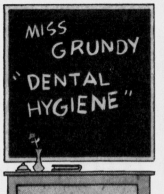

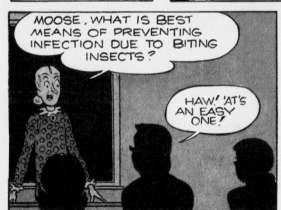

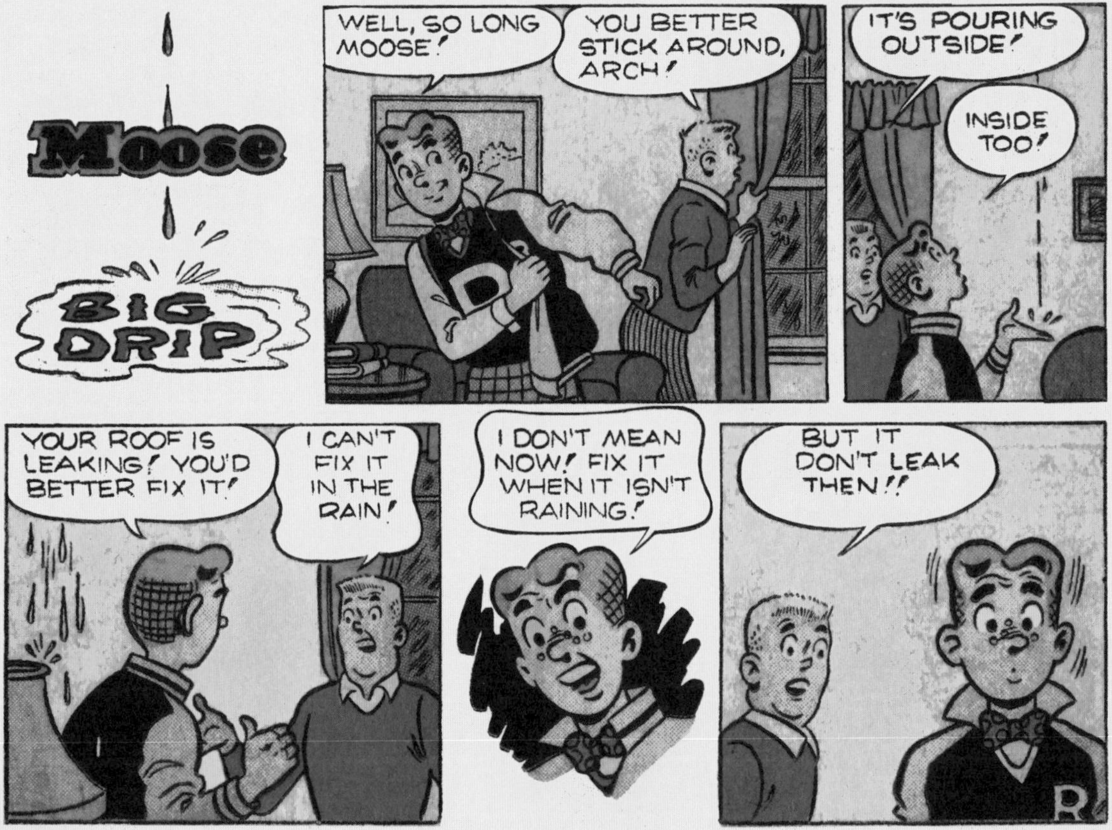
Moose
BIG DRIP
WELL, SO LONG MOOSE!
YOU BETTER STICK AROUND, ARCH!
IT'S POURING OUTSIDE!
INSIDE TOO!
YOUR ROOF IS LEAKING! YOU'D BETTER FIX IT!
I CAN'T FIX IT IN THE RAIN!
I DON'T MEAN NOW! FIX IT WHEN IT ISN'T RAINING!
BUT IT DON'T LEAK THEN!!

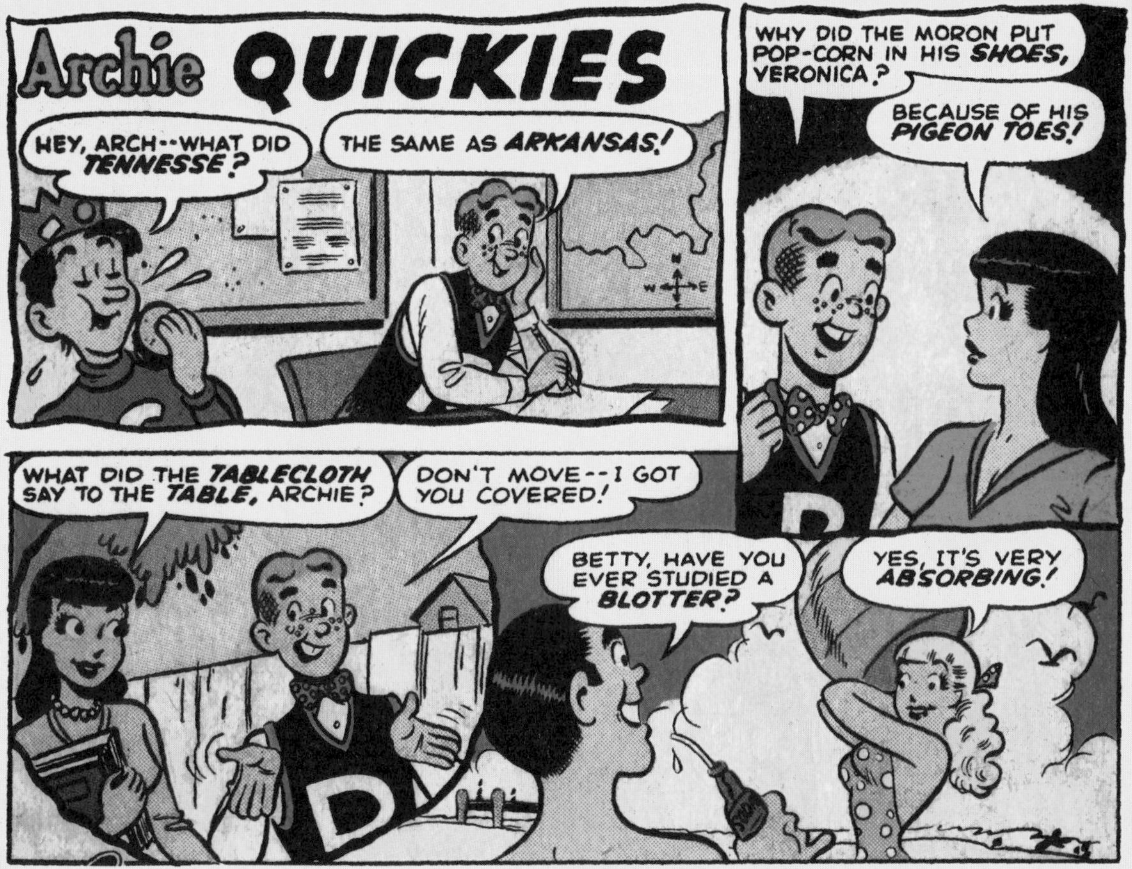
Archie QUICKIES
HEY, ARCH--WHAT DID TENNESSE?
THE SAME AS ARKANSAS!
WHY DID THE MORON PUT POP-CORN IN HIS SHOES, VERONICA?
BECAUSE OF HIS PIGEON TOES!
WHAT DID THE TABLECLOTH SAY TO THE TABLE, ARCHIE?
DON'T MOVE--I GOT YOU COVERED!
BETTY, HAVE YOU EVER STUDIED A BLOTTER?
YES, IT'S VERY ABSORBING!

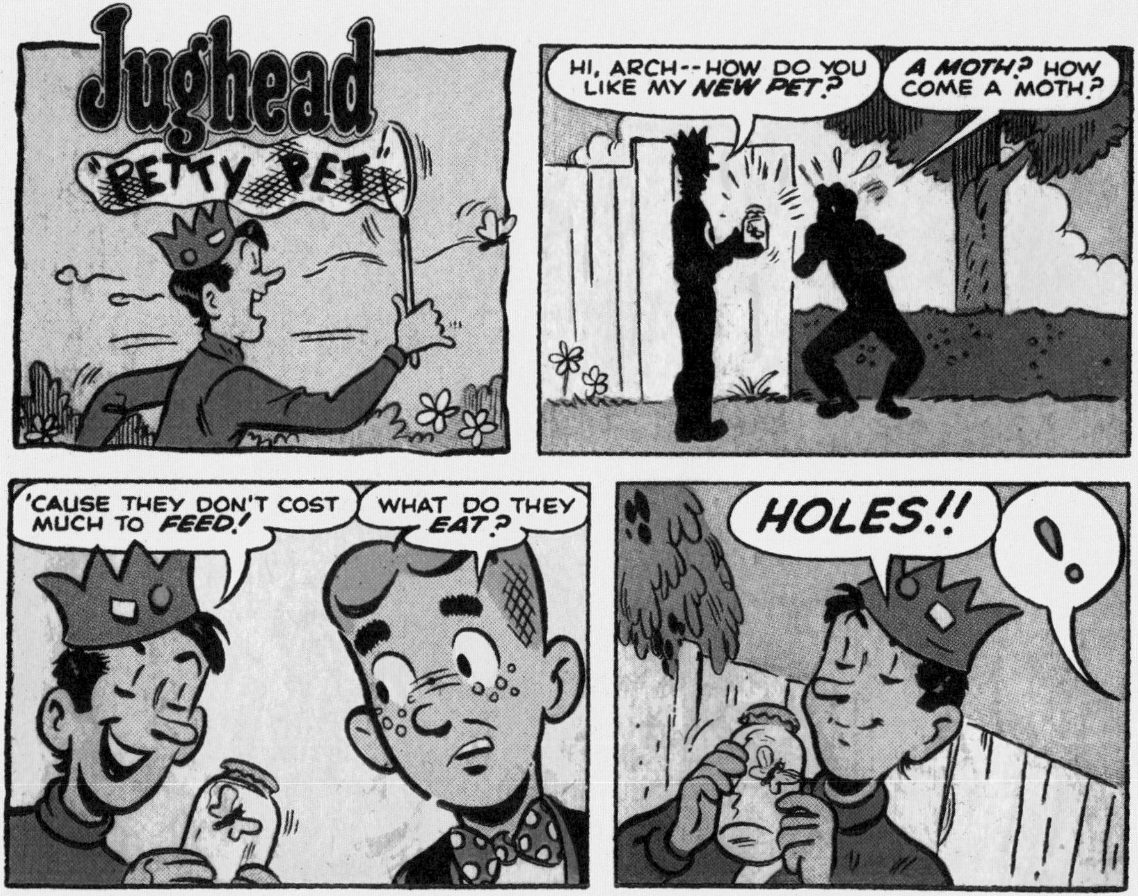
Jughead
"PETTY PET"
HI, ARCH--HOW DO YOU LIKE MY NEW PET?
A MOTH? HOW COME A MOTH?
'CAUSE THEY DON'T COST MUCH TO FEED!
WHAT DO THEY EAT?
HOLES!!
!

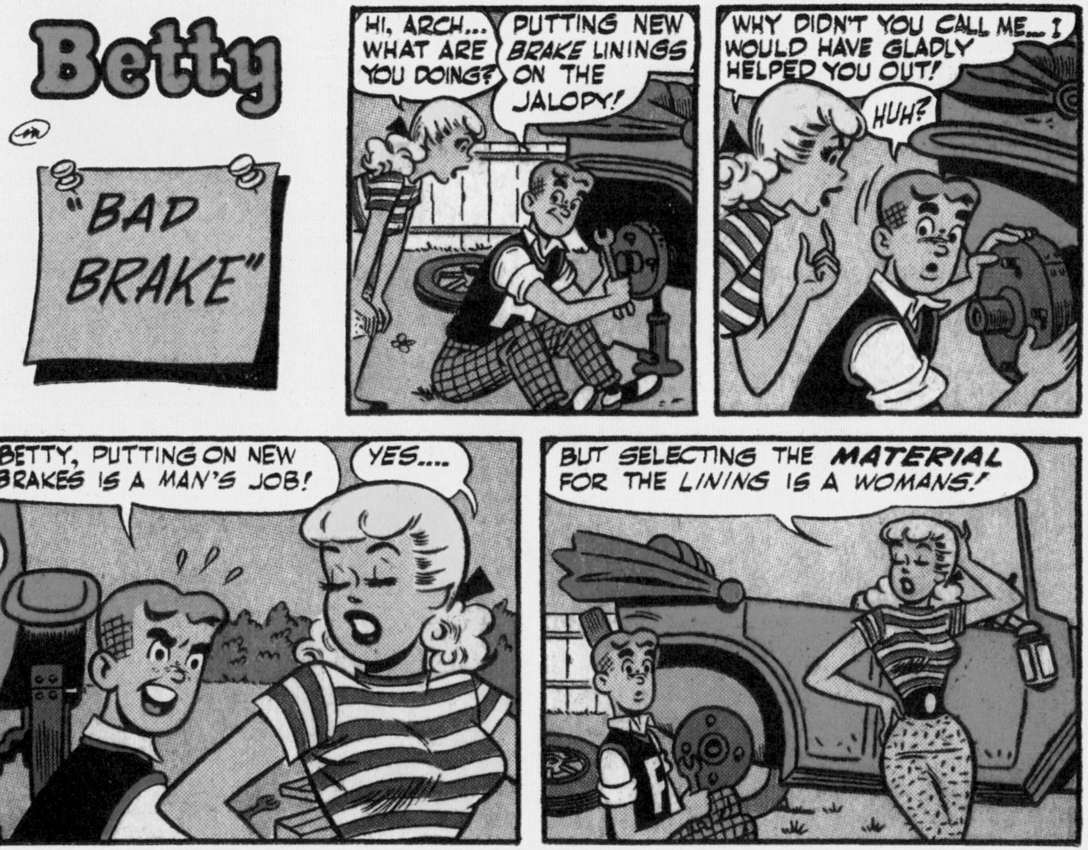
Betty
in
"BAD BRAKE"
HI, ARCH... WHAT ARE YOU DOING?
PUTTING NEW BRAKE LININGS ON THE JALOPY!
WHY DIDN'T YOU CALL ME... I WOULD HAVE GLADLY HELPED YOU OUT!
HUH?
BETTY, PUTTING ON NEW BRAKES IS A MAN'S JOB!
YES....
BUT SELECTING THE MATERIAL FOR THE LINING IS A WOMANS!

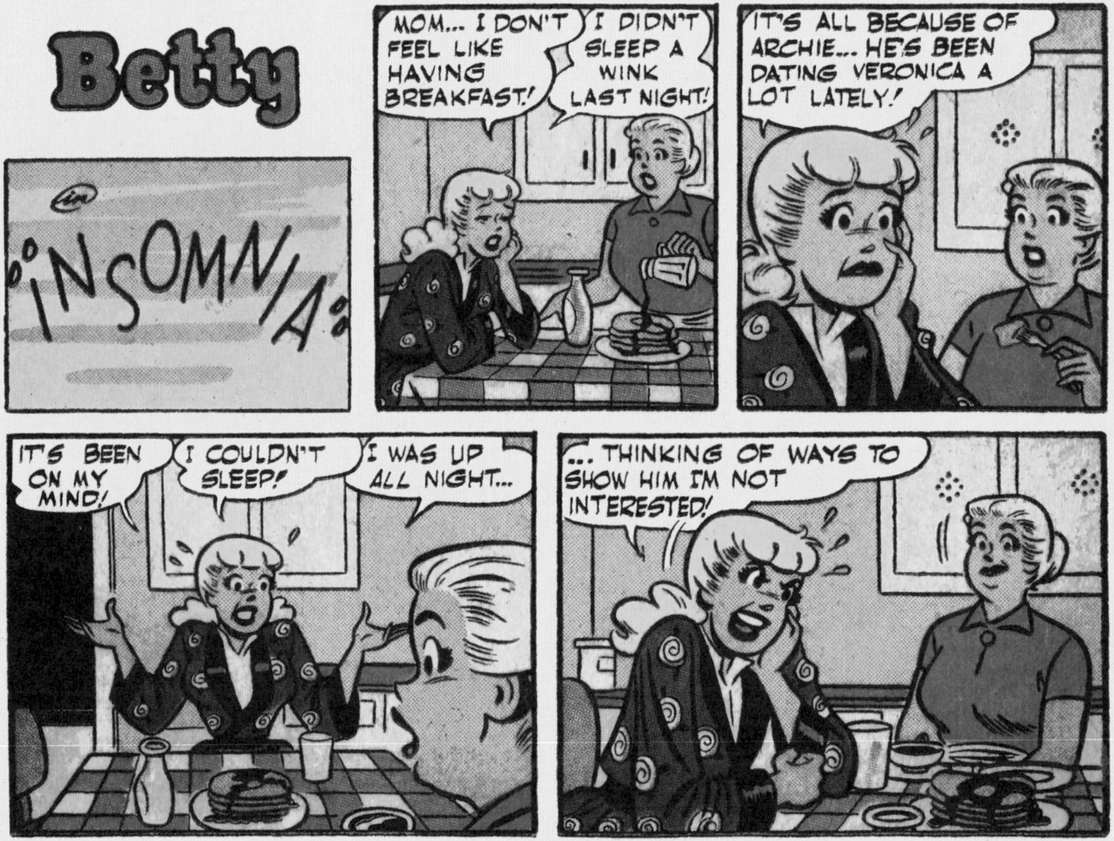
Betty
in
INSOMNIA
MOM... I DON'T FEEL LIKE HAVING BREAKFAST!
I DIDN'T SLEEP A WINK LAST NIGHT!
IT'S ALL BECAUSE OF ARCHIE... HE'S BEEN DATING VERONICA A LOT LATELY!
IT'S BEEN ON MY MIND!
I COULDN'T SLEEP!
I WAS UP ALL NIGHT...
... THINKING OF WAYS TO SHOW HIM I'M NOT INTERESTED!

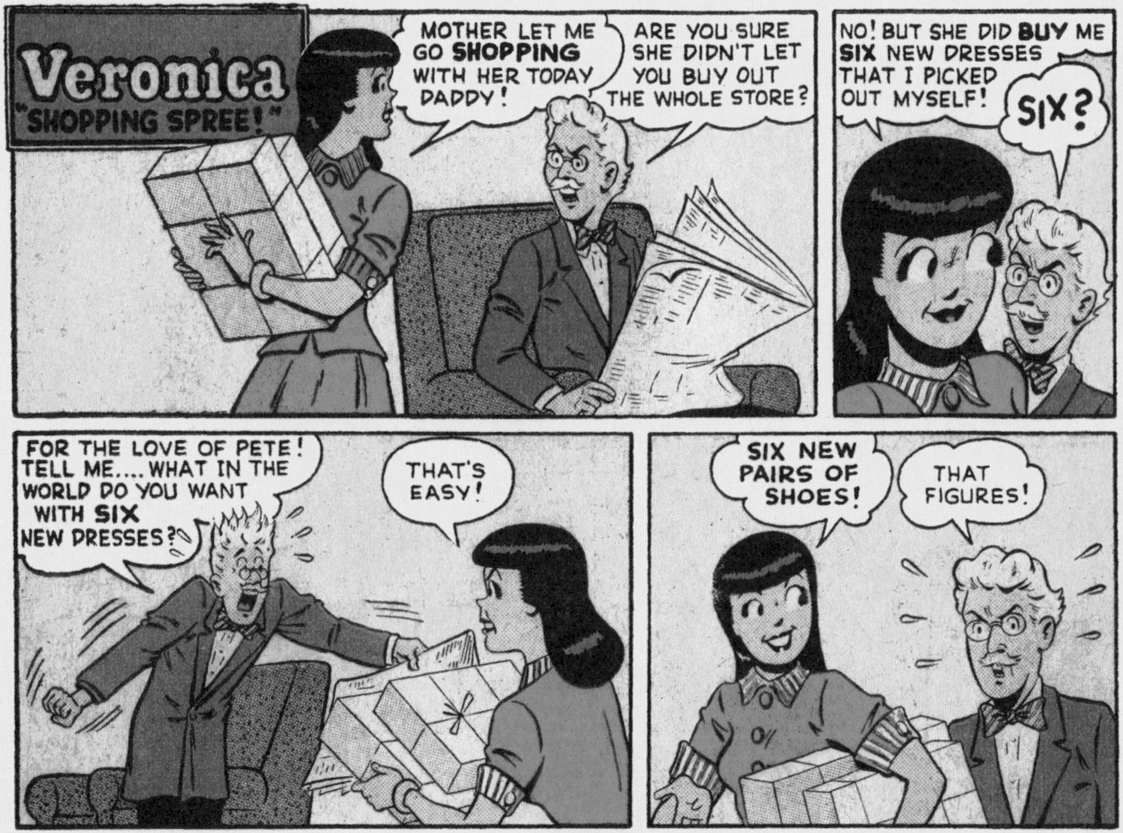
Veronica
"SHOPPING SPREE!"
MOTHER LET ME GO SHOPPING WITH HER TODAY DADDY!
ARE YOU SURE SHE DIDN'T LET YOU BUY OUT THE WHOLE STORE?
NO! BUT SHE DID BUY ME SIX NEW DRESSES THAT I PICKED OUT MYSELF!
SIX?
FOR THE LOVE OF PETE! TELL ME.... WHAT IN THE WORLD DO YOU WANT WITH SIX NEW DRESSES?
THAT'S EASY!
SIX NEW PAIRS OF SHOES!
THAT FIGURES!

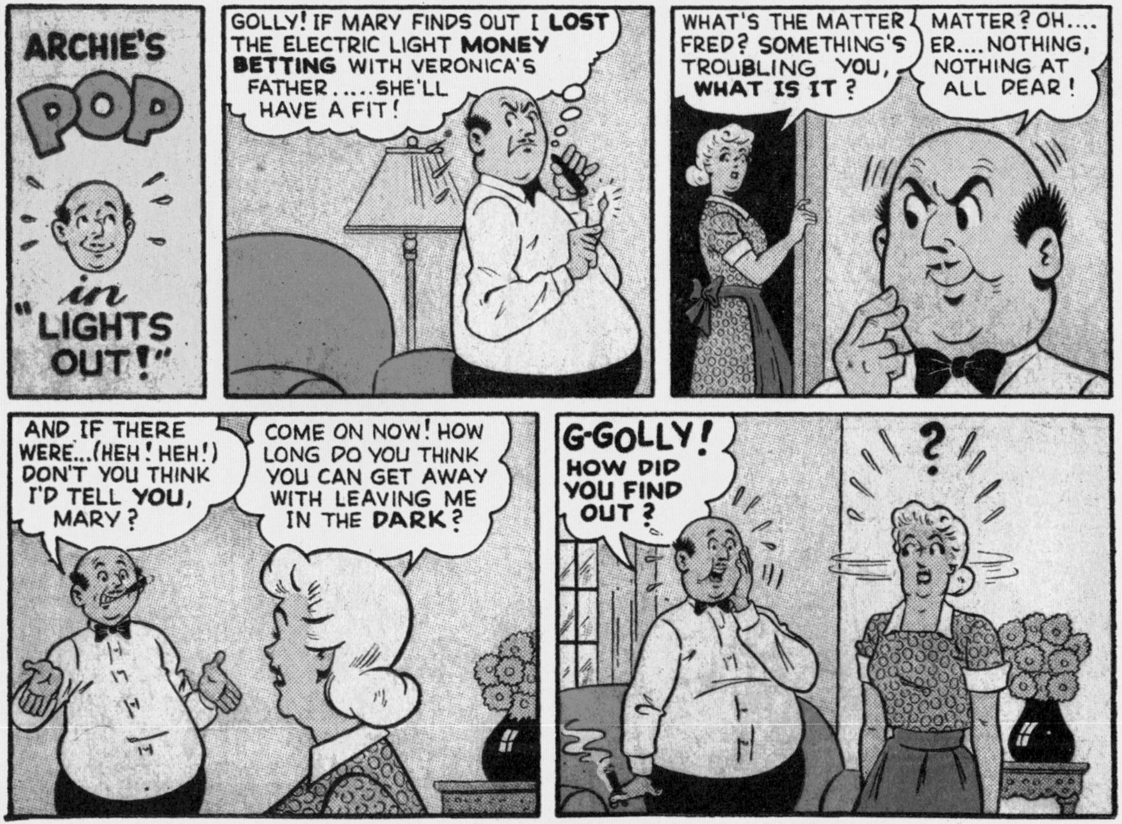
ARCHIE'S
POP
in
"LIGHTS OUT!"
GOLLY! IF MARY FINDS OUT I LOST THE ELECTRIC LIGHT MONEY BETTING WITH VERONICA'S FATHER.....SHE'LL HAVE A FIT!
WHAT'S THE MATTER FRED? SOMETHING'S TROUBLING YOU, WHAT IS IT?
MATTER? OH.... ER....NOTHING, NOTHING AT ALL DEAR!
AND IF THERE WERE...(HEH! HEH!) DON'T YOU THINK I'D TELL YOU, MARY?
COME ON NOW! HOW LONG DO YOU THINK YOU CAN GET AWAY WITH LEAVING ME IN THE DARK?
G-GOLLY! HOW DID YOU FIND OUT?
?

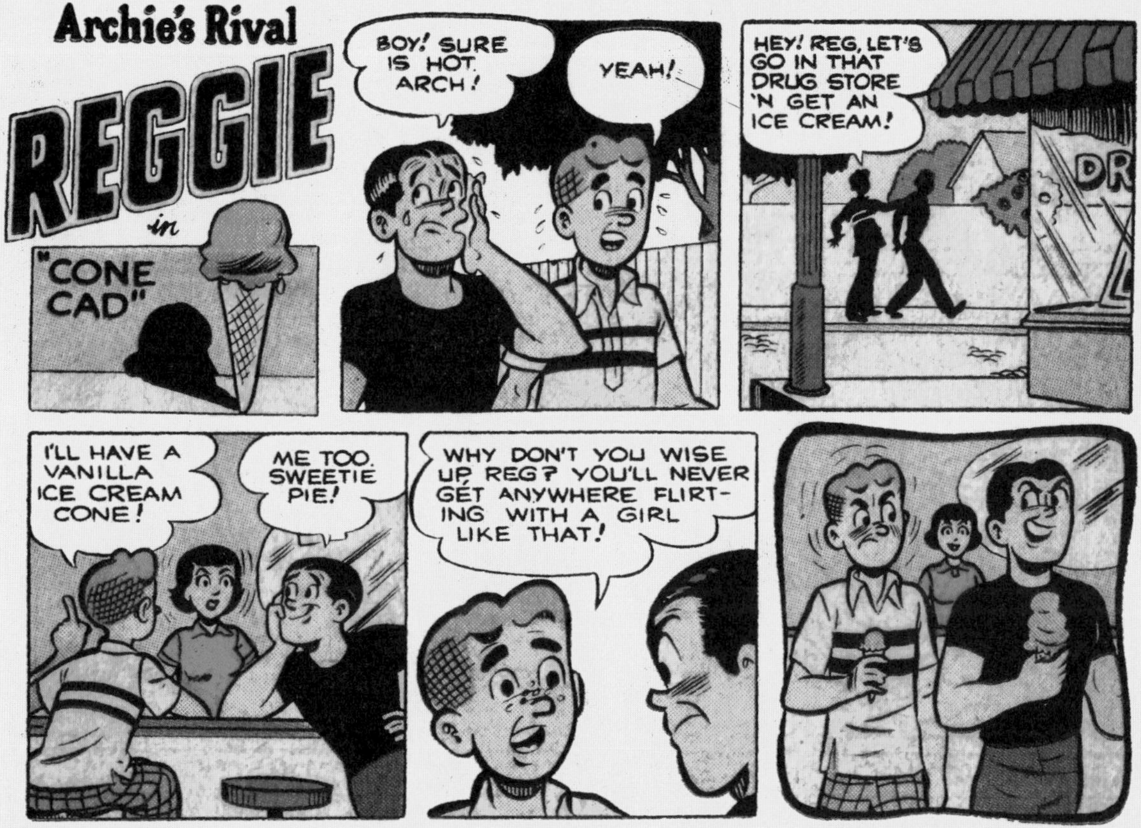
Archie's Rival
REGGIE
in
"CONE CAD"
BOY! SURE IS HOT, ARCH!
YEAH!
HEY! REG, LET'S GO IN THAT DRUG STORE 'N GET AN ICE CREAM!
I'LL HAVE A VANILLA ICE CREAM CONE!
ME TOO, SWEETIE PIE!
WHY DON'T YOU WISE UP, REG? YOU'LL NEVER GET ANYWHERE FLIRT-ING WITH A GIRL LIKE THAT!

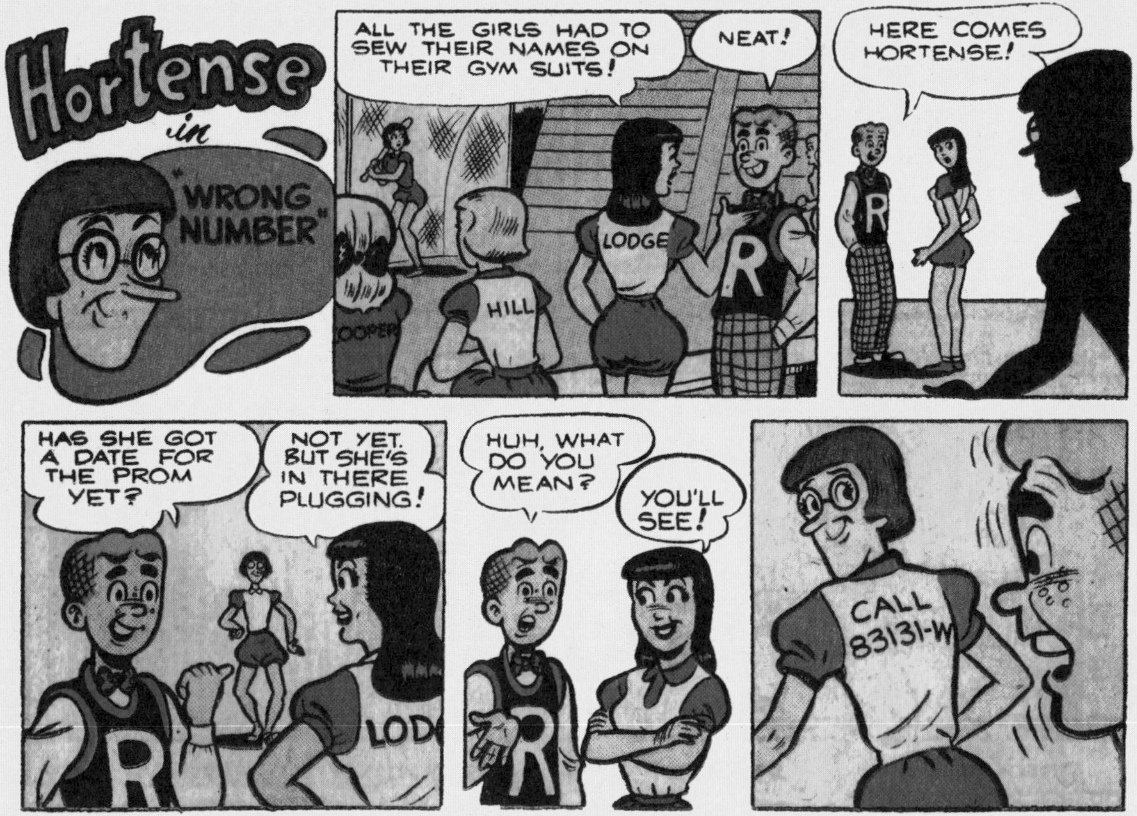

Hortense
in
"WRONG NUMBER"
ALL THE GIRLS HAD TO SEW THEIR NAMES ON THEIR GYM SUITS!
NEAT!
LODGE
HILL
COOPER
HERE COMES HORTENSE!
HAS SHE GOT A DATE FOR THE PROM YET?
NOT YET. BUT SHE'S IN THERE PLUGGING!
HUH, WHAT DO YOU MEAN?
YOU'LL SEE!
CALL 83131-W

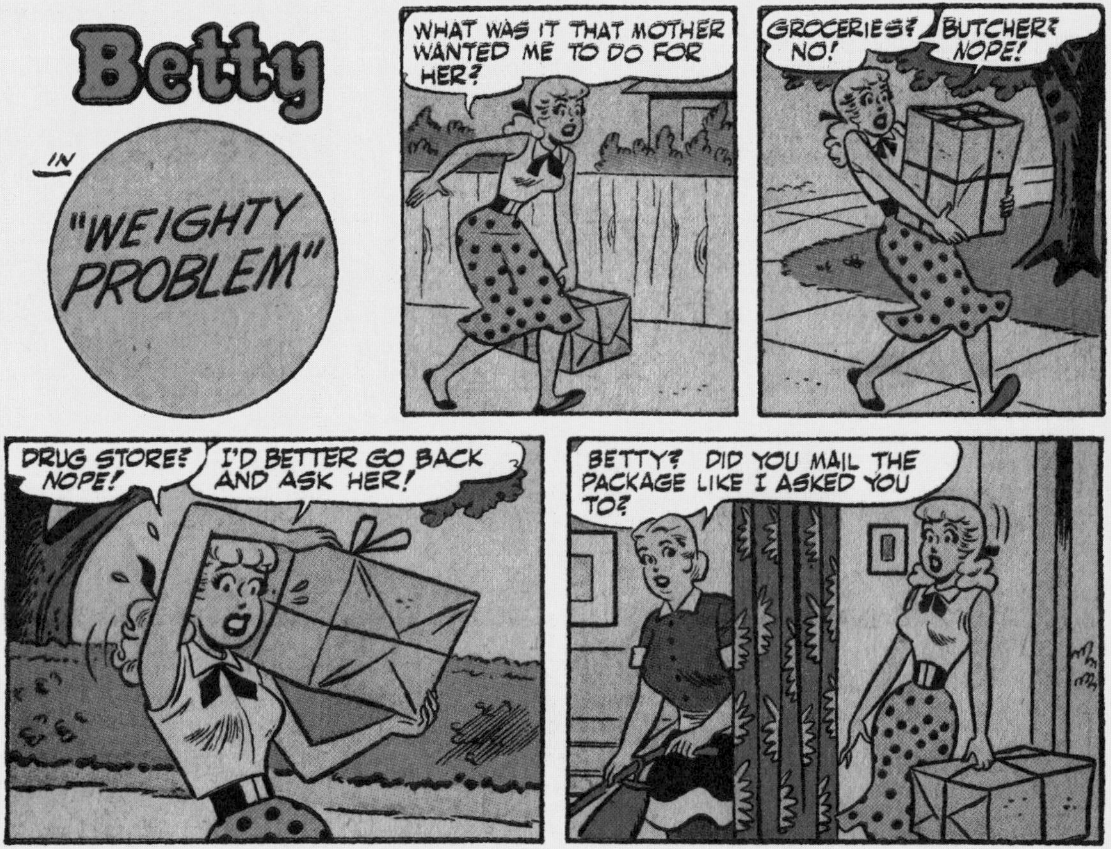
Betty
IN
"WEIGHTY PROBLEM"
WHAT WAS IT THAT MOTHER WANTED ME TO DO FOR HER?
GROCERIES? NO!
BUTCHER? NOPE!
DRUG STORE? NOPE!
I'D BETTER GO BACK AND ASK HER!
BETTY? DID YOU MAIL THE PACKAGE LIKE I ASKED YOU TO?

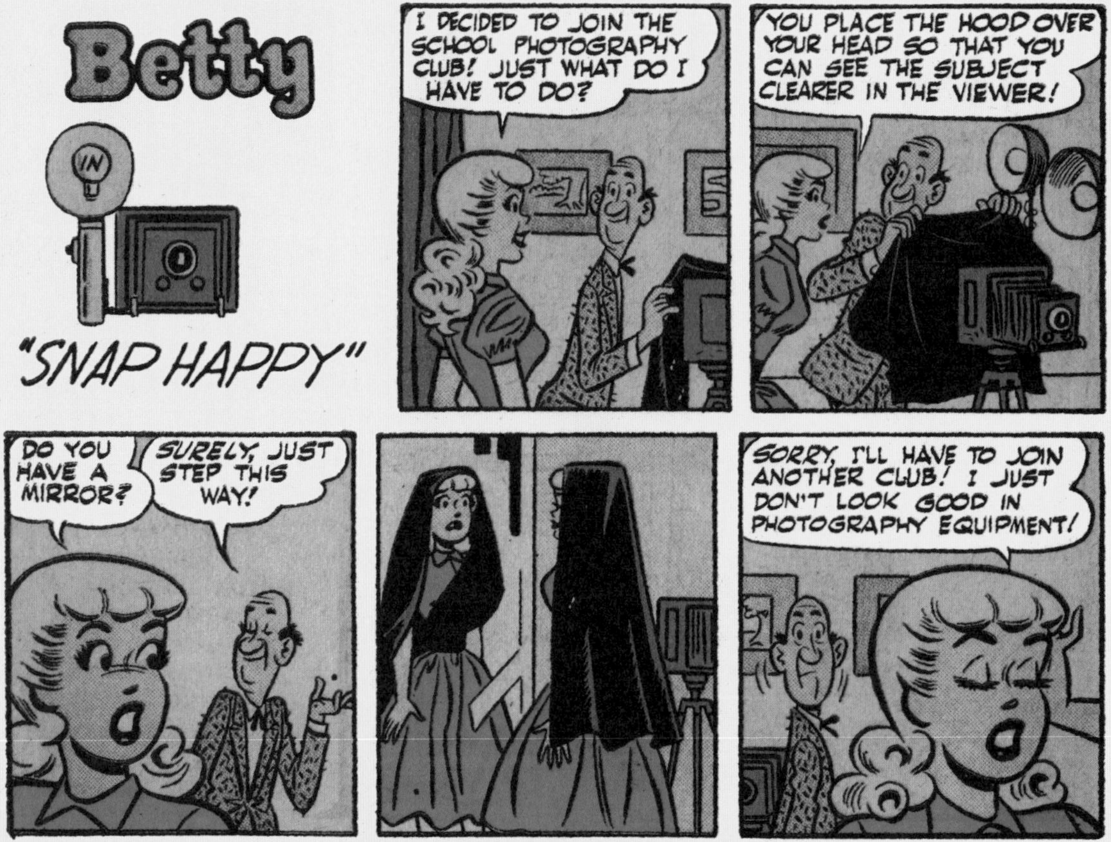
Betty
IN
"SNAP HAPPY"
I DECIDED TO JOIN THE SCHOOL PHOTOGRAPHY CLUB! JUST WHAT DO I HAVE TO DO?
YOU PLACE THE HOOD OVER YOUR HEAD SO THAT YOU CAN SEE THE SUBJECT CLEARER IN THE VIEWER!
DO YOU HAVE A MIRROR?
SURELY, JUST STEP THIS WAY!
SORRY, I'LL HAVE TO JOIN ANOTHER CLUB! I JUST DON'T LOOK GOOD IN PHOTOGRAPHY EQUIPMENT!

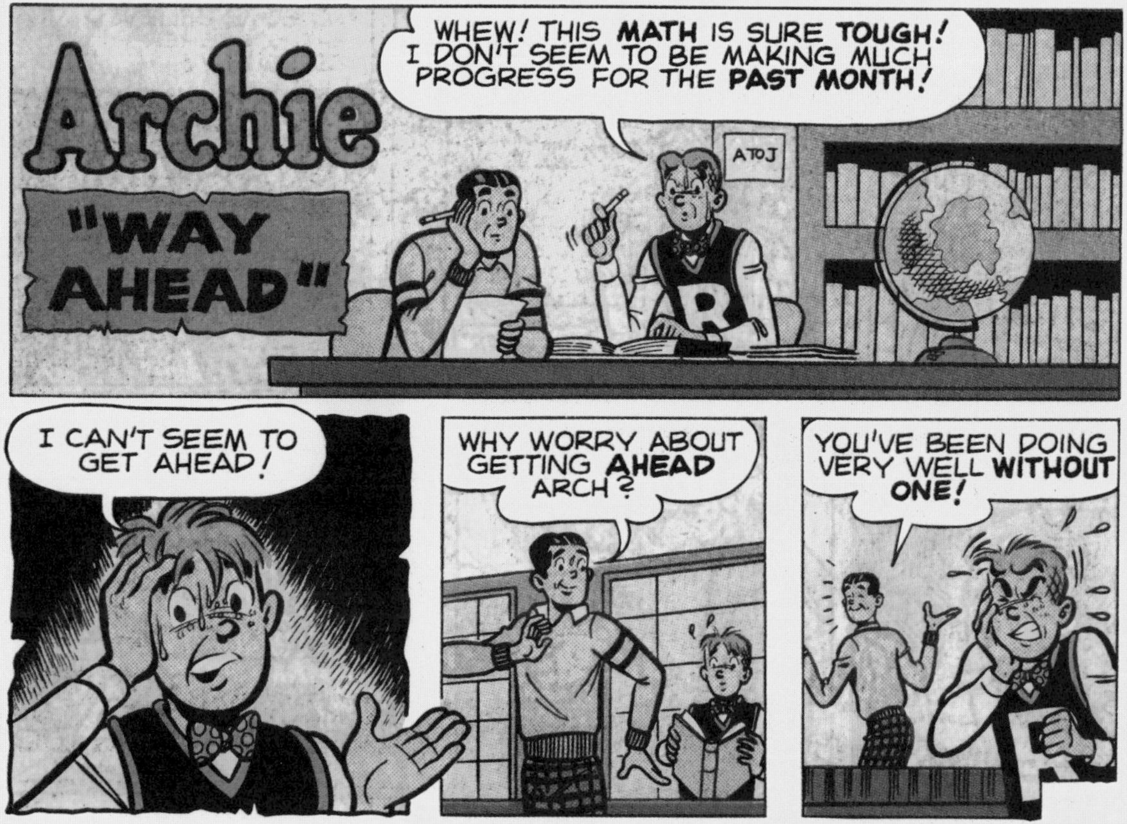
Archie
"WAY AHEAD"
WHEW! THIS MATH IS SURE TOUGH! I DON'T SEEM TO BE MAKING MUCH PROGRESS FOR THE PAST MONTH!
A TO J
I CAN'T SEEM TO GET AHEAD!
WHY WORRY ABOUT GETTING AHEAD ARCH?
YOU'VE BEEN DOING VERY WELL WITHOUT ONE!

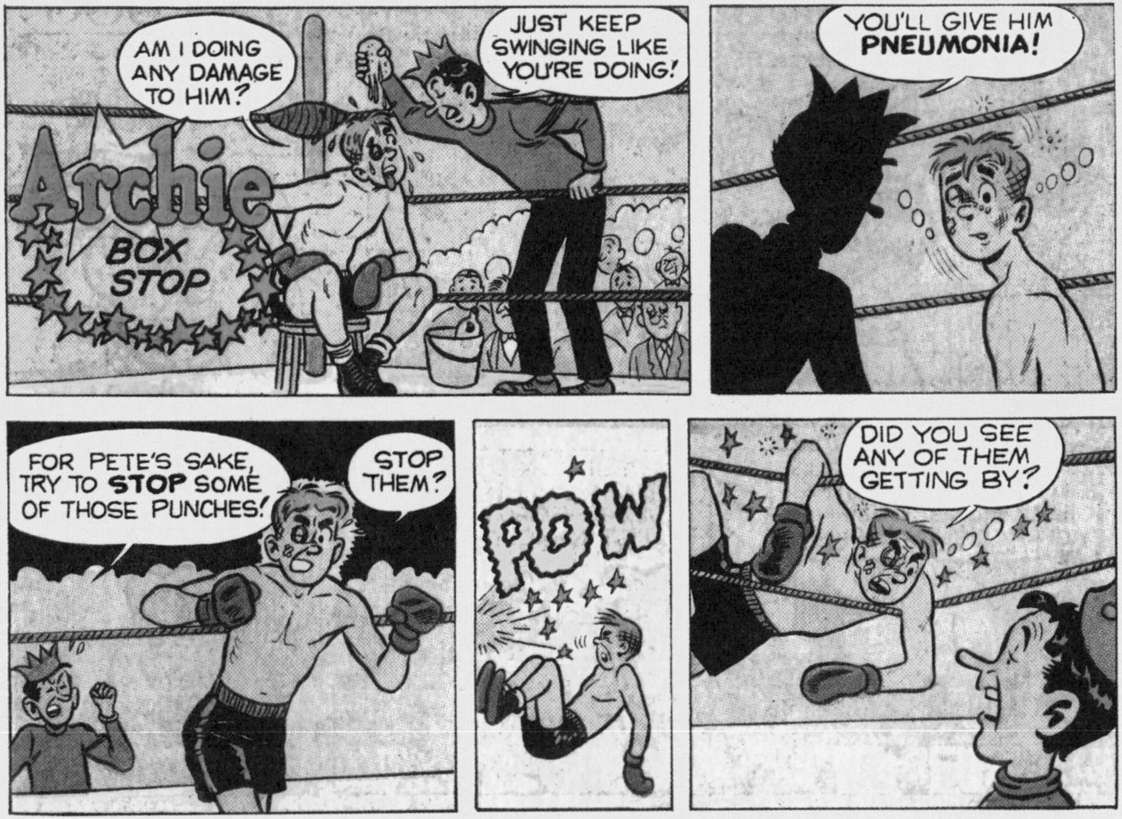
Archie
BOX STOP
AM I DOING ANY DAMAGE TO HIM?
JUST KEEP SWINGING LIKE YOU'RE DOING!
YOU'LL GIVE HIM **PNEUMONIA!**
FOR PETE'S SAKE, TRY TO **STOP** SOME OF THOSE PUNCHES!
STOP THEM?
POW
DID YOU SEE ANY OF THEM GETTING BY?

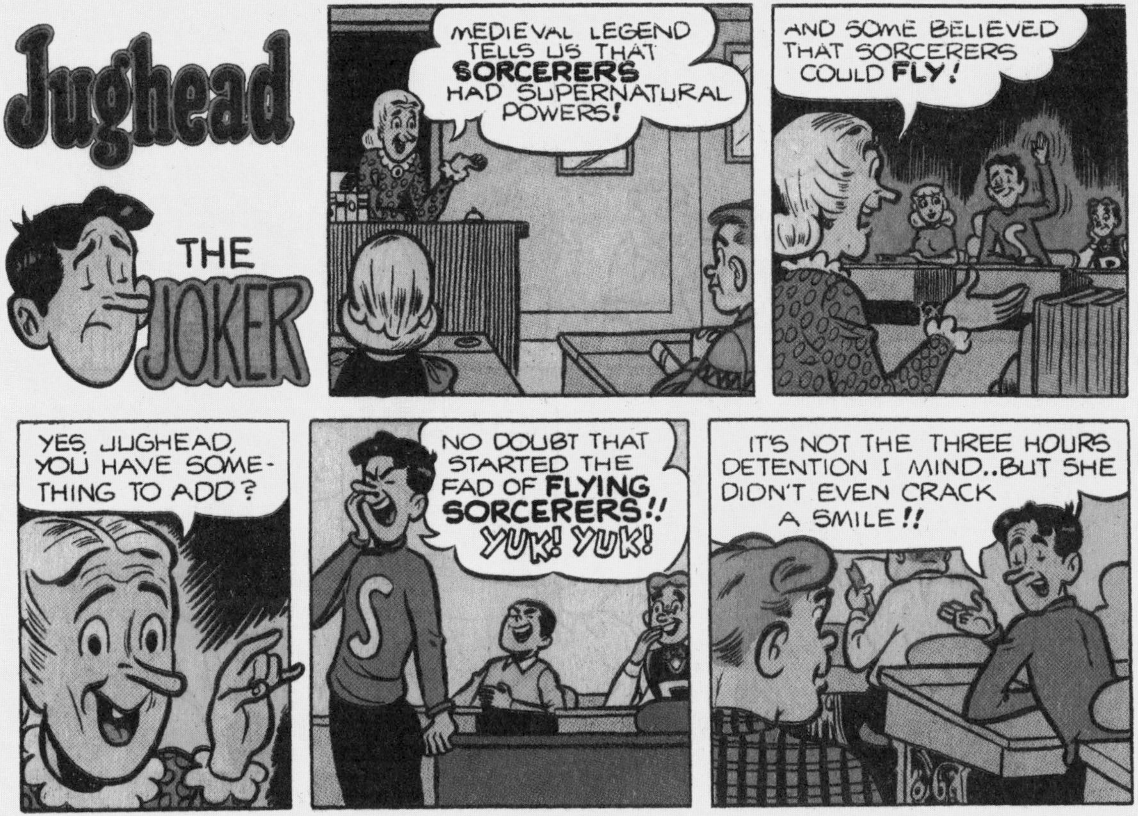
Jughead
THE JOKER
MEDIEVAL LEGEND TELLS US THAT SORCERERS HAD SUPERNATURAL POWERS!
AND SOME BELIEVED THAT SORCERERS COULD FLY!
YES, JUGHEAD, YOU HAVE SOME-THING TO ADD?
NO DOUBT THAT STARTED THE FAD OF FLYING SORCERERS!!
YUK! YUK!
IT'S NOT THE THREE HOURS DETENTION I MIND..BUT SHE DIDN'T EVEN CRACK A SMILE!!

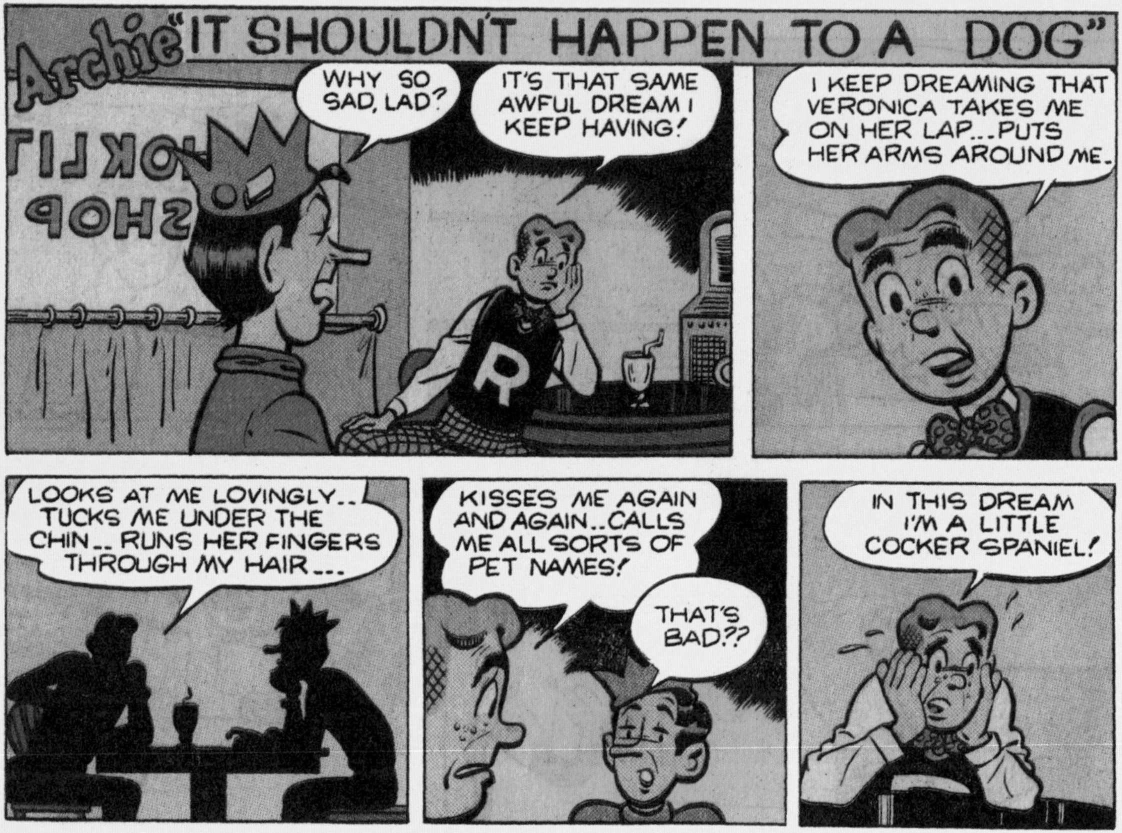

Archie
"IT SHOULDN'T HAPPEN TO A DOG"
WHY SO SAD, LAD?
IT'S THAT SAME AWFUL DREAM I KEEP HAVING!
I KEEP DREAMING THAT VERONICA TAKES ME ON HER LAP...PUTS HER ARMS AROUND ME.
LOOKS AT ME LOVINGLY.. TUCKS ME UNDER THE CHIN.. RUNS HER FINGERS THROUGH MY HAIR...
KISSES ME AGAIN AND AGAIN..CALLS ME ALL SORTS OF PET NAMES!
THAT'S BAD??
IN THIS DREAM I'M A LITTLE COCKER SPANIEL!

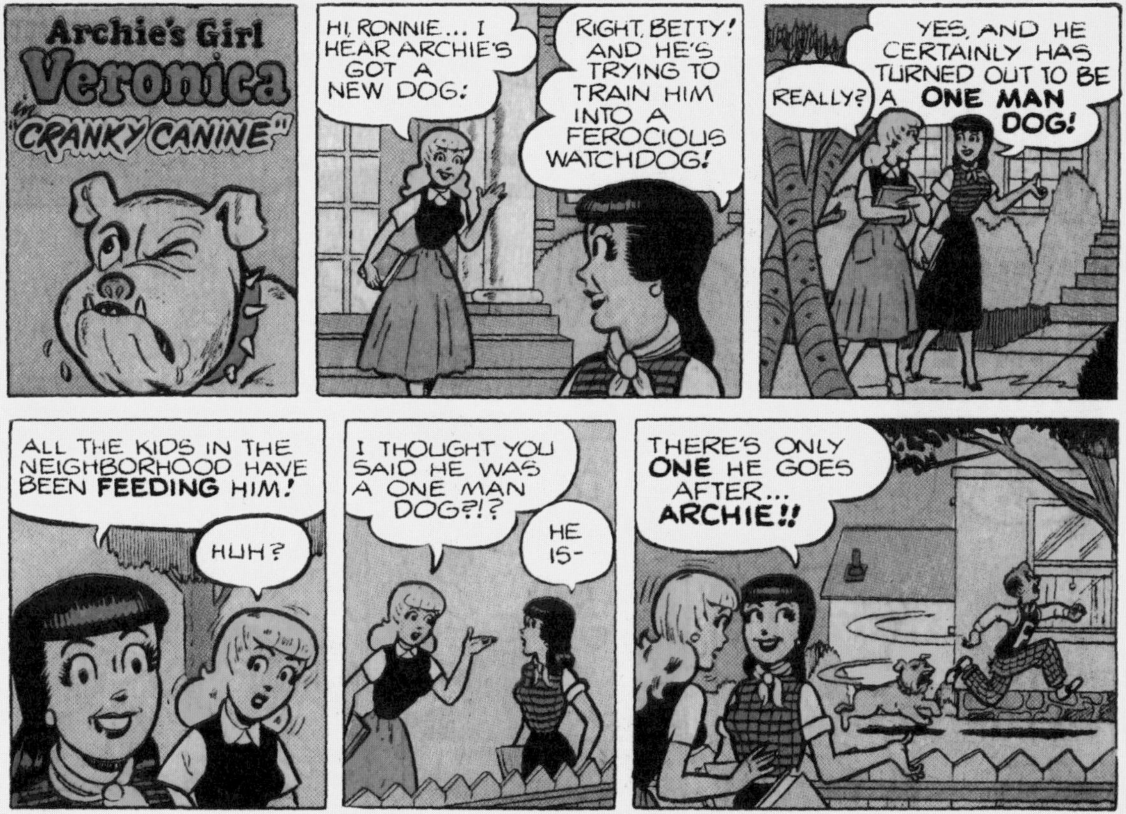
Archie's Girl
Veronica
in "CRANKY CANINE"
HI, RONNIE... I HEAR ARCHIE'S GOT A NEW DOG:
RIGHT, BETTY! AND HE'S TRYING TO TRAIN HIM INTO A FEROCIOUS WATCHDOG!
REALLY?
YES, AND HE CERTAINLY HAS TURNED OUT TO BE A **ONE MAN DOG!**
ALL THE KIDS IN THE NEIGHBORHOOD HAVE BEEN **FEEDING** HIM!
HUH?
I THOUGHT YOU SAID HE WAS A ONE MAN DOG?!?
HE IS-
THERE'S ONLY **ONE** HE GOES AFTER... **ARCHIE!!**

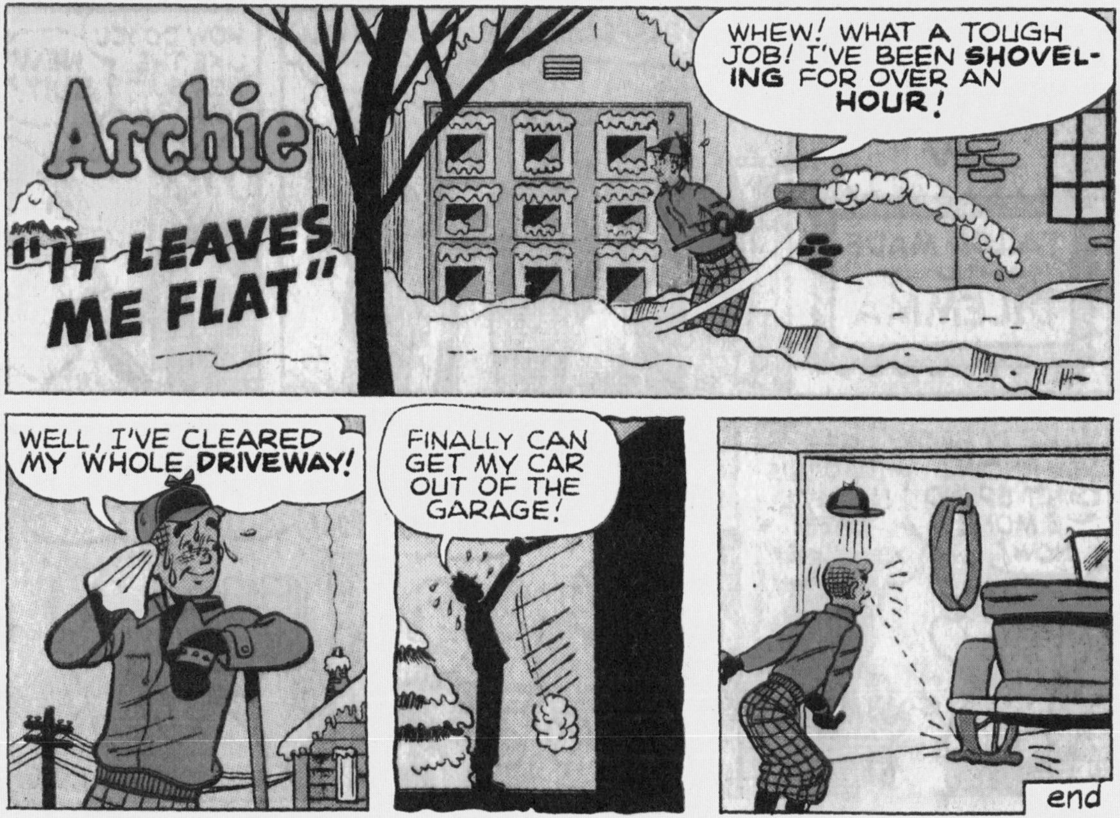
Archie
"IT LEAVES ME FLAT"
WHEW! WHAT A TOUGH JOB! I'VE BEEN SHOVELING FOR OVER AN HOUR!
WELL, I'VE CLEARED MY WHOLE DRIVEWAY!
FINALLY CAN GET MY CAR OUT OF THE GARAGE!
end

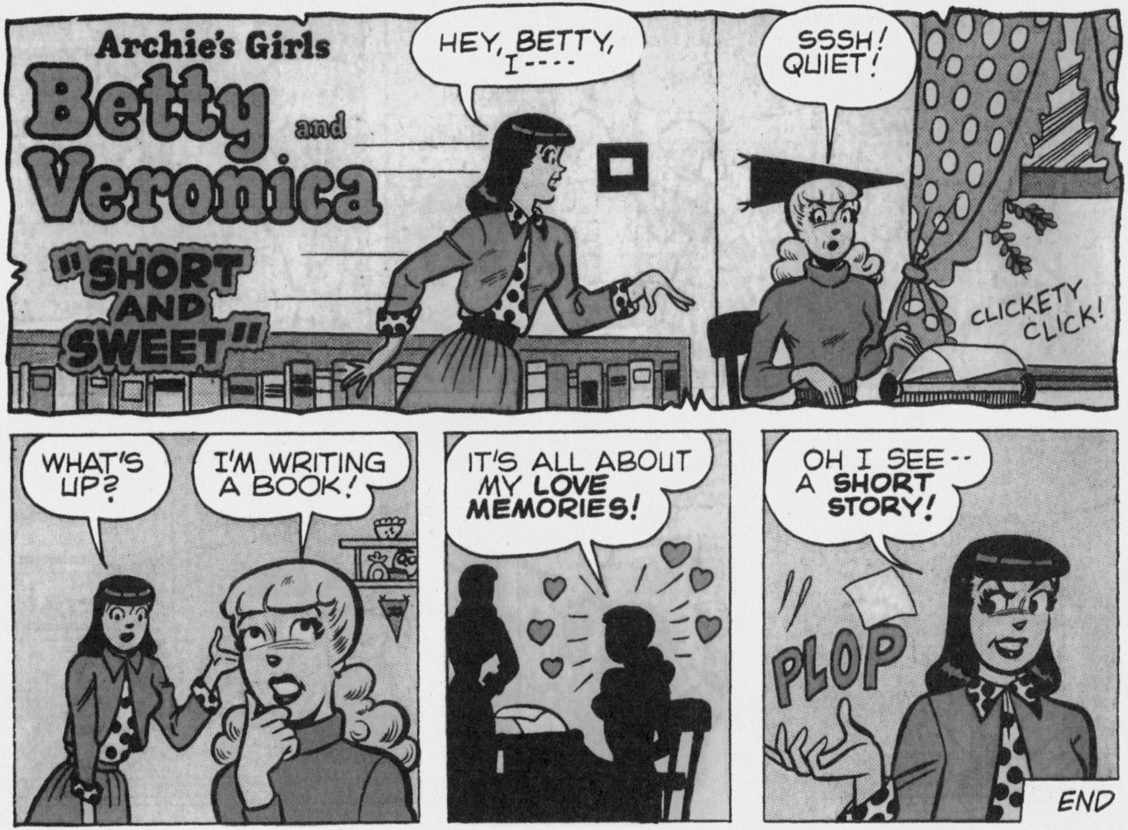

Archie's Girls
Betty and Veronica
"SHORT AND SWEET"
HEY, BETTY, I----
SSSH! QUIET!
CLICKETY CLICK!
WHAT'S UP?
I'M WRITING A BOOK!
IT'S ALL ABOUT MY LOVE MEMORIES!
OH I SEE-- A SHORT STORY!
PLOP
END

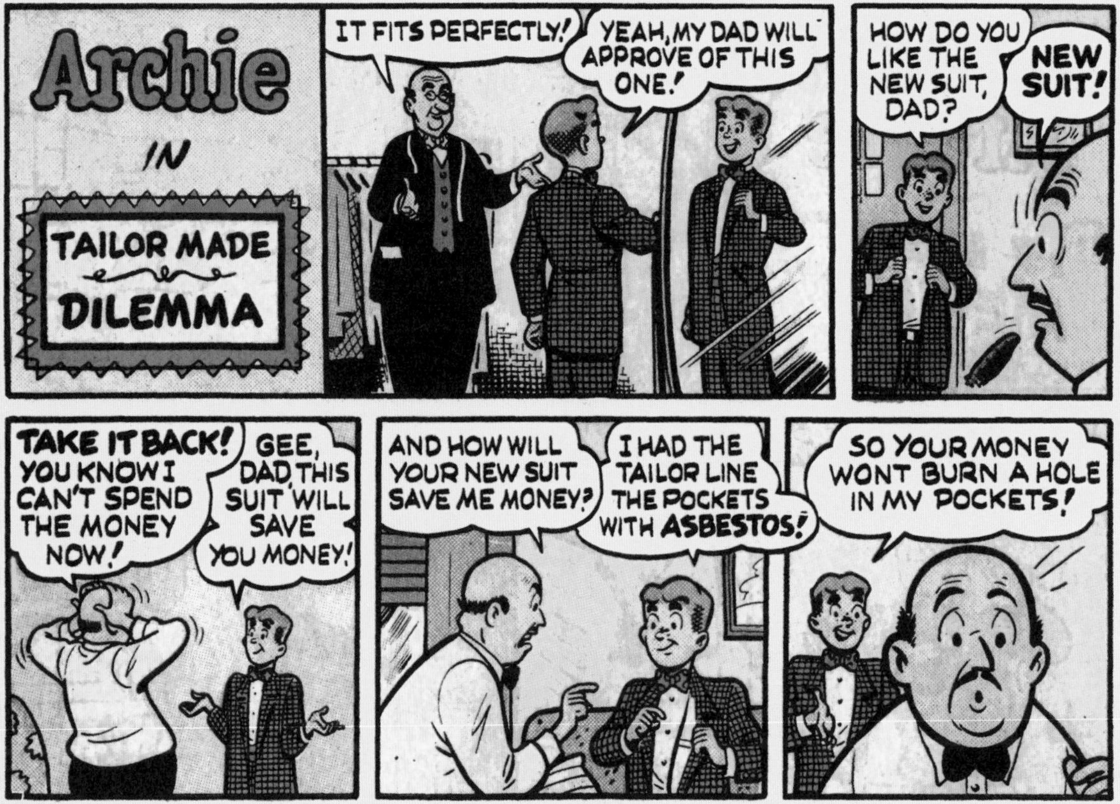
Archie
IN
TAILOR MADE DILEMMA
IT FITS PERFECTLY!
YEAH, MY DAD WILL APPROVE OF THIS ONE!
HOW DO YOU LIKE THE NEW SUIT, DAD?
NEW SUIT!
TAKE IT BACK! YOU KNOW I CAN'T SPEND THE MONEY NOW!
GEE, DAD, THIS SUIT WILL SAVE YOU MONEY!
AND HOW WILL YOUR NEW SUIT SAVE ME MONEY?
I HAD THE TAILOR LINE THE POCKETS WITH ASBESTOS!
SO YOUR MONEY WONT BURN A HOLE IN MY POCKETS!

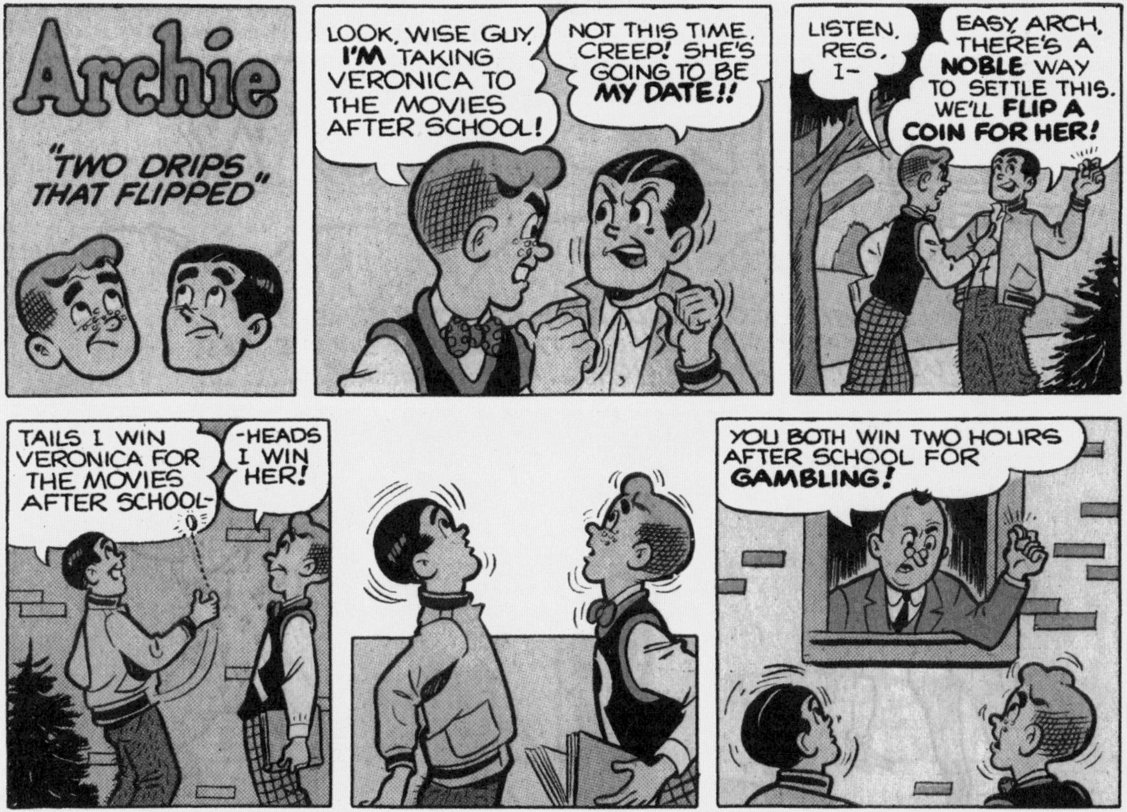
Archie
"TWO DRIPS THAT FLIPPED"
LOOK, WISE GUY, I'M TAKING VERONICA TO THE MOVIES AFTER SCHOOL!
NOT THIS TIME, CREEP! SHE'S GOING TO BE MY DATE!!
LISTEN, REG, I–
EASY, ARCH, THERE'S A NOBLE WAY TO SETTLE THIS. WE'LL FLIP A COIN FOR HER!
TAILS I WIN VERONICA FOR THE MOVIES AFTER SCHOOL-
-HEADS I WIN HER!
YOU BOTH WIN TWO HOURS AFTER SCHOOL FOR GAMBLING!

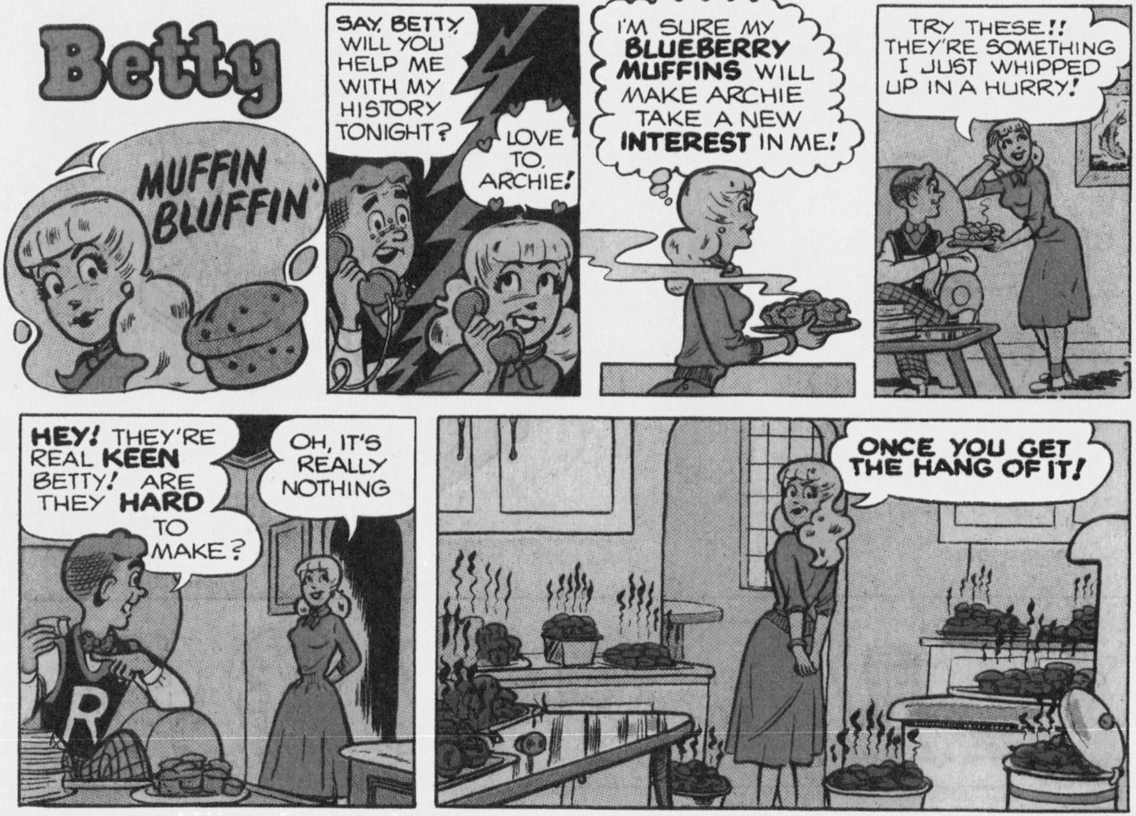
Betty
MUFFIN BLUFFIN'
SAY, BETTY, WILL YOU HELP ME WITH MY HISTORY TONIGHT?
LOVE TO, ARCHIE!
I'M SURE MY BLUEBERRY MUFFINS WILL MAKE ARCHIE TAKE A NEW INTEREST IN ME!
TRY THESE!! THEY'RE SOMETHING I JUST WHIPPED UP IN A HURRY!
HEY! THEY'RE REAL KEEN BETTY! ARE THEY HARD TO MAKE?
OH, IT'S REALLY NOTHING
ONCE YOU GET THE HANG OF IT!

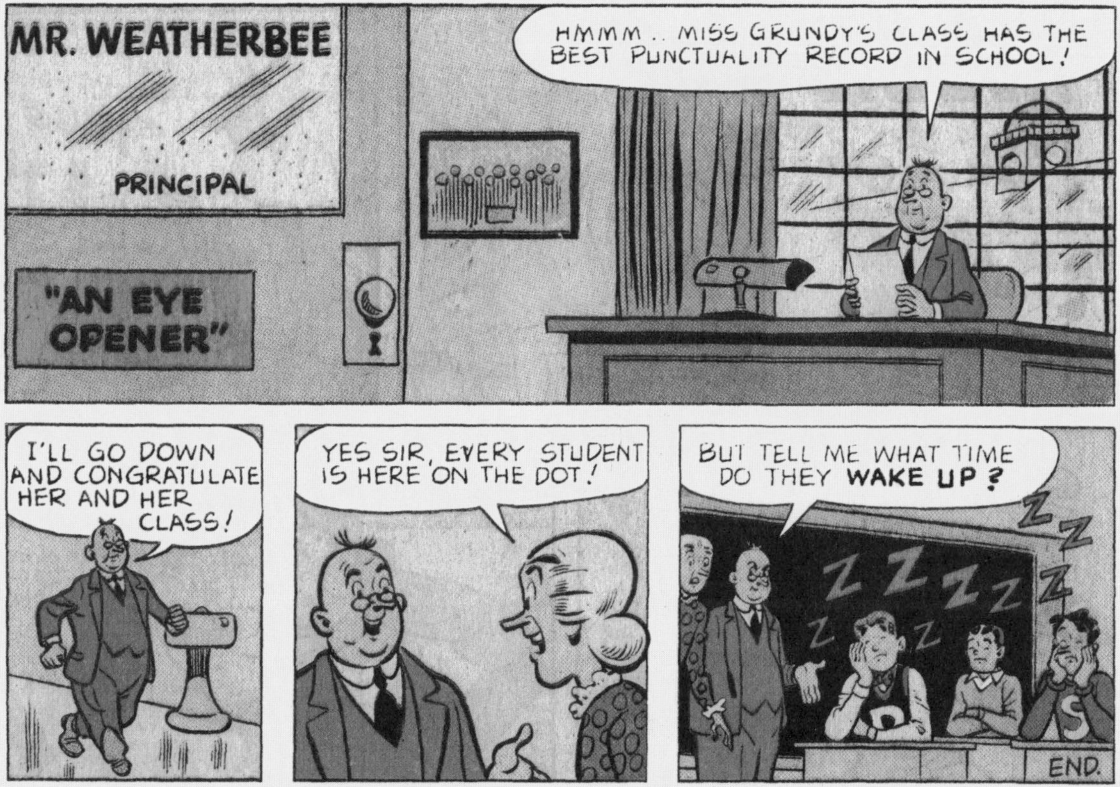
MR. WEATHERBEE
PRINCIPAL
"AN EYE OPENER"
HMMM .. MISS GRUNDY'S CLASS HAS THE BEST PUNCTUALITY RECORD IN SCHOOL!
I'LL GO DOWN AND CONGRATULATE HER AND HER CLASS!
YES SIR, EVERY STUDENT IS HERE ON THE DOT!
BUT TELL ME WHAT TIME DO THEY **WAKE UP**?
END.

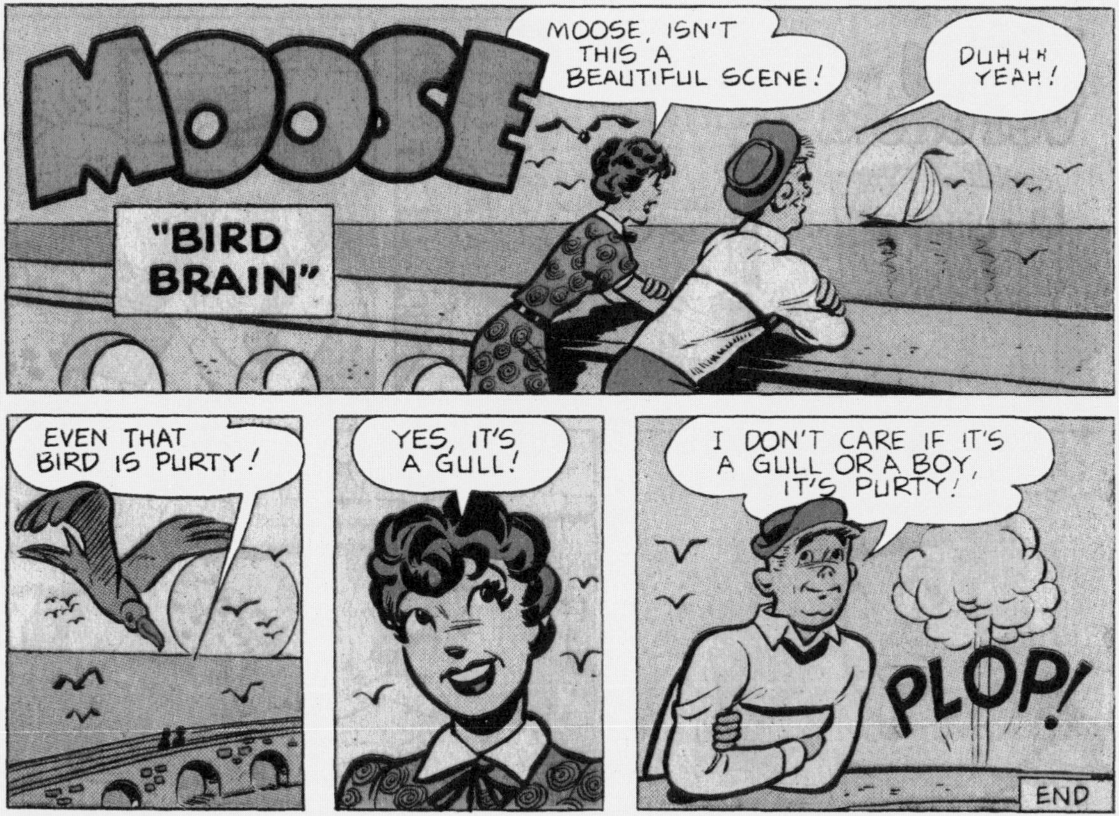
MOOSE
"BIRD BRAIN"
MOOSE, ISN'T THIS A BEAUTIFUL SCENE!
DUHHH YEAH!
EVEN THAT BIRD IS PURTY!
YES, IT'S A GULL!
I DON'T CARE IF IT'S A GULL OR A BOY, IT'S PURTY!
PLOP!
END

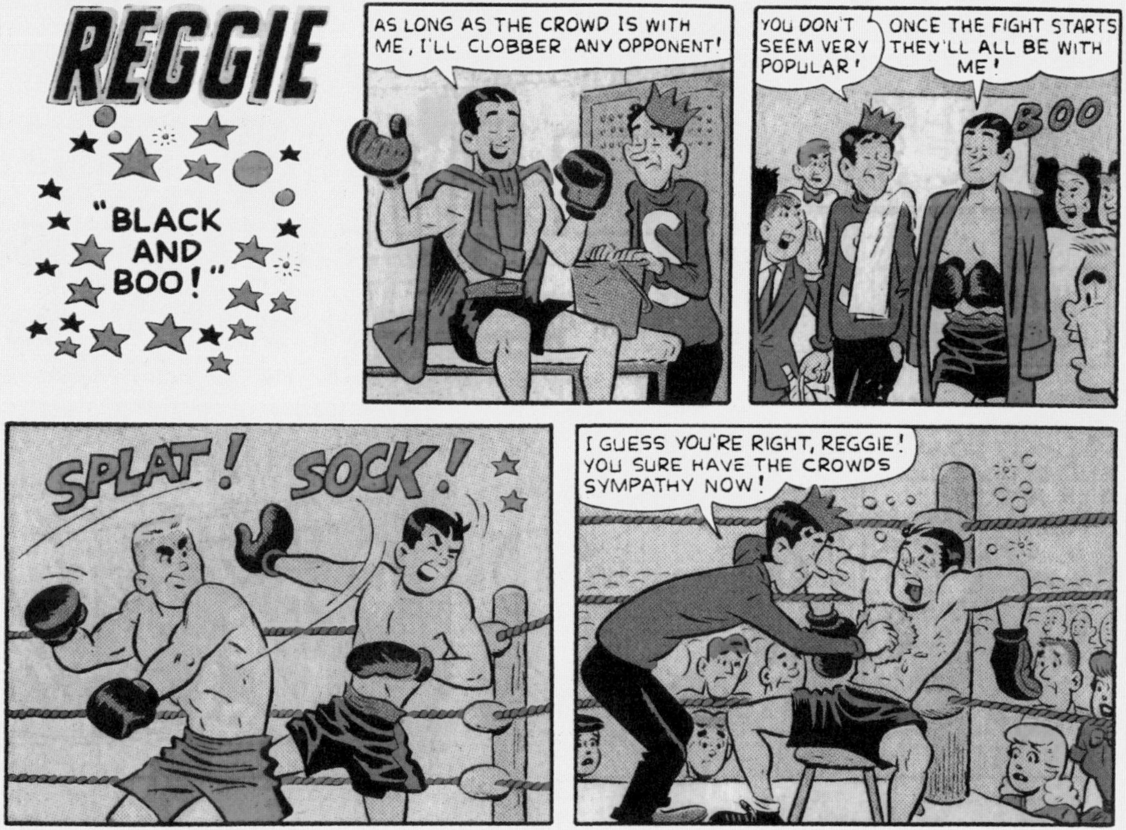
REGGIE
"BLACK AND BOO!"
AS LONG AS THE CROWD IS WITH ME, I'LL CLOBBER ANY OPPONENT!
YOU DON'T SEEM VERY POPULAR!
ONCE THE FIGHT STARTS THEY'LL ALL BE WITH ME!
BOO
SPLAT!
SOCK!
I GUESS YOU'RE RIGHT, REGGIE! YOU SURE HAVE THE CROWDS SYMPATHY NOW!

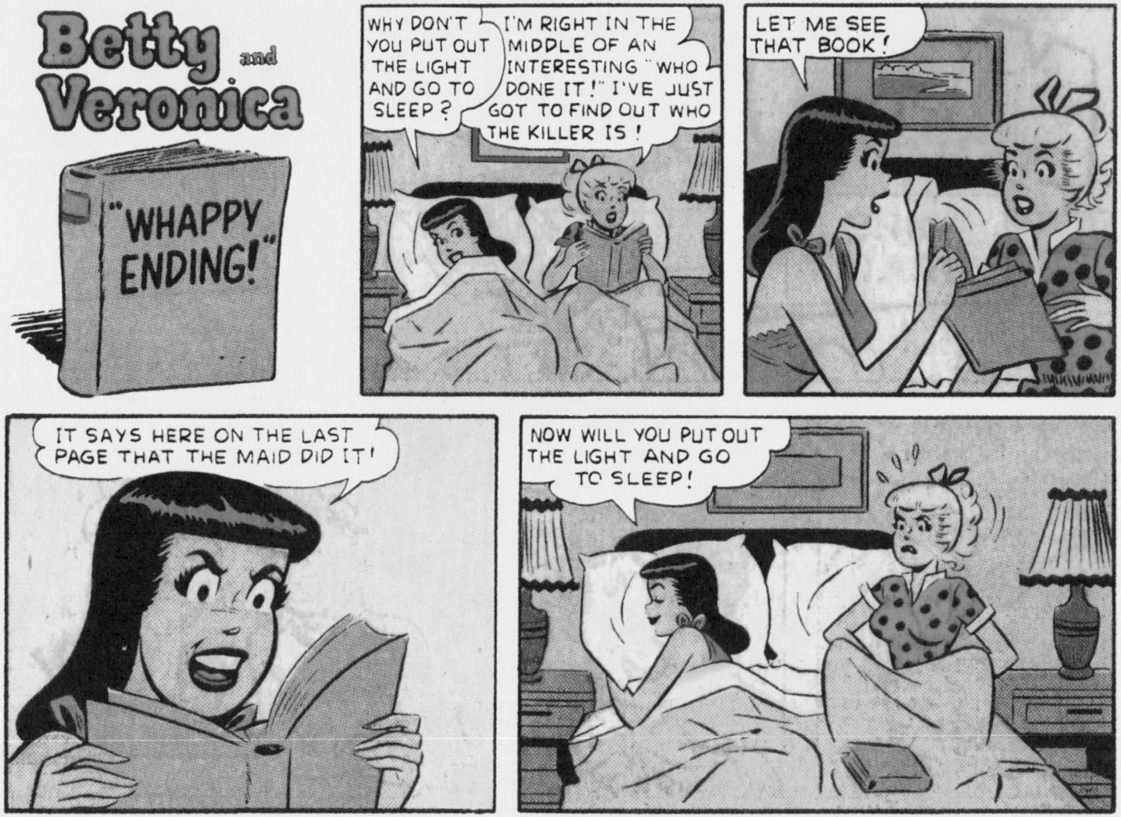

Betty and Veronica
"WHAPPY ENDING!"
WHY DON'T YOU PUT OUT THE LIGHT AND GO TO SLEEP?
I'M RIGHT IN THE MIDDLE OF AN INTERESTING "WHO DONE IT!" I'VE JUST GOT TO FIND OUT WHO THE KILLER IS!
LET ME SEE THAT BOOK!
IT SAYS HERE ON THE LAST PAGE THAT THE MAID DID IT!
NOW WILL YOU PUT OUT THE LIGHT AND GO TO SLEEP!

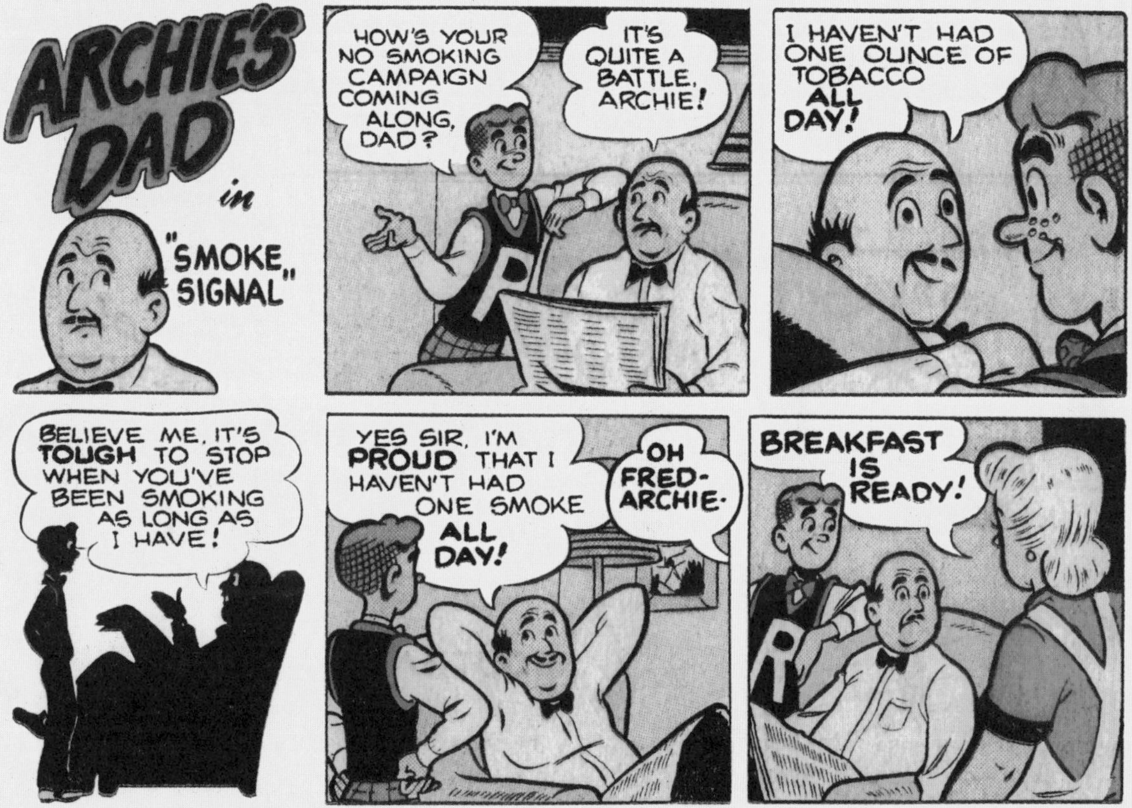
ARCHIE'S DAD
in
"SMOKE SIGNAL"
HOW'S YOUR NO SMOKING CAMPAIGN COMING ALONG, DAD?
IT'S QUITE A BATTLE, ARCHIE!
I HAVEN'T HAD ONE OUNCE OF TOBACCO ALL DAY!
BELIEVE ME, IT'S TOUGH TO STOP WHEN YOU'VE BEEN SMOKING AS LONG AS I HAVE!
YES SIR, I'M PROUD THAT I HAVEN'T HAD ONE SMOKE ALL DAY!
OH FRED-ARCHIE-
BREAKFAST IS READY!

HORTENSE in "DOG NAB IT"

THAT HORTENSE IS REAL CLEVER... SHE'S MET MORE BOYS SINCE SHE BOUGHT AND TRAINED A DOG!

WOW! IT MUST BE A CUTE DOG!

NAW, HE'S A HOMELY LITTLE MUTT!

THEN HOW—

LOOK OUT! HERE COMES HORTENSE NOW!

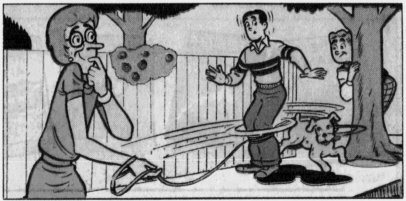

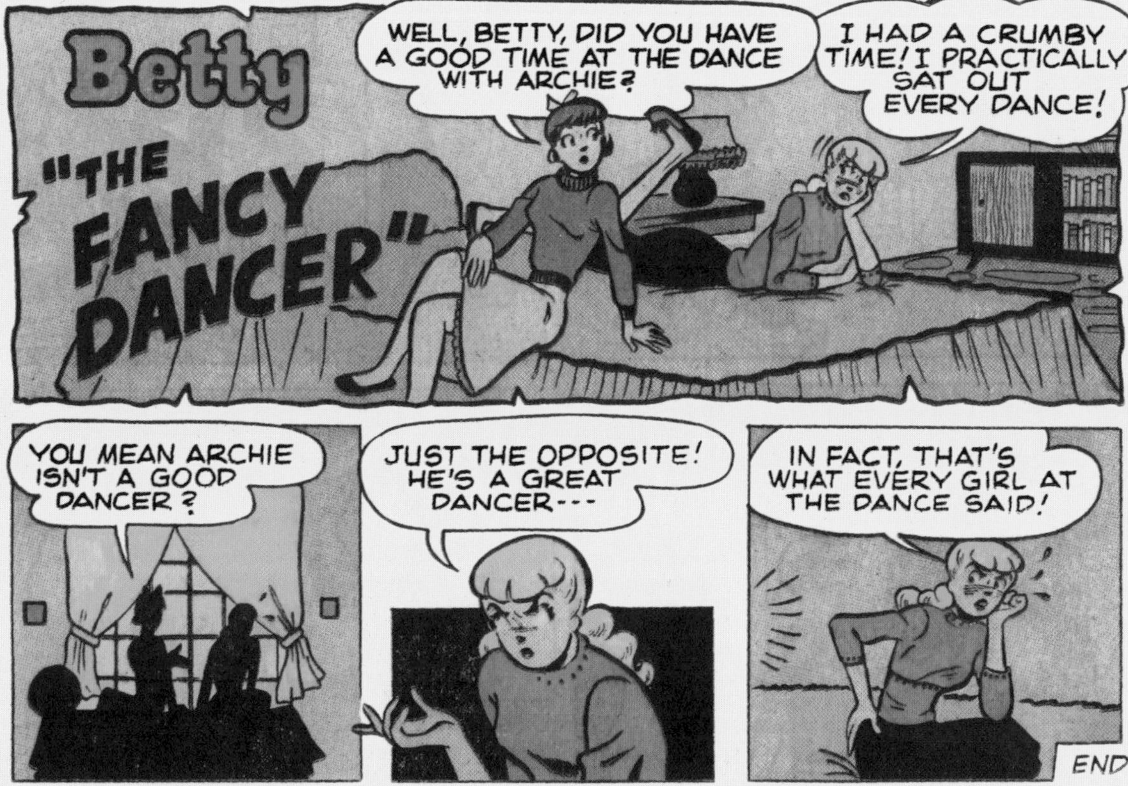
Betty
"THE FANCY DANCER"
WELL, BETTY, DID YOU HAVE A GOOD TIME AT THE DANCE WITH ARCHIE?
I HAD A CRUMBY TIME! I PRACTICALLY SAT OUT EVERY DANCE!
YOU MEAN ARCHIE ISN'T A GOOD DANCER?
JUST THE OPPOSITE! HE'S A GREAT DANCER---
IN FACT, THAT'S WHAT EVERY GIRL AT THE DANCE SAID!
END

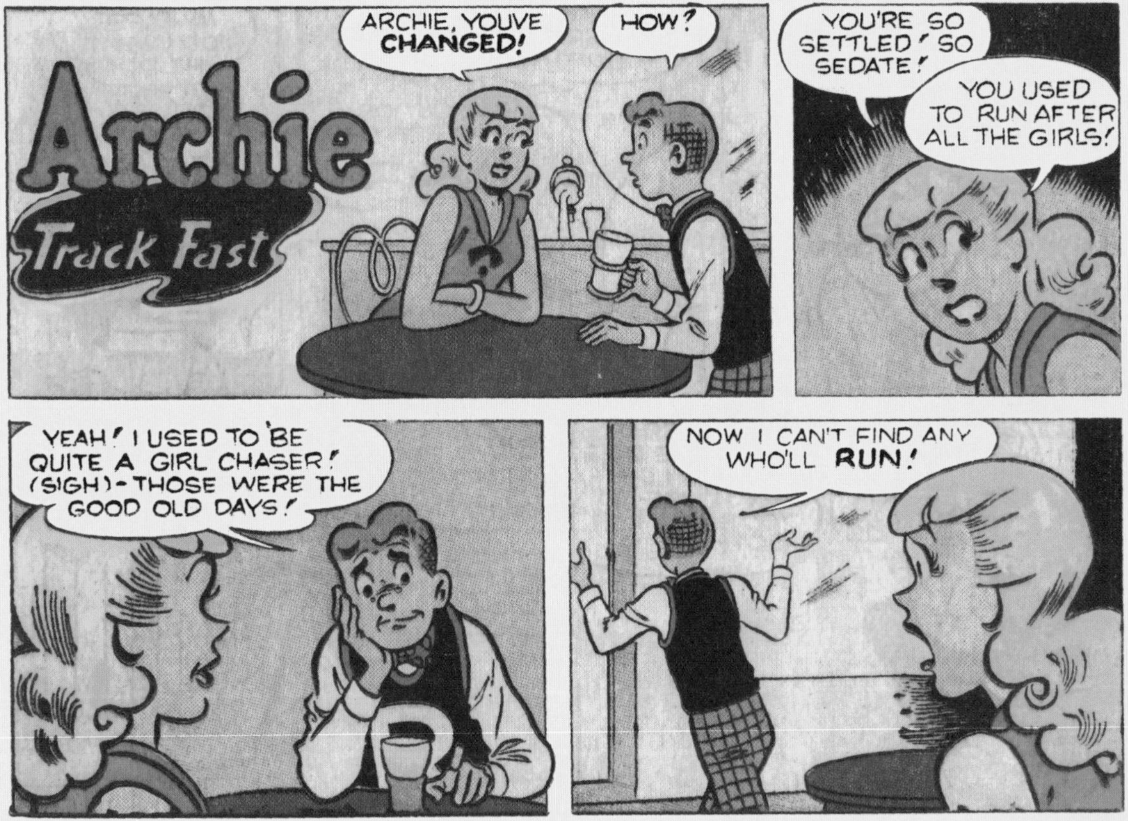
Archie
Track Fast
ARCHIE, YOUVE CHANGED!
HOW?
YOU'RE SO SETTLED! SO SEDATE!
YOU USED TO RUN AFTER ALL THE GIRLS!
YEAH! I USED TO BE QUITE A GIRL CHASER! (SIGH)-THOSE WERE THE GOOD OLD DAYS!
NOW I CAN'T FIND ANY WHO'LL RUN!

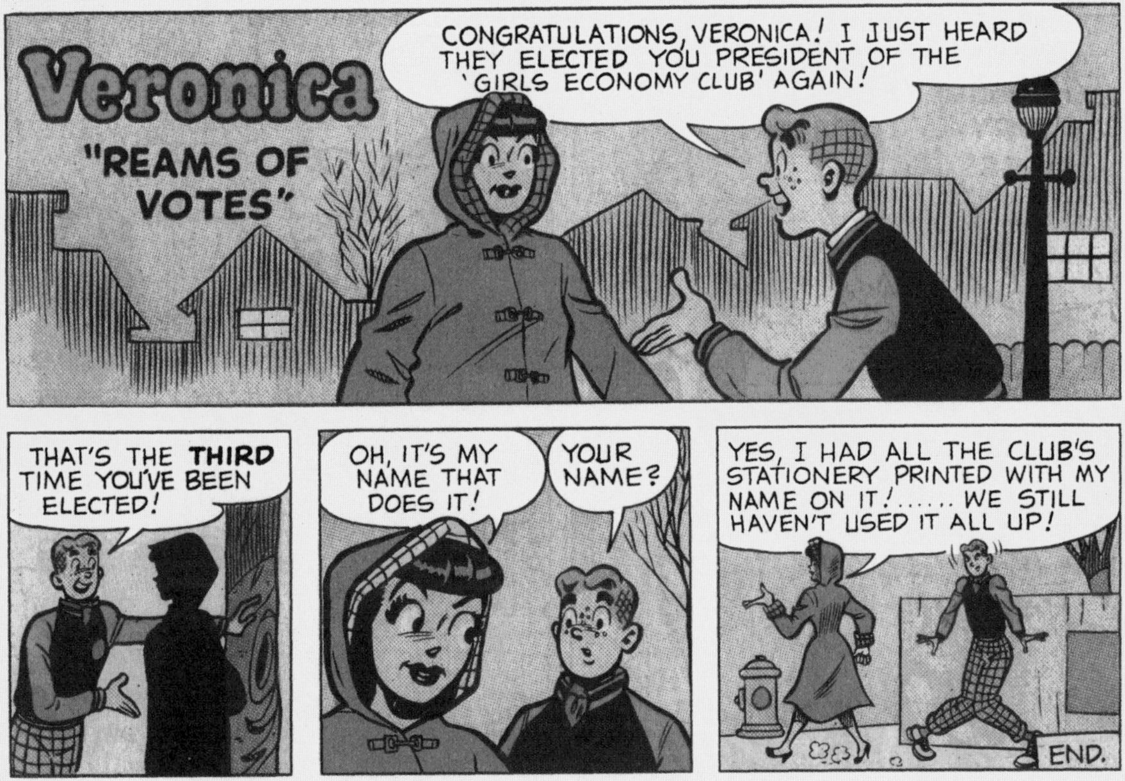
Veronica
"REAMS OF VOTES"
CONGRATULATIONS, VERONICA! I JUST HEARD THEY ELECTED YOU PRESIDENT OF THE 'GIRLS ECONOMY CLUB' AGAIN!
THAT'S THE **THIRD** TIME YOU'VE BEEN ELECTED!
OH, IT'S MY NAME THAT DOES IT!
YOUR NAME?
YES, I HAD ALL THE CLUB'S STATIONERY PRINTED WITH MY NAME ON IT!...... WE STILL HAVEN'T USED IT ALL UP!
END.

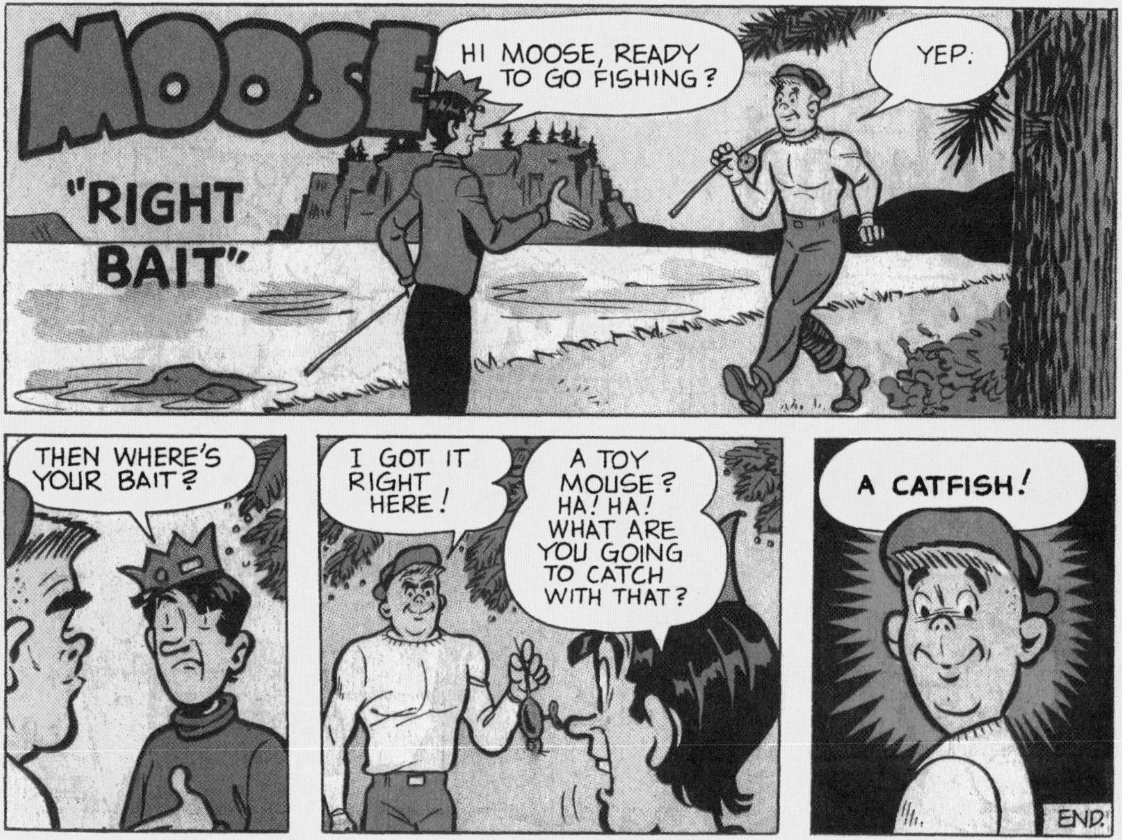
MOOSE
"RIGHT BAIT"
HI MOOSE, READY TO GO FISHING?
YEP:
THEN WHERE'S YOUR BAIT?
I GOT IT RIGHT HERE!
A TOY MOUSE? HA! HA! WHAT ARE YOU GOING TO CATCH WITH THAT?
A CATFISH!
END.

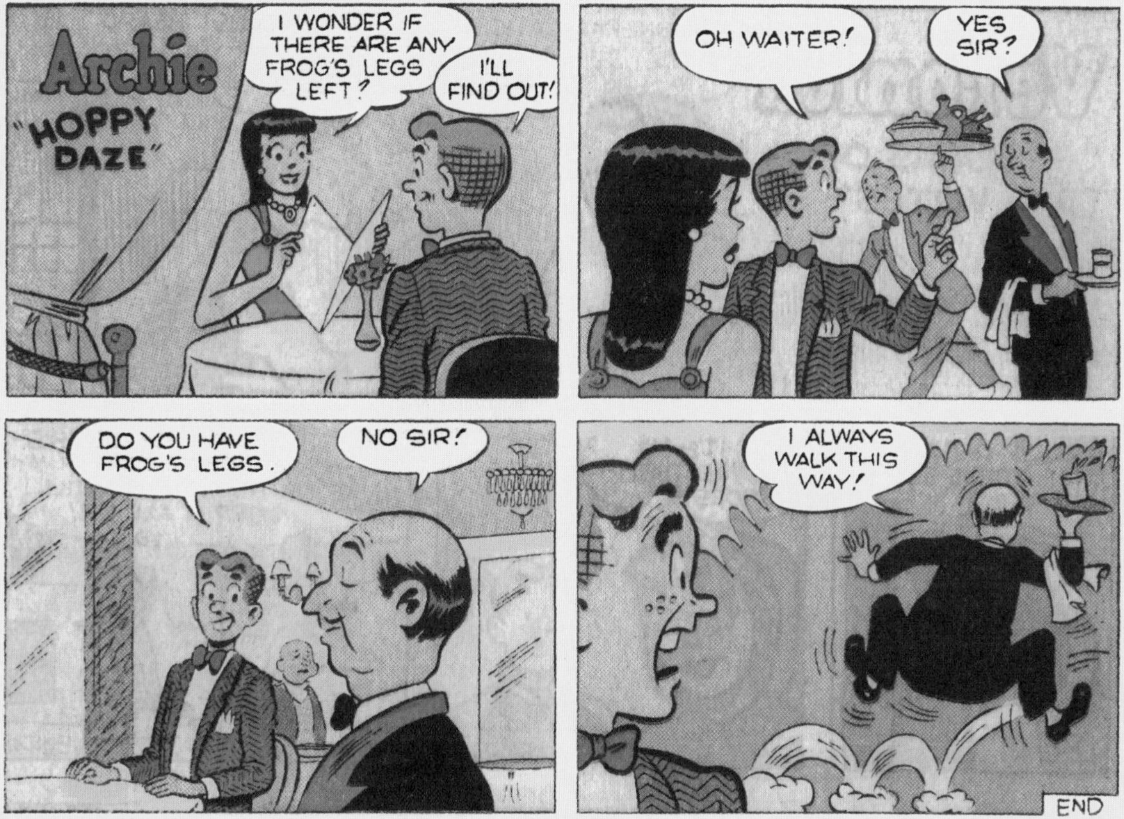
Archie
"HOPPY DAZE"
I WONDER IF THERE ARE ANY FROG'S LEGS LEFT?
I'LL FIND OUT!
OH WAITER!
YES SIR?
DO YOU HAVE FROG'S LEGS.
NO SIR!
I ALWAYS WALK THIS WAY!
END

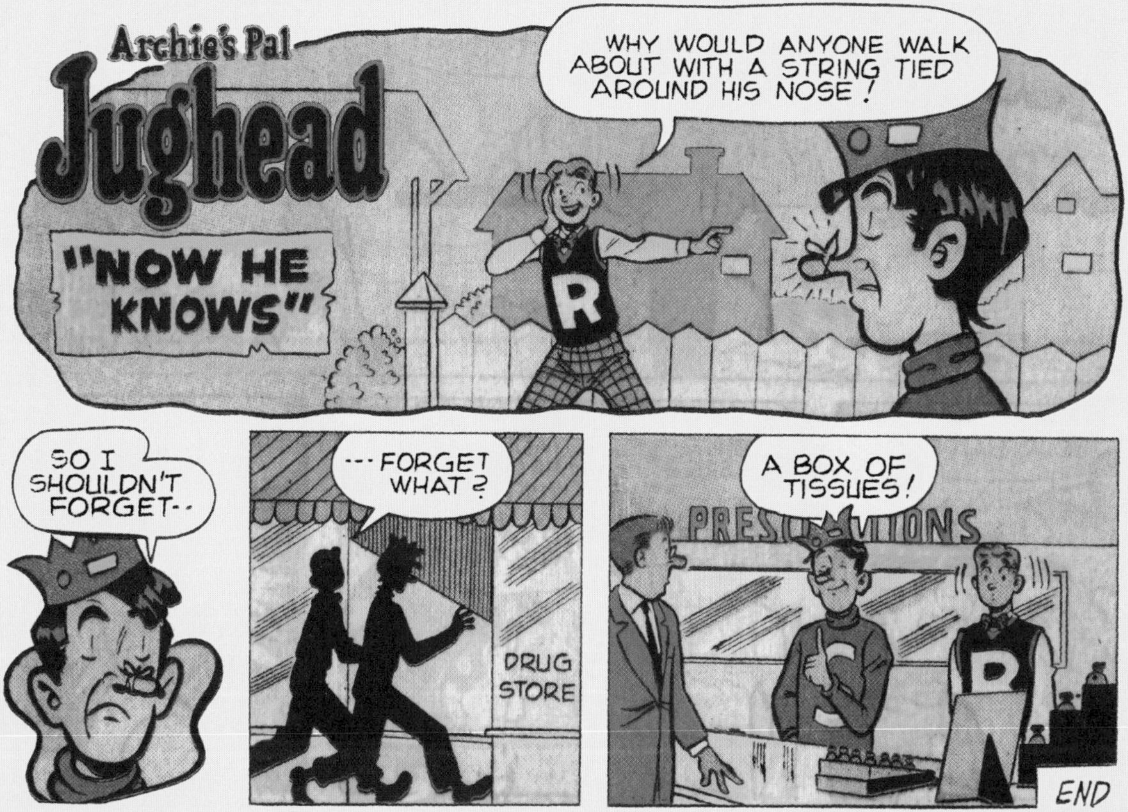
Archie's Pal
Jughead
"NOW HE KNOWS"
WHY WOULD ANYONE WALK ABOUT WITH A STRING TIED AROUND HIS NOSE!
SO I SHOULDN'T FORGET--
--- FORGET WHAT?
DRUG STORE
A BOX OF TISSUES!
PRESCRIPTIONS
END

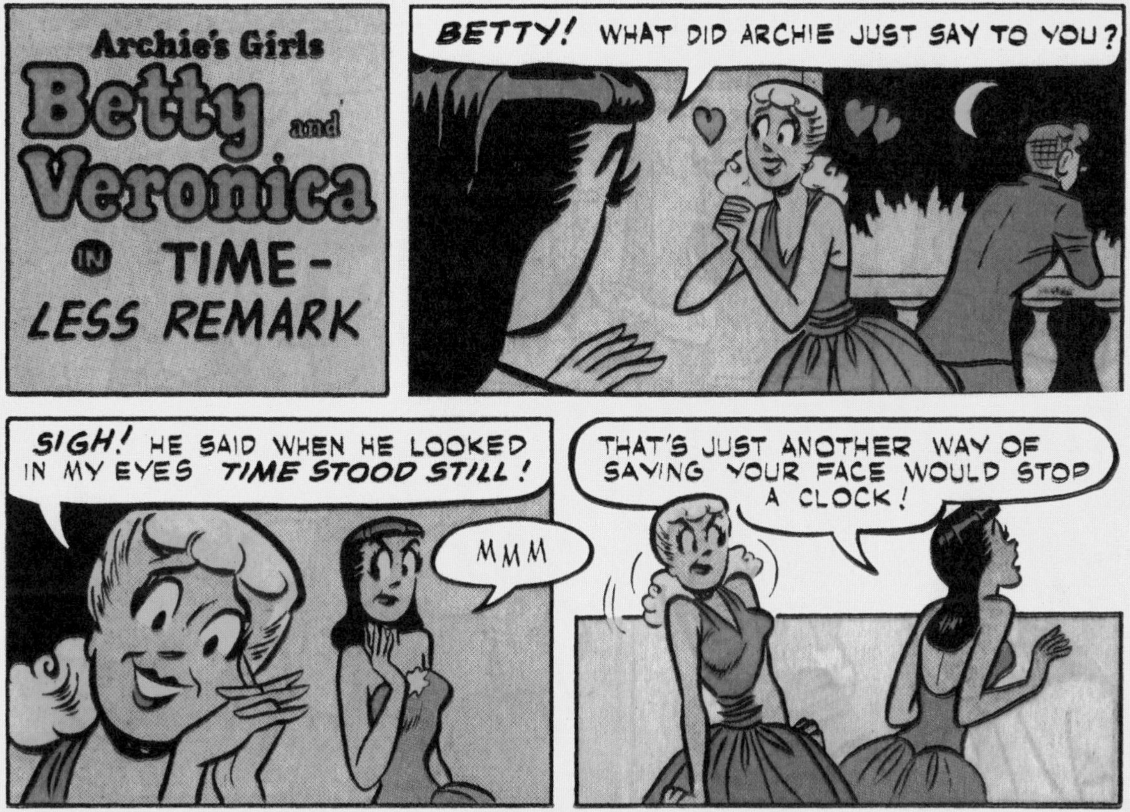
Archie's Girls
Betty and Veronica
IN TIME-LESS REMARK
BETTY! WHAT DID ARCHIE JUST SAY TO YOU?
SIGH! HE SAID WHEN HE LOOKED IN MY EYES TIME STOOD STILL!
MMM
THAT'S JUST ANOTHER WAY OF SAYING YOUR FACE WOULD STOP A CLOCK!

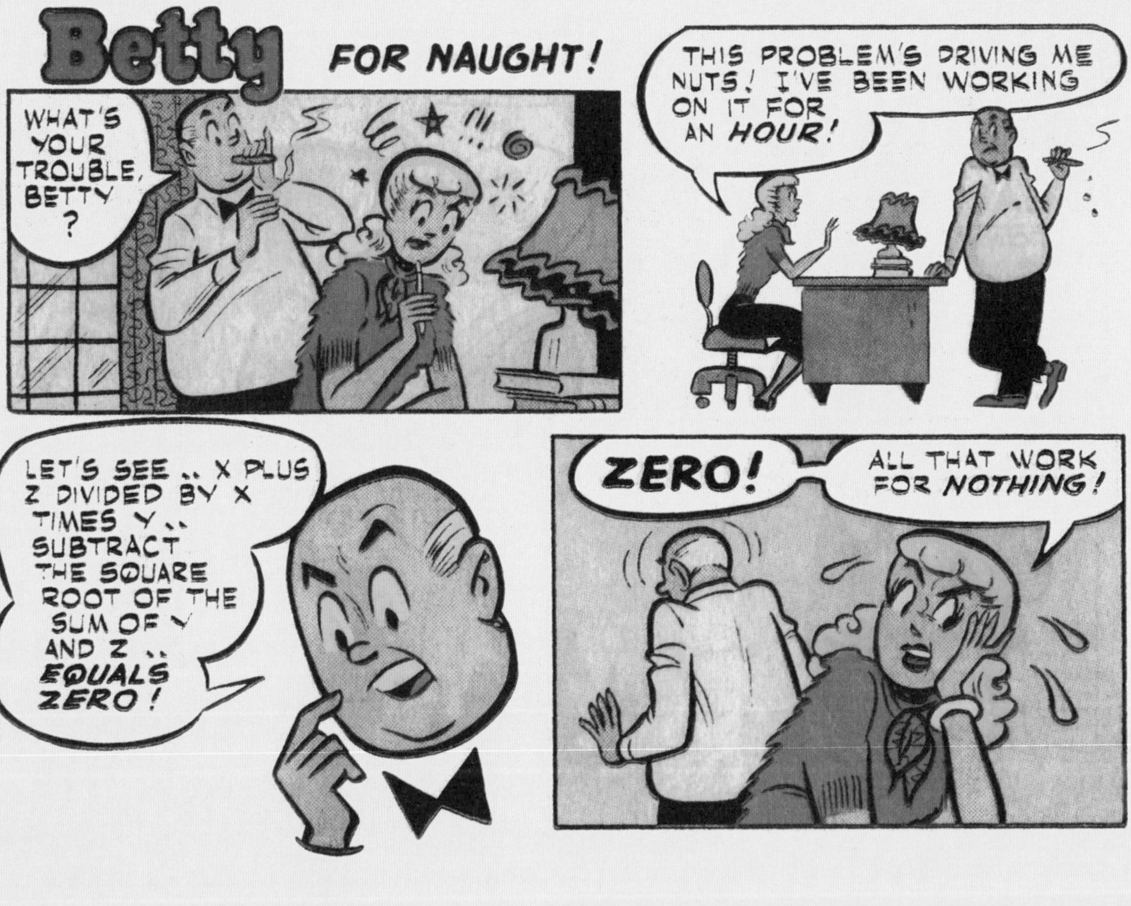
Betty
FOR NAUGHT!
WHAT'S YOUR TROUBLE, BETTY ?
THIS PROBLEM'S DRIVING ME NUTS! I'VE BEEN WORKING ON IT FOR AN HOUR!
LET'S SEE .. X PLUS Z DIVIDED BY X TIMES Y .. SUBTRACT THE SQUARE ROOT OF THE SUM OF Y AND Z .. EQUALS ZERO!
ZERO!
ALL THAT WORK FOR NOTHING!

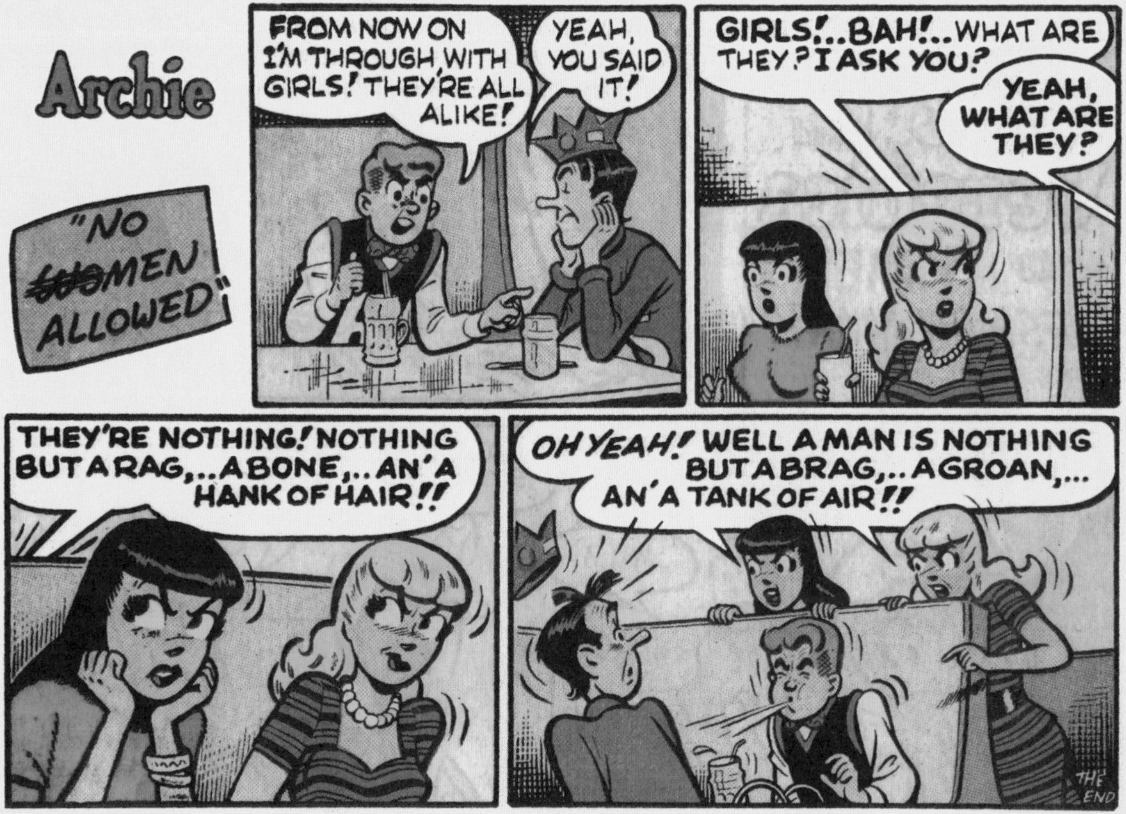
Archie
"NO WOMEN MEN ALLOWED"
FROM NOW ON I'M THROUGH, WITH GIRLS! THEY'RE ALL ALIKE!
YEAH, YOU SAID IT!
GIRLS!..BAH!..WHAT ARE THEY? I ASK YOU?
YEAH, WHAT ARE THEY?
THEY'RE NOTHING! NOTHING BUT A RAG,..A BONE,..AN' A HANK OF HAIR!!
OH YEAH! WELL A MAN IS NOTHING BUT A BRAG,..A GROAN,... AN' A TANK OF AIR!!
THE END

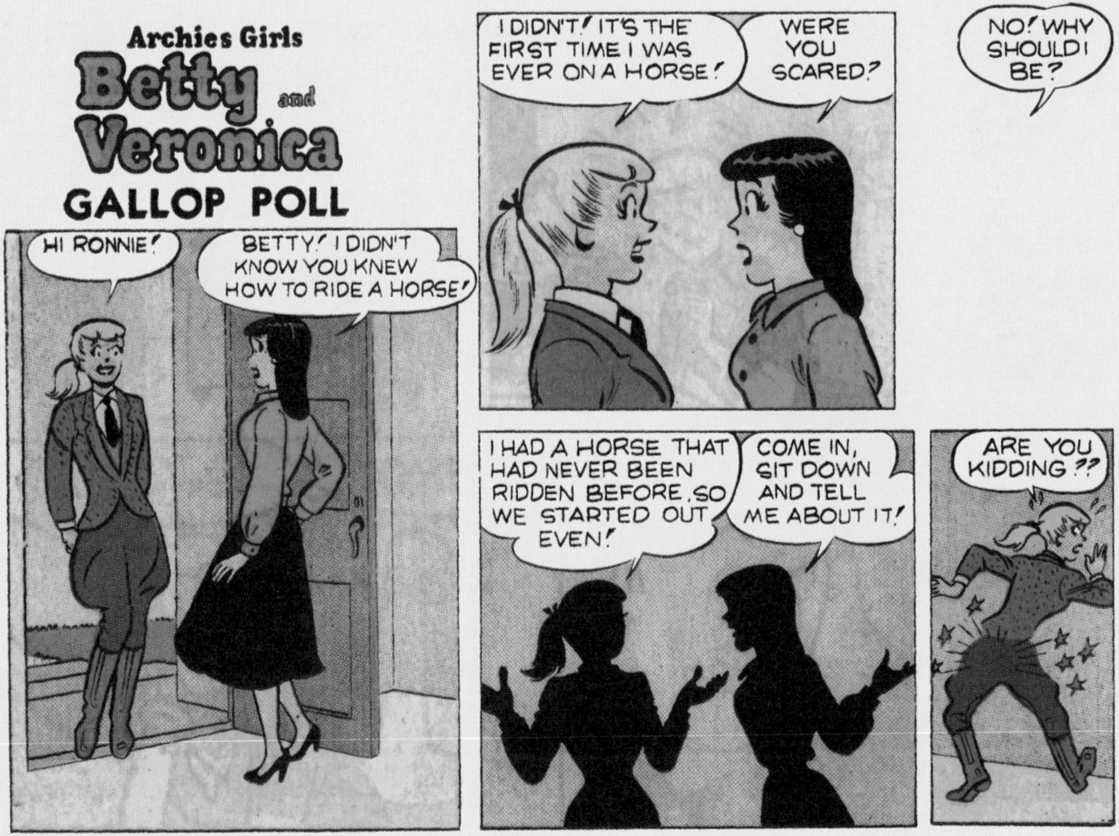
Archies Girls
Betty and Veronica
GALLOP POLL
HI RONNIE!
BETTY! I DIDN'T KNOW YOU KNEW HOW TO RIDE A HORSE!
I DIDN'T! IT'S THE FIRST TIME I WAS EVER ON A HORSE!
WERE YOU SCARED?
NO! WHY SHOULD I BE?
I HAD A HORSE THAT HAD NEVER BEEN RIDDEN BEFORE, SO WE STARTED OUT EVEN!
COME IN, SIT DOWN AND TELL ME ABOUT IT!
ARE YOU KIDDING??

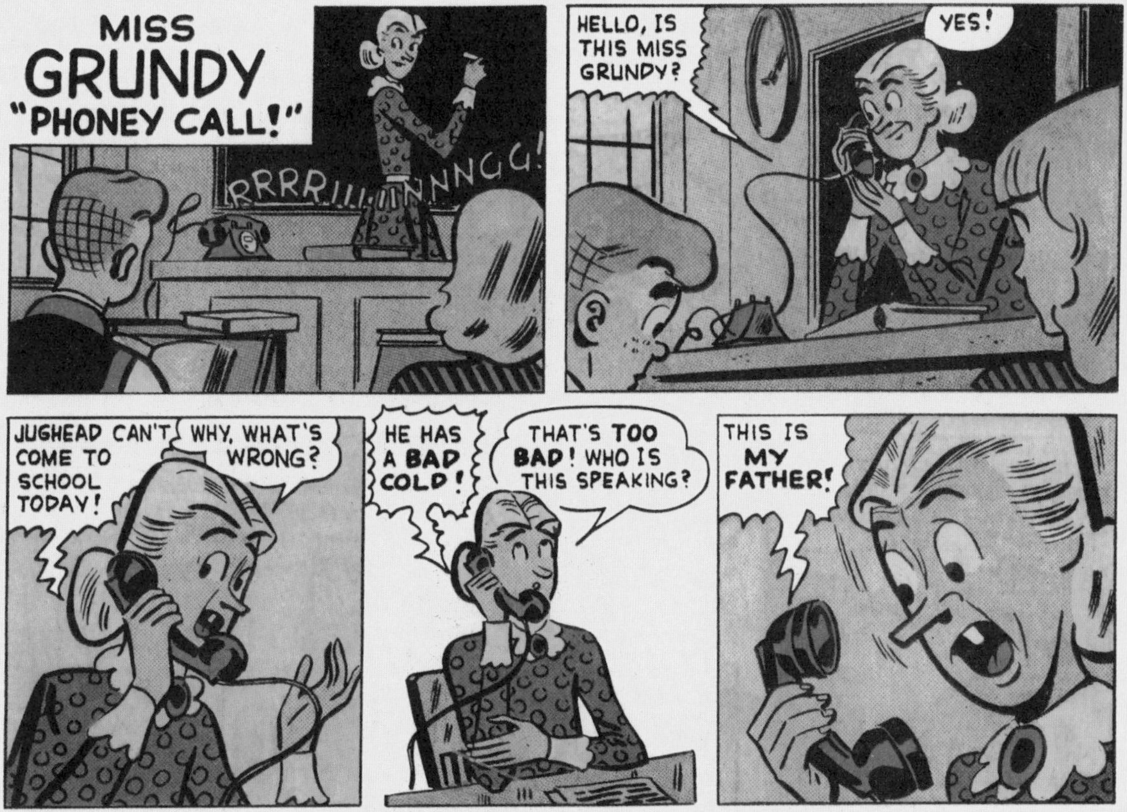
MISS GRUNDY
"PHONEY CALL!"
RRRRIIIINNNGG!
HELLO, IS THIS MISS GRUNDY?
YES!
JUGHEAD CAN'T COME TO SCHOOL TODAY!
WHY, WHAT'S WRONG?
HE HAS A BAD COLD!
THAT'S TOO BAD! WHO IS THIS SPEAKING?
THIS IS MY FATHER!

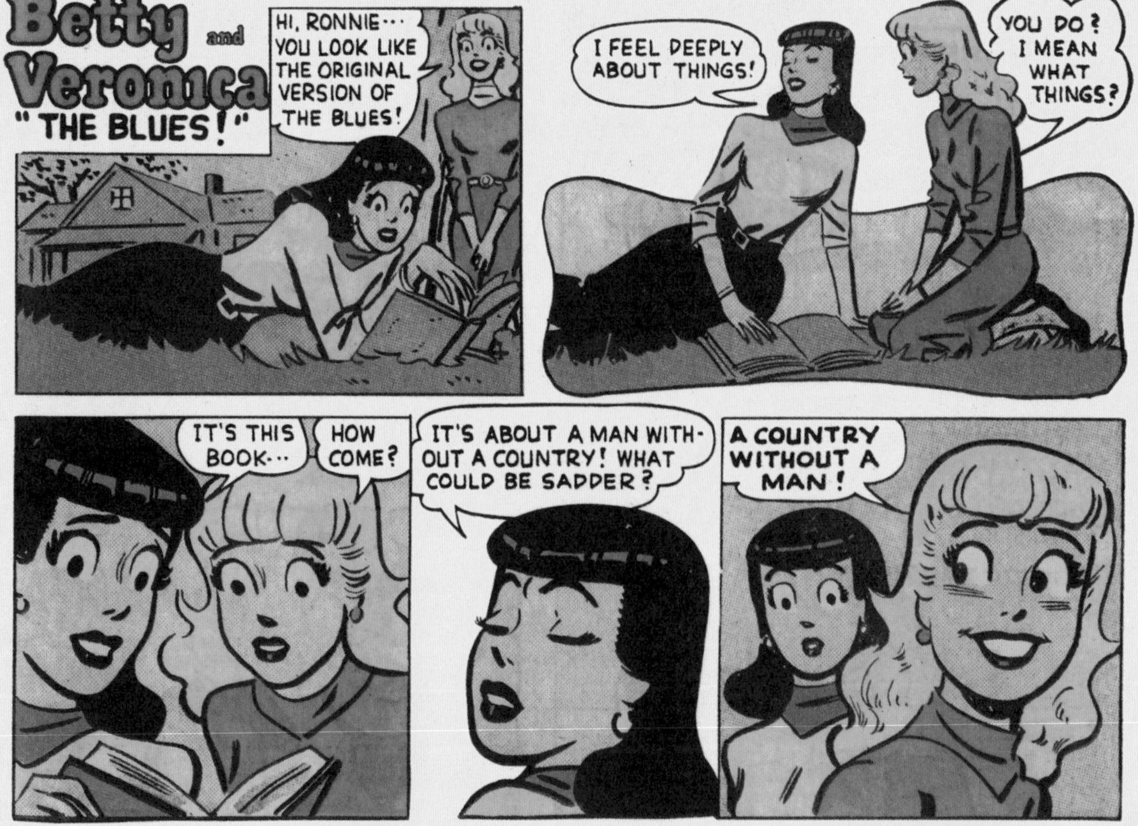
Betty and Veronica
"THE BLUES!"
HI, RONNIE··· YOU LOOK LIKE THE ORIGINAL VERSION OF THE BLUES!
I FEEL DEEPLY ABOUT THINGS!
YOU DO? I MEAN WHAT THINGS?
IT'S THIS BOOK···
HOW COME?
IT'S ABOUT A MAN WITH-OUT A COUNTRY! WHAT COULD BE SADDER?
A COUNTRY WITHOUT A MAN!

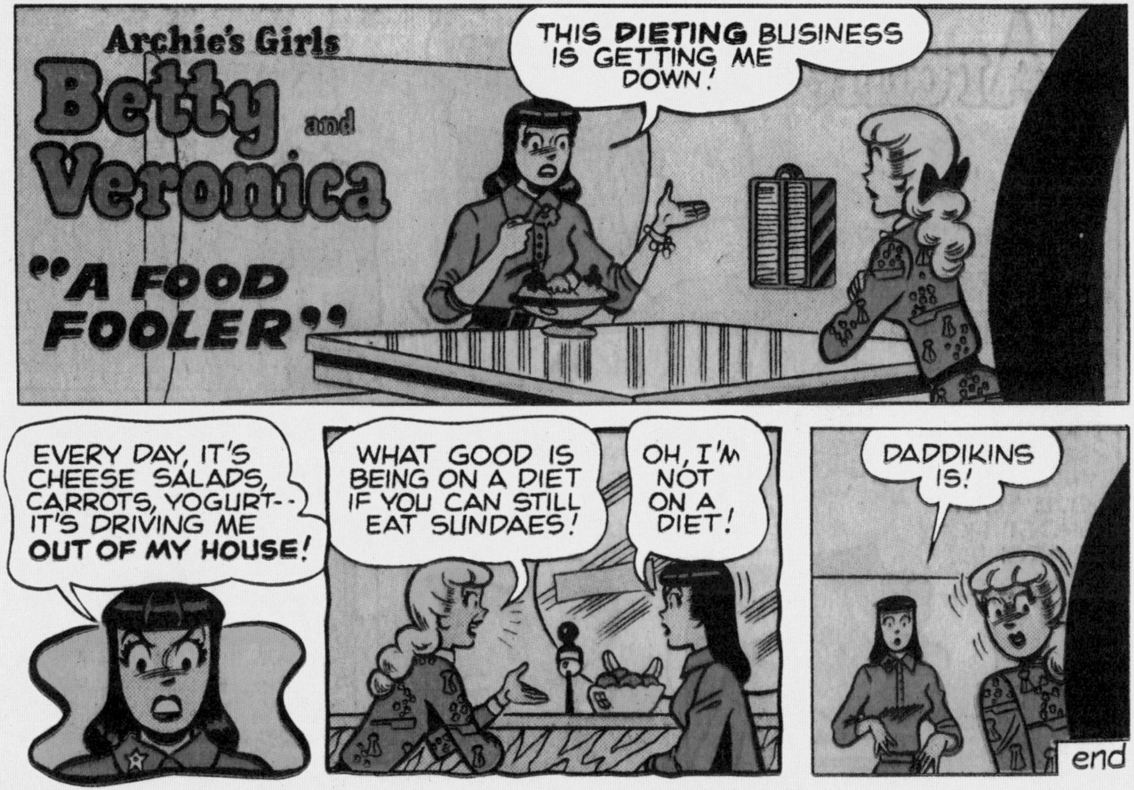
Archie's Girls
Betty and Veronica
"A FOOD FOOLER"
THIS DIETING BUSINESS IS GETTING ME DOWN!
EVERY DAY, IT'S CHEESE SALADS, CARROTS, YOGURT-- IT'S DRIVING ME OUT OF MY HOUSE!
WHAT GOOD IS BEING ON A DIET IF YOU CAN STILL EAT SUNDAES!
OH, I'M NOT ON A DIET!
DADDIKINS IS!
end

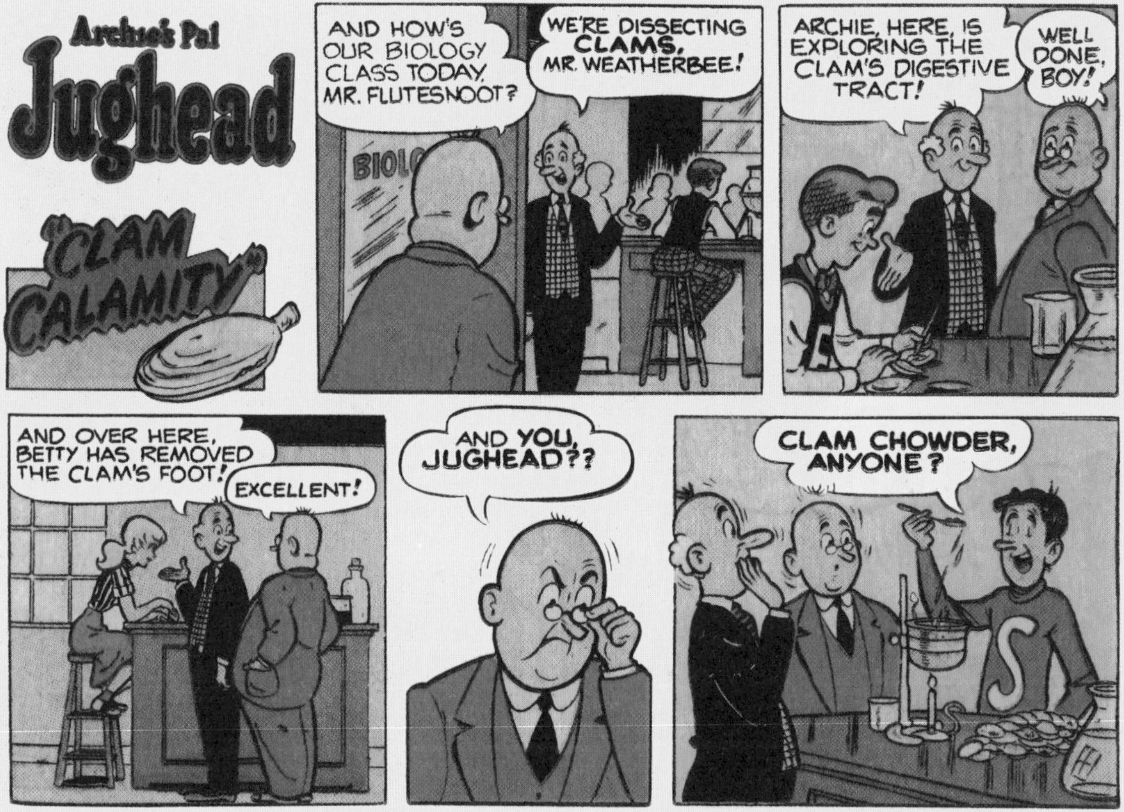
Archie's Pal
Jughead
"CLAM CALAMITY"
AND HOW'S OUR BIOLOGY CLASS TODAY, MR. FLUTESNOOT?
BIOLO
WE'RE DISSECTING CLAMS, MR. WEATHERBEE!
ARCHIE, HERE, IS EXPLORING THE CLAM'S DIGESTIVE TRACT!
WELL DONE, BOY!
AND OVER HERE, BETTY HAS REMOVED THE CLAM'S FOOT!
EXCELLENT!
AND YOU, JUGHEAD??
CLAM CHOWDER, ANYONE?

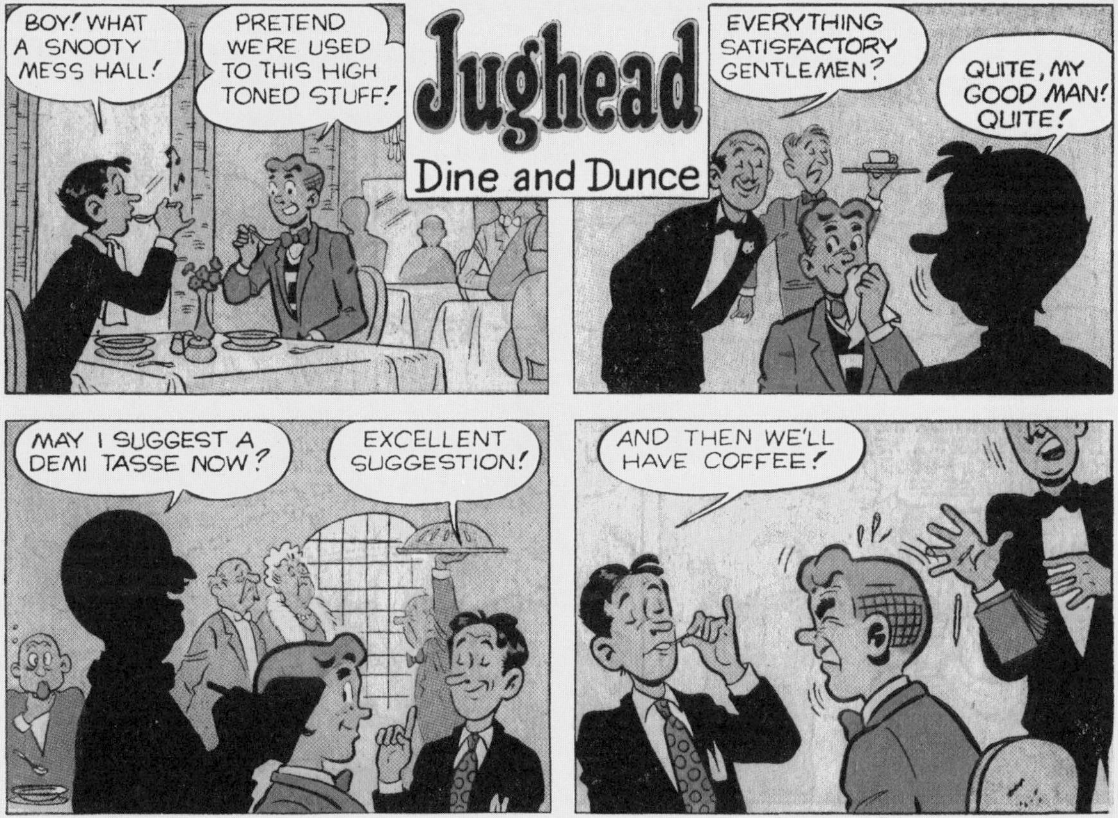
BOY! WHAT A SNOOTY MESS HALL!
PRETEND WE'RE USED TO THIS HIGH TONED STUFF!
Jughead
Dine and Dunce
EVERYTHING SATISFACTORY GENTLEMEN?
QUITE, MY GOOD MAN! QUITE!
MAY I SUGGEST A DEMI TASSE NOW?
EXCELLENT SUGGESTION!
AND THEN WE'LL HAVE COFFEE!

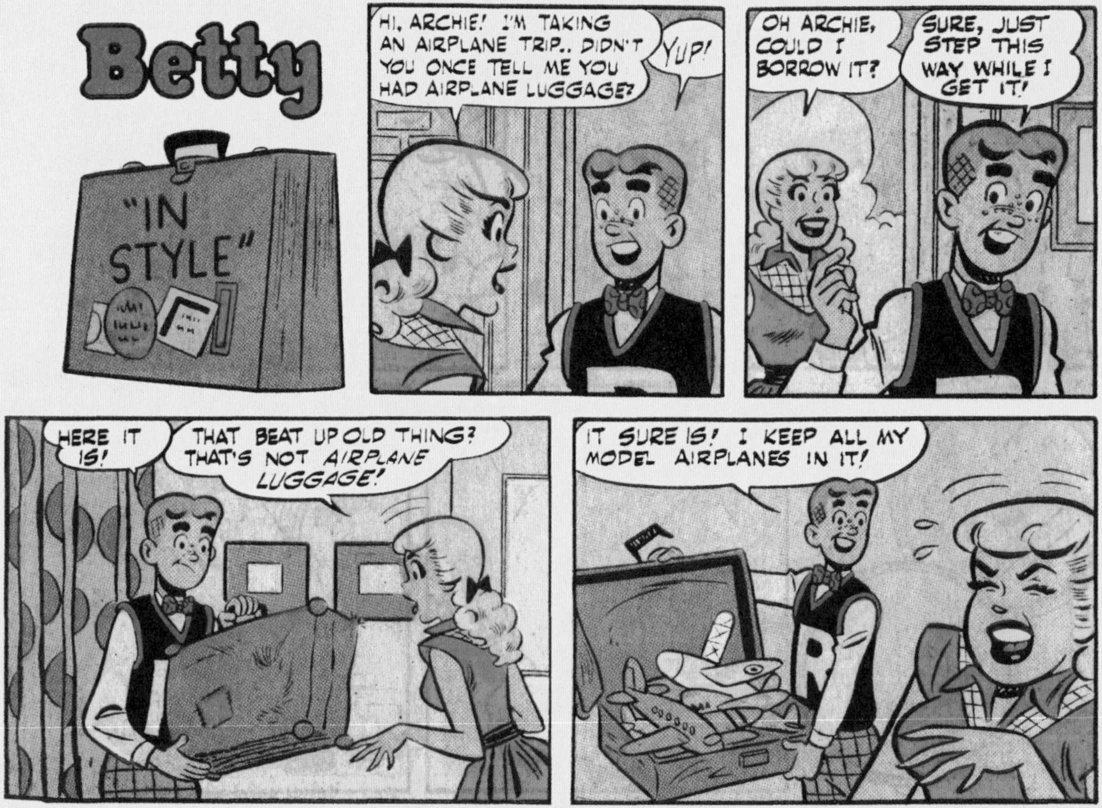
Betty
"IN STYLE"
HI, ARCHIE! I'M TAKING AN AIRPLANE TRIP.. DIDN'T YOU ONCE TELL ME YOU HAD AIRPLANE LUGGAGE?
YUP!
OH ARCHIE, COULD I BORROW IT?
SURE, JUST STEP THIS WAY WHILE I GET IT!
HERE IT IS!
THAT BEAT UP OLD THING? THAT'S NOT AIRPLANE LUGGAGE!
IT SURE IS! I KEEP ALL MY MODEL AIRPLANES IN IT!

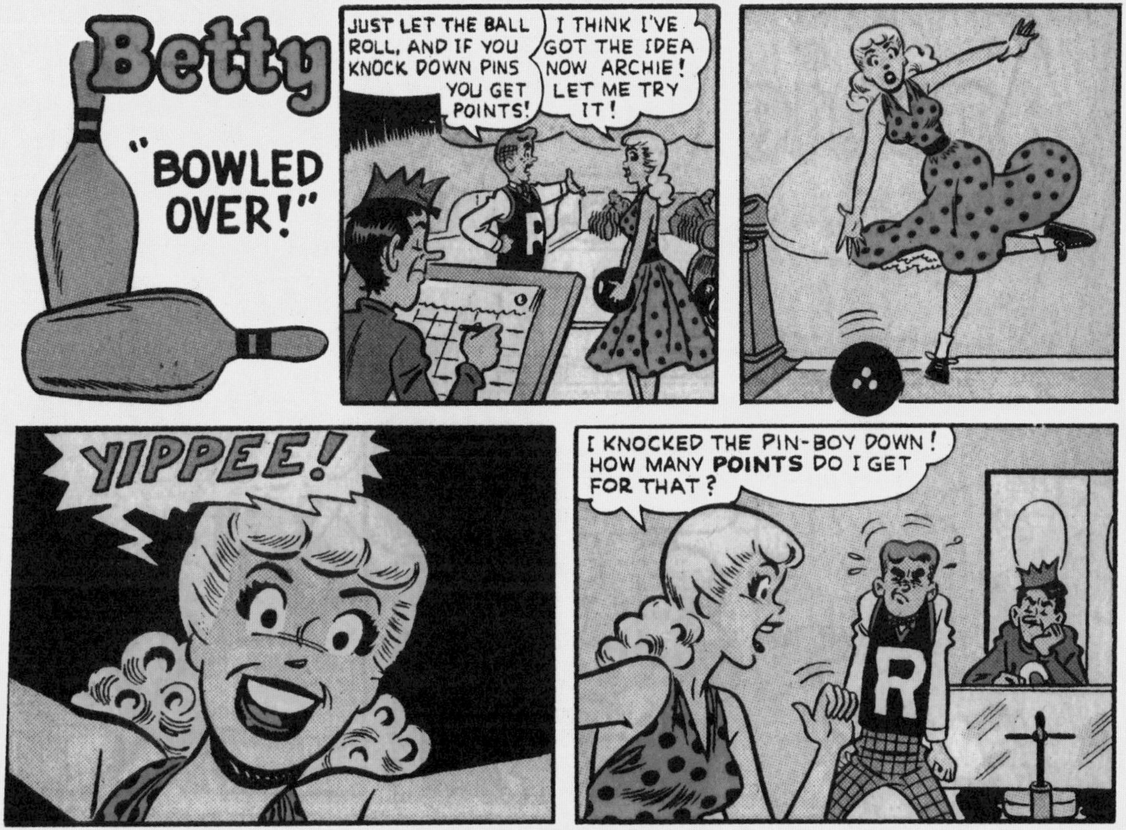
Betty
"BOWLED OVER!"
JUST LET THE BALL ROLL, AND IF YOU KNOCK DOWN PINS YOU GET POINTS!
I THINK I'VE GOT THE IDEA NOW ARCHIE! LET ME TRY IT!
YIPPEE!
I KNOCKED THE PIN-BOY DOWN! HOW MANY POINTS DO I GET FOR THAT?
R

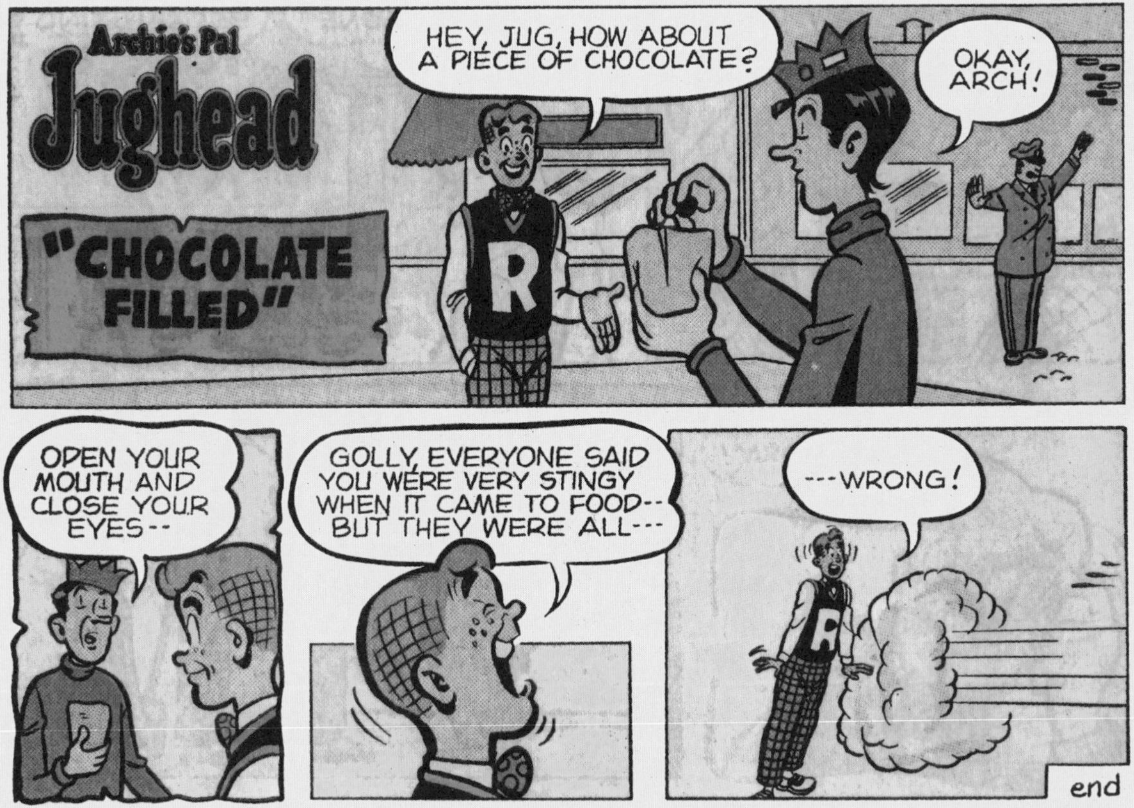
Archie's Pal
Jughead
"CHOCOLATE FILLED"
HEY, JUG, HOW ABOUT A PIECE OF CHOCOLATE?
OKAY, ARCH!
OPEN YOUR MOUTH AND CLOSE YOUR EYES--
GOLLY, EVERYONE SAID YOU WERE VERY STINGY WHEN IT CAME TO FOOD-- BUT THEY WERE ALL---
---WRONG!
end

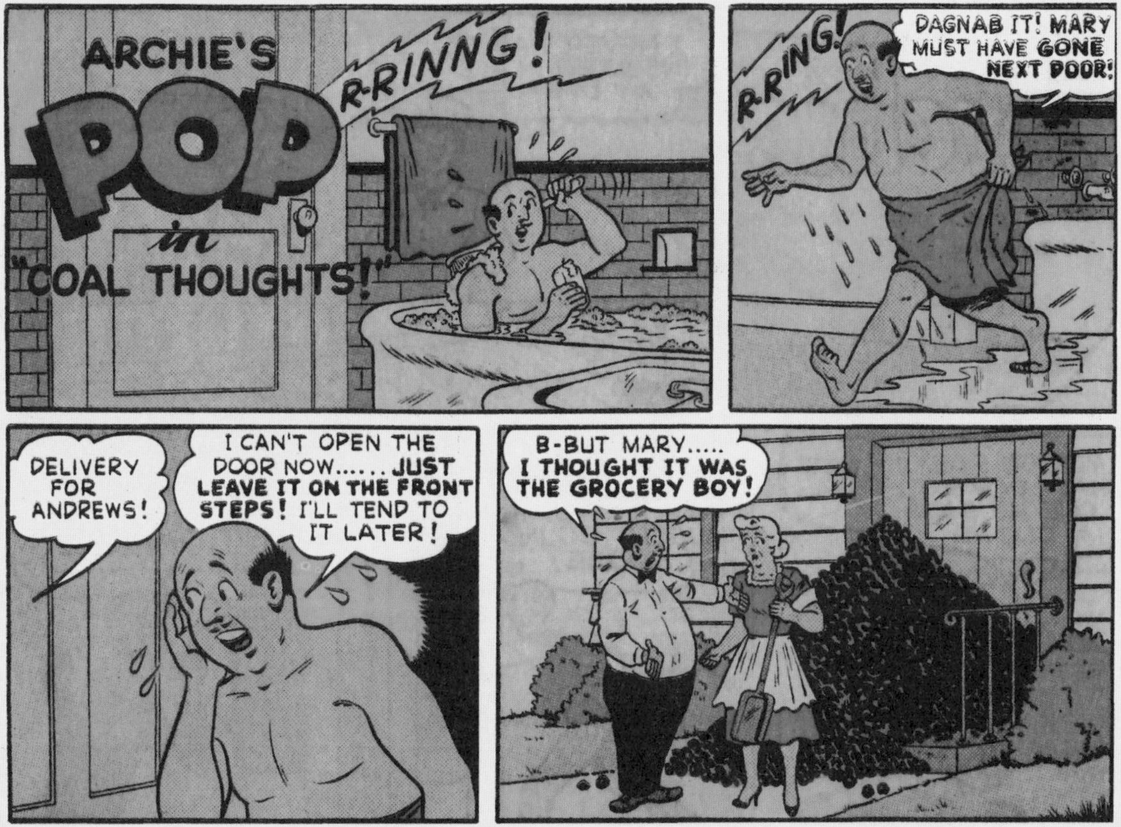
ARCHIE'S
POP
in
"COAL THOUGHTS!"
R-RINNG!
R-RING!
DAGNAB IT! MARY MUST HAVE GONE NEXT DOOR!
DELIVERY FOR ANDREWS!
I CAN'T OPEN THE DOOR NOW...... JUST LEAVE IT ON THE FRONT STEPS! I'LL TEND TO IT LATER!
B-BUT MARY..... I THOUGHT IT WAS THE GROCERY BOY!

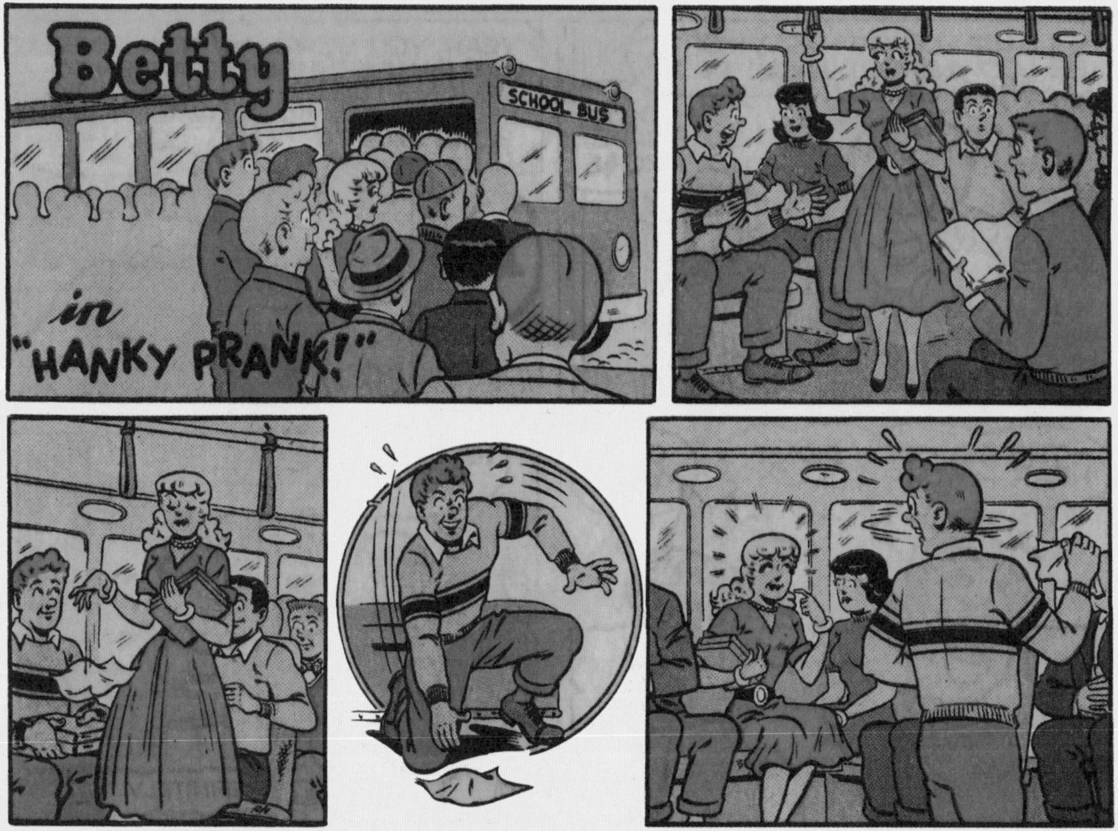
Betty
SCHOOL BUS
in
"HANKY PRANK!"

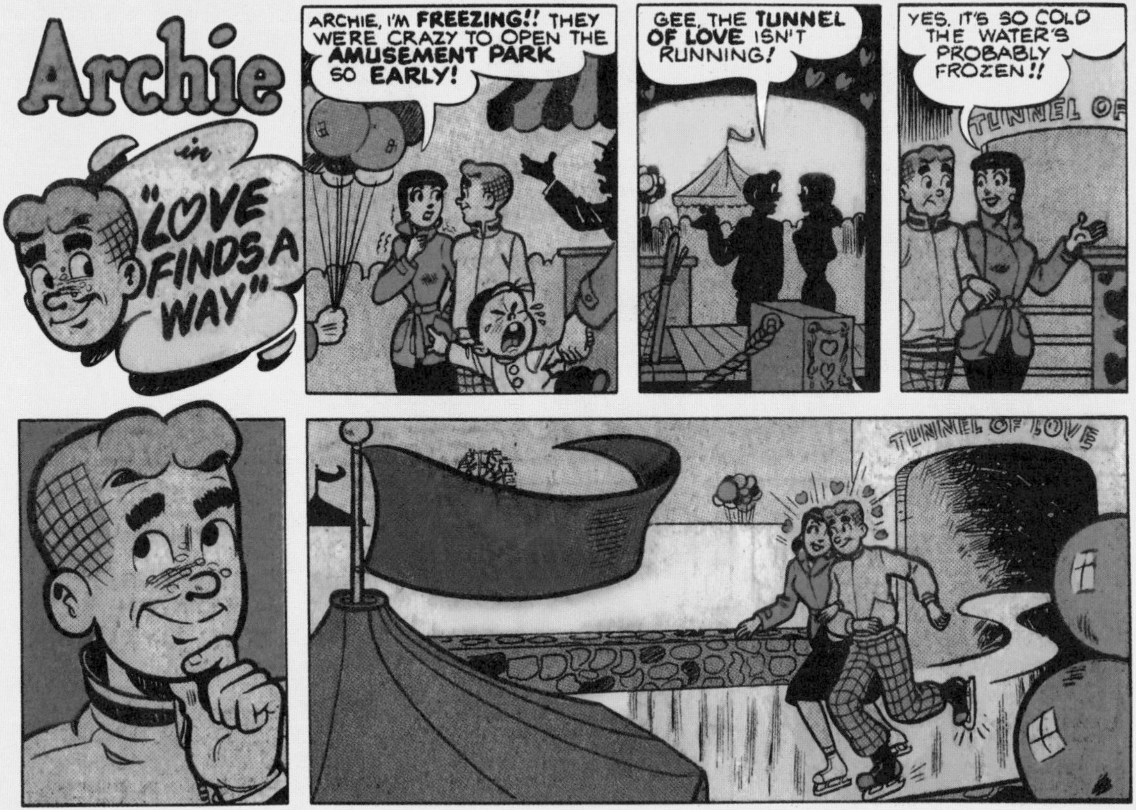
Archie
in
"LOVE FINDS A WAY"
ARCHIE, I'M FREEZING!! THEY WERE CRAZY TO OPEN THE AMUSEMENT PARK SO EARLY!
GEE, THE TUNNEL OF LOVE ISN'T RUNNING!
YES, IT'S SO COLD THE WATER'S PROBABLY FROZEN!!
TUNNEL OF
TUNNEL OF LOVE

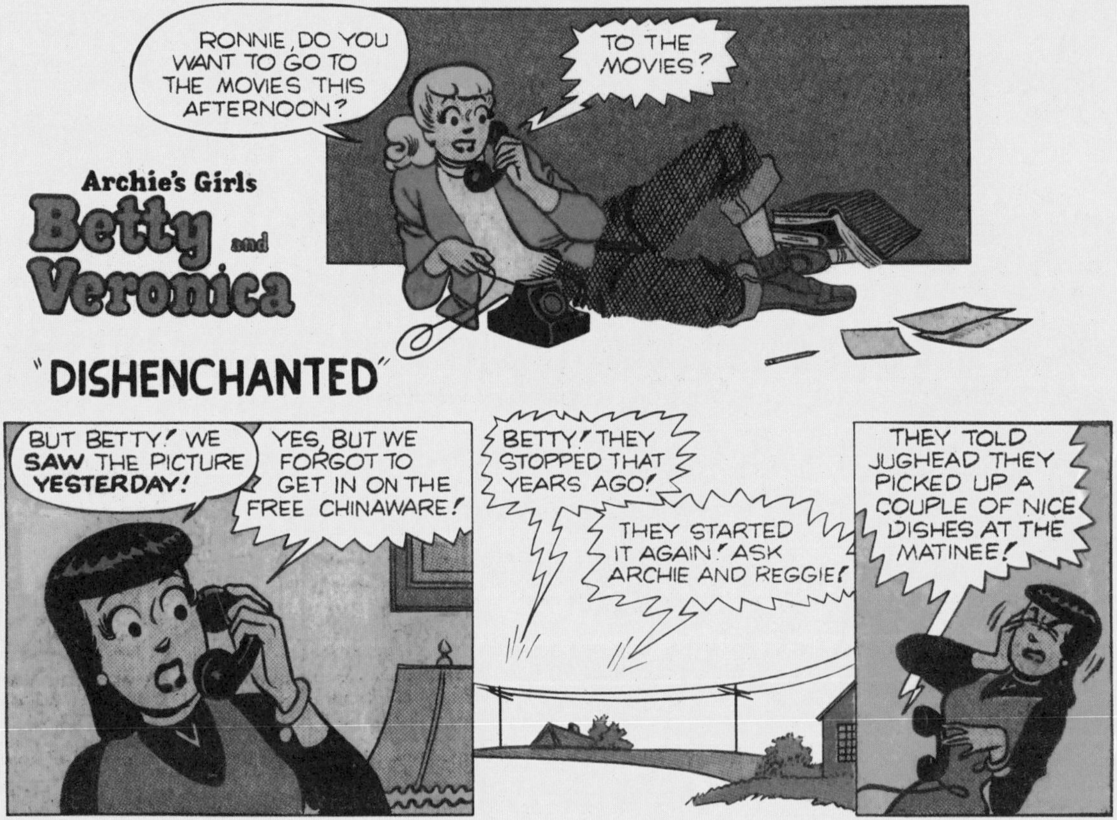
RONNIE, DO YOU WANT TO GO TO THE MOVIES THIS AFTERNOON?
TO THE MOVIES?
Archie's Girls Betty and Veronica
"DISHENCHANTED"
BUT BETTY! WE SAW THE PICTURE YESTERDAY!
YES, BUT WE FORGOT TO GET IN ON THE FREE CHINAWARE!
BETTY! THEY STOPPED THAT YEARS AGO!
THEY STARTED IT AGAIN! ASK ARCHIE AND REGGIE!
THEY TOLD JUGHEAD THEY PICKED UP A COUPLE OF NICE DISHES AT THE MATINEE!

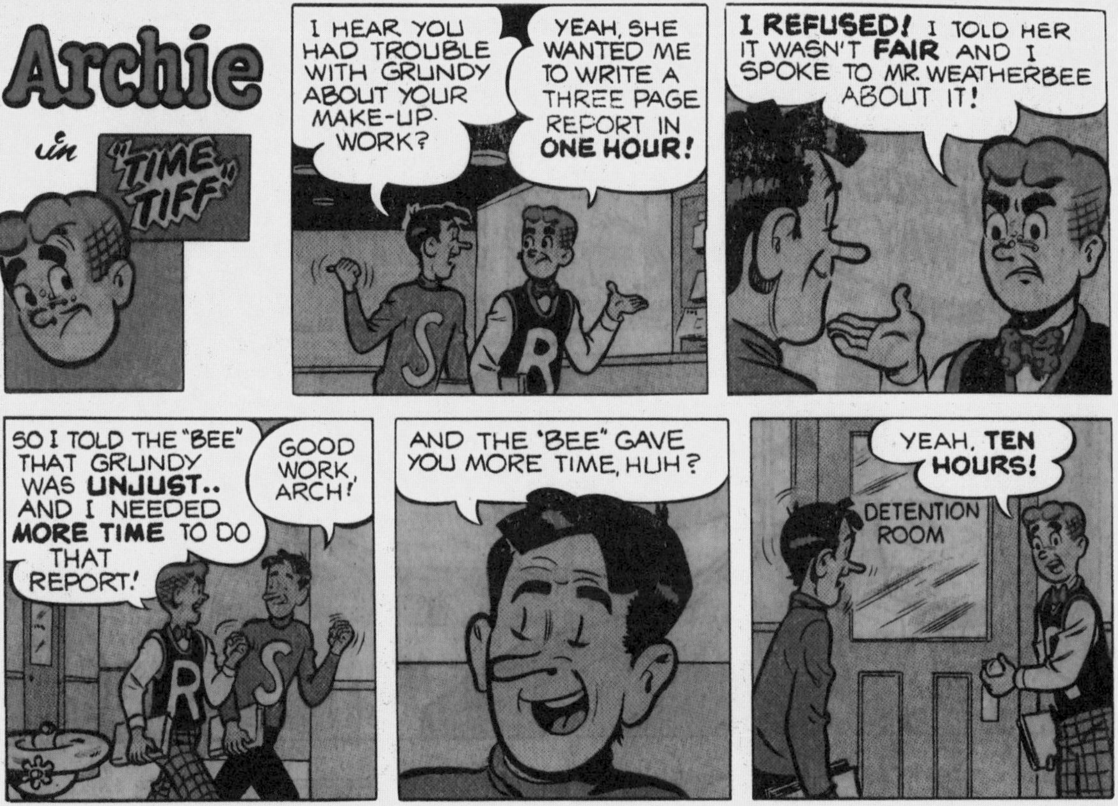
Archie
in "TIME TIFF"
I HEAR YOU HAD TROUBLE WITH GRUNDY ABOUT YOUR MAKE-UP WORK?
YEAH, SHE WANTED ME TO WRITE A THREE PAGE REPORT IN **ONE HOUR!**
I REFUSED! I TOLD HER IT WASN'T **FAIR** AND I SPOKE TO MR. WEATHERBEE ABOUT IT!
SO I TOLD THE "BEE" THAT GRUNDY WAS **UNJUST..** AND I NEEDED **MORE TIME** TO DO THAT REPORT!
GOOD WORK, ARCH!
AND THE "BEE" GAVE YOU MORE TIME, HUH?
YEAH, **TEN HOURS!**
DETENTION ROOM

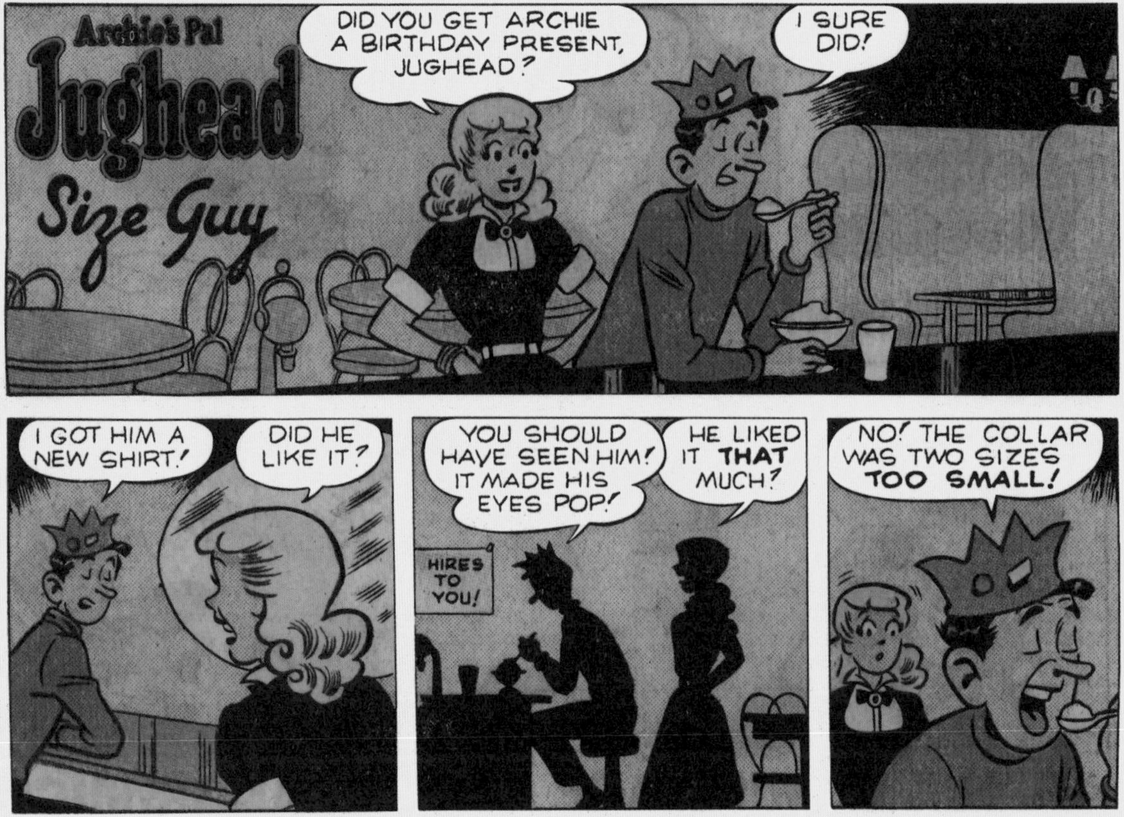
Archie's Pal
Jughead
Size Guy
DID YOU GET ARCHIE A BIRTHDAY PRESENT, JUGHEAD?
I SURE DID!
I GOT HIM A NEW SHIRT!
DID HE LIKE IT?
YOU SHOULD HAVE SEEN HIM! IT MADE HIS EYES POP!
HE LIKED IT THAT MUCH?
HIRES TO YOU!
NO! THE COLLAR WAS TWO SIZES TOO SMALL!

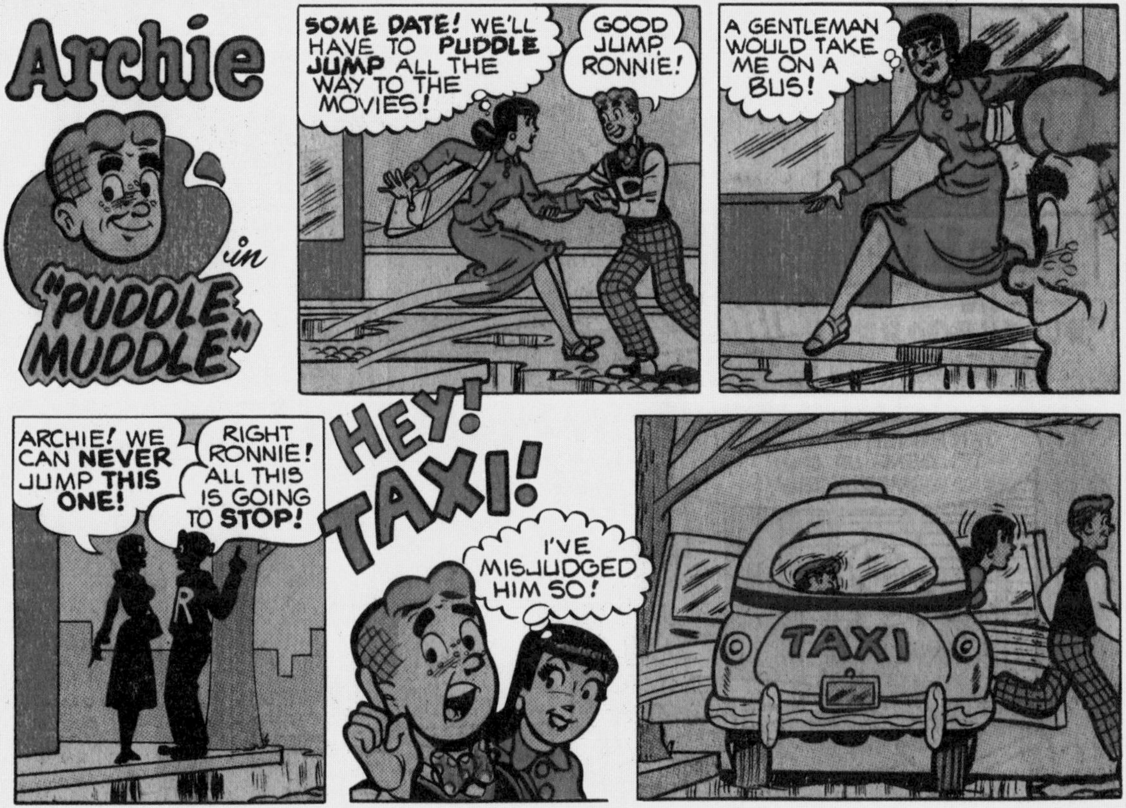
Archie
in
"PUDDLE MUDDLE"
SOME DATE! WE'LL HAVE TO PUDDLE JUMP ALL THE WAY TO THE MOVIES!
GOOD JUMP, RONNIE!
A GENTLEMAN WOULD TAKE ME ON A BUS!
ARCHIE! WE CAN NEVER JUMP THIS ONE!
RIGHT RONNIE! ALL THIS IS GOING TO STOP!
HEY! TAXI!
I'VE MISJUDGED HIM SO!
TAXI

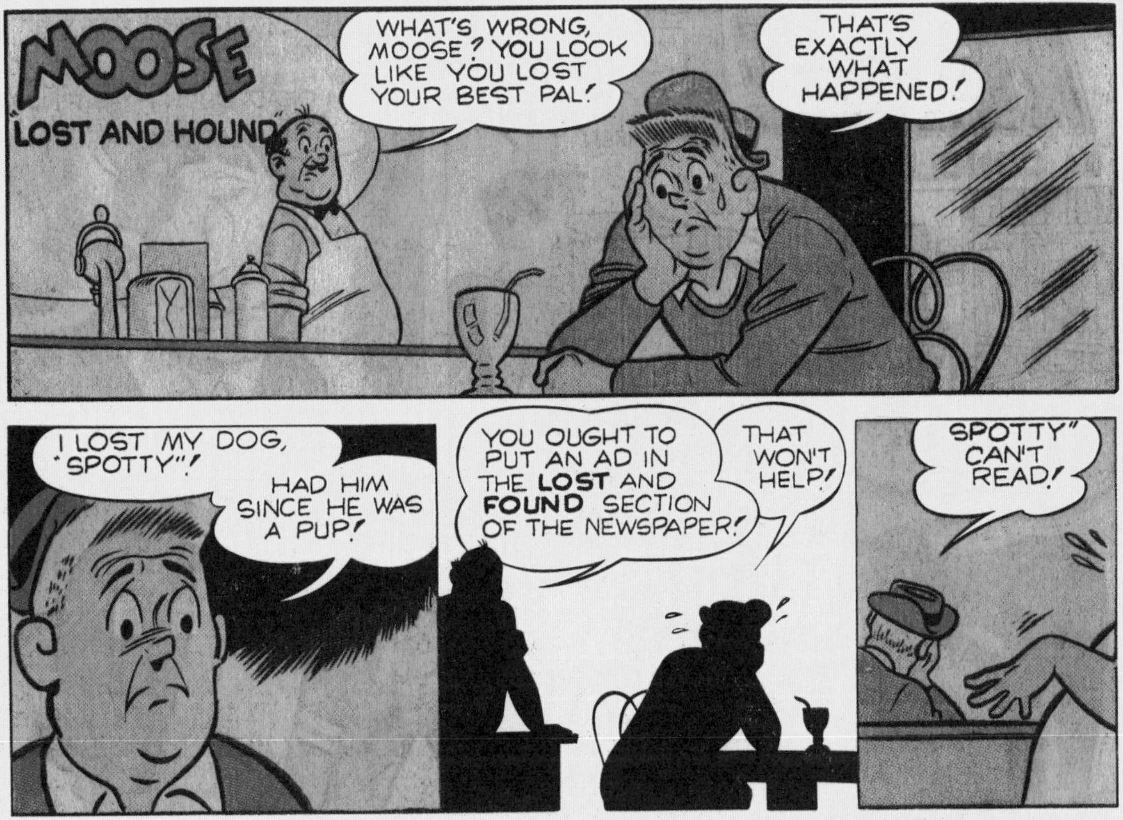
MOOSE
"LOST AND HOUND"
WHAT'S WRONG, MOOSE? YOU LOOK LIKE YOU LOST YOUR BEST PAL!
THAT'S EXACTLY WHAT HAPPENED!
I LOST MY DOG, "SPOTTY"!
HAD HIM SINCE HE WAS A PUP!
YOU OUGHT TO PUT AN AD IN THE LOST AND FOUND SECTION OF THE NEWSPAPER!
THAT WON'T HELP!
"SPOTTY" CAN'T READ!

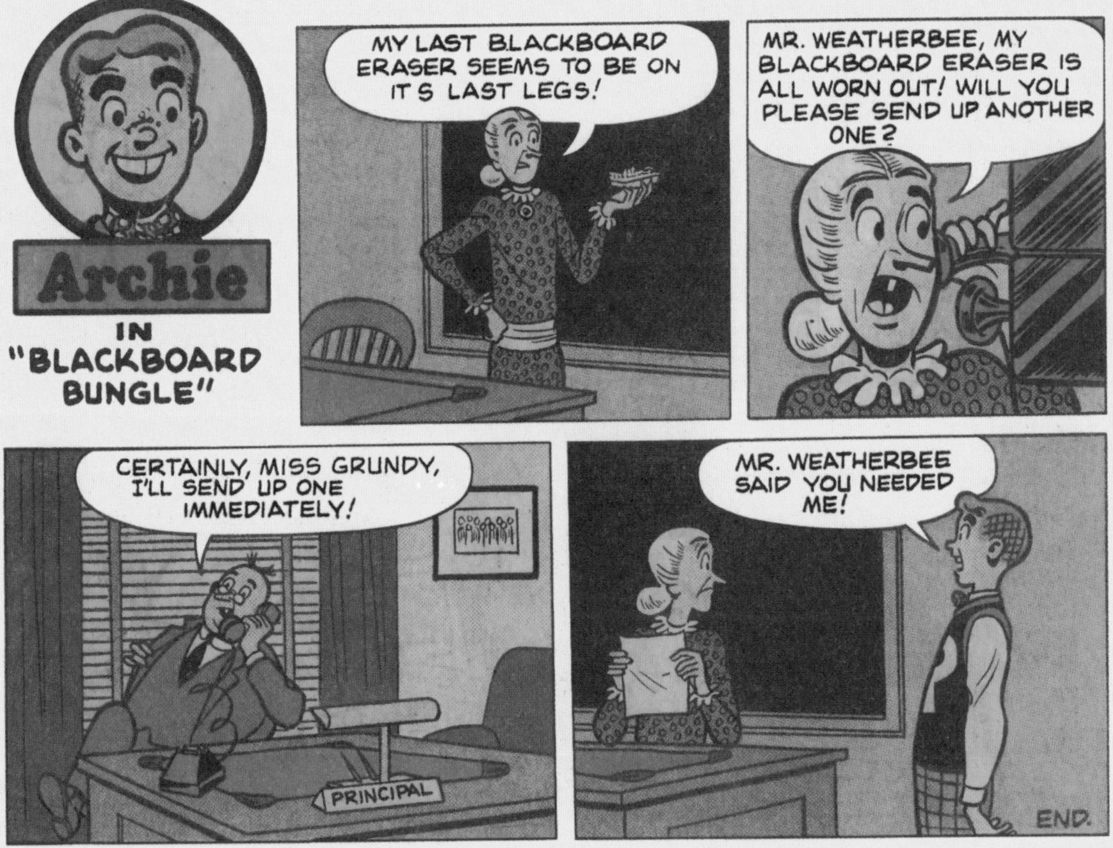
Archie
IN "BLACKBOARD BUNGLE"
MY LAST BLACKBOARD ERASER SEEMS TO BE ON IT S LAST LEGS!
MR. WEATHERBEE, MY BLACKBOARD ERASER IS ALL WORN OUT! WILL YOU PLEASE SEND UP ANOTHER ONE?
CERTAINLY, MISS GRUNDY, I'LL SEND UP ONE IMMEDIATELY!
PRINCIPAL
MR. WEATHERBEE SAID YOU NEEDED ME!
END.

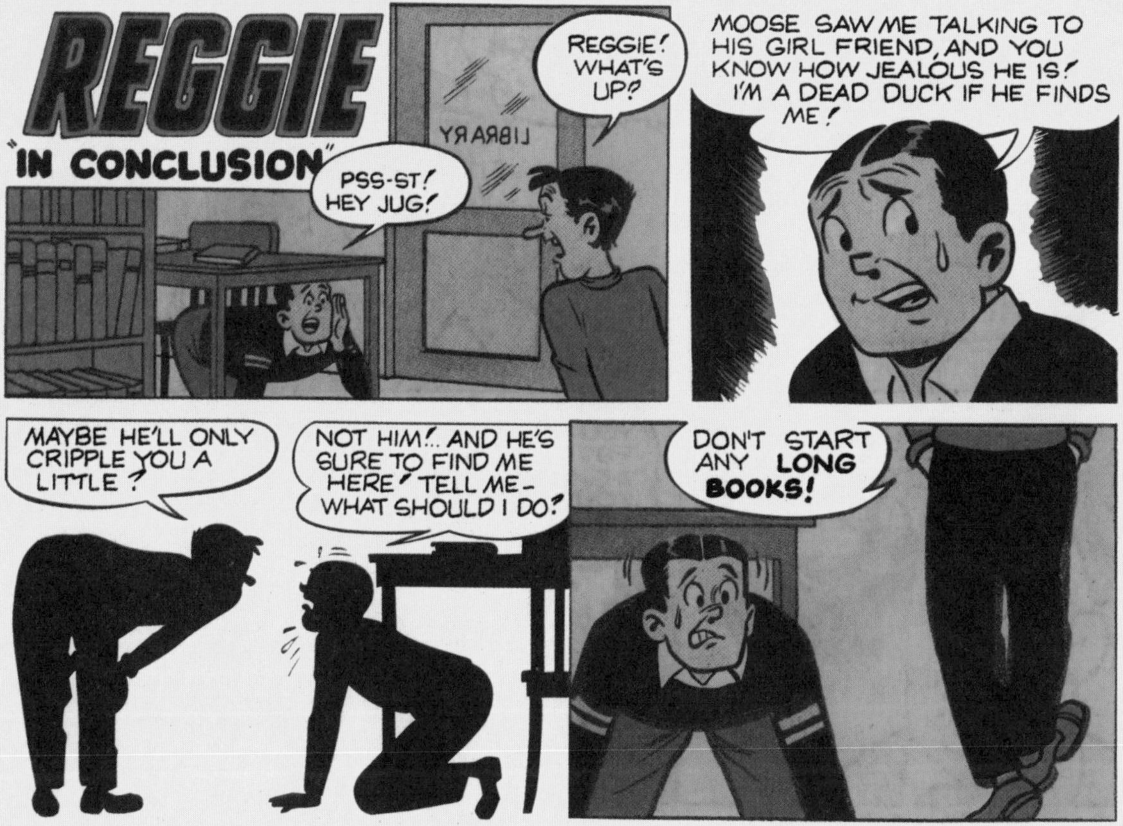
REGGIE
"IN CONCLUSION"
PSS-ST! HEY JUG!
LIBRARY
REGGIE! WHAT'S UP?
MOOSE SAW ME TALKING TO HIS GIRL FRIEND, AND YOU KNOW HOW JEALOUS HE IS! I'M A DEAD DUCK IF HE FINDS ME!
MAYBE HE'LL ONLY CRIPPLE YOU A LITTLE?
NOT HIM!.. AND HE'S SURE TO FIND ME HERE! TELL ME- WHAT SHOULD I DO?
DON'T START ANY LONG BOOKS!

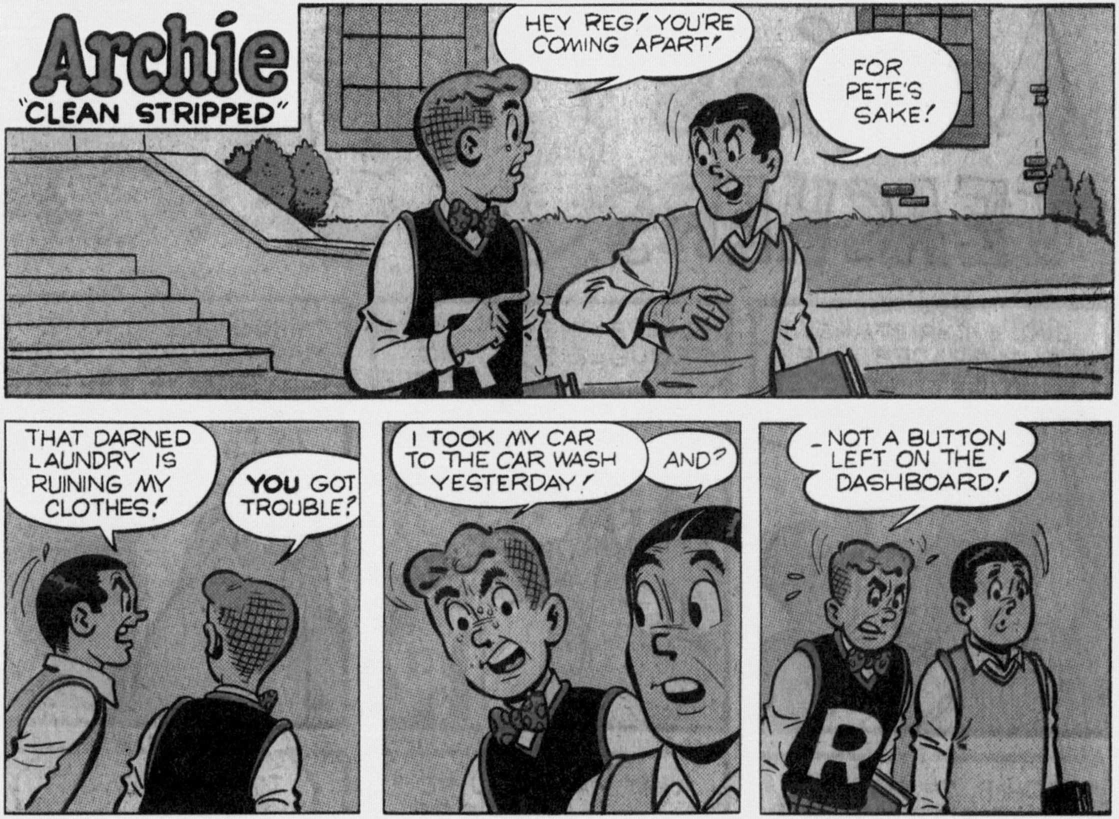
Archie
"CLEAN STRIPPED"
HEY REG! YOU'RE COMING APART!
FOR PETE'S SAKE!
THAT DARNED LAUNDRY IS RUINING MY CLOTHES!
YOU GOT TROUBLE?
I TOOK MY CAR TO THE CAR WASH YESTERDAY!
AND?
_NOT A BUTTON LEFT ON THE DASHBOARD!

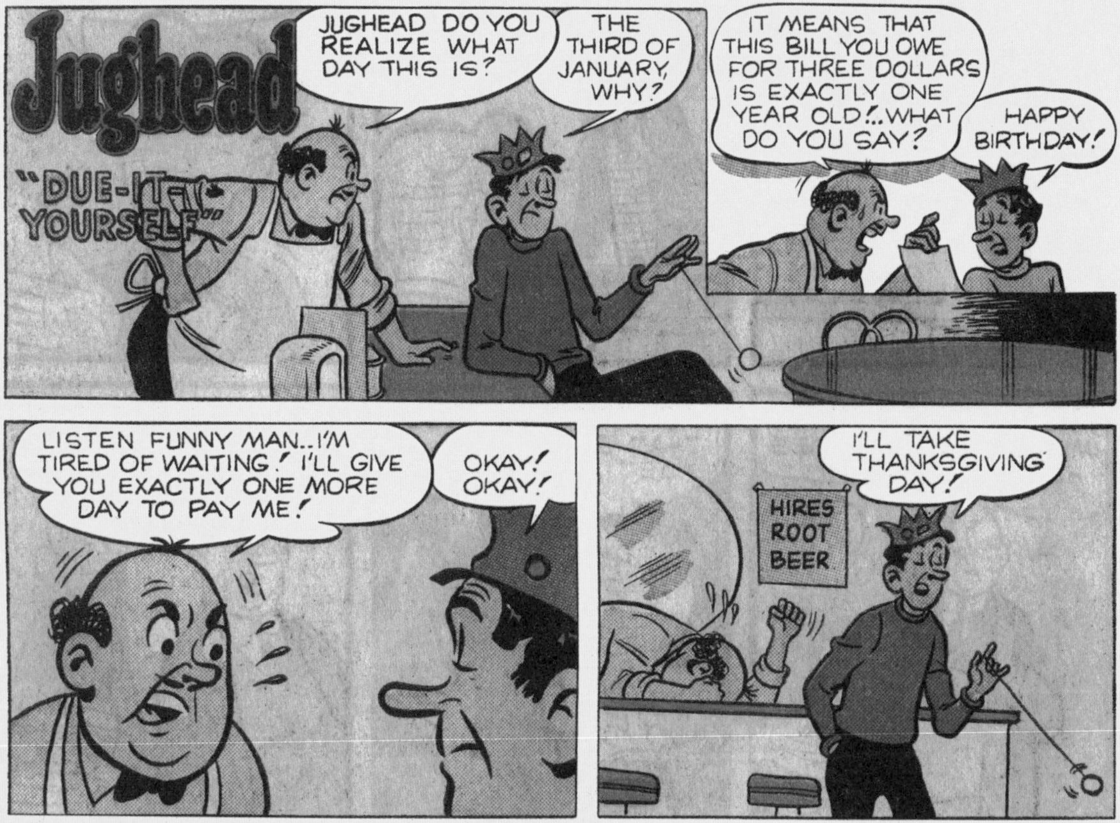
Jughead
"DUE-IT-YOURSELF"
JUGHEAD DO YOU REALIZE WHAT DAY THIS IS?
THE THIRD OF JANUARY, WHY?
IT MEANS THAT THIS BILL YOU OWE FOR THREE DOLLARS IS EXACTLY ONE YEAR OLD!..WHAT DO YOU SAY?
HAPPY BIRTHDAY!
LISTEN FUNNY MAN..I'M TIRED OF WAITING! I'LL GIVE YOU EXACTLY ONE MORE DAY TO PAY ME!
OKAY! OKAY!
I'LL TAKE THANKSGIVING DAY!
HIRES ROOT BEER

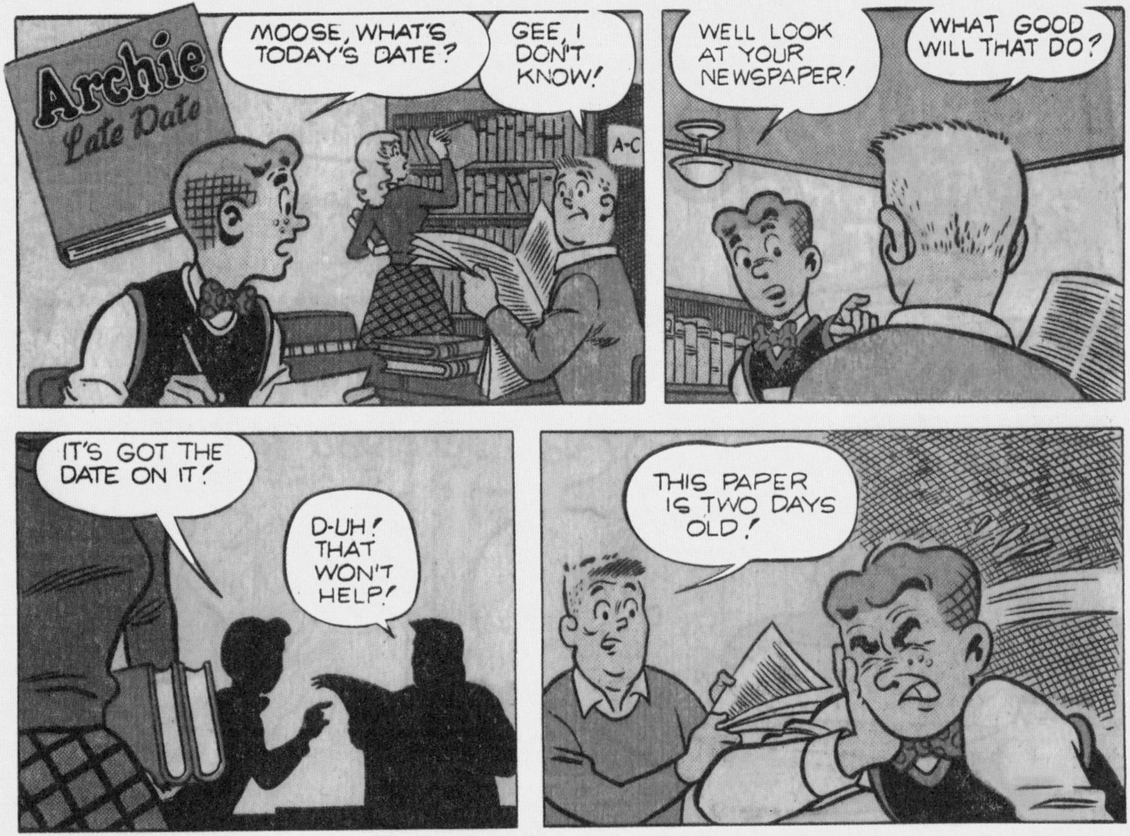
Archie
Late Date
MOOSE, WHAT'S TODAY'S DATE?
GEE, I DON'T KNOW!
A-C
WELL LOOK AT YOUR NEWSPAPER!
WHAT GOOD WILL THAT DO?
IT'S GOT THE DATE ON IT!
D-UH! THAT WON'T HELP!
THIS PAPER IS TWO DAYS OLD!

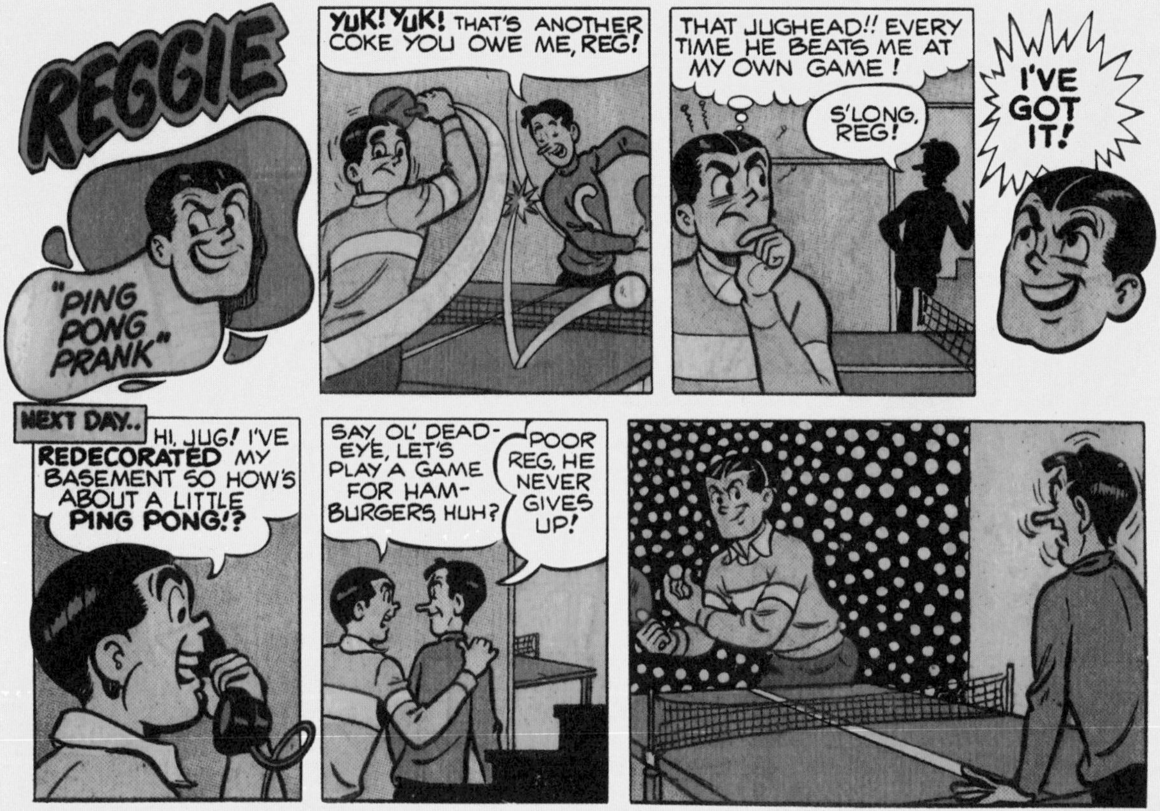
REGGIE
"PING PONG PRANK"
YUK! YUK! THAT'S ANOTHER COKE YOU OWE ME, REG!
THAT JUGHEAD!! EVERY TIME HE BEATS ME AT MY OWN GAME!
S'LONG, REG!
I'VE GOT IT!
NEXT DAY..
HI, JUG! I'VE REDECORATED MY BASEMENT SO HOW'S ABOUT A LITTLE PING PONG!?
SAY, OL' DEAD-EYE, LET'S PLAY A GAME FOR HAM-BURGERS, HUH?
POOR REG, HE NEVER GIVES UP!

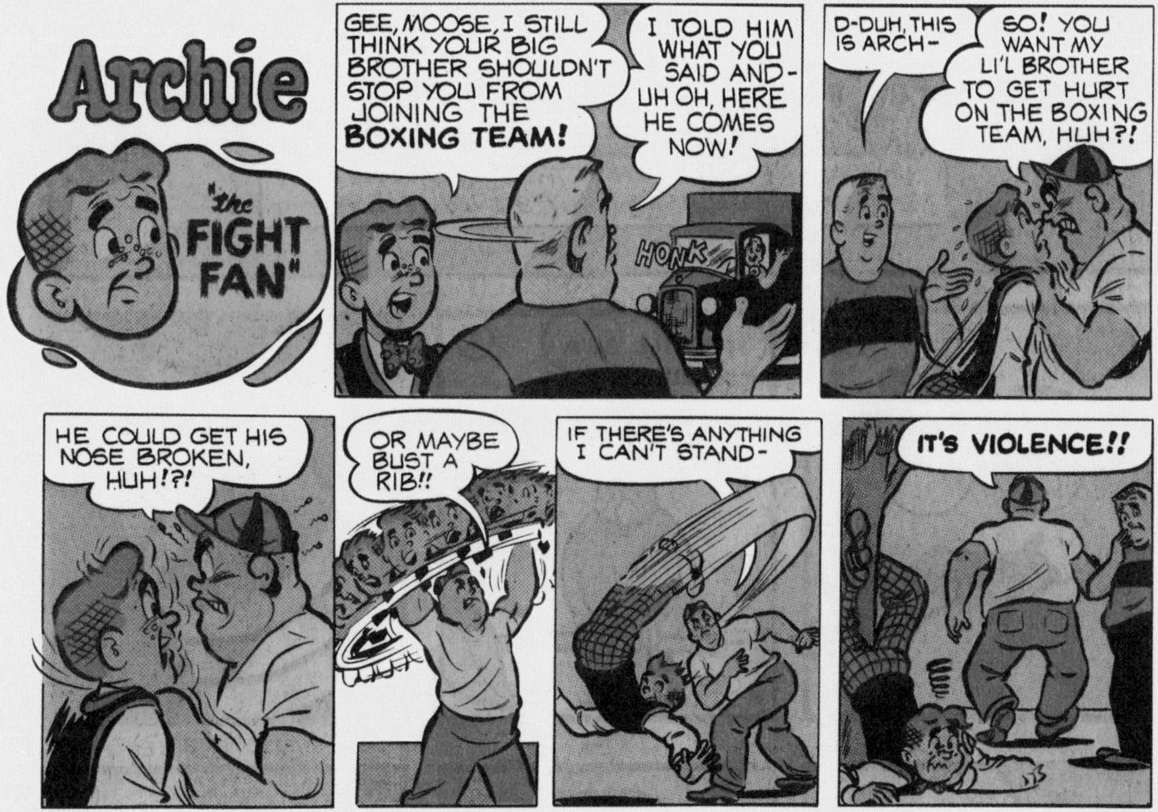
Archie
"the FIGHT FAN"
GEE, MOOSE, I STILL THINK YOUR BIG BROTHER SHOULDN'T STOP YOU FROM JOINING THE BOXING TEAM!
I TOLD HIM WHAT YOU SAID AND- UH OH, HERE HE COMES NOW!
HONK
D-DUH, THIS IS ARCH-
SO! YOU WANT MY LI'L BROTHER TO GET HURT ON THE BOXING TEAM, HUH?!
HE COULD GET HIS NOSE BROKEN, HUH!?!
OR MAYBE BUST A RIB!!
IF THERE'S ANYTHING I CAN'T STAND-
IT'S VIOLENCE!!

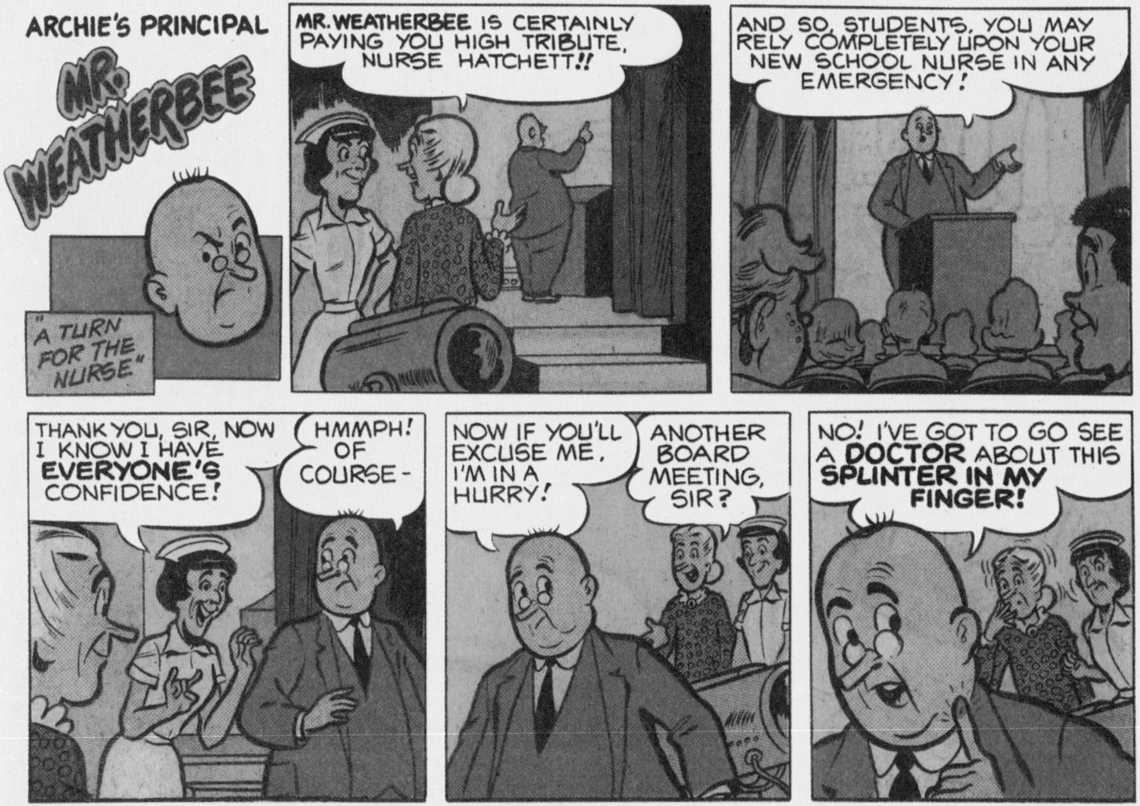
ARCHIE'S PRINCIPAL
MR. WEATHERBEE
"A TURN FOR THE NURSE"
MR. WEATHERBEE IS CERTAINLY PAYING YOU HIGH TRIBUTE, NURSE HATCHETT!!
AND SO, STUDENTS, YOU MAY RELY COMPLETELY UPON YOUR NEW SCHOOL NURSE IN ANY EMERGENCY!
THANK YOU, SIR, NOW I KNOW I HAVE EVERYONE'S CONFIDENCE!
HMMPH! OF COURSE-
NOW IF YOU'LL EXCUSE ME, I'M IN A HURRY!
ANOTHER BOARD MEETING, SIR?
NO! I'VE GOT TO GO SEE A DOCTOR ABOUT THIS SPLINTER IN MY FINGER!

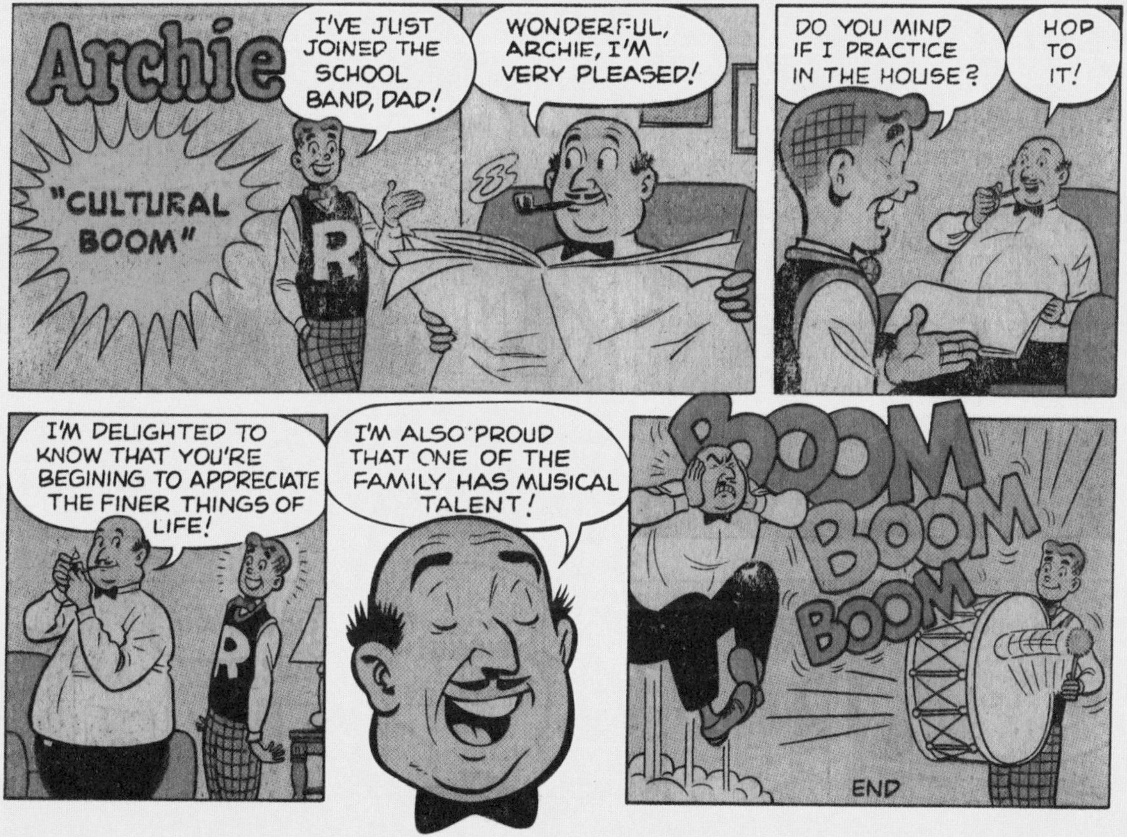

Archie
"CULTURAL BOOM"
I'VE JUST JOINED THE SCHOOL BAND, DAD!
WONDERFUL, ARCHIE, I'M VERY PLEASED!
DO YOU MIND IF I PRACTICE IN THE HOUSE?
HOP TO IT!
I'M DELIGHTED TO KNOW THAT YOU'RE BEGINING TO APPRECIATE THE FINER THINGS OF LIFE!
I'M ALSO PROUD THAT ONE OF THE FAMILY HAS MUSICAL TALENT!
BOOM
BOOM
BOOM
END

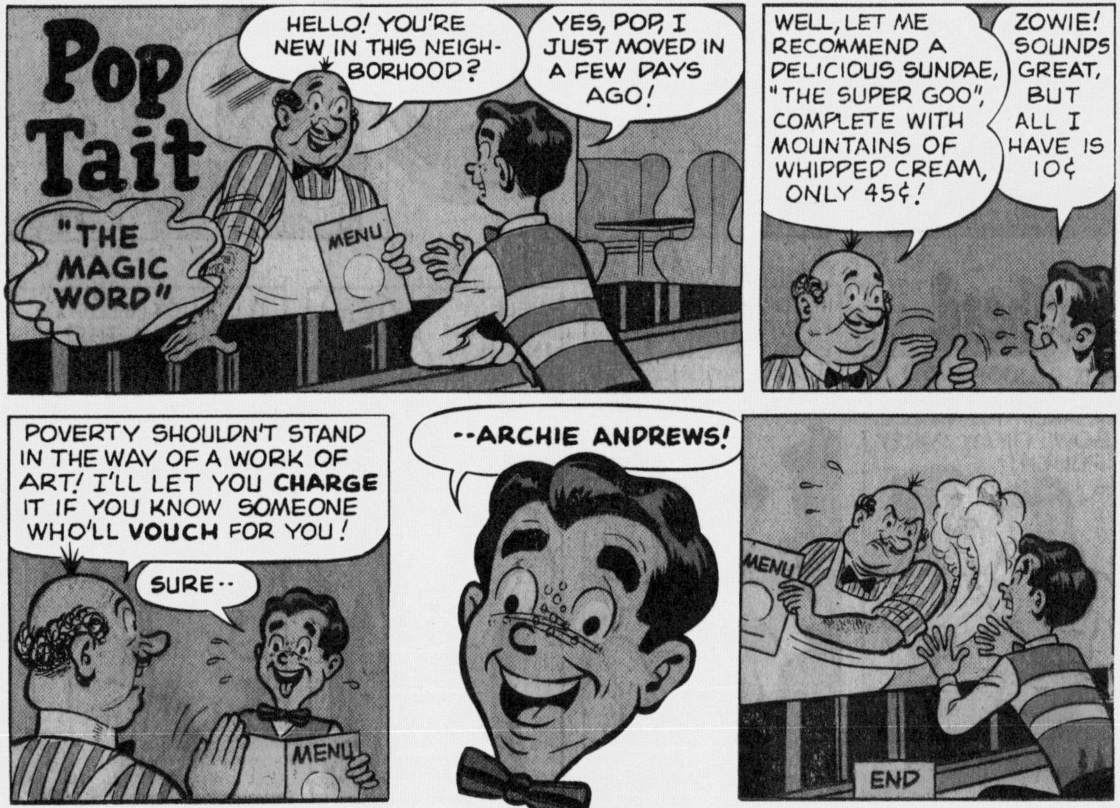
Pop Tait
"THE MAGIC WORD"
HELLO! YOU'RE NEW IN THIS NEIGH-BORHOOD?
YES, POP, I JUST MOVED IN A FEW DAYS AGO!
MENU
WELL, LET ME RECOMMEND A DELICIOUS SUNDAE, "THE SUPER GOO", COMPLETE WITH MOUNTAINS OF WHIPPED CREAM, ONLY 45¢!
ZOWIE! SOUNDS GREAT, BUT ALL I HAVE IS 10¢
POVERTY SHOULDN'T STAND IN THE WAY OF A WORK OF ART! I'LL LET YOU CHARGE IT IF YOU KNOW SOMEONE WHO'LL VOUCH FOR YOU!
SURE--
MENU
--ARCHIE ANDREWS!
MENU
END

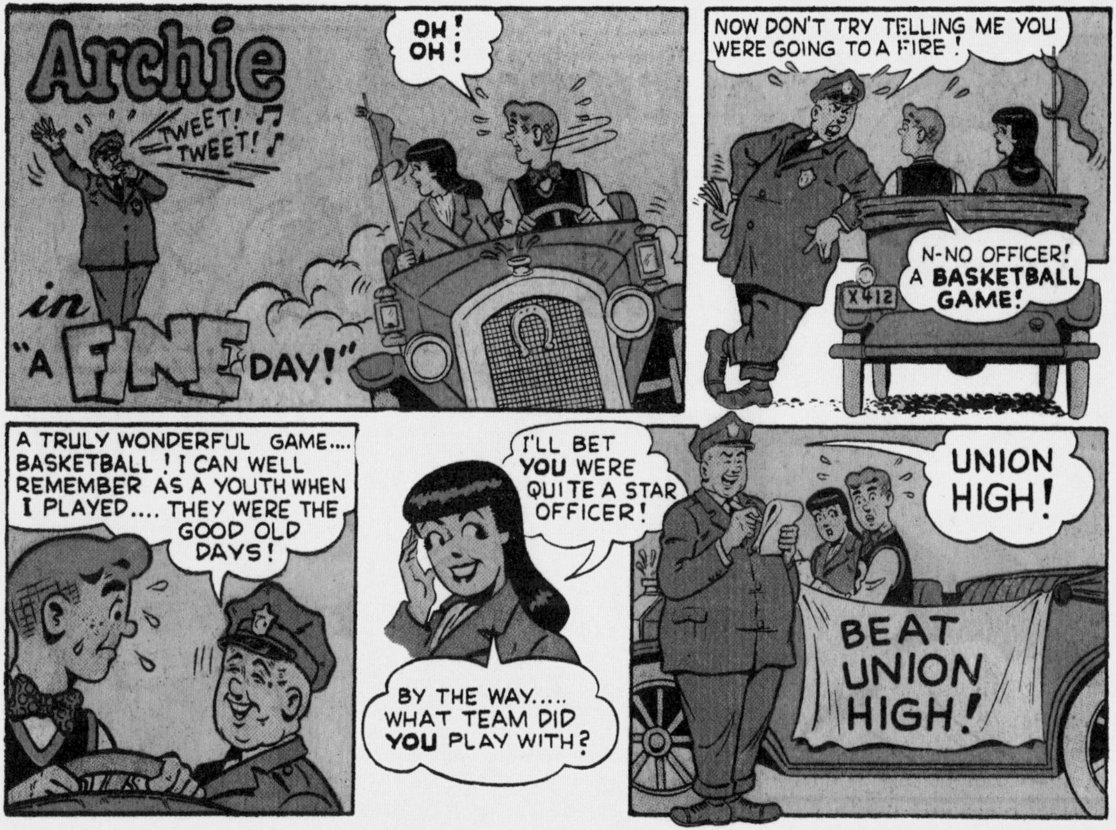
Archie
TWEET! TWEET!
in
"A FINE DAY!"
OH! OH!
NOW DON'T TRY TELLING ME YOU WERE GOING TO A FIRE!
N-NO OFFICER! A BASKETBALL GAME!
X412
A TRULY WONDERFUL GAME.... BASKETBALL! I CAN WELL REMEMBER AS A YOUTH WHEN I PLAYED.... THEY WERE THE GOOD OLD DAYS!
I'LL BET YOU WERE QUITE A STAR OFFICER!
BY THE WAY..... WHAT TEAM DID YOU PLAY WITH?
UNION HIGH!
BEAT UNION HIGH!

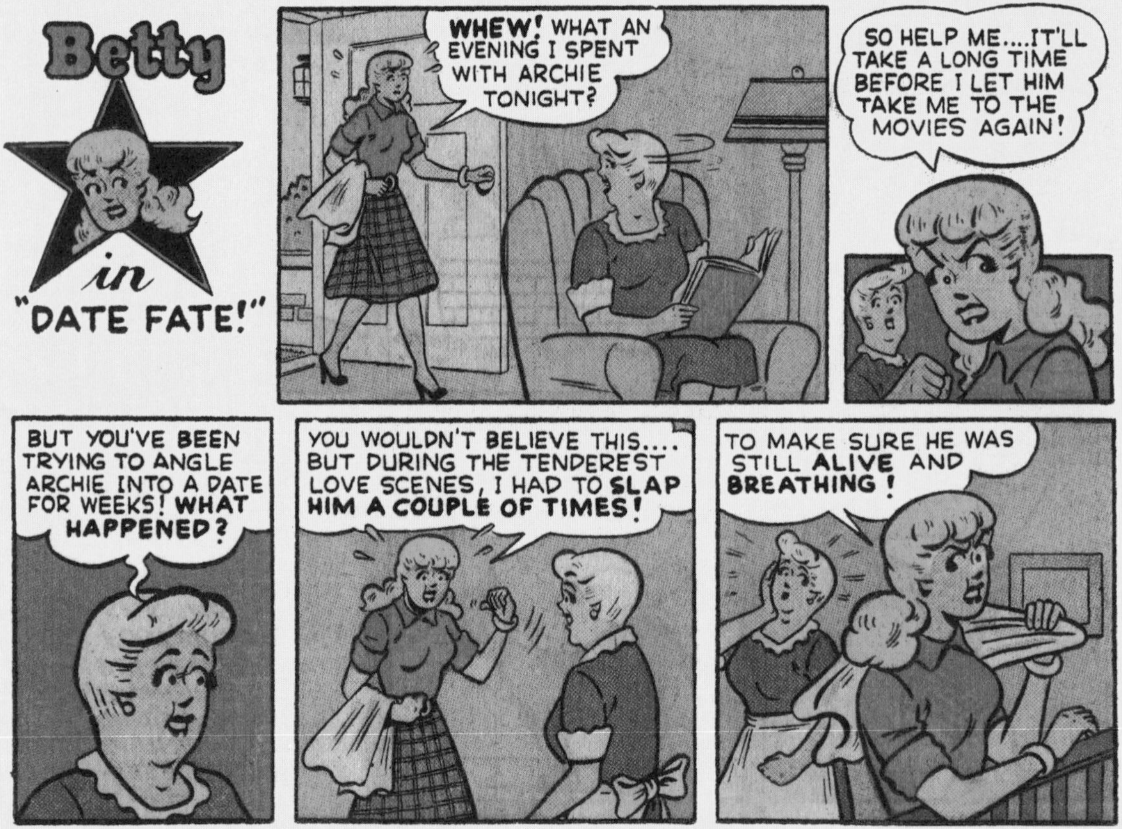
Betty
in
"DATE FATE!"
WHEW! WHAT AN EVENING I SPENT WITH ARCHIE TONIGHT?
SO HELP ME....IT'LL TAKE A LONG TIME BEFORE I LET HIM TAKE ME TO THE MOVIES AGAIN!
BUT YOU'VE BEEN TRYING TO ANGLE ARCHIE INTO A DATE FOR WEEKS! WHAT HAPPENED?
YOU WOULDN'T BELIEVE THIS.... BUT DURING THE TENDEREST LOVE SCENES, I HAD TO SLAP HIM A COUPLE OF TIMES!
TO MAKE SURE HE WAS STILL ALIVE AND BREATHING!

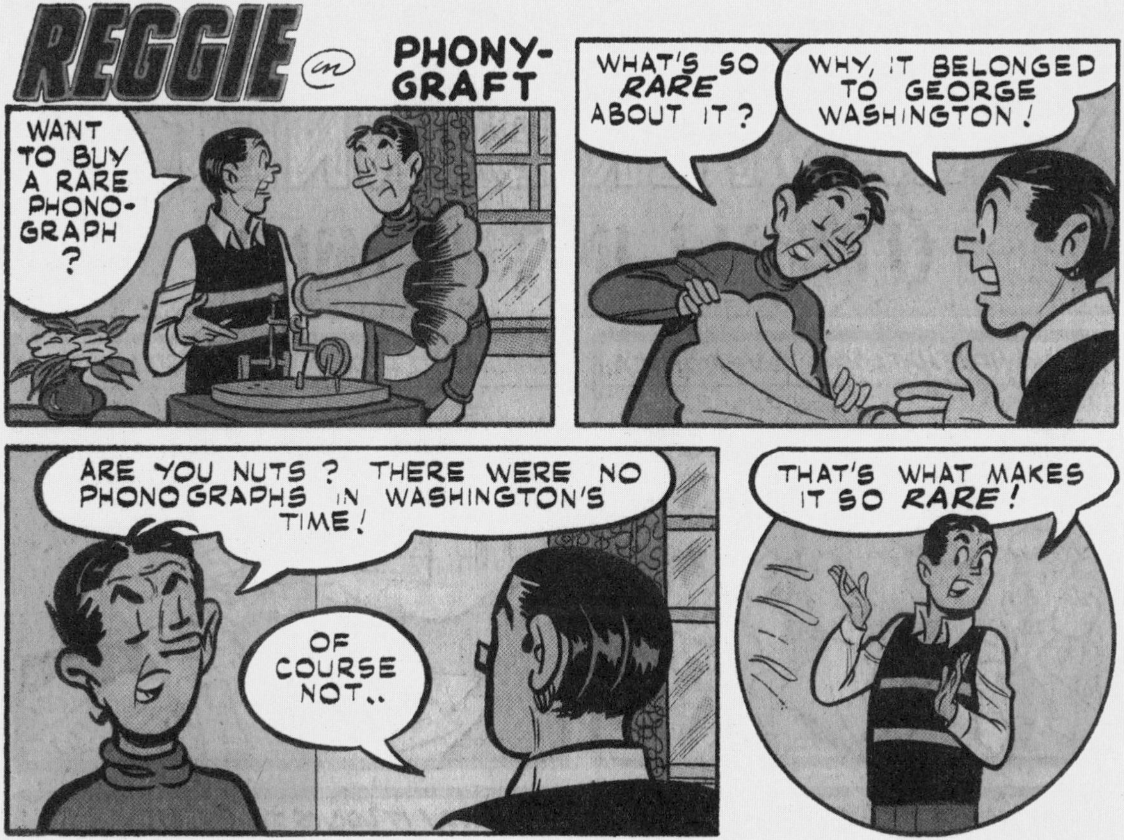
REGGIE in PHONY-GRAFT
WANT TO BUY A RARE PHONOGRAPH ?
WHAT'S SO RARE ABOUT IT ?
WHY, IT BELONGED TO GEORGE WASHINGTON !
ARE YOU NUTS ? THERE WERE NO PHONOGRAPHS IN WASHINGTON'S TIME !
OF COURSE NOT..
THAT'S WHAT MAKES IT SO RARE !

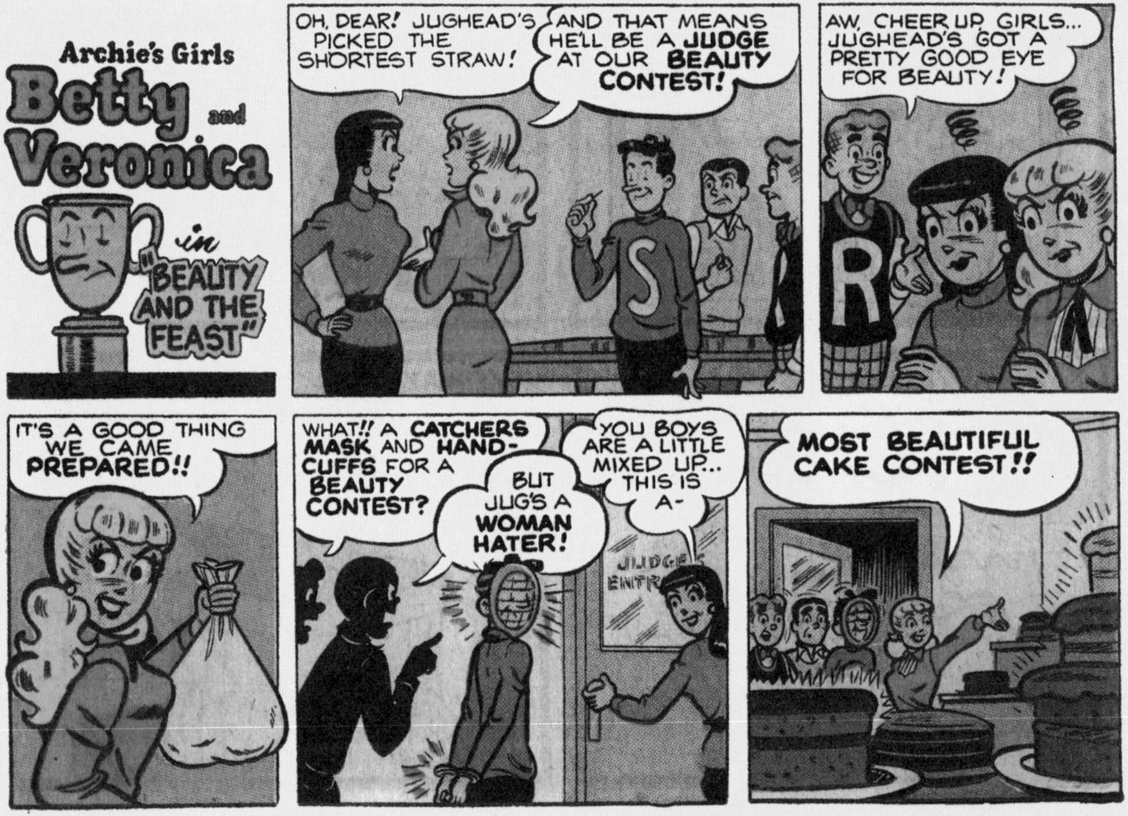
Archie's Girls
Betty and Veronica
in "BEAUTY AND THE FEAST"
OH, DEAR! JUGHEAD'S PICKED THE SHORTEST STRAW!
AND THAT MEANS HE'LL BE A JUDGE AT OUR BEAUTY CONTEST!
AW, CHEER UP, GIRLS... JUGHEAD'S GOT A PRETTY GOOD EYE FOR BEAUTY!
IT'S A GOOD THING WE CAME PREPARED!!
WHAT!! A CATCHERS MASK AND HAND-CUFFS FOR A BEAUTY CONTEST?
BUT JUG'S A WOMAN HATER!
YOU BOYS ARE A LITTLE MIXED UP... THIS IS A-
JUDGE ENTR
MOST BEAUTIFUL CAKE CONTEST!!

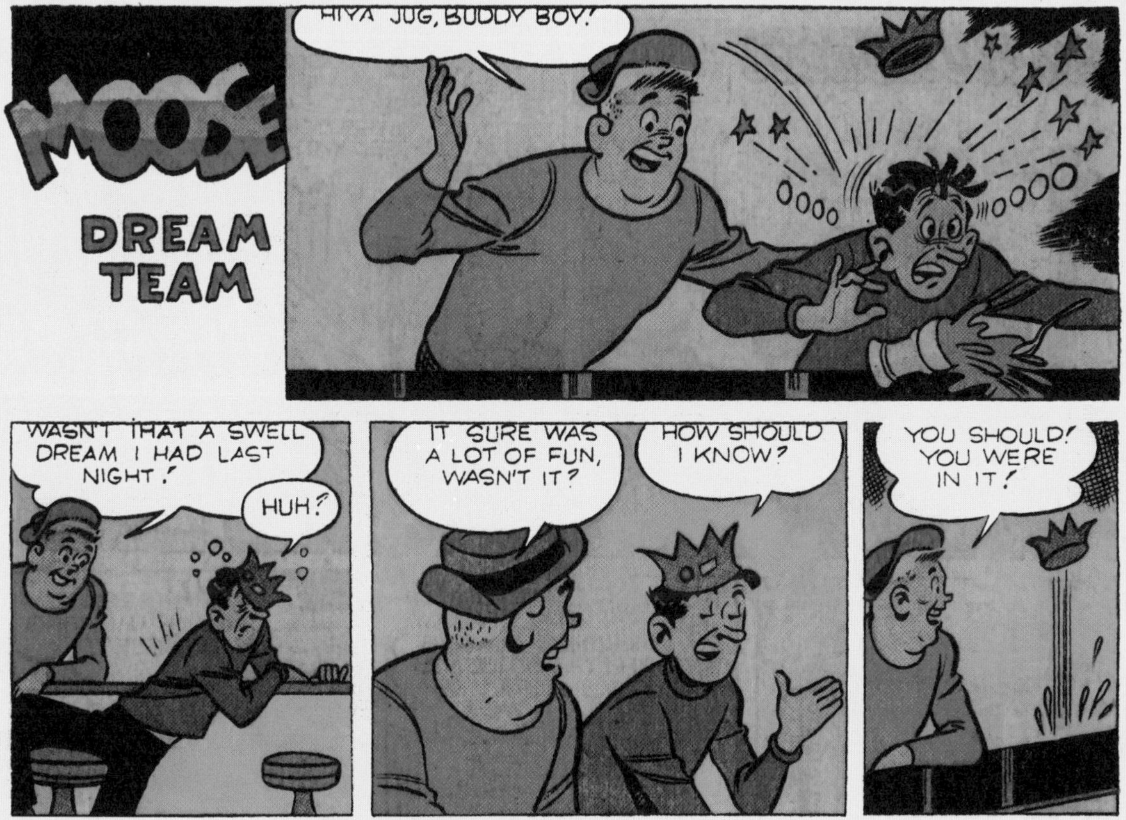
MOOSE
DREAM TEAM
HIYA JUG, BUDDY BOY!
OOOO
OOOO
WASN'T THAT A SWELL DREAM I HAD LAST NIGHT!
HUH?
IT SURE WAS A LOT OF FUN, WASN'T IT?
HOW SHOULD I KNOW?
YOU SHOULD! YOU WERE IN IT!

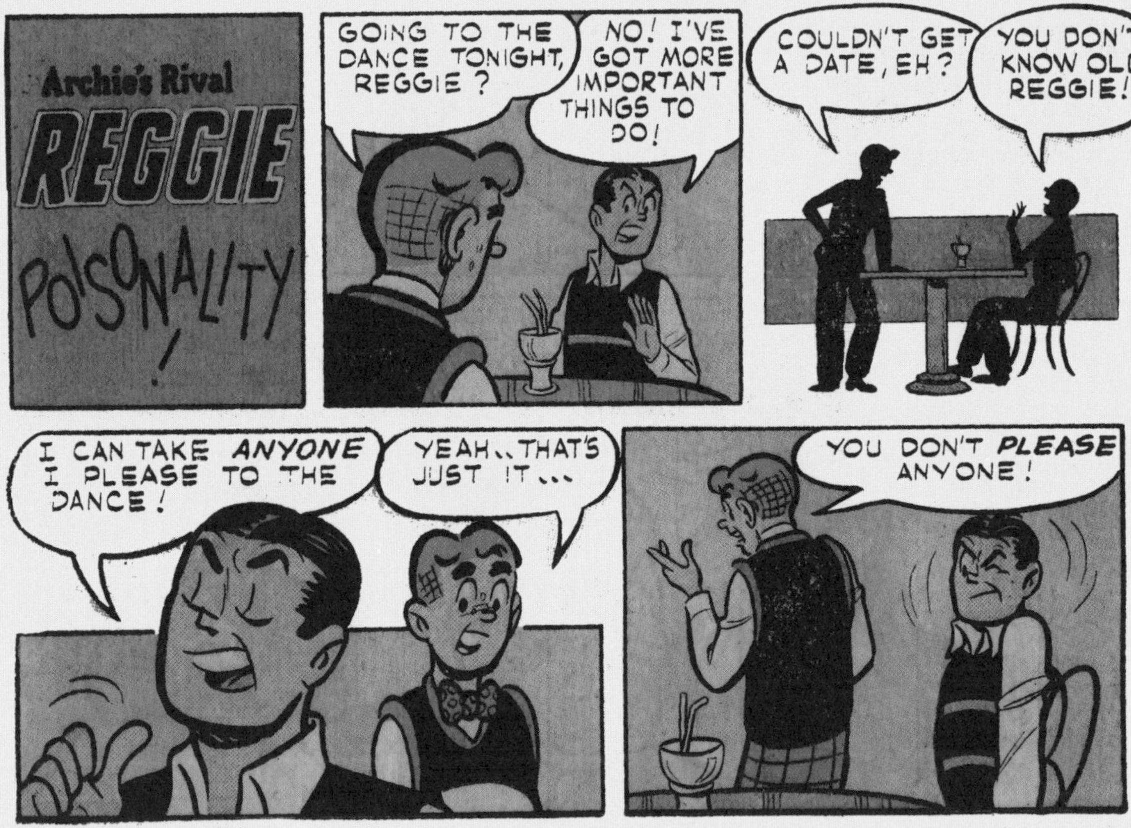
Archie's Rival
REGGIE
POISONALITY!
GOING TO THE DANCE TONIGHT, REGGIE?
NO! I'VE GOT MORE IMPORTANT THINGS TO DO!
COULDN'T GET A DATE, EH?
YOU DON'T KNOW OLD REGGIE!
I CAN TAKE ANYONE I PLEASE TO THE DANCE!
YEAH.. THAT'S JUST IT...
YOU DON'T PLEASE ANYONE!

Archie in TRADE WIND

FOR IT

Jughead in TECHNICOLOR

ENGLISH... | YES MA'AM?

TOO COLORFUL!

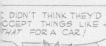

I DIDN'T THINK THEY'D ACCEPT THINGS LIKE THAT FOR A CAR!

WELL, IN THIS CASE IT WAS DIFFERENT--

--THE CAR DEALER WAS MY NEXT DOOR NEIGHBOR

WHAT DO YOU MEAN.. TOO COLORFUL, MISS GRUNDY? | LISTEN TO THIS..

IN THE FIRST 5 PARAGRAPHS YOU HAVE THE HERO TURN **PURPLE** WITH RAGE, THE RIVAL TURN **GREEN** WITH JEALOUSY, THE MAIDEN GO **WHITE** WITH FEAR AND THE COACHMAN TURN **BLUE** WITH COLD!

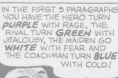

..AND IS HIS FACE RED!

Archie's Pal Jughead in MILLION-ERROR

AND THAT, STUDENTS, SUMS UP OUR DISCUSSION ON GEOLOGY TODAY...

IN CLOSING, I'D LIKE TO SAY THIS, GEOLOGISTS THINK THE WORLD WILL COME TO AN END IN 50 MILLION YEARS

Archie's teacher MISS GRUNDY in The Dickens To Pay!

WHAT ARE YOU BOYS DOING? | OH, NOTHING MUCH RIGHT NOW!

NEITHER AM I/ WHAT SAY WE GO INTO THE LIBRARY AND RAISE THE DICKENS?

GO

WHA'—/?? HOW MANY?!!

I SAID 50 MILLION YEARS, JUGHEAD.. | BOY! WHAT A RELIEF!

I THOUGHT YOU SAID 15 MILLION

SURE I MEAN IT!

I NEVER THOUGHT YOU'D WANT TO RAISE THE DICKENS! SHALL WE BEGIN BY THROWING SPITBALLS?

QUIET | LIBRARY

NO/ WE'LL BEGIN BY RAISING THIS SET OF **DICKEN'S WORKS** FROM THE BOTTOM SHELF TO THE TOP!